"A fascinating study of a turning point in the history of anthropology—arguably the moment that launched nineteenth-century anthropology into the twentieth. . . . *Coming of Age in Chicago* also puts a very human face on this crucial occasion and highlights the diverging and competing interests and visions that made it the kaleidoscope that it was."

    JACK DAVID ELLER, *Anthropology Review Database*

"This splendid volume brings together seven substantial essays, which, taken together, treat the 1893 Chicago World's Fair as 'a catalytic event in the professionalization of American anthropology,' as the editors put it. . . . These seven essays by themselves would constitute an important contribution, but the editors have contextualized them by adding key documents of the moment."

    RICHARD HANDLER, *Journal of the Royal Anthropological Institute*

"Both an intellectual history of anthropology and a snapshot of a turning point. It describes a moment when old ideas and practices were confronted with new ways of thinking about the nature of being human and what methods were best suited for that study."

    RORY G. MCCARTHY, *Michigan Historical Review*

"Will be of interest to historians of anthropology, of course, but also to scholars grappling with visual and material representations, museums and cultural institutions, and the politics of cultural exhibition."

    ADAM FULTON JOHNSON, *History of Anthropology Newsletter*

"*Coming of Age in Chicago* is at once a major contribution to the burgeoning literature on Chicago's 1893 World Columbian Exposition as well as a critical examination of a crucial phase in the development of American anthropology. . . . Such notable personalities as Frederic Ward Putnam, Franz Boas, Daniel Garrison Brinton, and especially Frank Hamilton Cushing, as well as lesser luminaries, all come alive and shine forth in this sparkling, multifaceted volume."

    RAYMOND D. FOGELSON, professor emeritus of anthropology at the University of Chicago

"In this richly detailed account of anthropology at the fair—and of the fair's exhibits in the minds of anthropologists—the authors deepen our understanding of the cultural origins of the anthropology profession."

ROBERT W. RYDELL, professor of history at Montana State University and author of *All the World's a Fair*

"*Coming of Age in Chicago* presents an account of the interplay of anthropology and the public spectacle of the 1893 Chicago World's Fair that is both authoritative and engaging. Original documents and photo essays heighten the reading experience and help convey the material realities of anthropology at the fair, just as the discipline was coalescing."

FREDERIC W. GLEACH, curator of the Anthropology Collections at Cornell University and founding coeditor of *Histories of Anthropology Annual*

Coming of Age in Chicago

Souvenir Map of the World's Columbian Exposition at Jackson Park and Midway Plaisance. Chicago, 1893. Creator unknown. Courtesy of the Chicago History Museum. ICHi-27750.

Coming *of* Age *in* Chicago

The 1893 World's Fair and
the Coalescence of
American Anthropology

Edited by
CURTIS M. HINSLEY
and
DAVID R. WILCOX

University of Nebraska Press
Lincoln

© 2016 by the Board of Regents of the
University of Nebraska

All rights reserved
The University of Nebraska Press is part of a land-grant institution with campuses and programs on the past, present, and future homelands of the Pawnee, Ponca, Otoe-Missouria, Omaha, Dakota, Lakota, Kaw, Cheyenne, and Arapaho Peoples, as well as those of the relocated Ho-Chunk, Sac and Fox, and Iowa Peoples.

First Nebraska paperback printing: 2023

This volume has been published with financial support from the Christine Callan Trust and assistance from The Southwest Center of the University of Arizona.

Library of Congress Cataloging-in-Publication Data
Names: Hinsley, Curtis M., editor. |
Wilcox, David R., 1944– editor.
Title: Coming of age in Chicago: the 1893 world's fair and the coalescence of American anthropology / edited by Curtis M. Hinsley, David R. Wilcox.
Description: Lincoln: University of Nebraska Press, 2016. | Includes bibliographical references and index.
Identifiers: LCCN 2015033577
ISBN 9780803268388 (hardback: alk. paper)
ISBN 9781496236852 (paperback)
ISBN 9780803284470 (epub)
ISBN 9780803284487 (mobi)
ISBN 9780803284494 (pdf)
Subjects: LCSH: Anthropology—United States—History. | World's Columbian Exposition (1893: Chicago, Ill.)—History. | BISAC: SOCIAL SCIENCE / Anthropology / Cultural. | HISTORY / United States / 19th Century.
Classification: LCC GN17.3.U6 C66 2015 | DDC 301.0973—dc23 LC record available at http://lccn.loc.gov/2015033577

Set in Minion Pro by L. Auten.

To George W. Stocking Jr.
Model, Mentor, Friend

CONTENTS

List of Illustrations xi
List of Tables xiv
Authors' Note xv
Introduction: The Chicago Fair and
American Anthropology in 1893 xvii
    CURTIS M. HINSLEY AND DAVID R. WILCOX

Abbreviations.. xlv

Essay 1. Anthropology as Education and Entertainment:
Frederic Ward Putnam at the World's Fair 1
    CURTIS M. HINSLEY

>   DOCUMENT A. Franz Boas, "Ethnology at the
>   Exposition" (1893)... 78
>   DOCUMENT B. Frederic Ward Putnam, "The Columbus
>   Memorial Museum: Address to the Commercial Club
>   of Chicago" (1891).. 84
>   DOCUMENT C. "Man and His Works: Ethnological
>   Exhibit at the Fair" (1893) 91

Essay 2. Ambiguous Legacy: Daniel Garrison Brinton
at the International Congress of Anthropology 99
    CURTIS M. HINSLEY

>   *Appendix:* Analysis of Registered Members of the
>   International Congress of Anthropology, World's
>   Columbian Exposition, 1893 110
>   DAVID R. WILCOX

DOCUMENT D. William Henry Holmes, "The World's
Fair Congress of Anthropology" (1893) 120

Essay 3. Anthropology in a Changing America: Interpreting
the Chicago "Triumph" of Frank Hamilton Cushing 125
DAVID R. WILCOX

DOCUMENT E. Excerpts from the Diary of Frank Hamilton
Cushing at the World's Fair (June 16–September 12, 1893) 153

DOCUMENT F. Monthly Report of Mr. Frank Hamilton
Cushing (September 1893)................................. 212

DOCUMENT G. "The Pueblos at Home" (September 1894).... 232

A Visual Interlude: Popular Images of Anthropology and
Its Subjects at the Fair 239
CURTIS M. HINSLEY

Essay 4. Refracting Images: Anthropological Display at the
Chicago World's Fair, 1893 261
IRA JACKNIS

Essay 5. Relic Hunters in the White City: Artifacts, Authority,
and Ambition at the World's Columbian Exposition.............. 337
JAMES E. SNEAD

DOCUMENT H. Cushing's Analysis of the Hazzard Cliff
Dweller Collection (1895) 362

DOCUMENT I. Warren King Moorehead, "The Ancient Man:
The Anthropological Exhibit at the World's Fair"
(June 22, 1893) 369

Essay 6. Patrons, Popularizers, and Professionals: The
Institutional Setting of Late Nineteenth-Century Anthropology
in Chicago.. 375
DONALD MCVICKER

DOCUMENT J. "Heir of the Big Fair: Field Columbian
Museum Opened" (1894) 405

Essay 7. Going National: American Anthropology Successfully
Redefines Itself as an Accepted Academic Domain 413
   DAVID R. WILCOX

   Appendix: Comparison of Primary Contributors to the
   American Anthropologist, 1888–1925 455
      DAVID R. WILCOX

      DOCUMENT K. Daniel Garrison Brinton, "The Aims of
      Anthropology" (1895) 459
      DOCUMENT L. Franz Boas, "The Limitations of the
      Comparative Method of Anthropology" (1896) 476

Afterword: The Ironies of the Fair, the Uncertainties
of Anthropology. 489
   CURTIS M. HINSLEY

Acknowledgments 497
Bibliography. 499
Contributors 547
Index. 549

ILLUSTRATIONS

Souvenir map of the Fair . . . . frontispiece
1. John Wesley Powell portrait, 1889 xxvii
2. Frederic Ward Putnam in his Peabody Museum office, ca. 1890 xxviii
3. Daniel Garrison Brinton, portrait by Thomas Eakins, ca. 1900 xxix
4. Frank Hamilton Cushing, portrait by Thomas Hovenden xxx
5. Thomas Hovenden, *Breaking Home Ties*, 1890 xxxi
6. Willard Leroy Metcalf, *Sunset Hour on the West Lagoon*, 1893 xxxii
7. Daniel Hudson Burnham, portrait, 1912 xxxiii
8. *Cairo Street Waltz*, sheet music lithograph, 1893 xxxiv
9. Putnam's Penobscot Village under the elevated rail 27
10. Eskimos at the World's Columbian Exposition 41
11. Esther and Columbia (Palmer) Eneutseak 43
12. Bertha Honoré Palmer 44
13. Illuminated White City at night 49
14. The Ferris Wheel on the Midway 65
15. The Midway Plaisance looking eastward from the Ferris Wheel 66
16. Stewart Culin 133
17. Sara Yorke Stevenson, 1917 134
18. Sarah Tyson Rorer, ca. 1886 137
19. "Mrs. Rorer's Corn Recipes Cookbook" 138
20. Daniel Burnham with Exposition architects and officials 139
21. Francis Davis "Frank" Millet, ca. 1891 140
22. Charles Deering, ca. 1908 142
23. Henry Blake Fuller, ca. 1896 143
24. "In the Cairo street," from *World's Fair Puck*, 1893 245

25. "A privileged race," from *World's Fair Puck*, 1893............246
26. "Travels on the Midway," from *World's Fair Puck*, 1893.......247
27. "A pre-Columbian shell game from Peru," from *Herald*, 1893..248
28. "A victim of long and continued riding in suburban trains" (Chac Mool), from *Herald*, 1893........................248
29. The Anthropology Building, from *Herald*, 1893.............249
30. "I'm not crazy yet," from *Herald*, 1893 250
31. "Great excitement—Indian lady throwing out dishwater," from *Herald*, 1893............................... 251
32. Mary Dookshoode Annanuck (Eskimo), from *Portrait Types of the Midway Plaisance* 252
33. Antonio (Apache Indian), from *Portrait Types*............. 253
34. William (Samoan), from *Portrait Types*....................254
35. Monahan Levi, Isaac Cohn, and H. Hondon (Turkish Jews), from *Portrait Types* 255
36. Northward from center of Wooded Isle, from *Vistas of the Fair in Color*...256
37. Totem poles and Kwakiutl Indians, from *Vistas of the Fair* ... 257
38. Statue of Industry, Court of Honor, from *Vistas of the Fair* ... 258
39. *Humors of the Fair* by Julian Hawthorne, 1894..............259
40. The cosmopolitan future: Strolling on the illuminated Midway 260
41. Smithsonian Institution display, U.S. Government Building, World's Columbian Exposition..........................270
42. Anthropology Building general view, World's Columbian Exposition... 271
43. Miniature model of the Haida village of Skidegate 279
44. Model of Captain Gold's house, Queen Charlotte Islands, ca. 1892..280
45. Captain Gold's house, Queen Charlotte Islands, 1884........ 281
46. Cosmos and Victor Mindeleff working on models of Peñasco Blanco Pueblo Indian village, 1885 282
47. Model of Serpent Mound, Ohio, by Charles Willoughby, 1893...284
48. Serpent Mound, Ohio, 1887 285
49. Plaster casts of Mayan ruins from Uxmal and Labná, Yucatán, 1893...288

50. Vaulted archway, northwest façade, Labná, Yucatán, 1888–91 289
51. Alfred Maudslay's team molding the Great Turtle, Quiriguá, Yucatán, 1883 291
52. Photographs and casts of Mayan ruins, Anthropology Building 292
53. Hopi bread makers life group, U.S. National Museum, ca. 1894 296
54. Hopi bread makers, Hano, Arizona, 1893 297
55. Navajo silversmith life group, World's Columbian Exposition 302
56. Navajo silversmith (Pesh-'lákai-ilhini), Ganado, Arizona, 1892 303
57. Mannequin of Comanche mounted chief, World's Columbian Exposition 311
58. Frank H. Cushing posing for mannequin of Comanche mounted chief, ca. 1892 312
59. Mannequin of Ojibwa scribe, World's Columbian Exposition 313
60. Walter J. Hoffman posing for mannequin of Ojibwa scribe, ca. 1892 314
61. Powhatan quarry life group, World's Columbian Exposition . . 320
62. Powhatan quarry life group, Rock Creek Park, Washington DC, ca. 1895 321
63. Powhatan quarry life group, expanded version, Smithsonian Institution, ca. 1920 322
64. Richard Wetherill at Round Tower, Mesa Verde 341
65. Warren K. Moorehead and workers in the field at Fort Ancient 344
66. The "Cliff Dwelling," World's Columbian Exposition 349
67. Frederick Starr "at home," in mid-career at the University of Chicago 378
68. George A. Dorsey with Patagonian (Tehuelche) "Giant" Colojo, 1904 382
69. Edward Everett Ayer, portrait by Elbridge Ayer Burbank, 1897 391
70. Harlow N. Higinbotham 392
71. Marshall Field 393

TABLES

1. Comparison of membership levels in the Anthropological Society of Washington and the American Anthropological Association for selected periods and places 432

2. Members of the AAA, 1902–1915, by category of interest. 435

Authors' Note for the Paperback Edition

Three of the contributors to *Coming of Age in Chicago* are no longer with us. Don McVicker (1934–2015) passed away just before its original publication in 2016. More recently, Ira Jacknis (1952–2021) died unexpectedly in Berkeley at age sixty-nine. David Wilcox (1944–2022), the coeditor and a major contributor to the volume, passed in May 2022 at seventy-eight. We take the opportunity of the appearance of the paperback edition to express our deep gratitude and respect for these fine scholars and dear friends. The book would not have been possible without them. We know they would be pleased to see their work again in the hands of the public.

CURTIS M. HINSLEY, Sedona, Arizona

JAMES E. SNEAD, Northridge, California

INTRODUCTION

The Chicago Fair and American Anthropology in 1893

CURTIS M. HINSLEY AND DAVID R. WILCOX

> The science of anthropology is so young in this country that the question is often asked: What is anthropology?
> —F. W. Putnam to George Davis, March 1893

> A new intellectual center has formed.... A dozen years ago those who note psychic signs perceived that an intellectual sun was rising on the city by the saltless seas.... The scientific culture of Chicago is young but vigorous.
> —W. J. McGee, "Review of W. H. Holmes, *Archaeological Studies,*" 1896

The 1893 World's Columbian Exposition, or Chicago World's Fair, has long been recognized as a major event in American cultural history. After three years of planning and feverish preparation, the Fair opened on May 1 along the transformed lakeshore of Jackson Park, unfortunately at the onset of a severe four-year nationwide economic depression. With little trace of irony the sponsors of the Fair presented to the world the vision of a future urban utopia, a "White City" of classical, hygienic harmony, and of a peaceful, humanly diverse global order premised on the hegemony of open capital markets. A few weeks after the close of the Fair on October 30, angry unemployed workers from the Pullman corporate settlement set fire to the former fairgrounds along Lake Michigan, destroying most of the buildings and reducing the White City to rubble. But while the physical structures of the Fair proved as ephemeral as those of other fairs and expositions before and since (Harris 1993), the Chicago events profoundly impacted the imaginations of millions of visitors and thousands of sponsors and exhibitors. The Chicago Fair affected subsequent developments in many directions: architecture, urban planning, music, painting—and the young field of anthropology.

Viewed from today, the transatlantic world's fairs of the late nineteenth and early twentieth centuries stand on the historical horizon as assertions of political ambition, displays of economic power and pretension, and expressions of cultural imagination. While they presented utopian dreamscapes of an urbanized, bourgeois future, the industrial expositions that were constructed at great expense and effort by North Atlantic elites in government and business between 1850 and 1920 were intended to demonstrate the global reach of Euroamerican power. Cultural historian Tony Bennett observed that in these decades of maturing imperialism and capitalism, and by means of industrial expositions and museums, social, economic, and political power "manifested itself precisely in continually displaying its ability to command, order, and control objects and bodies, living or dead" (Bennett 1988). Historically rooted in traditions of pilgrimage and market days, the numerous expositions in the capital cities of Europe and America morphed after 1850 into metropolitan displays of the human and material resources of region and empire. They functioned as intermittent but insistent ideological tools of public persuasion—what Walter Benjamin labeled "triumphal processions" of treasure and trajectory.

Inherently or intentionally, every exposition was an anthropological event, and none more so than Chicago's. Beginning in Paris in 1878, the major industrial fairs—among them Paris (again) in 1889 and 1900, Chicago in 1893, Buffalo in 1901, and St. Louis in 1904—featured human exhibitions drawn from global possessions. Cultural historian Paul Greenhalgh (1988) suggested that taken as a whole, the exposition phenomenon amounted to "a propaganda ground for imperial justification," at once promoting current imperial arrangements and placing recently conquered and colonized peoples on display as both resources and products. Recent scholarship has further implicated practitioners in the young fields of anthropology—in Germany, France, England, the United States, and elsewhere—in the ideological and sometimes self-serving promotion of these "human zoos" (Blanchard et al. 2008; cf. Rydell 1984, Conn 1998, Adams 2001, Strain 2003, Parezo and Fowler 2007, Ames 2008).

It was the Paris Exposition of 1889 that provided both model and stimulus for the Chicago Fair, and for its anthropological exhibits in particular. Inspired by both the 1876 Centennial Exposition in Philadelphia and the 1878 Paris International Exposition, and anticipating the Universal Exposition announced for Paris in 1889, in mid-1888 a group of prominent Chicago businessmen resolved to promote a World's Fair in their city to mark the upcoming 400th anniversary of Columbus's first voyage across the Atlantic. The following July, Chicago mayor DeWitt C. Cregier appointed a committee to organize and promote the exposition, and the state of Illinois chartered a company, "The World's Columbian Exposition of 1892," with an initial $5 million stock issue. Competing against New York, Washington, and St. Louis, the Chicago men proceeded to lobby Congress successfully, and in April 1890 (by which time the company's subscription had doubled to $10 million), Congress passed "An Act to provide for celebrating the 400th anniversary of the discovery of America by Christopher Columbus, by holding an International Exposition of Arts, Industries and Manufactures, and products of the soil, mine and sea, in the City of Chicago." Avoiding conflict with Spanish celebrations in Seville scheduled for late 1892, Congress delayed the opening to the following May and authorized $1.5 million for the federal government exhibits (Collier 1969).

The Paris Exposition exerted more specific anthropological influences as well. Otis T. Mason (1838–1908), curator of ethnology at the U.S. National Museum, found the Paris Expo a personal revelation: stunned by the experience—"my intellectual life has been in a bag," he lamented transatlantically to his wife (Mason 1889b)—Mason reported back to Washington that the entire Paris Exposition was the "most thoroughly anthropological" ever assembled, teaching the history of human cultural development through models of domestic and working life, from African villages to Tonkinese temples with Buddhist priests performing rites in the shadow of the stunning new Eiffel Tower along the Seine. He attempted to convey the spirit of Paris to his Smithsonian colleagues: "It was an exposition whose presiding Genius was a teacher, a professor of history, whose scholars were the whole world" (Mason 1889a; cf. Mason 1890, Smith 1994). Anticipating the Columbian celebration, Mason returned to Washington convinced that it was America's turn to teach the world: "all that Europe will ever know of [indigenous America] will be what we tell her." With the American site still not chosen, Mason began planning the National Museum's anthropology exhibits for the affair (Mason 1889a).

In his determination to create a major anthropological exhibit at Chicago, Mason could rely upon the enthusiastic support of the man who had sent him to Europe, Smithsonian colleague George Brown Goode (1846–96). Already the critical figure of his generation in the theory and development of museum anthropology, Goode had been a protégé of Spencer Fullerton Baird, secretary of the Smithsonian Institution from 1878 to 1887. After the Smithsonian inherited large collections from the Philadelphia Centennial, its U.S. National Museum grew exponentially, and in 1881 Baird placed Goode in charge of organizing the new museum. From that point until his death in 1896 Goode oversaw Smithsonian involvement in numerous regional, national, and international expositions—Louisville in 1884, New Orleans in 1885, Paris in 1889, Seville in 1892. As the dominant figure on the American museum scene, Goode was asked by the Chicago men to devise the classification scheme for their entire Fair.

In his quiet way Goode encouraged a system of public museums throughout the United States. His unabashedly democratic vision was adapted "to the needs of the mechanic, the factory operator, the day-laborer, the salesman, and the clerk, as much as to those of the professional man and the man of leisure" (Goode 1895a, 71).[1] The Smithsonian's National Museum, he told a visitor, "takes man as its central pivot, and around this is to revolve everything that man has done in the past or in the present in the world he lives in." For Chicago in 1893 this became the intellectual rationale and organizing principle as well. As historian Robert Rydell observed, in all his museum and exposition work Goode posited a single, all-embracing theme of social evolution: the Chicago Fair "would illustrate 'the steps of progress of civilization and its arts in successive centuries, and in all lands up to the present time.' With special attention to the history of the western hemisphere and the marvels of American civilization, the Chicago Fair would become 'an *illustrated encyclopedia of humanity*'"(Rydell 1984, 45–46).[2] As it happened, Goode's phrasing and his evolutionist vision for anthropology at the Chicago Fair captured the highwater mark of social evolutionism in 1890s America. The country was already undergoing a tidal wave of large-scale, unregulated incorporation and imperial ambitions; for the second time in a generation, it was also about to experience four years of deep, painful economic crisis (Wiebe 1967, Trachtenberg 1982). The Fair stood with one foot on the heights of nineteenth-century progress and the other on the threshold of calamitous events.

Anthropology before the Fair: Institutional Flux, Intellectual Tremors

The Chicago World's Fair was a catalytic event in the professionalization of American anthropology. After 1893 the landscapes of the embryonic fields of American anthropology—ethnology, archaeology, physical anthropology, linguistics, and folklore—displayed new patterns of organization, discourse, standards of training, and levels of private support and public awareness. These post-Fair initiatives did not occur overnight, of course; some signs of change appeared before the Fair, and some ideas and relationships sparked during the Fair bore fruit only years later—or not at all. Still, our hypothesis of the Fair as catalyst leads naturally to a series of "before, during, after" queries: What did the contours of American anthropology look like by 1893? What do we know of the experiences of anthropologists, exhibitors, the exhibited, and the general public at the Fair? Did new disciplinary and professional forms emerge as a result of the events in Chicago— were there unforeseen possibilities on the horizon? While we do not presume to answer all these questions, the essays in this volume pose them by presenting anthropology at Chicago through both contemporary eyes and current scholarship.

Franz Boas once remarked that there were three fathers in the genealogy of American anthropology: John Wesley Powell, Frederic Ward Putnam, and Daniel Garrison Brinton. Boas's oft-quoted observation reflected not only certain assumptions about scientific patriarchy but also the common post–Civil War conviction that institutions in any field of knowledge or industry were necessarily the creations of exceptional men and invariably bore the stamp of individual will and personality. In the words of government geologist-anthropologist W. J. McGee, who co-founded the American Anthropological Association in 1902 and briefly co-owned the *American Anthropologist* with Boas, "the inspiration and the brain must precede the organization and give character to it; and the organization can only provide means to ends already clearly perceived." With Powell in mind, McGee added that it was necessary to have "the genius of a born leader among thinking men" for an effective scientific institution to arise (McGee 1888). Accordingly, such institutions as museums (Putnam's Peabody Museum), scientific bureaus (Powell's Geological Survey and Bureau of Ethnology), and journals (Edward L. Youmans's *Popular Science Monthly*, W. W. Newell's *Journal of American Folklore*, Stephen D. Peet's *American Antiquarian*) were often identified with individual visions and careers. By the same token, aspirants seeking institutional support, affiliation, or merely recognition for their efforts and ambitions naturally pursued personal contact and approval; in the personal and unstable world of American science, including the embryonic fields of anthropology, men of institutional power functioned as the gatekeepers of others' dreams.

The United States in the last quarter of the century was, further, a world of jealous localities and expansive urban power centers competing with one another while resisting the growing political and cultural influence of the federal government (Flack 1975; Wiebe 1967).[3] At the same time, as Thomas Bender has shown, Gilded Age Americans experienced an "erosion of public culture" as the locus of intellectual discourse began to shift from a set of antebellum, small-town institutions (libraries, historical and philosophical societies, local colleges) to the new urban universities, led in the 1870s by Johns Hopkins, Cornell, and Harvard (Bender 1993).

Taking these personal, regional, and institutional factors into account, the past generation of workers in the history of anthropology have established a fairly coherent narrative of professionalization in the *fin de siècle* decades (Darnell 1998; Cole 1999; Baker 1998 and 2010; Conn 1998 and 2004). Boas's comment of the "three fathers," it now seems, contained much truth. Briefly stated, the predominance enjoyed in the 1880s by three centers—the "government men" of Powell's Bureau of Ethnology and the Smithsonian's National Museum, Putnam's Peabody Museum in Cambridge (increasingly conjoined with Harvard), and the Philadelphia institutional nexus associated with Daniel Brinton (University of Pennsylvania, Academy of Natural Sciences, American Philosophical Society)—began to give way in the decade after the Chicago Fair to a more varied landscape of competitive institutional centers in Chicago (Field Museum/University of Chicago), New York (American Museum/Columbia University), Berkeley (University of California), and a few years later Santa Fe (Edgar Lee Hewett's School of American Archaeology).

Professionalization is a complex process, but events singly or collectively can create significant conditions that open possibilities or produce constraints on behavior, or both—at once opening gates, for instance, but also "raising the bar" for what is judged to be good work. The decade prior to the Chicago Fair is suggestive in this regard, and the year 1879 is of particular import. That year the formation of the Archaeological Institute of America (AIA) in Cambridge and, in the nation's capital, both the Anthropological Society of Washington (ASW) and the Bureau of Ethnology (BAE) of the Smithsonian Institution seemed to promise new concentrations of energy for anthropology. Powell and Putnam both expressed disappointment with the strong preference for classical, Old World archaeology within Charles Eliot Norton's young Cambridge organization (Hinsley 1985, 55).[4] Yet in its first years the AIA did at least provide a base for Americanist Lewis Henry Morgan to develop a research design for the North American Southwest, which Adolph F. Bandelier subsequently implemented (Fowler and Wilcox 1999a; Lange and Riley 1996, 29–53). Powell was president of the American Association for the Advancement of Science (AAAS) that year, and he played a central role in establishing both of the Washington organizations (and many others). The initiatives in Boston and Washington presented, at a minimum, forums in which new contributions could be critically discussed and evaluated.

The unformed nature of anthropological inquiry created a sense of democratic openness as the eighties began. In the same significant year of 1879 Otis T. Mason, curator of ethnology at the National Museum, drafted the constitution of the Anthropological Society of Washington, and while women were initially excluded, Mason's paper "What Is Anthropology?" set a broad agenda and open policy for participation in anthropology. "Who may be an anthropologist?" he asked, and quickly answered: "Every man, woman, and child that has sense and patience to observe, and that can honestly record the thing observed"

(Mason 1883; cf. Mason 1884).⁵ Powell's Bureau of Ethnology created jobs for the largest contingent of proto-professional anthropologists anywhere in the country, with an annual budget (shared with Spencer Baird's U.S. National Museum) that reached forty thousand dollars. National publication outlets were few: Youmans's *Popular Science Monthly*, *Science* (published after 1900 by the AAAS), and papers in government reports or Peabody Museum annual reports had some claim to wide distribution. Still, when Franz Boas was hired in 1887 as assistant editor for *Science*, it was merely a "scientific newspaper" that spread its attention and resources across many fields (Cole 1999, 107).

The Washington men were nothing if not ambitious. The original *American Anthropologist* appeared in 1888 as the publication organ of the ASW—which had incorporated in the nation's capital the previous year "for one thousand years" (Flack 1975). The new journal, the first editor (1888–93) of which was government biologist Henry Weatherbee Henshaw, provided a new publication outlet for individual contributions, many of them first read as papers at ASW meetings (Lamb 1906).⁶ Under Henshaw's editorship most members of the editorial committee, like the ASW itself, could best be described as avocational anthropologists: government scientists, military men, Patent Office employees, physicians. But the society also served in effect as a "national seminary" (Lacey 1979), or what sociologist of science Nicholas C. Mullins has called a "theory group" (Mullins 1973), for the primary purpose of articulating, in the nation's capital, an American alternative to the more deterministic aspects of Spencerian philosophy. The Washington vision retained the framework of cultural evolutionism but emphasized "mental" rather than biological development: the creative potential of humans to shape their futures through new inventions and an activist government (Lacey 1979, 9; Hinsley 1996c, 127–33).

By 1888, a decade into its existence, the capital city's Anthropological Society was well established. Among the honorary, contributing, and active members that year, the dominant birth year was 1846 (also the year of the Smithsonian's founding), though Powell (b. 1834) and a few other "elder statesmen" and honorary members were well into their fifties or even older.⁷ The most striking characteristic of the membership, however, was the wide array of interests and primary careers, which prominently included military service, medicine, geological and geographical survey work, and civil service. Ever the anthropological promoter, Mason claimed that the ASW, along with its sister institutions in Washington, was creating a "modern anthropology" and a "wonderful reformation" by turning the "rambling and disorganized labor" of previous years into "systematic and rational employment."[8] Still, the path to anthropology was neither straight nor clear, Mason recognized; he advised one young and hopeful student: "Very few of us walked a bee line into our present work. We just fell in love with it and by and by the doors opened.... Write for the papers. Be seen about the societies. Take a hand in the drudgery" (Mason 1883; 1906).[9]

The main alternatives to government anthropology in the decade before the Chicago Fair lay in the Boston/Cambridge region, specifically the Peabody Museum of Archaeology and Ethnology, founded in 1866. The remarkable variety of individuals involved with the Peabody—and thus with Putnam, despite his lack of formal teaching at Harvard before the 1890s—has recently been outlined by David Browman and Stephen Williams (2013). The majority of workers in Putnam's circle served as unpaid fieldworkers or museum volunteers. While Putnam always struggled for even modest financial support—to set aside the Serpent Mound in southern Ohio in the late 1880s, for instance—occasionally private benefactors, such as Mary T. Hemenway and Charles P. Bowditch, sponsored pioneering archaeological expeditions to specific regions (Hinsley 1984 and 1985; Casler 1976; Wade and McChesney 1980; Hinsley and Wilcox 2002). In addition to these efforts and those of Putnam's widespread archaeological "correspondence school," in 1888 Cambridge also became the home of the American Folk-Lore Society (AFS). For years the AFS suffered a serious internal division between those who saw folklore study as a branch of literature and those, such as Boas, who viewed it as a vital part of scientific anthropology (Zumwalt 1988; Bendix 1997). The early membership of the AFS, like that of the Anthropological Society of Washington, reflected an amazing variety of motives, professions, and styles: according to one historian, "authors, politicians, administrators, philanthropists, physicians, army officers, lawyers, and clergymen" found reason to join (Bendix 1997, 122). Still, an early and congenial alliance between Boas and William Wells Newell (1839–1907), founder of the AFS and first editor of the *Journal of American Folk-Lore*, made the

AFS and its journal an effective anthropological instrument, a kind of "second trumpet" for Boas's unfolding vision of anthropology. From the beginning the two men collaborated to "keep folklore under the wing of anthropology" (Zumwalt 1988, 97). After the formation of the American Anthropological Association in 1902, the two societies held their annual meetings concurrently, even though the majority of AFS members were not AAA members.

Philadelphia, the third nexus of anthropological activity in the years leading up to the Chicago Fair, enjoyed a long and respectable history of scientific and literary societies and activities, beginning with Benjamin Franklin's American Philosophical Society (1743), the University of Pennsylvania (1740), and the Peale Museum (1786), and continuing in the nineteenth century with the Pennsylvania Academy of the Fine Arts (1805), Academy of Natural Sciences (1812), and Franklin Institute for the Promotion of the Mechanic Arts (1824). In 1880 William Pepper became provost (chief officer) of the University of Pennsylvania, marking a new and vigorous phase of growth and prominence for the university—as witnessed by the Babylonian Expedition Fund of 1887, the new university library of 1888, and in 1889 the university's Free Museum of Science and Art (later the University Museum; Fowler and Wilcox 2003; Kuklick 1996). Pepper was a vital (though controversial) force in the development of anthropology until his untimely death in 1898, but without question it was Daniel Brinton who for decades reigned as the dominant Philadelphian in all fields of anthropology: ethnology, Amerindian linguistics, and physical anthropology. In his early years he was even one of the first to dig in the prehistoric middens of the Florida coast. But Brinton never trained any students and dispersed his remarkable energies across a range of local institutions, to questionable effect (Baker 2010, 117–55). By the early 1890s he was the widely recognized "sage of Philadelphia"—Walt Whitman admired him as "eminent, "the best of them all" in anthropology (Traubel 1961, 129, 321)—but he was also growing out of touch with developments in the field. His honorific position as keynote speaker and president of the Executive Committee of the World's Fair Congress of Anthropology in Chicago spoke more to the past than to the future—both his own and that of American anthropology. As a consequence, Philadelphia would wait more than

FIG. 1. John Wesley Powell (1834–1902), explorer and geologist, 1889. Oil on canvas, 121.9 x 96.5 cm. National Portrait Gallery, Smithsonian, and Art Resource, New York. SIRIS #: NPG.70.21.

xxvii

FIG. 2. Frederic Ward Putnam in his private office, Peabody Museum, ca. 1890. © President and Fellows of Harvard College, Peabody Museum of Archaeology and Ethnology, Harvard University. PM #2004.24.1790, digital file #130650002.

FIG. 3. Thomas Eakins, *Portrait of Daniel Garrison Brinton*, ca. 1900. Oil on canvas, 41 x 36 in. From the collection of the American Philosophical Society, gift of friends of Brinton, 1900.

FIG. 4. Thomas Hovenden, *Portrait of Frank Hamilton Cushing*. Smithsonian American Art Museum, #1985.66.312,6, gift of Mrs. F. H. Cushing.

FIG. 5. Thomas Hovenden, *Breaking Home Ties*, 1890. Oil on canvas. Philadelphia Museum of Art, gift of Ellen Harrison McMichael in memory of C. Emory McMichael, 1942.

FIG. 6. Willard Leroy Metcalf, *Sunset Hour on the West Lagoon, World's Columbian Exposition*, 1893. Courtesy of Chicago History Museum. ICHi-62515.

FIG. 7. Daniel H. Burnham, portrait, 1912.
Daniel H. Burnham Collection, Ryerson
and Burnham Archives, The Art Institute of
Chicago. Digital file #194301.081001–13.

FIG. 8. *Cairo Street Waltz,* sheet music, lithograph, 1893. Courtesy of Chicago History Museum. ICHi-51022.

a decade after the Chicago Fair to begin to attain a place of respect in the field (Essay 7, this volume).

The anthropological dominance of Washington, Boston, and Philadelphia did not survive the turn of the century. A gradual but critical intellectual realignment, closely tracking the rising career of Boas, accelerated the coming changes. Writing as the century turned, Henry Adams recalled the powerful certainty of Gilded Age evolutionism:

> For the young men whose lives were cast in the generation between 1867 and 1900, Law should be Evolution from lower to higher, aggregation of the atom into the mass, concentration of multiplicity in unity, compulsion of anarchy in order. (Adams 1961, 232)

On the other hand, William James famously found the atmosphere of evolutionism in his early manhood dangerously suffocating—"certainty was moral death" for him, according to Louis Menand (2001, 75). Still, cultural evolutionism in various forms promoted by Herbert Spencer, William Graham Sumner, and their acolytes seemed to drive all before it in the 1880s; one has only to recall E. L. Youmans's preachings in *Popular Science Monthly* or the enthusiastic American celebration of Spencer during his tour of the East Coast in 1882 (Boller 1969, 47–69).[10]

By the 1890s, even as it seemed to gain popular hegemony, cracks were beginning to surface in the edifice of unilinear cultural evolutionism as accepted and preached by Powell, Brinton, and (less strenuously) Putnam. George Stocking has pointed out that by the mid-1880s, despite youthful marginality and insecurity, Boas insistently raised diffusionist and historicist objections to the precepts and practices of the cultural evolutionists; by 1896 he had gathered together strong arguments (Stocking 1974, 129–30; Document L, this volume).

"The Limitations of the Comparative Method of Anthropology" appeared only two years after Boas's humiliating departure from Chicago a few months following the Fair. Boas intended it as a direct riposte to Brinton's 1895 statement of evolutionist beliefs, "The Aims of Anthropology" (Document K, this volume)—his AAAS presidential address, which in turn had challenged Boas's AAAS paper of 1895, "Human Faculty as Determined by Race."[11] Boas's muted responses to the aging but revered Philadelphian effectively began the overt dismantling of the assumptions of the evolutionist generation, a process that culminated in Boas's immigrant head form study of 1910 and publication of *The Mind of Primitive Man* the next year (Boas 1910, 1911). By then he had become a forceful voice, pronouncing in the seventh chapter of *Primitive Man*: "It appears that serious objections may be made against the assumption of the occurrence of a general sequence of cultural stages among all the races of man." Logic and recent anthropological data had "shaken our faith in the correctness of the evolutionary theory as a whole." Boas was in effect announcing a new program, gradually under construction for twenty-five years, for a historicist and relativist cultural anthropology (Boas 1911, 192–93).[12]

Framing these *fin-de-siècle* institutional and intellectual ferments were the appearances of a new, expanded *American Anthropologist* in 1898 and a new professional organization, the American Anthropological Association, in 1902. Both signaled that the world of locally defined identities that had prevailed before the Chicago Fair was growing insufficient and obsolete. Without agreeing on all points Boas, McGee, and their colleagues began the process of establishing new national patterns of identity, audience, and standards of scholarship for the coming generation of university-trained students (Stocking 1960). In the previous quarter century, only Section H (Anthropology) of the American Association for the Advancement of Science had provided, in August of each year, a national gathering and forum for all students of anthropology. Putnam had served tirelessly as permanent secretary of the AAAS since 1873 (and continued to do so during and after the Chicago Fair), creating an impressive personal network across the natural sciences, folklore, anthropology, and archaeology (Kohlstedt 1976; Kohlstedt et al. 1999). The annual AAAS gatherings, which rotated among northeastern cities, served as vital yet still infrequent opportunities for contact and exposure between the established Fellows and the broader membership in a two-tiered organization; yet loyalties and identities remained dispersed and largely local. Similarly, the Archaeological Institute of America (1879) and the American Folk-Lore Society (1888), both founded in Cambridge, presented variant models of organization, but each assumed that semi-independent local branches would most reliably draw loyalty and enthusiasm. The results were as divergent as individuals and locales.[13]

No formal training existed in any field of anthropology before the end of the nineteenth century. Powell brought with him to the BAE men whose characters and capacities he trusted; like Powell himself, men such as McGee, Mooney, Henshaw, or Cushing were minimally trained but, it was presumed, would learn through experience. Nominally Brinton held the first university post in American anthropology in 1886, but as already mentioned, he neither taught consistently nor trained a single student. Putnam became a Harvard professor of anthropology in 1887 but had neither time nor inclination to teach until his return from Chicago in 1894 (Essay 1, this volume). In sum, the world of American anthropology at the time of the 1893 Fair was professionally inchoate: three centers of institutional power provided few outlets for publication and fewer opportunities for meeting and networking; a highly personalized environment depended on subjective assessments of "character and honesty" rather than formal training or credentials; and its apparently hegemonic intellectual structures were on the verge of collapse.

Most of the papers in this volume began as contributions to a symposium at the Society for American Archaeology 1999 annual meetings in Chicago. All have since been greatly expanded and revised, and we are deeply grateful to the participants for their patience as the project has slowly developed over more than a decade. Some time ago we invited Ira Jacknis to join the conversation with his important piece on anthropological displays at the Chicago Fair; and we have added introductory and substantive materials as seemed appropriate. The structure of the project changed, too, as we came to envision it as a dialogue between the immediate voices of the 1893 Fair and the views of contemporary scholars. Those historical voices come to us in various textual and visual forms: speeches, articles, cartoons, and photographs. We have interspersed these contemporary documents throughout the volume, matching them loosely with the essays; we have also added a special visual interlude of images from the Fair.

The first section of the volume addresses the status of American anthropology in 1893 by examining the three dominant figures of the moment: Powell, Putnam, and Brinton. An intellectual and organizational watershed was approaching for the field. Curtis Hinsley opens with Frederic Putnam's career as a naturalist and anthropologist, his difficulties and successes in managing the Department of Ethnology at the Fair, and his disappointments in the aftermath. Putnam struggled to satisfy his aims for both scientific integrity and popular education. Despite the overt racism in some of the cartoons and commentary of the time, at the anthropological exhibits on the Midway Plaisance—over which Putnam exercised nominal control—and those in and around his Anthropology Building, there may have grown greater tolerance in the strolling crowds than has been generally recognized. Accompanying the essay are Franz Boas's 1894 "Ethnology at the Exposition" (Document A) and two more texts from the time: Putnam's 1891 address to the businessmen of Chicago's Commercial Club; and a newspaper account of his Department of Ethnology (Documents B and C).

The puzzle of Daniel Brinton's position in anthropology, and particularly at the Fair's International Congress of Anthropology, is the central concern of the second Hinsley essay. Deeply respected for his multifield anthropological endeavors, Brinton nonetheless held by the final decade of his life theoretical positions that were increasingly open to challenge, especially by the young and outspoken Boas—Putnam's chief assistant at the Fair. The congress, held in the last week of August 1893, presented a remarkable moment of social and intellectual positioning, in which Brinton held a central place. Brinton's presidential address to the congress (described in Document D) serves as companion to the essay, and Wilcox provides a fascinating analysis of the people who attended the congress (Essay 2 appendix).

Next we examine the experiences of anthropologists on the fairgrounds. Frank Cushing arrived at the Chicago Fair with his wife, Emma, in late June and stayed until early September, keeping a daily diary of events, movements, individuals, and his own thoughts and reactions. In the third essay David Wilcox introduces the always fascinating anthropologist in "Anthropology in a Changing America: Interpreting the Chicago 'Triumph' of Frank Hamilton Cushing," followed by annotated excerpts of Cushing's diary of the Fair (Document E), an eyewitness account of activities in and around the exhibits and beyond the fairgrounds. Through Cushing's eyes appear the personalities not only of American anthropology but of Chicago society and commerce. His diary provides a rare and revealing look at the intersections of urban business, science, and culture at the height of the Gilded Age. Publication of the diary here for the first time also privileges us with insight into Cushing's private thoughts at a moment of professional and personal triumph for this unique, often misunderstood figure in the history of American anthropology. We explore Cushing's experiences further with his official account of these months (Document F) and a *Washington Post* description of his exhibits when they returned to the National Museum the following year (Document G).

Cushing's official function at Chicago was to finish several anthropological displays for the U.S. National Museum. In his close, fully illustrated study of the anthropological displays at the Fair, "Refracting Images" (Essay 4), Ira Jacknis examines the multiple visual representations of cultural objects, with special attention to architectural structures (buildings, villages, and ruins), costumed mannequins, and the use of photographs, casts, drawings and models in presenting to the fairgoing public these "museum-made surrogates" of cultural lifestyles. He places these practices in the multiple contexts of developing museum practice, the growth of anthropological and museological professionalism, the "second lives" or subsequent uses of these displays, and the influence of the Chicago experiences on subsequent exposition and museum display techniques. Jacknis suggests that the development of the "life group" should be understood in connection with the broader fascination, in photography and the nascent moving film technologies, with sequences of locomotion and the phenomenon of arrested motion—that is, the new challenge of producing narrative from single pictures of gesture, body position, and artifact. "All we have in culture and in cultural representation," he concludes, "are acts of interpretation"; the Chicago occasion offered, in anthropology and more generally, an "endless profusion of versions and simulacra."

A few anthropologists came to Chicago as institutionally established figures; most, however, came only with ambitions and dreams, hoping to network, show their collections or give a paper, and establish connections with patrons or professional gatekeepers. James Snead's "Relic

Hunters in the White City" (Essay 5) draws our attention to two such lesser known but revealing figures in early southwestern archaeology: Richard Wetherill and Warren King Moorehead. Their distinctly different experiences at the Fair—Moorehead ran into serious, debilitating conflict with Putnam, while Wetherill laid the groundwork for a decade of patronage with the brothers Talbot and Frederick Hyde—had both long- and short-term effects on their careers. While tracing their separate trajectories, Snead also raises the curtain on two other issues of significance at the Chicago Fair: the relationship between science and commerce—display and sale of collections—and the important but often overlooked factor of personal friendship or dislike. The Chicago Fair, he concludes, was an arena in which "complex interactions over artifacts and collections grew particularly sharp and clear," and where the differences between the ideology of professional science, as frequently expressed by Putnam, Boas, and others, differed markedly from the circumstances and dreams of some lesser known individuals. Snead's essay is paired with Frank Cushing's previously unpublished catalog of the C. D. Hazzard collection of artifacts (Document H), which were displayed in the popular model cliff dwelling near the Anthropology Building, and with Moorehead's on-the-spot description of the anthropology exhibits (Document I).

The early and halting growth of anthropology in Chicago in the wake of the 1893 Fair is the subject of Don McVicker's "Patrons, Popularizers, and Professionals" (Essay 6), in which he gives special consideration to two individuals: Frederick V. Starr and George A. Dorsey. McVicker explains that Starr, cut off from acceptance by Putnam, Boas, and the main currents of professionalization, built a career on travel and popular presentation of anthropology but failed to develop a viable program at the new University of Chicago; while Dorsey, who was Putnam's first doctoral graduate and who in 1897 succeeded Holmes as curator at the Field Museum, became an "avid collector and patronage seeker" for the Chicago business elite. McVicker's essay demonstrates as well the differing interests and styles among early Chicago patrons who were inspired by anthropology at the Fair, notably Allison V. Armour and Edward E. Ayer. We have included as well (Document J) excerpts from a newspaper report recounting the popular story of Marshall Field's million-dollar gift to establish the Field Museum and presenting the opening day speech of the museum's first director, Frederick J. V. Skiff.

In the final essay, "Going National," David Wilcox extends our analyses of anthropology at the 1893 Chicago World's Fair (and its immediate aftermath) by means of a series of five-year "structural moments" reaching well into the first quarter of the twentieth century. While, as he notes, the stability and paradigmatic clarity that had been reached by 1925 in the various subfields of anthropology could not possibly have been imagined at the time of the Fair, geographic and institutional patterns began to emerge by the turn of the century that can be traced forward to these developments. Wilcox employs four indices of maturation: competing research agendas; firmer institutional structures in universities and museums; a cadre of like-minded individuals; and regularized professional organizations, meetings, and publication outlets. In the end, he demonstrates, it can be argued that the Chicago Fair stood as the historical fulcrum, a point of leverage, that moved nineteenth-century anthropology from a relatively inchoate world of ambitions and interests to a recognizably modern condition of professional organization and disciplinary coherence. The accompanying items (Documents K and L) present the dueling visions of Daniel Brinton and Franz Boas in 1895 and 1896 as a focused demonstration of the impending changes in anthropology that emerged from the Fair.

While the substantive scholarly essays of our volume shed new, fascinating historical light on anthropology at the height of Gilded Age America, for fairgoers of the time the Chicago Fair was an intensely visual experience; accordingly we have included a selection of visual impressions that both reflect and augment (and possibly complicate) our literary accounts. Additionally, the appendices and tabular information present rich new material for further analysis of the backgrounds, social and professional identities, and levels of engagement of the hundreds of individuals who attended the Fair and chose to associate themselves with the diverse fields coming to be known collectively as the new social science of "anthropology." Finally, an afterword and consolidated bibliography provide further suggestions regarding today's scholarly status quo and future directions for inquiry into the complex institutional and intellectual roots of American anthropology.

Notes

1. In recent years Goode has been both revived and criticized. For a particularly useful and trenchant critique of Goode's notion of museums as vehicles of social control or, as he termed them, "passionless reformers," see Bennett 1995, 20–21, 24; cf. Kohlstedt 1991 and Genoways and Andrei 2008.

2. Rydell's emphasis.

3. For a revealing case study of local resentment of Washington's intrusive "government science," see McCusick 1991.

4. Several years later Powell complained regretfully that "our archaeologic institutes, our universities, and our scholars are threshing again the straw of the Orient for the stray grains that may be beaten out, while the sheaves of anthropology are stacked all over this continent; and they have no care for the grain which wastes while they journey beyond the seas." For his part, Putnam advised the AIA that "the widest field for the study of Ethnology is in America, where the study ought to begin" (Powell 1890b, 652).

5. The Women's Anthropological Society of America (WASA) was formed in 1885 and existed independently until merging with the all-male ASW in 1899. Forty-nine women joined at that time (Lurie 1966; Lamb 1906).

6. From the beginning of the BAE until his health collapsed in 1890 and he moved to Hawaii in 1893, Henshaw served as Powell's closest colleague in the Bureau, largely responsible for the early versions of what became (under Frederick Hodge's editorship) the *Handbook of American Indians North of Mexico* (1907, 1910) and the linguistic classification around which Mason organized the Smithsonian's anthropological exhibit in Chicago. Powell felt that Henshaw's training in biological taxonomy was essential to his new science of anthropology. Many years later C. Hart Merriam (a lifelong friend of Henshaw) wrote that Powell intended Henshaw to succeed him as director of the Bureau of Ethnology (Merriam 1930).

7. The list is in *American Anthropologist* o.s. 1 (1888): 4.

8. Between 1879 and 1892 Mason provided an annual review of anthropology to the Smithsonian's *Annual Reports*. Today these reviews are invaluable sources of names, publications, and events for the period. In his report for 1891 Mason listed eighteen journals for "those who desire to commence a course of anthropological studies"; fourteen were European, while only four were American: *American Anthropologist, American Naturalist, Popular Science Monthly,* and *Science*.

9. The year 1888 also saw the formation of the National Geographic Society by Alexander Graham Bell and his father-in-law Gardiner Greene Hubbard, and the launch of its journal, *National Geographic*, under the editorship of geomorphologist William Davis. However, the society and the journal dealt largely with issues of geography and geomorphology; they did not become allied with anthropology until well into the twentieth century, when they increased public awareness of human diversity—though it was a sometimes skewed awareness (Lutz and Collins 1993).

10. On Powell's critical adaptation of Spencer's principles, see Hinsley 1996c, 125–43.

11. On the ambiguous Brinton-Boas relationship, see Darnell 1988, 64–81; a recent review of Boas's positions in counterpoint to Brinton (and a severe critique of Brinton) is Baker 2010, 117–55.

12. The indispensable source on Boas's trajectory in this regard remains Stocking 1974; more specifically, see Stocking 1968.

13. The standard history of the American Folk-Lore Society is Zumwalt 1988; see especially her informative account of the conflict between the national organization and the Chicago Folk-Lore Society over the representation of folklore studies as science or literature at the International Folk-Lore Congress during the Chicago Fair (22–30). On the "bewildering mixture" of professions, interests, and motivations that constituted American folklore studies in this period, see the insightful and careful analysis in Bendix 1997, 119–53 (quoted phrases on 119 and 122). On the AIA, see Snead 2002b and Dyson 1999.

ABBREVIATIONS

AA *American Anthropologist*
AAA American Anthropological Association
AAAS American Association for the Advancement of Science
AES American Ethnological Society
AFS American Folk-Lore Society
AIA Archaeological Institute of America
ANB *Anthropology News Bulletin*
AMNH American Museum of Natural History, New York
AMS *American Men of Science*
ASW Anthropological Society of Washington
BAE Bureau of American Ethnology, Smithsonian Institution
CDAB *Cambridge Dictionary of American Biography*
DAB *Dictionary of American Biography*
DNB *Dictionary of National Biography*
FMA Field Museum of Natural History Archives
FWPP F. W. Putnam Papers, Harvard University Archives
IDA *International Directory of Anthropologists*
NAA National Anthropological Archives
NCAB *National Cyclopedia of American Biography*
NLA Newberry Library Archives, Chicago
SIA Smithsonian Institution Archives
SWM Southwest Museum, Los Angeles
USGS United States Geological Survey
USNM United States National Museum, Smithsonian Institution
WASA Women's Anthropological Society of America
WCE World's Columbian Exposition
WCEI *World's Columbian Exposition Illustrated*
WWWA *Who Was Who in America*

ESSAY ONE

Anthropology as Education and Entertainment
Frederic Ward Putnam at the World's Fair

CURTIS M. HINSLEY

> Until the close of the Fair Chicago will be the centre
> of the United States, the only place at present where
> brains can be turned into money.
>
> —Kate Field to Phoebe Hearst, August 27, 1893

In 1909 Franz Boas identified three men as the "fathers" of American anthropology—Major John W. Powell, Daniel G. Brinton, and Frederic W. Putnam. At the opening of the Chicago World's Fair, though, only Putnam stood in a position of professional strength and vigor. By 1893 Powell was approaching a decade marked by physical decline, loss of political and scientific influence, and intellectual sclerosis; he would soon lose control of the U. S. Geological Survey and enter a final, long period of drift in his sinecure at the Bureau of American Ethnology, to his death in 1902. After shepherding the major around the Chicago fairgrounds for four days, William Henry Holmes wrote to his wife: "He is quite weak and I had to take great care not to let him get tired out" (Fernlund 2000, 149). Brinton was the eldest of the three and already in poor health by the time of the Fair, but he still held the esteem and consideration of his contemporaries: he delivered the presidential address to the International Congress of Anthropology in late August at the Fair. However, while he stalwartly upheld the tradition of the nineteenth-century independent scholar, as Regna Darnell has observed, Brinton had already moved toward popular audiences, was wedded (like Powell) to an increasingly outdated evolutionism, and could not in any case call upon the institutional power of museum, university, or government agency to bolster or amplify his positions (Darnell 1998, 105–7, 114, 246–48).

By contrast, Putnam came to Chicago with a growing sense of confidence and position based upon years of museum and field experience. Just over fifty years old, he was veteran curator of the Peabody Museum and recently appointed (1887) professor of anthropology at Harvard when he was named chief of the Department of Ethnology in 1891 for the projected World's Fair. Putnam had every reason to anticipate respect and success in Chicago—his entire career seemed to point to this moment of personal and professional prominence.

Salem, north of Boston in Essex County, Massachusetts, was the pre–Civil War home of Fred Putnam, as it had been home to his family since John Putnam arrived in America in 1640. Three generations of male Putnam forebears had graduated from Harvard, but Fred grew up first under the scientific tutelage of Henry Wheatland, curator of the Essex Institute (now part of the Peabody Museum of Salem), and Putnam always considered Wheatland his first "father in science": "I joined in all his schemes with the enthusiasm and hope of youth," he recalled many years later (Putnam 1893a). The boy's initial work in natural science involved birds and fishes, and his first publication, for the Essex Institute when he was sixteen, was a catalog of the fishes of Essex County. That year he chanced to show Louis Agassiz the institute's collections, after which the nation's most prominent naturalist invited the young man to serve as his assistant at the Museum of Comparative Zoology at Harvard. For the next eight years Putnam studied with Agassiz, Asa Gray, and Jeffries Wyman. He always treasured the experience: "I had a perfect and thorough training under Agassiz, Wyman, and Gray, and it has been my pride in manhood to be able to say that I was their student. . . . The thorough methods of research that I learned during those eight years have given me power in my later undertakings; and it is such methods that I have endeavored to teach to others" (Putnam 1898; cf. Lurie 1960, Dexter 1965a and 1966a).

Putnam's early education deeply impacted his subsequent career at Harvard, Chicago, and elsewhere. First, at the suggestion of Agassiz he attended the Lawrence Scientific School rather than undertaking the standard Harvard curriculum; second, he played a major role in the 1863 student revolt against Agassiz, which sent him back to Salem and Henry Wheatland for ten years; and consequently, Putnam never received an academic degree. He came to regret some of his decisions: as he later explained to Harvard President Charles W. Eliot, regarding the lack of a degree, it was "simply one of those cases where one omits to do in youth what would have proved advantageous later" (Putnam 1898). The suspicion that Putnam possessed an insufficiently broad formal education shadowed him throughout his life, instilling insecurity and caution at critical moments in his professional relationships (Salisbury 1875).

His education was intensely personal and tutorial. As Ed Lurie pointed out some years ago (Lurie 1974), mid-nineteenth-century American natural science education was a hands-on, largely observational and descriptive experience, with little formal classroom instruction and much concentrated, one-on-one field and laboratory demonstration. Robert Bruce further suggested that for such men, "learning on the job under a senior scientist might be called a sort of graduate education" (Bruce 1987, 90). Putnam certainly thought so, and he carried forward the tradition in which he was trained. Joan Mark noted Alfred Kroeber's observation that Putnam was always a natural historian, more comfortable with specimens than with books; she also rightly remarked that Putnam stood "at the end of the natural history tradition in nineteenth-century American anthropology, at the turning point between nineteenth-century archaeology and natural history and the twentieth-century sciences of man" (Mark 1980, 15, 54).

As Margaret Rossiter and others have pointed out, an education like Putnam's was typically male, both paternally and fraternally—a matter of fathers, sons, and brothers (Rossiter 1982). Indeed, "for a woman to aspire to serious scientific work was deemed especially grotesque, unseemly, hopeless, and impermissible" (Bruce 1987, 76). Even a cursory reading of the *National Academy of Sciences Biographical Memoirs* of the period suggests that this educational process served to create alternative fatherhoods and brotherhoods—male professional lineages—that complemented or supplanted biological relations. Men of science adopted other men, and they became mutually integral to identities and careers: Adolph Bandelier referred frequently to his "father [Lewis Henry] Morgan"; late into his life Putnam viewed

Wheatland as his father in science, writing to him at one happy point as "the boy you took under your wing," and was deeply affected at his death just a few months before the Chicago Fair opened in 1893; at a particularly painful and dependent period of his immediate post-Chicago career, Boas signed himself as Putnam's "orphan boy." Putnam's relations with younger (and some older) students were strongly paternal and personal, especially for those without formal training. "Putnam," Douglas Cole observed, "was as concerned with the personal welfare of his protégés as with their scientific work" (Cole 1999, 176), so much so that he loaned emergency funds—to Boas, among others—even when his own finances were uncertain. Dependence sometimes bred expectation, disappointment, thin skin, and strong reactions, as seen in the revolt of Agassiz' young students in 1863 (Lurie 1974) or, several decades later, Putnam's explosive relations with fieldworker Charles C. Abbott (Meltzer 2003; cf. Hinsley 1985, 62–69). In a world of close dependence, sometimes the line between opportunity and exploitation was hard to draw.

To his credit, Putnam largely outgrew the limiting gender bias of his own upbringing, personally encouraging and promoting women in anthropology over the years. From Cornelia Studley (1855–87), whom he eulogized at her early death as "our gentle and gifted associate" (Putnam 1887), to Alice Fletcher (1838–1923), Putnam became "one of the few late nineteenth-century men who facilitated the careers of female investigators" (Rohde 2004, 271; Mark 1988). By 1893 Putnam was pleased to report that "several of my best students are women, who have become widely known by their thorough and important works and publications; and this I consider as high an honor as could be accorded to me" (Dexter 1978, 5). David Browman has demonstrated that the list of Putnam's female students and co-workers was impressively long (Browman 2013 and 2002a, 222–35; cf. Rossiter 1982).

With his appointment as curator of the Peabody Museum in Cambridge in 1874, Putnam began to develop the fieldwork practices that would establish his reputation as a demanding field archaeologist. The first half of the 1880s was the crucial and probably the most enjoyable phase of Putnam's career in field archaeology. In 1880 he was forty-one. His wife, Adelaide, had died the previous year, ending fifteen years of marriage and leaving him with three young children:

daughters Alice and Ethel and son Eben. That summer Putnam joined Charles L. Metz, a physician in Madisonville, Ohio, and Metz's coworker Charles F. Low, at prehistoric Madisonville Cemetery, which Metz had discovered in 1878 (Dexter 1977). Over the next five summers Putnam deepened and extended his collaboration with Metz and Low to include Fort Ancient, the Turner Group, and other sites in the valley of the Little Miami River. He worked incessantly, too, to have both Fort Ancient and the Serpent Mound permanently protected by the state of Ohio, since "all students of American archaeology know [them] to be as important to the history of America as the pyramids of the Nile Valley are to that of Egypt." They became the first two Ohio State Memorials, in 1891 and 1900 (Dexter 1982, 27).

The dynamic of his collaborations with Metz and Low demonstrated Putnam's idea of pursuing and teaching archaeology. Through summertime on-site fieldwork in person and wintertime letters of instruction and encouragement, Putnam taught Metz to clear a site; to "slice and trench" through a mound; to photograph and note relative positions of artifacts and skeletal remains in situ; to handle a working crew; to avoid competitors, curious locals, and especially journalists; to write up field and accession notes; and to pack and ship collections. The following excerpt from one letter to Metz in September 1882 provides a good sense of Putnam's instructional and exhortatory style. Ecstatic over Metz's discoveries in what they were calling the "Turner Group," Putnam advised strongly against collaboration or sharing with any other parties (especially the Smithsonian):

> Don't take any partnership in the work. You know that I have always said that the contents of a mound must be kept as one lot. There are no such things as duplicates. Take away one bead even from a bushel & you have destroyed the fact or rather the evidence to pass down for all time that a bushel of beads was found. The dividing of the contents of a mound between two parties is like dividing a volume of Shakespeare. Each would have some of his plays, but would not know about the others. . . . [A]s long as you stick to me stick close & tight and it will be better for science & for your credit as an archeologist & for this Museum. . . . There are hundreds of mounds in Ohio & I have purposely kept out of the state for years so as to give local societies the

first chance, but you know that they have not done much & that science has not been advanced by their work, except your own society at Madisonville, which has done more through you & Low, than all the rest of the west put together. Now the turn of the wheel has brought you to working in connection with this Museum & you know enough of me by this time to feel sure that what is done through the Museum is done for the one end of scientific advancement of American Archaeology. (Putnam 1882)

In April 1882 Putnam married Esther O. Clarke of Chicago; they honeymooned in southern Ohio, and for the next several years she and the children joined him in summers at the Ohio excavations (Dexter 1982, 24). While he never published a text on archaeological field methods, by 1885 Putnam felt that his Ohio fieldwork had shown the importance of "conducting explorations in a thorough and systematic manner" and "the great advance which had taken place during the last few years in American archaeology, which was at last being studied in a way due to its importance, by a few earnest workers pursuing the investigation with all the methods of science" (American Antiquarian Society 1887, 10)—or as Metz put it more colloquially: "Featherbed archaeologists ought to be squelched" (Metz 1884a). Putnam's phrases indicated the essentials of his new scientific approach: quietly serious workers rather than showy popularizers; purposeful exploration rather than serendipitous, backyard digging; and rigorous, defined contours of investigation devoid of preconceptions.

From this point onward Putnam argued that through his model and sponsorship of field exploration and collecting, the popular image of archaeology as a playground for men of "rashness" and "haste" in judgment was being replaced by a model of caution and moderation (American Antiquarian Society 1885, 22). Others recognized this and agreed: before his departure to Arizona on the Hemenway Southwestern Archaeological Expedition in January, 1886, Frank Cushing wrote to Putnam's close friend Alpheus Hyatt:

I do not think the wonderful systems of research which [Putnam] has been the first to develop in mound exploration, can be too often commented upon. His work in the Ohio mounds must take rank as the first of its kind. . . . No man ought to be allowed to push spade or pickaxe into a western mound or earth-work except as, at least, disciple to the system of research of Prof. F. W. Putnam. (Cushing 1886, cited in Hinsley 1999, 147)

On visiting the Ohio excavations in 1884, Metz reported, even Putnam's arch-competitor W. H. Holmes of the Smithsonian agreed, in somewhat milder terms, that Putnam's work was "very complete & it was done in the only way it should be done" (Metz 1884b; Dexter 1982). Browman has suggested that Putnam's "Peabody Museum method" of stratigraphy laid the groundwork for what later became known as the "Chicago method" of excavation, associated with Fay-Cooper Cole (Browman 2002b). At the same time, Putnam's enthusiastic support of networks of fieldworkers in Ohio and elsewhere was a major stimulus to activity: in 1897 Brinton marveled that "there are now in Ohio 310 persons interested in its archaeology! Can any other state equal this record?"(Brinton 1897, 763).

Putnam's concept of a new scientific practice extended beyond excavation techniques. In letters of instruction and advice to fieldworkers as well as in the detailed instructions he issued to his Chicago Fair field assistants (Johnson 1897–98, 2:320–23), he stressed careful notation, with photographs if possible, and complete retrieval of all elements of an assemblage in relative positions as found (Dexter 1982). Two years after the Fair, for instance, he wrote to Adolph Bandelier, who was exploring in the Andes for Putnam's anthropology department at the American Museum of Natural History, to remind him of the new standards for collecting and of his vision for an exhibit at AMNH. Putnam's close instructions to Bandelier differed little from his advisories to Metz fifteen years before; referring specifically to George Dorsey's Peruvian mummy materials that had been so popular at the Chicago Fair, Putnam was encouraging and respectful but clearly directive to the veteran Bandelier:

> You know what we are after at the American Museum is a thoroughly scientific collection; and we are very anxious that you should make a very large collection from each burial place; it is only in this way that we can illustrate the whole subject. Specimens picked up here and there ... really give us little information of the life history of the people, whereas objects found in each grave when kept together tell

a wonderfully interesting story, and if we thus have the contents of a large number of graves we can reconstruct the past life of the people in a way that never can be done with a heterogeneous collection.

I am very anxious that we should have at the American Museum a collection similar to that I had made for the World's Fair where I showed the contents of over fifty graves from Ancon alone. Each grave had its mummy done up in its wrappings, and all things found about it were arranged around the mummy bundle, just as found in the grave. Each grave was photographed before the bundle & other things were disturbed & thus we were able to rearrange the objects & show them just as they were found. We also placed the mattings, etc., which formed the roof of the grave in proper position; and in this way we gave to the public a pretty good idea of the burial customs as shown by our exploration of that necropolis. (Putnam 1895)

Clearly, the epistolary mode of instruction of the 1870s and 1880s—Putnam's "correspondence school" of anthropology, combined with occasional face- to-face instruction in the museum—remained Putnam's preferred teaching mode well after his appointment as professor in 1887 (Hinsley 1999, 144; cf. Browman 2002a, 217–19). The Harvard professorship did not change the tutoring style with which he was most familiar and comfortable. Classroom teaching was secondary. In the fall of 1890, however, Dorsey and John G. Owens (along with three undergraduate students, including Marshall Saville) forced the issue by enrolling for instruction with Putnam despite the fact that no formal undergraduate or graduate program of anthropology existed at Harvard. Whether this was his idea or theirs is unclear, but Harvard responded by creating the Department of Archaeology and Ethnology. In reality, with his attention soon divided between Chicago and Cambridge, Putnam could give little attention to formal teaching, and both of his graduate students (and Saville) spent the greater part of the next two years collecting in the field for both the Fair and the Peabody. Putnam had great hope and affection for his first students, and while Owens died in Copan three years later, Dorsey brought home important Peruvian collections to Chicago and received the first Harvard PhD in anthropology in 1894. After his return in 1894 from Chicago, and with the important help of Dorsey for two years (until Dorsey's move to the Field Museum in 1896), Putnam began to develop courses of instruction to be effectively melded into the Harvard curriculum.

While formal classroom teaching came slowly, Putnam saw early the need for organization, communication, and publication outlets in science. For more than a quarter century he was indefatigable in promotional activities for natural history and anthropology. From the time he "seceded," as a young man of twenty-four, from Agassiz and the Museum of Comparative Zoology in 1863, Putnam displayed a broad conception of career that included not only fieldwork, museum building, scholarship, and public lecturing but also organization and communication among like-minded natural scientists. Putnam's sense of scientific community was always exceptionally strong. On returning to Salem in 1863 he invited fellow secessionists Alpheus Hyatt, A. S. Packard, and Edward S. Morse to join him as curators at the Essex Institute and, a few years later, the new Peabody Academy of Science in Salem. These young comrades in Darwinian natural science comprised the core of a new national organization, the American Society of Naturalists, and in 1867 Putnam began publishing their journal, the *American Naturalist*. Simultaneously he initiated two related projects: the Naturalists' Directory and the Naturalists' Agency, which were designed respectively to put natural scientists in the United States and overseas in touch with one another, and to serve as a library and clearing house for laboratory and field supplies and scholarly resources.

There were, too, his own commercial ambitions. As one scientific or business activity led to another, Putnam founded the Essex Institute Press in 1866; three years later he took it over personally and renamed it the Salem Press. Over the next twenty-five years Putnam's publishing house printed works of natural historians and scientific reports for, among others, the Peabody Museum in Salem, the Peabody Museum in Cambridge, and the American Association for the Advancement of Science (of which Putnam served as executive director for a quarter century).

In 1873 the Salem Press, employing sixty people, became a privately held stock company, with the majority of stock in the hands of Putnam, his son Eben, cousin Henry W. Putnam, and Salem mentor Henry Wheatland. In 1889 Eben took over management of the press, and after its incorporation the following year he became its treasurer. The press was never a financial success, and as part of his appointment to the Chicago Fair in 1891 Putnam arranged for the anticipated publications of his Department of Ethnology to be printed by his son's company. But just one month before the opening of the Fair, Wheatland suddenly died, throwing the press and Putnam into a financial tailspin. The press failed in a few months, and with its demise—just as the Chicago Fair was opening—Putnam lost his entire investment in the printing enterprise he had founded and became suddenly indebted for an additional ten thousand dollars (Dexter 1985, 7).

Thus as he approached the Chicago prospect in 1891, Putnam was undergoing transitions in his own career while helping to effect a much larger one in the course of American anthropology. His fieldwork years were closing behind him, but partly on the basis of his experiences in field and museum he felt confident that a new scientific enterprise was on the horizon. Moreover, he believed, as he had since the early days with Wheatland, Agassiz, and Wyman, that museums of science were emerging as a vitally important cultural institution for America. Museum exhibits offered the public enlightening and uplifting narratives of human variety and progress; in his constant phrase, valuable "object lessons" were inherent in the artifacts assembled by the curatorial hand and eye. Historian Steven Conn has usefully identified a belief in "object-based knowledge" as a core assumption of the intellectual life of Putnam's generation (Conn 1998); it was certainly a fundamental piece of Putnam's own thinking. In his view, field methods and public instruction in the museum were closely linked, because only rigorous field methods of excavation, recording, and collection could create the rich sets of objects that made reliable and believable narratives possible within the halls of the museum; the same could be said of ethnographic observation and collection. These would be the narratives of the new science of anthropology; as George Brown Goode described them in 1888, the narratives of anthropology lay somewhere between the traditional fields of art and natural history—they told, in Goode's words, "the natural history of civilization" (Conn 1998, 76–77). Or as Putnam put it to Bandelier, the object lessons of museum anthropology would tell the "past life history" of each people, and collectively of humanity.

Putnam thus brought to Chicago a vision rooted in his early education; it wedded field method, museum display, and ethical purpose. After years of marginality in the shadow of Louis Agassiz at Harvard, and constant struggle for even minimal funding in New England, the Chicago Fair beckoned to Putnam as his great opportunity to educate the American public. He would deploy an unprecedented army of fieldworkers throughout the Americas; create a display of the world's peoples, past and present, modeled on the Peabody Museum's principles and practices; and simultaneously lay the cornerstone of a new cultural institution for the city of Chicago. He could hardly have known that he would confront in Chicago conditions that would seriously complicate his intentions.

Chicago and Its Fair

"I shan't go to Chicago, for economy's sake—besides I *must* get to work," William James wrote from Chocorua, New Hampshire, to his expatriate brother Henry in England in September 1893. "But *everyone* says one ought to sell all one has and mortgage one's soul to go there; it is esteemed such a revelation of beauty. People cast away all sin and baseness, burst into tears and grow religious, etc., under the influence!" (Skrupskelis and Berkeley 1997, 286). James's private aspersions on the "windy city"—so labeled by New York newspapers for its social and political bluster, not its weather—were only too common in East Coast circles in the two decades between the Great Fire of 1871 and the Exposition of 1893. The remarkable phoenix-like rebirth of Chicago was grounded in a determination among Chicagoans, almost from the day after the conflagration, to resume their rise to overtake New York and Boston in the East, and St. Louis in the Midwest, as the urban standard for post–Civil War America (Boehm 2004, 23–24; cf. Cronon 1991, 345–50, and Miller 1996, 176–98). There was certainly no disputing the fact of growth: between 1870 and 1890 Chicago was the fastest growing city of America, rising from fifth to second largest in population. At the same time the dizzying expansion in commerce, industry, and immigration came at a time of growing concern, largely expressed by eastern magazines and newspapers, over the corruption, poverty, and social dislocations of America's urban centers in the Gilded Age. Accordingly, Chicago became a constant and easy target of criticism aimed at its supposed penchant for corruption, greed, and growth at any social price—and at its apparent indifference to cultural refinement (Boehm 2004, 31; Horowitz 1976).

The rising business class of Chicago was not insensitive to raised eyebrows in Boston and New York, as demonstrated by the origins of the Commercial Club of Chicago. Cultural historian Lisa Boehm relates that in the fall of 1877 Chicago shoe wholesaler Henry MacFarland had dinner with some Boston business friends at the Boston League Club on Beacon Hill. Anxious to reciprocate but without a corresponding social business club, on his return to Chicago MacFarland raised three thousand dollars from fellow Chicago merchants as an "entertainment fund" and invited the Boston men to visit Chicago. The businessmen from Beantown saw the stockyards, Board of Trade, and business offices and returned to Boston, presumably well impressed. With their remaining funds the Chicagoans formed the permanent business group that became the Commercial Club—dedicated, according to its charter, to "advancing, by social intercourse, and by a friendly exchange of views, the commercial prosperity and growth of the City of Chicago." Over the next two decades the Commercial Club not only expanded into a culturally progressive and engaged organization but also spawned others, such as the Civic Federation (1894) that arose in the heady progressive moment immediately after the World's Fair (Boehm 2004, 72–73). Thus there must have been mixed reactions when, in 1891, another New Englander, Frederic Putnam, made a point of presenting his plans for anthropology at the Fair, and for the museum as a vital cultural institution, to a luncheon meeting of the Commercial Club. On this occasion Putnam pointedly exhorted the businessmen of Chicago that "for the City to longer remain without such a museum seems impossible; and not to take advantage of the golden opportunity now offered for its foundation would simply be choosing to remain in the darkness of ignorance when one of the brightest lights for culture is within reach" (Document B, this volume).

Fairs always seemed a promising strategy of growth and recognition for Chicago. Indeed, throughout the constantly expanding United States of the later nineteenth century, periodic commercial and industrial fairs became a favored means of attracting investment and shaping positive regional images. Determined not to be surpassed, between

1873 and 1890 Chicago held the annual, two-week Inter-State Industrial Exposition every September in a specially designed Exposition Building (modeled on London's Crystal Palace of 1851), on the lakefront where the Chicago Art Institute would later stand. The annual expo was intended primarily to promote regional trade and revenue, and to promote a progressive image for Chicago in the wake of the 1871 fire. While it probably failed in the latter purpose, it did attract some outside revenue (Boehm 2004, 34–35); but the greater service was as an ongoing model and precedent for the 1893 Exposition. Aware that too often "fairs," in Chicago and elsewhere, had been little more than opportunities for encouraging real estate speculation, Chicago business leaders were determined to use such public vehicles for cultural as well as business leverage—and the Inter-State Expo in fact received positive reviews for exhibiting over the years such artists as Whistler, Sargent, Millet, Monet, Pissarro, and Degas.

By the mid-eighties the directors of the annual Inter-State Expo, along with some Chicago politicians and businessmen, began seriously discussing the greater challenge of a world's fair. Energy waxed and waned until the summer of 1889, when Mayor De Witt C. Creiger sponsored the formation of a group of more than two hundred Chicagoans to lobby the U.S. Congress for the anticipated national Columbian celebration. From this group a central organizing committee of thirty-five eventually formed a corporation, initially named the "World's Exposition of 1892," to offer stock in the proposed enterprise (Boehm 2004, 41).

Few took Chicago seriously at first. Andrew Carnegie recalled that "the mention of Chicago as a possible site generally created a smile on the face of the citizens of New York" (quoted in Boehm 2004, 42). But the winter of 1889–90 saw a fierce competition arise among Chicago, New York, St. Louis, and Washington DC for congressional approval to hold the Columbian Exposition. The competition, which culminated in presentations before a Senate Select Committee in January 1890, marked Chicago's open bid for recognition, primarily against New York, as the premier American city. Beneath a veneer of mutual urban respect lay animosities and stereotypes that would persist through the Fair and ultimately contribute to significant structural complications. Both before and after Congress gave its blessing to Chicago on February 24, 1890, the attacks on Chicago's abilities, resources, and pretensions were withering, with East Coast commentators anticipating nothing more than a "cattle show" in the "far-away frame-shanty metropolis, spreading like dandelions over the prairies of Illinois." Charles A. Dana of the New York *Sun* (who also was chairman of the New York group's Building and Site Committee and had personally invested ten thousand dollars in his state's failed effort) editorialized that the people of Chicago "could not build a World's Fair even if they won it" (Brooks 1952, 170; Boehm 2004, 42, 44; Badger 1979, 146). New York was "at first incredulous then exasperated.... She did not love her pushing, energetic sister," suggested another observer (quoted in Badger 1979, 148). But Dana and the critics turned out to be quite wrong: Chicago was coming of age, and from the vantage point of a half century later literary historian Van Wyck Brooks caught well the sense of arrival:

> With the World's Fair of 1893, the old frontier village of Chicago had become a metropolis, a cosmopolis as it were overnight, and there were not wanting those who said it was the heart of the nation already and would soon be the national centre of letters and art. Only thirty years before a wilderness of mud-flats strewn with shanties along the silent lake-front, with a few flimsy stores and wooden sidewalks ... it had passed rapidly through the phase of a struggling, straggling prairie town and was now a city of canyons and towering cliffs. (Brooks 1952, 163)

Still, Brooks was amused to note, there were those transplanted New Englanders in Chicago who at least for a season "refused to change their clocks from Boston time"; more important, some Washington politicians continued to doubt Chicagoans' abilities to put together a respectable fair. Congress had been swayed chiefly by the prodigious initial fundraising among Chicago's business elite, but still the financial promise did not seem sufficient. The grudging tone of President Benjamin Harrison's first pronouncement of April 25, 1890, did not go unnoticed, and Congress expressed its own doubt by insisting on funding a National Commission for the Fair—to represent the "national interests" and to oversee the local Chicago World's Fair committee structure and its decisions. This was a fateful insistence, for the arrangement promised to create endless dilemmas of dual authority—and it did (Badger 1979, 53–61). Not until November 1890 did the National Commission (made up of one Republican and one Democrat from each state) give its approval to the plans of the Local Commission—at which point Harrison finally, on December 24, issued his presidential proclamation that the World's Columbian Exposition would open in Chicago two and a half years hence, on May 1, 1893, and close on October 31.

The political process had taken nearly a year, pushing the Fair back accordingly. Ominously, from this point the Chicago World's Fair went forward under a dual authority structure: on the local level, the directorate of the Local Commission (headed by President Harlow N. Higinbotham), which was in turn derived from the stockholders of the World's Columbian Exposition Company (the Chicago investors); and a national oversight structure, the Executive Committee (including Director-General Colonel George R. Davis) of the congressionally appointed National Commission. As Lisa Boehm concludes, "Congress' continued interest in the most mundane aspects of the fair reflected a distrust of Chicago fair officials, and a continued disbelief that this seemingly backwater town had the cultural resources to produce such an important spectacle" (Boehm 2004, 49). Right to the close of the Fair, the split authority would complicate and delay hundreds of decisions—from opening on Sunday and placement of buildings to the management and character of the human exhibits.

Putnam's Vision of Anthropology at the Fair

From his earliest presentations in 1890 and through all the changes and challenges of the next three years, Putnam's original vision for anthropology at the Fair remained clear and consistent, even as his strategies toward implementation changed. The core of Putnam's vision advanced three related arguments. The first presented an evolutionary and historical framework for anthropology at Chicago. Putnam contended that in order to understand and appreciate the astounding material and moral progress of American civilization (and by extension European civilization as well) in the four hundred years since Columbus first made landfall in 1492, the Chicago Fair required a comparative demonstration of the cultural state of the western hemisphere in Columbus's time. Laying out his vision to the Exposition

Company's Committee on Liberal Arts in September 1891, Putnam urged that a celebration of the heights of nineteenth-century civilization would be unconvincing and hollow without simultaneously demonstrating the low cultural baseline of North, Central, and South America at the time of contact. Only through such comparison, by means of the descendents of the American indigenes of Columbus's time, could contemporary fairgoers comprehend how far American civilization had come:

> What, then, is more appropriate, more essential, than to show in their natural conditions of life the different types of peoples who were here when Columbus was crossing the Atlantic Ocean and leading the way for the great wave of humanity that was soon spread over the continent and forced those unsuspecting peoples to give way before a mighty power, to resign their inherited rights, and take their chances for existence under the laws governing a strange people? We know the results, and we know well that four hundred years has [sic] brought the last generation upon the stage of action, when it will be possible to bring together the remnants of the native tribes, with probably a few exceptions in South America, in anything approaching purity of stock, or with a precise knowledge of the ways of their ancestors. These peoples, as great nations, have about vanished into history, and now is the last opportunity for the world to see them and to realize what their condition, their life, their customs, their arts were four centuries ago. The great object lesson then will not be completed without their being present. Without them the Exposition will have no base. It will show the material prosperity and the development of our race in the arts and in culture, but it will have no beginning; it will be a monument standing upon nothing, so far as concerns America of 400 years ago; for it will be showing simply America of today. (Putnam 1891h)

Putnam then painted for the Liberal Arts committee the picture of a charming "ramble through a wooded isle" on the fairgrounds, with Natives from the Americas working quietly in their houses, far removed from the modernity of the Machinery Building and the bustle of the industrial, civilized parts of the exposition. Models of Central American and southwestern ruins would grace the pathways. "After such a stroll amid the scenes I have only briefly sketched," the professor concluded, "one will visit the other departments of the Exposition with singular feelings and with an appreciation which could only be aroused by such contrasts" (Putnam 1891h).

Putnam's second argument hit closer to Chicago sensibilities. In various forums, public and private, he made it clear that the Chicago World's Fair must not come across as a strictly commercial enterprise. Sufficient attention and funding must be devoted to higher, disinterested human affairs, especially the concerns and advances of science, in order to rise above the predictable East Coast accusations of cattle- town provincialism. Putnam positioned himself, in fact, as a Boston spokesman for the Chicago Fair who would reassure eastern audiences of the higher purposes of the Chicago Exposition (Putnam 1891l); to the same end, he consistently defined his Department of Ethnology as the only truly disinterested division of the Exposition, a locus of higher study and noble purpose in a display world of commercial self-promotion. Commercial exhibits he labeled the "material" aspects of the Fair, and he lectured Director-General Davis (a fellow Massachusetts native) that because of his Department M (Ethnology), "notwithstanding the immense material involved in the Exposition, . . . the higher aims of life as represented by pure science are not to be omitted at the World's Columbian Exposition" (Putnam 1892a). He reminded Davis, too, that the motto finally chiseled into the Anthropology Building, "Man and His Works," was chosen as a way of "acknowledging the claims of pure science on the Exposition grounds" (Putnam 1893e). And even though the Department of Ethnology officially included the exhibits on what became the controversial Midway Plaisance (discussed later in this essay), Putnam assured Davis in the heady and idealistic summer days of 1891 that "schemes for private ends" would not be considered in his department, and those "of the popular amusement character could not be tolerated" (Putnam 1891d). The Department of Ethnology would hold aloft the torch of science on the shores of Lake Michigan (see Documents A and B).

The third part of Putnam's vision was a new museum of natural history and anthropology for Chicago. As early as May 1890 he imagined a new institution that would emerge from the Exposition, just as the South Kensington Museum had grown directly from the Crystal Palace in 1851 and the U.S. National Museum had formed from the massive collections inherited after the Philadelphia Centennial of 1876 (Dexter 1970, 21). Indeed, Putnam made clear that establishment of a museum was the major condition of his accepting the position of chief of the Department of Ethnology in 1891: he could not devote three years of his career, he reminded Davis more than once, to putting together a six-month display—a temporary "bazaar" or "tableau" of anthropology, in his words (Dexter 1970, 23–24) —without reasonable assurance that the collections would become central to a permanent public institution for Chicago. Like his museum contemporary, Goode of the National Museum, Putnam subscribed to the belief in museums as "passionless reformers," vehicles of mental and spiritual improvement for America's growing industrial class (Bennett 1995, 20–21; Kohlstedt 1991). But as we have seen, it was also a question of cultural pride for the business class of Chicago. Expanding his case for the museum as a cultural and educational institution, Putnam gave heartfelt expression—in words that could have been as readily spoken by the first secretary of the Smithsonian, Joseph Henry—to a firm belief in the edifying and civilizing influence of science museums:

> It is beyond question that a love of nature is inherent in mankind, and is shown alike by the savage, the child, and the cultured man and woman. Through this natural tendency, properly fostered and directed, a people may be led to feel an intelligent interest in all the forms, existing and extinct, of the animal and vegetable kingdoms; as well as in the structure and formation of the earth on which we live. Many an indifferent idler straggling into a well-arranged museum goes forth with new ideas and fresh interests. When this intelligent interest is once aroused, it incites enquiry and research and often brings energy and brightness into an otherwise aimless and weary life. By a series of object lessons, often taken unknowingly at first, the person becomes a student to a greater or lesser extent and the process of a refining culture is begun which cannot fail to result in benefit to the community. (Putnam 1891k; cf. Hinsley 1996c, 38–39)

Putnam reminded Chicago's business leaders, too, that an early opportunity had been lost with the destruction of the Museum of the Chicago Academy of Sciences in the fire of 1871, and he did not hesitate to say that it was the city's "disgrace" that the academy's collections had not received a new museum home in two decades. Putnam knew the history well, for his mentor Agassiz had spurred the development of the Chicago Academy in 1857, a fellow student of Wheatland and Agassiz had been its museum director before the 1871 fire, and at a later point Putnam himself had been invited to Chicago to reorganize and direct the academy. Chicago natural science already had deep Boston roots (Putnam 1893c).

The response of the Exposition Company—and, importantly, all of the prominent Chicago newspapers—was strongly positive and gratifying, at least through 1891. Chicagoan William T. Baker, president of the World's Columbian Exposition Company, took up the project as his own cause, promising to gather financial support and predicting "the greatest collection of its kind in the world." To his wife Putnam exuded confidence: "I have carried the fort by storm. The committees have agreed to all my plans, have backed me up right through and said that I have hit the nail on the head" (Dexter 1970, 22). Unfortunately, with the illness and resignation of Baker in August 1892, and the onset of economic depression as the Fair neared, the road to a museum would become more difficult; but initially at least, the way seemed smooth.

Putnam's correspondence and speeches reveal that at every stage of promotion and preparation beforehand, and active direction of the Department of Ethnology during the Fair itself, the Harvard professor tirelessly advanced his final goal of a museum for Chicago. "I have from the very first worked with this plan in view," he reminded Davis at the end of September 1893, "never for an instant forgetting it in my correspondence or on any opportunity which occurred for furthering the cause, and have always insisted that the museum is a certainty . . . a Museum of Natural Science which is to be established in Chicago as a memorial of the Exposition" (Putnam 1893d). By the time the anthropology exhibits were stabilized in late summer, the Fair was already half over, and Putnam began turning his attention to arrangements for keeping the collections, through gift or purchase, for the new museum of natural history and anthropology. At the end of August 1893 he circulated a letter to all foreign and state exhibitors assuring them that any exhibits donated to the proposed museum would be safely preserved (Dexter 1970, 24). In September Davis became chair of the committee to secure the Exposition exhibits; he immediately appointed Putnam in his place. By the end of September, with the close of the Fair still a month away, cards of commitment began to appear on the displays, indicating an intended destination that did not yet exist: the Columbian Memorial Museum of Natural History. The museum idea was always at the forefront of Putnam's thoughts.

Did Putnam expect to become director of the new Columbian Museum? In his thoughtful review of the history of Putnam's campaign for the institution that became the Field Museum, Ralph Dexter suggested that Putnam "secretly hoped" to become its first director but "never committed himself on that point" (Dexter 1970, 21). Douglas Cole similarly suggested (1999, 157) that Putnam's desire for the directorship of the new museum crossed the intentions of the new trustees. But neither Cole nor Dexter actually cited evidence of such a desire, in either Putnam's or Boas's records. The truth is, Putnam was ambiguous and coy on the matter, and consequently there is evidence both to support and to doubt the surmise. On the one hand, on several public occasions Putnam described an ideal director whose experience and qualities closely resembled his own. For example, in the last month of the Fair Putnam wrote to Charles L. Hutchinson, president of the Corn Exchange Bank of Chicago, member of the powerful Exposition Directory, and chairman of its Committee on Liberal Arts, once more outlining a vision for the museum, reminding Hutchinson that he (Putnam) had originated the museum idea, and even appending a draft set of by-laws. On this occasion Putnam emphasized that the museum must be planned with care, with no false steps at the outset, that "its base must be science and its purpose the giving of knowledge pure as crystal," and that leadership of men "who are known to be worthy and capable of the great work entrusted to them" was the key to success. Interestingly, retained with a copy of the Hutchinson letter in Putnam's papers at Harvard, and presumably originally attached to it, was a laudatory recommendation of Putnam by "J. H. H." (possibly Chicago journalist James H. Haynie) that rhetorically asked: "What brain [is] better fitted to guide this immense undertaking than that of the Chief of Anthropology, Prof. F. W. Putnam of Harvard University?" (Putnam 1893f).

On the other hand, Putnam displayed genuine reservations about

Chicago. He delayed moving with his wife (a native of Chicago) and children from Cambridge and shifting his World's Fair base from the Peabody Museum until October 1892—only six months before the opening—and he went with a specific, one-year leave of absence from Harvard that required his return at the start of 1894. When the Fair closed—but months before the museum directorship was given to Frederick J. V. Skiff—Putnam worked strenuously to meet that deadline, turning down most social engagements in Chicago from the end of the Fair through the Christmas holiday season. Most tantalizingly, in mid-October, about the same time as the letter to Hutchinson, Putnam raised the issue with Harvard president Charles W. Eliot (who had written to complain of the high cost of Harvard's display at the Fair!):

> I presume you have noticed various items in the papers relating to my staying in Chicago and taking charge of the Columbian Museum. All that I have done thus far is to act as the head of this new institution in getting it properly organized and in securing material for it from the various exhibits.... I have not committed myself in any way as to the future. Of course the temptation is very great, but so is my love for the Peabody Museum. As soon as I can leave things here after the close of the Fair I shall go to Cambridge, although I may have to return here again. (Putnam 1893t)

Despite the coyly balanced language to Eliot, Putnam's attachment to the Peabody was sincere and profound. Four years later, when Morris K. Jesup tried to hire him away to the American Museum of Natural History in New York, Putnam negotiated for a half-time split with the Peabody (Freed 2012, 145–46). This time he explained to President Eliot that the Peabody was, after all, the work of his life: "I look on it as my child and cannot be parted from it, however it might be for my personal advantage to do so" (Putnam 1897). Less than a decade later he arranged similarly to divide his time between the Peabody and Phoebe Hearst's new anthropology department at Berkeley. Whatever the temptations, and however great may have been his personal or professional ambitions for institutionalizing anthropology, Putnam could never abandon his museum child.

Putnam came to Chicago with a strong and appealing vision for putting the advances of anthropology on display. In the early months, when ambitions for the Fair ran freely, he persuaded the local business and political patrons of the Chicago enterprise of the importance of a commitment to the "higher ideals" of science in Jackson Park, and he launched an effective campaign for a new natural history and anthropology museum that would be worthy of Chicago's pretensions to urbane culture. In the twenty-seven months between his appointment and the opening of the Fair, however, Putnam learned the painful difference between vision and actualization.

Putnam's Anthropology Exhibits

For most of the 27 million visitors who came to the Chicago World's Fair the experience was a matter of days, perhaps a week. But for Putnam and dozens of other organizers and officials, the Fair was a phase of life, an "event" that began sometime in early 1891 and ended about three years later. Furthermore, even into its middle period, and for months on end of preparation, the Fair was always a work in progress, with constant adjustments, additions, deletions, and bewildering changes in policy and personnel. Putnam's Department M (Ethnology) was no exception—indeed, it was arguably among the most tumultuous divisions of the Fair. Five decades ago Ralph Dexter reviewed the hindrances and insults of Putnam's time in Chicago (Dexter 1966c) and concluded, rightly, that they were maddeningly many.

In accord with his vision for the Fair, and with a promised budget of $100,000 (Rosenberg 2008, 253), Putnam formulated plans for an ambitious indoor-outdoor exhibition of the ethnography and archaeology of the Americas. The indoor anthropology exhibits were originally intended to occupy 160,000 square feet of the immense, centrally located Manufactures and Liberal Arts Building. Following the display techniques he had developed at the Peabody Museum, here Putnam planned to include privately owned collections, exhibits contributed by U.S. states and foreign governments, and most important, the new materials gathered by his force of more than one hundred fieldworkers dispersed throughout the hemisphere—the Department of Ethnology's "special exhibits." After circulating a call for exhibits in June 1892, Putnam became the victim of his own success: an immense amount of material flowed into Jackson Park for his Department of Ethnology. Together with the even greater mass of largely commercial exhibits in the Liberal Arts Department that battled for space in the Manufactures and Liberal Arts Building, this situation eventually forced construction of a separate structure, which Putnam named the Anthropology Building—placed, however, in the southeast corner of the fairgrounds, easily overlooked by most visitors. Fair officials hoped to relieve the potential congestion of Manufactures by removing all the Liberal Arts and Ethnology exhibits to the new building. In the end, though, only certain overflow Liberal Arts exhibits—including natural history and American history, which thereby became officially catalogued in the Department of Ethnology—joined Putnam's anthropology exhibits in the new edifice.

Due to the complex decision-making processes of the Chicago Fair—always bedeviled by the divided and competing authorities of Director-General Davis and Exposition Director Higinbotham—all of these decisions were badly delayed, and both Putnam and Boas showed increasing anxiety and anger. In November 1892—only six months before the opening—Putnam was protesting vigorously against delays, lack of workrooms, and especially the uncertainty surrounding the ultimate location of his anthropology exhibits. Under intense pressure from his exhibitors—who naturally wanted some sense of the placement of their collections—Putnam began to feel his own honor and reputation at stake, as time seemed to be "just slipping away" (Putnam 1892a). As the last weeks of 1892 came and went, Putnam still thought that his always expanding indoor anthropology exhibits, stashed on arrival in various holding places in Jackson Park, would have to be squeezed into a steadily diminishing space in Manufactures and Liberal Arts.

He was thrilled to learn in December, then, that he would have a separate Anthropology Building, for which he had been lobbying since August. But for the next six months the Construction Department drove him to further distraction as work delays (including a strike) kept the new building from being ready for visitors until July 4, when the Fair was already one third gone. To make matters worse, within one eight-month period Putnam was forced to move his own office nine times; desperate for storage space, he managed to secure a dairy barn as an annex, but was later displaced for a cheese exhibit. As spring passed, the Fair opened, and construction of his building still dragged on, Putnam became uncharacteristically sarcastic: "Feeling confident that a detailed report of the trials and struggles of the Chief of Department M during the month of May would prove very harrowing to the nerves of those who might take the trouble of reading it," he reported to Davis in early June 1893, "I think best to make the story brief. If it were not in defence of my own reputation I would not trouble you with any complaints" (Putnam 1893a, 1). A month later the story was even worse: "Never before have I had to contend with such difficulties, such inefficiency of workmen and lack of cooperation. I have never in all my experience seen so little accomplished by workmen and so much time wasted by correspondence and by requisitions" (Putnam 1893b, 1). As a consequence, visitors in the first two months of the Fair saw only the outdoor anthropology exhibits—construction of which was also delayed, however, because the Construction Department had not graded the shoreline of South Pond. "The construction department," moaned Boas, "*always* leaves us in the lurch" (Cole 1999, 154). Disgusted, some of Putnam's private and government exhibitors withdrew; but even halfway through the six-month Fair others took their places. In the final days before opening his Anthropology Building, Putnam reported with outrage that "college professors and their wives, and other gentlemen and ladies" did the final dusting and cleaning preparations. Putnam particularly praised Boas's indefatigable physical labor (Putnam 1893j).

The Anthropology Building finally opened on July 4—one of the most crowded days of the Fair—with a first-day building visitation of more than 25,000. Anthropology's interior exhibit space was 60 percent less than originally promised, however; and the Fair was already one third over. After reviewing the chaotic story of the Anthropology Building and its exhibits, it is difficult to disagree with Douglas Cole's conclusion, in his study of Boas's early career, that "Putnam had been squeezed out, buffeted about by more worldly and self-assertive chiefs of departments and disliked by Director Harlow N. Higinbotham, who never bothered to visit the building" (Cole 1999, 156; cf. Fagin 1984, Jacknis 1991). Still, by the beginning of August, when he was at last given direct responsibility for the Anthropology Building, Putnam felt that the building was finally under his control: "Every ship needs a captain, and now that the Chief is something more than a title there is hope that the remainder of the voyage will be a calm and prosperous one," he reflected to Davis. Now, halfway through the six-month Fair, Putnam's customary optimism had returned:

> The department as a whole, so far as exhibits are concerned, is now very satisfactory to me and I feel rewarded for all the time and labor and patience which have been expended upon it. I feel that long after the troublesome financial difficulties have been overcome and forgotten, and the Exposition itself has become a memory, this department will still live in the annals of science, and its good work will still go on by the development of interest which it has awakened in this science; and it is hoped that the larger part of the collections will be preserved as a museum of natural sciences in Chicago which shall be an everlasting memorial of the Exposition. (Putnam 1893k)

The indoor displays of the Anthropology Building were not even the major part of Putnam's plan, though. It was the outdoor exhibits that Putnam considered his personal contribution to exposition anthropology, his "pet scheme" and deepest commitment, in which he invested a great deal of money, energy, and reputation (Putnam 1891g). He called the proposed ethnographic village his "Sub-department for the Representation of the Native Peoples of America" and promised that it would be "an exhibit illustrative of all the native peoples of America (so far as possible) by a representation of their actual home life, their dwellings with full equipment, etc," with groups of artisans—silversmiths, weavers, potters—from throughout the western hemisphere on active display. This was to be the heart of his "great object lesson" for modern America; as he predicted to the Exposition's Committee of Liberal Arts in 1891, the ethnographic village "will prove to be of the greatest popular interest and at the same time be regarded as an essential and appropriate display," the necessary basis for understanding and fully appreciating the industrial and aesthetic accomplishments of modern life on display everywhere else in the park.

Like so many aspects of Putnam's department in the two years leading up to the Fair, here again simply determining a location for the ethnographic village proved daunting, despite Putnam's repeated pleas for a clear decision—which only added to his sense of uncertainty. As mentioned, he originally envisioned his outdoor village occupying the Wooded Isle, in the center of the fairgrounds and across the lagoon from the Manufactures and Liberal Arts Building, where the Department of Ethnology exhibits would be housed. Along the shores of the romantic isle, set off from the busy scenes of modern industry, he would display the indigenous peoples of the American hemisphere on a north-south axis along the water's edge, with appropriate plantings for each cultural or geographic area. Putnam was particularly anxious and insistent that his live exhibits have access to water, since he also hoped to have many distinctive coastal and lacustrine groups. Furthermore, water demonstrations—rowing, racing, kayaking—would be appropriate as featured events on the edge of Lake Michigan. As early as the summer of 1891 Putnam felt great concern that the anthropology exhibits be centrally located on the fairgrounds; he admitted to Davis that he was "heartsick" at the thought that the Department of Ethnology would be "overlooked and shadowed" by the "more stirring accomplishments" of American civilization (Putnam 1891g). He had his heart set on the Wooded Isle.

It was not to be. As space became increasingly precious in the lead-up to the Fair, the Wooded Isle became the most prized and protected location in Jackson Park. Frederick Law Olmsted had specifically designed the Wooded Isle as a key part of his plan for the transformation of Chicago's lakeshore swampland into the Jackson Park fairgrounds, and the nation's most prominent landscape architect wanted it left free of buildings. After fierce struggles it remained largely as Olmsted intended, with two exceptions: the Japanese or Nippon Teahouse, and a small log cabin on the south end (Badger 1979, 65). Putnam's village was consigned instead to a thousand feet of shoreline on the east bank of South Pond, well out of the main traffic of the Fair and close to the southern edge of the park, backing upon the Leather and Shoe Trades building and the south loop of the noisy elevated railway. It was an unpromising and unimpressive spot—and, as the editors of the *World's Columbian Exposition Illustrated* (WCEI) commented in the last month of the Fair, just as Putnam had feared, "liable to be overlooked by the ordinary visitor" (WCEI 1893, no. 8, 219). New York State contributed to Putnam's village with fifty-five feet of additional shoreline for an Iroquois bark council house. Although it was only a few yards north of the Anthropology Building, the ethnographic vil-

FIG. 9. Putnam's Penobscot Village on South Pond, under the elevated rail. Courtesy of Paul V. Galvin Library.

lage was hardly the quiet but central retreat for reflection that Putnam had envisioned: Boas found it necessary to block out the Leather and Shoe Trades Building with white sheets behind his Kwakiutl dancers' outdoor performances (Jacknis 1984; Hinsley 1991, 349, 353). A year before the Fair opened Putnam was complaining that the clacking elevated railway "greatly mars the picturesque effect" of his village (Putnam 1892g). He was right.

Immediately upon approval and appropriations for his original departmental plan in the spring of 1891, Putnam began sending out agents to locate and negotiate with willing Native peoples in North and South America. Here as elsewhere Putnam had to learn as he went, changing strategies as disappointments and opportunities emerged. For the outdoor village he wanted a special ethnographic assistant—analogous to Boas (who was in charge of anthropometry and physical anthropology more generally)—to gather and take charge of the various groups being brought to Chicago for display. His first choice for ethnographic assistant was a well-known Tuscarora Indian and Civil War veteran, army captain Cornelius C. Cusick (Putnam 1891e), whom Putnam had come to know through the American Association for the Advancement of Science (Cusick 1900; Hauptman 1993). "I have a very broad scheme on foot," he confided to Cusick in midsummer of 1891. "I have not given out the details of my work in this connection as I do not care to have it known until it is sure of execution" (Putnam 1891f). For months Putnam negotiated with the army to have Cusick assigned to the Fair; when this failed Cusick resigned his commission, after a lifetime of military service, in early 1892 to work for Putnam and the Exposition. He moved to Cleveland and traveled from there to collect materials, and also take anthropometric measurements for Boas's display, in the Iroquois regions of upstate New York and the Canadian border. But he never assumed the broader responsibilities Putnam anticipated for him; New York State ultimately sponsored the Iroquois group (and Canada brought a representation of Cree Indians). In early 1892 Putnam wrote to his wife: "I am Chief of the natives as I intended to be," but actually the position was being forced upon him by default (Dexter 1966c, 321). A few months later Putnam tried again, turning to a young man named Antonio Apache (fig. 33), who dubiously claimed (Howard 2002, 160–90) to have been left orphaned on the battlefields of the Southwest. Antonio offered to bring families of southwestern tribes (Navajo and Apache) to the Fair and to take Boas's obligatory measurements in the field. Putnam arranged for him to learn the fundamentals of field anthropometry briefly with Boas and hoped Antonio would oversee not only the promised southwestern groups but the entire outdoor village as it formed. While he did eventually deliver and, controversially, watch over a Navajo group for the second half of the Fair (discussed later), Antonio also disappeared for months in the Southwest and failed to account for expenditures. He reappeared just as the Fair was opening. Army Lieutenant E. H. Plummer later wrote to Putnam from Fort Defiance, Arizona Territory, that Antonio "has been unfortunate in this part of the country in making people distrust him, both white and Indians, everywhere that he has visited" (Plummer 1893). Putnam's original experiment with Antonio ended as an expensive failure.

As financial pressures mounted on all sides and the Fair drew closer, Putnam realized that his original plan of having a special assistant to oversee a corps of agents, who would in turn bring small groups of Native artisans to Chicago for strictly noncommercial, "scientific" displays of indigenous life, was not going to succeed. Rather, he would have to depend upon a combination of his own workers (notably Boas), state and foreign governments, and individual entrepreneurs to create the ethnographic village. Furthermore, commercial intentions could not simply be forbidden—a major concession for Putnam—because both Native peoples and their sponsors expected to make money and because the directors of the Fair were increasingly anxious for revenue from concessionaires. As the Fair was opening Putnam explained to anthropologist Jesse Fewkes how circumstances had changed:

> At first I had in mind the plan of having him [Antonio] take charge of representative families of these tribes to the Exposition, but no arrangement was made for this, and after it was decided that this Ethnographical Exposition on native peoples could be brought about largely by means of State Commissioners and private parties who would undertake the matter at their own expense, relying upon the sale of articles of native manufacture to refund their expenses, I did nothing further about having Antonio bring the people. The State of Colorado is to represent the Navajo and probably the family of Apaches also; the State of Minnesota will represent the Chippewa and Sioux, and so on (Putnam 1893g).

As we have seen, Putnam's entire scheme for the outdoor village was predicated on the possibility of presenting contemporary Native peoples, from Tierra del Fuego to the Arctic, living in completely or largely "traditional" ways—he was fond of saying, living "as in olden times." As attractive as it might have been as an attempt at enacting the ethnographic present, in his effort to create a cultural-historical "baseline" for the Americas Putnam was attempting to elide four hundred years of historical change. Moreover, it was not an easy position to maintain at a moment of strong assimilationist sentiment in the country, impelled by the first flush of the Dawes Act of 1887 and the dark shadows of Wounded Knee. As historian George Moses recognized in his study of Wild West shows of the period (1996, 131), Putnam's concept of an ethnographic village at Chicago inserted a third factor—scientific purpose—into an already fierce ongoing cultural battle over Indian images in public space and consciousness, a struggle between assimilationist reformers and commercial showmen such as "Buffalo Bill" Cody.

In this struggle the Indian Affairs Bureau was a key player, and like W. J. McGee at the Louisiana Purchase Exposition a decade later, Putnam sought a necessary alliance (Parezo and Fowler 2007, 135–37). Unfortunately, the government office switched sides with political winds. As it happened, during the months of preparation for the Fair Thomas Jefferson Morgan was serving as commissioner of Indian Affairs in the Republican administration of Benjamin Harrison (1889–93). Morgan, who knew little of Indian affairs when he took office, was a Baptist minister and educator who became, according to historian Joan Mark, "after Alice Fletcher, the second most influential person in the late-nineteenth-century campaign to Americanize the Indians" (Mark 1988, 194). He believed in Indian education as firmly as he disliked Cody's Wild West business, and he kept close data on the treatment of "Show Indians"; at one point he even proposed a ban on all displays and shows involving Indians for any purpose (Moses 1996, 142). But with the Fair he saw an opportunity in Chicago to counter Cody's commercialism with the government's own alternative version of "show" Indians on the road to civilization.

Putnam agreed with Morgan about banning "wild west" showmen and their Indians from the fairgrounds (Cusick 1891), and he certainly wanted to keep his exhibits free of commercial motive. He was pleased to report to Director-General Davis that Commissioner Morgan sanctioned the exhibit plan of the Department of Ethnology "with the understanding that the Commissioner will not authorize any money-making exhibit of Indians or anything bordering on a wild west show to be made by any party. This agreement will put a stop at once to all the schemes for making money by Indian shows which would be derogatory to the Indian and to the Columbian Exposition, and all the Indians as well as other native peoples from America will then be under the immediate charge of the chief of Department M" (Putnam 1892e).

But Putnam sought an even closer understanding with Commissioner Morgan, and he worked assiduously for an amicable division of labor. Putnam traveled at least three times to Washington to confer with Morgan, partly to be assured of the field cooperation of the Indian bureau's reservation agencies and partly to clarify the distinctive purposes of their respective exhibits. For his part, Morgan was mainly concerned to present the bureau's educational and civilizing mission to the nation's Indians as a success story: the bureau's central exhibit in Chicago (as later at St. Louis) would be a schoolhouse, with rotating groups of Indian children in attendance during the course of the Fair. The location of the schoolhouse in Jackson Park, and its spatial and ideological relationship to Putnam's "traditional" village of presumably unassimilated indigenes, became a matter of considerable sensitivity and ongoing negotiation.

Putnam always professed to see no contradiction between the distinct but complementary purposes of the Indian Affairs Bureau and his Department of Ethnology: "I am working in perfect harmony with the Government Department," he wrote in June 1891, "and it is my desire to do so in every way. The grand exhibition we are to have in Chicago gives enough for us all to do, and there is not the slightest reason why there should be any confliction" (Putnam 1891c). The next month he and Morgan reached agreement to divide efforts between the "civilized" and "indigenous" Native exhibits (Putnam 1891g). But Putnam still needed the bureau's cooperation for his fieldworkers, and the potential for "confliction" persisted; so early in 1892, Putnam again met with Morgan in Washington, this time with Alice C. Fletcher attending, to clarify their understanding.

At the meeting in January 1892 Putnam sought the bureau's assistance in bringing Native people, houses, and implements to Chicago as well as explicit permission, especially on Boas's behalf, to measure schoolchildren and adults at reservation agencies and schools. Morgan countered that all Indians brought to Chicago under such arrangements must be clearly labeled as "Indian Office Indians" in Putnam's live village. And he wanted his schoolhouse to be portrayed as the culmination of an historical development, to which Putnam's village would serve as background:

> The desire is to have [the Indian industrial school] put in such relation to the other that while it will be a distinct thing—that is, there is the

> Government school, the work done by the United States for the civilization of the Indian through education—it should be so related to the others that it [Putnam's village] will furnish a sort of back-ground for it. There are the native Indians, customs, etc.; here are the educated Indians, and it is to be so arranged that everything shall put forth the school in its best light. (Morgan 1892, 2)

In contrast to Putnam's plan for a hemispheric, north-south geographical arrangement of Native peoples along the edge of the water, Morgan urged an evolutionary progression, at least for the U.S. reservation tribes under his care: "If we take the school as the apex—as the culmination—you might want to vary the geographical by the progress in civilization. As for instance suppose you have some of the Yumas there. Follow these with those that are a little higher, until here is a group of people living very much as white people live, and from that to the school would be only a step" (Morgan 1892, 2; cf. Moses 1996, 134).

Putnam was conciliatory but noncommittal, choosing to ignore the divergent visions. Morgan promised cooperation in measuring schoolchildren and bringing people and their household materials to Chicago; and he appointed Fletcher as his "confidential secretary" to take charge of the Indian Affairs Bureau exhibit and to "do all the thinking" (Morgan 1892, 3). Fletcher, who at this point hoped to be Putnam's chief ethnographic assistant at Chicago (Mark 1988, 211), readily agreed to serve as liaison between the two men. Under this still vague but workable understanding, the development of the two exhibits went forward over the next year—albeit with little help from Fletcher, who later came to feel distanced and "put on a shelf" by Putnam and fell into a prolonged illness (Mark 1988, 212). Putnam followed through with the geographical plan for his outdoor village, which ultimately was spread out along the South Pond at a short distance south of the bureau's schoolhouse.

Historians have differed in interpreting Morgan's intentions for the Indian Affairs Bureau exhibit at the Fair, but it does appear that the commissioner originally, and perhaps independently, had conceived of a government exhibit that would contrast a "primitive" group encampment with "civilized" or government-educated Natives, mainly children. He envisioned the Indian encampment, possibly on the Midway, with the contrasting schoolhouse nearby, filled with educated Indians and their handiwork. "To be picturesque and impressive, to satisfy the curiosity and philanthropic and scientific interest of people, the primitive Indian must be presented, living in his own habitation and carrying on his own avocations, such as making baskets, blankets, jewelry, bead work, pottery, etc. This part of the exhibit is not to be omitted" (quoted in Moses 1996, 133). After the January meeting with Putnam he explained to Interior Secretary John W. Noble that the bureau's lack of expertise and funds had made him "very glad to accept the suggestion of Professor Putnam" (Moses 1996, 309). Still, as historian Fred Hoxie astutely noted, the radically different messages of the encampment and the schoolhouse reflected the "confliction" and the confusion that in fact characterized the intentions of Fair officials toward Native peoples in the American republic (Hoxie 1984, 88–89).

As it turned out, by the opening on May 1, 1893, Morgan was gone. The Democratic administration of Grover Cleveland that came into office in March immediately replaced him with a political hack: Daniel M. Browning, an Illinois judge with even less experience or interest in Indian matters than Morgan had had, and who was "indifferent" (Moses 1996, 141) to the derogatory images of Wild West shows and uninterested in Putnam's scientific purposes—but quite sensitive to political appointments. The loss of his working relationship with Morgan on a potentially controversial issue—display of "primitive" or "savage" Indians for the purposes of scientific study—cost Putnam considerable embarrassment a few months later in a public dispute with Emma C. Sickles. Since the Sickles affair has been repeatedly cited by scholars, usually to the discredit of Putnam (Dexter 1966c, 326–28; Rydell 1984, 63; Moses 1984, 80; Baker 1998, 59–60; Conn 2004, 186; Fear-Segal 2007, 45–46), it deserves brief reconsideration here for the light it throws on the larger issues under discussion.

Emma Sickles was a former teacher at Pine Ridge reservation in South Dakota who had played an intermediary role at Wounded Knee in 1890 and had provided ethnographer James Mooney with the Lakota ghost dance songs he later published (Mooney 1896; Baker 2010, 104–05). A Chicago native, in subsequent years she was also prominent in lobbying for a federal "Bureau of Domestic Science" to enhance women's cooking skills. Sickles had been hired in September 1891 into the

Department of Ethnology by Director-General Davis (a former Illinois congressman), over Putnam's objections, in payment for previous lobbying efforts on behalf of the Fair. She disapproved of Putnam's fundamental purposes, specifically the display of traditional peoples and ways of life, as well as Morgan's schoolhouse and the division of labor and purpose between the two men. After several months of conflict Putnam fired her for insubordination, but she stayed on at the Fair with the Board of Lady Managers and publicly attacked his department as "one of the darkest conspiracies ever conceived against the Indian race" (Dexter 1966c, 327).

During the Fair Sickles's outrage came to center on Boas's Kwakiutl troupe. Working through his long-term informant and friend George Hunt, Boas had arranged to bring fifteen adults and two children to Chicago to live in two great houses as part of Putnam's outdoor village. Camped along the shore of South Pond, the Indians would perform various ceremonials and live their lives as normally and realistically as possible. One performance involved the use of red paint to give the appearance of violent conflict. Sickles accused Putnam and Boas of sponsoring the "Indian Sun Dance" and other degrading spectacles. As head of the Indian Committee of a reform organization, the Universal Peace Union, she publicly circulated a resolution protesting the presentation of "low and degrading phases of Indian life." The *New York Times* printed her accusation that Putnam's village exhibit "has been used to work up sentiment against the Indian by showing that he is either savage or can be educated only by Government agencies" (Dexter 1966c, 327). While the Kwakiutl dance was not repeated, Commissioner Browning admonished Putnam, personally bringing Sickles's complaints to his attention. Placed on the defensive, Putnam responded at length and with vigor, reminding the new commissioner that the Kwakiutl did not perform the Sun Dance and that, in any case, they were not under the control of the American government:

> There has been no representation of the Indian Sun Dance, and there has not been a single Indian belonging to the United States who has taken part in any exhibition under my direction except the Navajo, who have been quietly sitting in their hut weaving and making silverwork.

> The Indians from Vancouver Island, who are entirely outside the jurisdiction of the United States, have every Thursday evening an exhibition on one of the floats, when they perform ceremonial songs and dances, as it is our wish to have these Indians appear in a manner purely native. One of these ceremonies consists of jugglery when the Indians pretend to beat themselves with clubs and appear to become covered with blood. . . . Even this exhibition (which is pure jugglery and of the same class as the jugglery of the Hindoos and others, and is in itself of considerable scientific importance and interest as illustrating a custom which has been in existence with these people from time immemorial) was only performed once and then by the wish of the Indians themselves without our previous knowledge and they were at once directed not to give the exhibition again. Like many other letters and communications over the signature of Miss Emma C. Sickles, the Circular Letter is, as I have stated above, simply a tissue of misrepresentations and false statements. (Putnam 1893i)

Accepting the legitimacy of neither Putnam's scientific purposes nor Morgan's educational assimilation, Sickles presented a third alternative: that Native Americans would find their own path of progress without government "guidance" or interference and that they were capable of self-government and landholding on their own. She accused Morgan directly, and Putnam implicitly, of collaborating with speculators ("land rings") in promoting a vision of Native peoples as either savage or childlike in order to take their land (Baker 2010, 109–12).

Before the end of the Fair Sickles was reinstated in the Department of Ethnology, but by then Putnam was too tired and harried to respond further. The clash had exposed the delicate relations with the Indian Affairs Bureau in a changing and unpredictable political environment; but it was only one of the sets of concerns that continually absorbed Putnam in Chicago. There were countless others, some of which came more directly from the Native groups themselves.

Display, Desire, and Indigenous Agency

Until recently students of human exhibits at world's fairs and expositions in Europe and the United States generally assumed that lack of direct verbal testimony from those on display indicated relatively passive, even victimized acceptance of conditions. The operating assumption has been that the privileged voices of (usually) white male power—possibly even well-meaning ones such as Putnam's—more or less had their way, and with generally unfortunate results: a "torrent of abuse and ridicule" (Rydell 1984, 63) for those observed, and confirmation of illiberal, ethnocentric bigotry among visitors. Recent scholarship, however, has challenged or modified these assumptions through closer attention to the individuals and groups on display, to the often indirect but revealing voices and actions of those on the other side of the display ropes, and to audience responses. In this essay the issue is discussed with regard to the Midway exhibits, but it is important to recognize that anthropology at the Chicago Exposition—on or off the Midway—was a complex affair of multiple agency, in which control and power were constantly subject to challenge and limitation and in which vectors of desire and purpose constantly crossed at many levels. As Julie K. Brown firmly demonstrated some years ago with respect to photography at the Chicago Fair, even the most strenuous efforts at top-down control of imagery could not prevail in the unpredictable, heterogeneous and free-flowing environs of Jackson Park (Brown 1994). In the end, in contradiction to Putnam's preferred belief, money was the one ubiquitous desire and common denominator in the cross-cultural encounters of the Fair. To demonstrate the complexity of agency among those "on display" in Jackson Park proper (excluding here the Midway Plaisance), let us consider more closely, to the degree that the current historical record permits, two cases: the small Navajo group who arrived during the Fair; and the twelve families of Inuit entertainers (fifty-seven individuals) who set up their "Eskimaux Village" in Jackson Park in early 1893.

Antonio Apache and the Navajos

Putnam's notion of ethnographic "types" owed much to Lewis Henry Morgan's belief, expressed most fully in his final work, *Houses and House-Life of the American Aborigines* (Morgan 1881), that domestic structures were strong markers of cultural distinctiveness and relative "progress." Accordingly, Putnam was anxious to have representatives from throughout the hemisphere, including several southwestern tribes (he usually mentioned Navajos and Apaches) living in traditional structures. His plan was that these would be built in the field and then disassembled, shipped to Chicago, and reassembled by the Natives themselves. In mid-1892 he dispatched Antonio Apache to Fort Wingate, New Mexico, "for the purpose of interesting the Apaches and Navajos in the objects of the Exposition and for securing from those tribes as thorough collections as possible illustrating their method of life, their customs and manufactures." Like all of Putnam's field agents, Antonio was given multiple tasks: he was to take head and body measurements of as many individuals as possible, based on his brief training with Boas and on-site instruction at Fort Wingate from army ethnologist Washington Matthews. He was also instructed to secure "a habitation with all its appurtenances of a purely Indian character"—no white-manufactured pans, dishes, or utensils were wanted. Putnam instructed Antonio that clothing of men, women, and children "should in all cases be such as were used long ago or should be made as they were in old times; old styles entirely, of native material with native decorations"; finally, he should collect bows, arrows, shields, weapons, and "ornaments of every kind." Regarding people, Putnam was equally specific: an arrowmaker with his family, or a basketmaker, weaver or potter, for a total of one or two "honest and reliable" Navajos and their families; and the same with Apaches. He provided Antonio with full-color bird's-eye view prints of the proposed Chicago Fair for trade and inspiration. Antonio was urged to cooperate with representatives of the Board of Lady Managers, who were also in the area looking for female Navajo weavers for the Colorado State exhibit and for the Woman's Building (Putnam 1892c).

During the summer of 1892 Antonio reported from New Mexico on his progress and dilemmas, and his letters revealed significant problems with Putnam's assumptions. Putnam had imagined that the Indians, once situated along the edge of the water in Jackson Park, would merely exist as *tableaux vivants* for popular and scientific observers. Antonio found, though, that they feared homesickness above all; and he discovered expectation of monetary profit from sales of wares: "Navajo Jack," recently returned from an unprofitable appearance in Albuquerque, demanded that he receive a regular salary if he came to Chicago. Moreover, Antonio reluctantly reported that the Navajos no longer wore nor knew how to make the yucca fiber clothing of the Columbian period—Putnam's notion of "traditional" wares and clothing would have to be adjusted at least a century forward in time to embrace woven wool (Apache 1892a). Still, by midsummer Antonio thought he had persuaded as many as *two hundred* to come to Chicago, including silversmiths and weavers. "I cannot make them realize," Antonio explained, "the importance to manufacture [sic] articles ahead to take with them" (Apache 1892b). Shocked, Putnam was quick to respond that such numbers were out of the question: he could only afford five Navajos and perhaps two hogans; and they needed to bring "all the fixings for the house" themselves, and must not show up before April. "I expect the four or five who do come to pay their living expenses while in Chicago, and all they make over that will be for themselves," he conceded. They could sell their wares, but only under Putnam's direct supervision (Putnam 1892d).

By the end of the summer of 1892 Antonio had exhausted his allotment of funds without any definite commitments for the Navajo and Apache display, and he decided to stay at San Carlos to learn fluent Apache (Apache 1892c). The winter passed without further word, while Putnam's funds dwindled and he came to depend more heavily on collaborations with other exhibitors. In March 1893 he reached an agreement with the Colorado State Exhibit to have Colorado pay for a group of Navajos to come and live in a hogan in Putnam's village and sell their manufactures under his direction. On Putnam's recommendation and with approval from Commissioner Browning, Antonio (who had been silent most of the winter) was now hired once again to recruit, deliver, and supervise the group—for fifty dollars a month plus "10% of all sales made by him outside of booths and tents." The members of the group—one silversmith (Peshlakai, fig. 56), two weavers (Mrs. Walker and Cheeno), and two children (Ned and Mary Manning)–were to receive salaries ranging from ten to twenty-five dollars a month (Greenberg and Greenberg 1984).

The small Navajo contingent arrived around the first of June, but almost immediately at least two were taken from the village on South Pond and up to the Midway in the hope of better profits—for them and for their sponsor, the State of Colorado. By August, it appears, they had entirely abandoned Putnam's village and decamped to the

Midway, presumably to a lot where a mixed group of Plains Indians had been gathered under a concession to showmen Thomas Roddy and Henry "Buckskin Joe" De Ford (Rydell 1993, 160). This exhibit, which apparently was arranged after the Fair opening (and therefore does not appear on most maps of the grounds), was located on the north side and west end of the Midway between a military encampment and an ostrich farm, "a very large enclosure protected against the view from the outside by a high board fence," and dominated by a group of sixty Sioux, Pawnee, Blackfeet, and Cheyenne (Buel 1894, n.p.). "These Indians [the Navajos] are now on the Midway Plaisance in connection with other Indians," Putnam reported to Commissioner Browning, "but they are rather restless, I understand, and wish to come back to their Hogan. They have unquestionably been a little homesick at times, as are all the Indians who are here." Matters devolved from there. Having brought them to Chicago early in the summer, in September the Colorado Board refused to continue paying for them. As Colorado official A. F. Wilmarth ambiguously advised Antonio: "It was a mistake to keep them so long, but it was done in the hope that they might have some faint glimmering of what was decent and right" (Wilmarth 1893). At the same time, Antonio was accused of molesting the Navajo women—a charge that Putnam personally pursued and found baseless: "I and my wife and daughters as well as all my assistants, both men and women, have perfect confidence in the man and trust him implicitly. His behavior here and his never failing courtesy have won him a host of friends, and we all see in him the capability of the Indian" (Putnam 1893l). Six months later, long after the Fair had closed and the Navajos had returned to their homes, Putnam was still trying to convince Higinbotham and Skiff to honor the Fair's obligation to them. Lieutenant Plummer of Fort Defiance personally advanced them funds "to keep them quiet."

Even in this brief summary the Navajo case demonstrates that human displays were already understood as a contractual business and that it was no longer possible (if it ever had been) to draw a line between strictly "scientific" and "commercial" motives and practices. Of course, expectations and desires did not always yield fair results—the Navajo group went home angry and still poor—although Peshlakai, one of the outstanding silversmiths of his generation, also returned home with a lifelong commitment to westernized education for his children and grandchildren (Greenberg and Greenberg 1984, 8).

The Secession of the Inuits

Issues of conflicting desires and agencies emerged even more clearly in the experiences of the Inuits in Jackson Park. In 1892 the Arctic World's American Exposition Company, a private enterprise headed by J. W. Skiles of Spokane, Washington, obtained a concession from the Committee on Ways and Means of the Chicago World's Fair to bring a Labrador Inuit group to establish an "Esquimaux Village" in Jackson Park. The village was not to be on the Midway Plaisance but located on Northwest Pond, far away from but officially in association with Putnam's ethnographic village. Unlike the rest of Putnam's live ethnographic displays, the Esquimaux Village was one of only three exhibits within the fairgrounds—the "Isolated Exhibits" —that charged separate admission fees. (The other two in the park were the Nippon or Japanese Teahouse on the Wooded Isle and the H. Jay Smith Colorado Cliffdweller Exhibit outside the Anthropology Building; each charged twenty-five cents.) Robert Peary's early expeditions and previous displays of Arctic groups in European venues had raised American awareness and curiosity about the peoples of the far north, and Putnam was anxious and pleased to have their representation as part of his ambitious hemispheric outdoor ethnography. He also made well-publicized arrangements with Peary to bring back Arctic collections (WCEI 1891, 4:23).

After conferring with Putnam and obtaining his approval in June 1892, Skiles's agents W. D. Vincent and Ralph G. Taber set off for Labrador (Putnam 1892f). Four months later they arrived back in Boston harbor with a troupe of fifty-nine Inuit individuals and thirty-five dogs from Labrador. The Boston press responded with front-page headlines of the "Strange People" who "eat fish raw" and whose dogs "howl like wolves" (Zwick 2006, 11). Ten of the twelve recruited families were from established settlements near Moravian missions and Hudson's Bay Company outposts and thus were familiar with Euroamerican practices and spoke English; the other two families were deliberately recruited from farther north and had had much

Fig. 10. Eskimos at the World's Columbian Exposition. "Eskimaux Village," World's Columbian Exposition, Midway Plaisance, Chicago IL, 1891–1893. Reuben E. Denell, designer. HALIC, Ryerson and Burnham Archives, The Art Institute of Chicago. Digital file #M525840.

less contact. The *Boston Globe* was particularly thrilled to see these "heathen aborigines" who were "unsullied by the touch of civilization" (Zwick 2006, 12).

By the end of October—fully six months before the opening of the Fair—the families were settled in Jackson Park and the concession was charging admission to the "first and one of the most celebrated attractions at the Fair" (Zwick 2006, 16). The Northwest Pond was in a secluded corner of the fairgrounds, behind the state buildings of Kansas, Nebraska, and North Dakota. Most of Jackson Park was still under construction, but the group drew the fascination of the Chicago public from the births of three Inuit babies within their first month in the city: Columbia Susan Manak, named "the World's Fair Baby"; Kotuktooka, or Evelina Cooper; and a boy who was named Christo-

Anthropology as Education and Entertainment

pher Columbus Palliser. In mid-January 1893 a third girl arrived, this time to Esther Eneutseak, an unwed fifteen-year-old. No father was identified. For unknown reasons Bertha Honoré Palmer, the head of the Board of Lady Managers of the Fair and the most prominent woman of Chicago, took immediate and very public interest in this child and became her godmother; Mrs. Palmer named her Nancy Helene Columbia Palmer, or "Columbia."

It is probable that the Labrador Inuit families were deliberately brought early to Chicago in order to acclimate them to a strange environment. If so, the strategy failed, for tragedy struck repeatedly in the brutal Chicago winter of 1892–93. The "World's Fair Baby" Columbia Susan lived only a week; her parents held a funeral service in the Esquimaux Village, and she was buried in a Chicago cemetery; in April a boy who had been born before leaving Labrador also died in the village from "a bad cold and the climate." Except for the Administration Building, the Exposition buildings were unheated and intended only for temporary habitation in mild weather. The Inuit families were housed in flimsy bark-covered sheds; they suffered severely from cold, a measles epidemic, and inadequate food. During February and March a dispute with the Skiles Company ended up in the courtroom of Justice Porter of the Hyde Park Police Court. Porter took the side of the Inuits and began to track their living conditions. Matters came to a head in late March, when Chicago temperatures suddenly rose above seventy degrees. The concessionaires, anxious not to lose their pre-Fair business due to the appearance of having "inauthentic" Esquimaux, forced the group to wear their fur clothing; when they resisted, the company locked recalcitrants in the sheds and instructed the new Columbian Guard and, later, a private enforcer to keep them locked in. The Natives sued successfully in Porter's court for their freedom from confinement, testifying that their village had literally become a prison: "When they coaxed us from Labrador they told us we would be fed well and only have to wear the skin clothes half the day; but when they got us here they made us wear them from 9 in the morning until 6 in the evening. No man can stand that here" (Zwick 2006, 20).

Finally on April 20, just ten days before the opening of the Fair, thirty-seven of the fifty-nine-member troupe walked out of Jackson

FIG. 11. Esther and Columbia (Palmer) Eneutseak. Courtesy of Them Days, Inc., Newfoundland.

FIG. 12. Bertha Honoré Palmer, 1849–1918. Source unknown.

Park and into a hotel on Hope Avenue. A few days later Inuit leaders Peter Mesher and Tom Deer, along with Chicagoan Charles F. Duke, incorporated the Esquimaux Exhibition Company and established an independent Esquimaux Village outside the fairgrounds—only a few feet outside, near Buffalo Bill's Wild West show. Justice Porter was the largest stockholder in the new corporation. Historian Jim Zwick argued that the Inuits' successful challenge "set precedents that empowered other groups exhibited in the anthropological displays and Midway shows at the Exposition" (Zwick 2006, 21).

Only two Inuit families remained in the original Jackson Park Esquimaux Village for the duration of the Fair, and at times the spot seemed deserted; but they became a popular attraction through games of "snap-the-whip" (touching coins placed on the ground by visitors) and paddling their kayaks on the pond. "Prince" Pomiuk, a young boy who stayed, became a favorite of fairgoers and appeared on postcards and in souvenir albums. Sadly, he injured his hip at the Fair and the wound became infected; after his return to Labrador in 1894, he spent months in a hospital. He died there of influenza in 1897.

By refusing to provide transportation home to Labrador at the end of the Fair, Vincent and Taber were able to reassert control over the rebellious families and ultimately reorganize them into groups for exhibition around the country, including the California Midwinter International Exposition in San Francisco, which began in January 1894 as a West Coast extension of the Chicago Fair. Here they lived in white plaster "igloos." Another baby girl was born and, after a contest among San Francisco schoolchildren, was named after the city newspaper: Francisca Examiner Deer. But she too died after a few weeks. Twelve days later, little Christopher Columbus Palliser, who had been born just after arrival in Chicago, died of malnutrition (Zwick 2006, 23–24). He was seventeen months old.

In contrast to these tragic and disturbing stories, the attentions of Bertha Potter Palmer gave advantages and renewed prominence to Esther's "Columbia," who later inherited the titles of "World's Fair Baby" and "first Eskimo born in the United States." After the Fair she, her mother, grandparents, and ten others were exhibited at a Boston dime museum in early 1894, then toured with Barnum and Bailey's short-lived "Grand Ethnological Congress of Strange and Savage People" for the 1894 and 1895 seasons. Over the next quarter century Columbia Palmer's remarkable career led her to appearances in at least eight more expositions (among them Jamestown, Pan-American, and Panama-Pacific) and travel throughout the United States, Europe, and even North Africa. She became the first Inuit to write and star in a Hollywood film with an Inuit cast, *The Way of the Eskimo* (1911).

Columbia lived until 1959; her mother Esther outlived her by two years (Zwick 2006, 142–43).

Because of its early start in the winter before the Fair, and despite the secession, the Skiles Company's Esquimaux Village was lucrative. Concessionaire contracts at the Chicago Fair generally called for the Chicago Exposition Company to receive between 25 and 33 percent of the concessionaire's gross receipts; the Esquimaux Village concession paid in more than $38,000 to the Exposition company. The Inuits' contract paid them $50 each per year plus room and board—and supposedly transportation back home. While figures are not available, the rebel Esquimaux Village outside Jackson Park was probably not a financial success. After appearing in San Francisco the leader of the rebellion in Chicago, Zacharias, summarized his feelings and probably those of the group: "We are glad to be at liberty once more, and not to be continually looked at as if we were animals. We shall never go again" (Zwick 2006, 31).

Even thus briefly considered, the cases of the Navajos and Inuits demonstrate why generalizations about the experiences of the indigenous peoples in Putnam's ethnographic village come at some risk. In the end Putnam had only a handful of groups, each of whom operated under unique conditions and understandings: the government of British Guiana sponsored a small group of Arawaks; in addition to the Fort Rupert Kwakiutl shepherded by Boas and George Hunt, Canada sent a Cree delegation from Saskatchewan; New England woodlands cultures were represented by four families of Penobscots from Maine, whose wigwams occupied a patch of bare ground beneath the intramural elevated railroad (Buel 1894, n.p.) ; the five Navajos, three adults and two children, arrived in July and left in September, probably living in their hogan on South Pond at night but by day selling merchandise on the Midway; and the Inuits, at the far north end of the Park, split and seceded before the start of the Fair.

What can one conclude from such diverse experiences? In the opening weeks of the Fair, Putnam contributed a descriptive chapter on Department M to a semi-official history and guide (White and Igleheart 1893, 415–35) in which he characterized his work in Chicago as an effort to display the "first rude attempts in human art and industry" in the Americas, the result of years of "scientific investigation in relation to prehistoric life" in the hemisphere. In describing the outdoor exhibits he remarked: "This little colony of native people is not intended for a side show for the amusement of the visitor, but for a scientific study of the first historic people of America. Moreover these people are treated with kindness and consideration and are allowed every opportunity for improvement by observation of the benefits of civilization and education. The Indian Schoolhouse nearby, which is conducted by the United States Government, shows to the world what the Indian is capable of when allowed such advantages" (White and Igleheart 1893, 424). In other words, he saw the outdoor ethnographic village as an experiment in mutual exposure: the Natives might profit and improve from exposure to kind sponsors and serious, civilized visitors; while fairgoers would be edified by "scientific study" of their hemispheric ancestors. It is hard to know to what degree Putnam's intention for the "serious visitor" was realized, since accounts written during the Fair or retrospectively paid scant attention to the little village of exotic peoples on South Pond—and hardly more to the exhibits in Putnam's building. But the evidence with regard to the human displays is not encouraging and was probably disappointing all around. Boas came away swearing "never again to play circus impresario," and on the last evening of 1893 he looked back bitterly on the year: "A rushing rat-race, great uneasiness, and unsatisfactory work have been its watchwords." As Douglas Cole observed, the exhibition ended up being "more quaint than coherent." Shoved to the southernmost margins of the fairgrounds, Putnam's efforts at a serious, scientific anthropology were—as he had always feared—simply overwhelmed and overshadowed (Cole 1999, 155–56).

But not entirely. The outdoor exhibits also featured Edward H. Thompson's remarkable full-size casts of Mayan structures from Labná and Uxmal on a space a short walk from the Anthropology Building—forming, in effect, the southern boundary of the ethnographic village (fig. 49). As a result of Putnam's support and Thompson's efforts, Mayan culture and architecture first came to North American public attention at Chicago—with stimulating results for future research and patronage (Llorente 1996; Evans 2004). Louis Aymé, who had preceded Thompson as U.S. consul in Mérida, Yucatán, and now lived in Chicago as a journalist for the *Inter Ocean*, had predicted that Mexico would show her "Castles of the Dark Ages" at the Fair (Aymé 1892, 20). In addition to casts of Mayan stelae inside the Anthropology Building, and case after case of specimens, near the entrance stood the impressive full-size Mayan reproductions, set back on a manicured lawn and separated from wide and pleasant walkways by chain fences. "Everyone who visited the Exposition," reported the Massachusetts Board of World's Fair Managers, "will recall the weird effect produced on the imagination by these old monuments of an unknown past standing in stately grandeur amidst all the magnificence and beauty that landscape art and architecture of today could devise" (Thompson 1929, 41–42).

Edward Thompson traveled to Chicago to oversee the molding and installation but then returned to Mexico, at Putnam's request, to select and ship appropriate tropical plantings for the Mayan monuments. He and Putnam were engaged in domesticating Mayan prehistory for the American public with green lawns and metal fences—perhaps a foreshadow of Sylvanus Morley's reconstruction of the Maya site of Chichén Itzá (which Thompson personally owned for many years) for the Carnegie Institution of Washington between 1915 and 1945. Popular photo albums of the Fair found these photogenic and mysterious "Relics of a Nameless Race" irresistible (Anon. 1894c, 153), and one watercolor artist imaginatively repopulated them with modern Mexicans in sombreros (Hinsley 1996c, 131–32). Putnam could justly enthuse that his Chicago exhibit "contains a more complete collection of Central American archaeology than ever before available for the study of these old ruins and their unknown builders," with their hieroglyphs offering a mystery and puzzle for future scholars (Putnam 1893h, 429–30). Along with the southwestern Cliffdweller Exhibit—a private concession—a few yards away, Thompson's Mayan architecture received wide popular attention. Deeply pleased with the effect, Putnam suggested that the Columbian Museum might feature a Mayan front portal.

The Midway as Ethnic Marketplace

The World's Columbian Exposition came to American consciousness in three stages: before, during, and after the Fair. From the beginning of 1891 to mid-1893 the American public enjoyed increasingly romantic and alluring visions of the never- to-be-forgotten, evanescent experiences to be had in the coming White City (e.g., Ralph 1893). During

FIG. 13. The illuminated White City at night, by amateur photographer Hunter Bartlett. Courtesy of the Chicago History Museum.

the six-month Fair proper, reporting included an astounding array and volume of text, photos, and drawings emanating from the printing presses of Moses Handy, the Exposition's director of publicity; at the same time, local and national journalists and artists set up permanent shop at the Fair: Julian Hawthorne and Will Chapin (*Humors of the Fair*), William Dean Howells (*Letters of an Altrurian Traveller*), Kate Field (*Kate Field's Washington*), and Julian Ralph (*Harper's Chicago and the World's Fair*)—not to mention the editors of *World's Fair Puck*, who opened their editorial offices and presses for daily publication in a gingerbread building that became a tourist destination in the center of the park. Their tones were considerably more skeptical and ironic than the official sources but nonetheless admiring. Finally, well before the gates closed for the last time on October 30, a bewildering variety of souvenir photo albums and Fair histories were already in production (Putnam contributed to several), effectively consolidating and exploiting the national market in memories. In this process, from 1891 through 1894 publicists of the Fair constructed a coherent, watertight narrative, running from anticipation through nostalgia and embedding the White City in local and national remembrance.

In the construction of expectations the Midway received special attention, and visitors were cued about what to expect well before it existed. Three themes emerged and overlapped: that the earth's remarkable human and cultural diversity would appear on the Midway in microcosm; that fairgoers would consume an entire world of pleasurable and exciting entertainments, along with effortless education; and that it would be a commercial affair, an international marketplace, a "bazaar of nations." In 1891, for instance, the *World's Columbian Exposition Illustrated* predicted that the Fair would be "a gigantic and brilliant reunion of the people of all nationalities; a grand spectacular and realistic bazaar, within whose capacious and magnificent booths and squares will be met natives from all countries under the ethereal dome—persons speaking all the different tongues that spread indescribable confusion at Babel's base." Furthermore, it promised to be "a place where visitors will expect amusement rather than profound education; amusement such as can only be afforded by attractive object education; attractive education obtained by object lessons at once conspicuous and delightful" (WCEI 2, no. 5: 3). A year later the popular *Harper's* journalist Julian Ralph forecast that the Midway would be "a jumble of foreignness—a bit of Fez and Nuremberg, of Sahara and Dahomey and Holland, Japan and Rome and Coney Island. It will be gorgeous with color, pulsating with excitement, riotous with the strivings of a battalion of bands, and peculiar to the last degree" (Ralph 1893, 207).

Ralph's terms suggested constructed confusion and fractured experience: the Midway would offer a chaos for the senses, a kaleidoscopic passing of scenes too quick for valuation or judgment; the visitor would be invited to a sensual feast of sound, sight and smell, encouraged to suspend rational faculties and simply consume the sensual stream. For some, the disorientation could be truly frightening. In her popular novel of the Fair, *Sweet Clover*, Clara Louise Burnham's character Miss Berry expressed the sense of relief on emerging from the Plaisance into the White City:

> In the Midway it's some dirty and all barbaric. It deafens you with noise; the worst folks in there are avaricious and bad, and the best are just children in their ignorance, and when you're feelin' bewil-

dered with the smells and sounds and sights, always changin' like one o' those kaleidoscopes, and when you come out o' that mile-long babel [sic] where you've been elbowed and cheated, you pass under a bridge—and all of a sudden you are in a great, beautiful silence. The angels on the Woman's Buildin' smile down and bless you, and you know that in what seemed like one step, you've passed out o' darkness into light. (Burnham 1894, 71)

The constructed chaos of the Midway had been anticipated at earlier expositions. An English reviewer of the Paris Exposition of 1889 remembered experiencing the "phantasmagoria of colonial empire" along the Seine and coming away with "a pleasing sense of bewilderment and magnificence" (quoted in Greenhalgh 1988, 66). Strolling through the bazaar of global exotica at Chicago, the fairgoer would step from the linear concourse of history (the Midway boulevard) into side streets of clamor and sensual overload. In his multi-volume account of the Chicago Exposition, historian and publishing impresario Hubert H. Bancroft vividly recaptured the Midway experience in language reminiscent of both Ralph and Burnham:

> Entering the avenue a little west of the Woman's Building, [fairgoers] would pass between the walls of medieval villages, between mosques and pagodas, Turkish and Chinese.... They would be met on their way by German and Hungarian bands, by the discord of Chinese cymbals and Dahomeyan tom-toms; they would encounter jugglers and magicians, camel drivers and donkey boys, dancing-girls from Cairo and Algiers, from Samoa and Brazil, and men and women of all nationalities, some lounging in oriental indifference, some shrieking in unison or striving to outshriek each other in the hope of transferring his superfluous change from the pocket of the unwary pilgrim. Then, as taste or length of purse determined, for fees were demanded from those who would penetrate the hidden mysteries of the plaisance, they might enter the Congress of Beauty with its plump and piquant damsels, might pass an hour in one of the theaters or villages, or partake of harmless beverages served by native waiters. (Bancroft 1893, 4:835)

As the editors of the 1894 memorial volume *The White City (As It Was)* effused: "The Midway Plaisance was the play-ground of the

Fair, and in that eighty acres could be found more novel and entertaining sights than a journey around the world could disclose to the most observant traveler" (Peabody and Wood 1894, n.p.).

The reporting during the Fair suggested a more complex reality. Julian Hawthorne's *Humors of the Fair*, for example, was a collaboration over the six-month period with popular Chicago political cartoonist Will E. Chapin. "The Fair has three parts," Hawthorne instructed: "the architecture, the exhibits, and the foreigners" (Hawthorne 1893a, 44). Following their fictional female visitor, Hildegarde, as she experiences Jackson Park and the questionable enticements of the Midway, Hawthorne establishes a tone of detached bemusement, mild criticism, and occasional irony: "I was talking with a girl on the veranda of the Woman's Building yesterday [says Hildegarde], and mentioned the Plaisance. She said, 'Don't speak that name, please; I've got to go home to Boston tomorrow'" (Hawthorne 1893a, 77). He took seriously, though, the possibilities of edification through exposure to cultural difference, as he mulled over the nature of American curiosity: "We are perhaps more interested in stranger people and their ways, than in any other thing, so that Cairo Street is jammed every day, and the various Asiatic natives are stared at whenever they appear on the [Midway] Walk, and are surrounded by intent groups whenever they stop to speak to an acquaintance.... In the course of time [the Fair] will leave us a wiser and broader people than it found us" (Hawthorne 1893a: 36). He also suggested that the Midway might provide a corrective to the native skepticism and provincialism of Americans:

> A third of the visitors to the Plaisance think that every show is a fifty cent, or a twenty-five cent, or a ten cent fake, as the case may be, and that the Turks, Arabs, Persians, Fijians, Soudanese, Dahomeyans, and for aught I know the pygmy Javanese also are bogus.... It is a pity that we cannot believe that the world contains anything except the things we are familiar with; and one of the best uses this Fair can serve will be to disabuse us of that idea. It is the cheapest and most exhaustive journey over the earth that ever was made. (Hawthorne 1893a, 77)

Hawthorne's on-the-ground reflections suggest that fairgoers' experiences of the Midway may not have been as chaotic and thoughtless as the initial language predicted. Looking beyond the overtly racist caricatures of the time, one can see that artists and cartoonists repeatedly portrayed exactly the type of cross-cultural contact, across and outside exhibit boundaries, for which Hawthorne hoped. Further evidence can be found in many long, descriptive captions to hundreds of photographs of individual "Midway Types" in the numerous souvenir albums (some published as serials during the Fair and available to visitors), revealing unexpected familiarity with named individuals, families, and especially children in the human displays (see A Visual Interlude, this volume). In short, for some visitors the Midway experience involved close, commercial-free encounters. On this point Julian Hawthorne's observations tend to confirm much visual imagery from the Fair that depicted a pattern of eclectic mixing of peoples in close proximity. Here Hawthorne strolls down the crowded, "enchanted" Midway:

> You cannot spare your eyesight at any step of the journey down this enchanted avenue. For not only are there unfamiliar spectacles in the way of buildings on either hand, but the strange people themselves have escaped from their proper abiding places, and are out walking and looking, almost as much interested in you as you are in them. There are Musselmans of all tribes, and Cingalese, and wild Arabs in their bournouses [*burnouse* = hooded cloak] and swathed heads, and Javanese in skirts and jackets, and stately Soudanese, with their black hair braided in strings, and dirty white togas bellying in the breeze; and Algerians and Persians and unspeakable bashi-bazouks, and the more familiar figures of Chinese and Japanese, and perhaps a savage Dahomeyan or two, and Numidians and Nubians from the tropical interior. Ever and anon, as you pass, you will see an interested, craning group ringed round some object of fascination in the center, and if you peep over their heads or between their shoulders, you will always find a swarthy, smiling face and a queer costume in the midst, with whom the local American is striving to hold converse. Cigars or cigarettes are given or exchanged, there is a dropping fire of humorous remarks, and then the group breaks up, and the swarthy ones continue on their way. The ends of the earth are meeting, and finding one another good fellows. (Hawthorne 1893b, 571)

The Midway produced in texts and cartoons a particular kind of humor that expressed uneasiness and uncertainty about boundaries—

the tourist's sympathy at a safe distance—recognizing the common humanity of other peoples and yet preserving the option of unbridgeable difference. In this discourse the appearance of babies, the blooming of romance, and presumed family structures within the exhibit groups became reliable themes of universal humanity, while differences of aesthetic appreciation (dance, music, female beauty) signaled cultural distance.

In the end, commercial more than cultural exchange was the central logic of the Midway. Early in its development from a dusty, tree-lined country road of 1890, the Plaisance was envisioned as a covered arcade, an attempt to combine the interiority of the department store with the exteriority of the street or promenade (Lewis 1983; cf. Harris 1978). And despite officials' initial misgivings about the effect on Chicago's image, the distinctively commercial nature of the Midway—and its contrast with the central, free-admission domains within the White City—was inescapable for reporters of the Fair. After visiting the Fair for a week in September at the invitation of Daniel Burnham, author and editor William Dean Howells informed the readers of *Cosmopolitan*, through the eyes of his visiting "Altrurian Traveller," that while the White City may provide visions of a more advanced, commerce-free American future, the global present was to be found on the boisterous Plaisance:

> The competitive life of the present epoch is relegated to the long avenue remotest from the White City . . . where a hundred shows rival one another in a furious advertisement for the favor of the passer. . . . In the Fair City, everything is free; in the Plaisance everything must be paid for. You strike at once here the hard level of the outside western world; and the Orient, which has mainly peopled the Plaisance with its theaters and restaurants and shops. . . . The lascivious dances of the East are here, in the Persian and Turkish and Egyptian theaters, as well as the exquisite archaic charms of the Javanese and the Chinese in their village and temple. One could spend many days in the Plaisance, always entertainingly, whether profitable or unprofitable; but whether one visited the Samoan or Dahomeyan in his hut, the Bedouin and the Lap in their camps, the delicate Javanese in his bamboo cottage, or the American Indian in his teepee, one must be aware that these

citizens of the Plaisance are not there for their health, as the Americans quaintly say, but for the money that is in it. (Howells 1961, 24)

Howells saw the commercial characteristics of the Midway as inherently and unfortunately a part of the "outside western world," but in fact they were the culmination of a set of representational practices that had been nearly a half century in development in the transatlantic community. For our purposes it is important to note that they were largely alien to Frederic Putnam; he had little personal or professional interest in them. Nonetheless, they were significant for American anthropology both at the Chicago Fair and beyond. Since most studies of human exhibits at the 1893 Chicago Fair have focused on the Midway, and since the Midway exhibits were officially part of Putnam's Department of Ethnology, accusations of racism and ethnocentrism on the Midway have sometimes fallen on his shoulders. There is considerable irony in this criticism since, due to the complex administration of the Fair and his own distinct concerns, Putnam had little to do with the formation or daily administration of what became the most popular, memorable, and controversial section of the Fair. Yet neither was he completely distanced or divorced from the Midway; and he undoubtedly used his official status to put the best possible face on what today may seem questionable language, practices, and attitudes. The challenge today is to specify the nature of his relationship to this heterogeneous and still fascinating phenomenon.

The roots of the Midway Plaisance reached deeply into nineteenth-century metropolitan centers of empire and the international trade in human diversity. In his probing account of "human showcases" at international expositions and world's fairs, Paul Greenhalgh (1988, 82–111) traces the genre of live human displays in the second half of the century, with special attention to the several Paris fairs (1867, 1878, 1889, 1900). He argues that initially at the 1867 Paris Exposition "exotic" individuals appeared primarily as waiters and vendors in various North African (Egyptian, Tunisian, Algerian) cafés, or as camel handlers or barbers; on a smaller scale, at the Philadelphia Centennial of 1876 Chinese, Arab, and Japanese craftsmen (constructing the exhibits) appeared, along with a Turkish Bazaar and Café. Again at the 1878 Paris Exposition, North African and Arabic themes predominated—an Algerian Bazaar and the Cairo Street (which had made the first of its many appearances at London's Crystal Palace in 1851) comprised part of a larger colonial thematic. In the same period English fairs began to feature Ceylonese and Indian Teahouses with Asian waiters. In 1883 the International Colonial and Export Trade Exhibition in Amsterdam featured a kampong, or Javanese village, situated behind the Rijksmuseum—the first of many changing appearances of the Javanese (Indonesians) at international fairs, including Chicago's Midway (Bloembergen 2006). Comparable human displays were part of expos in Brussels, Berlin, and a half dozen other European cities in the seventies and eighties. But the Exposition Universelle of 1889 in Paris saw a change in the logic and purpose of human display: "colonial peoples were not brought to serve as exotic vendors, waiters and servants, but simply to be looked at" (Greenhalgh 1988, 86). What caused this consequential difference in 1889?

Greenhalgh attributes the new pattern of simply "gazing" at exotic peoples to two related factors. The first was the growth of French anthropology in the 1880s—a period that saw new scientific and popular curiosity throughout Europe and especially in France about the "primitive" peoples of the imperial systems (German, Dutch, Belgian, and English as well as French). The second was the popular new Parisian practice, begun in the late 1870s with the encouragement of prominent Parisian academics, of displaying human groups—Lapps, Fuegians, American Indians, Ashantis, and others—along with plants and animals at the Jardin d'Acclimatation (Paris Zoological Gardens). Almost immediately commercial pressure overtook anthropological interest and "the atmosphere around began to change from one of learning to a circus parade." The move to association with animals produced a marked degradation of the humans on display: "Regardless of its motives, the anthropological community had invented a genre at the Jardin d'Acclimatation destined to debase and defile non-Western cultures in a way barely conceived of before" (Greenhalgh 1988, 87). Moreover, the imperial reach of the 1889 Paris Exposition extended more deeply into sub-Saharan Africa, Asia, and the Pacific: the popular human villages along the Seine in 1889 were from Senegal, the Congo, Gabon, Dahomey (Benin), Indochina, New Caledonia, and Java. The lesson seemed clear enough: Europe's imperial and exhibitionary reach was becoming increasingly global, reflecting an emerging consensus that the metropolitan intellectual system and its scientific elite could rightly claim space and time—the entire earth and the full range of human social evolution—for their domain: all the human world, from the lowest "savagery" of the peripheral regions upward, might be gathered and displayed for the entertainment and edification of urban western fairgoers. One visitor described the Paris displays this way: "In the back settlements behind all the gorgeous finery of the pagodas and the palaces of the further East the ingenious French have established colonies of savages whom they are attempting to civilize" (Greenhalgh 1988, 88).

Display of human groups for science, entertainment, and profit was a global phenomenon with a long genealogy, but recent scholarship makes abundantly clear that it reached a peak of activity with the unprecedented global imperium of western Europe and the United States between 1875 and 1915 (Blanchard et al. 2008; Ames 2008). French anthropologists alone between 1873 and 1909 published more than eighty articles based upon measurements and observations of human groups at their exhibitions. Science, entertainment, and profit thus became closely intertwined in the new visual economy of the exposition. But the phenomenon was even more powerful and influential than these terms suggest. In her recent thorough study of Dutch expo presentations of colonial Indonesia (Java), Marieke Bloembergen stresses the air of cultural authority emanating from the language and imagery of the international expositions as spectacle:

> World exhibitions were the new media of the nineteenth century. They aroused high expectations, in much the same way as the arrival of the internet at the end of the twentieth century. These highly modern, spectacular events attracted huge crowds of visitors from every walk of life, for the first time in history. Since the national political, economic and cultural elite was involved in designing world exhibitions (or in organizing entries), the events radiated an air of authority. And with their audacious combination of delight and instruction, they made an enduring impression on all who saw them. (Bloembergen 2006, 13)

Perhaps "delight and instruction" through cultural authority account for anthropologist Paul Topinard's comment in 1888 that "for about fifteen years, the public has developed a taste for savage races" (Boetsch and Ardagna 2008, 118–19). But it was hardly a French phenomenon alone. As Eric Ames has recently demonstrated (Ames 2008), German animal collector, trainer, and entrepreneur Carl Hagenbeck figured prominently in these developments. In 1874, with his international business in exotic animal collection and display sagging from the global economic depression, Hagenbeck fortuitously discovered the popular appeal and profitability of ethnographic troupes when he brought a group of six "Laplanders" (Sami) to accompany a herd of thirty-one reindeer for display in various European capitals.

The public loved what Hagenbeck labeled his "anthropological-zoological *tableaux-vivants*." He soon hired Johan Adrian Jacobsen as his full-time ethnographic recruiter or collector (his title was "Traveler"); henceforth Hagenbeck's ethnographic collecting and display provided him with a new income stream, and he vigorously pursued the innovative display genre—humans together with animals and cultural objects—over several decades (Ames 2008, 18–62). Jacobsen later wrote that animals would have been easier: "Collecting peoples alone—there are so few occasions to do so, and so few peoples who allow themselves to be collected" (quoted in Ames 2008, 33). To Chicago's Midway Hagenbeck brought only animals and, on the floor above them, a rarely visited collection of cultural artifacts (which Putnam valued highly). Although Hagenbeck never displayed human groups at a world's fair, his success throughout the urban centers of Europe further encouraged the association of "exotic" humans with animals in popular thinking.

Because expositions took place virtually nonstop in western Europe and North America in the last quarter of the century, entrepreneurs with human groups for display could simply move year after year from one venue to another, with only minor adjustments in the exhibits. In tandem with the exposition phenomenon, then, grew an experienced international network of private businessmen and government agents who could at once claim to bring forward representative groups from the diverse imperial world and also make sizable profits; more often than not, the people they brought together for display were themselves experienced, even well-traveled troupes of contracted individuals or families—anything but "raw savages" or "primitives." As with Putnam's ethnographic village, on the Midway each of the concessions for displaying humans had a unique history and set of conditions. Many had appeared elsewhere previously and would go on to fairs in San Francisco, Buffalo, St. Louis, and other venues.

The Street in Cairo

The Street in Cairo was one of a group of "Oriental" exhibits that had been in circulation for several decades—including a Turkish Village (Robert Levy, concessionaire), Egyptian Temple (Prof. Demetrius Mosconas, concessionaire), Persian Palace of Eros (G. K. Debbas, manager), Moorish Palace (Columbian Moorish Palace Company, concessionaire), and Algerian and Tunisian Village (Ela Ganon and A. Siflico, concessionaires; Sol Bloom, manager). They clustered near the middle of the Plaisance on either side of the promenade. The Egyptian Temple was an architectural replica of Luxor with facsimiles of mummies, while the Moorish Palace was a truly eclectic combination of Alhambra-like castle, garden of palms, harem guarded by a eunuch, and a truly bizarre upstairs wax museum that among other things featured scenes of Little Red Riding Hood, the beheading of Marie Antoinette ("with the original guillotine"), Martin Luther and family, Jesus at the Well, and wax figures of forty-four "reigning monarchs and poets" (Bidlake 1893d, 17). The Turkish Village compound housed between 200 and 350 residents and included a mosque, café, bazaar (carpets, silver and brass, antiques), 400-year-old Persian tent, artisan cottages, Turkish theater, and Bedouin encampment with camels and horses. The latter encampment, although associated with Levy's Turkish Village, was in fact owned by a wealthy Syrian newspaperman and financed by the Sultan of Turkey. Originally set up in a baseball park outside the fairgrounds as a "Wild East Show," the Bedouin group in the last months of the Fair moved onto the Midway, where their performances of mock desert warfare were highly popular and endlessly photographed (Scott 1991, 231–32).

Although they were similarly multifaceted enterprises (theaters, bazaars, cafés), the Persian Palace and the Algerian-Tunisian Village became most popular and notorious for introducing the *danse du ventre* or belly dance, and the mythical Little Egypt, to the American public (Carlton 1994; Scott 1991, 195ff). The Persian Palace in particular, with its upstairs rooms filled with raucous "college boys and 'prematurely grey men'" lounging around ethnically questionable dancing girls, threatened to evoke memories of Philadelphia's sinful "Centennial City"; after stories appeared as far away as the *New York Times*, the Persian Palace was briefly shut down and cleaned up (Scott 1991, 193).

The Street in Cairo appeared at several fairs from 1851 onward and had won a gold medal at Paris in 1889. The Chicago version, which was the most popular and profitable exhibit on the Midway (two and a half million visitors in six months, by one estimate), was operated by an Egyptian banker named George Pangolo and became home to several hundred North Africans during the course of the Fair. In the view of Fair officials, Pangolo was the ideal worldly businessman of the future: a mixture of English, Greek, and Italian born in Turkey, he had been educated in an American Congregationalist school in Constantinople before moving to Egypt and rising to be manager of the Anglo-Egyptian Bank in Cairo. Attracted by the possibilities of the American exposition environment, Pangolo moved to Chicago in 1890 to devote himself to the Cairo Street project. He walked away handsomely rewarded. In American eyes Pangolo was quintessentially a man of the world who understood global exchange values. As the authors of *Portrait Types of the Midway Plaisance* captioned him, Pangolo seemed "a forerunner of that final race who are [sic] to possess the earth when all the nations of [the] globe shall be of one blood" (Anon. 1894d, n.p.).

Much of the appeal of the Street in Cairo lay in its construction: the narrow streets, multistoried and balconied building fronts, small shops, street vendors and performers—conjurors, mind-readers, jugglers—created a sense of enclosure, exoticism, and noisy excitement and exchange, even an edge of daring and danger. Through the streets strode camels, donkey boys, and daily wedding processions. For twenty-five cents Achmet the Donkey Boy would help the visitor ride his donkey for five minutes; Achmet went home with five hundred dollars. Five minutes on a camel cost fifty cents. In the Cairo Street occurred a constant and close mixing of Fair crowds with the village people, and some fairgoers and writers took great interest in the personal lives of the villagers. They also crossed personal boundaries, as some felt that the price of admission justified intrusive gawking and touching (Scott 1991, 165–66). Hawthorne was hardly alone in his fascination with the closeness of human and animal smells and sounds of the Cairo Street:

> The colors [of the buildings] are sunny and warm, with harmonious blendings of pale yellow and pink and purple; there are projecting balconies and airy loggias and mysterious archways; and everywhere are tiny shops, overflowing with things you want to buy. . . . But you inevitably turn from the shops and houses to the crowd in the street. Right beneath us, as we sit, is the donkey- and camel-stand—that is, the donkeys stand and the camels lie down, in the peculiar fashion possible for camels only. Their drivers, living pieces of human Egypt, in long caftans, fez and turban, brown-skinned and black-eyed, and with naked feet lounge about, or lean upon their beasts, and let no possible customer escape them. And customers are plenty, men, women, and children. The donkeys are very small and the camels very large, so that whichever the rider selects, he or she is sure to be the object of attention to the laughing, cheering, surging, good-humored American crowd that presses together everywhere, and follows them on their course down the narrow thoroughfare, or dodges to escape the too precipitous onset of their career. (Hawthorne 1893b, 575)

Like the rest of the Midway, the Street in Cairo stayed open late into the romantic, illuminated evenings. On the last night of the International Congress of Anthropology, Cushing and a group of friends visited "Cairo" where, Cushing recalled, they watched the "strange coarsely sensuous contortionate dances with head carried level, belly and hips extraordinarily jerked about and various plays with swords and vases of water" (Cushing Diary, September 2, in Document E, this volume). After their closing banquet the anthropologists moved on to the Javanese (Cushing's favorite display) and the Samoans, ending up at midnight at Dahomey Village for a final show. Sadly, the Africans were all asleep.

The Dahomey Village

The village of sub-Saharan Fon people, or Dahomeyans—ceaselessly caricatured by the Chicago press as a group of savages, Amazons, and cannibals—was only one version of an exhibit that had appeared at the Paris Exposition of 1889 and would reemerge after 1893 at several more venues, ending with London's Imperial International Exhibition of 1909. Like the Senegalese villages that also traveled widely in these years, the Dahomey Village phenomenon was a direct outgrowth of French colonial ambitions in Africa. It began under the sponsorship of the French government, which was still engaged in a war of conquest and "improvement" of the sub-Saharan region; in 1894 France finally succeeded in replacing the traditional Fon royalty of the territory of present-day Benin with its first colonial administration.

There were actually two Dahomey groups on the road in the nineties: "Both groups," Paul Greenhalgh recounts, "decided to take their fates into their own hands by placing themselves under the control of various entrepreneurs, leasing out their services to exhibitions and holiday resorts, although they still appeared in a more official role as part of French imperial sections" (Greenhalgh 1988, 94). The group that came to Chicago was under the direction of a French geographer, labor contractor, and ivory trader in West Africa named Xavier Pené (Hill and Hatch 2003, 137). As Rydell relates the negotiations of his concession, Pené realized from the popularity of the African exhibits at Paris in 1889 that an opportunity was appearing in Chicago for another form of "trading in human beings." After initially turning him down, the Exposition Company's Ways and Means Committee reversed itself in July 1892, having heard that the French government enthusiastically supported Pené's plan. The Chicago contract called for Pené to provide a "faithful" representation of a Dahomeyan village with at least sixty individuals, half of whom were to be women—explorer Richard Burton's legendary "Amazons," or bare-breasted women warriors. Fair officials required as well a "king" or "chief," performance of regular military exercises and religious ceremonies, and a "museum" or colonial gift shop in which the Fon would sell gold and silver jewelry and other wares made on site (Rydell 1999, 138–40).

Pené returned to Africa and recruited sixty-seven individuals from French Congo, French Guinea, and Benin—Fon people from the traditional kingdom of Abomey ("Dahomey"). Although the troupe included a mixture of tribal and regional groups, in Chicago they all became "savage Dahomeyans," and the women became "Amazons," a people advertised as occupying one of the lowest rungs of social evolution.

Located toward the western end of the Plaisance, between the Laplanders and the Austrian Village and across from the Brazil Concert Hall, they were the Fair's only major black exhibit. African-American spokespersons Frederick Douglass and Ida B. Wells were doubly incensed that while black Americans were deliberately denied any meaningful presence at the World's Columbian Exposition, "African savages were brought here to act like the monkey" (Bay 2009, 162). "As if to shame the Negro," Douglass wrote, "the Dahomeyans are also here to exhibit the Negro as a repulsive savage" (Reed 2000, 221; Greenhalgh 1988, 99). For his part, Pené boldly reminded French officials that he was less concerned with personal profit than with impressing the Africans with "the grandeur of France" and the irresistible power of Euroamerican civilization (Rydell 1999, 140).

Some American reactions to these Africans were predictably virulent: "Sixty-nine of them are here in all their barbaric ugliness," reported *Frank Leslie's Popular Monthly*, "blacker than buried midnight and as degraded as the animals which prowl the jungles of their dark land." A Boston woman noted "the gulf between them and Emerson." Others thought they made even Native Americans look attractive (Rydell 1984, 66). The cartoon caricatures and jokes in *World's Fair Puck* were sometimes brutal. However, the larger reality of cultural contact between Dahomeyans and fairgoers was considerably more ambiguous than is suggested by *Puck* ridicule, with elements of curiosity and even admiration intermixed with revulsion and fear. If some fairgoers were repulsed by the tom-tom rhythms, others were entranced. Christopher Robert Reed is persuasive, in his important study of black experiences at the Columbian Exposition, that the Fon—including their babies and children (like the Inuits)–became individuals to some reporters and observers, as they mixed on the Midway and reached across barriers: "All of a sudden," Reed notes, "Chicagoans were introduced on a personal level to Butagalon, Amessang, Sosolangago, Ipoke, Umbibi, Cogabi, Aballo, and Adajemus, rather than the impersonal 'the Dahomeans'" (Reed 2000, 148).

At the end of the Fair Pené and the Dahomeyan troupe went on to the Midwinter Fair in San Francisco, where according to Rydell the show became considerably more sexual (Rydell 1999, 141); for the 1901 Pan-American Exposition in Buffalo Pené put together an even more ambitious show, "Darkest Africa," bolstered by commissions from the Smithsonian and the Buffalo Society of Natural History for material collections; here he again produced a large group of West Africans (Rydell 1999, 142). Undoubtedly many were veterans of Chicago's Midway.

The Street in Cairo and the Dahomey Village were only two of more than twenty ethnic exhibits on the mile-long Midway, augmented by foreign and state pavilions in Jackson Park that sometimes included indigenous or colonial displays. As every Midway map shows, the human displays were spread out beneath the original Ferris Wheel—the world's first, Chicago's answer to the Eiffel Tower—and interspersed with an incoherent array of business and entertainment exhibits, rides, and restaurants (e.g., Libbey Glass, Adams Express Company, Diamond Match, an ostrich farm, French Cider Press, Electric Scenic Theater, Captive Balloon, Panorama of the Alps, Venice Murano Glass, Hagenbeck Animals, and a New England Log Cabin). The Midway exhibits were arranged in no discernible geographical or evolutionary order—although as already noted, the Mediterranean and North African exhibits did cluster in the middle, under the Ferris Wheel. This was probably a reflection of Sol Bloom's influence (discussed later) and the extended process whereby the ground allotments and placements for exhibits were determined.

In the most thorough study to date of nineteen human performance exhibits on the Midway, Gertrude Scott labels the Plaisance a "sustained, six-month theatrical event" (Scott 1991, 14). She divides this "village environment" into four levels of performance: formal events (such as dance or music) on a stage or in a room or café, for which visitors paid entrance (twenty-five or fifty cents); street performances such as juggling, sword swallowing, or camel or donkey riding, which the observer experiences with some immediacy (e.g., the Street in Cairo); special public performances of significance to the troupe, such as weddings, funerals, dedications of buildings, or holidays; and "work/life" displays, in which visitors simply gaze over the fence as natives move around their village encampment going about daily chores.

Each level or form of performance had its own history of development: for instance, Scott reveals that Hagenbeck was among the first to overlay simple work/life displays with formal performances and

FIG. 14. America's answer to the Eiffel Tower: the Ferris Wheel on the Midway. H. H. Bancroft, *The Book of the Fair* (Chicago, 1893, 860).

social outings: in London his "Nubians" from North Africa attended Wimbledon and the theater, mixing up close with the crowds, both observing and observed.

Managing the Midway: Putnam, Bloom, Bidlake

Chicago's officials, as already emphasized, were determined that the city's reputation be enhanced by an edifying Exposition. Rudyard Kipling had written that Chicago was "inhabited by savages," and the city elders were determined to "outgrow vulgarity" (Scott 1991, 43). Moreover, certain lessons from Philadelphia still loomed large less than twenty years later: the 1876 Centennial officials had banned "honky-tonk" business from the fairgrounds, only to see "Centennial City"—a shantytown of beer halls, sideshows, and notorious crime—mushroom outside the walls. (The fathers of the City of Brotherly Love demolished it.) Still, most agreed that education for the masses

FIG. 15. The Midway Plaisance, looking eastward toward Lake Michigan from the Ferris Wheel. H. H. Bancroft, *The Book of the Fair* (Chicago, 1893, 834).

required amusement in order to be palatable. So the Midway Plaisance came about as a spatial and conceptual compromise, neither fully in nor fully outside the Exposition. It was easily recognized and ridiculed as an unhappy hybrid: when it was announced that the tree-lined carriage road known locally as the Midway Pleasure Drive (now 59th Street) would become the Fair's "Midway Plaisance," Chicago writers joked of the pretentiousness of the "Royal Road to Gaiety," the "Mudway Plaisance," and the "Mudway Nuisance"(Scott 1991, 49–51; Burnham 1992, 71).

Born of hesitation and compromise, the Midway concept still required integration into the Exposition's classification scheme. Fair officials enlisted George Brown Goode, Smithsonian assistant secretary in charge of the National Museum, who exhorted that the Chicago Fair be a thoroughgoing school of public instruction through object lessons of the progress of humanity (Rydell 1984, 43–46; de Wit 1993, 62–63)—essentially, an exposition of history and anthropology. Goode's vision meshed well with Putnam's. Not surprisingly, Goode produced through several iterations a scheme that placed all the exhibits of the Midway Plaisance in Putnam's department, which was fully and awkwardly titled "Ethnology, Archaeology, History, Cartography, Latin-American Bureau, Collective and Isolated Exhibits." (Goode's classification also placed all U.S. state pavilion exhibits under Putnam, but only seventeen agreed to comply, and Putnam never exercised any control.) However, as we have seen, Putnam had minimal interest in developing a commercial Midway: over more than two years of monthly reports to his boss, Director-General Davis, Putnam virtually never mentioned the Midway concessions under development. Rather, all prospective concessionaires first applied to the Exposition's Ways and Means Committee, which negotiated contracts and issued the concessions; after contract approval, actual space allocation, building design, and construction schedules were in the hands of Daniel Burnham's Department of Buildings and Grounds. Though there were exceptions (such as the Skiles Esquimaux enterprise), in general Putnam, operating from Cambridge until six months before the Fair, played little role in determining the contracts or the physical space on the Midway. Rather, the figure who emerged to shape the Midway was Sol Bloom—and his story sheds a final unique light on Putnam, the Midway, and human exhibits at the Fair.

Sol Bloom was born in Illinois in 1870, the son of Polish immigrants who soon moved to San Francisco. Fascinated even as a boy with theater staging and production, by the time he was a teenager Bloom had left his boyhood work in a brush factory and was arranging boxing matches and managing the Alcazar Theater owned by Michael H. De Young, scion of a prominent San Francisco family and publisher of the *San Francisco Chronicle*. With De Young's blessing, nineteen-year-old Bloom undertook a world tour in search of new shows to sponsor or produce on his own. His first stop was New York; his second was the 1889 Exposition in Paris.

For Bloom, as for Smithsonian curator Otis Mason and so many others, the exhibits of French colonial peoples arrayed below the Eiffel Tower along the Seine were an eye-opener—but in his case of a decidedly non-anthropological sort. The young man returned again and again to the Algerian Village and Café, where the dancers, acrobats, glass-eaters and scorpion-swallowers fascinated him, not as ethnography but as profitable entertainment: "He saw the strange, yet enchanting dances of the Algerian women, who moved in sensuous and hypnotic rhythms. He was sure that nothing like it had ever been seen before in the Western hemisphere. It occurred to him that he could make a fortune with them" (Carlton 1994, 3; cf. Bloom 1948, 107). With an eye to the Columbian celebrations rumored for Chicago in 1892, Bloom paid a thousand dollars to the manager of the troupe of Algerians and Tunisians for exclusive rights to bring the show across the Atlantic. The contract had a two-year limit.

On returning to New York at the close of 1889 Bloom heard that Chicago was favored as the venue for the Columbian fair. His proposals for the Algerian concession were premature, though, so he continued to San Francisco. For a year he arranged prizefights and resumed local theatrical promotions. In the meantime Congress awarded the Exposition to Chicago, President Benjamin Harrison issued his official pronouncement, and in early 1891 Putnam was appointed chief of the Department of Ethnology (including the proposed Midway). Bloom's two-year Algerian concession clock continued to tick, and with the dates for the fair now pushed to 1893, Putnam's plans for Department M (Ethnology) began to take shape. But commercial exhibits had little place in his thinking, and the National Commission to whom he reported generally agreed. Determined to create a non-commercial, educational tone for the fair, the commission resolved that "when the gates to the Fair are opened . . . , the admission fee collected at the entrance should entitle the visitor to see everything on exhibition within the enclosure. In other words, there should be no side shows of any name or nature—theatres and snake charmers alike must be barred out" (Boehm 2004, 59). Most of the boosterism in the months of preparation emphasized that the Chicago Fair would be an unprecedented educational opportunity for American visitors from every region. Indeed, the theme of education and uplift remained strong to the end of the Fair: even novelist Henry B. Fuller (fig. 23), who moved to Chicago at about this time and promptly excoriated the greed and philistinism of the city's business class in such novels as *The Cliffdwellers* (1893) and *With the Procession* (1894), predicted that the Chicago Fair would someday be seen as "not a mere 'business college,' qualifying us narrowly for a narrow life and its narrow purposes, but a real and broad university—one to advance us in the arts, the sciences, the amenities, the humanities" (Boehm 2004, 55).

As the projected costs of the upcoming Fair steadily rose in 1891 and 1892 and fears of a serious national economic depression took hold, a strong countercurrent of commercial profit began to blur the distinction between intramural high culture and extramural low-brow entertainment. The Midway had always been the potential ground of contest. Consequently, "by the time [the Midway] was in full operation . . . , the fair's management had given up—under financial pressure—all expectations of a 'dignified and decorous' ethnological display under the control of Professor Putnam" (Badger 1979, 107). As historian George Moses concluded, "it was along the Midway, the marketplace of pleasure, that the educational ideals of ethnological villages competed for attention and dollars with snake-oil salesmen" (Moses 1996, 135).

Just as this contest between edification and commerce was beginning, Sol Bloom returned to Chicago in the summer of 1891 to resuscitate his pending Algerian concession. "I found things very poorly organized," he recalled years later, since "no single person appeared to have been placed in charge of taking care of people like myself who wanted to set up amusement concessions"—but he was assured that "plans were being drawn for a great avenue to be known as the Midway Plaisance" (Bloom 1948, 117). Bloom retreated to San Francisco for a conference with his influential friend Michael De Young—a national commissioner from California—to complain of the disorganization in Chicago and discuss his concession.

Less than a week later De Young asked Bloom to manage the entire Midway. The young man accepted and left for Chicago. Since Putnam was still in Boston, Bloom met with Harlow Niles Higinbotham (fig. 70), financial officer with the Marshall Field Company, president of the Chicago Exposition Company, and the man most responsible for the financial stability of the Fair. Higinbotham referred Bloom directly to Daniel Burnham (figs, 7, 20), architect and powerful chief of works for the Exposition. Working under Burnham's direction, Bloom began construction of the Midway in the spring of 1892; half the structures were ready by summer, nearly a full year before the opening of the Fair (Bloom 1948, 118–20). His own Algerian troupe arrived six months early, took construction jobs on the fairgrounds, and performed in local hotels. Like the Inuits of the Esquimaux Village, the North Africans were an immediate hit in pre-Fair Chicago.

Bloom appears nowhere in official accounts of the Chicago Fair; but perhaps that is not as odd as it appears. Scholars are fond of citing the comment, from his 1948 autobiography, that putting Putnam in charge of the Midway was akin to "making Albert Einstein manager of the Ringling Brothers and Barnum and Bailey Circus" (Bloom 1948, 106). It is a clever but misleading remark made decades later. In actuality, while Bloom was important in organizing the Midway vendors and shows, neither he nor Putnam directly supervised the Midway (although it was Putnam's formal responsibility). Two months before the opening of the Fair all of the fee-charging exhibits, categorized and referred to as the "Isolated and Collective Exhibits"—that is, all the Midway concessions and the three fee-charging exhibits in Jackson Park proper (Cliffdweller, Esquimaux Village, Japanese Teahouse)—were placed under the direction of a man from North Dakota named John Bidlake.

Born in Hereford, England, in 1858, John Bidlake had migrated to the United States in 1882, settled in North Dakota, and become a naturalized citizen in 1887. After military service he served in both houses of the North Dakota legislature, but his main business interests lay in mining exploration in Minnesota and the Dakotas. It is not clear how he came to Putnam's attention, but it probably occurred through William E. Curtis of the State Department's Latin American Bureau, who was working closely with Putnam. Six months after the Chicago Fair Bidlake took charge of the U.S. consular office in Barranquilla, Colombia. He served for many years as American consul in that country, eventually purchasing a coffee plantation and mining interests. He died on his Colombian plantation in 1917.[1]

However he came to be supervising the Midway, in March 1893 Bidlake undertook a review of the records and receipts of the concessions, which were in considerable disarray (Bidlake 1893a). From this point on, Bidlake reported every month to Putnam (and Putnam to Davis) about such matters on the Midway as new concessions and applications for space, which continued as late as August; wild behavior in the Bedouin encampment (five men received one-way tickets back to Beirut); lewd dances in the Persian Theater, which was temporarily closed, on Putnam's recommendation; and access to liquor among Native Americans, which was restricted after one month (Bidlake 1893b, c). In short, while Bloom oversaw construction of the Midway in the year before the Fair, by the time it opened he was merely managing (and presumably enjoying) his Algerian Theater. Bidlake had taken charge of the Midway daily management, with Putnam's oversight. Briefly thrown together, Bidlake and Putnam continued a genial correspondence after the two had moved on from Chicago. For his part, Bloom left no correspondence with Putnam but went on to a long career in musical production and national politics as the U.S. congressman from Manhattan's Silk Stocking District. The onetime impresario of the exotic capped his career by helping to draft the United Nations Charter at the end of World War II. He died in 1948.

Putnam after the Fair: "A Used Up Orange"

The gates of the World's Columbian Exposition closed and the American flag was lowered for the last time at sunset on October 30, 1893, amid a general sense of sadness and despair that even the most avid boosterism could not hide. The Fair that had begun six months earlier with the onset of nationwide economic depression ended with the assassination, on October 29, of Chicago's popular new mayor, Carter Harrison IV. The mayor had hoped to keep the Fair open through November and reopen it in the spring as a form of public works for the desperate working men of Chicago. Instead, within a few weeks most of the Exposition buildings in Jackson Park had been burned to the ground by disaffected Pullman Palace Car Company workers (Miller 1996, 531–32).

Putnam spent the last weeks of the Fair scrambling to claim collections for the new Columbian Museum that he had been promoting since 1890. In mid-October Chicago lumber baron and private collector Edward E. Ayer (fig. 69) showed department store magnate Marshall Field through the Anthropology Building; Field finally pledged a million dollars to the new museum, assuring its future (Essay 6 and Document J, this volume). Putnam and Boas worked day and night through November and December to transfer the collections from the Anthropology Building and other sites in Jackson Park to the Palace of Fine Arts, the prospective home of the museum. However, as plans for leadership and staffing took shape it became clear to both men that they were being marginalized. "The people here treat Putnam, who has worked two years on behalf of the museum, unspeakably rudely, and make their final arrangements completely behind his back," Boas wrote to his parents in mid-December (quoted in Cole 1999, 157).

Several factors conspired against Putnam. During the Fair he reported directly to Director-General Davis, not Chicago Exposition Company president Higinbotham. Unfortunately for Putnam, Higinbotham was the key figure in arranging financing for the Columbian Museum—he personally contributed $100,000—and served as the first chair of its board of directors. He and the other directors had a broader vision for the museum than Putnam, one that embraced not only natural history and anthropology but the entire range of exhibits represented at the Fair (Brinkman 2009). It was an understandable position, since many collections related to the businessmen's various commercial interests. Putnam had argued from the beginning for a permanent building for his Department M that would become the new museum—and not incidentally would give him substantial control of the new institution. Higinbotham took an early dislike to Putnam (Collier 1972, 8), resented his ambitions, and probably blamed him, unfairly, for inefficient administration and opening the Anthropology Building two months late (McVicker 1999, 40). Indeed, he made a point of telling Putnam that as president of the Chicago Exposition, he had never entered the Anthropology Building. It is likely, as suggested by Paul Brinkman, that Putnam's occasional casting of aspersions on Chicago as a culturally inferior city, together with assertions that his own Exposition work would elevate the city above mere commerce and lift the Chicagoans from the "darkness of ignorance" (Document B, this volume), had grown tiresome and offensive to Higinbotham and his circle. Brinkman also argues that Ayer, the first president of the Columbian Museum, was probably the only Chicago philanthropist with an interest in advancing serious anthropology by means of the new museum; the others were chiefly concerned with commemorating the Fair and with local pride and cultural self-esteem (Brinkman 2009, 88).

At this sensitive juncture, furthermore, there were external actors positioning themselves for Chicago's new cultural institutions. As Donald McVicker outlined some years ago (1999, 39–40), Thomas C. Chamberlin, former member of Powell's U.S. Geological Survey and former president of the University of Wisconsin, was anxious to staff the Columbian Museum and his new home, the young University of Chicago, with USGS colleagues—namely Charles D. Walcott in geology and William H. Holmes in anthropology: these Washington men would make a "glorious team," he thought, to lead Chicago science to "the highest and best things" (Chamberlin 1894). Putnam and Boas had no chance against this accomplished political and academic infighter, who was operating as well on behalf of William R. Harper, the president of Rockefeller's new University of Chicago. Even C. Staniland Wake, the English bibliophile who served as Putnam's secretary for the International Congress of Anthropology, who organized and transferred Department M's library of twelve hundred volumes (donated from all over the world) to the Columbian Museum, and who hoped for a permanent librarian position, was frozen out of the new museum (Wake 1894a). As Boas discovered in the dismal year of 1894, association with Putnam opened no doors in Chicago (Hinsley and Holm 1976; Cole 1999, 159–66).

For his part, Putnam was exhausted and increasingly bitter in the last weeks of 1893. He worked nonstop through the year-end holidays in order to return to Harvard in the new year, as stipulated by his leave of absence: "Stern duty is my taskmaster," he responded in turning down one Christmas invitation (Putnam 1893m). He left Chicago stung by a sense of disrespect and ingratitude and feeling that "after squeezing all the juice out of me they threw me aside as a used up orange" (Cole 1999, 158; Putnam 1894). He had always realized, he confided to his close State Department colleague William E. Curtis, that "the great difficulty in Chicago is to get hold of men long enough to get them to consider any subject, every one is in such a rush and drive" (Putnam 1891j). By the end of the Fair he feared that the new museum would suffer from the shortsighted ambitions of a business-oriented board intent on collecting artifacts rapidly and competitively. On the last day of 1893 he even presumed to warn Ayer that a scientific and educational institution requires care and foresight to permit "a healthy, steady growth" —it must not be too rushed, haphazard, and overcommitted—so that "the next generation will honor their predecessors" (Putnam 1893n). To little avail, Putnam was delivering a message from conservative New England to the rich urban upstart on the lake. All would be half-baked, shabby work in Chicago, he advised Edward H. Thompson a few months later: "You need a quiet, conservative, scientific life in order to do your best work" (Putnam 1894a). Thompson stayed in Chichén Itzá, on his Yucatecan plantation and near his Mayan sacred *cenote*—but even he later contracted with Chicago interests.

The personal disappointments were substantial and bitter, to be sure; but from the longer perspective of his career, and even in the short run, the Chicago World's Fair solidified Putnam's preeminent position in American anthropology until his retirement in 1909. Whatever Chicago's business elite thought of him, over a three-year period of incessant activity Putnam had created a massive national and international network, overseen dozens of fieldworkers throughout the hemisphere, prosecuted successful working relations with political and cultural leaders in the Americas and Europe, and established himself as the central institutional force in American anthropology. On returning to Harvard he taught his first introductory graduate course in anthropology; granted his first PhD to George A. Dorsey; and began to shepherd the first generation of Harvard graduates in anthropology: Roland B. Dixon, William C. Farabee, John R. Swanton, and Frank Russell. In these years of constant manipulation of small but vital fellowships, salaries, and staff at Harvard and the Peabody Museum, first Dorsey (until his move to Chicago in 1897) and then Dixon and Russell (until his death from tuberculosis in 1903) became the workhorses of Putnam's young department (Hinsley 1992, 135–39). When Alfred Tozzer received his PhD in 1904 and joined the teaching staff, his arrival marked the beginning of a new generation for the Harvard museum and department (Browman and Williams 2013, 302–5).

Putnam's return to Cambridge was anything but a retreat or retrenchment. Rather, from his increasingly solid positions in Cambridge he reached out in mid-1894 to accept Morris K. Jesup's offer to establish anthropology on a more solid footing at the American Museum of Natural History in New York; and a few years later he accepted Phoebe Hearst's invitation to place her new program at Berkeley on a firm foundation as well. Each of these initiatives, along with his prescient and reliable support of the brilliant and sometimes prickly Boas, presents a complex story in itself; but it is hard to imagine they would have occurred without Putnam's prominence and activities from 1890 through 1893. Chicago established Putnam.

And in a sense, Putnam established Chicago in anthropology. Unquestionably embittered, Putnam nonetheless left Chicago convinced that anthropology at the Fair, both on and off the Midway, had taught Americans important lessons about global diversity in aesthetics and values—although he hardly used those words. In a fascinating introduction to *Portrait Types of the Midway Plaisance*—the 1894 album of captioned photos that had first appeared as a serial publication during the Fair (see Visual Interlude, this volume)—Putnam mentioned the unprecedented and controversial variety of music and dance that fairgoers had encountered. Like Boas he viewed all such performances as data for ethnological study, but he also saw the more broadening effects of such exposure for an American public on the edge of world markets and nascent imperialism. Returning readers once again to the exotic side streets of the Midway's Cairo, Putnam recalled in an embracive first person plural the shared sense of wonder and curiosity that marked this unique blend of education and entertainment:

> What shall we say of the "Street in Cairo" with its confusion of life: Arabs, Egyptians, Nubians and Soudanese in varying and characteristic costumes; jugglers, swordsmen, venders, donkey boys, and camel drivers. How we dodged from under the camel that pushed on regardless of anyone who stood in the way; and how we laughed at those who rode the beast as he lurched to his feet with his load. Here indeed we met with life such as never before was seen in America and here was the opportunity for a study of national character of great variety. At one end of the street the old Temple of Luxor reminded us of ancient Egypt, while the architecture of the street and the Mosque at the other end told of Cairo in its splendor. Here in the playhouse of the street were gathered the dancing women, and here was to be witnessed the national *dans du ventre* which not being understood was by many regarded as low and repulsive. What wonderful muscular movements did those dancers make, and how strange did this dance seem to us; but is it not probable that our waltz would seem equally strange to these dusky women of Egypt? What is a dance, is a question one was

forced to ask after a trip through the Midway. Every nation had its own form. With some it was a rhythmic movement of the hands and arms; with others of the feet and legs; and with others of the body; some were ceremonial, others for amusement, according to national traditions and customs. (*Portraits,* "Introduction," n.p.)

Perhaps Putnam's hopes for popular education were not misplaced after all. The ubiquitous Julian Hawthorne had predicted, or at least hoped, that Americans would emerge from the Fair "a wiser and broader people" (Hawthorne 1893a, 36). The artist for Poole Brothers' *Vistas of the Fair: A Portfolio of Familiar Views* (Anon. 1894e) painted colorful cosmopolitan scenes of cultural strolling and mixing on the Wooded Isle, in the Kwakiutl Village, and beneath the Yucatan ruins. The *Harper's* magazine representation of evening on the illuminated Midway chose to see the world on promenade through the eyes of a young American couple (fig. 40). We do not see their expressions, but the confrontation is unmistakable. Like this strolling couple, young America was already facing a new and puzzling set of global realities.

The dilemma was as old as Columbus and his caravels. Claude Lévi-Strauss described in *Tristes Tropiques* (1955) "that crucial moment in modern thought when, thanks to the great voyages of discovery, a human community which had believed itself to be complete and in its final form suddenly learned, as if through the effect of a counterrevolution, that it was part of a great whole, and that, in order to achieve self-knowledge, it must first contemplate its unrecognizable image in this mirror" (quoted in Green 1979, 102). At their quotidian best, the on-the-ground experiences at the Chicago Fair—on the Midway, in Putnam's building and ethnographic village, at the Cliffdwellers exhibit—undermined the Fair's larger hegemonic intentions, providing space for a reflective exercise in reconsidering self, other, and totality. A few certainly thought so. Looking back after twenty-five years on the effects of the Fair on his city, Chicago banker and historian William Hudson Harper had no doubt of the profound and positive changes that the human exhibits at the Fair had wrought on his still-provincial community—and perhaps on America, too:

> Chicago people who had drunk the blending of golden and brown elixir out of the two teapots of the gentle Ceylon representative, or had taken

coffee with the Costa Ricans, or in "Old Vienna," or from the "Hot, Hot" coffee-pot of the white-petticoated Turk, who had watched the batik-making of the Javanese, observed the completeness of Japan's defensive equipment, sanitary and otherwise, been cheered by the lifegiving quality of French art, or depressed by certain decadent tendencies in the German—Chicago people who came in contact with all this daily and intimately could never be accused of provincialism again. They would feel at home in the real "Streets of Cairo," quite at their ease in a village of the South Sea Islanders, and in return they knew that the name of Chicago and the entire feasibility of dealing with us had been made known to the uttermost parts of the earth. It is needless to say that the memory of all this will have a decided effect in stimulating interest in foreign trade, which can never seem so "foreign" since the World's Fair. (Harper 1921, 57)

Notes

Epigraph: Scharnhorst 2008, 211.

1. Information on John Bidlake comes from the National Archives and Records Administration, College Park, Maryland, General Records of the Department of State, Record Group 59 (1910–1929), decimal file 321.113, box 3872. Thanks to Dave Ellison of Reston, Virginia, for locating and retrieving these records.

DOCUMENT A

Ethnology at the Exposition

FRANZ BOAS

At great expositions the achievements of individuals and of nations may be set forth in two ways: either by competitive exhibits, in which each individual and each country endeavors to show to best advantage the points of eminence of its products; or by selected exhibits, which are arranged with a view of giving a systematic series of exhibits covering a certain field. The latter method gives the best result for the student of the history of civilizations; the former is unavoidably pursued in all portions of an exposition which have a commercial interest, as the producer considers the exhibition of his works a profitable investment, and as the consumer or trader is given an opportunity to find the best source of supply for his demands. This method cannot be avoided even in art exhibits which rely upon contributions of living artists. It is the method which subserves best the interest of the exhibitor; it is the exposition method. The method of selected exhibits is more advantageous to the student; it is the museum method.

Many departments of the World's Columbian Exposition have a series of exhibits arranged from the latter point of view; but it is the distinctive feature of one only: of the Department of Ethnology. If the department had relied upon contributions of exhibitors only, there would have been danger of an accumulation of heterogeneous collections, arranged according to the fancy and taste of collectors; a systematic representation of the present status and methods of ethnology would have been almost out of the question. Besides this, the

From *A World's Fair, 1893: A Special Issue of Cosmopolitan Magazine*, December 1893 best available material is massed in museums, which naturally can send a small portion of their collections only to an exposition.

The abandonment of the plan to bring together isolated ethnological collections, and the effort to create a systematic and comprehensive exhibit, characterize the ethnological department of the World's Columbian Exposition. The lines on which the exhibit was to be developed were laid down in the request of the World's Fair committee to Professor F. W. Putnam, of Harvard University, to present a plan for a department which should illustrate early life in America, from remote ages down to the period of Columbus. Thus the anthropology of America was made the leading point of view and determined the direction in which the department developed.

Professor Putnam was selected chief of the department, and at his suggestion a considerable sum of money was set apart for original scientific work on the anthropology of America. The results obtained by means of these funds form the nucleus of the ethnological exhibits at the World's Fair.

First in importance stands the work in American archaeology. Four subjects, which cover some of the most important problems in this field, were selected for special studies: the age of man in America; the culture of the mound-builders; the archaeology of Central America; and the ancient culture of Peru. Therefore, these subjects are most fully represented in the exhibits of the department. The work has been favored by good fortune, and it may safely be said that some of the most important finds have been made during those investigations.

The much-disputed paleolithic implements are fully represented, together with material relating to their stratigraphical position. The question of the antiquity of man hinges upon the undisputed find of rude stone implements in undisturbed layers, the geological age of which can be determined beyond doubt. Disputed ground has been subjected to a new examination, and a number of new finds have been made, which seem to favor the theory that man inhabited the Delaware valley at the time when the glacial gravels were being deposited. Incidentally, numerous remains of the Indians of this region have been found, and a series of well-preserved graves have been opened, the contents of which are shown in the collections of the department. The culture of the mound-builders of the Ohio valley is represented by a magnificent collection. Models of a series of earthworks illustrate a number of types of those structures. The beautiful implements and ornaments made of stone, copper, bone and shell, the clay altars on which burnt offerings were found, the variety of objects buried with the dead, convey a most vivid idea of the arts, industries and customs of those people. They also show that we must not imagine the mound-builders to have been a people very far in advance of the Indian tribes at the time of their discovery, but that their culture was on a similar level.

The results of those systematic explorations form the nucleus of the exhibits on North American archaeology. They are supplemented by a series of collections which give a comprehensive review of types found in certain regions. Ontario, Ohio, Missouri, Wisconsin, Tennessee, Arkansas and California deserve special mention in this connection.

The archaeological exhibit of the state of Colorado is also the result of special exploration, and the ancient culture of the cliffdwellers is one of the best represented subjects at the exposition, as, outside of the Anthropological building, where the department collections are exhibited, the "cliffdwellers exhibit" is devoted entirely to this subject.

Perhaps the most impressive exhibit of the archaeological section is the one devoted to Central America. Never before has so complete a collection of sculptures of the ancient peoples of this region been attempted. In front of the Anthropological [sic] building are found facsimiles of some of the most remarkable edifices of Yucatan—the famous portal of Labna, the Parade of the Serpents, the arch of Uxmal, and several others. The moulds which served for the construction of these facsimiles were taken by agents of the department. The collection of sculptures in the Anthropological building contains casts from Mexico, Guatemala, Yucatan and Honduras, and is supplemented by an excellent series of photographs. The achievements of the Central American Indians, and the stage which their civilization had reached in early times and long before it was so ruthlessly destroyed, is forcibly illustrated by these works of art. Costa Rica has furnished a collection of beautiful stone carvings, of pottery and gold ornaments, which shows another side of the varied arts and industries of Central America.

The civilization of the highlands of South America is well represented through collections made under the direction of the department. Explorations in the necropolis of Ancon have yielded a large series of mummies, with which are found specimens of pottery and wonderfully preserved textile fabrics, woven in highly artistic designs. The exploration was not confined to this region, but covered all the more important centers of South American culture.

Another section of the department is devoted to ethnology and endeavors to set forth the customs and arts of various people before they were influenced by the whites. Naturally, American collections predominate in this section as well as in archaeology. Although nowadays it is difficult to obtain good collections which show native industries entirely unaffected by our civilization, they have the advantage over archaeological collections that the implements can be seen in actual use and that the meaning of ceremonial objects and of ornaments can be learned from the people who use them. The Eskimo of North Greenland and of Alaska, the numerous tribes of the North Pacific coast, the Indians of the northwest territories of Canada and the tribes of Wisconsin are best represented. The Indians east of the Rocky mountains have been so much modified by contact with the white that, taken as a whole, a small amount of material only has been gathered. A number of excellent collections from South America represent the ethnology of parts of that continent quite exhaustively. Brazil sends a large collection of its curious pottery, dancing masks and drums and stone implements. Paraguay has a magnificent display of feather ornaments, weapons and utensils of the tribe of the Gran Chaco, of Paraguay and of southeastern Brazil, which can hardly be equaled by any other collection. British Guiana and Venezuela, Bolivia and Peru add their share to the ethnological exhibit, which illustrates the recent status of the Indian. All this material is arranged in geographical groups, in order to convey to the mind as clearly as possible the culture of each tribe. This tribal exhibit is supplemented by a few very good collections illustrative of certain manufactures of the American Indians. There are collections of basketry, of beadwork and of pottery, gathered from all over North America.

The meaning of the ethnographical specimens is made clearer by the presence of a small colony of Indians, who live in their native habitations near the Anthropological building. The most striking among these buildings are the houses from British Columbia, with their carved totem posts. The collection from this region is particularly strong in paraphernalia used in religious ceremonials, and their use is illustrated in the dances which the Indians perform. Another instructive group of dwellings are the bark-houses of the Iroquois Indians, which are inhabited by a number of members of the various tribes composing that stock. Other tribes and dwellings represented in this group are the Eskimo, Cree, Chippewayan, Winnebago, Navajo, and the Arawak of British Guiana. In this connection must be mentioned the highly instructive villages of Midway Plaisance, in which a great variety of races are found. A mere enumeration will give an idea of the scope of these exhibits: Java, the South Sea Islands, Dahomey, the Soudan, Lapland, Arabia, Turkey and Algeria are represented here.

The ethnological collections from foreign continents are not numerous. Those from Australia, the South Sea Islands, and from parts of Africa, are fairly good, but cannot be compared with those of the great museums of Europe.

One section of the Department of Ethnology is devoted to religions, games and folk-lore. In this section the historical development of a number of games is illustrated by an elaborate series of specimens. Naturally, the games of the Old World, the history of which can be traced through long periods and through many countries, have received fullest attention, but homologous games of primitive people are not wanting. In the arrangement of this section the wide spread of ideas as well as the recurrence of similar ethnic phenomena among a great variety of people, is brought out with great force. Objects of worship, idols and amulets form another attractive group in this section.

The anatomical laboratories. The methods of studying the anatomy of races are illustrated by means of a series of the principal apparatus used in anthropological investigations. The results of researches on certain races, and on people of the same race living under different conditions, exemplify the scope and the objects of these researches. In order to attain this end more satisfactorily, a number of instruments are shown in operation, and measurements of visitors who present themselves are taken. A very full collection of crania and skeletons illustrates the anatomy of human races. A second section of the laboratories is devoted to the anatomy of the nervous system. The growth of the brain and its anatomy are set forth by means of specimens, casts and diagrams. The third section of the laboratories is devoted to experimental psychology. There a very full collection of psychological apparatus is found, and the methods of investigation are illustrated in a working laboratory, in which a number of the simpler tests are shown. These laboratories serve to explain the objects of psychological and anthropological research, but at the same time the accumulating material will prove to be of considerable scientific interest.

The remaining parts of the laboratories are devoted to two special subjects: the development of children, and the anthropology of the North American Indians. In the former section the results of special investigations on the physical and psychical development of American children are exhibited. This collection of material will be of special interest to educationists who believe that the experimental study of children is the true basis of the art of education. There also are found Dr. D. A. Sargent's statues of the typical American man and woman, the dimensions of each being derived from an extensive series of measurements of college students.

This brief sketch of the ethnological exhibit at the World's Fair shows that its strong side lies wholly in a full representation of American anthropology. Its great merit is the large amount of material, new to science, that has been accumulated and which has considerably advanced our knowledge of the history and characteristics of man in America.

DOCUMENT B

The Columbus Memorial Museum

Address to the Commercial Club of Chicago, November 28, 1891

FREDERIC WARD PUTNAM

The City of Chicago is now nobly provided with libraries, and is to have an Art Museum of the highest character in connection with its Institute of Art, and has also an Historical Society. The lovers of literature, art and history are thus assured of essential aids in their studies. But how is it with the multitude of students and lovers of nature? Should not they be given equal opportunities for observation and investigation in the natural sciences?

To this great City is now offered an exceptional opportunity of establishing a grand Museum of Natural History, as a permanent result of the World's Columbian Exposition. Surely this opportunity must not be lost. Arrangements should be made without delay to thus add . . . the means of culture in the natural sciences to the present attractions and importance of the City.

It is beyond question that a love of nature is inherent in mankind, and is shown alike by the savage, the child, and the cultured man and woman. Through this natural tendency, properly fostered and directed, a people may be led to feel an intelligent interest in all the forms, existing and extinct, of the animal and vegetable kingdoms; as well as in the structure and formation of the earth on which we live. Many an indifferent idler straggling into a well-arranged museum goes forth with new ideas and fresh interests. When this intelligent interest is once aroused, it incites enquiry and research and often brings energy and brightness into an otherwise aimless and weary life. By a series of object lessons, often taken unknowingly at first, the person becomes a

Typescript, F. W. Putnam File, Field Museum Archives

student to a greater or lesser extent and the process of a refining culture is begun which cannot fail to result in benefit to the community.

That museums of science and art, as well as libraries, are a social and intellectual benefit to a great city cannot be denied; and in every city they should be fostered and sustained. In fact, such museums now exist in nearly all prominent cities; and certainly when searching out the general culture of a city, one asks for its libraries, museums and galleries and judges fairly well of its intellectual life by what he finds therein. Once Chicago had a splendid beginning for a Natural History Museum, which in the ordinary course of events would have furnished to the City what is now so markedly and lamentably wanting; but the great fire swept away the Museum of the Chicago Academy of Sciences; and it has often been held up to the disgrace of the City that this once important Academy,—which so well performed its work of education in the City, and was known throughout the world by its publications,—was not sustained when renewed prosperity came to Chicago. That the collections of the Academy of Sciences may still form a nucleus for a new museum on a grander scale than dreamed of by founders of the Academy, can but be the wish of all who knew that institution before its sad fate. But in whatever way the museum, now so much needed, is to be formed, the necessity of its speedy coming into existence on a scale equal to the demands of the day is imperative for the culture and fame of Chicago. For the City to longer remain without such a museum seems impossible; and not to take advantage of the golden opportunity now offered for its foundation would simply be choosing to remain in the darkness of ignorance when one of the brightest lights for culture is within reach.

Of what then should such a Natural History Museum consist, and what should be its organization?

First, there should be a building of considerable size, so designed as to admit of additions in future years as the growth of the museum demands.

Second, the building should be planned at once, that every one may know it is to be; and the organization of the administration board should be such as to inspire the greatest confidence in the community.

With those two important matters assured, there would be given to the museum thousands of objects, exhibited at the Columbian

Exposition, which would otherwise be sent elsewhere. In relation to this it is well to remember that the National Museum in Washington owes its existence largely to the Centennial Exposition, at which time so much was secured for the Government by the foresight of the late Professor [Spencer] Baird. Just such an opportunity, but a hundred times greater, will be offered to Chicago by the coming Exposition, if it is known that there is to be a permanent museum, where everything will be properly arranged and cared for.

As to the organization of the Museum,—two methods are common in this country, each of which has its advantage. One is to have the museum owned by a society which would also have a library, hold meetings for the discussion of scientific subjects, give lectures in order to encourage scientific thought and instruction in the community, and publish papers read at its meetings. Such a society would elect its council or governing body, who would appoint the paid officers and designate their duties. All property would be invested in a Board of Trustees elected by the Council. Such in general is the organization of the Society of Natural History in Boston, and of the Academy of Natural Sciences in Philadelphia, two of the oldest societies in the country which have sustained large museums forming important institutions in their respective cities.

The other common plan is the formation of a Board of Trustees who hold the property, given or raised by stock subscription, for the specified purpose of the trust, and who appoint all officers and confirm all plans to be carried out. The American Museum of Natural History in Central Park is one of the largest and most important museums managed somewhat on this plan. It has received very important aid from city and state, and has a long list of influential subscribers to its funds, including Patrons, Life Members and Annual Subscribers.

The Peabody Museum of American Archaeology and Ethnology of Harvard University is also an example of successful management upon the Trustee system, although it is a constituent part of the University.

Modifications of these general plans have come into existence as the many museums in the country have grown to importance under various circumstances. Whatever may be the source of the power making a governing body, such a responsible body, with corporate [powers], must exist in order to hold property and give permanence to the museum. A large amount of property in buildings and in collections as well as in funds will be in time accumulated, by gifts and bequests, as the museum is shown to be worthy of aid, by the advantages it afford[s] to the people. In fact, a carefully arranged museum, properly sustained and officered, will necessarily sooner or later become a school of natural science, just as every great art museum falls short of its usefulness unless there is connected with it a school of art.

Let us then assume that there is a Board of Trustees organized and a building erected or at least planned, and that officers are wanted to take care of the specimens of all kinds which must be properly catalogued, labelled and exhibited according to the most critical demands of science today; so that every object in the Museum shall be there as the exponent of a certain fact in nature and all these parts shall be so arranged as to teach great truths. Such a corps of officers should consist of the following:—

A *Director*, who should plan the general arrangement of the museum, assign each department to its proper place and oversee the work in all departments. He should be a man not only of thorough scientific attainments but also in sympathy with the presentation of the economic side of scientific research. His powers should be absolute within specified limits agreed to between him and the Board of Trustees; and all Curators, Assistants and Employees should be appointed by the Trustees only on nomination by the Director. This would be necessary in order to maintain proper discipline and system in the Museum. The Director should hold his position as a life appointment, subject only to removal for serious offence.

The other principal officers should be appointed for specified terms or for life, subject to removal for sufficient cause to be determined by the Trustees.

Next in rank to the Director should be the *Curators*. Each Curator should be the head of the special department to which he is appointed, and should have entire and free management of the department, under the general plans of the Director.

Next to Curators should be *Assistants* in the several departments, working under the direction of the respective Curators. There should also be a *Chief Assistant* who should be under the orders of the Director and who should act as his executive officer. Other employees should be clerks, messengers, a janitor to take care of the building, and watchmen.

Having thus arranged for the Governing Board and the officers there is now to be considered the departments into which the museum should be divided. At the start there should be as few as possible and their increase should depend on the special requirements of the museum as its development progresses. Primarily there should be the following departments:—

1. *Geology.* This should include the structure of the earth, illustrated by the structure of the rocks and the methods of their formation; the structure of the mountains and valleys and the formation of lakes and rivers. This department should also include Economic Geology with special reference to rocks used in the arts; ores, coal, petroleum, natural gas, salt, clays, and other products of the earth used by man; with illustrations of the methods by which they are obtained from the earth, including mining, smelting, etc., etc.

2. *Mineralogy.* This would include a collection of minerals, ores and gems exhibited in such a way as to show their structure and constituents, their occurrence in nature, their uses, etc. Under this department the economic division would also be large and of great practical value.

3. *Botany.* This would include the vegetable kingdom, both living and fossil, also an economic section showing the use of plants to man. This economic collection would be of great size and importance as can readily be imagined by recalling the many thousand plants essential or more or less useful to man in various parts of the world. Another section would contain injurious plants. Another would show all the lower and microscopic forms of plant life.

4. *Zoology.* This would include all animals, both living and fossil. In this division would be stuffed skins and alcoholic specimens, skeletons and various anatomical preparations. This department would also have its economic sections to show the animals used by man for food and various other purposes.

5. *Anthropology.* This would include Archaeology and Ethnology and the Physical Structure of Man. This department would illustrate man in his organic parts and as a physical being; the evidence of his existence in geologic time, through prehistoric times; and his distribution by races and peoples over the earth.

In addition to the Structural, Systematic and Economic groups or arrangements in the five departments, there should also be a Synthetic or type collection of the principal forms of rocks, minerals, plants and animals, and another similar collection of the various formations of the earth from the oldest known rocks to the present time and showing the characteristic fossils of each period; thus illustrating in a concise manner the structure of the earth and the development of plant and animal life upon it. There should also be a collection illustrative of the great geological, mineralogical, botanical and zoological conditions of each continent and of the several groups of islands; and also of the characteristic plants and animals of the Pacific and Atlantic oceans. Thus, in one hall would be shown features of North America, with examples of the principal animals, plants and minerals. Another hall would be devoted to South America, and so on, for all large divisions of the world. In each of these halls would be placed an ethnological collection, illustrating the native peoples with their habitations and their arts, surrounded by the native fauna and flora, and the natural scenery of the country.

In a museum thus arranged, it can easily be imagined that a series of object lessons would be presented which could not fail to give the people a knowledge far greater than could be obtained in any other way. As to the desirability of establishing in Chicago such a carefully arranged museum, as a suitable and enduring memorial of the Exposition, there can be but one answer,—science and culture demand it. The only question is, Are the people of Chicago ready for such an undertaking, and have they the desire to carry it out? The grand opportunity is here, and the financial support can certainly be obtained if the men and women of culture and of means, in this great and wealthy city, will enter heartily into the work.

There are two features in connection with this plan for a permanent museum which should be considered but which are not specially alluded to in the preceding pages.

One is that the central hall could well be a memorial hall of Columbus in which could be placed a statue of the discoverer of America, with portraits of Columbus and other worthies of his time, with the model of the Santa Maria and all such relics and reproductions illustrative of his time as can be secured from the Columbian collection of the Exposition and from other sources.

The other is the use of the museum by all the colleges and other educational institutions in and about Chicago. By an arrangement with such institutions, the officers of the institution could receive their classes for instruction in the natural sciences and thus secure a portion of their salaries from such sources. The museum would remain entirely independent of such institutions while its facilities and resources could be used for their benefit under proper regulations. Now that the only approved method of teaching the natural sciences is by instruction in laboratories and lecture hall from the objects themselves and not from text books as formerly, every important university, college or high school must have access to some large museum. The independent maintenance of such a museum by each institution would be too great a financial burden in most cases. Now, if all the educational institutions of Chicago and vicinity should unite in using the laboratories and collections of the Museum, it would become of greater importance to itself and could be maintained in a manner equal to all demands upon its resources.

DOCUMENT C

Man and His Works

Ethnological Exhibit at the Fair

Models of Mounds, Ruins of Yucatan, Indians of Every Tribe, Eskimos, South Sea Islanders, Columbian Relics and Many Other Interesting Things

There is at least one world's fair exhibit that is without commercial purpose. Professor Putnam's department of ethnology is in one sense the basis of all the rest of the fair exhibits. In the other departments the works of man are studied. In ethnology man himself is studied, and the world's progress is denoted by a comparison of customs and periods. As a background to the modern exhibits the ethnological exhibit will have a peculiar value. Modern ways of living will be placed in direct comparison with the manners of life in all ages. Especially appropriate will be the exhibition of the customs of native American tribes at the time of Columbus' landing.

The value to scientists of the remarkable ethnological exhibits now being collected scarcely needs recounting. Long after the world's fair has become a matter of history these collections will be kept in museums for the edification of students and scientists.

But the popular features of the ethnological exhibit are of more immediate interest. There will be colonies of all the principal families of native American Indians living on the fair grounds in the exact way that their forefathers lived before the white man's face was ever seen in their hunting grounds. The space set apart for this outdoor exhibit is on the bank of the south pond in the southeastern por-

Chicago Herald, March 18, 1893

tion of the grounds. Here will be native Indians with canoes, fishing and hunting tackle, costumes, and all the appurtenances of Indian life. The Indians will cook, make trinkets, hold their councils and go through the ordinary routine with which their tribe has been familiar from time immemorial.

Interesting Columbian Relics

Another exhibit of great popular interest will be the Columbian relics in the convent of La Rabida. This structure, one of the most interesting on the grounds, has been placed in a comparatively isolated spot. It is close, however, to the general ethnological exhibit and is within easy reach of the great casino pier at the main water entrance to the grounds. The old-fashioned convent itself will form a striking contrast to the magnificent modern architecture on the fair grounds. Its quaint wall and roof and general ensemble of the middle ages will give the visitor a correct idea of the religious architecture of old Spain in Columbus' time. Inside the convent will be the most valuable relics on the fair grounds, with the possible exception of the American declaration of independence and one or two other priceless possessions of the government. Illustrations of the life history of Columbus and relics of the court of Ferdinand and Isabella and of the early history of this continent in Columbus' time will be shown in profusion. The Columbian relics have been gathered from every quarter of the globe for a special exhibit at the world's fair.

Another very popular exhibit will be archaeological specimens showing, by steps familiar to all scientists, the successive periods of human habitation on this continent. Long before Columbus' time, and probably long before the period when written history began to take up the ethnological record, the civilization of American peoples or tribes left enduring monuments. In Central and South America, and in some parts of North America, ruins have been frequently unearthed that leave no room for doubt in the scientist's mind that the early inhabitants of America were skilled in some of the arts.

Ruins of Yucatan

Peculiarly interesting will be the famed ruins of Yucatan, which will be reproduced in staff [a composite substance used for casting from molds] at the world's fair exhibit, forming an exact duplicate of the original. Then there will be mummies in the Peruvian exhibit, and a vast collection of archaeological specimens that have for the first time been brought to public notice since the world's fair ethnological exhibit was planned.

Entering the ethnological region the visitor will first reach the government Indian school, where he will have an opportunity of studying the red man in his semi-civilization and, in the case of the younger generation of Indians, in their fuller civilization. Passing on he will go through the Indian village, where the methods of tribal life 400 years ago will be duplicated, forming a complete contrast to the government's exhibit of the Indian in his later development. The visitor will then pass through the famous portal of Labna, 25 feet high and 40 feet wide, into the outdoor exhibit of Yucatan ruins. After examining the architecture of early Mexican and Central American civilizations he will pass on to the regions of the cliff dwellers, and if he desire he may ascend the artificial rock on the back of a mule. Close by he may enter the anthropological building, which will be the climax of the ethnological and archaeological exhibits, containing the most valuable scientific and historical collections ever brought together at a similar exposition.

Man and His Works

Although called the ethnology exhibit, Professor Putnam's department embraces anthropology with all its important subdivisions. It includes ethnology, archaeology, history, cartography, the Latin-American bureau, collective and isolated exhibits. Other divisions are physical anthropology, primitive religions, games and folk-lore, and anthropological library and various minor departments.

The building for the ethnology exhibit is the new one erected since manufactures and liberal arts building proved too small. The new building is called, over the main entrance, "Anthropology—Man and His Works." It is 415 feet long and 225 feet wide. The ground floor will contain 430 square feet for exhibits, aisles, offices and lavatories and the gallery 52,804 square feet. In the southern part of the ground floor 30,000 square feet will be taken up by two sections of liberal arts—the bureau of charities and corrections and the bureau of sanitation and hygiene. The rest of the ground floor will contain the general archaeological and ethnological exhibits. The north end of the gallery will contain the laboratory of physical anthropology. Here will be illustrated the sciences of anthropometry, psychology, and neurology. The visitor may have his measurement taken and learn his place on the charts showing the physical characteristics of man. Along the sides and southern end of the gallery will be specimens of the animal kingdom as an exhibit in natural history.

On the ground floor one of the largest spaces is given to the ethnological exhibit from Spain, which includes the interesting collection shown at the recent Spanish exposition. Greece has a large space on the ground floor, in which will be shown valuable specimens of Grecian art and archaeology. The latter will include gods, goddesses and many other idolatrous relics of the most ancient periods in Grecian history.

Greatest Exhibit Ever Made

No previous exposition can be said to have approached the world's fair in a comprehensive collection of ethnological specimens. Chief F. W. Putnam is professor of American archaeology and ethnology in Harvard university. Since he took charge of the exhibit there have been perhaps seventy volunteer assistants, who have penetrated every part of North and South America to collect specimens for the world's fair. Many Harvard students spent last summer's vacation in aiding Professor Putnam to bring together the data from which comparative ethnology may be studied. Although a world's ethnological exhibit in the highest sense, the early history of America is to be made a specially prominent feature. By this means foreign visitors will be able to gather much information that has heretofore been confined to scientific collections. Americans will learn much more of the early history of their own country than the schools teach, and the striking comparison between aboriginal customs and the splendors of modern civilization will be one of the principal features of the fair.

Universal ethnology will be illustrated in the exhibit from foreign countries. The principal foreign countries that will have space are: Brazil, Canada, England, France, Greece, Honduras, Mexico, Peru, Russia, Spain, Costa Rica, Paraguay, New South Wales, Argentine Republic and a special foreign exhibit from the minister of public instruction in France. From the Vienna museum will come one of the most valuable European collections. Canada will be represented in the outdoor exhibit and indoors by valuable specimens. British Guiana will send a colony of the Arrawak [sic] tribe of Indians, who will live in thatched huts in the outdoor exhibit. Norway will send a Viking ship, which will be one of the marina exhibits in the south pond, affording an interesting comparison with modern sailing methods.

Professor Putnam's Great Work

The main American collections have been brought together as a special departmental effort under the personal supervision of Professor Putnam. Besides the special department collections there will be valuable loans made to the department by state boards or historical societies and museums. Among the principal states sending exhibits are: California, Maine, Pennsylvania, New York, Missouri, Indiana, Kansas, Ohio, Utah, Wisconsin, Colorado, North Dakota, Louisiana, and Washington. Among the individual exhibitors will be Armand de Potter, who will send a valuable collection of Egyptian antiquities.

The department of archaeology will contain many important collections. The outdoor exhibits of Yucatan ruins will include six sections. The first will be the central structure from the ruined group of Labna, showing the Labna portal. The second section will be the straight arch of Uxmal reproduced from the east facade of the so-called "house of the governor," from the ruins of Uxmal. The third section will include the famous facade of the "serpent-house" from the ruins of Uxmal. The fourth section will be the north wing of the "house of the nuns," from the ruins of Uxmal, and the fifth and sixth sections will be other wings of the same famous ruins. There have also been reproduced two monoliths and several loose specimens of sculpture. The casts for these Yucatan ruins were made . . . by means of papier-mache molds and were taken from the original ruins by Edward H. Thompson, the United States consul to Yucatan, under Professor Putnam's instructions. Mr. Thompson has gone back to Yucatan to collect tropical plants common to the ruins. He will bring, in part at least, the plants that are now actually growing upon and over the original structure buried in the jungle.

The indoor archaeological exhibit will include objects enabling the visitor to draw comparisons between the various prehistoric periods on this continent.

From Earliest Ages

The glacial period will be illustrated by several valuable archaeological specimens, mainly from the Ohio and Trenton valleys. These specimens are dug out of the gravel, and include implements and utensils used in remote periods. Their ancient character is familiar to all geologists. Following the glacial period comes a second prehistoric period of the continent. To illustrate this there will be objects from shell heaps, mostly from Maine and Florida. Ancient villages will be shown by models, the localities being mostly in the Ohio valley. Burial places, mainly in the Ohio and Trenton valleys, will be shown by models, maps and photographs. Earthworks, also from the Ohio valley, will be shown from models made from papier-mache, molds and by photographs. The contents of mounds will be shown in the form of skeletons, implements, ornaments and various treasures which the aborigines were in the habit of burying with their dead. From these same mounds will be shown specimens of altars which the ancient natives used to put inside their burial places. Ancient pueblos will be shown, mostly from Arizona, New Mexico and Colorado. Connected with these will be portions of skeletons, pottery and other valuable archaeological finds. The ancient cliff and cave dwellers of the south will be studied by means of all manner of relics. The ruined cities of Mexico, Central and South America will be illustrated in the collection lent to the world's fair by the Peabody museum. This will include models of sculptured stones, human heads, hieroglyphics, etc. From Wisconsin there will be shown a group of effigy mounds, in the shape of animals. The remarkable mound at Cahokia, Ill., nearly 100 feet high, will be illustrated by photographs, and the Serpent mound of Ohio, an earth structure 1400 feet long, will have much of its actual contents brought to the fair.

Other Great Collections

Besides the Yucatan ruins, there will be shown a loan collection of casts from molds taken by [Désiré Charnay] while on the Lorillard

Expedition. This collection is sent to the world's fair by the department of public instruction in France. From further south the results of the explorations of G. A. Dorsey in the island of La Plata, Ecuador, Peru, Bolivia, Chile and other South American states will be seen at the fair. The Peruvian exhibit, which is a part of the Dorsey collection, includes the greatest find in mummies yet made on the continent. Mr. Dorsey will show in this exhibit the peculiar methods of burial of the ancient Peruvians. Taken from the burial places along with the mummies were furnished work baskets, bags of peanuts, beads, flags, and other unique objects, all of which will be shown in the exhibit.

From New York, besides the Iroquois exhibit, there will be exhibits in archaeology and natural history. In the latter will be shown a skeleton of a mastodon 6½ feet high and 9 feet long, not including the head, which overhangs five feet, making the creature 14 feet by 6½ feet in length and height. In the historical exhibit from Wisconsin will be shown the silver altar ornaments of Perrot. From Ohio will come the valuable archaeological collection by Dr. Metz, Mr. Moorehead, and others, and from the Delaware valley similar collections by Mr. Volk.

In the department of ethnology the customs of the native American tribes from the earliest times to the present will be illustrated. The handiwork of the natives and photographs of themselves and their habitations will be sold as souvenirs. There will be canoes in plenty, and at various points through the lagoons the world's fair visitor may occasionally see a stray Indian in aboriginal costume paddling around among the electric launches and fourteenth century gondolas.

Indians of Every Kind

Professor Putnam will arrange the tribes geographically. The details of the actual extent and variety of this exhibit are not yet settled, but the promises of state boards and commissions are sufficient to guarantee that all the leading native tribes will be represented. Beginning with the Eskimo, from the extreme north, the groups by latitudes will descend somewhat as follows: The Cree family, from the Canadian northwest; Haida and Fort Rupert tribes, from British Columbia; Iroquois, from the eastern states; Chippewas, Sioux, Menominees and Winnebago tribes, from the middle and northwestern states; Choctaws, from Louisiana; Apaches and Navajos, from New Mexico and

Arizona; Coahuilas, from southern California; and the Papagos and Yakuis, from the extreme southern border of the United States.

South of the United States the ethnological specimens will include valuable mementoes of the time of Cortez, which were collected in Europe by Mrs. Zelia Nuttall. These objects were taken to Europe at the time of the Spanish conquest, and include a series of Mexican shields. From the South Sea islands there will be a unique collection, made directly from the natives by Otto Finsch, of Germany, during several years' residence on the islands. This collection will include objects showing the methods of life, customs and dress used by the natives long before the adoption of civilization.

From Egypt and Palestine there will be an interesting collection, and from Africa there will be enough to give the world's fair visitor an idea of how explorer Stanley's protégés live in various parts of the dark continent.

ESSAY TWO

Ambiguous Legacy

Daniel Garrison Brinton at the International Congress of Anthropology

CURTIS M. HINSLEY

On Monday morning, August 28, 1893, at the Memorial Art Institute in downtown Chicago, the president of the International Congress of Anthropology, Daniel G. Brinton, welcomed the attendees to Chicago, the World's Fair, and the Congress. Following the first day of opening ceremonies and addresses, the participants moved to two venues on the fairgrounds; the next five mornings were devoted to papers and discussion, with afternoons reserved for visiting the anthropology exhibits in the Government Building, the Anthropology Building, the Midway, and elsewhere. A convivial banquet closed the congress on Saturday night, September 2. As with dozens of other congresses sponsored through the summer and fall by the Congress Auxiliary of the Chicago Fair, the Congress of Anthropology had two primary goals: to demonstrate genial collaboration among American institutions, and to present an account of the current state of knowledge and critical questions in a field that was still only vaguely understood by the public.

In his review of the congress for the *American Anthropologist* (Document D)—published even before the Fair closed—William Henry Holmes struck an apologetic tone, explaining that haste of preparation and the organizers' busy schedules had produced a respectable but hardly outstanding set of papers, and that a number of key figures, especially Europeans, did not attend. "The meeting did not, therefore, rise fully to the dignity expected of an international congress," Holmes concluded, "but there were enough earnest workers on hand to fill out the week's program and bring out of the heterogeneous elements results of very considerable importance" (Holmes

1893, 423). As Frederica de Laguna noted some years ago, Holmes was wrong about the insignificance of the meetings (de Laguna 1960). But the expressions of his disgruntlement ("earnest workers," "heterogeneous elements") were due in part to the timing of the congress, which conflicted with the annual meetings of the American Association for the Advancement of Science (AAAS) in Madison, Wisconsin, where debate over Paleolithic humans in America—in which Holmes was deeply involved—became quite heated.[1]

Undoubtedly, too, there was the shadow of comparison with previous congresses of international scope, such as the biennial International Congress of Americanists (nine European sessions since 1875) and, more recently, the anthropology gatherings at the Paris Expo of 1889. While Americans were largely absent from such meetings, they still looked overseas for approbation, and the paucity of Europeans at Chicago was taken as rebuke. But as de Laguna suggested in 1960, Holmes was too close to it to see that the 1893 Congress of Anthropology "not only summarized past accomplishments but directly stimulated further advances" in the young field (De Laguna 1960, 99).

The organization of the congress reflected its goals: coordination and coverage. Brinton chaired an executive committee of *ex officio* institutional representatives from the AAAS (Holmes), the Anthropological Society of Washington (Otis Mason), the Women's Anthropological Society of America (Alice Fletcher), and the U.S. Army Medical Museum (Louis LaGarde). Boas served as secretary. Putnam chaired the local organizing committee and served, along with Boas, Brinton, Holmes, and C. Staniland Wake on the publication committee as well (on attendees and affiliations, see appendix to this essay).[2] Paper sessions fell into six categories, reflecting an emerging consensus on anthropological fields: physical anthropology, archaeology, ethnology, folklore, religion, and linguistics. As Brinton proudly reflected in reviewing the published volume from the congress, "an effort was made to consider the history of the [human] species as an aggregate, and to lay down the principles for its scientific analysis"—with at least two papers representing each area, he noted (Brinton 1895b, 100–101).[3] Breadth and inclusiveness were the intended watchwords of the congress.[4]

Brinton appeared prominently at the congress, and his presence was clearly considered crucial to the seriousness and dignity of the proceedings. Yet today he presents a puzzle, since on the key intellectual and institutional issues of the time the "fearless critic" of Philadelphia stood for commitments and practices of a receding time; he was already viewed as a man of the past more than the future.[5] What was Brinton's unique status in 1893, and what can it tell us of conditions in anthropology?

Like those of Boas's other two "fathers" of anthropology—Powell and Putnam—Brinton's adult life was disrupted and divided by the Civil War. Born in Chester County, Pennsylvania, in 1837, he graduated from Yale in 1858, returned to Philadelphia for medical school for two years, then traveled and studied medicine in France and Germany. Returning in 1862 to a country embroiled in civil war, Brinton enlisted in the Union Army as a surgeon; over the next year he served at key battles (Chancellorsville, Gettysburg) and, while he escaped battle wounds, in late 1863 he did suffer serious sun-stroke. For the rest of his life Brinton (who in any case never welcomed the rigors of fieldwork) strictly limited his exposure to the sun, effectively restricting him to "armchair" status. Still, he served out the war as surgeon-in-charge of a military hospital in Illinois.

After leaving the military in 1865 Brinton devoted himself to medical practice for a decade in the Philadelphia area. He also began editing several medical and surgical periodicals. Brinton stopped practicing medicine in 1874 but continued the medical publishing until 1887, when he retired completely from medicine at age fifty, to devote the rest of his life to pursuing and promoting anthropology—to become, in his words, "an observer, a thinker, and an unpaid writer" (Brinton 1893).

If medicine constituted Brinton's formal training and early career, the indigenous peoples of the Americas became his enduring intellectual fascination. As a student at Yale in 1858 he traveled to the Florida coast for his health, and while he avoided visiting a coastal mound due to mosquitoes, the trip resulted in his first book, *Notes on the Floridian Peninsula, Its Literary History, Indian Tribes and Antiquities* (1859). As Regna Darnell has pointed out, in *Notes* and an early article on the moundbuilders controversy (Brinton 1866) Brinton set a pattern of inquiry that came to rely not on ethnographic field experience but on deep library research in English, German, French, Italian, and Spanish language sources. Darnell notes that for Brinton the term "fieldwork" meant comprehensive library work, delving into original documents—although occasionally for linguistic work he did have contact with Native informants visiting Philadelphia (Darnell 1988, 2, 21–23).

Brinton's preference for library "fieldwork" requires some intellectual context. At the methodological heart of nineteenth-century anthropology lay a dilemma of evidence. From George Bancroft and William H. Prescott in the 1830s through Frank Cushing and Adolph Bandelier in the 1880s certain questions persisted. To what degree could the documentary history of the European conquest (particularly in the early historic period, 1500–1700) be trusted? How were the early Spanish, French, or English records to be interpreted, and what did they reliably reveal about Native communities, their interrelationships, belief systems, land patterns, relations with settlers, and much more? Most important, could they be reconciled with contemporary Indian accounts, myths, and tales? And most centrally, could a place be found—or created—in the practice of American history for the Indians' unwritten versions of events? Who would transform these into historical source material? How expansive could the definition of "history" be?

For at least half a century—most of Brinton's lifetime—in one way or another most antiquarians, ethnologists, and historians of the conquest and colonial periods struggled with these questions.[6] In doing so each found some balance (or blend) of interest and occupation between, on one hand, the cultural worlds of Native language, lore, and accounts of the past and, on the other, the puzzling, contradictory, sometimes simply vague historical documents of the European contact. Cushing, for example, struggled to discover if the Spaniards' "Seven Cities of Cibola" were Zuni pueblo and its surrounding settlements; while he became familiar with the Spanish chronicles, over time he came to trust Zuni accounts as well and developed new methods accordingly. Bandelier famously walked through the ancient and modern pueblos of the Rio Grande in the 1880s, but then with his remarkable multilingual skills (French, English, Spanish, German) he also worked for years in the archives of Seville and the Vatican, trying to make sense of the human history and prehistory of the Southwest through documentary studies.[7] His "fieldwork" became a balance between pueblo and library. In the end dissatisfied that either form of history could adequately convey reality, he wrote a novel of prehistoric pueblo life, *The Delight Makers* (1890).

In sum, the line between the armchair and the field notebook was not always clear. Brinton's eight-volume, personally published *Library of Aboriginal American Literature* (1882–90), which was a costly disappointment to him, demonstrated the importance he placed on making available to scholars the rich sources of indigenous North and Central America—in effect, expanding the definition of legitimate history for the continents.

And yet, despite his attentions to indigenous languages and narratives, Brinton was far more the evolutionist than the historicist—and increasingly so with time. His basic convictions were established early, and they tended to become permanent fixtures of his thinking. Like his near-contemporary and fellow armchair theorist Lewis Henry Morgan, he became fascinated by the development of the human mind rather than the experiences of specific human groups, their languages, practices, or beliefs—in the parlance of the day, his forte was ethnology rather than ethnography. And although he ranged widely through the languages and mythologies of the Americas, it was neither migration nor historical contacts and experiences of peoples so much as the spontaneous and parallel inventiveness of the human mind (psychic unity and independent invention) that impressed him.

After the initial Florida and moundbuilder work Brinton paid little attention to archaeology and, before the late 1880s, little to physical anthropology either. But beginning around 1890, as Lee Baker has emphasized, Brinton began a shift "away from antiquarian and academic focus on Native American linguistics and grammar to a broader, more popular focus on racial classification and ethnography" and developed a reactionary defense of racial hierarchies. The sad paradox of Brinton's last decade was that he attained new popularity as a lecturer by appealing to the racist predilections of his listeners, weaving "the authority of science into the tapestry of contemptuous images" of racial difference in popular media (Baker 2010, 133–35).

The direction of Brinton's anthropology was on full display in the three papers he delivered at the International Congress of Anthropol-

Ambiguous Legacy

ogy in 1893. In his presidential address, "The 'Nation' as an Element in Anthropology" (1894a), Brinton had several purposes. He wished first to demonstrate, through examination of the concept of the nation and its evolutionary development, that all branches of anthropology, as represented at the congress, must be embraced and pursued together: physical anthropology, archaeology, ethnology, folklore, religious histories, and linguistics. All, he insisted, were equal and equally necessary to a full understanding of the science of man.

The bulk of the address he then dedicated to distinguishing between two stages of social evolution: the tribal or consanguineal stage of political organization, and the territorial or national phase in the contemporary industrial world. As Brinton explains it in the address, the nation as concept and organizing principle is not only a necessary product of evolution but itself a major causal factor in human progress, as can be seen across the fields of anthropology. The "dissolving potency" of the nation encourages linguistic homogeneity, reduces disturbance from religious differences, even brings about increased racial mixing and loss of the desire for "purity" that had been so determinative in the tribal stage of evolution (Brinton 1894a, 26–27). While tribal survivals certainly persisted into the modern world, he noted, inevitably "the Nation breaks down the walls of narrow tribal animosities; it increases the number of those whose patriotic interests are in common, and thus widens the area of duty and the conceptions of ethics"—even though, for example, we still admire the murderous military man as heroic. To be sure, progress was uneven and imperfect, and Brinton pointedly remarked on the lack of full rights for women in modern America: "At first she was but a slave and a beast of burden; at present, so far as the enjoyment of civic rights in modern states is concerned, she has risen to be classed among idiots and children" (Brinton 1894a, 29, 33).

The striking aspect of Brinton's presidential address is that it derives almost wholly from Morgan's schema of social evolution, as first suggested in *Systems of Consanguinity and Affinity in the Human Family* (1871) and fully developed in *Ancient Society* (1877).[8] This was, as all knew, the classic American framework of social evolutionism championed as well by Powell but already under suspicion, if not outright attack, by a younger generation of scholars such as James Mooney,

Frank Cushing, and cautiously, Boas. It is particularly notable that in this address Brinton approvingly cited seven contemporary scholars: three French, two German, one Swede—and Morgan, the sole American. Brinton thus brought to his relatively traditional argument little new field information but the prestige of Morgan and European scholarship.

Presidential addresses are often summary performances, of course, and Brinton's was probably received with polite assent. Not so with his second paper, delivered two days later, which provoked considerable discussion and some consternation. "On Various Supposed Relations between the American and Asian Races" (Brinton 1894b), which later appeared in the ethnology section of the published volume, was a combative and sometimes snide attempt to dismiss through ridicule all arguments for prehistoric connections between indigenous America and Asian peoples. After refusing even to consider Hermann F. C. Ten Kate's theory and evidence of "alleged Mongoloid resemblances," Brinton took aggressive aim at three groups of "mental products" employed to suggest migration and contact: the supposed similarity of the Mexican calendar to the Tibetan calendar system; similarities between the parchisi game of India and the pre-Columbian Mesoamerican game of patolli; and the alleged presence of Asiatic jade in the Americas. In the first two cases Brinton contradicted the authority of luminaries Alexander von Humboldt and Edward B. Tylor and invoked the recent work on comparative games by Cushing and Brinton's fellow Philadelphian, Stewart Culin. Having demolished the first two arguments, Brinton then turned to the question of Asiatic jade, "a favorite subject with our distinguished member, Professor Putnam." Citing recent papers from the International Congress of Americanists by Rudolph Virchow of Berlin and two other German scholars, as well as recent discoveries of jade deposits in the Americas, Brinton offered his final word on the matter: "no variety of jade whatever, from a purely mineralogical point of view, can attest ethnic wanderings" (Brinton 1894b, 149).

Judging from the printed version at least, Brinton's "attack" (his term) was an unkind performance, and it brought forth vigorous responses. Cushing arrived late—as did Putnam—but in time for the discussion, and his diary account for August 30 indicates serious disagreements among the participants. Mason of the National Museum saw clear Asian influences, while Japanophile Edward S. Morse of Salem sided with Brinton; Stephen D. Peet, founder and editor of the *American Antiquarian*, disagreed strongly with Brinton, citing the migration of the swastika symbol. When his turn came, Cushing spoke in general support of Brinton but then attempted to bridge differences, as reported by Holmes, "by taking the position that foreign influences have certainly not been *sufficiently strong to seriously affect* the trend of purely American cultural development" (Holmes 1893, 425–26).[9] Cushing privately congratulated himself: "My speech was well received." But not by Putnam, who followed and "claimed that my [Cushing's] idea was pernicious—of having Am[erican] Cult[ure]s studied without ref[erence] to Asiatic connection." Brinton, having the final word, noted approvingly Cushing's expression of "the growth of culture in water tight compartments."[10]

The autochthonous nature of the Americas—its "water-tight compartments" of culture—which Brinton was so aggressively championing was an old idea already in retreat by the 1890s; within a decade it would be seriously undermined by the American Museum's Jesup North Pacific Expedition (1897–1902), led by Boas and supported by Putnam (Cole 1999, 188–203, 254–60; Freed et al. 1988a, 97–103). As with the earlier presidential lecture at the congress, again Brinton favored his readings of European scholars and papers delivered at the International Congress of Americanists over the closer groundwork of American colleagues—or so it must have seemed to Putnam and others.

This was no small matter. By the last quarter of the century Americans in the young field sciences of geology, geography, paleontology, and anthropology, especially in the western regions of the continent, felt an inductive superiority to European savants who had so long dominated opinion. In the hemisphere of the Americas lay the book of earth's history, and the book of humanity's history as well, open for reading. As Powell repeatedly expressed the sense of coming of age, America had been revealed as the laboratory of the earth sciences, and the invigorating experience of camaraderie in the field was closely bound to a sense of having achieved empirical, grounded knowledge. Otis Mason thus spoke for a generation when, on returning from the Paris Expo of 1889, he predicted that the Chicago Fair would be America's emergence: "all that Europe will ever know of [indigenous America] will be what we tell her" (Mason 1889a). American fieldworkers wanted recognition, not lectures.

Brinton's third and probably least controversial paper was a review of recent work in American Indian linguistics. Still, it contrasted sharply with the other linguistics paper published from the congress: Boas's "Classification of the Languages of the North Pacific Coast" (Brinton 1894c, 335–38; Boas 1894, 339–46). Together with Powell's linguistic map of North America that was being featured in the Government Building at the Fair, Brinton's brief survey of the field marked the culmination of a tradition of vocabulary gathering that extended back into the nineteenth century through such figures as Albert Gallatin, Horatio Hale, William W. Turner, George Gibbs, and Powell (Haas 1969, 239–55; Fowler 1975, 16–32). Surveying the hemisphere from south to north, Brinton displayed his considerable familiarity with the legion of students of Amerindian languages in Europe, South America, Mexico, Canada, and the United States—most of whom were engaged in the usual comparative vocabulary collecting. Once again, Brinton stood astride the field, pronouncing accomplishments and lacunae.

Boas, on the other hand, concentrated his paper on seven languages of the Northwest Coast, grouping them through analysis of sound, grammar, structure, and vocabulary into four groups which, he suggested, were generically distinct from each other. While he was still cautious in his phrasing in 1893, Boas left no doubt where he stood: while vocabulary collecting would continue to be a basic aspect of Indian linguistics, the future of serious language study and classification lay with the close, tedious structural analysis he was demonstrating:

> Etymologies of Indian languages, the histories of which we do not know, is a subject of the greatest difficulty, and must be based on investigations on the structure of the languages, if it shall not sink to the level of mere guessing. In the present state of linguistic science, a classification ought to take into account structure as well as vocabulary. The former will give us valuable clues where the comparison of mere words ceases to be helpful (Boas 1894, 346).

Through the rest of the decade, until his death in 1899, Brinton would find himself engaged in a rear-guard action against the ascendant and increasingly bold Boas—and not only in linguistics (Essay 7, this volume). Regna Darnell has noted that the Boas-Brinton relationship was particularly fraught: Brinton early recognized Boas's serious intelligence, and Boas appreciated both Brinton's position of prestige and his efforts at gathering indigenous literatures—even though privately he found the Philadelphian "very arrogant but not very deep" and disagreed fundamentally with Brinton's commitment to the comparative method in anthropology (quoted in Cole 1999, 263). "Their interaction," Darnell observes, "clarifies the paradox of Brinton's simultaneous isolation from the developing science of anthropology and his prestige among its practitioners, even among younger men who did not draw theoretically or substantively on his work" (Darnell 1988, 64).

The "paradox of Brinton" at the time of the Chicago Fair reveals several polarities and tensions within the ranks of American anthropology. In the first place, the home-grown nature of the young field created a desire for recognition by Europeans but also an instinctive dismissal of transatlantic theory—and as I have demonstrated, Brinton took pleasure in his cosmopolitan knowledge and probably his role as interlocutor. Equal parts resentment and admiration were his rewards. Secondly, the ethnographic ground shifted beneath Brinton, who remained primarily a library scholar as emphasis on fieldwork became irresistible. Finally, the theoretical principles of his early years—psychic unity, independent invention, comparative method—were in the process of profound challenge and change as the new century approached, and Brinton chose to move in even more conservative directions, toward racial hierarchies. Notwithstanding these misfits, the institutional flux of the moment maintained Brinton as a necessary figure of leadership, a reference point for scientific status, the respectable "fearless critic" who could be relied upon to speak up for anthropology—at least as he understood it.

In the final evenings of the congress and during the week following, Cushing and Culin dined frequently with Brinton, discussing the drama and occult of the Midway late into the illuminated evenings on the fairgrounds. In his diary (Document E, this volume) Cushing confided that he was thrilled with these late summer nights. He felt that he had "won" Brinton as an admirer, and on their final evening together Brinton encouraged the younger man to write a popular book on his Zuni life and a dictionary of the language. For the moment at least, the mutual pleasure of fresh acquaintance and kindred spirit masked the wide gulf that already separated Brinton from the coming world of anthropology. Perhaps simple loneliness also played some part. In any case, there is poignancy in imagining the two men, strolling past midnight beneath the giant illuminated Ferris Wheel and on through Jackson Park, sharing memories and plans, unaware that Brinton would not live to see the new century, and Cushing would soon follow him into history.

Appendix

ANALYSIS OF REGISTERED MEMBERS OF THE INTERNATIONAL CONGRESS OF ANTHROPOLOGY, WORLD'S COLUMBIAN EXPOSITION, 1893

DAVID R. WILCOX

The International Congress of Anthropology was held at the World's Columbian Exposition on August 28 to September 2, 1893 (see Cushing Diary, Document E, this volume, for a firsthand account). The Local Committee of Organization included F. W. Putnam as chairman and Charles Staniland Wake, who edited the published volume (Wake 1894b) as secretary. Other members included the bibliophile and philanthropist Edward Everett Ayer (1841–1927), who claimed that he persuaded Marshall Field to endow the Field Columbian Museum (Ayer 2003; see also Wilcox 2002); Illinois Indian historian Hiram William Beckwith (1833–1903); banker and bibliophile James William Ellsworth (1849–1925), who was one of the principal organizers and supporters of the Fair; Frederick Starr (1858–1933), who had just been hired at the University of Chicago (Essay 6, this volume); and Stephen Dennison Peet (1831–1914), editor of *American Antiquarian*. On the Executive Committee for the Congress, Brinton served as president, Boas was secretary; and Holmes represented the American Association for the Advancement of Science. The committee was filled out with William Wells Newell of the American Folk-Lore Society, Otis Mason of the Anthropological Society of Washington; Alice Cunningham Fletcher of the Women's Anthropological Society of America, and Louis Anatole LaGarde (1849–1920) of the U.S. Army Medical Museum. Brinton, Boas, Holmes, Putnam, and Wake also served as the Publications Committee.

There were 247 registered members of the congress (not counting 5 duplicates). Of these, 46 (19%) can be identified as "practicing anthropologists" who either worked for institutions as anthropologists or sociologists or were privately engaged in the study of anthropology or folklore. Google, the Biographical and Genealogical Master Index, and other sources produced information about 93 (38%) additional individuals, while the rest (43%) appear to be "ordinary citizens" who had some kind of interest in the meetings. Further inquiry using local sources for the latter individuals might turn up additional information.

Practicing anthropologists or folklorists at the World's Fair International Congress of Anthropology

Name	Dates	AAA Membership dates; Comments
Cyrus Alder	1863–1940	03/40; AES member; librarian of Smithsonian
Frank Baker	1841–1918	AES member; BAE; anatomist; soon to be editor, *American Anthropologist*
David Prescott Barrows	1873–1954	Completed Pomona College, 1894; PhD 1897, University of Chicago under F. Starr
Franz Boas*	1858–1942	02/42; anthropologist
John Gregory Bourke*	1846–1896	AES member; anthropologist
Daniel Garrison Brinton*	1837–1899	ASW member; anthropologist
Gustav Brühl*	1826–1903	02/03; physician; explorer
Robert Stewart Culin*	1858–1929	02/27; University Museum PA
Frank Hamilton Cushing*	1857–1900	ASW member; archaeologist; BAE
William Healy Dall	1845–1927	ASW member; geologist; USGS
Henry Herbert Donaldson	1852–1938	08/36; Head, Dept. of Neurology, Univ. of Chicago; close friend of Boas
George Amos Dorsey**	1868–1931	02/16, 25/30; archaeologist
Jesse Walter Fewkes*	1850–1930	02/30; archaeologist
John Comfort Fillmore**	1843–1898	Musicologist with Alice Fletcher
Alice Cunningham Fletcher*	1838–1923	02/23; WASA member; anthropologist
Mary French-Sheldon	1847–1936	African explorer

Essay Two Appendix

Franklin H. Giddings	1855–1931	03/27; sociologist; Bryn Mawr
Emil Hassler	1864–1937	Paraguayan commissioner
William Henry Holmes	1846–1933	02/27; archaeologist; BAE
Walter Hough*	1859–1935	02/35; archaeologist; USNM
George Hunt		Boas collaborator; Tlingit Indian
Johan Adrian Jacobsen	1853–1947	Norwegian sailor and adventurer; collected over 3,000 NW Coast artifacts, 1881–1882, and over 2000 Yup'ik artifacts in Alaska, for the Ethnologisches Museum, Berlin
Joseph Jastrow	1863–1944	Psychologist; Univ. of WI
Morris Jastrow Jr.*	1881–1921	Univ. of PA, Semitics professor
George Frederick Kunz*	1856–1932	02/03; mineralogist; Tiffany's
Pierre Emile Levasseur	1828–1911	Professor of geography, history and statistics, College of France
Carl Sophus Lumholtz	1851–1922	02/15; archaeologist
Anita Newcomb McGee	1864–1940	WASA member; physician/nurse
William John McGee	1853–1912	02/12; AES; anthropologist; BAE
Otis Tufton Mason*	1838–1908	02/08; ASW member; anthropologist; USNM
Henry Chapman Mercer	1956–1930	Archaeologist
Emilo Montes		Archaeologist, Peru
Edward Sylvester Morse*	1838–1925	ASW member; geologist; Peabody-Essex Museum director
William Wells Newell*	1839–1907	Founder American Folk-Lore Society and editor
Zelia Maria Magdalena Parrott Nuttall	1857–1933	02/31; anthropologist
Stephen Dennison Peet	1831–1914	Archaeologist; editor, American Antiquarian
George Henry Perkins	1844–1933	02/27; archaeologist; zoologist; geologist; entomologist; Univ. of VT
Frederic Ward Putnam*	1839–1915	02/15; archaeologist; Peabody Museum
Albion Woodbury Small	1854–1926	Sociologist; Univ. of Chicago
Harlan Ingersoll Smith	1872–1940	02/35; archaeologist

Mrs. Cornelius [Sara Yorke] Stevenson	1947–1921	Anthropologist; University Museum PA
Matilda Coxe Stevenson*	1850–1915	WASA member; anthropologist; BAE
Ernest Volk	1845–1919	Archaeologist
Charles Stanisland Wake	1835–1910	Secretary of the congress; folklorist
Gerald Montgomery West		Assistant, Dept. of Ethnology, World's Columbian Exposition; curator of physical anthro., Field Columbian Museum, 1894
George Frederick Wright	1838–1921	Geologist; Oberlin College

Key: * = member of the American Folk-Lore Society in 1893; ** = member by 1896; AAA = American Anthropological Association; AES = American Ethnological Society; ASW = Anthropological Society of Washington; BAE = Bureau of American Ethnology; WASA = Women's Anthropological Society of America.

Persons interested in or supportive of anthropology for whom information is currently available are indicated in the following biographical notes, in alphabetical order.

Karl Abel (1837–1906) published *Linguistic Essays*. Mary Newbury Adams (1837–1901) was born in Peru to missionaries; her home in Dubuque, Iowa, was an avant-garde salon for intellectuals of the period; her husband was chief justice of the Iowa Supreme Court and her sister was the wife of John J. Bagley, the governor of Minnesota. She was instrumental in founding the Federation of Woman's Clubs and the Association for the Advancement of Women; she was chair of the Historical Committee of the Chicago Fair. She and her husband were friends of W. Bronson Alcott of Boston (*People in History*).

Charles Friedrich Sebastian Artes (1947–1916) was Evansville's leading and most successful jeweler and an avocational archaeologist. Robert Michael Ballantyne (1825–94) was a Scottish author of books for young people. Lt. Fletcher Stewart Bassett (1849–93) planned and organized the International Folk-Lore Congress and was chief interpreter and translator at the Fair. Elizabeth Burns Battle was a member of the Theosophical Society. Dr. Robert Bell (1841–1917) was a pioneer in the geography and geology of Canada; Frederick Berchtold (1857–1942) was a professor of modern languages, physics, and history at the Oregon State Agricultural College, where he became dean in 1896.

Mrs. Boas attended with her daughter Marie (Cole 1999); Emanuel Roth Boyer (1851–1900), a graduate of Harvard University, published a *Laboratory Manual in Elementary Biology* in 1894 (*Who Was Who in America* 1:76, hereafter WWWA).

James E. Brady (1858–1903) worked for a meat and grocery business, eventually buying it. Max Braverman was a gem and mineral collector who gave many specimens to museums. Born in Norway, Gustav Olsen Brohough was a professor at Red Wing Seminary, Minnesota, who later wrote about the Sioux and Chippewa individual script. Clark H. Bronson was a blind phrenologist and physiologist. Mrs. William Wallace Brown (d. 1919) was an Indian agent and student of Passamaquoddy folklore.

Walter I. Cauldwell was a high school professor in 1894 and a graduate in 1891 at Shelbyville, Tennessee. Heli Chatelain (1859–1908) was a missionary and U.S. commercial agent in West Africa who founded the Philafrican Liberator's League; in 1894 she published the first Memoir of the American Folk-Lore Society, *Folk Tales of Angola*. Carlos Carleton Closson Jr. (b.1869), a Harvard University graduate in 1892, was an instructor of political economy at the University of Chicago; Richard T. Colburn (1832–1908) was vice president of Section I (Social and Economic Science) of the American Association for the Advancement of Science in 1897 and left $300,000 to be evenly divided between the Carnegie Institution of Washington and the AAAS. John Hoeny Copeland was the editor of the *Texas Tribune* and the *San Antonio Tribune*; E. H. Crane, from Niles, Minnesota, was a professor of taxidermy and embalming and an avid avocational archaeologist and collector; Edward Estlin Cummings, who graduated from Harvard College in 1883, was an instructor of sociology who became the minister at Old South Church, Boston (he was the father of the poet e. e. cummings). Mrs. Stewart Culin also registered.

Robert E. Cutler was a school principal in Chicago who published *Outline of Civil Government in Illinois and of Chicago Municipal Government* in 1898; James Deans (1821–1905) studied the Haida, 1869–70, for the Hudson's Bay Company (*Dictionary of Canadian Biography*); Chris F. Dittmer (1857–1943) was a postal clerk, mail carrier, and wagon maker. Thomas Dowling Jr. was a member of the Anthropological Society of Washington whose father had run an auction house in Washington DC; Henry Magiford Echlin (1864–1913) was a student at

Northwestern University in 1892, but did not graduate, and was the western representative of Charles Scribner and Sons; Charles Lincoln Edwards (1863–1937) was a biologist who became a professor at the University of Cincinnati in 1894 and then J. Pierpont Morgan Professor of Natural History at Trinity College in Hartford, Connecticut; he was president of the American Folk-Lore Society in 1899.

W. E. Gaston was the author of *Looking through the Microscope* in 1901; William H. Gillard was a geologist; Mary E. Gouldy (1843–1925) was a graduate of Mount Holyoke Seminary and a missionary to Japan; Henry E. Graham was the author of *Where We Got the Bible*; William Brooks Greenlee (1872–1953) was a Chicago businessman and a trustee of the Newberry Library; he gave them his extensive library on Portuguese and Brazilian history (*National Cyclopedia of American Biography* 41, hereafter NCAB).

Emile Herman Grubbe (1875–1960), who graduated from Valparaiso College in 1894, became the first person to use X-rays in the treatment of breast cancer in 1896. C. M. Grumbling was a professor of natural science at Iowa Wesleyan University; João Verissimo Mendes Guerreiro (d. 1911) was an architect and served as engineer and chief of the public works of Lisbon, Portugal (Bull. Int. Railroad Congress Assoc., 1911); Frederic Putnam Gulliver (1865–1919) was a topographer with the U.S. Geological Survey until 1891, when he resigned to pursue independent studies; he published *The Geographical Development of Boston* in 1903. Carter Henry Harrison (1825–1893) was the mayor of Chicago who was assassinated on October 28, 1893.

Ernest Abraham Hart (1836–98) was a physician and editor who was the author of *Hypnotism, Mesmerism, and the New Witchcraft*; Alice Palmer Henderson was the author of *The Rainbow's End: Alaska*, in 1898; Frederick Charles Hicks (1875–1956) was an economist who went to the University of Missouri in Columbia in 1892, where he defended the gold standard, to the consternation of locals.

Rev. F. L. L. Hiller, like his brother C. C. P. Hiller, was a minister; he built a church in East Pueblo, Colorado, in 1891. John Hans Hjetland (1861–1934) graduated from the Divinity School at Yale University in 1895; he was to have many Congregational pastorates in North Dakota and Montana.

Bayard Taylor Holmes (1852–1924) was a noted physician who became

Populist Party candidate for Mayor of Chicago in 1895 (*Anthropology News Bulletin*, hereafter ANB; *Dictionary of American Biography*, hereafter DAB; NCAB 10; WWWA 1); Helen Sarah Norton Howell (1839–1923) was a native of Minnesota; John L. Jackson was a Baptist and Christian Socialist who believed in the Social Gospel, which he preached at the Fountain Street Church, 1890–96.

Ulrich Jahn (1861–1900) was the author of *Volkssagen aus Pomern und Rugen*, 1889; Arthur Kaiser (1870–94) graduated from Cornell University and became principal of one of the schools in Buffalo, New York, but soon died of consumption; Henry Frederick Kallenberg was known for having refereed the first unofficial basketball game with five players on each side between the University of Iowa and the University of Chicago in 1896; Nellie Sawyer Kedzie [Jones] (1858–1956) started a program of Household Economy and Hygiene at Kansas Agricultural College in 1881 (*Woman's Who's Who of America* 1914; WWWA 3; Google: K-State Libraries); Dr. Charles Anselm Kersey (1845–1945) was a physician; Samuel S. Lewis (1824–1921) was president of the University of Missouri in Columbia, 1876–89.

John Gill Lemmon (1832–1908) was a pioneer botanist in California and botanist to the California State Board of Forestry, 1887–91 (*Appleton's Cyclopedia of American Biography*; DAB; WWWA 1); Sara Allen Plummer Lemmon (1836–1923), his wife, was also a botanist and artist and successfully led the campaign to have the golden poppy named the California state flower. Mt. Lemmon near Tucson, Arizona, is named for her (WWWA 5; *Artists of the American West* 1).

Montegue Richard Leverson (1830–1925) was a supporter of European revolutions who also later was involved in the Lincoln County War in New Mexico (WWWA 4). Born in Lanark, Illinois, Charles Sumner Lobingie(r) (1866–1956) received his AB in 1888, AM in 1892, and LLB in 1894 from the University of Nebraska; he later became a judge of the Philippine Court of First Instance, 1904–14, and judge of the U.S. Court of China in Shanghai, 1914–24. William McAdams (1835–95) was a geologist who prepared and sold numerous collections of antiquities and fossils; he was superintendent of the Archaeology Exhibit for the State of Illinois at the Chicago Fair. Frank Addison Manny (1868–1954) was a student of John Dewey at the University of Michigan (WWWA 5).

Wilfred Hamilton Manwarren graduated from the University of Michigan in 1895 and became a superintendent of schools in Battle Creek. Edward Laurens Mark (1847–1946) was director of the Zoological Laboratory, Harvard College, where he had frequent power struggles with Alexander Agassiz; he became Hersey Professor of Anatomy at Harvard and later director of the Harvard Bermuda Biological Station for Research, 1903–31. P. J. Miniter was a labor agitator and president of the United Order of Bricklayers and Stonemasons in Chicago; Georg Wilton Moorehouse was a physician who received his 1897 MD from Harvard University and who was interested in medical folklore.

Manuel Antonio Muniz, who was several times surgeon general of Peru, was a physician who published on leprosy and trepanning in Peru (with W. J. McGee). Althea Abbey Ogden (1850–1919) was the author of *Bugle Notes of Courage and Love* in 1912. Alice Edmands Putnam (b. 1865) was the oldest child of F. W. Putnam. Jerome Hall Raymond (1869–1928) graduated from Northwestern University in 1893; he became the youngest university president in America as president of the University of West Virginia, 1897–1901. Before that he had been secretary to Frances E. Willard, George M. Pullman, and Bishop James M. Thoburn. His first love was teaching in University extension programs (NCAB 25; WWWA 1).

Frank C. Rex was on the staff of the West Chester Normal School in Pennsylvania; Rev. W. A. Ryan (b. 1856) was educated at St. Joseph's College, Buffalo, New York, and St. Joseph's Seminary, Troy, New York, where he graduated in 1882. Stephen Salisbury III (1835–1905) was a businessman and president of the American Antiquarian Society, 1887–1905; he opened a museum in Worcester, Massachusetts, in 1898 (NCAB 7).

Ariana Scammon's two scrapbooks from the Chicago Fair are at the University of Chicago, Special Collections Research Center; Charles Hubbard Sergel (b. 1861) was owner of a publishing house in Chicago (*The Book of Chicagoans*, 1911). Thomas Edward Shields (1862–1921) received a degree in biology from Johns Hopkins University and taught biology at a diocesan seminary in Minnesota before going to the Catholic University of America in 1902 (ANB; DAB). Herbert Wood Smith was a member of the American Folk-Lore Society. Charles Warren Spaulding was a judge and banker whose love scandal with his stenographer (and later wife), Sara Louise Ervin, sent him to jail; she also registered for the congress. Benjamin F. Steinmates was a prominent attorney in Clinton, Illinois.

Isaiah Mulligan Terrell (1859–1931) was a "colored" educator who in 1891 became superintendent of Colored Schools in Fort Worth (*Who's Who of the Colored Race*, 1915); Yates P. Thruston's book *The Antiquities of Tennessee and Adjacent States* was reviewed in *Science* 7, no. 172: 539 by Daniel Brinton. Z. A. Weidler was with the United Brethren Church in Pennsylvania. Born in Wisconsin, Henry Solomon Wellcome (1853–1936) established the pharmaceutical company of Burroughs, Wellcome and Company in 1880 and became a British subject in 1910; upon his death the Wellcome Trust was established, becoming one of the largest biomedical charities in the world. He made a large collection of medical artifacts and had the site of Jebel Moya in Sudan excavated for many years.

Henry S. White (1829–1915) was an active chaplain throughout the Civil War and was Methodist pastor at Romeo, Minnesota, for some forty years. Eliza Lawton Whiteley, an English naturalized citizen, was a homeopathic physician who opened an office in Chicago in 1886.

Henry Payne Whitney (1872–1930) was the oldest son of William C. Whitney, who was king maker for Grover Cleveland at the 1892 Democratic Convention. He graduated from Yale University in 1894. As a sportsman and explorer, Whitney published *Hunting with the Eskimos* in 1910. In 1904 he inherited $24 million from his father and in 1917 another $12 million from his uncle. He married Gertrude Vanderbilt (ANB; DAB; NCAB 21).

George Durand Wilder (1869–1946) enrolled in Oberlin College in 1891 and received his bachelor's of divinity from Yale University in 1894. He was also ordained at Oberlin in 1894 and went to China, retiring in 1938. He was the author of *Analysis of Chinese Characters* (*Obituaries on File*).

G. P. Williams DD was superintendent of the American Sunday-School Union and superintendent of missions, Chicago Presbytery, and active with the American Tract Society. Hannah S. Wingate (1838–1930) taught for forty-two years at Public School 50 in the Bronx,

New York, retiring in 1902; her brother was George Wood Wingate (1840–1928), a Civil War general who later constructed the elevated railways in Brooklyn. His rules for rifle practice led to the formation of the National Rifle Association in 1871 (*Appleton's Cyclopedia of American Biography*; WWWA 1:806).

Albert Edward Yerex (1860–1908) became a professor of sociology and literature in Oregon, 1889–94, and then was president of the Historical Society of Southern California, 1900–7; his wife was Clara B. Garrison Yerex (1859–1940).

Notes

1. Holmes had been a prominent force against Paleolithic evidence at the 1892 AAS meetings, but in 1893 his colleague W. J. McGee took up the cause and read Holmes's contribution for him. David J. Meltzer discusses the explosive 1892 and 1893 meetings of Section H of AAAS in Meltzer 2010.

2. Charles Staniland Wake (1835–1910), who edited the *Memoirs of the International Congress of Anthropology* and saw it efficiently to publication in 1894, was an Englishman who had participated in the transatlantic debates between Lewis Henry Morgan, Lorimer Fison, and others in the 1870s over the evolution of marriage and morality. Approaching sixty, at the end of the Fair he hoped to become librarian in the Department of Ethnology in the new Field Museum. See Gardner 2008.

3. Only two papers each in physical anthropology and linguistics appeared in the *Memoirs*.

4. The Chicago Folk-Lore Society had, however, insisted on its own congress, which met in July and was modestly attended. For an account of its struggle with the larger American Folk-Lore Society, see Zumwalt 1988, 22–30.

5. The standard biography of Brinton is Darnell 1988.

6. Two particularly stimulating recent studies have thrown new light on these nineteenth-century struggles: Michaelson 1999; and, most pertinently, Conn 2004.

7. See, e.g., Bandelier 1892. It should be added that Bandelier was deeply concerned to preserve the documentary records. For Cushing's fascination and struggle with the Cibola problem, see Green 1990 and McFeely 2001.

8. Just as Morgan had closed *Ancient Society* (1877) with the ringing assertion that "a mere property career is not the final destiny of mankind" —a socialist future lay ahead, he seemed to suggest—Brinton closed his address with a prophecy of internationalism: "at no very distant future the human race will outgrow the limits of Nationality and will demand and find some guiding principle which will break down the barriers which the Nation, under present conditions, must perforce erect around itself" (Brinton 1894a, 34).

9. Emphasis added.

10. Cushing diary, August 30,1893; see Document E, this volume.

DOCUMENT D

The World's Fair Congress of Anthropology

WILLIAM HENRY HOLMES

The scheme of calling together a comprehensive series of congresses as an auxiliary of the Columbian Exposition at Chicago was worthy of the great occasion, and on the whole, so far as realized up to date, the undertaking has proved a decided success. In some cases, notably the Congress of Anthropology, the task of unfolding and carrying out the scheme fell to the lot of very busy men already overburdened with executive duties pertaining to the exposition. There was consequently in this particular case a lack of pre-arrangement and preparation, and the program was made up of such papers and materials as could be prepared or assembled on very brief notice. It could not be expected that a congress called together under such circumstances would be signalized by the presentation of a large number of papers of the highest order. Many prominent American students of anthropology were unable to be present, and foreign countries were necessarily in large part unrepresented. The meeting did not, therefore, rise fully to the dignity expected of an international congress, but there were enough earnest workers on hand to fill out the week's program and bring out of the heterogeneous elements results of very considerable importance.

The opening ceremonies, on Monday, August 28th, were conducted in the Assembly Hall of the Art Palace, where an address of welcome was delivered by Mr. C. C. Bonny, President of the Congress Auxiliary, and responses were made by Prof. F. W. Putnam, Director of the

From *American Anthropologist* old series 6 (October 1893): 423–34

Department of Anthropology [*sic*], and Dr. D. G. Brinton, President of the Congress of Anthropology.

The Congress then assembled in the hall assigned to it in the Art Palace, and was opened by Dr. Brinton, who, in an address on "The Nation as an Element in Anthropology," presented a thoughtful and able exposition of the methods and purposes of modern anthropology. In illustration of his theme, the author traced the development of mankind and social institutions from the primitive state through successive stages to the present condition, in which development proceeds rather through institutions inspired by the mind of man than along the lines of organic evolution. It was shown that sociology, one of the most intricate branches of modern anthropology, is destined to greatly modify, if not to replace, the more primitive statecraft based on superficial studies of individuals; for sociology is the real science of human institutions which themselves express the emotions, convictions, and experiences of the human species. The especial aim of the address was to exhibit the profound changes brought about by the transition of the social condition from the totemic, gentile, or tribal stage to that of national existence. This was shown to be necessarily associated with far-reaching modifications of the physical man, through the destruction of clan marriages and of matriarchal and patriarchal systems, as well as through other causes; and to lay the foundation for a true ethnic (in place of tribal) psychology, based on new and often contrasting conceptions of religion, ethics, and jurisprudence. The speaker closed with an expression of belief that the national is not the ultimate stage in sociological evolution, but that it will be followed by an international regime, when neither races nor States will be in antagonism, and that like aims, directed to the benefit of the whole species, will be recognized and pursued by leading minds everywhere. . . .

Ethnology.—One morning session was devoted to the reading of papers on ethnologic subjects, the opening paper, by Dr. Brinton, treating of the "Alleged evidences of ancient contact between America and other continents." It was confidently affirmed that tangible evidences of such contact do not exist in any department of American physical or cultural phenomena, and that the analogies on which the theory of contact is based are purely adventitious, arising from correspondences in man and his environment. In the discussion that followed, this view was combated by Professor Putnam, who presented cases in which the resemblances of phenomena were so marked and the conditions of occurrence so peculiar as to warrant serious challenging of the conclusions reached by the author. Prof. O. T. Mason, Mr. F. H. Cushing, and others took part in the discussion. Professor Mason opposed the view of Dr. Brinton, maintaining that contact was a constant condition to-day in the Behring Sea region, and that interchange has probably not been entirely interrupted for a considerable period of time since the occupation of the American continent began. Mr. Cushing supported Dr. Brinton, taking the position that foreign influences have certainly not been sufficiently strong to seriously affect the trend of purely American cultural development, and pointing out the fact that as a rule the striking features of native art and institutions can be traced back to their ultimate sources in America.

The arguments, on the whole may be regarded as inconclusive with respect to the particular analogies to which attention is most frequently called, but there is little doubt that American arts and institutions are flavored with elements, recognizable or not, of the culture of Asia and the Pacific islands, infused from time to time during the occupation of the western continent. . . .

Consideration of Collections.—The Congress devoted its afternoon sessions to the discussion and study of the extensive collections of anthropologic materials brought together by the exposition. Discussions relating to collections of the Department of Anthropology included papers and addresses by a number of gentlemen connected with the exhibits and others especially qualified to discuss them. Professor Putnam reviewed the history of the department and the progress of the great series of explorations and investigations conducted under his direction. He passed hurriedly over the more important features of the multitude of exhibits brought together by agents of the department and by individuals, states, societies, educational institutions, and foreign governments, and concluded by explaining to the congress his plans and hopes with respect to the prospective outcome of his prolonged and arduous labors—a great anthropologic museum to be established in Chicago. . . .

Concluding Remarks.—The Anthropologic Congress of itself probably marks no epoch in the history of the science of anthropology, taking rather the character of a suitable and withal satisfactory feature of the Columbian Exposition, serving an important function in giving emphasis to the value of the great assemblage of anthropological material there brought together. The great richness of the American field of investigation was made apparent to all. The importance of the outcome of the whole group of anthropologic features connected with the fair depends largely on the action of Chicago with respect to the opportunity of the century in museum-making....

ESSAY THREE

Anthropology in a Changing America
Interpreting the Chicago "Triumph" of Frank Hamilton Cushing

DAVID R. WILCOX

What is most fascinating about the diary that Frank Hamilton Cushing kept during his time at the World's Columbian Exposition (WCE) is the light it sheds on the relationship of late nineteenth-century American anthropology and the American public's aspirations at a moment when America was on the verge of actively assuming the role of world economic and political power.[1] On its face, anthropology at the Fair was merely another entertainment, but Cushing's diary shows that at a deeper level, many American people then began to recognize it had a more profound importance to them. This essay introduces excerpts from the Cushing diary (Document E) and two related documents (Documents F and G), analyzing the "electricity" Cushing generated among those with whom he interacted, stimulating new public interest in the study of American anthropology, and contrasting this "coming of age" moment with the journey both Cushing and American anthropology would take in the following decades—a story pursued further in Essay 7 of this volume.

America and American Anthropology at the Time of the Fair

Breaking Home Ties (fig. 5), a painting by Thomas Hovenden of Philadelphia that won him top honors at the 1893 WCE, brilliantly encapsulates the moment in American history also symbolized by the White City in Chicago and its Court of Honor, the architectural core of the Fair (fig. 13).[2] His tableau shows a boy about to leave his loving, rural home for the unknown dangers of the big city. The American democratic experiment, so long expressed largely in terms of rural and small-town values, was now rapidly taking up the challenges of urban life and would soon address those of world power (Kennedy 1987; Zimmermann 2002; Bender 2002; Morris 2005). Urban universities multiplied more rapidly, grew larger, and established graduate programs to train the administrators and entrepreneurs of the coming American empire. Chicago stepped forward with the University of Chicago, founded in 1892 and located immediately north of the Midway Plaisance at the Fair (Storr 1966).[3] Museums, too, proliferated about this time as places to educate the urban masses about this new world (Conn 1998). Chicago joined in following the Fair, establishing a major new museum when dry goods mogul Marshall Field provided the necessary funding (Nash and Feinman 2002; Brinkman 2009; see Document J). Science curricula in both universities and museums flourished, displacing the traditional preoccupation with Greek and Roman civilization as ideals of what Americans should know and become, much to the dismay of "the arbiter of America's taste," Charles Eliot Norton (Horowitz 1976, 1; Turner 1999). New conceptions of the good life were being born that would have to contend over the next several generations for the soul of America.

Nowhere was the promise of progress through science and technology more evident than at the World's Fair, where electricity lit up the night sky (Berg 1976, 98) using the scientific breakthrough of alternating current, which soon would bring electricity to both urban and rural households (Nye 1990; Jonnes 2004). Yet the decision of the architects and artists at the Fair was seemingly Janus-faced, looking both backward to classical models in the White City and forward in Electricity Hall toward a new vision of what America could become. Daniel Hudson Burnham, the Chicago architect who was appointed chief of construction and later director of works at the Fair (fig. 7), well understood the high stakes for the Fair.[4] On January 10, 1891, he told the architects he had selected to build the White City (see Karlowicz 1970) that

> the material progress and commercial supremacy of the country seemed conceded, but, though the city of Chicago was one of the greatest centers of power in finance, commerce, and manufactures, our cultivation in higher and more refined interests, and especially regard-

ing the fine arts, was denied; and there existed, however, a growing appreciation of these interests, and that this feeling would not be satisfied with merely the extent and abundance of the Exposition, but that the designers would be strongly supported by the people in an endeavor to attain a superior result in the fine arts themselves; and that the Chief of Construction would therefore use all his power to remove this stigma placed upon our country and especially upon the West (Burnham 1895, ii–ii).

Burnham also sought to motivate the makers of the Fair by telling them that it was the third greatest event in American history after the Revolution and the Civil War (Berg 1976, 77). The World's Columbian Exposition was to be no less than a coming of age of American civilization, when its sponsors would set out to show the world that America was the equal of any other nation—that it had its act together (Berg 1976; de Wit 1993).

Drawing upon a European neoclassical Beaux Arts design vocabulary, Burnham's architects created a preeminently American ideal that was a "showcase of American urban possibilities" in terms of its immensity, rapidity of construction (albeit with temporary cheap building materials), unity and harmony among adjacent buildings, landscape plan, and sanitation facilities, including more than three thousand water closets (Wilson 1989, 62–63; Berg 1976, 87). Cities, too, Burnham believed, could be civil places. The City Beautiful movement quickly followed the Fair, adding a sense of centeredness to many American cities (Burnham 1902; Wilson 1989; Cigliano and Landau 1994; Schaffer et al. 2003). A few years later, working with several of the same people from the Fair, Burnham helped to beautify Washington DC, making it a worthy symbol of empire in the coming "American Century" (Hines 1974; Longstreth 1991). His Union Station there reiterated many of the values of the Fair (Hines 1979). Burnham's final contribution was a bold regional master plan for the Chicago metropolis—the first in the country (Hines 1974; Wilson 1989; Condit 1973; Smith 2006). When Burnham died in 1912, President William Howard Taft told the *New York Times* that "there was no man in the professional life of the United States who has given more of his life to the public without having filled public office than Daniel Burnham."

On March 25, 1892, before the Fair opened, Burnham's success in building it was celebrated by many of America's cultural elite in New York City. Charles Eliot Norton (Turner 1999) was effusive in his praise of the White City: "a splendid display of monumental architecture. They show well how our ablest architects have studied the work of the past; and the arrangement of buildings according to the general plan produces a superb effect in the successful grouping in harmonious relationships of vast and magnificent structures" (cited in Hines 1979, 115). Ironically, the structures were an illusion of lath and plaster on wood or steel frameworks that would burn to the ground immediately after the Fair (de Wit 1993).[5]

As Burnham's story suggests, in the last decade of the nineteenth century enormous changes were happening in American society, brought on by the growth of corporate economic power, unprecedented migration from abroad, and the struggle between the haves and have-nots for their version of the American dream. The *avant-garde* movement of the generation before World War I (Brooks 1915; May 1994 [1959]; Stansell 2010) launched a vigorous challenge to the cultural assumptions of the confident nineteenth-century "genteel tradition" (Brooks 1952) and its beliefs in uplift for the masses and the brotherhood of man—on elite terms. Genteel motivations underwrote the building of great American museums, where the working masses could be educated—if only they would be opened on Sundays when working people had a day off (Kennedy 1969, 104–6; Freed 2012, 58–59).

It is now clear that the turn-of-the-century ideological and institutional struggles for the future of anthropology were preceded by several decades of seeming confidence and stability that reached a high point with the Chicago Fair. The dominant anthropological vision of the last quarter of the nineteenth century was premised upon values both similar to and different from those Franz Boas and his students would later advocate (Stocking 1968; Darnell 2001). The center of that vision and power was the nation's capital, specifically the new federal bureaus of that Gilded Age city (Flack 1975; Lacey 1979; Hinsley 1981). With the establishment in 1879 of the Anthropological Society of Washington (ASW) and the Bureau of Ethnology within the Smithsonian Institution, a small group of Americans began a transatlantic conversation with European colleagues about human evolution, differentiating themselves from the philosophy of Englishman Herbert Spencer (1880) by arguing that humans were different from animals in having a mind (and its cultural inventions) no longer subject to natural selection but only to cultural selection (Lacey 1979; Hinsley 1981, 125–31). Such figures as Lester Ward (1968 [1883]),[6] John Wesley Powell (1882–83), and W. J. McGee, although believing in the evolutionism of Lewis Henry Morgan (1877), took issue with Spencer, whose evolutionism attracted great interest in America in the 1870s and 1880s (Hofstadter 1944): "The starting point for the reconstruction of the Spencerian cosmology had to do with Spencer's assessment of the role of mind in human evolution. The Spencerians did not feel it played a major role. The Washington circle believed it was the decisive factor, the sine qua non in the story of social development" (Lacey 1979, 191).

As historian Michael Lacey (1979, 243) explains: "Powell and the other Washington anthropologists believed for the most part that biological change within the human species had been relatively insignificant since the advent of man." These views are strikingly similar to those of another American anthropologist, Daniel Brinton (Darnell 1988, 74–75; Document K), and to arguments that later Boasians would erect against the biological determinism of eugenicists and some environmental determinists (see Wilcox, Essay 7). Both sets of anthropologists apparently believed in what more recently is being called "human agency," but whereas the Boasians would advocate a "cultural relativism," the Washington anthropologists and Brinton believed in progress based upon human invention and the ineluctable development of innate ideas (Lacey 1979, 244; Darnell 1988). At the Chicago Fair, progress, especially technological advancement, was also the central message (deWit 1993).

With the establishment of the *American Anthropologist* in 1888, the Washington men advanced their views in provocative articles and book reviews that could be sent to European colleagues. They also had ideas about the special collaborative coalition of anthropological specialties required to solve current anthropological problems: the peopling of the New World; the independent development of civilization in the Americas (see Gallatin 1845, 1848; Brinton 1890; Kidder 1936); and the "unity or diversity" of the American Indian (Putnam 1901; see also Cushing 1890a; Fewkes et al. 1912). Solving these problems required consideration of data from all parts of the New World and the research domains of ethnology, archaeology, linguistics, and physical anthropology (Brinton 1892a, 1892b; Hallowell 1960; Darnell 1988; see also Cole 1974). This conviction, together with a belief in the relevance of folklore, had crystallized as a foundation consensus by the time of the Fair (Brinton 1892a, 1892b; Fowler and Parezo 1999; see introduction, this volume). It found expression there in multi-vocal ways.

When Chicago won the contest for the Exposition, Frederic Ward Putnam boldly told the *Chicago Tribune* that this was an opportune moment "to create a perfect ethnological exhibition of the past and present peoples of America" (Putnam 1890).[7] The board of the Exposition agreed, and they hired Putnam to do it, accepting his condition that original field research be supported. Accordingly, he was able to put at least fifty-five men and women in the field (Johnson 1897–98, 2:319–23)—nearly twice that, according to others—multiplying several times the number of active American archaeologists (see Powell 1890b), and even guiding their efforts with a written set of instructions. The display of the findings achieved by the nascent profession of American anthropology at the Fair, which included images of aboriginal sculpture from Yucatán and artifacts and mummies from South America as well as the Powell linguistic map of the distribution of North American Indian languages (Shaul 1999), for the first time attracted the attention and interest of millions of Americans and numerous foreign visitors—and potential wealthy patrons.

At the Fair this Americanist program began to resonate with the values and interests of the American business elites, resulting in the founding or elaboration of institutions with purposes that Boasians and others would later, in part, redirect to achieve different anthropological ends. The consensus about what would later be called the four-field approach (plus folklore) would be embraced by Boas and others (Boas 1909; McVicker 2012; see also Cole 1976).

The Fair of 1893 was the moment in the history of anthropology when a consensus was first expressed to a national audience of middle-class Americans and they seemed to respond favorably to its messages. The young Franz Boas was at the Fair, as Frederic Putnam's principal assistant, but he was then little more than a participant observer, dutifully measuring the heads of visitors and serving as impresario to his Kwakiutl troupe—although he did speak up vigorously at the Congress of Anthropology (Holmes 1893, Document D). His time of major influence would come later (Lesser 2004). In 1893 the generation of Powell, Brinton, and Putnam still defined the agenda. Their interest in a specifically Americanist agenda would endure, however, even after the Boasian transformation of American anthropology and continues to be of great interest today (Kidder 1936; Greenberg et al. 1986; Greenberg 1987; Ruhlen 1991; Meltzer 1993, 2009; Wilcox et al. 2008; cf. Foster 1996). It was their consensus about what the domain of American anthropology should be that was embraced and used effectively by Boas (1909) when he later toasted them as the "three fathers" of American anthropology (see also Freed 2012).

Frank Hamilton Cushing at the Fair

The Chicago Fair was a crucible of bubbling activity involving—among others—anthropologists, business people, and even social critics contesting the meaning of what was being displayed there. No anthropologist was more suited than Frank Hamilton Cushing, by personality and charisma, for what we today call networking and participant observation to report on the human chemistry at the Fair. He kept a fascinating and detailed diary of his experiences.

One of the boy wonders brought to the Smithsonian by Spencer Baird in the 1870s, Cushing at age nineteen was a curator at the 1876 Centennial Exposition in Philadelphia.[8] He then conducted two brilliant methodological explorations, first to define the role of ethnologist at Zuni Pueblo, 1879–84, by learning the Zuni language as a way to understand the culture, and second in the role of ethnological archaeologist in the Salt River Valley and again at Zuni, 1886–89, applying his knowledge of Zuni culture to interpret the archaeological record. The ethnology was for Powell's Bureau of Ethnology (Green 1979, 1990) and the ethnological archaeology for the Boston philanthropist Mary Hemenway (Hinsley and Wilcox 1995, 1996, 2002). As the director of the Hemenway Expedition, Cushing had had a paper read at the meetings of the International Congress of Americanists held in Berlin, Germany (Cushing 1890a)—the first time an American anthropologist had done so.

Cushing's exploits at Zuni and during the Hemenway Expedition were brought to the general public by his friend Sylvester Baxter, an editor for the *Boston Herald,* in articles published in *Century Magazine* and the *Herald* (Hinsley and Wilcox 1995, 1996), and in Cushing's own "My Adventures at Zuñi," illustrated in part by his friend Willard Metcalf (Cushing 1882–83), and *Zuñi Breadstuff* (Cushing 1884–85). Unlucky in his enemies, however, Cushing had to leave Zuni in 1884 after irritating Illinois senator (and vice-presidential candidate) General John H. Logan, one of Powell's principal supporters in the U.S. Congress (Green 1990). The Hemenway archaeological expedition collapsed, too, after Cushing's field secretary and future brother-in-law, Frederick Webb Hodge, made mean-spirited and self-serving accusations against him (Wilcox 2003b).[9] Finally, Cushing suffered seriously and repeatedly from severe health problems brought on by a deformed stomach that caused diverticulitis and a tapeworm infection that nearly killed him in early 1890 (Cushing 1890b).[10] As his health recovered, Powell took him back as an ethnologist in the bureau in January 1892. Under the dunning attentions of William Torrey Harris, the president of the Hemenway Expedition board (and U.S. commissioner of education), Cushing wrote three installments of an itinerary about his archaeological experiences (Hinsley and Wilcox 2002).[11] But he finally gave up that work in May 1893 when Mary Hemenway's son Augustus refused any further payments. Thus liberated, he became free in the summer of 1893 to seek new challenges for his anthropological vision (see Cushing 1890a). As his diary reflects, in Chicago Cushing would find intellectual and social renewal and a kind of triumph over recent adversities.

Among many other matters, Cushing's Chicago diary traces in some detail the beginnings of his close anthropological friendship with Stewart Culin, then secretary of the newly launched Free (University) Museum in Philadelphia. Their close collaborative relationship lasted to the end of Cushing's life and resulted in the publication by Culin (1975 [1907]) of his classic, *Games of the North American Indians.*[12]

Cushing's diary also records contacts with other Philadelphians, including Brinton and Sara Yorke Stevenson.[13] The latter, with Culin, would later introduce him to William Pepper, provost of the University of Pennsylvania—which in turn led to his Florida expedition in the middle 1890s (Cushing 1897; Gilliland 1975, 1989; Wilcox 2003b;

FIG. 16. Stewart Culin (1858–1929). National Anthropological Archives, Smithsonian Institution, Portrait 19.

Kolianos and Weisman 2005a, 2005b). More surprisingly, the diary documents intimate contacts with some members of the Chicago business elite, centrally including Daniel Hudson Burnham—providing us important clues as to why American archaeology and ethnology became established in enduring institutional nexuses such as the Field Columbian Museum (Nash and Feinman 2002).

Cushing had planned with Mary Hemenway to create a "Museum of

FIG. 17. Sara Yorke Stevenson, portrait by Leopold Seyffert, 1917. Courtesy of Penn Museum, image #151005.

Humanity" in Salem, Massachusetts, with the moral goal of fostering the brotherhood of man (Hinsley and Wilcox n.d. a). He communicated his conception of this plan to Powell and to Otis Tufton Mason, curator of anthropology at the National Museum.[14] They encouraged him to carry out his exhibit ideas for lifelike displays at the WCE, under the direction of his friend William Henry Holmes (but see Essay 4, this volume). It was to complete this assignment that he was dispatched to Chicago with his wife.

Their first sight of the Fair was the 250-foot Ferris Wheel (fig. 14), America's commercial and entertainment answer to the Eiffel Tower. Arriving in the Exposition wonderland of high ritual, national symbolism, and "competitive potlatches" (Benedict 1983), Cushing had such a good time with family and friends, constantly meeting new people and sharing his ideas, that he almost forgot to complain about his health problems. In the somewhat strained competition between the U.S. government exhibits and Putnam's Anthropology Building exhibits, Cushing's realistic figures (Essay 4, fig. 41, this volume) did well, ironically more closely realizing the methodological goals called for by Putnam's chief assistant, Franz Boas (1887), than either the approach of Mason or the exhibits presented in the Anthropology Building (Fagin 1984). A year later Cushing again worked under Mason to create a Pueblo exhibit at the National Museum that took his ideas several steps further (Anon. 1894a). The success of his exhibit ideas (in the opinions of Powell and Holmes) was Cushing's first triumph at the Fair—but that was only the beginning.

The Congress of Anthropology at Chicago

Urged by Powell and Holmes to stay on at the Fair for the Congress of Anthropology in late August, even after his wife Emma went back to Washington, Cushing had a second brilliant success, presenting several talks and ably discussing others (Holmes 1893, Document D). Brinton was president of the congress, and he and Cushing found that their ideas about the autonomy of aboriginal American culture history were simpatico (see Brinton 1890, 1891). Two of Putnam's protégés whom he met at the Congress of Anthropology, Alice Cunningham Fletcher (Mark 1988) and Zelia Nuttall (Parmenter 1966), both warmly praised him, saying— perhaps with some feminine amusement—that he "had put them on new trails & was a sort of Sun in Anthropology illuminating the ways of all of them" (Cushing 1893a).[15] Although Holmes would later claim that the congress "did not . . . rise fully to the dignity expected of an international congress" (Holmes 1893, 423; Document D, this volume; cf. Zumwalt 1988, 27–28), Cushing (1893a) had a perfectly delightful time.

Highly stimulated by Cushing's performances at the congress, many were won over to him and his ideas. Culin by then was already an ally, and now Brinton eagerly walked with and talked at length to Cushing, as did Fletcher and Nuttall. Even Putnam, who may initially have been cool toward Cushing, was impressed. Later, while rushing around making his final contacts before leaving the Fair for Washington, Cushing made a point of looking for Putnam to say goodbye. Not finding Putnam, he left a card, but he did see Putnam's wife, who was most cordial to him. By forging these friendships Cushing later successfully brought about an alliance between the University of Pennsylvania's Free (University) Museum, and the Bureau of American Ethnology to sponsor his expedition to Florida (Gilliland 1975, 1989). When terrible charges were made against him of forging artifacts, it was Putnam who came to his defense, and he survived the scandal (see Wilcox 2003b).

Cushing's Unique Experience at the Fair

The interactions Cushing had with several new friends he made at the Exposition provide important clues about the basis for the intellectual alliance that was then forming between both women's elites and some elements of the American business class and the nascent cadre of anthropologists. First, in the Illinois Building, where Sarah Tyson Rorer of Philadelphia ran a Corn Kitchen, Cushing supplied her with Zuni maize recipes.[16] Several women on the Board of Lady Managers were intent on persuading the American public that maize was a good human food, not only fit for animals, as was then widely believed. They also wanted maize to become a national American symbol. Cushing gave a talk on maize at the Woman's Building on July 22, with Mary Cantrill, who was on the Executive Committee of the Board of Lady Managers, as toastmistress (Weimann 1981, 459–63, 568).[17] Cushing's ethnography of corn at Zuni Pueblo, *Zuñi Breadstuff* (originally 1884–85), was then being partially reprinted by D. H. Ranck in his new magazine, *Milling*; it was the underlying text for this movement. Even Mary Hemenway was briefly attracted to it.

Second, Boston artist Francis Davis "Frank" Millet,—whose sister Lucia had married Cushing's close friend Sylvester Baxter in 1893—stopped by with his wife to greet Cushing on July 24. Mil-

FIG. 18. Sarah Tyson Rorer, ca. 1886. From *Mrs. Rorer's Philadelphia Cook Book: A Manual of Home Economics* (Philadelphia: Arnold and Company, 1886.

let had been hired by Burnham to be director of decoration for the Exposition; he was Burnham's "friend and advisor . . . in everything" (Berg 1976, 99).[18] Because Burnham and his wife Margaret were with the Millets, Cushing met them as well. On August 4 they met again. Cushing found that Burnham was a most lovable man, and a Sweden-

FIG. 19. "Mrs. Rorer's Corn Recipes Cookbook," distributed at her "corn kitchen" in the Woman's Building at the Chicago World's Fair.

FIG. 20. Daniel Burnham and Exposition architects and officials: (*left to right*) Burnham, George B. Post, M. B. Pickett, Henry Van Brunt, Francis D. Millet, Maitland Armstrong, Col. Edward Rice, Augustus Saint-Gaudens, Henry Sargent Codman, George W. Maynard, Charles F. McKim, E. R. Graham, and Dion Geraldine. World's Columbian Exposition, architects and officials, Chicago IL, 1891. Daniel H. Burnham Collection, Ryerson and Burnham Archives, The Art Institute of Chicago. Digital file #194301.worldsfairgroup.

borgian,[19] the cousin by marriage of Cushing's friend Joseph Worcester, the founder of the Swedenborgian church in America, whom Cushing apparently met in 1887 or 1888 in San Francisco. The families soon were spending much time together, and on August 19 the Cushings were invited out to the Burnhams' Evanston home, where they stayed up talking until past one o'clock at night. Cushing (1893a) reports that "Mr. Burnham discussed Museum of World's Fair project. Grand scheme of his own original'y. His idea[s] all excellt"—suggesting that Putnam may not have been alone in grasping the post-Fair possibilities of a natural history museum in Chicago.

Burnham stood at the very heart of the Chicago Fair and had close ties to many in the Chicago elite as well as those critical of that elite.[20] He was close friends with Edward Everett Ayer (Essay 6, fig. 69, this volume), who later claimed *he* was the one who persuaded Marshall Field to put up a million-dollar endowment for what quickly became the Field Columbian Museum (Ayer 2003; but see Wilcox 2003a), and Ayer served as its first president of the board.[21] Harlow Niles Higinbo-

FIG. 21. Francis Davis "Frank" Millet (1848–1912). Francis Davis Millet, portrait, ca. 1891. Ryerson and Burnham Libraries Book Collection, Ryerson and Burnham Archives, The Art Institute of Chicago. Digital file #000000_millet.

tham (Essay 6, fig. 70, this volume), Field's bookkeeper and partner, who served as president of the local Exposition Board, was the second president of the museum, thus maintaining a close control of this institution by this group of the Chicago upper class, who had their own ideas about what the museum should be (see McVicker 1999; Wilcox

2003b).²² Among Burnham's other friends whom Cushing met were industrialist Charles Deering, wholesale druggist George S. Lord and his wife Eda, art critic and novelist Henry Blake Fuller, muckraking author Henry Demarest Lloyd and his wife Jessie, and archaeological collectors Walter C. and Edward F. Wyman and Walter Alison Phillips.²³ If we can credit Cushing's diary, he wowed them all with his engaging style and esoteric knowledge about Zuni ethnology and spiritual interests—adding them to his "conquests," as he notes. While none of these people later kept in touch or directly supported Cushing's work, his ability to reach out to wealthy patrons (especially the Burnhams, Lords, and Lloyds), whose homes he visited, is a striking illustration of how the interests of such people resonated with the fascinating field of anthropology.

What was the secret of Cushing's charm? Two factors may be suggested. First, people were fascinated by the firsthand exotic knowledge he possessed in such abundance, his experiences living with Native Americans, and his ability to sing to them in the language of the Zuni. Central to his knowledge was interesting information about Zuni religion and its "correspondences" to their own. While we do not know the precise nature of Cushing's conversations with the Burnhams, Millets, and others in Chicago, they were probably along the lines reported in a newspaper account of 1894 about a lecture Cushing gave at the People's Church in Washington DC. In this lecture Cushing shared his ideas about "Primitive Religion" with a general audience. His evolutionary thesis began with religion in animals and how it became human; he then discussed what he regarded as similarities between "primitive" religions and their own "more advanced" Christianity:

> Prof. Cushing then emphasized the idea that primitive religion was in unity with the last religion, the Christian religion. Man is one with animal blood and nature, he said, the first religion is connected with the last religion, and there is no greater or more instructive religion than the primitive ones, showing as they do the [e]ffect of environment on man, and leading up to the complicated systems of to-day. These religions, he continued, are a part of those of to-day in substantiation of which he instanced the fact that a most remarkable feature of all

FIG. 22. Charles Deering, ca. 1908. Courtesy of the Chicago History Museum, ICHi-18104.

FIG. 23. Henry Blake Fuller, ca. 1896. Courtesy of the Chicago History Museum, ICHi-10342.

primitive religions was the places in which the Gods live, these being the places from which come the winds. The back and face, as well as the right side and the left side of this supreme being was a discovery among all, even the lowest of the savage races, and from this reasoning a connection was found with the winds that blow from these four quarters as the breath of a living being. The upper and lower regions then were added and again the all-containing God, or po-shai-an-kya, as the Zunis styled him, who was the center of all.

The septenary system, thus arising, was evidenced in all religions of the day and especially in the Christian religion. From it, he declared, we have the seven sacred numbers of the Eastern nations, the week of seven days, and the sabbatical years. In the New Testament Christ called the disciples together and sends them two by two into the regions of the world, making six sets, while he remained the master of all of them. When Judas Iscariot perished after the betrayal another was chosen in his place to preserve the sacred number, and after Christ was crucified, Paul became the head, from whom emanated the later Gospels.

Prof. Cushing then showed the parallel to this in the custom among the Zuni Indians, which was also true, he said, of other primitive peoples, of having a dual god in each of the six quarters referred to. The Zunis styled them the father and mother priests with one great center, the all-containing-one, which is the sun (Anon. 1894b).

In conclusion, Cushing told his listeners, "He hoped the day would come when all religious teachings and sayings could be traced back to their early origin in this manner, *for we should know that the heart of religion [is] true and sincere*" (Anon. 1894b; emphasis added).

A second reason for Cushing's allure is simple but is often overlooked: he was a nice man. His obituary published in the *Bulletin of the Free Museum of Science and Art* (Anon. 1900) concludes that "he was a man of rarely sympathetic personality, courteous, warm-hearted and generous. His early death will be lamented, not only by his scientific associates, but by every man, woman, and child with whom he ever came in intimate contact." The portrait of Cushing painted by the Philadelphia artist Thomas Hovenden in 1894 (fig. 4) wonderfully captures that conception of him.[24] It is also the dominant impression that emerges from transcribing his personal diaries.

As noted, at the Fair Cushing began a lifelong friendship and close collaboration with the man who probably wrote that appreciation of him, Stewart Culin. The beginnings and growth of their anthropological friendship are documented in Cushing's diaries (see Cushing 1893a). His avid discussions with Culin about games led to his hypothesis that many American games, including patolli, were derived from arrow divination, and evolved autonomously and anciently in the New World (see Cushing's September 1893 Monthly Report, Document F). Culin's extensive knowledge of Chinese was complemented by Cushing's experience attending the Chinese Theater in San Francisco during his visit there in 1887, accompanied by the reporter Henry Burden McDowell and journalist Kate Field (*Daily Examiner*, San Francisco, November 20, 1887, p. 9, cols. 3–5).[25] Cushing expounded to McDowell, who already knew a lot about the Chinese, the similarities between Zuni mythic drama and the Chinese drama.

The insights realized by Cushing and Culin contrasted with a theory propounded by the famous English ethnologist Edward Burnett Tylor, who posited a connection between patolli and India's game parchisi (Culin 1893).[26] In November 1894 Cushing wrote to Culin about a dinner party at Powell's during which a communication was received from Tylor about their work. Powell read it aloud:

> Tell Frank Cushing that I understand he regards American Games as autochthonous and believes he can even prove patolli to be so. Tell him that I love him; but that if he undertakes to prove his position before the Scientific World, I shall fight him to the bitter end—until one or the other of us breaks his lance!
>
> [Cushing then continued to Culin:] Here is my [en prise]—for I hold Tylor's messages as in the highest degree chivalric—considering his well known feats in the arena of Scientific Tourney. Powell was fired to a high degree and counted off on his four fingers the men who, like himself are—if I may venture the term—Indiginists of America,— himself and Brinton and *ourselves*! He discoursed magnificently on the theme thus introduced, saying that one after another the strongholds of the Alienists had been taken; that one alone remained—one which no one had yet dared to attack save by general siege,—Games; but that the *arrow of Divination* had pierced its most vulnerable part

and it too must fall—and gentlemen, said the Major— "Cushing here, fired the arrow & he has a quiver full—" ["]yes, and Culin gave me the sheaf" said I. Then the Major spoke so fervently of the importance of the work that my zeal has been renewed and you shall not have much longer to wait. (Cushing 1894).

It seems likely that for many of these same reasons Daniel Brinton was drawn to Cushing. A proponent of the anthropological theory of the "pychic unity of mankind" as an explanation for cultural similarities (Darnell 1988; Brinton, Document K), Brinton discovered in Cushing at the Congress of Anthropology a person with firsthand knowledge of a Native American group and their language who had reached very similar explanatory ideas to his own. The folklore of games also seemed to confirm Brinton's extreme "Americanist" views about the independent development of American Indian culture (Darnell 1988). Thus, in his 1895 publication of "The Arrow" in the *American Anthropologist*, Cushing (1895a) seemed to support Brinton's ideas about the aims of Americanist anthropology (Brinton 1895a; see also Culin 1902, 1975 [1907]; Lyman 1982, 1990). Only a year later, however, Franz Boas (1896b; Document L) took deadly aim at the foundations of the "psychic unity" methodology—an early step in redefining the directions American anthropology would take in the twentieth century (Lesser 2004).

Notes

First thanks go to Curtis Hinsley for his friendship and criticism. We began a project to publish a documentary history of the Hemenway Expedition in 1983, which has become a long odyssey that has moved well beyond our original goals. Many institutions have helped us to gain knowledge about that expedition and about its leader, Frank Hamilton Cushing. They include the National Anthropological Archives, Peabody Museum at Harvard University, Southwest Museum (now part of the Autry National Museum), Brooklyn Museum Library, Huntington Free Library, Cornell University, University Museum of the University of Pennsylvania, and Arizona State University Library and Archives. I want to thank the Christine Callen Trust for support for four research trips that contributed to this essay. I also thank Jim Collette, Jeannie Greiner, and Marlene Conklin for reading the essay and providing helpful criticism, and three readers for the University of Nebraska Press for their comments or criticisms. For any errors or ambiguities that remain, I alone am responsible.

Reference works such as dictionaries of biography are not in the bibliography but are identified in full at first use in these notes and thereafter abbreviated. An abbreviations list appears at the front of the book. Biographical detail not otherwise sourced comes from supplementary Google searches.

1. Jesse Green was given Cushing's diaries by a member of the family and has since deposited them at the National Anthropological Archives (NAA). He gave copies of the diaries dating from 1888 to 1897 to Curtis Hinsley and David Wilcox, and the latter transcribed them into the computer and wrote extensive endnotes about the people and other points found in them. A version of those transcriptions has also been placed in the NAA by Wilcox.

2. Born in Dunmamwan, County Cork, Ireland, Thomas Hovenden (1840–August 14, 1895) came to the United States in 1853, where he studied art at the National Academy of Design; later he studied in Paris at the Ecole des Beaux Arts under Cabanel, returning to the United States in 1880. He won the grand prize at the WCE in 1893 for his painting "Breaking Home Ties," which now hangs in the Philadelphia Museum of Art. In 1894 he painted a portrait of Cushing. "Hovenden was mortally injured in a heroic effort to save a child from a railroad train in the station of Germantown" (Terhune and Johns 2006).

3. William Rainey Harper, the first president of the University of Chicago, hired Frederick Starr as its anthropologist in a Department of Sociology (see McVicker 2012). The university had its own museum, but it would only be after Starr's death in 1923 that a strong anthropology graduate program began there under the direction of Fay-Cooper Cole. Meanwhile, the Oriental Institute also began to grow within the university, led first by James Henry Breasted (see C. Breasted 1943; Abt 2011). In the 1960s, when the faculty of the Oriental Institute were teaching in the anthropology department, a synergy was created that produced the "new archaeology" of the 1960s, and at long last a relationship between some of those students, several of their professors, and the curator of anthropology at the Field Museum, Paul Sidney Martin, had a significant impact on southwestern archaeology—and on my life! (Wilcox 2003a).

4. Daniel Hudson Burnham (1846–1912) was chief of construction and director of works for the World's Columbian Exposition. Applying his experience at the Fair, and working with friends made there, Burnham later successfully pioneered in city planning for Washington DC. in 1902 and Chicago in 1909. His wife Margaret was the daughter of John B. Sherman, a Chicago stockyards magnate, for whom Burnham built a mansion in 1874—his first big commission (Hines 1974).

5. Even more ironically, Burnham was also one of the pioneers in the architecture of skyscrapers, which would soon overwhelm the Beaux Arts classicism of the White City and the kind of order envisioned by the City Beautiful movement with a twentieth-century vision of urban possibilities, linked to suburbs via railroads or electric streetcars (but see Bender 2002, who found that in New York City these different conceptions continued to coexist for some time, and true skyscrapers came later than in Chicago; in a further irony, the first skyscraper in New York was Bur-

nam's 1902 Flatiron Building). Looking today at some of Burnham's conceptions in his Plan of Chicago (Smith 2006), we may even be disturbed by how much they present a stifling uniformity; we can be thankful that in the contest between private interests and public aspirations, this was rejected by the democratic eclecticism of American society.

6. Born in Joliet IL, Lester Frank Ward (1841–1913) received an AB from Columbian University in 1869 and an AM in 1873. A Civil War veteran, he was a geologist and sociologist who worked for the U.S. Geological Survey (USGS) for many years and was a founding member of the Anthropological Society of Washington (ASW). See *Anthropology News Bulletin*, hereafter cited as ANB; *National Cyclopedia of American Biography* 13:112, hereafter NCAB; *Who Was Who in America* 1:1293, hereafter WWWA). He was the father of American sociology (Lacey 1979) and president of the ASW in 1896 (*American Anthropologist* 9:220, hereafter AA).

7. Born in Salem MA, Putnam (1839–1915) received his early training there under Henry Wheatland at the Essex Institute. In 1863 he founded and edited the *American Naturalist*, moving to the Peabody Museum, Harvard, in 1874 as director and curator; he served until 1909. He became Peabody Professor of American Archaeology and Ethnology in 1887, retiring in 1909. From 1873 to 1898 he was the permanent secretary of the American Association for the Advancement of Science, becoming president in 1898–99. He was one of the founders of the Archaeological Institute of America (AIA) in 1879. After serving as head of the Anthropology Building at the WCE, 1891–93, he became curator of anthropology at the American Museum of Natural History, 1894–1903, hiring Boas as his assistant curator. In 1903 he founded the Department of Anthropology at the University of California, Berkeley. He was elected to the National Academy of Sciences in 1884 (WWWA 1:1002; Curtis Hinsley in *International Directory of Anthropologists*, hereafter IDA; *New York Times*, August 15, 1915, p. 13, col. 6) and was the second president of American Anthropological Association (AAA) in 1905–6.

8. For an interesting account of Cushing's brief time at Cornell University before joining the Smithsonian, see Gleach 2007.

9. Born in Plymouth, England, Hodge came to the United States at age seven and attended but did not graduate from Columbian University. A clerk in the USGS, 1884–86, he became field secretary under Cushing on the Hemenway Expedition, 1886–88. He then joined the Bureau of Ethnology, becoming chief, 1910–17. From 1899 to 1915 he was the editor of the *American Anthropologist*, becoming president of the AAA in 1915–17. He was president of the ASW in 1911–12 (AA 13, 177–178). In 1917 he joined the Museum of the American Indian in New York City, excavating at Hawicuh near Zuni NM, 1917–23. On January 1, 1932, he became the director of the Southwest Museum in Highland Park CA (AA 34:170; IDA, 293–295; WWWA 3:406).

10. While recovering in his hometown of Albion NY, Cushing met and befriended Talcott Williams (1849–1928), who was an editor of the *Philadelphia Press* for thirty-one years, beginning in 1881. Williams's wife, Sophia Wells Royce (1850–1928), was from Albion. Williams was a close friend of William Pepper (1848–98), the provost

of the University of Pennsylvania, and was a member of the board of its Free (University) Museum, 1888–1914, which Pepper headed. He was also a close friend of the artist Thomas Eakins, who would do Cushing's portrait in 1895; note, too, that Eakins's portrait *The Black Fan* in the Philadelphia Museum of Art is of Mrs. Williams (http://www.philamuseum.org/collections/permanent/42511.html; NCAB 15:306–7; *New York Times*, January 25, 1928). Talcott Williams and his wife were thus the first of what at the WCE would become a series of key friendships that Cushing forged with Philadelphia intellectuals.

11. Dr. William Torrey Harris (1835–1909), philosopher and U.S. commissioner of education from 1889 to 1906, was the leader of the St. Louis Hegelians, the superintendent of schools in St. Louis from 1868 to 1880, and editor of the *Journal of Speculative Philosophy*, which provided a forum for the philosophical début of Charles Sanders Pierce, Josiah Royce, William James, and John Dewey. In 1880 Harris helped to found the Concord (Massachusetts) School of Philosophy and through these activities came to the attention of Mary Hemenway. He became her trusted advisor on issues of educational reform and was appointed chairman of the Hemenway Expedition board. "Hardly any American philosopher was more widely acclaimed in his own time" (*Dictionary of American Biography* 8:330, hereafter DAB; see also NCAB 15:1–2).

12. Born in Philadelphia, Culin (1858–1929) had engaged in mercantile business in Philadelphia until 1890. In 1888 he founded the Oriental Club of Philadelphia and was its secretary from 1888 to 1902. He learned some Chinese, read the *I Ching*, and was a participant observer of the Chinese community in Philadelphia (Lyman 1982). The anthropological importance of their friendship is analyzed later in this essay.

13. Sara Yorke Stevenson (1847–1921) was the vice-president of the jury of awards for ethnology at the Fair. A founder of the Archaeological Association of the University of Pennsylvania, which soon became the Free (University) Museum, she was its secretary for ten years and then president of its board of managers. A woman with wide-ranging intellectual interests, she was elected to membership in the American Philosophical Society and was the first woman given an honorary degree by the University of Pennsylvania. Impressed by Cushing's performance at the Congress of Anthropology at the Fair, when in Washington in November 1893 Mrs. Stevenson told Cushing that "all Philad[elphia were his] Friends—since Expos'n," which probably helped pave the way for his hiring by the university museum to conduct an archaeological expedition to Florida two years later.

14. Born in Maine, Mason (1838–1908) graduated from Columbian College in 1861 and then became principal of its preparatory school, 1862–84. In 1872 he became connected to the Smithsonian Institution, where he was a collaborator for twelve years, becoming curator of the Department of Ethnology, U.S. National Museum in 1884. His paper "What Is Anthropology" was the working plan for the Anthropological Society of Washington, which he helped to found, and he served on its journal *American Anthropologist* for many years (WWWA 1:786; *New York Times*, November 6, p. 7, col. 4). He wrote the ASW constitution. For eighteen years he also

served on the U.S. Board of Geographical Names (Hough 1908). He was president of the ASW in 1893 (AA O.S. 6:221).

15. Born in Havana, Cuba, Fletcher (1838–1923) was abused by a stepfather early in life. Her friend Claudius Conant made her financially independent. In 1873 she helped organize the Association for the Advancement of Women, led by Julia Ward Howe, Mary Livermore, and Maria Mitchell. Converted by F. W. Putnam to an interest in anthropology in 1879, she went west in 1881 to live with the Sioux and to visit the Omaha, where the son of Chief Joseph La Fleshe, Francis, became her field assistant; in 1890 she adopted him as her son. In 1887 she helped write and lobbied for the Dawes Act, which disastrously allocated Indian land so that it could be alienated to whites. In 1888 she published *Indian Education and Civilization*. Mary C. Thaw (mother of the man who murdered the architect Stanford White) in 1890 founded a lifetime fellowship for Fletcher at Harvard's Peabody Museum. "She was an early proponent of the preservation of archaeological monuments in the United States" (Joan Mark in ANB 8:108–9).

Born in San Francisco, Zelia Maria Magdalena Parrott Nuttall (1857–1933) was educated in Europe, marrying the French geographer Alphonse Pinart in 1880 (separated 1884, divorced 1888). She first visited Mexico in 1884; she lived in Dresden, Germany, 1886–99, and then in the Coyoacán suburb of Mexico City, 1902–33, at Casa Alvarado, the site of the mansion of the Spanish conquistador Pedro de Alvarado. She was awarded a gold medal at the WCE in 1893. She found and authenticated the Codex Maglibecchiano and the Codex Nuttall (IDA, 513–14; SW Museum bio file). She was one of the first to realize that the Mayan glyphs contained historical information (Bernal 1980, 151). The character "Mrs. Norris" in D. H. Lawrence's *The Plumed Serpent* is based on her (*Cambridge Dictionary of American Biography*, 540; *American Men of Science* 1921, 512).

16. Sarah Tyson Rorer (1849–1937) was the author of *The Philadelphia Cookbook* and the founder of the Philadelphia Cooking School (Weimann 1981, 459). She and Cushing became friends; he later often stayed with her at Mt. Gretna PA, and she would help him find a stenographer in Philadelphia to type his Florida report for the American Philosophical Society (Cushing 1893a).

17. From Georgetown KY, Mary Cecil Cantrill (d. 1928) was a friend of Mrs. Bertha Honoré Palmer (1849–1918), the president of the Board of Lady Managers at the Fair. Cantrill was a member of the Executive Committee of the Board of Lady Managers and acted as toastmistress after Cushing gave a talk on corn in the Corn Kitchen on July 22 (Johnson 1897, 1:207; Weimann 1981, 84, 105, 568).

18. Francis Davis "Frank" Millet (1846–1912) was a popular Boston artist, war correspondent, and critic who became close friends with Daniel Burnham at the WCE (DAB 1928; Hines 1974). Millet "had charge of all coloring inside and outside the buildings, the flags, banners, and woven-fabric effects of the processions and ceremonies inside of the grounds, and later of all the music and illuminations and fireworks; directed and controlled the sculpture and mural paintings, and was the friend and adviser of the Chief of Construction [Daniel Burnham] in everything"

(Burg 1976, 99). In July 1893 he was made director of functions as well as director of decorations (Johnson 1897, 1:478). He later tragically drowned with the sinking of the *Titanic* (Hines 1974, 358–59).

19. For a detailed modern discussion of this version of spiritual Christianity, see Crompton 2005.

20. Burnham did become an organizer and early board member of the Field Columbian Museum (Nash and Feinman 2002), but he was not one of the most important "cultural philanthropists" in Chicago (Horowitz 1976), such as Charles Hutchinson, Martin Ryerson, or Frederick MacVeagh, all of whom, interestingly, had become the leaders of the Chicago Society of the AIA in 1890.

21. Ayer (1841–1927) made a fortune in producing railroad ties and once owned a lumber company in Flagstaff AZ, which he sold to the Riordan brothers. He was a bibliophile who in 1911 presented his library of ca. 49,000 items to the Newberry Library. He gave many antiquarian collections to the Field Museum, including its Egyptian collection. He was a trustee or director of the Newberry Library, 1891–1911; Art Institute of Chicago, 1891–1927; and Chicago Historical Society (NCAB 20; Lockwood 1929).

22. Higinbotham (1938–1919) rose from being a bookkeeper at Field, Palmer & Leiter to a partnership at Field, Leiter & Company, resigning in 1901. He was then president of the American Luxifer Prism Company, Portland Cement Company, and National Grocery Company and was a director of the Northern Trust Company (NCAB 18; Gilbert and Bryson 1929, 736). His daughter Florence married Richard Teller Crane Jr. (1873–1931), a wealthy plumbing and iron and brass industrialist. Higinbotham was a founder of the Chicago Home for Incurables (see *New York Times*, July 29, 1949, p. 21, col. 1).

23. Charles Deering (1852–1927) was the son of William Deering, who founded a major harvester company in Chicago that later merged with International Harvester, for which Charles Deering became the chairman of the board. He built an estate in Florida, was a member of the Jekell Island Club in Georgia, and founded the Deering Library at Northwestern University.

24. Terhune (2006, 149) says the portrait was painted in 1890; however, Cushing's diary (1894) make it clear that this occurred after the Fair in 1894, another of his successes in Philadelphia. The more famous portrait of Cushing by Thomas Eakins (Rosenzweig 1977, 153–58) came about in 1895.

25. Born in San Antonio TX, Henry Burden McDowell (1857–1928) graduated with an AB from Harvard University in 1878, studied law there, 1879–80, and also studied Sanskrit and Chinese. He was a chemist with his grandfather's Burden Iron Company in Troy NY, 1882, and later a consulting engineer in New York City. In San Francisco he was editor and proprietor of the Ingleside newspaper, 1883–85; a member of the editorial staff of the *Daily Examiner*, 1885; and a correspondent for the *Daily Examiner* who wrote "The Chinese Theater" in *Century Magazine* (November 1884: 27–44) and "A New Light on the Chinese" in *Harper's Magazine* (December 1892). McDowell "made extensive researches in Chinese mythology and religion

and [was] author of the 'Chaldaeo-Chinese hypothesis.'" He went to Arizona and reported on the Hemenway Expedition in a series of articles in the San Francisco *Examiner* (Hinsley and Wilcox n.d. b), and as a result of that he "published maps of prehistoric irrigating ditches of Salt River Valley, Ariz, leading to building of Roosevelt Dam." At Cambridge MA he later organized the Roosevelt Club and later yet supported Roosevelt's candidacy for the U.S. presidency (WWWA 1:809). McDowell's father was the Civil War general Irvin G. McDowell (1818–85), who lost the first battle of Bull Run (and the second). He retired from the army in 1882 and became a park commissioner for San Francisco, planning the park improvements of the Presidio reservation and laying out the roads overlooking Golden Gate Bridge (WWWA 1, 416).

26. Born in Camberwell, England, to a Quaker brass maker, Tylor (1832–1917) entered his father's foundry at age sixteen but abandoned business in 1855 to travel for his health; he accompanied Henry Christy on an expedition to Mexico, authoring *Anahuac, or Mexico and the Mexicans, Ancient and Modern*, in 1861. He is best known for his 1871 book *Primitive Culture*. He led the movement to create an anthropological section in the British Association and in 1884 acted as its first president. He taught at Oxford from 1883 and successively was keeper of the University Museum, 1883; reader in anthropology, 1884; and professor of anthropology, 1896; he retired in 1909. He was also the first Gifford lecturer at Aberdeen University in 1888; was president of the Anthropological Society, 1891; and was knighted in 1912. "The secret of Tylor's eminence lies in his infinite respect for facts"; a stout Darwinian, to him the psychological method in understanding humans was paramount (*Dictionary of National Biography* 24:539–541; and see Thomas and Freire-Marreco 1907). In October 1884 Tylor spoke to the ASW on the theme "How the Problems of American Anthropology Present Themselves to the English Mind" (Lamb 1906, 570).

DOCUMENT E

Excerpts from the Diary of Frank Hamilton Cushing at the World's Fair

June 16–September 12, 1893

Part I: June 16–25, 1893

With the collapse of the Hemenway Southwestern Archaeological Expedition in June 1889 Frank and Emma Magill Cushing retreated for more than two years to Albion, his boyhood home in northwestern New York State. During this period, in deep poverty and serious illness he struggled, and ultimately failed, to complete an account of the expedition; at the same time he experimented with the sources of pottery making on the shores of Lake Ontario (published in the *Memoirs of the International Congress of Anthropology* [Wake 1894b]) and composed the brilliant "Outlines of Zuñi Creation Myths," which he presented to great acclaim at the August 1891 meeting of the American Association for the Advancement of Science (the spelling Zuñi was an accepted variation at the time). At the end of 1891 the Cushings finally returned to Washington DC, moving in with Emma's sister Nell and her husband George Payne. Emma's eldest sister, Catherine, had died in childbirth the preceding year. The youngest Magill sister, Margaret, and her husband Frederick Webb Hodge had recently moved a few miles outside the district to Garrett Park, Maryland, and were expecting their first child.

On February 1, 1892, Cushing resumed work at the Bureau of Ethnology, concentrating at Powell's request on two areas: exploring Native American mythologies, and helping to design the Smithsonian's anthropology exhibits for the Chicago Exposition. For another year, though, he continued his efforts to compose an "Itinerary" of the Hemenway

Transcribed and annotated by David R. Wilcox, with commentaries by Curtis M. Hinsley

Expedition, finally giving up the project in March 1893 and turning his efforts fully to the Exposition work.

We pick up the diary eight days before Cushing and Emma ("Emalie") departed for Chicago. Under the general direction of William Henry Holmes, Cushing was working daily on exhibits from the bureau and the U.S. National Museum to be installed in the Government Building at the Chicago Fair. The exhibits were to illustrate industries and ceremonials of southwestern tribes, specifically Navajo silversmithing, Zuni bead making and drilling, Navajo spinning and weaving, Zuni tapestry weaving, Hopi (Oraibi) basket making, Zuni pottery making, Hopi ceremonial bread making, and a Zuni kiva with priests (Essay 4, this volume).

Although the Fair had been well under way since the beginning of May, none of these exhibits was finished—in fact, most elements of the displays were still being gathered and designed in the National Museum under the eyes of Holmes and curator Otis Mason. Cushing would continue to work on them, and gradually install them at the Fair, well into September. After the Fair the exhibits returned to Washington and were installed in the National Museum as the new exhibit of "Pueblos and Allied Tribes," to great fanfare (Document G, this volume). Throughout this work, both in Washington and Chicago, in his diary Cushing gave personalities and names to the mannequin figures as he adjusted their faces, wigs, postures, and clothing.

Excerpts from Cushing Diary, June 16–17 and 22, 1893

FRIDAY, 16TH JUNE

Slept until near 1/2 after two; heavy air awoke both Emalie and me.[1] Cold was better, but had attack of gas.[2] Emalie massaged me and afterward I her. Succeeded in sleeping just before morning until half past seven, when awoke greatly refreshed and better; cool air and breeze making vast difference. Still very cloudy. After breakfast sorted out papers, then went down to Museum and Bureau. . . . At Bureau saw Holmes who had directed fig'rs painted again and asked me about pecking stones & implt[?] manf.[3] Saw wig makers. Another wig finished. Met Dr. Dorsey who wants to know what I will contrb to World's Fair Anth Cong.[4] Saw Major Powell and explained about papers. Said take until Monday if liked. Got Peperaziull[?] from Thompson's, and malt from Burchell's for trial. Went to Museum and arranged about Silversmithing costumes. No news about orders to Exposition. Came back via Bureau, home. Wrote until four—Heavy rain and cool. Slept until half past five. Wrote again until dinner, and after, till ten o'clock—accomplishing 69 pp in all—best for many months I believe. Emalie better, I also except for cold. Still raining. Bed at eleven. Letter this morning inviting us to Chicago (from "Aunt Mary").[5]

SATURDAY 17TH JUNE

Rest much interrupted last night. Cooler but dank and cold (infl. troublesome again). In morning hours slept fairly, and tho ill on arising still soon rallied and after breakfast better than for several days. Finished Article (—ecpt Authorities & Cross refce's) before leaving (at 10 with Emalie via Market) for office. There turned Mss. over to Miss McChesney, and went to Museum.[6] Learned that final orders for my Chicago trip & work had come, and decided on Thursday (22nd Jne). Attended to figure work in Bergmann's shop—ordering remaining (pot polish'r Pueblo) head up to wig makers, then returned to offce.[7] Mr. Croffutt submitted his poem on—[?] in Champlain to me, and gave him points and Deity names.[8] Saw woman and reptd Ms. Went to wig makers and banged hair of "Belt weaver." Lunched. Went up to Nell's & told Emalie of marching orders.[9] Came home and worked at Pueb's and Rñs Artcl [Pueblos and Ruins article] until 5—then went back to Offce and got typecopy and thce to Nell's for Dinner. We examined corner Sr Payne House; not admirable.[10] Later I learned would be givn us reduced to $3500. We'll take it if possible. Letter from Uncle Ferd giving up "Cobb's Island" trip of "Family" with him. We came home at 8:30. Wrote all evgng, on article . . . Made very fair progress. Tired but fairly well at bed time—tonight at near 12.

Very clear this evgny but some warmer.

THURSDAY, 22ND JUNE

Had good rest (though troubled) last night, and awoke early—before six. Arose and wrote—with success—on article (Puebls & Rñs). Much better; morning close and hot, midday cooler, after noon shftng, and in evening storm. Went to Museum early. Arranged (there and at R. R. office), to leave for Chicago, on Monday,—not Saturday. Gave Mss to Misses Davison and Thomas for copying. Came home to lunch. Went back immediately [?] after and had Miss Davison start copying, meanwhile writing further. Saw Holmes and arranged to consult tomorrow ("take stock") of World's Fair matters, learned Profr McGee is virtually [in] charge of Bureau.[11] Congratulated him and arranged for future typewriting. Wrote all afternoon. Bought 8 mds, paper, and got book for Emalie. Came home. Wrote till dinner. Had letter about Citizenship Prizes from a Mr. Matturson (Pittsburg Dispatch) which replied to and referred his letter [?] to Col. Flint.[12] Wrote all rest of evening at "Religion of Pueblos," hardest remaining part. Rain ceased at 9.30. Cooling at 10, and prepare for bed at abt 11—

Part II: June 26 to July 3, 1893

On June 26 Frank and Emma took the overnight train to Chicago, arriving on the morning of June 27. The U.S. Geological Survey had rented a cottage on Woodlawn Avenue, and here the Cushings had reserved a room. In his first week at the Fair, Cushing divided his time between work on the Smithsonian anthropology exhibits in the Government Building and seeing the Fair with Emma. They spent time with Emma's uncle and aunt, Charles and Mary Magill, and cousin Ned Magill. In an initial flurry of activities Cushing toured the Midway—he was especially impressed with the Javanese Village dances—the Anthropology Building and the Kwakiutl performances, and the Hazzard-Smith cliffhouse exhibit (Essay 5, this volume). He immediately recorded his intention to study the cliffhouse exhibit carefully. The Cushings particularly enjoyed the company, too, of old gemology and geology friends of the Tiffany Company, George F. Kunz and William Phipps Blake.

Excerpt from Cushing Diary, June 26–30, 1893

MONDAY 26TH JUNE

Passed a bad night—a thunderstorm at three o'clock with torrents of rain, having arisen and wakened us. I suffered from severe attack of gas but succeeded in sleeping again until five o'clk. Awoke with excruciating headache, but worked steadily correcting Zunian article until 8 o'clock. Finished! And completed packing and setting my room in order, Betty being very good and helpful.[13] Leaving Emalie (at ten) then came down to office. Enquired at Swiss Laundry for linen,—which found. At office submitted my Mss. to Miss Davison and Mr. Hodge for copying.[14] Latter suggested illustration. Saw Major Powell with reference to it. He was very good and genial. Wants article on Pueblos and ruins to be illustrated and made two. Told me to get Hodge to pick out material and send me and bade me good speed. Gave Miss Clark fetish.[15] Saw Profr McGee and expld alt papers for moving—if office shifted during my absence. Saw Dr. Croffut and satisfactorily arranged about my Ms for 13th Annual.[16] He gave me last page. Emalie telephoned, met me at Station. Got some tobacco and went thither— very ill, but had good luck getting train and our section is very comfortable. Near us a party of eternally loquacious Prussians and on oth[e]r side of silent Mins. We followed all day the superb route (on the B & O) thro the Mountains via Harper's ferry. This side of latter beautifully cool and sweet also. Headache until after dinner. Read a little then, and retired (Emalie first) after the wonderful sight of the Pittsburgh fires, at midnight. A superb moon light and lurid lights in the natural gas regions which are extremely picturesque. Most comfortable bunks but the germans still talkative as ever.

TUESDAY 27TH JUNE 1893

Awoke at between three and four o'clock, having rested delightfully. Got up and went to smoking room then returned to berth and slept almost un[in]terruptedly until nearly eight o'clock. Arose wholly well of headache and lassitude. We were speeding through a country much like Western New York in both topography and trees and other growths. Not able to get breakfast until between 9 and 10, but it was delicious and abundant. We arrived at the edge of the city nearly an hour and a half before reaching the Grand Central. Miles away the first object of the great Exposition was the gigantic wheel [fig. 14] and the towering dome of the Administration Building gleaming through the mist and smoke.[17] The new depot is magnificent with long rows of cloudy buffs and yellow marbleshaft columns and checked fine tile floors. A fine restaurant opens into it from above at the end, but not stopping to eat, we sought the Elevated South Side R.R., and came up to Lexington avenue (in half an hour), where, after some search, we found the Survey cottage. It is small, but very nice and they had very kindly reserved a nice front, double room for us. So, after resting we went back into the city for our baggage. Forgot number and they would not take my order, but went to Central trfr Offce and arranged to leave exact address (6235) at Parmlee Branch offce; paid $1.25 for two pc's and then Emalie and I called on Uncle Charles [Magill] Printer etc., Cor. Clark [and] Van buren. Thence we came home to Woodlawn Cottage. Emalie remained to rest whilst I went to Brch Trsptatn Offce. Passed Midway Plaisence.[18] Saw towers, minarets, Great wheel and that wonderful Javanese Village thro knotholes in board barrier. It alone worth coming to see. Returned at six aftr arrg for bagge, & wrote (in our room) letters to Messers Beattie, Stone, Hodge, Professor Mason and Mr. Karr.[19] Went to get water (arcadia at corner druggists; Great Domes of fair visible—illuminat[ed] with electric lights). Beautiful night, and cool. Came up at once, wrote mema, read little & retired. Tired Both.

WEDNESDAY, 28TH JUNE

Up at between 6 and 7 and went out to arrange breakfast at the Leonard. Emalie made ready soon after whilst I wrote at Article on Creation myths, doing seventeen or eighteen pages. After breakfast we immediately started for the fair and on entering, rode around on the Intramural road to Govt Building—where I left card for Mr. Earll then went to have photograph for pass made.[20] En route we passed over to Wooded Island and saw Japanese Temple. Those pieces of wood work—railings honed up just enough at crossing corners, metal buildings, great kakemonos flower boxes—hoppes [?] strapped on billets of wood are superbly decorative. In Horticultural Hall their exhibit and the Australian there are wonderful. But most of it is the usual thing. From there we went over to the Public Serv'ce building near which is the photograph gallery. There my portrait was taken in considerably less than a second. We came out and at once went to the Art Gallery where we looked at the endless sculptures—of all ages (reproductions mostly—Japanese art exhibit, British which is in part good; some superb,—and Holland which is all admirable). Cannot record details now—At one o'clock we were literally tired out and went nearly around grounds to the Casino near the Peristyle—which also must describe later. There we had lunch; not very good for very much money, but it refreshed us marvelously. Then we went slowly, resting now and then through the grandest of all squares ever built [the White City]—for impressiveness and beauty, the Peristyle at one end with its aspiring columns, statues etc. against the blue sky and endless lake, the gigantic golden statue of the Republic in front facing the Administration Bdg and fountain at the opposite end of the walled in Lagoon, the Liberal Arts Bdg at the right, Agricultural at the left, and an endless vista of superb classical structure beyond. We gazed at and wandered amongst these for more than an hour, avoiding the other (especially industrial) exhibits, then I went back to our exhibit where I set [to] work on cleaning up figures, into action and went up to report to Mr. Earll. Found my mail there—sent by self— and secured a messenger to take it over. Took Emalie up and introduced her. She was cordially invited to come to head office and sit whenever she liked. Ordered some material for work and then Emalie & I took intramural RR. to exit. Got return check, then we went home. Took fare to go again for baggage, as found it had not yet been delivered. Learned that it would not come until tomorrow morning ("on wagons," they said). Crossed Midway Plaisance—wonderful conglomeration of villages of all nationalities: Javanese Village especially grand—an orangontang [sic] in bamboo cage remarkable,—facial expressn especially. Came home late very tired. We went to Leonard to tea—which was quite good. Had nice visit with all our fellow cottagrs in hall; after I wrote. Went to bed early.

THURSDAY, 29TH JUNE

Up at little before seven and quite well. Another beautiful day, but warmer. After breakfast went alone to the fair grounds reporting at once to Mr. Earll. There had more mail for me. Asked for a pass for Emalie in order that she might come every day and help me with the sewing and painting. Mr. Earll said he'd do what could but had little hope of success. Thence went down and at work getting out material, getting up and dressing figures until quarter after 12, when went out and down to cottages to take Emalie out to lch. We went to the Leonard and had miserable lunch. Came back, Emalie with me, at two and worked until half past four on same as in morning—Was just about to leave when Uncle Charles and Aunt Mary (Magill) found me out and sent after me. We therefore did not see much. Sat with them on shore of the lake until nearly dusk. Then went to ride with them on Intramural as far as the Electrical build'g neighborhood. There we left and went to lunch at one of the Wellington Cafe's. The meal was expensive, but good. After eating and seeing illuminations inside, went out to see electrical and searchlight illuminations (with fireworks) of the statues and of the Fountain and Peristyle. That was in presence of thousands and of a great band (giving admirable music). At a time when the columns of the Peristyle were illumined (agst. the dark sky and lake) of a burning red rose color, the central portion warm silver, and the Triumphal group of Columbus surmounting in a blaze of white search light, the waters of the court lake lightened up [fig. 13], and the golden colossus of the Republic ablaze thus was divided into three on as many sides, and exquisitely echoed one another. We left them, passing through Machinery Hall and seeing the gigantic eng'ns and Westinghouse Electrical generators playing then the half-nite more or less of firey-furnaces. We left the grounds at about ten through the collonaded terminal near the obelisque and court of Mountain lions, and reached home at about eleven, so very tired that we at once went to bed.

FRIDAY, 30TH (LAST OF) JUNE

Was up at seven and after breakfast Emalie and I visited the grounds ... apart, but later she rejoined me so tired that she remained nearly all the morning in the division of the exhibit where I was working. Had the plastering of the case (nearly all by myself) done. Went to lunch at the "Banquet Hall," a place near the state buildings S. W. of Govt Bdg.—where we found better fare for the money than yet. Met Miss Hamiegton[?] of Albion there.[21] She lunched with us. Had fuss with waitress about price—this overcharging being a common thing here. It began to rain before we had finished. Went back for Emalie's wraps etc. On returning found she had gone. Searched through Hayti, German and other bdg's but not finding her, returned, being met by her in the ramada. Resumed work on the figures, Emalie helping with the painting of Navajo Spinner, but found eyes had to be modelled down so left for morning. Had Woltz go at work repairing paint on Kyäklu and Anahoho masks, then had finished plastering Estufa [kiva] floor in case. At four o'clock (or little after) Emalie and I went over to Art Building and looked hastily through Italian and Austrian Exhibits. Not altogether satisfactory. Passing thro: United States (which must claim our attention for two or [more] days—went on to the French Annex. It is fine—must be gone over more carefully. At seven o'clock we took the cars (elevated) for White-Horse Inn to get supper and be near the "Cliff-House" & Ethnological Exhbts to rendezvous with Mr. Kurtz and his friends.[22] We had a nice meal, tho being insolent Britishers the people who wait there are none the best. (While we were eating Mr. Kunz & Professor Blake—whom I knew at Centennial in 76, at Prescott in '87–came in.)[23] We appointed to meet them at Cliff and went to examine ruins of Yucatan full size models. They are remarkably realistic, but not so impressive as might have been made. Saw some Navajos. Advis'd man in his own language but he was utterly impassive. Went on down thro: Yucatecan buildings to very excellent N.W. Coast Settlement of Vancouver Indians—quite Japanese looking these—in two large houses, fronts and dozen totem posts, all genuine. Beyond Earth and Chippea bark lodges etc. Sat down near Cliff Dwellings on returning to rest and wait. Soon joined by Profr Blake and Kunz. Later several others came in (our cottagers and some of the Tiffany Exhbtrs). Was introduced to Mr. [H. Jay] Smith, the originator of the Exhibit. Met also his assistant, Mr. Henderson.[24] Very nice, all of them. Cliff villages admirable—$\frac{1}{10}$th size and entirely faithful. Museum finest I ever saw. Must make sketches in future and refer to fuller special notes. Is worth working up at least for the magazines, and shall attempt it if possible. At about 9 o'clk we were all taken by Messrs. Smith and Kuntz to the Kwali-ut (and other Vancouver) settlement, to witness dances. They took us in to a very large house, the ridge poles supported by collossal idols (two at rear, one at front end). In the middle they built a large fire and meanwhile, in the adjoining house we heard a long drumming and song for all like the Zuñi=Moqui shield dance-song. Presently the dancers, men, women and girls filed (shuffling to drum-beats) in with carved rattles, feather-fans, conventional N.W. Co'st-mantles kilts etc. and began to dance jerkily and contortedly around fire, singing loudly and with deafening beat of tamboureen-drum. The first dance was not very characteristic except leader who posed with his feather wands as Japanese do with fans, changing instant to double drum beats. Second dance ended in fire performance of one particular member. He threw coals etc. about, took embers betw' his teeth and blew them about—Handfuls at a time, not however until he had been enclosed in a magic cedar bark "hoop of rebirth," and held by it—in hands of attendants had circled howling several times around the fire.

The next dance was that of the "Dog Eaters" (evidently), in which a special member began to grow frantic and call for blood. He at last had to be captured and hooped by two attendants—all others retiring and beating a loud racket on drum rattle sticks and carved chests—He evoluted as other had [bef]ore at, all and at last seized the arm of half-breed Chief George (George Cook) with his belt and bit it frightfully—clinging two or three times around the fire.[25] This was followed by a single dancer circling around after the carved and inlaid sky serpent ingeniously suspended and worked back and forth, up and down on strings until he suddenly disappeared and was apparently swallowed by dancer who then contorted and began to spit blood as tho: being gnawed internally by the myth-reptile. There was a talk and laugh dance and a head scratching dance. Then, it being late—last train time, we had to come home—tired and ready at once for bed at eleven.

Clouding slightly.

Part III: July 4 to July 18

Independence Day was the most crowded day of the entire Fair; it was also the day of the delayed opening of Putnam's Anthropology Building—two months late. The Cushings spent part of an exhausting day and evening (complete with fireworks over the lake) with Holmes and his wife Kate; notably, they did not visit Putnam's building. Over the next two weeks, while working daily on the government displays, Cushing deepened his relationships with H. Jay Smith and business partner Charles Hazzard, making plans for study and publication of their cliffhouse collections. Importantly, he met up again with Stewart Culin—their friendship, based upon common interests in cross-cultural indigenous games, blossomed at the Fair and remained strong for the remaining seven years of Cushing's life. Over the next two weeks Cushing met, dined, and toured with a wide group of visiting anthropological workers, including Harlan Smith, Antonio Apache, and Warren King Moorehead. Activities continued to center on his own exhibit work and the Hazzard-Smith cliffhouse exhibit.

Excerpt from Cushing Diary, July 6–13, 1893

THURSDAY 6TH JULY

Became very warm before seven, air heavy—awoke with fearful headache. Pumping no good. Off for grounds nevertheless at between eight and nine. Put little Basketmaker in place temporarily and later Mr. Fitz came to get label for it—which [I] wrote. Worked remainder of morning at Ceremonial group but made sorry and hard work of it, being too ill to command nerves. Emalie came over at noon and we lunched as usual at Banquet Hall, and took stroll, for sake of my head, on beach. Returning worked at ceremonial group until three; a new man (Mr. Gerrett, a young student) having been brought in as my Assistant—which he really proves already to be. Emalie decided not to accompany me to Mr. Smith's house and camp, but went with me as far as midway through the Liberal Arts Bdg. Reached Cliff House [fig. 66] at between three and four. Mr. Smith welcomed me heartily. Introduced me to Mr. Aliot (a nephew of Broca), his Secretary.[26] We went into his private den and they gave me some whiskey and ginger for my head which made it better. Talked over a possible Expedition (from Durango, Colorado to Zuñi country) to exhaustively follow out Cliff cultus. Went out to rest on Pier near Forestry Building. Came back through Anthropological Bdg. *Very* incomplete but most extensive collection have ever seen, comprising all countries. Plains, Mexican and Central American Colls. wonderful, but put up in poor taste and with restorations too gaudy. Returned to Cliff, and at six awaited Messrs Kunz and Walker.[27] Former came but Walker did not. Am sorry as he was thinking of having me write for his Cosmopolitan. Smith, Kunz, Aliot & Self went out to Camp of Smith party in beautiful grove on lake S.E. of Grounds. They live in fine large tents. Smith took us to drive along lake. At eight we returned and sat down to a liberal family dinner, Mr. Smith's mother, and his Assistants Mr. & Mrs. Henderson being present.[28] After dinner we examined Navajo blankets and I talked (and sang) Zuni until nearly eleven o'clock. Kunz, Aliot & Self then beat retreat. Too late for cars. Kunz & I had to walk miles to find our way back. Got home for bed at near one o'clock. Head better, but still bad. Growing hotter and stuffy.

FRIDAY, 7TH JULY

Up late, but much better. Warmer at 8'oclk than at any midday heretofore. Very humid. Still after breakfast continued comparatively well. Went to Gov't Bdg at nine and at once set at work on Ceremonial Group—Emalie not accompanying me. Nearly finished main work by two o'clock. Mrs. Holmes brought note from Emalie written in Zuñi and saying that she was too unwell to join me. Had a call after lunch (at Banquet Hall) from a Captain (of Scouts) Parker, of Walla-walla. He wished to see battle blankets and had some to show. Was quite wild to learn I was the Cushing. Promised to bring pictograph examples. Mr. Fitz came in to offer aid and promised to get "fixstiff," after which group can be taken out. Worked until after five steadily helped by Mr. Gerrett who has cleaned up our work place beautifully. Came away (leisurely) at six. Very tired at supper time. Found Emalie better. We went to call on Cousins Ned and Julia (Magill).[29] Home at ten and in bed by half past. Frightfully close, hot evening, but threatens storm.

SATURDAY, 8TH JULY

A heavy thunderstorm during night cleared air and made me well at last of headache. Emalie better too, but unable to accompany me to Grounds. Went out at eight and worked hard until one'oclock completing group and all accessories except shell gorget inlaying representation which am affecting with a paint—paste. At betw 1 and 2, Emalie not coming, went to Banquet Hall and had lunch. After that (having been delayed by calls from Messrs Gill and Trill[30]) went over to Cliff dwellers to get umbrellas etc. Mr. Smith not readily seen, and was about to leave when he came out bringing a Mr. [blank,] President of the [blank.] He was in haste to leave, but sat drinking in all I had to say of Cliff dwellers and Anthropology in America in general to Doctor Lambern and Mr. Culin, who opportunely came in.[31] They were very eager, insisting on my writing up the Cliff dwellers from the standpoint of Zuñi etc. Later we went into the den and drank selzer and looked over some of Mr. Smith's treasures. Dr. Lamborn brought out some Smithsonite and on my saying that I had sentimental interest in it gave it [to] me much to my discomfiture. He also gave Mr. Smith a "chrysophrase" intaglio of great beauty. We had a most pleasant time.

Met there, Riggs also a Mr. Hoskins—City inspector of Electric lights, who was hunting for me and extraordinarily enthusiastic.[32] Washington Matthews had just been there before me, but could not find him.[33] Went over with Mr. Culin to examine some u'än k'o lo kya tubes. They were sacrificial as I told him, and how the game was played. He was delighted. When I told him of the Gods of war and Chance (*Games as well*) he was still more interested and immediately introduced me to the Chinese regional and game-war worship system identical to (tho more elaborate than) that of Zuñi. The thing is fascinating; must give days to it and kindred collections. As I was carrying out (with Mr. Kunz's and my own umbrella, to take through Liberal Arts Bdg.). Met Holmes then Gill. Latter told me Capt. Bourke was in La Rabida.[34] We went at once to call on him, but were too late. Returned via Tiffany's to Govt Bdg, touched up Ceremonial case and had it moved out. Then began inlaying of shell with a kind of turkois paste and black. Holmes happened around and was highly delighted with the ingenuity of it, having much to say. Did not [get] home until before six. Emalie at dinner already. Hurried me to take drive with Cousins Ned and Julie. They came soon after and drove us miles and miles through Grand Boulevard, the parks etc. This is a far more magnificent city than I ever imagined. Cousin Ned has done much better than I had supposed. Returned at 9.30. Found that Mr. Hill had arrived. Went to bed almost at once. Cool, fine night.

SUNDAY, 9TH JULY

Awoke quite refreshed at six this morning and decided to get up and write memda. Wrote continuously until eight. Aroused Emalie who was very sleepy, and went to order breakfast. Emalie, then Messrs. Hill and Kunz joined me soon after. Mr. Kunz gave us an amusing account of the Dinner of Concessionaires last night. Said also that Mr. Smith had a trip thro: Cliff house and S.W. with me earnestly and much at heart. Waited quite a while for him, then we went together to Grounds, I entered Govt Bdg and there finished Kyaklu's gorget shell, put it on, touched up group and left it in my Garrett's charge. Came home at between 12 and 1 and made ready for our dinner with Cousins Magill. It was plain Roast beef dinner but ample and good. At three o'clock I apologized and left for the grounds to visit anthropologic building and take notes and help Mr. Culin set up game. Had to go back for change. Then came again here to shift coats and in process left pass-book in room so that on reaching grounds had to return a third time and this made me late (half past four). One guard told me Mr. Culin was in and another challenged me. I told him I came to assist Mr. Culin and showed pass. He said all right, but remarked that it was "a strange time for a man to be coming by so late to work." I told him it made no difference when I came if I had business and went down to Culin's department. He was not there. While I was looking the guard came. I said I could'nt find Mr. Culin and asked if he knew where he was. He said he guessed I could be getting out of that building. I had little argument him but left word on card for Mr. Culin and came away—(perforce—madder than for many days). They thought it an outrage when, after dinner I told them of it here. Want me to report it, Dr. Day particularly.[35] Mr. Gill came in evg., Kunz also, Holmes & Mrs. Holmes, so we had quite little visit. Shower this evening which cooled and lightened air considerably. Much damage to glass in Exposition Bdgs. Mrs. Day's birthday. Read note from Mrs. Fanny enclosed in Emalie's letter from her yesterday.[36] Make ready for bed at eleven. Am out of sorts—spirits rather. It is dreadful to be so poor and in ill health too with so much to lose forever thereby!

MONDAY 10TH JULY

<Our wedding day—the eleventh>

It was not a bad night for sleeping but my fearful supper was upsetting and I awoke at 3 o'clock full of gas. Emalie rubbed me. We slept until seven. Feel pulled down. Cloudy but with signs of clearing. Had long wait at breakfast. Emalie came at last bringing letter from Mr. Hodge—fresh as usual. Left Emalie and went to grounds directly from Café (Leonard). Saw some beautiful Exhibits in German Section of Liberal

Arts—especially porcelain. Went directly to Govt Bdg however, and started setting up warrior garter loom. Met Lieut. DuPray. Aide on Grounds. Invited me cordially to his tent. Got warp laid out by noon, when Emalie came. We went to lunch at the Banquet Hall, then visited the Art Gallery, U.S. Ehbts today. Many wonderful and beautiful pictures not to be mentioned in detail. Coming out we visited Costa Rican and Ceylonese Bdgs. Fine woods in one; Superb carving and interesting masks in other. Went back tired and worked until six on Garter weaving. Came home to bed. Supper at Leonard's. Better times later as the dear Cottagers got up a little entertainment—with tea (of Russia) for Emalie who was beautiful in her white dress. Had Profr. Decker of Yale and Mr. Phiphant Geol. Stand. Oil Co. Mr. Smith and Antonio Apache—also invited, did not come. Messrs. Hill, Holmes, Day, Kuntz and bdrs all present.[37] Much lively conversat. Went up to bed at 12. Growing warmer and closer—.

Fire burned entire cold storage Bdg today and at least Fifteen or twenty brave firemen & some others.

TUESDAY 11TH JULY

Up at dawn. Had another bad attack of gas. Emalie rubbed, but with little benefit. Close morning prospectively hot. Left for work at nine. Finished loom, but by noon was utterly worn out. Emalie joined me, and we lunched at Banq Hall. After went thro: Manf's Bdg toward La Rabida. Down at Great Wharve rode out on . . . R.R. walk. Rested little. Examined La Rabida and the Caravals. Then we went through the Shoe and Leather Exhb to Anth Bdg, but Emalie so tired could not see much. The Polynesian exhibit magnifict. Saw glimpse of mounds and some of N.W. Coast but a bad tout ensemble. Met Holmes & wife. Came away with them on Intramural. Went back to Govt bdg & worked until half past five. A Mr. Desseler called to learn abt Indians—as wishes to make painting of them a life work. Mr. Hatmaker called earlier, also a German who has hammered a remarkable lot of imitative vessels from cents & dimes and wishes to exhbt with us.[38] Mr. Kunz sent him. Had calls also from others to weariness. In evening went down town for tobacco. Long trip. Emalie ill. All spent evg on porch. Prof. Gilbart with us & Mr. Gill went out at eleven—Retired little later—Both worried about money.

Diary of Frank Hamilton Cushing

WEDNESDAY 12TH JULY

Up at little after seven. Gas in night again and Emalie rubbed me very little. She is still unwell, but wished me to visit her little while before going to breakfast. Did'nt feel able to accompany me. Went over to Governmt building immediately after 9 & Bkfst. Set at work dressing and finishing up figure of garter-maker. Finished and had out in case next to little basketmaker at 3.30. Very fine. Holmes came around at about ten and went with me to see Lt. Emmons Alaska Collections.[39] Superb and must study more. We also looked ovr Exhbt of Am Republics—which are not so good. Both in Galleries of our Bdg. Holmes helped me out (temporarily $20.00) with money, and said depend on him. After finishing Weaver girl Mr. Ives from the Tiffany's came with invitation of Mr. Kunz, to dine with H. I. Smith, Antonio Apache and others—meet at Pavilion in Lib. Arts Bdg at 5.45—Then went to Banqt. Hall for Lunch and came home to see about Emalie,—via Cottage Grove.[40] She was better, but not quite able to go with me to the Dinner we were invited to by Mr. Kunz. Bathed, shaved and "Dressed up" for the occasion, then went to keep the appointment with Kunz. He was at the Tiffany Pavilion, & tho: late, I was ahead of Mr. Smith, Dr. Cronan & Antonio Apache. Dr. Cronan (a German Archaeologist). Mr. Smith and Antonio all came by six. We then went to the [blank] Hotel, and had a very nice dinner, meeting many people. After dinner we met Mr. & Miss Weeks, Dr. and Mrs. R. W. Gilder.[41] A dance at which Walter Bezant is to be invited tomorrow night.[42] We came,—at nine, to the Cottage. Emalie at Cousins. Dr. Carrington Bolton and all our people here.[43] Went after Emalie. Met her with Cousins. We came and spent pleasant evening. Talked of origin of pottery with Mr. Smith & gave him my book. With Holmes about Anct man (glaciall) in Ohio as discussed with strangers. Antonio sang—Spanish Apache—& Moqui imitation song. I sang Incantan rain song and told Folk tale. Antonio told folk-tale also, both of Cliff ruins. Mr. Smith spoke more of my joining him. Evening passed (to late hour) interestgly so that we did not get to bed until one. Has been an excessively hot day and is still close and warm tonight. Emalie better.

THURSDAY 13TH JULY

Up at half (past) six & in spite of hot night good rest, and fairly well. Very hot and rather close weather growing more so as day advanced.

Emalie much better today but did not accompany me as wished to call on Aunt Mary and to save strength for this evening. Went to building early—but had to return for pass. Soon after nine however reached Govt. building and at once began work on weavers and Spinners. Wrote up labels making a *Pueblo series.* Holmes came in bringing Mrs. Seidmore and little Miss Curtis.[44] Had pleasant chat. Trill and a German Exhibitor by name, also. Got group all prepared by lunch time, then went to Banquet Hall. Returning, examined the Viking ship, which is admirable, and wholly finished up weavers which put out. They make a striking group. Was very badly used up by the exertions and drenched by the heat which is greater than at any time hitherto. Came home at little after four and arranged with Emalie for our trip to the grounds and to the Dance tonight. After tea, it clouded so loweringly, that Emalie feared going with me, so had to go alone. Did not reach rendezvous until after half past eight, but found party still there. Who should come forth from the gloom of one of the caverns suddenly but Miss Kate Field with a girl, interesting Miss Armstrong. Mr. Smith's cousins—Mr. Aliot, Mr. Oliphant, Mr. & Mrs. Richard Wilson [sic] Gilder, Mr. Besant, Doctor Spriggs the New York Commissioner and his wife, Mr. and Miss Weeks and many others were present.[45] All were nearly as enthusiastic as I over the Cliff house & Zñ resemblñs [Zuni resemblances], And highly commendatory. They were reluctant to leave for the KwaKul Indian dances which were announced for nine. We all went however. The same Drum and club clatter, the same wild singing, weird fine shadows and lights on [?]ges and rough in tenor, same dance too,—[?]ing men and women. Fire setting, arm [?]ing laughing and scratching dances, and finally the skewer dance which was fine—superbly performed, and impressive. We came away at between ten and eleven. Mr. [blank]—one of the Launchmen brought us around by lake and lagoons by his boat—only breath of fresh air today. Came back with the guests of honor and had talks with all. Home at half pst 11. bed at once. Storm gather'g. Emalie unwell.

Part IV: July 19 to August 14

On his birthday Cushing gave a talk at the Woman's Building on the Zuni myth of the creation of corn. Short of money, at the end of July the Cushings moved to Aunt and Uncle Magill's house for several weeks. As the pace of the Fair quickened and the World's Fair Congress of Anthropology approached at the end of August, the pace of Cushing's life increased as well. He continued to work on the exhibit figures and met regularly with anthropology acquaintances new and old—especially with Powell and Powell's sisters and daughter—but Frank and Emma now began to enjoy the social circle of the Burnhams, Millets, and Deerings—a sector of the industrial and cultural elite of Chicago. In this period, too, his father, Thomas, having attended the funeral of Uncle Milo Cushing in Oregon, passed through and stayed a few days at the Fair.[46]

Excerpt from Cushing Diary, July 21–29, 1893

FRIDAY, 21ST JULY

Up early. Went to Buffalo Bill's. Saw Salisbury off for New York. He was very courteous but vented a terrific tirade on Putnam!![47] At Govt Bdg soon aftr Had directns to "fix everything" and take charge (instead of my few groups only). Up set me somewhat. Holmes anxious about my time as wants me to come back. Plan for my three years (work) to come made by Major Powell and him today. Wants me to write Religion of Am. for Anth Congress. Worked hard until time to join Emalie (at Uncle Charles' at dinner), making good progress. Had pleasant dinner. Called on Dr. Matthews. Not at home; on Bourke whom found. He was jolly and friendly. We came home quite late. Very warm. Bed before midnight and quite well.

22ND JULY

My Birthday,

Saturday.

Awoke at six and was unable to sleep longer, hence we both arose and had a fairly early breakfast. Dressed for the lecture occasion and went to grounds in time to get corn-wand and to go to woman's building, and, with Mrs. Rorer's and her sons' assistance, to arrange examples of Zuñi corns and wafer breads; before half past ten Mrs. Gould, Lady Manager for Illinois, came in and asked me to give her Board all grace I could.[48] At quarter of eleven began my lecture to a quite large audience. Had much applause although the talk (on the Myth of the Creation of corn) was made against fearful odds of noise. Met many distinguished people, ladies especially. Gave some corn grains to plant. Altogether good occasion. Fearfully hot. Went back to Govt Bdg. Unable to work on acct of heat. Had call from Mr. Mott who will start for the W[est] in two or three days. Emalie and I had delightful lunch at the Banquet Hall. Then went to Colombia Building and saw collection of gold and Terracotta objects—finest from Bogota yet seen. Lieutenant Wendey showed to us. Wishes to sell for $30,000. Worth it. Gave me privlge of studying it. Came back to Govt Bdg joined by Holmes to bid me good bye. Hurries me. Must go back within a week. So sorry as but light prospect of return. Fixed up some frames & went over Collctns with Holmes. Went up to Office to bid him goodbye. Dr. Matthews came in. Very much brokn but pleasant reunion. Miss S[e]idmore & Gardnrm called. Miss Kate Field later. Introduced me to Mr. Hunt, Chge of State Dept Exhibit.[49] We all went out & talked (on lake front) of old times. Came away at six to go to Mrs. Rorer's dinner. Had enjoyable evenng. Home at Elevn.

SUNDAY, 23RD JULY

Awoke at half past five, much rested. Very cool, sweet air. Slept again until nearly eight. We arose and made ready to go to the Culins. While awaiting Emalie, went to get shoes blackened and to see Major Powell. Told that Mr. Smith besides calling yesterday had come last evening here and appointed to meet me. He had talked a little while with Major Powell. Latter said he had not much more than we had suggested, to be told relative to the Cliff dweller urns. We went to [?] and thence easily to the Culins'. Found them ready, in a delightful little flat. We had a jolly time getting breakfast, which we all enjoyed delightfully. Mr. Culin and I went on to Grounds later leaving ladies together. Closed. Intramural not running. We had to walk to S.W. corner of Grounds. Left Culin at Cliff dwellers. Went in and met Mr. Smith's cousin; Smith himself came in little later. We examined basketry finding sieves, colanders, vizor-runs and an anklet. Fine specimens on every hand. Cautioned Smith about the misrepresentations his guides were making. He gave orders for them to stop telling exaggratd tales. Discovered weaving was of all kinds, virginal shields—moccaisin or sandal stones, plume-working sticks—not plume sticks simply. Ancient stones etc, etc. Took lunch (excellent one) at Big Tree. Smith wants me at own price to explore with him. Told him hardly thought would be able. Insists it can be arranged. We worked [on?] collections until five—nearly, then rushed to keep our engagements. Smith went after Emalie. I called on Culin. Not in Anthro: Bdg. Wrote note to him apologising, then went out to Mr. Smith's camp. Rested there and drew plan of checker board. Emalie and Mr. Smith soon came. We all had supper, then more subject of joint exploratn res[ume]d. Came home at ten, after beautiful rides. Fine, bright, cool day. Quite well. Bed betw 11 & 12.

MONDAY, 24TH JULY

My meals yesterday gave me trouble in night, but awoke fairly well this morn at seven. Saw Major Powell. He had no need of me except to take pkg Mss. to Profr. Clark. Wrote Croffutt abt Ms.—take home to him. Came to grounds (leaving Emalie to come later) at nine & took Intramural for Anth. & Cliff Bdg's to fix game for Mr. Culin and see H. J. Sm[ith]. Found Mr. Culin not arrived, so cut out the lines of game and was about to leave when he appeared with Mr. Jastrow.[50] We then laid out the game and Culin discovered that it was identical with the Chinese game of surrounding, the Assyrian, Egyptian etc., etc.

Visited Mr. Smith's place; not there, but his secretary was. Had him mark the little flat piece as probably a wood card. Gave him the Pueblo corn for Mr. Smith. Took Intramural for Govt Bdg and worked on Potter group until after noon. Emalie and I went to lunch at various places but ended at the Banquet Hall. Fearsomely hot—boiling day. Had to give up work early therefore. Came home (alone) by Midway to dress for our dinner with Culins and Williams.[51]

Had money (or check today. Also hairstring by post). Emalie went on to rendezvous in Anthropological Bdg. I followed later at after six only arriving there. Culin, the Williams' and Mrs. Wharton, a new judge—the Historian, were there waiting with Exception of latter we all went to the 51st St Restñt at once and had a delightful little dinner being joined there by delightful Mrs. Culin.[52] Immediately after, it was nine o'clock, we went over to the midway, and first to the Chinese theatre. The acting and singing were characteristic, the juggling good, and the tassle swinging excellent. Afterwd we went through the Joss [Chinese Joss House and Wah mee Exhibit] and saw the pantheon and the Bhuddistic [Hall], then the Restaurant under the guidance of Mr. Culin who speaks Chinese. Thence we visited the Arabs. We were overwhelmed with welcomings through Willms who speaks the language like a native. Had dances, coffee, presents & played games. Met the Millets and Burnham; invited to tea with them Wednesdy. Came home at one well worn out.[53] Splendid experiences.

Had talk with Major Powell about the Cliff matter. He advises six months [leave?] for the Exploration and is very kind.

TUESDAY, 25TH JULY

Arose very early—oppressed by the shortness of my time here and the amount of work. Another excessively hot day. In Govt. Bdg by half past eight. Worked at dressing and placing of new figures all of which found and had unpacked. Charley Wotts helped and built up mills most creditably. Emalie came over afternoon, bringing a letter from Mrs. Fanny to me. Provd to be a very sweet Birthday letter from the Lake![54] Emalie and I went (out of grounds) to Vendome. Had expensive bad lunch. Was not well—It was later that she joined me with letter and we went to the Reception in the Illinois state Bdg. Mrs. Gould recd us with Mrs. Sewall and Mrs. Preston, both Lady Managers.[55] Saw the art works under their guidance and heard some very pleasant music. Left there quite ill. Took an egg phosphate in Midway—via which we went home—which made me worse. Joined [our?] cottagers in dinner at the Vendome. It was excellent and not so expensive as the lunch. We all passed the evening until late, on the porch, talking. Major Powell present and very talkative with Emalie. Cooler but as rainy as we had anticipated it would be.

WEDNESDAY 26TH JULY

Slept delightfully and woke at near seven. Made ready for the call on the Millets and Burnhams before going to breakfast, then went directly to grounds and went at work on Potter group. With Wotz fixed up Travois, hearth in Kitchen-case, and broken hand on figure

Diary of Frank Hamilton Cushing

of Toaster girl. Wrote large label for the Powell Rain maker picture. Major Powell called and was pleased. . . .

Painted the two potters and made papier mixture for closing up joints on figures and for completing pot making adjuncts. Went to late lunch alone, then over to Anth Bdg for moment, thence to Cliff Dwelling Exhibit. Met Mr. Hazard there; he was exceedingly glad to see me.[56] Asked many intelligent questions about Exhibit. Told me of his life—run-away, rise, health, Explorations, illness and plans for South Seas. That he had paid everything. Thought it a losing game and little of Smith's finances. Did not see latter. Came back to Govt Bdg. to keep appointmt with Emalie. Mr. Earll talked about finishing groups. Too indifferent to correctness. Cannot himself make extra allowance. Emalie joined me soon. We both went to Wooded Island to take tea with the Milletts, but sat awhile under the trees to see if our friends might come.

THURSDAY, 27TH JULY

Awoke at a little after six. Fine cool morning. Rested until betwn sevn and eigt. Emalie and I went at once from the Leonrd to Grds. She painted figs & I dressed and arrangd othrs. Had potter case brot in, Bread-mak'g case worked at, and partly set up group. Mrs. Culin called on us and later went to lunch with us at Banquet Hall. Afterwrd we went to Art Gallery. Saw Metcalf's picture and many oth'r fine things (in Gallery proper).[57] Met the Williams. Arrgd to go with them through Indian Village & Cliff House. They called later. Mr. Graham also.[58] Fixed up Spinner, Travois, and Other potter. Then went with Mr. Talcott Williams, (appointing to meet Emalie and rest of their party at Midway) to Morrocco Exhibit and Cliff. Met party at Damascus Pavln five o'clk. Emalie not there. Wms & I went to Soudanese Village in Cairo, and saw the Cowrie owner Ahmed. He cast lots and told that I had loving handsome (fair) wife, jealous enemies, White heart, sister or near friend pregnant who would have girl child, etc. Came away near six. Emalie still missg. Culins joined us. Had to leave Turkish dinner. Came home & found Emalie had been to dinner with Major Powell. Visited cousins Ned & Julie. Home at ten. Talk awhile abt Emalie's judgeship. . . . Bed at eleven.

FRIDAY, 28TH JULY

Awoke in night betwn 2 and 3. Found air heavy and close, sounds carried remarkably by it so that all locomotives were audible. Was ill with acid stomach. Took soda and slept. Awoke better—at six and again slept until aftr seven. Delightfully fresh morning. After breakfast at Leonard Emalie went to Uncle's, I to grounds. Before leaving closet heavy rain but for only few moments. At ten it became close and hot increasing steadily all day. Finished fixing up Pottery group. Working at this and Kitchen case all day,—nearly. Had calls from Graham, Uncle and Aunt Magill—who came to see Emalie, from Mrs. Henderson and a friend Miss [blank,] Mr. Culin, Professor Goodyear and Mr. Morehouse.[59] Mrs. Rorer's son also came to invite us to a tea at the Ceylonese Pavillion on lake front at four. Miss [blank] and Mrs. Henderson again came back bringing autograph album for me to write and sketch in. Mr. Graham came to see abt venture of bringing on Zuñis and Moquis. Mr. Morehouse to appoint to see Major Powell. Mr. Culin to see about a withlakna game. He said Putnam and others called my games etc. *inventions*! *Let pass*!

Telegraphed Stone to know if furniture could remain week or so longer. Had answer it could by 3 P.M.; cost $1.29 but can remain now next week! Emalie came at noon. Lunched with Uncle & Aunt. I at Banqt. Hall. We a'ragd to go to Uncles tomorrow evg., to remain few days. At four went to tea having finished case. Met the Williams & Party,—Mr. [blank] and his Croft—and Mrs. Rorer. Culin came also. Had pleasant time. Came away at five. Got jar for little cousin; saw finish of preparatns of Case for Exhbt tomorrow and came home. After dinner all visited on lawn evg. Fixed coral necklace meanwhile. Mr. Morehouse called but not encouraged by Major. Emalie worked for today on jury. Came up for bed at eleven. Still hot, and close.

SATURDAY, 29TH JULY

Hot and rather close all night. Up at half past six. Packed and after breakfast ordered Express and arranged for our leaving at once to go to Uncles & Aunts' a few days. Brot papers & satchel to Bdg—Dr. Day coming part way. They are loveable people. Reachd Bdg at 9.15 and at once had case of potters moved out. It makes a splendid exhibit! Placed

Mooney's boys and old burden bearer on top of cases—where they show to greater advantage than yet. Shall put more up,—Redcloud and Rose.[60] Had a call from Graham and dear old Dr. Matthews. While he was there Emalie came. Pleasant little chat. Thinks my exhibits finer. Soon after he left Emalie & I went to lunch at Banquet Hall. We were shortly joined by Mrs. Culin. She remained and lunched along with us. Dr. Matthews came and sat. Afterward we separated; but all went to Art Gallery. After examining Gallery Collectns (saw Metcalf's Mexico & Japanese falcons etc.). Met Talcott Williams party and engag'd for Monday afternoon to see the Cliff Dwellings & Indians. I then went back to Govt. Building and worked awhile. Met Colonel Waring and showed him about. Had very pleasant visit. Went as engaged to meet Emalie & Mrs. Culin at Anth Bdg. Had visit with Antonio & engagd to bring the Millets Tuesday aftrnoon. Went back to Culin's. Mrs. Culin there without Emalie. She had gone back to get sa[?] (which I had brot). So had to take them back. Mesg from Mrs. Millett to get Mrs. Willms address. Took him back with me to Govt Bdg. Engaged (by letter to Mrs. Millett) to go with them Tuesday, 4 o'clk to Inds & Cliffs. Returned to Elevated with luggage. Reached Uncles at seven. Time for dinner. Met Cousin George.[61] Talked with them all evening; they were very pleast. Warm close night. Bed 11.

Part V: August 15 to September 2

On the 15th Powell left Chicago, and the Burnhams invited the Cushings to come out to their Evanston home for the coming weekend. It was a high point of the Cushings' Chicago sojourn, marked by late evening talks and stories, and exchanges that included Zuni experiences and Swedenborgian sharing. On the 24th the Cushings received notice that they must give up their rental home in Washington immediately. Accompanied by Mrs. Culin, Emma left two days later to supervise the move. Cushing stayed, at Holmes's insistence, to attend the International Congress of Anthropology, which took place from August 28 to September 2.

The congress was a grand success for Cushing personally and was the most extensive gathering of anthropologists in America to that time. Particularly gratifying to Cushing in this period was the time spent with Daniel Brinton and Stewart Culin—further strengthening his growing ties to Philadelphia—and the flattering remarks of Alice Fletcher and Zelia Nuttall, to the effect that Cushing was "a sort of Sun in Anthropology illuminating the ways of all of them." Cushing's diary reflections on the papers of the congress, and the last evening of celebration on the Midway, are particularly revealing.

Excerpt from Cushing Diary, August 19 to September 2, 1893

SATURDAY, 19TH AUGUST

Cool, and at first cloudy morning, better rest last night, as slept until breakfast bell. Still cool but clearing when started for grounds at near 9. Went via State Strt. to get tobacco & paprs. On reaching Govt Bdg. saw Colonel Bickford in refce to the Corn Emblem table.[62] As expected could not be allowed in Govt. Exhbt Bdg. Saw Mr. Burnham's Secy & learned that our Statn would be Dempster Street. Went on to Govt. Bdg. and there with William's assistance set up the Silvermaker grp in case for building in ground work. Mrs. Rorer's elder son called to invite us to meet Mrs. Shoemaker of Philada but having arranged to meet Emalie at home (Uncle's where she remd) could'nt arrange. Said would see Mrs. Rorer on way out. Young Mr. Waters called to thank me for our Conversatns. Hopes to join me in field some time. Says can easily afford to pay all exps. Told him would have him in mind for it. He bade me goodbye with extremely grateful expresns. Left at half past 12. Called on Mrs. Rorer & appointed some time next week for meeting. She undertook to explain corn emblem matter to Mrs. Cantrill. Came out & had lunch at World's Inn then came home and made haste to prepare for the visit to the Burnhams at Evanston. We left on Cottage Grove cars. Went via Marshall Field Busses to N.W. Depot & reached Dempster St. Statn at betw four & five. Met there by Mrs. Burnham with Carriage. Drove down to their place—charming old house among old elm & maple trees near lake seen thro leaves in glimpses. Stopped for her sister, Mr. Woodyet, & all took drive along lake thro trees & grds of N.W. Univty & beyond.[63] Found camp sites in campus and a famous one on bluff at turn of shore N. of Village. Evanston a bit of Cambridge—little young as to trees—exquisitely beautiful. We returned at sunset. Dear old house. Our room looking twrd lake thro: trees. At home immedtely. Nice family of boys and girls (3 of former, 2 of latter; one grown, others small). Dinner at seven. Before over Mr. Burnham came home. More happy to know him than ever. After dinner old Mr. Hurd came in—his daughter Mrs. Lord, Mrs. Woodyet & son, Mrs. Taller & a former Wellesley girl, who saw Indns & self during Boston visit—and others. Wyman Bros. latter—local archaeologists.[64] After rest of compny gone they remained & Mr. Burnham discussed Museum of World's Fair project. Grand scheme of his own original'y. His idea all excellt. Discussions followed on Anct race of Auora. Swedenborgian correspond[ences] etc. Intensely interesting evg. Talked constantly until aftr one. Went to bed at abt 2. Lovely night, lake sounds & wind in trees. Not very well.

SUNDAY, 20TH AUGUST

Awoke quite early not withstanding lateness of retiring, and with one of my terrible headaches. Siphoned, but with little affect. Beautiful morning. Delightful family breakfast, Mr. Burnham & I drinking little to make up for loss of sleep at beginning of it. We went out to walk on own down Dempster street. Met Dr. Fuller.[65] Very intellectual man, but not spiritual. Mr. Burnham told him about my mention of Spirit of stone in grain, and the Swedenborgian correspondence he made of this. Met also Dr. Phillips.[66] Had fine visit in the sunlight. Dr. Phillips brot me home & gave me some Bromo camphor for headache which helped little. Mr. B & I had long and delightful conversatn on Swedenborg—of whom read some wonderful passgs. After lunch we all went out with Wymans, Dr. Phillips, Mr. Burnham and his boys, daughter & cousins to hunt relics. Made fair finds but was w[r]etchedly ill. Mr. B. left for fair at six. Dr. P & I follwed rest examining sand meddings [?] along way. Very late home (betw 7 & 8). Mrs. B. sweet about it; Emalie not ple[ase]d. After tea, head better. Large company in. Talked Zuñi all Evg. to immense delight of all—told stories. Authoress of Columbia ode proct [?] & other selected rites. Bed very late again but better. Cool, beautiful night among the trees.

MONDAY, 21ST AUGUST

Slept better and awoke refreshed this morning, to a clear and beautiful day. My cold, howevr—of some days' duration—very bad. We had eight o'clock breakfast; were too late for a 9 o'clk train, so had lovely little visit with Mrs. Burnham and family. Mrs. Woodyet & her young son came in. She played for us beautifully. She talked with me about Mr. Worcester & heard some of my expe[riences]s with him whilst Dear Emalie was making ready.[67] Mrs. Burnham took us to ten o'clk train. Lovely visit. Engaged to go again either to them or to the Lords. Reached city at midday (about). Took bus to Field's—thence Cottage Grove cars to 57 St. Entrance. Very hard trip. Found on reaching Govt. building that Mr. Holmes had returned and already had men at work. Emalie & I had lunch, then went to visit Anth Bdg as usual. Both of us very tired. And home at quite early hour. Very hot day. Fairly good hour to bed.

TUESDAY, 22ND AUGUST

Up early. Hot day. Went to Bdg. early, rolled up sleeves and worked hard on groups—Silver-Smiths especially. Holmes came in at about half past ten. Was very cordial and glad to see me, glad too, I had staid. Said I was on Program of International Congress for talk on our group exhibits and especially the Ceremonial group. Gave him title Illustration of Zuñi Dramatic Ceremonial. Mr. Burnham suddenly called genial and bright, bringing Col. [blank] and Mr. [blank,] scientist of the Pennsylvania Road, in chg of their Exhibit. They waited for me to change clothing and show them our groups. I devoted an hour or so to them. The lesson of correspondences in the ceremonial group was especially interesting to Mr. Burnham from the Swedenborgian point of view. He left me with cordial expression and the assurance we would continue in our acquaintance & friendship. Introduced them to Professor Holmes. With latter went afterwrd to lunch. In afternoon visited Anthropological Bdg. Met Dr. Fewkes there.[68] He was most cordial and anxious for my sympathy anent [regarding] the Hemenway. [?] . . . Emalie & family.

WEDNESDAY, 23RD AUGUST

Warm in morning but cooler as day went on. Up a little late, [so] that Emalie & I did not reach grounds until about ten. Went at work on group and also on packing up express box of idols, specimens etc. . . . Holmes engaged Melville yesterday and had him with all of us work on group of Anct [specimens?]. Went over to anthropological bdg. in

Diary of Frank Hamilton Cushing 179

afternoon. Saw Culin and Brintons there.⁶⁹ Had intrstg conversatn with them [regarding games]. They were astounded and arranged to have me read papr on [the games?] Folklore day. [A]llen (Phila), Wymans, Phillips & o[t]hrs met & saw collectn of Mr. Willow. Telegraph from Stone askg for house. Sent message [six lines illegible: written over underlying text] Month Exps.

THURSDAY, 24TH AUGUST

Awoke very early with headache. Siphoned a little and correspondgly relieved. Cool at first but rapidly grew warm. Emalie had started for Fair at half past eight, going by way of Cousn George's office (Bank) and having check cashed—Left Emalie on way in to call at Woman's buildg. When reached Gov't Bdg, found telegram askg for house at once. This makes move home essential! Alas. After doing all could Emalie and I went to lunch, then visited State buildgs. Mr. Holmes says I *must* stay to take advantage of Congress even "if they have to tie me." Am trying to arrange. Emalie, dear one, wishes for my sake to go alone and attend to moving. A letter came today inviting Emalie & I to visit the Lords,—(from Mrs. Burnham who tells of her sister's loss of a child) next Saturday & Sunday. Had to write could not go.

Emalie and I visited the State Buildings Washington, Idaho, Iowa, Florida, others and Utah. Small but very fine cliff collection which must sketch. Later we went to Anthropological Bdg. Met the Culins, Miss Fletcher, Mrs. Nuttall.⁷⁰ They all say I must not go [and] are wonderfully nice about this interest. In evening we dined together with the Culins at the World's Inn and afterward all went to Grounds; rode around the grounds on Intramural, talking about Arrow games, and then went through the Art Building. It was lighted up resplendently and the pictures are Oh so wonderfully beautiful in that light. They are beyond even their finest in that light, especially the French. We were late in going home, but Emalie and I very happy. Bed quite late.

FRIDAY, 25TH AUGUST

Very hot morning and day. We were up betimes, however, and off for the fair before nine o'clock. I started on ahead and called on Doctor Matthews. He was glad to receive me, and was much better than I had expected to find him. He introduced me to his stepmother (I had already met Miss Matthews) and to a couple of Sioux girls who were enthusiastic students, pianists & quite pretty. Doctor was packing to leave and could'nt be induced to stay to Congress. Goes by way Mt Vernon Brrks whre Lt. Witherspoon is comdg. He went with me to Illinois Central, where took train for Grounds. On arrival found telegram from Stone saying positively wanted house. Joined soon after by Emalie. She decided to go, but I did not consent to her going alone. Holmes once more urged necessity (for my own sake) of my remaining at Congress. Learned that I was down on Program for several things. We went to lunch at World's Inn, then to Anthropological Building. Emalie preceded me to the Culins' place, and when I arrived, found Mrs. Rorer with Miss Shomaker there to meet us. They were talking over our enforced leaving. Mrs. Rorer kindly offered her son James to go on with Emalie & help, but Mrs. Culin volunteered to go! I found her quite determined in this, Culin acquisent & raidiant [sic] over my staying. Took Mrs. Rorer, her Asst. Miss Crane and Miss Shomaker thro: the Nomed[?] Bdr., Cliff and Peruvian Exhibits.[71] Mrs. Rorer called my attention to a *hewe* stone she had discovered. Saw also a Spear thrower like the Mexican—wh. had been a puzzle to me before. Came back to the Culins' place at six—nearly—Mrs. Rorer sent her son off to get Sleeper tickets for Emalie and Mrs. Culin and to have her (Emalie's) baggage checked. We took dinner with the Culins at the World's Inn, then went home in good season and Emalie nearly finished packing. When we had been at home only little the Bourkes called to bid us goodbye (having heard we were going) and remained until after ten o'clock. Walked home with them and had amusing talks with John G. Bed at about midnight—slightly cooler.

SATURDAY, 26TH AUGUST

Hot again this morning. We finished packing and left Emalie's trunk ready for Parmlee, then went to Fair in good season, to Govt. building (whence I sent telegram to Stone saying would move Monday or Tuesday) and then to Woman's Building where we left luggage, to meet Mrs. Culin. We waited there until two o'clock and were about to give the dear little woman up, when she appeared and we all went to World's Inn and took our last lunch together. Came back through Midway that Emalie might look once more at the lions; but they were napping. The little monkeys in front of Hagenbeck's were however bunched together in a long double row—eleven of them—napping and were as like a comical Japanese carving of sleeping monkeys as anything we ever saw.[72] We enjoyed them for fully ten minutes—and in all the noise they slept peacefully on, only one, sleepily moving out of the line,—he, the twel[f]th one. I took the little ladies to the Illinois Central, and went after luggage at Woman's build'g. Came back and we took Express to City. My heart was very heavy to see my darling leaving and taking her last look at the wonderful World's fair but she and Mrs. Culin seemed happy withal. We reached depot (Grnd Centrl) an hour before train. Trunk not there. Went up to Parmlee's—several squares away—to see about it. Mistake made in number, they said. Would rectify tomorrow. Emalie fearfully disappointed—when, just in time for train, I came back. Saw them aboard. Two (2) minutes before time for it to go, Mr. Culin (whom I went to meet) came rushing down. We bade the poor little girls good bye—after placing them in car and giving them the bigger share of our money—and went back to see about luggage. Found trunk just there. Got checked and returned to give Emalie just as train was disappearing. Culin & I went up towrd City P.O. where we found a drinking room. Went in and had refreshmt. Whilst I wrote note & telegrm to Emalie and enclosed check. Culin volunteered to get regstrd & sent, and I set out for Evanston to visit the Lords. Had good fortune to catch 6.30 train—an Express—and found Mr. Lord & one of his boys waiting for me with carriage. We were late to dinner, but beautifully welcomed to a charming room where I sat down and gathered myself for a few moments. And here also trees and the cries of insects, very sweet and quiet. At dinner eight children at a great round table, young lady down to baby boy! We all sat until late on veranda talking. Several callers came—Woodyet & others. To bed at midnight. Cool and fresh.

SUNDAY, 27TH AUGUST

Brilliant, but very hot morning. Did not awake until nearly eight and was just a little late for breakfast. Immediately after breakfast Mr. and Mrs. Lord and I went out (with one of their boys) to drive Northwrd along lake road where I discovered the midding [midden] last Saturday evening. Found a camp in some woods on the way and then pointed out some bluffs four or five miles away as likely Indian places. They exchanged smiles & drove thither. It proved a superb beautiful spot high wooded bluffs,—the home of the Lord's friends formerly of the Goddards. They had visitors—who chanced to be delegates to the Labor Congress and to have introdnctns to me. One was Mr. Clarke of London, an old friend of Baxter's, the other a Theosophist of the Blavatsky lodge of Engd., Mr. Burrows who had an introduction from Mrs. Besant!![73] On their place here at Winetka I found a camp—flatland near lake—burial place—high head land—and fort signs further back, and found several relics. Met in the Lloyds very prominent and perfectly delightful people.[74] Mrs. Lloyd at once claimed Emalie and me to visit them saying she should write Emalie. We came home to a late dinner—after two. Then I was sent up to rest—by Mrs. Lord—needing it so badly that slept nearly two hours. Was very refreshed. We had Mr. & Mrs. Crown (Swedenborgians & old friends) at tea, and afterward, the Woodyats, Burnhams, Fullers and many others—a delightful, enthusiastic reception of me, all enjoying my Indian folk tales and Experces amazingly. It was very late when we broke up and I went to bed happy with the night's friendly conquests!

MONDAY, 28TH AUGUST

Was late again this morning, having rested so well! Mr. Lord had already gone to his business in the City. Mrs. Lord sat breakfast with me. She wished the Locust song (I told them the stories of the Locust & the coyote, the coyote and the woodpecker, last night) and I wrote it roughly for her,—but had to hurry off, promising to send it later, to catch nine o'clk train. She went with me saying very delightful things on the way. Caught train just moving out. Reached city in half hour. Met Mrs. [Anders] Zorn on way. She said Mr. Zorn was recovering from his serious fall from horseback riding. Took a car and went up to Illinois Central and took boat to grounds. Wrote Emalie on way. Sea was very rough and boat crowded; several seasick of course and ludicrous of course! Went to Govt bdg via Culin's whom saw, and learned from him Bourke and I were to speak tomorrow (Tuesday) afternoon. Congress organizing this morning. Visited Millett on way and had good luck to find him. He was very cordial, and said he had his books waiting for me. Wants me for a dinner and other entertainments. Went over to Government Bdg and worked all could on both my own and Holmes' groups. Came home early. Went, with Uncle Charley and cousin George, to call on Bourke and remind him he was to speak tomorrow. We came home a little late stopping on the way and taking some beer and other drinks. It is a little cooler tonight, and I am just tired enough to rest well. No letter yet from Emalie, but wrote her a little note. Bed at near eleven.

TUESDAY, 29TH AUGUST

Cloudy, dreary, and damp morning, but I awoke especially well and started off for the Congress—held today in Recital Hall at end of the Peristyle. Was too late to attend meeting of the morning, but fortunately nearly all of papers down for day laid over for later occasn. Mercer's excepted (See Program at opening of this.) Met Lumholtz and he is delightful; has brought back many dmt. of interesting information, and my Mss.[75] Went to World's Inn to lunch and felt ripe for the papers of afternoon. These were Culin's introductory which was nice and most highly commendatory of me. He showed the various arrow games I've discovered. Then I addressed them on the latter and American Games in general. Said Games began with "if" and the bow and arrow. This latter the true arbiter through chance of Primitive man's life hence arrows cast for winning. All games divinistic except plays of children—the Apocryphal truth, so to say of true games as folklore of myth. From casting and shooting of arrows to divine, step to the arrow cane game of Zunis—then to wood cane arrow game with counters, then parchisi & then game of draught chess of stone warriors the last development. The same with stone throwing shell or bone—with a people who use only clubs, slugs etc., and the ultimate result ending in dice-draughts etc. as before. All games to the four quarters—etc. etc. The speech was most enthusiastically received.[76] Bourke followed most entertainingly strengthening my address in almost every sentence. The meeting following a very bad beginning was a grand success, and there is no doubt for the outcome of the Congress being greater than any American meeting ever yet held. Brinton presides admirably and seems to becoming friendly. In ev'ng we all dined at table d'hote [at] German Village. An old gentleman—[fellow] with Spiritual ideas of extraordinary nature! Attached to me until dinner over. Then joined Culin and Lumholtz and we spent whole ev'g in Mexican Garden where the variety performance was extraordinary. We left not earlier than midnight. Cleared brightly at noon but remained cold. Only reached home near one. But wrote Emalie and am well excpt for cold which is dread[ful.]

WEDNESDAY, 30TH AUGUST

I awoke quite early, despite my late hours. It was clear but so cool, that I took my overcoat with me. Altho: I started before nine oclock, was half an hour late and did not hear first portion of Doctor Brinton's address.[77] But having been invited to discuss it—on Americanist side—paid most careful heed to latter portion. It was replied to first by Mason who asserted strong immigratns from Old World since Prehistoric times. Inst'ed Japanese Armor & Elk as Asiatic. Quite strong. Morse followed. Instanc'd no Asiatic (thumb) release. No titles even in Mexico. Made good reply to both speeches which were good also. Followed by Peet—who instancd fylfot & Swastika cross as Asiatic indubitably.[78] Followed finally by me. I called attention to fact that altho immigratn has existed it had counted for nothing in American Cults. That these—even tribally had developed in water tight compartments. I exampled the Teguanos who joined the Keres in 1640, yet who still retain language, social organization, religious customs etc. of their ancestors. Tewas of Hano in Tusayan, the same! and hundred other instances might be named. Sufficiency—as in the games of natural developmt to account for identity of custom and arts etc. The Swastica for inst (Peet) only the cross of the four quarters, encircled as one (the 5th & 1st). The ribbed armor of the Eskimo,—only the earliest form of Japanese steel & bronze rib-plate armor, etc. etc. My speech was well received.[79] But I was followed by Putnam (who came in late). He claimed that my idea was pernicious—of having Am. Cults studied without refce to Asiatic connection. He said that I would limit other enquirers by my own opinions—and made his argument on jade but spoiled it all by immediately claiming Heterogenesis for humanity. I was given no chance for replying to him; but Dr. Brinton did reply and he specially commended my expression of growth of culture in water tight compartments.

Miss Fletcher followed with paper on Sioux music, which was illustrated by a song and examples of harmonization along natural lines, by Mr. Fillmore.[80] Their theory is that the variations in Indian song are often to be explained as an unconscious seeking after harmony that the inconstancy of scale is to be explained in this way, which I think is the truth. I think this the first real work in Primitive music yet produced. (see clipping of former delivery of same lecture.)

After a hasty lunch at World's Inn (we had to adjourn early on acct. of rehearsal in Recital Hall) returned and Mason read his general paper on the Govt. Museum Exhibit—Holmes followed with a paper on the evolution of Chipped stone implements during whch he gave a very hasty acct of his own and our work in that Exhibit. Mr. Hiller read a paper of the collections illustrative of religious etc., which, from attaching too little importance to American Cults was defective, but otherwise good.[81] Last, I gave my lecture on the groups in our Exhibit, and in fact the groups in general, closing with the case illustrating the dramaturgic character of myth and ritual ceremonial and giving the myths of creation and the tale of Ky'aklu to indicate how these myths are symbolised not only in Dramatic acts, but in dramatic costuming etc. etc. The lecture was most highly well received.[82] Mr. Dorsey gave a brief acct of his colls and explorations in Peru, and Miss French Sheldon, of East African Tribes.[83] Mrs. Nutall [sic] also spoke and all refer[r]ed to my address, Mrs. Sheldon most flatteringly.[84] It was reported very well in substance, in the Record of [blank]. Mr. Green, formerly of Orleans County, called. Had in fact quite an audience of outsiders for my paper. Had long and intensely interesting talk with Mrs. Nutall and Miss Fletcher,—both of whom said I had put them on new trails & was a sort of Sun in Anthropology illuminating the ways of all of them. My lecture was attended by Messrs. Wyman and Dr. Phillipps. They were very enthusiastic. Explained to them influence of pit boiling and net fishing on origin of lacustrine pottery. Home at seven, and spent evening with family of Uncle.

THURSDAY, 31ST AUGUST

Clear in morning and cool—not very hot even at midday. Had letter from Emalie at early breakfast time—telling of her good progress and intention to visit Nellie as before. Was off to the Congress early. After Mrs. Nutall's paper on epoch making,—four other interesting papers—mostly on ritual and folk-lore or read Mr. Newell spoke first,—on Myth-dramas as derived from ritual and referred to my presentation of yesterday in support of this.[85] His paper was an excellent one—ending in a more hasty address which was itself cut short by the President.[86] And Doctor Boaz [sic] read his paper on the Ritual of the Kwakiutl Indians (by himself and George Hunt, their half-breed Chief).[87] It was interesting as giving the laws of the de[s]cent of medicines and ceremonies and accounts of the supposed possession of performers in the cannibal and other rites by demons and other spirits. It too was cut short for the paper of Doctor Fewkes on the Flute Ceremonials as a study of the Dramatization of the Snake & Antelope myth. This latter—as far as told for it too was cut short by the Presdt.—was a repetition rather crude but full of the Zuñi myth of the Snake soc'y origin.

In the discussion which followed I referred to the former universality of the Snake Ceremonials as (per Oñate) in Acoma, and in the Tchikyalikwe of Zuñi, saying that the Tusayan tho now more primitive, were really borrowers largely, from the Zuñis, citing the Sacred names imported from Zuñi etc.[88]

In rfce to ceremonial as dramaturgic, gave account of the Ceremonial killing and then reviving by means of paint and the yucca circlet of rebirth—the performer en maske. This was suddenly applauded—and I closed to give chance for the paper of Mr. Kunz on Folklore of Precious stones which he read mainly by little referring to his little book on the subject, for completing and offering to distribute it from their place (Tiffany's). Four other papers were read merely by title—and the meeting adjourned for 2 o'clk at the Assembly Hall of Agricultural Bdg. Went to lunch at the World's Inn, and had a nice quiet plain meal so as to be prepared for the afternoon.

On reaching the Assembly Hall was met by the Heaven girls (brought by Mr. Holmes).[89] Learned they were all well, that Mrs. Fanny was well and beautiful this summer, and all the rest of them, and that they including Uncle Walter were probably coming to Washington this Winter.[90] They had to leave. I was beseiged by acquaintances. All the Evanston friends had come to hear my lecture,—and many others—the Hall was filled—the largest and most general yet select audience we have had.

Professor Putnam spoke at great length on the Collections on Anthropology in the Anthropological Department—and on their illustration of American Archaeology—reviewing Glacial, Shell heap, Mound, South and Central American Archaeological Exhibits quite interestingly and clearly.

I was next called for my Cliff Dweller address. This was important considering its relation as to subject to the Prehistoric Civilizations—so called of America as apprtly indigenous growths. I presented the matter quite more easily than ever before, in the following order:[91]

I defined the race of Town builders however diverse of Stock as Aridian group of Culture peoples. Then showed the place of Cliff dweller in time and degree of advancement in Pueblo culture. Referred to this evolution as 1—scattered sand house tribes (who built with plastered and slab tiled wooden posts etc, and were so widely distribut'd as to favor theory of having been driven into Desert—. 2 Single House builders in little groups & relation to linguistics of "House" etc. of Zuñi during which irrigation, water storage and increased productiveness resulted—3 Then attacks from without for products and consequent massing in cliffs. The evolution (again linguistic) of the sect story from over-crwd'g. 4th the Mesa Dwelling as an agglomeration of Cliff or Caveate towns (as shown also by linguistics [(]& probably would be further shown!) in other than Zuñi languages) then the group towns (an enlargement of this idea into several as one), and finally the composite cities or Cities of Pueblos as in our Salado investigation.

I classified modrn Pueblos as descendants respectively of Cliff Dwellers and Caveate dwellers, the Zuñis & Moquis of the former (and to some extent the Keres) and the Tañoans & Keres of the other. That while all pueblos were at one time or at times Cliff & cave Dwellers, the Cliff-Dwellers were originally Zuñi—The Moqui Shoshonis adopting *their* life in S.W. Colo. & S.E. Utah & Arizona following it whilst the Zuñi and Cliff Dwellrs kept Southward & Eastwrd to present region.

Reasons:

Pottery of two kinds—Earliest Cibolan black & white as also Cliff Tusayan, Polychrome as later Zuñi (of the 7 cities). Zuñi therefore more primitive *as* cliff dwellers. Progress of this pottery developmt—with color decoratn introductn of open space—bands as symbolic etc.

The linguistic reasons as above. The domestication by herding of Cliff Dwlrs and after them of Zuñis alone = Turkey Houses in both.

Identity of games—Hidden ball—bone dart,—ball, & arrowgames including ta-sho li or block-arrow etc.

Thunder balls & their identity. Identical fetichs and phallic or increase sacrifices for game. Identity of symbolism & evdce of grwth from N. to S.

The T shaped mark in the wands of the Gods on the masks of granry god impersonators—in Corn mild cups of Cliffs and in granery doors of Cliffs as explaining this survival. The women's shields (cliff (vaginal)) and the term of parting the bark, of weaning the bark (during chastity observce) in Zuñi as survivals. The meaning therefore of this study as a unique example of the survival of the materials of a remote period of development, of the life as shown by the Pueblos today of a later period, and of the meaning of survivals among more southern tribes of even the Pueblo phase as their phase necessarily of development.

The lecture was much applauded—was discussed by Putnam, the Presdt & others as finely reasoned out & forcibly presented. My friends gathered in force & were very complimentary—but more than all was the fact that this day I have won over mine enemies even. Thank God! Mrs. Nutall spoke a moment on Mexican archaeology, Manuel de Peralta on Centr Am (by Title) and Mr. Dorsey very delightfully on Peruvian Archaeology.[92] Mr. Volk closed with a paper on the Village finds of New Jersey which settles I think the Abbott question!—[93]

I took quite a party through the Cliff Exhibits all except Peet who does'nt agree with my line of thought being wonderfully pleased. In evening Culin, Brinton and I after trying other places dined at the Wrld's Inn and sat until very late afterward, talking. I have won Brinton by this (So Culin told me), and am most happy that this is so!

Went home very late; very cold too, but wrote Emalie just before retiring. It is a little heavy tonight but very cold—

FRIDAY, 1ST SEPTEMBER

Warmer and a little closer today. Went directly to the Congress—as was late, too late to hear Mr. Jastrow's paper on the Historical Study of Religions.[94] I heard however, a little of the discussion—by a person (grey bearded and pompous) thoroughly unqualified. The next paper was by Mrs. Sarah Y. Stevenson of Philadelphia—the Egyptologist.[95] She described the Ceremonial Rites of the dead—the incarnating as it were of Spirits in the Mortuary Statues by means so like the Zuñi dance possession Ceremonies as to be striking—in the use of paint etc. to open the eyes of the corpse & statue, that the mind is captivated by it—indeed she made reference to my papers on similar subjects and constantly lectured to me in the course of her talk. This was followed by a "Chapter in Zuñi Mythology" by Mrs. Matilda Stevenson—a poor effort, rambling, superficial, and in its differences from my well known statements, really silly and somewhat venomous. I was called on to discuss it, but stated that I could not discuss the paper as it needed, rather than deserved—but that I would explain the apparent differences of statement between the authoress and myself. As she was absent—Profr. Mason read for her—I would have from considerations of courtesy, to refrain from doing more. Stated that necessarily the Social organism of the Zuñis was mother-clan, not father & mother as stated. That there was a slight tendency to the Patriarchal instns but that it could hardly be regarded as an Institutn. That the Women did propose marriage by customary signs—and that the rain makers (among the Gods) did not use vessels for Sprinkling the world but their breaths & the breaths of the ancestrl souls were regarded as the means of making clouds & rain. Her statement of all curing by sucking ridiculous; repeated impossibility of further correction from consideratns of courtesy.

Brinton read fine paper on linguistics in afternoon. Boaz on N.W. Coast simplifying it considerably. Mason gave his splendid paper on Industries etc. of N. Am. Peoples—in which he quoted me much—I discussed it—with others—favorably & told of shell orientation. Went home early—not very fine night . . . hot & close.

SATURDAY, 2ND SEPTEMBER

Awoke very early and was at fair between nine and ten. Somewhat warm still, but not so uncomfortable as yesterday. Having given up all thought of returning home tomorrow (and thus written Emalie) devoted day to the Congress. Meeting in the morning was most poorly attended; but Mason's paper—the principal one, was very interesting.

I spoke only to fill in some allusions he made. Dorsey also confirmed his statements about great prehistoric quarrying operations in Peru. Paper by Boaz was very interesting, tho: indistinct and the paper by [blank] was equally so tho: most unscientific. After luncheon I went to afternoon session to make remarks on Doctor Lumholtz's paper. There were so many papers to present, however, and so little time that no discussions were possible. Lumholtz paper not finished but admirable on the Tarahumaries. The papers preceding on the German Museum and on the Ceylonese inhabitants were very interesting also. The meetings were quite hastily closed with a brief appropriate remark by Dr. Brinton—and the final gathering arranged for banquet at German Village. Went over to Gov't Bdg and did some work, arranging along with Mr. Holmes to have Melville kept on.

In evening we all went to German Village. Had cousin George as guest. Before dinner we went in a body to Cairo, visiting house there (of 16th Centy Moorish = Turkish dancers)—strange coarsely sensuous contortionate dances with head carried level, belly and hips extraordinarily jerked about and various plays with swords and vases of water. Stamping accented, but from hips downward only. Head jerked but kept level, and time marked by [snapping?] finger and [?] castinets. Only one dancer—others sitting on devans—little child trying to crawl out under curtain. Suppressed by dancer adroitly spiriting it under drapery. Thence we went to Mr. Balantynes Hindoo jugglers. The most extraordinary series of performances ever saw. Thumble rigging money changing, serpent charming. Turban burning and finally basket trick. Impossible to understand. Banquet followed. Three long tables filled with members and guests. Speeches by Putnam, Brinton, Mason, Paterson, Peris and Italian delegate—all quite apt. At close I called Cheers and gratitude to Putnam, Brinton. It was most extravagantly responded to. After dinner we went to Javanese theatre. Elaborated my thought regarding evolution of drama from ritual out of Secret Societies 1st by shadows of sacred performers on tent or screen wall—then screen shadow then puppets or Marionettes then figures in stiff but beautiful pantomime. Next we visited the Samoans. Club drill marvellous. The songs and timed gestures same as before. Marvellously fine. Near 12 we went to Dahomey Village. All in bed but we saw the houses. Hieroglyphs & phallic (family) figures on mud walls of great interest. Stopped after we came out to correct article by Rev. Mr. Hovey on "Cliff Dwellers" for Scientific Amercn.[96] Fairly good tho by no means exhaustive. After twelve and very cold when George and I went home. We both got bad cold. Wrote Emalie after reaching home and some notes. Sleep very late—betw one & two. Culin left Early appointing rendezvous for Brinton, Mrs. Nutall and self at Anthropological Bdg. Had letter from Emalie today. She is up in mountains at Wellington Prce. William Co., with George & Nell, and urges me still more to stay.

Part VI: September 3 to September 15

Cushing's final ten days in Chicago were marked by important, even intimate discussions with Brinton—"He expressed gratification that he knew me"—Culin, Fletcher, Nuttall, and Holmes, with whom he shared a tent in the final week. Regretfully turning down Frank Millett's invitation to a Samoan pig roast, Cushing took the 4:55 pm train back to Washington on September 11, arriving on September 12.

Excerpt from Cushing Diaries, September 3–9, 1893

SUNDAY, 3RD SEPTEMBER

It is a cool, very fine day, clear and breezy. But was so tired from hard neck and lateness to bed last night, that over slept and did not get to Anthropological Bdg. until between ten and eleven. No one was there. Seems to have been a misunderstanding. So I passed morning sketching in Colorado Cliff exhibit most profitably. At noon, went to see Miss Cummins in California Bdg. Her mother was with her. Greatly pleased with meeting me again. Had envied me always more or less she said, my good luck in place of her Husbd's who lost all his work in dying. But when I told her some of my life she acknowledged it was only at suffering price one could win. Believer in reincarnation. Had interesting long talk and sang over the two Zuñi songs several times for Miss Cummins. She gave me Frayer's song to interline. Went to lunch at the World's Inn and then back to Utah Bdg, where worked until after five—being permitted to sketch there to heart's content. Knee pads, mountain goat decoy, grains of various kinds etc of great interest; also foot shape pot (half coiled ware, half painted) and polychrome vase like Chihuahua Casa Grande style.

Went home quite early. Had nice long visit with the family and went to bed quite seasonably. Very fine night.

MONDAY, 4TH SEPTEMBER

Grew warm and some close, during the night, nevertheless slept well and was much rested this morning. A little late arriving at Government just in time to see Culin and learned he was very ill. Satdy night lost lot of money too—and so used up yesterday, had to sleep nearly all day. Holmes and I, with aid of the boys, packed up everything preparatory to opening out alcove where I have worked at the figures so long. At noon, having got note from Mrs. Rorer about a "National Cup" (for the corn) which Mrs. Cantrill is going to have made, went over to see her. Engaged to meet the designor—Miss. [blank] tomorrow morning, at half past nine. Went to World's Inn for lunch, and afterward, to Anthropological Building where I spent the afternoon. Met Mr. Allen, Librarian, of Philad. Worked some at getting up games for Culin, and had talk with Wyman about a new copper adge . . . from which inferred wider fastening & told him of it. Went for comprson to S. Sea Coll, & found an identi[c]al specn even to braiding at top and bottom. Communicated all to him to his unbounded delight. Arranged possible trip but fear cannot make it. Suddly saw origin of trigram of Corea Japan etc. in cane arrow games. He was wild as it is *named* divining sticks or canes in Chinese. One of my finest generalisations & hit also. Had long talk with Miss Fletcher over the pipes—without pipes—of peace. Told her they were the flute and smoking cane combined in one. She was intensely interested. In the Evening Culin, Brinton and I all dined at the World's Inn (after finding German Village impracticable for it was stiflingly hot) and afterward we sat until very late talking over Primitive Drama—in which I told Brinton of my Javanese discov'ry—and also talking over Indian Occultism. Got an insight into a strange and very human phase of his mind. We went from World's Inn to a place beyond Midway where we drank some liquor then separated. Culin accompyd me long way; warned me to publish what had been talking else would lose—even if others did not consciously steal. A great night. Bed at between 12 and one as sat up to write Emalie.

TUESDAY, 5TH SEPTEMBER

Not so hot today, & was up early and in fairly good condition. Reached Govt Bdg. betw. nine and ten. Figures were still not ready, so I spent most of day in Anthropological Bdg, studying collections and talking—with Mrs. Nutall, Miss Fletcher, Culin and Brinton particularly. Lunched with the latter at Log Cabin. On my way into the grounds called (as engaged) at the Woman's building and there met Mrs. Frachetie—who is to be the artist of the Corn-Cup for the Natl festival. She proposes a vase with standard so that the cup shall necessarily be passed to seven in course of round (as loving cup). So I told her of the Seven Corn maid and Youth for precession around cup, and that would send her sketches therefor as soon as could find after my return. Suggested also she visiting Anth Bdg to see Peruvian and other vases. She went with me and I showed her some of the water vessels and our groups in Govt Bdg. Later she joined me at the Anth Bdg, and I took her to see Peruvian colls.—the water bottles of whc. she approved. Had long talk with both Miss Fletcher and Mrs. Nutall on the correspondences of the calendar. And we arranged (Mrs. Nutall and I) on this subject, in parallel columns, she the Mexican of it, I the Zuñi, which I hope may be done.[97]

Met Brinton & others during day. Brinton was very pleasant and courteous. Saw Mr. Wyman and told him I feared could not take Archaeological trip with them and Dr. Phillipps. Met and talked with Mr. Willoughby, also with Mr. Rust and Wyman again.[98]

In the Evening, Culin and I went down [to] town to get buckskin for the Sho li we game, and to consult books in the Public Library. We had dinner at the Grand Central Restanrt then went to Library. He found abundant proof of arrow influence I have discovered, in early Chinese games. Found Owens paper on Zuñi games and tried to buy it 2nd hand stores but failed. We came home late, both of us very tired and I not very well.[99]

WEDNESDAY, 6TH SEPTEMBER

In spite of my lateness in retiring last night, was up early but not very well as it has been an excessively hot and oppressive day. Was hindered by crowded cars from getting to work in Govt building. On arriving there found a note from Mrs. Rorer stating Mrs. Cantrill expected me to lecture before Board of Lady Managers on Corn (but Title not statd!) in her room, at elevn o'clock. Went over immediately to refuse; but on arriving there found posters in Woman's Building stating I was to lecture on "Zuñi Symbolism of Indian Corn Our one True National Floral Emblem"—at 2 o'clk P. M. at Assembly [?] of Brd Ldy Mgrs. So decided, in as much as Mrs. Rorer (who was delightfully apologetic) told me it had been announced in the papers, to accept. Went back and worked at both Holmes' and my own groups (Silver Smiths) until noon, then went to lunch at the World's Inn in no very good mood over Mrs. Cantrill's "management." Lunch bettered me, and I made headings afterward sitting in veranda fixing them in my mind as follows—The Creation of World—of men, & their Journeys, of the Raven and the Macaw—of Corn by men and the Gods of Dawn, fire and Time—The universality of its symbolism. Its place in Myth, in the History and cults of America—its appropriateness as symbol of American Indian (Its Creator High Priest)—my Ancestor's use of Indn in Mass Arms for corn; our use of Corn from Indian as the one True American Home of the Golden Rod and other plants sprang from it, etc. etc. I was preceded by a Kansas lady on Domestic Industrial Education of our girls which nearly destroyed my audience; but after I started, many came in and at the last I had a beautiful audience. The lecture was successful far beyond my expectation. It was encored and a vote requesting me to publish it and supplement it with more was unanimously passed. Mrs. Cantrill gave a splendid speech at the end of it. Went to Govt Bdg then to Anth. Saw (merely Holmes, Culin & Lumholtz). Home early. Wrote late. Still close.

THURSDAY, 7TH SEPTEMBER

Again in spite of short hours, was up early and well rested. Still quite a warm morning tho: cooler late in night. Finished a letter to Emalie which took until nine o'clock, then left for Fair-Grounds. But the crowd today was excessive, more so, than yesterday so that could not reach entrance for over two hours. On way in, met Colonel Hazzard and had long, quite satisfactory talk with him. He is very friendly and has offered me photographs and other favors again. Went from him (in front of New York Bdg), to Utah Bdg., where bought two photographs (for 60c), one of relics from Utah Cliff Bdgs, other of Pictographs of unusual interest. Worked, after reaching Govt Bdg., all the rest of the morning on my group as well as Holmes'—which is nearly completed and of which I fixed some of the dress and wigs. Went a little late to World's Inn and had lunch, then to Anth: Bdg. Was announced in papers to lecture again before the Ladies' Assembly but did not. Heard of it several times during day, from people who had come in to hear me. I saw Hartman (fixing the Tarajumari colls), but not Lumholtz.[100] Also met Rust & Wyman, giving final decision about impossibility of my going archaeologising with them. Told Rust the significance of his talk about ceremonial of Girl Ripening—its significance and connections,—also identified his cup and boulder specimen and a terra cotta pepper bowl from Mexico. Met Mrs. Culin sitting at their table and glad to see me, then Mr. Culin. Did but little on the games but arranged to go on with them tomorrow.

My Kinsman (& Correspondent) Mr. Cushing called, having come to hear my lecture and left with me early to return and make ready for dining with Cousin George and his family, who returned yesterday.[101] Was nearly on time in spite of bad trains, and had pleasant evening. I met their Cousins Blanche Bowman (a teacher & cultivated girl) and Linda Davis—who stays winters with Uncle & Aunt and is studying Elocution etc. George & I went out and bot stockings; also a fishpole & some corn husks as mat[eria]ll for some of Culin's games. Roughed out the canes and borrowed tools for finishing.

FRIDAY, 8TH SEPTEMBER

Was up early, and feeling quite well at first. Arranged with Uncle and Aunt to leave them and accept Good Old Holmes' invitation to pass remainder of my nights with him at the Cottage on Woodlawn Avenue—in his tent! Thus made this arrangement to enable them to have some visitors tomorrow night & Sunday. Went to Building to finish groups at about ten o'clk, but again no progress had been made by Melville, so did merely what I could and left to another day—working on Culin's games. Blocked out the Tipcats also the cane arrow slips, and the top and shinny stick. Went to late lunch, then to Anth: Bdg. Found dear Mrs. Culin there and had a nice talk with her about Emalie, meanwhile working at the games. As soon as Culin came about, went out and finished the canes (by burning) in the Cookery Building of New York. Had difficulty in finding fire. Had tried Intramural Power house, a manufacturing building power house, and the Garbage Cremating house. But here Mrs. Joliet Corbes the celebrated Cookery authority recognised me; [she] was very complimentary and nice.[102] Went to the Kentucky Distillery to get some oil and found suitable corn-cobs, also for Tan-ka la game tht Culin and I put up a day or two ago. Oiled the sticks all marked properly and gave to Culin. He was delighted beyond measure—put them into his pocket immediately and he and Mrs Culin invited me to dine with them at the World's Inn. So with Mrs. Culin's help I made up the husk pads of the Zuñi shuttle cock game. Mr. Newell came around and had a long conversatn with us on our generalizations (which he but half believes in) about arrow derivation of Amcn games. But he was pleasant and friendly and fearfully in earnest. He asked my opinion of Fewkes. I gave as good as I could. Culin invited him also, and we all went to dinner at the World's Inn, then wandered about the Beautiful never forgettable illuminated grounds until late. A high wind & mighty surf on lake. Cold also. Home at midnight, & wrote until one o'clk.

SATURDAY, 9TH SEPTEMBER

I arose in good season, again very well. It has been very bright and more comfortable than usually. I packed first thing (finishing after breakfast) and bade Uncle and Aunt Magill good bye. Took my luggage (by help of one of Aunt Mary's shawl straps), to Gov't building, for repacking. It was fearful work but it solves much of my difficulty about getting all I have of papers, tools and specimens home. Went by 31st St. cars, Illinois Central and the Intramural. On reaching the Govt Bdg, worked very hard as well as at packing box for Expressage—well nigh finishing both. Telegraphed Emalie that I could not return until Monday. All this so rushed me that I was unable to keep my engagement with Culin, Dorsey, Col. Hazard and others at Anthropological Bdg. Did not reach there, in fact, until at about five o'clock. One cause of delay was the call of Profr. Norton,—who repeated his invitation that I visit him in Cincinnati,—and a struggle of Holmes and myself with Earll to extend our man Melville's passes—which he wouldnt do—thinking it wrong! ... Arranged with Gary to take my valise to 6255 Woodlawn Ave. for me. He gave me his letter to the newspaper of his place, with request that I recommend him for a place with us. Went to Anthropological Bdg. too late for Culin. Called on Col. Hazzard and saw him just as he was leaving, appointed to meet him tomorrow morning. Back to Anth Bdg., and not findg Culin went to call on Dorsey in Peruvian Sectn. Mrs. Dorsey there.[103] She said how disappointed she was she had not met Mrs. Cushing and that she (Emalie) was not coming back. She told me Culins and Brinton were to dine together at the French Restaurant. Engaged to visit them Monday. Then as had two hours before going to join Brinton and the Culins, went out to call on H. I. Smith. He was so much better as to be absent in Minneapolis. Mrs. Smith would have me stay to supper. Boiled mutton alas which did not agree with me over well. Left with rembrances to Smith, at about half past seven. Took Illinois Central to 51st Street and after a considerable hunt found the Culins at the French Restant dining with Brinton, who immediately ordered coffee and cordial for us. After sitting awhile, we all went home to the Culins where Stewart brought Whiskey and Cigarettes and we all had a long talk. Brinton was most friendly. We talked of Madrid Expositn and many other things. They are disappointed in Anth Exhbn. When Brinton came away he accompanied me many squares. Told me of writing—said I must write a popular work on my life in Zuñi[,] Studies there and so on, and a Dictionary of the Language. He expressed gratification that he knew me. It was aftr midnight when I reached tent. Holmes good old fellow had kept light burning for me and was awake. Very tired and beginning to get ill. Cold night.

Notes

The diaries are transcribed from copies provided by Jesse Green, since deposited in the National Anthropological Archives, Washington DC. Cushing's many abbreviations have been preserved except that very slight editing has been done for clarity. Words that could not be read are marked with [?]. In these notes about individuals mentioned, biographical detail not otherwise sourced is from supplementary Google searches (with additional search terms noted in a few cases).

1. Emma Tennison Magill Cushing (1860–1920) married Frank on June 10, 1882 (*National Cyclopedia of American Biography* 15:27, hereafter cited as NCAB). She was the daughter of John Whitehead Magill (1830–79), who was born in Meadville

PA, and joined Lewis Johnson & Company, Bankers, as a junior clerk, rising to be a partner (*Washington Post*, June 4, 1879, p. 4). Her mother was Catherine Cecilia Magill (1838–91).

2. Cushing had a deformed stomach and suffered continually from diverticulitis.

3. William Henry Holmes (1846–1933) was a curator at the U.S. National Museum and in charge of preparations by the Bureau of American Ethnology (BAE) for the World's Columbian Exposition (WCE). On Holmes at the WCE, see Meltzer 2010. For a biography of his fascinating life, see Fernlund 2000.

4. Rev. James Owen Dorsey (1848–95) was an ethnologist at the BAE who made extensive studies of the languages and sociology of numerous Plains tribes (Hewitt 1895).

5. Emma Cushing's Aunt Mary and her husband, Charles Magill, a printer, lived at the corner Clark and Van Buren, Chicago.

6. Augusta McChesney was a clerk at the BAE (Smithsonian Institution Archives, RU31, box 74, folder 3).

7. Carl F. W. Bergmann was the preparator for the Bureau of Ethnology and the fabricator of exhibits; he later worked with Cushing on his Florida Expedition for the University Museum of the University of Pennsylvania (Gilliland 1989).

8. Born in Redding, Connecticut, William Augustus Croffut (1835–1915) was a private in the U.S. Army during the Civil War. He was then a phonographic reporter and correspondent of many leading journals: sometime editor of the *Minneapolis Tribune, New York American, Rochester Democrat, New Haven Palladium, American Architect, Hearth & Home*, and the *Daily Post* of Washington DC. He was regarded as "one of the most brilliant writers that ever appeared on any stage" (*Washington Post*, March 22, 1878, 1). He was the executive officer of the U.S. Geological Survey, 1888–94. A poem entitled "The Prophecy" by William Augustus Croffut (1835–1915), of Washington DC, was read at the Chicago World's Fair opening ceremonies. One stanza was, "He [Columbus] saw an empire radiant as the day,/Harnessed to law but under Freedom's sway,/Proudly arise, resplendent in array,/To show the world the way" (for the whole poem, see Johnson 1897, 1:345–46). He organized the Anti-Imperialist League in 1899, was president of the Liberty League, and was a conspicuous member of the Secular League; early on he wisely invested every penny in Mergenthaler stock, and so became wealthy (*Who Was Who in America* 1:227, hereafter cited as WWWA); *Washington Post*, August 1, 1915, 16).

9. Nell and George C. Payne, Cushing's sister- and brother-in-law, lived near the Cushings in Washington. George Clay Payne (1862–1901), of the law firm Taylor & Payne, was married to Emma Cushing's sister Eleanor ("Nellie") Magill Payne. He came to Washington at age four, graduated from Columbian University law school, and was admitted to the bar in 1883 (*Washington Post*, October 16, 1901, pp. 3, 7; October 17, 1901, 3).

10. Col. James G. Payne, the father of Cushing's brother-in-law George Clay Payne (1862–1901), lived on Massachusetts Avenue and served as auditor of the Supreme Court of the District of Columbia.

11. William John McGee (1853–1912), geologist, anthropologist, and hydrologist, became Powell's chief assistant and heir apparent at the Bureau of Ethnology in 1893, following the departure of Henry W. Henshaw (Hinsley 1981, 162, 231–61). After nine years of service, McGee was passed over following Powell's death in 1902 when the bureau was reorganized. Holmes was appointed chief (not director). McGee went on to play a vital role at the St. Louis Exposition (Parezo and Fowler 2007) and in the development of the conservation movement in America; he was appointed by Theodore Roosevelt to the Inland Waterways Commission (Lacey 1979).

12. Weston Flint (1835–1906) was librarian of the Scientific Library, U.S. Patent Office, 1877–87; acting chairman of the Board of the U.S. Civil Service Examiners, 1884–87; Statistician in the U.S. Bureau of Education, 1889–95; and secretary of the National Statistical Association, 1895–98. He then was trustee, 1897–98, and then librarian, 1898–1904, of the Public Library of Washington DC (WWWA 1:407; *New York Times*, April 7, 1906, p. 9, col. 6).

13. Betty was the Cushings' young cook, whom they hired on April 11, 1892, and whose last day was November 14, 1893 (Cushing Diaries, National Anthropological Archives, hereafter cited as NAA).

14. Frederick Webb Hodge (1864–1956), Cushing's brother-in-law, had been his field secretary on the Hemenway Expedition, and married Margaret Whitehead Magill in 1891. Hodge later became director of the BAE, conducted archaeological excavations at the protohistoric Zuni site of Hawikuh (1917–23) for the Heye Foundation, and finally served as director of the Southwest Museum, 1932–56 (Wilcox 2003).

15. May S. Clark (1862–1952) was born in Davenport, Iowa, the daughter of Major General W. T. Clark. She was private secretary to J. W. Powell and continued in the Smithsonian until about 1932 (Washington *Evening Star*, March 2, 1952; vertical file, Southwest Museum, Los Angeles).

16. Cushing's "Outlines of Zuñi Creation Myths" appeared in the *13th Annual Report of the Bureau of Ethnology for the Years 1891–1892*, published in 1896 (Cushing 1896, 321–447).

17. This was Chicago's answer to the Eiffel Tower, the great wheel created by George Washington Gale Ferris that could take 2,000 paying customers at a time 264 feet into the air (Gale 1992, 122).

18. On the development and management of the Midway Plaisance, see Essay 1, this volume.

19. Born in New Orleans, William Wesley Karr (b. 1853) was the disbursing clerk for the Smithsonian Institution. Stone was the agent through whom the Cushings rented their Washington house. Otis Tufton Mason (1838–1908) became curator of the Department of Ethnology in the Smithsonian's U.S. National Museum (USNM) in 1884. His paper, "What Is Anthropology? " was the working plan for the Anthropological Society of Washington, which he helped to found; he served for many years on its journal, the original *American Anthropologist* (WWWA 1:786; *New York Times*, November 6, p. 7, col. 4). He also wrote the ASW constitution (Walter Hough in *AA* 10: 661–67).

20. Robert Edward Earll (1853–96) was chief of the Division of Fisheries, U.S. Fish Commission, 1883–88, and then joined the USNM as a curator. He was the executive officer in charge of the preparation of the Smithsonian exhibits at expositions in 1884, 1885, 1888, 1893 (WCE), and 1895.

21. Albion, on the Erie Canal in Orleans County in western New York, was Cushing's hometown.

22. The H. Jay Smith Colorado Cliffdweller Exhibit, also known as the Battle Rock cliffdweller exhibit, was across from Putnam's Anthropology Building at the southeastern corner of the fairgrounds. Charles Kurtz was assistant chief of the art department at the Exposition; in subsequent years he played a large part at many other World's Fairs (Harris 1978, 144–45).

23. George Frederick Kunz (1856–1932), an expert on gems, was employed by Tiffany's from 1879, becoming vice president in 1907. At the 1893 Exposition he was in charge of the department of mines. In 1890 he had published Cushing's controversial turquoise-encrusted toad (Wilcox 2003b). William Phipps Blake (1825–1910), geologist and mining engineer, had prepared the government's exhibit at the 1876 World's Fair on the mineral resources of the United States. In 1895 he became professor of geology and mining, and director of the school of mines, at the University of Arizona, where he published several articles of archaeological interest (Blake 1899, 1900) and was of assistance in developing Arizona State Museum (Wilcox 2005). At the Centennial Exposition at Philadelphia in 1876 Cushing was a curator for the Smithsonian Institution; he became reacquainted with Blake in Prescott in 1887, during the Hemenway Expedition (Hinsley and Wilcox 2002).

24. H. Jay Smith of Minneapolis created the Battle Rock cliffdweller exhibit, located opposite (west of) the Anthropology Building (Brown 1994, xv, 84). His business partner or financial supporter was Charles D. Hazzard. Palmer Henderson published an article on "Cliff-Dwellers' Houses" in the *American Antiquarian* (Henderson 1893) in which he recognized that groups of cliff dwellings formed villages and that the so-called estufas (kivas) were in fact living rooms.

25. This was probably George Hunt (Jacknis 1991a, 1991b).

26. Hector Alliot (1862–1919), nephew of French anthropologist Paul Broca (1824–80), came to the United States as a young man; he became H. Jay Smith's secretary, and later agent of C. D. Hazzard; officially he was director of the cliff dweller exhibit at the Fair. He lost everything in the San Francisco earthquake of 1906 and then moved to Los Angeles, working for a time as a reporter for the *Los Angeles Times*. He became the first curator of the Southwest Society of the Archaeological Institute of America and briefly director of the Southwest Museum.

27. Editor and publisher John Brisben Walker (1847–1931) introduced an entire issue of *Cosmopolitan* devoted to the Fair in his article, "A World's Fair, Introductory: The World's College of Democracy" (Walker 1893).

28. Alice Palmer Henderson, wife of H. Jay Smith's assistant, exhibited costumes of Alaskan tribes in the Anthropology Building (Johnson 1897–98, 3:423), and registered for the Congress of Anthropology (Wake 1894b, xii).

29. Samuel Edward Magill (1861–1913) was born in Erie County, Pennsylvania, the son of dentist William E. Magill (1825–96) and Louisa (Jones) Magill (1830–1911). He married Julia Groves (b. 1864) in 1887 and was engaged in the coal and real estate business in Chicago, 1882–97 (Google: *The Book of Chicagoans*). He served as U.S. consul in Tampico, 1897–1907, and Guadalajara, 1908, and as U.S. consul general in San Salvador, 1907–8.

30. DeLancey Gill was the chief staff artist at the BAE (see Darrah 1951, 392); Cushing to Culin, November 18, 1893, Cushing correspondence, 1.6.001, Culin Archival Collection, Brooklyn Museum of Art Library.

31. Metallurgist Robert Henry Lamborn (1836–95) made a fortune as a major owner of the Mexican Central Railroad and became a collector and philanthropist, sponsoring the citizenship prizes of the Anthropological Society of Washington (McGee 1895). Robert Stewart Culin (1858–1929), a protégé of Daniel Brinton, was the founder of Philadelphia's Oriental Club, and in 1892 he was placed in charge of the archaeology division of the University Museum (Jacknis 1985). Cushing first met him in early 1893 at the National Museum, but it was at the Chicago Fair that they became best friends. Cushing was enlisted by Culin in his study of all forms of games. In 1903 Culin left Philadelphia to become the first curator of ethnology at the Brooklyn Museum; after Cushing's death in 1900, Emma Cushing gave him Cushing's library of manuscripts and letters (three boxes of which Culin passed on to Frederick Webb Hodge in 1921 (NCAB 29:161; *New York Times*, April 9, 1929, 31).

32. Possibly Chauncey Wales Riggs (b. 1857), to whom Cushing had written on June 17, 1891 (Cushing Letter Book 7:317–18, Cornell University).

33. Washington Matthews (1843–1905), ethnologist of the Hidatsa and Navajo, was a close friend of Cushing. He published a study of the human remains recovered by the Hemenway Expedition (Matthews et al. 1893). At the Columbian Exposition he was one of the few American anthropologists to attend the International Folklore Congress, held the week of July 10 and sponsored by the Department of Literature; his paper was on "Navajo Songs and Prayers, as Recorded by the Edison Phonograph, with Sacred, Agricultural, Building, War, Gambling, and Love Songs" (Zumwalt 1988: 26–28).

34. John Gregory Bourke (1846–96), Capt., 3rd Cavalry, and ethnologist of the Hopi, Zuni and Apache, was another close friend of Cushing who discussed papers at the Exposition's Folklore Congress. La Rabida was a reconstruction of the La Rabida friary in coastal southern Spain, where Queen Isabella's agents called Columbus back to undertake his exploration to the New World.

35. David Fisher Day (1829–1900), member of a committee of the Buffalo Society of Natural Sciences, had invited Cushing to give a talk to the society on December 15, 1890 (Brooklyn Museum, Culin Collection). A lawyer, he served several times as president of the society. Just as he would soon do in Chicago, Cushing was remarkably successful in Buffalo while a patient at Invalides Hospital (November 1890–March 1891) in becoming intimate with the intellectual elite of that city; besides the

Days, he became friends with Dr. Lee Herbert Smith (1856–1935); William Clement Bryant and his brothers Bryant Burwell Glenny (1848–1917) and William Henry Glenny Jr. (1848–1929), and their families; Henry Raymond Howland (1844–1930); John Clark Glenny (1859–1909) and family; Gordon F. Wilcox; Daniel Newton Lockwood (1844–1906), a member of Congress who became the general manager of the Pan-American Exposition at Buffalo in 1901; William Learned, the librarian; and Frederick Boies Houghton (1866–1950), a grammar-school principal who became an avocational archaeologist (Robertson and Barcellona 1939).

36. Fannie E. Coann Curtis (1853–1931), the daughter of Ezra Titus Coann, a banker in Albion NY, was a close family friend of the Cushings. Her husband, Judson Curtis (1840–79), had passed away. She had two children, a son, Judson Coann Curtis (1877–1931) and a daughter, Pearl (b. 1877), also known in the family as Pearlita to distinguish her from her Uncle Pearl Coann (Google: Albion Cemetery).

37. Antonio Apache was allegedly a Chiricahua Apache captured as a boy by the U.S. military in 1877 and sent East to be educated. At Harvard he came to the attention of Putnam, who brought him to the Chicago Fair as a tour guide in the Anthropology Building and as a manager for five Navajos who were also on exhibit (Essay 1, this volume; Trennert 1987a). His ethnicity was repeatedly questioned and is still unknown.

38. Benjamin J. Hatmaker (b. 1870) was president in 1889 of the Christian Endeavor Society of the Presbyterian Church of Albion NY; in the 1892 census he was listed as a banker, aged twenty-two.

39. Lt. George Thornton Emmons (1852–1945) was a naval officer who in 1882 began making extensive collections among the Tlingit tribe of the Northwest coast. In 1891 he was given charge of the Alaskan exhibit at the Chicago Fair, which contained 2,700 pieces and took up 3,000 square feet. Putnam helped arrange to have it purchased for the Columbian Museum (Cole 1895; Dexter 1970; Low 1977).

40. Halsey Cooley Ives (1847–1911), from Tiffany's, was chief of the Department of Fine Arts at the Fair; he was responsible for choosing the paintings on exhibit. Harlan Ingersoll Smith (1872–1940) was one of Putnam's field assistants; he supervised the building of the model Ohio Mound for the Fair (*New York Times*, January 29, 1940, 15).

41. Joseph Dame Weeks (1840–96) was an expert on industrial relations and mining; at the Exposition he was judge of awards in the Department of Mines and Mining (*Dictionary of American Biography* 10:602–3, hereafter cited as DAB). Richard Watson Gilder (1844–1909) was editor of *Century Magazine* for twenty-eight years; he published Cushing's "My Adventures at Zuñi" (*New York Times* November 21, 1909, 13).

42. Walter Besant (1836–1901) was an English writer who participated in the Literary Congress of Writers in the English Language at the Fair (July 10–15); Besant's paper on "The Aims and History of the English Society of Authors" was well received (Besant 1894). His sister-in-law was Annie Besant, theosophist and woman's activist (see note 94).

43. Henry Carrington Bolton (1843–1903), chemist and bibliographer, was one of the founders of the American Folk-Lore Society, a regular contributor to its *Journal*, and a student of the history of science (see Zumwalt 1988, 24).

44. Eliza Ruhnmah Seidmore (1856–1928), a travel writer who visited Japan many times, became the first woman trustee of the National Geographic Society and was an early advocate for planting cherry trees in Washington DC. Pearl Coann Curtis (b. 1877), often called "Pearlita," was the niece of Pearl Clement Coann and daughter of Fannie Coann Curtis—all friends of Cushing from Albion (Google: N.Y. State Census).

45. Mary Katherine Keemle "Kate" Field (1838–96) was a journalist, author, lecturer, and actress whom Cushing had first met in San Francisco, and with whom he had gone to the Chinese theater (DAB 6:368; *Daily Examiner*, November 20, 1887, p. 9, cols. 3–5). They became good friends (Cushing Diaries for 1892 NAA). She was the editor of *Kate Field's Washington* (Scharnhorst 2008). S. S. Sprigge gave a paper at the Literary Congress on "Copyright and Lord Monkswell's Bill" (Besant 1894, 124–25).

46. Cushing met Charles Deering and his wife on August 4, 1893 (Cushing 1893a). A decade later Deering would become chairman of International Harvester (Scott and Harshe 1929).

47. We have not identified Salisbury. On Putnam, see Essay 1, this volume; on Buffalo Bill's Wild West show at Chicago and other fairs, see Warren 2005 and Rydell and Kroes 2005.

48. Sarah Tyson Rorer, author of *The Philadelphia Cookbook* and founder of the Philadelphia Cooking School (Weimann 1981: 459), is considered a pioneering American nutritionist. She was hired by the Board of Lady Managers to run the Illinois Corn Kitchen, which was intended to promote the use of corn as a food for humans as well as animals; Cushing provided her with Zuni recipes for Indian dishes made with corn. She later helped him find a stenographer in Philadelphia to type his Florida report for the American Philosophical Society (Cushing Diaries, NAA). Marcia Louise Towndrow Gould (1859–1936), president of the Illinois Woman's Exposition Board, was from Moline (Johnson 1897–98, 1:210).

49. Gaillard Hunt (1863–1924) held various positions at the State Department (1887–1909, 1917–24) and was chief of the division of manuscripts at the Library of Congress, 1909–17.

50. Morris Jastrow Jr. (1861–1921), who joined the faculty of Semitic languages at the University of Pennsylvania in 1893, presented a paper at the Fair's Congress of Anthropology on "The Historical Study of Religions: Its Method and Scope" (MS 6, BAE 6.5, Southwest Museum). He became one of America's foremost authorities on Semitic languages and Near Eastern religion (*New York Times*, June 23, 1921, 11). Alternatively, Cushing's reference may be to Morris's brother Joseph (1863–1944), who was a fellow of the AAAS, Section H (since 1887) and professor at the University of Wisconsin; he was head of the psychological laboratory at the Fair.

51. Talcott Williams (1849–1928) was editor of the *Philadelphia Press* for thirty-one years, beginning in 1881. Born in Turkey, he spoke fluent Arabic. A close friend

of William Pepper (1843-98), the provost of the University of Pennsylvania from 1888 to 1898, Talcott Williams was a member of the board of managers of the University Museum, of which Pepper was the founding director. Williams's wife, Sophia Wells Royce, whom he married in 1879, was from Albion, New York, and there they became friends with Cushing in 1891 (NCAB 15:306-7; *New York Times,* January 25, 1928; Cushing Diaries, NAA).

52. Anne Hollingsworth Wharton (1845-1928) was the author of *Through Colonial Doorways* (1893) and many other books. She served as a judge of the American Colonial Exhibit at the Fair. Helen Bunker Culin divorced Stewart Culin in 1905 (Don Fowler and Diane Fane, pers. comm., 1999); she then married Edgar Arthur Singer Jr. (1873-1954), professor of philosophy at the University of Pennsylvania. Culin married Alice Mumford (1875-1950), a Philadelphia portrait painter (*New York Times,* August 10, 1950, 25).

53. Francis Davis "Frank" Millet (1846-1912), popular Boston artist, war correspondent, and critic, became close friends with Daniel Burnham at the Fair (DAB 1928; Hines 1979) while serving as director of functions and decorations for the Exposition (Johnson 1897-98, 1:478). Millet "had charge of all coloring inside and outside the buildings, the flags, banners, and woven-fabric effects of the processions and ceremonies inside of the grounds, and later of all the music and illuminations and fireworks; directed and controlled the sculpture and mural paintings, and was the friend and adviser of the Chief of Construction [Daniel Burnham] in everything" (Burg 1976, 99). He drowned on the *Titanic* (Hines 1979, 358-59). Lucia Millet, Frank's sister, became the wife of Cushing's friend Sylvester Baxter in 1893 (Hinsley and Wilcox 1996). Daniel Hudson Burnham (1846-1912) was chief of construction and director of works for the Chicago Fair. Applying his experience and working with friends whom he made there, Burnham later successfully pioneered in city planning for Washington DC in 1902 and Chicago in 1909. His wife Margaret was the daughter of John B. Sherman, a Chicago stockyards magnate, for whom Burnham built a mansion in 1874—his first major commission (*New York Times,* June 2, 1912, Section II, p. 13, col. 5; Hines 1979).

54. At Lakeside, on Lake Ontario north of Albion, New York, the Coann family had a summer place where Cushing often stayed while recovering his health in 1891 (Cushing Diaries, NAA).

55. A suffragette active in the International Council of Women, May Eliza Wright Sewall (1844-1920), a Lady Manager for Indianapolis, chaired the Committee on Organization for the Congress of Representative Women that was held from May 15 to 21, 1893 (Johnson 1897-98, 1:210, 4:15-16; Weinmann 1981: 524-32). May Wilson Preston (1873-1949), a Lady Manager for Utah (Johnson 1897-98, 1:211), was an illustrator later associated with the Ash Can School in New York.

56. Col. Charles D. Hazzard, on behalf of the H. Jay Smith Exploring Company, in the spring of 1892 purchased the "second" Wetherill collection of "cliff dweller" material from the San Juan River region. After exhibiting it at the Sixth Minneapolis Industrial Exposition, they collected additional material and showed the whole

collection of about one thousand specimens at the Chicago Fair in the Battle Rock cliffdweller exhibit (McNitt 1957, 32–33; Blackburn and Williamson 1997, 25–26). In May 1894 negotiations were undertaken by Hazzard's agent, Hector Aliot, to sell the collection to the University Museum of the University of Pennsylvania. By March 1895 they reduced the original asking price from $25,000 to $15,000, and in February 1896 it was purchased for $14,500 for the museum by Phoebe Apperson Hearst. Cushing studied the collection for six weeks in September and October 1895, probably recommending its purchase (Administrative Records, American Section Curatorial, box 25, folder 13, University Museum Archives, University of Pennsylvania, Philadelphia). His previously unpublished report appears as Document H, this volume.

57. Willard Leroy Metcalf (1858–1925) studied art in Boston and at the Academie Julian, Paris. A close friend of Cushing from the early 1880s, he illustrated Cushing's "My Adventures at Zuñi." He won a medal for his painting at the Exposition and became recognized later as being among the foremost American Impressionist landscape artists (*New York Times*, March 10, 1925, p. 21, col. 1; see also Hinsley and Wilcox 1996).

58. Douglas D. Graham (1849–ca. 1920) was in Zuni in 1879 when Cushing arrived; he operated a store there from March 1881 and served as well as the Zuni postmaster. He sold out in 1898; four years later he became the first agency superintendent at Black Rock (McNitt 1962: 240; Lange et al. 1984, 425, fn 495; *Handbook of North American Indians*, 9: *Southwest*, 477).

59. William Henry Goodyear (1846–1923) was a classical archaeologist who in 1890 became the first curator of fine arts at the Brooklyn Institute of Arts and Sciences.

60. James Mooney (1861–1921) joined the BAE in 1885 and became a leading authority on the anthropology of the Cherokee and Kiowa. He helped prepare Smithsonian exhibits for many expositions, including the Chicago Fair (*American Men of Science* 1921, 483–84; Essay 4, this volume).

61. Frank Cushing's cousin by marriage, George L. Magill, was cashier at the Thirty-first Bank in Chicago in 1893 (*New York Times*, July 27, 1893, 2) and a member of the ASW in the following year. Six years later, as president of the Avenue Savings Bank, he was convicted of a crime and was in county jail; his sentence was later lightened (*New York Times*, April 7, 1900, 1; *St. Louis Republic*, January 1, 1901, p. 7, col. 1).

62. F. T. Bickford was secretary of the Board of Management for the Government Exhibits at the Exposition (see Bickford 1893; Weinmann 1981, 29).

63. Clara Lillian Burnham Woodyatt (1850–1939) was Daniel Burnham's younger sister; she married William H. Woodyatt in 1873 (*New York Times*, July 24, 1939, p. 13, col. 6; Hines 1979, 10).

64. Cushing later corresponded with Dr. Henry M. Hurd, father of Mrs. Lord (Cushing Letter Book, 8:334, Cornell University). Hurd (1844–1927) was a psychiatrist and first superintendent of the Johns Hopkins University Hospital (Schneck 1961, 353; *New York Times*, July 20, 1927, 23). George S. and Eda Lord were friends of the Burnhams (Hines 1979). He was the principal in Lord, Owens & Co., a wholesale drug company that in 1901 formed the Dearborn Chemical Company (*New*

York Times, February 13, 1901, 1). He declared bankruptcy in 1903 (Hines 1979, 231). The Wyman brothers Walter C. (1851–1927) and Edward F. (n.d.) mounted a private exhibit of copper and stone implements from Wisconsin, Illinois, and Missouri in the Anthropology Building (Johnson 1897–98, 3:419).

65. Henry Blake Fuller (1857–1929) was art critic for the *Chicago Record* and the *Art Amateur*; he was also author of the famous Chicago novel *The Cliff-Dwellers* (Fuller 1893; Hines 1979, 252; Weinmann 1981, 316, 353).

66. The identity here is difficult. Possibly it was Dr. J. Wallace Phillips of Northwestern University, Evanston. However, at the Exposition, in the Anthropology Building, an H. W. Phillips "showed a collection illustrating the methods of stone chipping" (Johnson 1897–98, 3:420). Most likely, though, Cushing is referring to Dr. William Abbott Phillips (b. 1861), who by 1908 lived in Evanston and was attached to the Field Museum of Natural History. He made an extensive study of the Mill Creek (Illinois) chert quarries from 1899; in 1901 he showed W. H. Holmes the quarries.

67. Joseph Worcester (1836–1913), a graduate of Harvard College, was ordained in 1867 by his father as a Swedenborgian minister. He moved to San Francisco and by the 1890s had become a spiritual leader to many young artists and intellectuals there; he introduced the idea of the rustic house to San Francisco. He designed the Lyon and Washington Street Swedenborgian Church (1894). He was a cousin by marriage to Daniel Burnham (Longstreth 1983, 111–13, 375; Schaffer 2010). Cushing apparently met him in San Francisco during visits there in 1887 or 1888.

68. Jesse Walter Fewkes (1850–1930) was a student of Louis Agassiz who also studied at the University of Leipzig (1878–80). He then began a career as an invertebrate paleontologist at Harvard's Museum of Comparative Zoology, 1881–89 (WWWA 1:394). A Harvard classmate of Augustus Hemenway, he replaced Cushing as director of the Hemenway Southwestern Archaeological Expedition in June 1889. Reacting to Cushing's criticism, he left the Zuni field for Hopi in 1891. After Mary Hemenway's death in 1894, he joined the BAE and in 1918 became its chief.

69. On Daniel G. Brinton (1837–99) see Darnell 1988 and Essay 2, this volume. His wife was Sarah M. Tillson, whom he married in 1865 (NCAB 9:265–66). Following his death, he was memorialized as the "Founder of American Anthropology" (*Journal of American Folklore* 13:152 [1900]). At first cool toward Cushing, he was won over during the International Congress of Anthropology (Essays 2 and 3, this volume).

70. Ethnologist Alice Cunningham Fletcher (1838–1923) gave papers at the Fair's congresses of music, anthropology, and religion. It was at the Fair that she first became friends with Zelia Nuttall who, like herself, was a protégé of Putnam (Mark 1988, 235). Beginning in 1886, Zelia Maria Magdalena Parrott Nuttall (1857–1933) was for forty-seven years an honorary assistant in Mexican archaeology at the Peabody Museum, Harvard University. She was one of the great pioneers of Mexican archaeology (Tozzer 1933, 480), who at the Columbian Exposition won a gold medal for her contributions. Cushing again avidly talked with her about calendars in Washington in November 1893 (Cushing Diaries, NAA); she published *A Note on the Ancient Mexican Calendar System* in 1894, and *Fundamental Principles of Old and New World Civilizations*

Diary of Frank Hamilton Cushing

in 1901, both of which benefited from Cushing's input. Like Sara Stevenson, Nuttall was a close friend of Phoebe Hearst, who also sponsored Cushing's Florida work in 1896. Nuttall and Fletcher worked with Hearst to set up the Department of Anthropology at the University of California, which opened up a job for Alfred Kroeber in 1901 (Parmenter 1966; Mark 1988, 282–88; Thoresen 1975; and Essay 7, this volume).

71. Erma Crane, Mrs. Rorer's assistant, graduated from her cooking school in Philadelphia and helped her with classes (Weinmann 1981, 459).

72. Carl Hagenbeck (1844–1913) was a German merchant of wild animals which he sold to zoos; at the Chicago Fair he presented Hagenbeck's Zoological Arena and Ethnological Museum, located near the east end of the Midway Plaisance (Ames 2008; Essay 1, this volume).

73. Sylvester Baxter (1850–1927), Cushing's close friend, was an editor for the *Boston Herald* and secretary-treasurer of the Hemenway Southwestern Archaeological Expedition (Hinsley and Wilcox 1995, 1996). Herbert Burrows (1845–1922) was a well-known theosophist and follower of his one-time lover, Helena Petrovina Blavatsky (1831–91). Annie Wood Besant (1847–1933), prominent English theosophist and woman's rights activist, in later years became an advocate for democracy and home rule for India. The *Washington Post* (February 12, 1893, 12) reported her visit to Washington, where Cushing met her at the home of his close friends Julia H. and George M. Coffin. Cushing (February 11, 1893, Cushing Diaries, NAA) said of Annie Besant that she was "of course extraordinary—a very clear thinker and undoubtedly in earnest. She held long conversation with me [?] to the exclusion of others." He was thrilled that she remembered him.

74. Henry Demarest Lloyd (1847–1903), a friend of Burnham (Hines 1979), was a social critic and journalist for the Chicago *Tribune,* 1872–85. In 1894 he published *Wealth against Commonwealth,* a five-hundred-page expose of the trusts. His wife was Jessie Bross Lloyd, the daughter of a lieutenant governor of Illinois.

75. Henry Chapman Mercer (1856–1930) received an AB at Harvard in 1879 and became curator of American and prehistoric archaeology at the University Museum of the University of Pennsylvania from 1894 to 1897. He was an associate editor of the *American Naturalist* on anthropology, 1893–97 (Hinsley 2003, 8–9; Meltzer 2003, 70–74). At the Chicago Fair he presented a paper on "The Discovery of an Artificially Flaked Flint Specimen in the Quarternary Gravels of San Isidro, Spain" (Wake 1894b, 61–68). Carl Lumholtz (1851–1922), Norwegian explorer, ethnographer, and naturalist, collected important anthropological materials from northwest Mexico for the American Museum of Natural History. His talk at the Congress of Anthropology was on "Cave Dwellers of the Sierra Madre" (Wake 1894b).

76. Holmes reported (1893, 431–32; Document D, this volume) that Culin's exhibit on games took "a foremost rank among the great group of collections in the Anthropology Department."

77. Brinton's talk was "On Various Supposed Relations between American and Asian Races" (Wake 1894b, 145–51). For discussion of this and his other papers, see Essay 2, this volume.

78. For more about the fylfot and swastika symbols see Document F. Rev. Stephen Dennison Peet (1831–1914) was the founder, editor and manager of the *American Antiquarian* from 1878 to 1910. His talk at the Anthropology Congress was on "Secret Societies among the Wild Tribes" (Wake 1894b).

79. Holmes (Document D, this volume) reported that "Mr. Cushing supported Dr. Brinton, taking the position that foreign influences have certainly not been sufficiently strong to seriously affect the trend of purely American cultural development, and pointing out the fact that as a rule the striking features of native art and institutions can be traced back to their ultimate sources in America."

80. John Comfort Fillmore (1843–98) was a collaborator of Alice Fletcher in musical studies. His talk at the congress was on "Primitive Scales and Rhythms," while Fletcher's was on "Love Songs among the Omaha Indians" (Wake 1894b, 153–75).

81. Rev. F. L. L. Hiller (Wake 1894b), like his brother C. C. P. Hiller, was a minister; he built a church in East Pueblo, Colorado, in 1891.

82. See Holmes, Document D, this volume.

83. As a graduate student at Harvard, George Amos Dorsey (1868–1931) was sent to South America in 1891 by Putnam to collect material for the Columbian Exposition. While working near Lake Titicaca, he met Harlow N. Higinbotham, the future director of the board of the Field Museum (Johnson 1897–98, 2:370). In 1896 he joined the Field Museum, becoming curator from 1898 to 1915. Fay-Cooper Cole (1931, 414) said of him that "no one of our generation has done more toward popularizing science." See Essay 6, this volume.

84. Nuttall's paper was on "The Mexican Calendar System" (Wake 1894b, vii; see also Document D, this volume).

85. Rev. William Wells Newell (1839–1907) founded the American Folk-Lore Society in 1888 served as longtime editor of its journal (Zumwalt 1988). At the Fair's Congress of Anthropology he read "Ritual Regarded as the Dramatization of Myth" (Chamberlain 1907).

86. At this point the diary is crossed out and illegible for fourteen lines (see Cushing Diaries, NAA).

87. George Hunt, the son of an English merchant and a Tlingit noblewoman, was raised as a Kwakiutl, and as Franz Boas's principal collaborator was coauthor of a paper at the congress on "The Ritual of the Kwakiutl Indians"—although the paper was not published (see Cole 1985; Jacknis 1991a,. 95, and 1991b).

88. Juan de Oñate was the first Spanish governor of New Mexico (Hammond and Rey 1953).

89. "Miss [Sophie] Heaven has spent several summers at Lakeside, and has many friends hearabouts" (*Albion Republican*, January 23, 1895, 3). The Heaven family lived in Washington, where they were friends of the Cushings (Cushing Diaries, NAA).

90. Uncle Walter Palmer was a Cushing uncle from Albion; the Heaven sisters were his nieces (Cushing Diaries, NAA).

91. Cushing presents another version of these ideas in his September 1893 Monthly Report (Document F, this volume).

92. Manuel M. de Peralta, of Costa Rica, was scheduled to give a talk on "Central American Archaeology" (MS 6, BAE 6.5, Southwest Museum).

93. Ernest Volk (1845–1919) a few days earlier at the meetings of the AAAS, Section H, in Madison, Wisconsin, had also given a paper titled "Observations in regard to the Use of Argillite by Prehistoric People, made from Explorations of ancient Village Sites in the Delaware valley (illustrated by specimens, diagrams, and maps)" (McGee 1893, 439). His talk at the Fair's congress was on "Cache Finds from Ancient Village Sites in New Jersey" (SWM Ms. 6 BAE 6.5).

94. Morris Jastrow Jr. presented a paper on "The Scope and Method of the Historical Study of Religions" (Wake 1894b, 287–97).

95. Sara Yorke Stevenson (1847–1921) was a forceful player; see Essay 3, note 13. For suggestive reevaluations of Stevenson's role in this period of both classical and Americanist anthropology, see Visweswaran 1998 and Danien and King 2003.

96. Horace Carter Hovey (1833–1914) was a Presbyterian minister and geologist (*New York Times*, July 28, 1914, 7) who in 1893 published "Homes and Remains of the Cliff Dwellers," *Scientific American* 28 (October): 279.

97. Cushing discusses many of their findings in his September 1893 Monthly Report (Document F, this volume).

98. Charles Clark Willoughby (1857–1943) was an artist whom Putnam regarded as a prodigy; he hired Willoughby to be one of his assistants at the Fair. He became chief assistant at the Peabody Museum, Harvard University, in 1894, assistant curator in 1899, assistant director in 1913, and finally Putnam's successor as director from 1915 to 1928 (*New York Times*, April 22, 1943, 23). Major Horatio Nelson Rust (1828–1906) was from an abolitionist family and, indeed, had been a "friend and companion of John Brown." After the Civil War he pursued commercial interests in Chicago, 1865–81, and then moved to California, where he established a ranch in South Pasadena and was a "warm friend" to the Mission Indians, being appointed government agent to them in 1889. He was largely instrumental in founding the Pasadena Public Library, of which he was president (*American Anthropologist* 8:737). His correspondence with Lummis is at the Southwest Museum, Los Angeles, and his papers are at the Huntington Library in San Marino (Kim Walters, pers. comm., 2005). He sold his collections from the Fair to Beloit College (Militello 2009).

99. Owens and Dorsey were Putnam's first graduate students in the fall of 1890 (Hinsley 1985, 134). Owens for two years held the Hemenway Fellowship. In the summers of 1890 and 1891 he was an assistant to Jesse Walter Fewkes on the Hemenway Expedition; in November 1891 he was sent by Putnam as director of the first Peabody Honduras Expedition to excavate and collect at Copán, partly for the Columbian Exposition. He died there of yellow fever in 1893 (Brown 1994, 41; Hinsley 1985, 1992).

100. The reference is apparently to Carl Vilhelm Hartman (1862–1941). A European-trained scholar, Hartman was curator of archaeology and ethnology at the Carnegie Museum, Pittsburgh; in 1909 he went to the Royal Ethnographical Museum, Stockholm, where he remained at least until 1915 (*American Anthropologist* 10:178, 17:426). Willey and Sabloff (1974, 82) write that "he was appreciative of grave lot

segregation and grave superposition" and "he was the best archaeologist except for Uhle" in South America.

101. The reference is probably to Marshall Cushing, whom Frank addressed in a March 24, 1894, correspondence as "Kinsman" (Cushing Letter Book 8:375, Cornell University). He was initially an editorial writer for the *Boston Globe*, becoming night editor. He then was private secretary for Henry Cabot Lodge and then for U.S. Postmaster General John Wanamaker. He founded the original *Washington Times* (*Washington Post*, April 29, 1984, 1).

102. Juliet Corson was a cooking-school teacher in New York (Weinmann 1981, 458–59).

103. Ida Chadsey Dorsey of Kansas City married George Dorsey on December 8, 1892 (WWWA 1:333).

DOCUMENT F

Monthly Report of Mr. Frank Hamilton Cushing

September 1893 (inclusive of July and August)

During latter June, the months of July and August, and the first two weeks of September, 1893, I was absent on duty with Professor W. H. Holmes installing and completing the general and group-exhibits of the Bureau of American Ethnology in [the] Government Building of the World's Columbian Exposition at Chicago. Aside from Professor Holmes' special archeological exhibit, in which my services were but incidentally required, the general exhibits consisting of collections displayed by the Bureau of American Ethnology and the U.S. National Museum, were designed to illustrate by means of material data, the character and distribution of the arts and industries of North America in Pre-Columbian times, according to the areas of the great linguistic stocks as determined by the researches of the Bureau of American Ethnology, and recorded by Powell in his linguistic families of North America. The group exhibits, while belonging to this more general series, were nevertheless in some measure distinct from it; since they were designed specially to illustrate the processes of the arts (shown in contiguous wall cases) such as the industries and ceremonies of special tribes. Of those groups I had more directly to deal with those illustrating phases in the life of the Pueblo and other southwestern Indian tribes, with which my extended residence amongst those tribes had made me familiar in a practical way.

The work of arranging, setting and costuming the figures of these

Manuscript MS 6, BAE 3.5, Frank Hamilton Cushing Collection, Southwest Museum; transcribed by David R. Wilcox, 1999, with minor adjustments for clarity groups was difficult and tedious, as many of them had to be remodelled and readjusted to suit conditions which it had been impossible to foresee and provide for in Washington. But the results were highly satisfactory and the series is now suited not only to this purpose of temporary exhibition for which it was primarily designed, but also, is so adapted to permanent exhibition in the National Museum, that it is the intention of Professor Goode to have the series greatly extended, after the return of the collections to Washington.[1] I have been requested to design and take charge of the construction of additional (related) figures and groups for this purpose, inasmuch as the permanent exhibit of the Bureau of American Ethnology in the National Museum may thereby be greatly augmented, and shall be pleased to do so if, in your judgment, the devotion of my time for this purpose during portions of each day or of stated days in the week throughout the coming winter will be of advantage to our service.

The groups as already arranged at Chicago, are as follows:

Illustrative of Industries.

Silversmithing. In large case, fitted up with ground work representing space near a native hut, and with stick supported adobe forge and primitive goatskin bellows, etc. in working order; three Navajo men; one, standing at the head of the forge, working the bellows and smelting; one, squatting at the foot of the forge and soldering by means of the blow-pipe, embers, and primitive grease lamp; one, sitting at the side of the forge shaping silver buttons and beads by means of rude punches and dies of iron.

Bead-making and Drilling. In small case representing sitting-bench along side of a Pueblo house, a Zuñi man fashioning shell and turquoise beads by chipping and grinding, and drilling by means of the primitive flint-tipped Pueblo pump-drill.

Spinning and Weaving. In large case fitted up with ground work representing space near native hut, two Navajo women; one, spinning, and twisting cotton-wool on the thigh, by means of a primitive whorl-spindle.[2] The second figure is a portrait of one of the most celebrated blanket-makers in the Navajo tribe, weaving a figured (woolen) serape, at an upright, crotch-supported loom.[3]

Tapestry weaving. In small case representing limited space in room of Pueblo house, a young Zuñi woman, weaving tapestry girdles with reed lap-loom supported by waist-yoke "cloth-beam" and foot-piece "yarn-beam."[4]

Basket-making. In small case representing limited space in a pueblo room, a young unmarried Tusayan maiden of Oraibe plaiting baskets of various kinds. The head dress of this figure is interesting, as representing in the two spiral chignons at either side of the head, the flower of the melon-, or squash-vine,—this symbolizing mature, but "unperfected" or virginal womanhood.

Pottery Making. In medium sized table-case, representing a portion of a pueblo room, two Zuñi women; one, fashioning a large clay vessel—by spirally building up with ropes of paste, (in a base-mould made to revolve on the floor) and by scraping with gourd-shell spatulae, the vessel thus made, to form and strengthen the sides and rim; the other, finishing and polishing smaller vessels, after drying by rasping with fragments of grit-rock, then applying white clay slip and polishing with smooth waterworn pebbles. It may be noted that the pueblo base-mould here shown, with its tapering yet concave bottom, so made as to revolve easily and steadily on an earthen or sandy floor, is the first stop in the evolution of the potters-wheel as seen in Egypt and the Orient; whilst the coating of slip, which is made of slightly silicious clays is also a first step in the process of glazing and enamelling.

Illustrative of Ceremonials.

Ceremonial Bread making. In a large case representing a section of a Pueblo kitchen, four Moqui or Tusayan women and girl; 1st, a married woman parching maize over a corner-hearth, in preparation for grinding; 2nd, an unmarried girl in ceremonial costume crushing and hulling the corn on the coarse tufa slab or metate of the family milling trough; 3rd, a little girl, also in ceremonial costume, reducing the samp or meal to fine flour, on one of the finer sandstone metates of the same milling trough, preparatory to its use for bread-making; 4th, an old woman, cooking wafer bread made from a paste of the fine corn flour, and of corn meal mush, (equally mixed) on a baking-stone at the side-hearth. Examples of the bread thus prepared (and variously colored to represent the seven kinds or colors of corn for use in ceremonials relative to the same number of sacremental color sign regions) are also shown.

Ceremonial ritual. In a large case, representing a portion of one of the Six kivas or sacred chambers of the Zuñi, three Zuñi Indian Priests ceremonially reciting the Ritual-epic of Creation; a quadrennial observance, in which many others of the chief priests (masked and unmasked), of the thirteen cult societies of Zuñi, also take part.

The principal figure, K'yak-lu, sits in the middle space on a litter-throne, reciting the epic. Over his head a representation of the midnight star (Sirius) and upon it the God of Thunder-bolts with his warriors and messengers, (the mountain lions and the martins of the four quarters); behind him, mantle of the four seasons; under his feet, the earth-, and cloud-terrace (represented in prayer meal on the floor); and surrounding him, the Ko'-lo-wis-si Á-tchi, or Twin Serpents of the Sea, (represented in dry powder painting, also on the floor). To the right sits a Master Priest of one of the Six kiva-houses responding to the ritual, and to the left stands the Chief or Master Priest of the Bow in the ceremonial regalia of his order, guarding, with his Wand of the Seven Regions, the Sacred person of K'yak-lu. On top of the case are shown the masks of one of the ten Clown-priests of the Zuñi Dramas (or Kâ-kâ Dances), and of A'-na-ho-ho the "Lifter up" or "Destroyer of Forms," who, with others, follows the Principal Priest, making sacrifices from the tops of the houses. The ceremonial (of which this case represents but a small part) is an exact dramaturgy of the "Middle"-Myth of Creation, and is fully explained in my current paper on the "Zuñi Myths of Creation and Migration."

The group illustrates a point more fully brought out in this paper, namely, that the duck effigy held in the hand of the principal actor, the baton held by the warrior, the plumed corn or medicine wand standing before the Priest, even the paintings of the Sea Serpents on the floor, and all the appliances and parts of costume employed are not only symbolic, but are also held to be *personalities* in the Drama, and are supposed to possess, as do the living actors, potentialities—powers of recreating or renewing the world, etc., by means of the ceremonial performances to which they pertain.

Additional Work:

Observations of Anthropological Collections;
Incidental Discoveries and Experiments.

By verbal request of the Director, I undertook to study, during such moments as could be spared from the duties above recorded, various of the many and important anthropological collections of the Columbian Exposition, with a view to further research, and possible publication in the future.

The Cliff-Dwellers. Especial attention was given to the Cliff-Dweller collections both in the Colorado section of the Anthropological building and in the contiguous exhibit of Messrs. H. Jay Smith and C. D. Hazzard, which led to important discoveries relative to the status and place in the development of the Aridian or Pueblo and other phases of culture in the Southwest and South held by the Cliff Dwellers and their identification ancestrally with particular pueblo Indian stocks. Whilst it has been generally conceded that the Cliff Dwellers were pueblo Indians, and that all or nearly all pueblo peoples have at one time or another been Cliff Dwellers or Cave- and Caveate-dwellers, it has not heretofore been possible to identify particular groups of cliff dwellings as the work of special Pueblo stocks or tribes.

My studies led to the inference that the original and probably oldest Cliff Dwellers represented in these collections from the San Juan and Mancos regions of southwestern Colorado were of the Zuñian stock; whilst the Cliff Builders further west in the same region and in northeastern Arizona were later, and were probably of the Shoshonean stock, represented today by the Tusayan or Moqui [Hopi] Pueblo Indians. These inferences were based, with other considerations, upon the following observations:

1st., The pottery of the older cliff collections of the Mancos region is either coiled-ware or smooth-ware, the latter being decorated in black and white only, and representing an early stage in the development of the painted Cibolan or early Zuñian earthenware, which, whilst being at the time of the Conquest polychrome and more elaborate in design, nevertheless presented identical forms and decorations. Moreover these decorations can be unbrokenly traced in the pottery of nearly all ruins lying north and northwest of the Zuñi region until those of the Cliff Dwellers in question are reached.[5]

On the other hand the pottery remains of the more westerly and southwestern cliff ruins is more or less polychrome, the earliest diverging but little from the Mancos types in black and white, but the latest approximating the Tusayan polychrome type more and more closely as the Tusayan region is neared.

From this it is to be inferred that the earlier pottery (of the eastern cliffs) was made by Zuñians whose art down to recent times remained so identical with it; and that late in the history of their occupancy of the Mancos cliffs, bands of Shoshoneans, their nearest neighbors to the west, adopted, perhaps by conquest, the Cliff-pueblo phase of life; developing of course, the peculiar forms of pottery decoration characteristic of the more westerly ruins, and continuing to diverge from the more primitive, borrowed art, until the Tusayan type of polychrome decoration was fully evolved.[6]

2nd. The symbolism of this pottery is especially significant as connecting the older Mancos Cliff Dwellers art with that of the Cibolan Zuñi. Amongst many examples of absolute identity in devices (their emblematic significance and their employment accordingly on vessels of special use), one only need here be given in detail. The handles on a series of mugs in the cliff dweller collection, designed for serving corn-atole, are characterized by large decorative T-shaped perforations. Such perforations are found in some other vessels of other shapes connected with the use of this peculiar corn-drink, in the Colorado exhibit. On vessels similarly used amongst the Zuñi today, this device may be found painted in black, but not cut. And again it is found painted on the mask of the impersonator of the God of graneries and ovens. An explanation of at once its origin and specific use in connection with the corn-drink or "The seed milk" may be found in the fact that the doors of all living-rooms leading to graneries and of graneries themselves, in the cliff ruins, were T-shaped, to enable the harvester to enter them without removing his basket or blanket-load of corn from his back. And whilst the use of the T-shaped granery door has long been abandoned by the Zuñi, nevertheless the painted form of it survives as a granery symbol replacing the cut form of it as an identical symbol amongst their cliff dweller ancestors.

3rd. Again, on certain vessels in the cliff dweller exhibit, evidently designed for use in Kiva ceremonials, occur paintings arranged according to the four directions and the above and below representing the birds of the four quarters and the animals of the above and the below—precisely as such symbols are now painted by the Zuñi, not on vessels but in the kivas themselves during ceremonials relating to the six-seven regions.[7]

4th. In correspondence with this are the genetically similar kiva arrangements of the Cliff Dwellers and of the Zuñi. Amongst the Cliff Dwellers, the Kivas were circular, and in the walls of each, corresponding to the north, west, south, east, northwest and southeast, were square niches for the reception of sacrificial wands, etc., during ceremonials.

The kivas of the modern Zuñi are square, it is true, but distributed throughout the pueblo itself, as were the square niches of the Cliff-Dweller kivas, and also designated according to the six directions.

5th. Among the Zuñi are preserved, as sacred relics, thunder balls. These were pot-hole stones containing natural cavities into which prayer meal and a heart of turquoise were, it is said, introduced, being secured by a plugging corn cob. The thunder balls were rolled down labyrinthine tracks cut in the rocks of the cliffs, "making thunder and emitting lightning" on their way. The stones now used in Zuñi lack the pluggings and other traditional characteristics and are merely rolled about on the floors of the estufas during very sacred rain ceremonials. But in the cliff collections I fortunately discovered very large and fine examples of these thunder stones, one still containing its original plugging of corn cob.

6th. In these collections too, I discovered both Hunter and Medicine animal fetiches common to the Zuñi today (see my contribution on Zuñi Fetiches, Second Annual Report, Bureau of Ethnology) and rude figurines of the mountain goat and other game animals such as are annually sacrificed in Zuñi at the close of phallic ceremonials for the increase of herds—wild and tame.

7th. The textile collections of the cliff dwellings were marvelously well preserved. Both the woven and knitted fabrics showed signs of manipulatory processes and the use of accessory devices identical with those of Zuñi. But the most significant examples found were in

[the] form of little circular, folded pieces of cloth made of bark and stitched with fiber. The signs of wear on these, no less than the eyelet holes for the attachment of cord-bands, two above and one below, gave unquestionable evidence as to their use by women as vaginal shields.

The regular use of such shields has long been discontinued by the Zuñi women. They are merely said to "Wear the bark fiber" during ceremonial observances separating them from the men. And in the old folk-tales and archaic rituals, first-marriage was spoken of as "The parting of the bark fiber" or "Removing of the bark." This series of allusions may be regarded as survivals of a usage such as that of the Cliff Dwellers and thus as indicating at least ancestral connection with the latter or a common ancestry.

8th. Probably one of the strongest evidences of the descent of the Zuñi from the northern Mancos Cliff Dwellers discovered by me was the finding of the herding-crooks, call-whistles, feather-cloth and various other remains in the collections, evidencing the domestication and herding of the turkey, and its use not only as a source of food but also and especially of feather supply. By reference to the notes, maps and restorations of buildings in the Cliff Dweller Exhibit, I learned also that the Cliff Dwellers (of the Mancos and San Juan at least), had in each village, small outlying houses furnished with perches made from smoothed sapling-poles, and leading up to these slanting rows of pegs fixed in the walls. In these little rooms two carcasses of young turkeys (exhibited) had been found.

Now in the traditions and folk-tales of the Zuñi, it is related how anciently the turkey was domesticated by the "Fathers of the Seven Towns," for the sake of their feathers, which were woven into robes and spreads. Their wings were maimed to keep them from flying away from those—slaves, male and female—who herded them over the plains by day, using crooks for seizing the straggling young ones by the neck, and bone whistle-calls for summoning the elder ones when bringing them home to roost, at night. As the turkeys were maimed, their houses had to be provided with "ladders, (pegs driven into the walls), to enable them to climb up to the perching poles.

In my excavations of the ruined Seven Cities I unearthed these little turkey houses everywhere in the outskirts of the towns, finding not only holes in the walls where pegs had been driven and poles had been inserted, but also the carcasses of young turkeys which had died and been trampled into the turkey-lime and thus preserved; showing that the turkey had been truly domesticated; that is, bred and reared by the original inhabitants of these seven Zuñi towns, no less than by the dwellers in the Mancos cliffs.

At the time of the Spanish Conquest of the Pueblos, in 1540-'41, the Zuñi alone, north of Mexico, are distinctly mentioned as having had "domesticated fowl" and as having reared them principally for the sake of their feathers, which were twirled around strands of fiber and woven into mantles, etc.

Aside from these special points of resemblance, there are many others not less striking, but which, in themselves could not be used as arguments for establishing the relationship ancestrally of the (Mancos) Cliff Dwellers to the Zuñi. Yet, they are worthy of mention. The games of the two peoples were identical, as shown by abundant remains. The agricultural and other industrial appliances were exactly alike, so much so that when I entered the Cliff Dweller Exhibit for the first time, it seemed as though I were witnessing the forms and appliances I had so often heard of in Zuñi tradition (but never had seen!) recreated, as it were, to illustrate the stone age stories of such things dating from the time of their common use.

The importance of these observations is great whether indicating connection or not; for they do indicate, in the most positive terms, the advantage of looking to the cliffs for material data in the study of the prehistoric condition of the Pueblos; and on the other hand, of studying these remains (as archeologic) only in the light of modern investigations amongst the pueblos themselves. Nowhere else in the world is a case parallel to this in these respects, presented; and I shall hope to continue for this office investigations not only ethnologic but also archeologic along those lines.

Ancient Peruvian collections. The collections of antiquities from Peru in the Department of Anthropology at the World's Columbian Exposition—both those of Mr. Dorsey, from Incan burial fields on the coast, and those of Señor Montez from Incan and Chancan sources in the Montaña regions, were of such extent and surpassing interest that they claimed a large share of my leisure attention. In both of these were everywhere to be traced striking analogies between the Andean and Aridian (or our own southwestern) cultures.[8]

1st. At a glance it was clear that the same Six-seven or Septenary system prevailed in Peru that characterized, as I have shown, the mythico-sociologic institutions of the Cliff Dwellers and of the ancient Zuñi. For example, on a stone plate, in the Dorsey collection, were carved in relief, the seven animal fetiches of the six regions and the middle synthesis of them all; as, in sacred medicine spoons of the Zuñi the same number of game-animal gods are painted. Again, I observed that the mummy of a Matron (probably priestess) had been buried with the seven ears of corn (of the different colors) laid across her breast, as would be the case in the burial of a Clan-priestess and Matron amongst the Zuñi (and possibly Moqui) of today. The stone idols and fetiches of the Montez collection offered also striking resemblances to the like objects of worship observed by me amongst the Zuñi and in the collections I made for the Hemenway Expedition from the ruined Pueblo Cities of the Salado in Arizona. For example, with the latter and the Zuñi, the Mountain lion (puma) was held to be the chief of the Prey gods and his fetich carved in stone and inlaid with turquoise and white shell was carried by both warrior and hunter. In these collections from the Andes, the most conspicuous fetich was that of the *Jaguar* (spotted puma), more beautifully carved but inlaid in an identical manner with turquoise, red shell, and little bands or plates of gold; and these fetiches, it was said, had been found in the burial towers of dead Warrior Chiefs. It was noteworthy that in both the southwestern carvings of the puma, and in the Andean carvings of the jaguar (his southern representative) the tail was indicated as laid lengthwise along the back, a conventional treatment nowhere else given so far as I know, in the ancient world, in representations of such animals. I call attention to these few of many resemblances,—striking, but not so constant as between the Cliff Dwellers and the modern Zuñi,—less with the idea of presenting them as evidences of far off connection or identity of culture derivation, than as suggestions for study of the possibility of such identical development,—even as to details like these,— amongst totally unrelated peoples, placed in, and slowly influenced during growth by, similar environmental conditions and suggestions.

2nd. Of greater specific moment were my observations of the textile art remains, in the Dorsey collection. These included not alone tapestry and other fabrics of great beauty, variety and perfection, but also the appliances by which they were wrought. Amongst the latter I observed that the small, long, double pointed spindles—hitherto so-called—found with the mummies of women never occurred singly; but in sets of from four or six, to thirty-six, and in one case to between *sixty* and *seventy*! On each of these was placed near the middle, (as on a string) a bead of terra cotta or stone, usually incised and painted with some conventional pattern. From the fact that along with these sets of little spindles were other spindles of the usual kind employed by primitive peoples—larger, longer, blunt at one end, and provided with heavier and flatter whorl-discs, it was obvious to me that the smaller specimens were probably not mere spindles, but accessories, perhaps, to weaving, as well as to spinning operations. More careful studies of the hundreds of examples shown, bore out this inference. For instance, on many of the specimens, were little sections of cane, one, two, sometimes three. Each section had wound upon it fine cordage of llama wool or cotton. It immediately occurred to me that these joints of cane were, when large, "warping-spools," and when small, probably "quills" for wool-threads; since, on the latter, the threads were almost always of different colors where two or more occurred on the same spindle. It at once became clear to me, also, that the bead-whorls were designed primarily to facilitate the rolling of the spindles on the thigh or a flat board with the palm of the hand, in the process of winding the spools and quills, as well as in the process of doubling and twisting for fine work; that the spindles thus furnished with full spools might be stuck up in rows to facilitate "warping-in," precisely as spools are placed in frames for the same purpose by weavers amongst ourselves today; that the spindles with beads of different colors directly, or with wound quills, were used as permanent bobbins, by being thrust into the warp at different points so as to at once retain their places between definite sets of the warp-threads, by means of the beads and at the same time to show the pattern or portion of the pattern the threads they were wound with pertained to, also by means of the patterns incised or carved and painted on, the same beads.

I may add that during numerous experiments in feather and tapestry weaving with primitive appliances, I have found some such devices most convenient, not to say indispensible; and that, with the original specimens, as well as since my return I have tested the fitness of these little instruments for the uses above indicated with most extraordinary and satisfactory results. With these hints as guides I find it may be quite possible to restore perfectly knowledge of the manipulatory processes in weaving of the ancient Peruvians; and it is most interesting to thus find that their acknowledged supremacy in the weavers' art was due not less to skill and patience in working than to their marvelous ingenuity in making hand-machinery embracing prototypes of nearly all mechanical contrivances and appliances used in the textile industries of modern civilization.

To indicate the significance of these observations in another direction, it may be stated that it would be quite possible to restore all the patterns and color-designs which any set of spindles found might have been intended, merely by a study of the different patterns engraved and painted on the rolling-beads with which they were provided and a classification and distribution of these according to their relations (in design) to one another. If, then, these studies and experiments may be continued by me in the presence of such colleections as those made by Mr. Dorsey, or as are gathered, I understand, in the Metropolitan Museum of New York, I am confident that I might go nearly as far toward monographing the Peruvian textile industries as though the ancient Andeans themselves were living today, and might be observed in the actual practice of those industries.

3rd. To some extent the figure-designs on Bannerettes of the Dead and in the tapestry-pieces of the Dorsey collection were of interest in elucidating the status of religious belief of the ancient Peruvians.

Of greater importance still, however, was a series of beautifully carved and painted wooden vessels and other objects evidently used in connection with sacred rites, occurring in the Montez collection and constituting almost unique examples of the kind in early Incan or Chankan art. The figures on some of these were so highly conventionalized as to be almost unrecognizable as representations of even idealized animals or men; but careful examination revealed the fact that they, like the less developed bannerett-, and textile-designs were mythic pictures; and that they represented many of the personified deities of the ancient Andeans, especially the genii or Gods of the Elements and of the Phenomena of Nature. The point of special significance in these pictures is this: that whilst, as amongst the Pueblo Indians, the Elemental and Physical gods were in a way identified with particular animals, these animals in the Peruvian paintings are in turn represented only as the disguises (masks, costumes and paraphernalia) of the gods themselves—who are invariably shown either in human form wearing these dramatic paraphernalia of an older phase of belief, or else are represented clearly as men behind, or by the side of, these paraphernalia. Of course this is an indication that ancient Peruvians had almost passed the transition phase of belief between Zoötheism and Physitheism represented by the Zuñi and other advanced Pueblo Indians; had in fact begun their development as pure Physitheists, having gods almost purely anthropomorphic, and to some extent idealistic. As a solitary exemplification of this particular phase of religious development, the art of these sacerdotal carvings is of greater interest, perhaps, than any other in America. The symbolism is still so close to that of the largely Animistic or Zootheistic Pueblos that it may be almost at once interpreted by one familiar with the conceptions of the latter. On the other hand, it is really so advanced beyond the Pueblo phase, that it distinctly constitutes the link between prehistoric religion hitherto so little understood, and the historic religions of the Old World so well recorded, but even less understood heretofore, because of the lack of all such links.

I made, therefore, a few sketches of these figures, slightly illustrating the points above set forth, but have since found them so unsatisfactory—through lack of color—that I have requested Mr. Sawyer of the Geological Survey, whilst visiting the Exposition, late this month (September), to make additional sketches in color, with a view when possible to carrying this study as much further as sketches will enable me to carry it.[9] I may add that I have been the more interested in this particular series of observations, as it seemed of importance to the Director—with whom I conferred on the subject during his visit to the Exposition.

Games: Observations on the Belomantic, or Arrow-origin, of American Games. No collections in the Anthropological Department of the Exposition were so suggestive or fruitful of significant results to my studies as those relating to games and divination gathered and arranged with extraordinary scientific skill, care and patience, by Mr. Stewart Culin of the University of Pennsylvania.

Although there were comparatively few American Indian games exhibited, yet, there was a sufficient number of them to make it at once obvious to me that they were, as a rule, much more primaeval than those of Asia and other portions of the Old World (more abundantly shown in the collections). Further examination led me to believe also that these American games might be regarded as practically archetypes of certain classes of the oriental games. It was my privilege to contribute a small series of Zuñi games to Mr. Culin's Division, which helped to explain other games of a doubtful kind in his main series; and, becoming imbued with his enthusiasm, I began to make a more serious study of not only these but also of my own games, than I had ever before undertaken. The results obtained by Mr. Culin and myself, jointly, have seemed of sufficient importance to justify my turning aside for a time from other work, in order to prepare in connection with him a paper on the subject. As it has been decided by this office, much to our gratification, that the paper in question shall be published speedily in one of the Bulletins of the Bureau of Ethnology, it will only be necessary for me here to briefly summarise my chief discoveries.

1st. Close study of all stick-, cane-, reed-, and other kindred games in the Culin collections indicated that they were developments from, or in many cases, survivals of, Belomantic, or Arrow-casting operations of a divinatory nature; and (2), that as a consequence of this earliest use of arrows or of sticks (or blocks etc. representing them), in divining, all games derived from such use by natural step, were played with reference to the four quarters, and were thus invariably developed along identical lines as to rules, formulae, counts etc., leading up gradually to even such elaborate dice-, and diagram-games as the hitherto mysterious Patolli or backgammon-game of Mexico, or to the still more elaborated and little understood game of "Stone Warriors," or checkers, in Zuñi. Increasing the importance of these observations of mine on the combined divinatory and arrow origin of games in America, were [sic] Mr. Culin's further development of the idea (gained from these studies of the American games) in its application to the games of China, Corea, Japan, Tartary and other oriental countries; with the startling result that it was found that nearly all games had passed through a like phase of development in the Old World, and that there even more elaborate diagram-games might be accounted for as belonging to this same family—as descended, in other words, from the arrow as used in divining.

Observations relative to the Origin of the Fylfot or Swastica. Whilst studying the pictographic designs representing game diagrams, etc., of the ancient Mexicians, I was struck by the symbol which stood for the world and the four quarters; (according to which, as above stated, all arrow-games or diagram-games derived from them, were customarily played). This consisted of a circle enclosing a simple cross (fig. 1) or a circle enclosing a central [area], and four surrounding circles of different colors (fig. 2). [All Cushing's figures are omitted here.]

Opposite the four extremities in examples of the cross, (or in the four quarters made by it in other examples) were little circular dots each of a different color—leaving no question as to the significance of the enclosed cross as that of the four directions on the plane of this world. This latter was further shown by a slightly larger dot or circle, parti-colored, and placed in the center of the circle at the intersection of the cross, as synthesis of course (or the "all-in-one") of the four regions represented by the external dots. Among the Navajos, the world and the four directions as one, is represented in an identical manner; although no dots are used, but a double circle (fig. 3.) is sometimes drawn. This is especially the case when the figure is drawn as a sacred diagram, a very significant varient, in which case, as with the Havasupais—is not infrequently to be observed, where in the points at which the arms of the cross join the inner circle, the latter is broken off at one side of each of them (fig. 4).

Yet further, amongst the Pimas of Arizona, the symbol of the four winds is made simply by leaving off the outer circle of this diagram and employing merely the cross with the four curved arms, (that is, the broken inner circle). This figure is common throughout ancient America, from Ohio to the ruins of Yucatan and the Andes. In a few instances the cross with these curved arms becomes the true Swastica, as among some of the pictographs of the southwest; and the copper remains of the Ohio mounds; and my observations of varieties of these have led me in connection with the known meanings of the Mexican, Navajo, and Pima devices, to the conclusion that the right-angle Swastica so to call it, was primarily the representation of the circle of the four directions, winds, and regions. It became a right angle figure by the above development or like steps and by the attempt finally to represent the circle of the four wind gods standing at the heads of their "trails" or directions, but necessarily represented at right angles to these trails in order to distinguish them therefrom. In the light of this observation the open spaces in the inner circle of the Navajo, and the broken circle of the Pima diagram, became conceivable as the gateway of the winds, thus symbolizing not only the world and the four quarters, but also the winds of the four directions all in one figure. That the true Swastica of the Orient and the Gammadion of Europe and their many varients (which I have since made a study of), had practically the same genesis as these early American forms seems to admit of little doubt. The examination of the Zuñi gammadio-form arrangement of the four sacred ancient spaces or terraces of the gods (of the four directions, fig. 6) and of the ancient fylfot-arrow symbol, of the thunder bolt (of all directions, fig. 7), would seem to add so much evidence to this conception of the orginal symbolic intent of the Swastica that further research and the presentation of other details seems desirable. The peculiar form of this symbol of the world and the two or four directions or quarters in it, used in game divinations and the heraldry of China, Japan and Corea in which the arms of the enclosed cross are double curved (fig. 8) but another variety of the Swastica, of which variety I also observed beginnings in the Mexican pictographs representing the celebrated mantle of the five roses on which the sacred game of Patolli was customarily played (fig. 9a, b).

It is possible, however, that this curved or volute form of the swastica, as apart from the simpler region symbol, was developed both in Mexico and in the Orient, in connection with cane (arrow) games, a section of a cane or reed at one of its joints representing the highest or all-count (as well as all the four quarters of divination or their synthesis) whilst the cane, divided into four differently crossmarked slips stood, according to the varying falls of these slips, for one or another of the four quarters apart, the counts being arranged according to the quarters each slip was marked for, as in the symbol of the four directions and the world within them, seen on Chinese compasses and on the National flag of Corea.

Observation on the Mexican Calendar as Developed from a Calendaric Sequence of Ceremonials like that of Zuñi. It was my privilege to participate in the Proceedings of the International Congress of Anthropology held during the latter days of August and the early days of September, at the Columbian Exposition; and to hear, and join in the discussion of Mrs. Zelia Nuttall's remarkably ingenious and judicious paper on the Mexican Calendar system. From the fact that the numbers thirteen and twenty and their various permutations are constantly employed in the arrangement of "months" and "weeks," as well as longer periods and cycles, etc., in this calendar, it occurred to me that there was a vague attempt in it to record not only the solar year (as consisting of eighteen months of twenty days each with five intercalary days), but also to record a lunar (more strictly ceremonial) year, of twenty-eight semi-months, of thirteen days each, with one intercalary day in addition to the still more strictly sacred inter-year of nine months or 260 days suggestive of the Southwestern agricultural season. Thus the Mexican (and related calendars of Central America), being a combined secular and sacred arrangement of empiric (twenty-day) periods, and of lunar (thirteen-day) periods, it would seem that the empiric periods had resulted from vigesimal methods of counting, and symbolically naming days; the lunar period, from counting and numbering days in sets conformably to the visible semi-monthly phases of the moon as correlated (mythically) to the duo-septenary system of (the thirteen) terrestrial and celestial space and time relations conceived of by most of the advanced tribes of the Southwest and South, and conformed to by them in the ranking and ordering of their Cult Societies and the ceremonials thereof.

With this idea in mind it can be shown, I think, that the calendar in question is primarily the resultant of an attempt to name and fix, and finally to symbolically record, the times in the year and the days in the months or semi-months, for such ceremonials as, in an orderly sequence, corresponding to the march of the seasons (and of their phenomena as supposedly derived from the Element-gods of Wind and Winter, Water and Spring, Fire and Summer, Earth and Autumn, localized in the four World-quarters) as are performed by the Priest members (for example) of the thirteen graded or successionally ranked Cult Societies of Zuñi. For these Societies are classified according to the supposed specific relationship of each (totemically) to one or another of the (animistic) Gods or Genii of the four different quarters and their severally associated elements and seasons. Hence each must have its specific time for ceremonial observances in the time (season as well as quarter thereof) to which it pertains, and the phenomena of which its dramatic operations are supposed to magically influence.

The system of Cult Societies in Zuñi contains one general or central society presided over by the seven tribal and regional Priests of the six kivas or estufas. It relates equally to all the other twelve special societies (six pairs, in four groups of three, each group associated especially with one of the four quarters and seasons, etc.), all of which are related to the central one as, for instance, the twelve months are to the whole year. It follows that the All-society has its special time at the end of the old and beginning of the new year (the "Middle time" or period of the Winter solstice), and that the other societies (each according to its rank or succession), have their special times throughout the rest of the year. These times being determined according to the remarkable correlation of the world spaces and the seasons above refered to, and being conformed to the associated movements of the sun, moon and chief constellations have resulted, merely or mainly the outcome of mythical and ceremonial requirements, in a system of calendaric combinations well nigh mathematically exact and astronomically correct.

The light which the threefold divisions of the Zuñi agricultural year into seasons corresponding to Winter, Spring, and Summer and Autumn combined, and the Zuñi natal months and nine-day ceremonials in celebration thereof, and other mythic time divisions might throw upon yet other features of the Aztec calendar (not herein discussed for lack of space), became evident during conversations it was my good fortune to have with Mrs. Nuttall. She proposed therefore that I collaborate with her in a fuller writing up of this subject from Zuñi, as well as Aztec sources. In view of the fact that a demonstration of the natural and simple *ceremonial* (and withal unconcious) development of this celebrated Mexican Calendar would serve to account for its origin independently, here in America, without recourse to the theory of Humboldt, Tylor and others, that such a system must necessarily have been derived from analogous Calendaric systems found in Tibet, China and other Oriental countries, it is my earnest hope that I may thus be enabled to work, in conjunction with Mrs. Nuttall, and that with this purpose in view, I may be permitted by the office, to visit Zuñi, at an early date, for the purpose of securing additional data therefor.[10]

Notes

1. Born in New Albany, Indiana, George Brown Goode (1851–96) was an ichthyologist who graduated from Wesleyan College in 1870 and met Spencer Baird in 1872, becoming his principal assistant. He was put in charge of the Smithsonian exhibits at the 1876 Centennial Exposition in Philadelphia, from which the U.S. National Museum emerged. On Baird's death in 1887 Goode was placed in charge of the museum. He died at age forty-five of pneumonia and overwork (Otis Mason, in *American Anthropologist* 9, no. 10: 353–54). He was the author of *The Origins of the National Scientific and Educational Institutions of the United States* (1890), and *The Smithsonian Institution, 1846–1896* (published posthumously in 1897).

2. [Cushing footnote:] It may be remarked that this figure is the first, either thus shown or shown in illustrated works, which represents accurately the well nigh universal method of primitive spinning with the whorl-spindle, the notion of the distaff having hitherto erroneously influenced observers and artists in such representations.

3. [Cushing footnote:] While costumed as a *woman*, this figure really represents a man belonging to a peculiar class of *"women-men"* who, when they do woman's work such as weaving and cooking, herding, etc., are dressed, and are spoken of, as "women."

4. [Cushing footnote:] This loom is practically that of the ancient Aztecs; although the Aztec loom was used, (as sometimes the Zuñi looms are, for larger work), with supports or with the warp itself attached to convenient posts or rafters, in the house. It is interesting to remark that I found a similar loom in use amongst the Javanese women of the Midway Plaisance at the Columbian Exposition; although the latter have the waist-yoke (or "cloth-beam") supported across the back, instead of in front and by means of a band around the waist, and the yarn beam with them is held by a frame work on the ground, instead of by the upturned toes as with the Zuñi. In Finland, too, identical belt-looms are used; but the reed-held is there cut out of a solid piece of wood instead of being made from parallel slips of cane as in our Southwest. The Navajo girdle-loom exhibited in the same case—which is supported on a frame work made from the trunk and long crotch of a piñon tree—is interesting as being of the Pueblo lap-loom, supported—as it is—by the body, (trunk), and the outstretched legs, (crotch).

5. In modern terminology, Cushing appears here to recognize that the Zuni were a part of the "Eastern Anasazi" cultural region, in contrast to the "Western Anasazi" one from which the Hopi derive (see Hawley 1936).

6. Ironically, perhaps, the modern name for the polychrome pottery found in the cliff dwellings of the Tsegi Canyon in northern Arizona is Tusayan Polychrome (Colton and Hargrave 1937).

7. Cushing here refers to kiva mural art, which he discussed in greater detail in an 1894 *Washington Post* article (Document G).

8. For Cushing's general exposition of his theory of an Aridian culture and its Peruvian connections see Cushing 1890.

9. Wells Moses Sawyer (1863–1960) enjoyed a long life and remarkable career. He was born on a farm in Iowa to a merchant father. He studied art with John O. Anderson, 1882–85; at the Chicago Art Institute, 1885–86; at the Corcoran School of Art, 1891–92; and at the Washington Art Students League, 1893–97. He was an artist in the division of illustration, U.S. Geological Survey and Bureau of American Ethnology, 1891–97. He worked for Cushing in Florida as both a photographer and artist, 1895–97 (Gilliland 1989). He then was with the office of the secretary of the treasury in charge of design and inspection of furnishings in federal buildings, 1897–1906; and then with the Bank of New York (president of the City Bank Club, 1914–15). He retired in 1926 and lived in Spain and Mexico until World War II, staging thirty one-man shows of his art (*National Cyclopedia of American Biography* 48; *Who Was Who in America* 5:635; *New York Times*, April 22, 1960, p. 37, col. 2).

10. Alas, Cushing was never able to make that trip to Zuni.

DOCUMENT G

The Pueblos at Home

New Exhibits Being Arranged at the National Museum to Be the Finest in the World. Mr. Cushing, Who Has Spent Many Years among the Famous Indians, in Charge of the Arrangement of the Splendid Ethnological Collection Which Is Being Rapidly Arranged in a New and Attractive Form—Their Pastimes and Religions

The National Museum has started within the past week into a new field of scientific and artistic display. It is a change that emphasizes the difference between the methods of this institution and the other great museums of the world, and which promises to develop in time one of the most complete and beautiful ethnological exhibits of the world. It is the construction of one of the great halls of the museum building of a complete department giving the national history of the Pueblo, or Southwestern village Indians of America, as far back as such history can be constructed from tradition, ceremonials, and archaeological research. The results aimed at are not only scientific accuracy and completeness, but artistic perfection as well, and from the manner in which the work has been commenced it would seem that both are to be obtained.

The plan in brief is to collect in the large hall all the material pertaining to the history of the Pueblos and the allied tribes, and to arrange this mass of matter so as to give even to the casual visitor a comprehensive idea of the manners and customs of the aborigines, their trades, sports, religion, and past times [sic], as far as possible without recourse to tables and dry tabulated statistics. It is such a plan as has never been attempted, even at any of the great expositions of the world, the nearest approach being in the various tribal villages

Washington Post, September 4, 1894

of the Midway Plaisance, the only difference in the present instance being that the villagers will be perfect models instead of live subjects of doubtful nationality.

Arrangement of the Museum

In speaking of the new work Prof. Otis Mason, the chief of the Division of Anthropology, said: "The National Museum has been long criticized by the old conservative museums of the world for the way in which it arranges its specimens. In the British Museum, the Museum of Berlin, the Danish Museum, and the Trocadero in Paris, the whole building is divided into stalls and alcoves, and all the material of one people is piled in there. Everything Dutch goes into a room labeled Holland, and so on with all the nations from which they have specimens, no matter how much or how little they may have. If there is only a nose plug from the Andaman Islands, they put it in an alcove and label it 'Andaman Islanders costume,' and let it go at that.

"Now the National Museum, on the other hand, tries to make the best disposition of its material according to the amount it has. If there is enough for a national series it is put together, but if we have only, say, a knife from some interior African tribe, it is not labeled according to the tribe, but put with the knives of other nations for comparative study. Now in the Pueblos we have our richest collection of any people, one of the greatest ethnological collections, in fact, in the world and the time has come when we feel that we can put it together for display and study. We have nothing else approaching it in completeness except the collection of the Esquimaux, and this is deficient in material from the East Greenland tribes but this we expect soon to make up by exchange with the museum of Denmark and then we will have another national series ready to set up, but that is a thing of the future. The Pueblos we have just commenced to work on, and they will be ready for exhibition in about three months, though it will be a year before the collection is thoroughly arranged."

Cushing's Life with the Tribe

The arrangement of the new collection under the direct supervision of Mr. Frank Hamilton Cushing, who through the long years of residence among the Pueblos is better qualified than any other man living to take charge of such a task. The story of Cushing's life among the Pueblos is too familiar to need more than mentioning. He struck into the heart of the then mysterious and almost unknown Southwestern desert just before the region was invaded by the settler and the railroad. Living among the Indians as one of their tribe, he picked up the language, their customs, and was initiated into their religious systems as has been the lot of no other white man. He lived with the tribes six years in all, and then returned to give the outside world the history of one of the most remarkable and picturesque races that ever lived.

When *The Post* man found Mr. Cushing he was in a costume of almost aborigine picturesqueness, consisting of a shirt, trousers, and embroidered moccasins, with a big red bandana folded about his neck. Before him were saucers of black, white, red, and green earth paints, and a dozen long-handled brushes, with which he was outlining the models for a series of religious drawings to decorate the interior walls of one of the Pueblo temples.

A Wealth of Material

"It is too early," he said, "to give more than a general outline of what we want to do in arranging the new collection. We have a wealth of material at command and it will be used with a view both to the general artistic effect of the Pueblo hall and to displaying to advantage the different sections of the exhibit. In the first place, we have accurate models of many of the noted Pueblos of the country, surveyed and modeled exactly to scale by Victor and Cosmos Mind[e]leff, and other field workers of the Bureau of Ethnology. Then we have the large cases of figures and other material that were on exhibition at the World's Fair. To these will be added many new ones for which we have all the material now in hand.

"In one section of the hall, which is a large one, I want to arrange a Pueblo house, comparatively small, of course, but large enough to give a life-sized presentation of the family at their household employments, the man making moccasins or arrows, the wife cooking tortillas in the adobe fireplace, and the children playing about them. You see, we have one case already," pointing to one of the large glass cases recently returned from Chicago, "containing the stone handmill for grinding corn and the fireplace with the woman cooking. It is accurate, for it is the model of my own kitchen in the house where I lived. There are a few more touches to be put to it before it is ready to go in with the rest of the exhibit.

"Besides this we shall have the blanket weavers, the potters making and baking their earthen vessels, the children at their games, the girls (and some of the Indian girls are beautiful of their type) winnowing grain in their big yucca leaf baskets, and as many more of the types and occupations of the Pueblo as we have room for. Up on one side of the hall above the rest of the collection we shall arrange a cliff dweller's home as large and complete as there is room for, with the ladders and brush awnings and other accessories reconstructed as nearly as possible from the remains, which give abundant material from which to work. From these remains I should say that we can carry the tribal history back 700 years before the invasion of the Spaniards.

Their Religious Paintings

"Then in some of the window arches above the hall there will be arranged a series of mural paintings from the religious ceremonials of the tribes, which will add both to the artistic decoration of the hall and to the ethnological value of the collection. It happened very fortunately when I went in among the Indians to live that I was able to paint very well, that is, they thought so, and in this way it fell to my lot to do a good deal of decoration on the walls of their religious houses. These religious paintings are a matter of tradition with them, and are reproduced year after year with unvarying detail and religious exactness. To one entering their religious houses during any time except in the midst of a religious festival they would seem the most dreary and deserted places in the world, but just before the ceremonies the walls are decorated with the most brilliant and complicated paintings, such as I am working on here. These remain only during the progress of the ceremonies, which last nine days, one day for each month of the gestation of the human being. It is thought that the gods whom the paintings represent come personally and invest their images with life during the religious festivals, so that the paintings take a real and active part in the ceremony. When that is over all the work, complicated and gorgeous as it is, must be washed out and only replaced at the end of the next year.

"The materials used in the paintings are really unequaled for that variety of work. The smooth adobe walls make an excellent background, and the brushes of long bunch grasses with the smooth earth paints mixed with a wonderfully perfect sizing made of the juice of the yucca plant, all combine to make the religious paintings a work of art. Every line has a meaning for the participants, and they are never at a loss where to put a mark or a dash of color. They paint with a long sweeping back-handed stroke, using the back of the hand as a meal stick to guide and steady the brush.

How He Learned the Language

"During the progress of the work the old men all sit about chatting and instructing the youths in the proper drawing of the symbols, and in this way I learned more of their religious observances than they would ever think of telling a stranger. How did I learn the language? Just as a baby would learn it, by reaching after things and being told their names. In nine months I began to talk fairly well, but when the old men had once made up their minds that they wanted to take me into the tribe and teach me their language and customs, they never let up or gave me a minute's rest. More than a year after, when I had learned the language fairly well and would be in the midst of telling them something, perhaps about some wonder of the outside world, they would stop me in the midst of a sentence to correct some mistake of language.

"Their mythology, as it will be illustrated in these paintings, is one of the most picturesque in the world. It is curiously like and unlike that of the other older nations. It follows these in the dramatization of the processes of nature, but with a local color of its own. The winds, the seasons, and all the forces of nature are personified. These two figures on which I am now working in these bright flat tints, are the youth and the maiden who brought the green corn to the earth. Every detail of the costume is a matter of law and tradition, some of the symbols they do not know the reason for themselves. This latchet on the heel of the moccasin, for instance, they do not tell the meaning of, but it is a necessary part of the costume of the ancient figures. But we can easily guess that it is a relic of the time when they were cave dwellers and wore sandals and that was the broad thong running over the instep to protect them from thorns of the cactus.

Mythological Figures

"This curious figure that looks like a mere decoration on the edge of the skirt has a meaning of its own. It is the rain symbol. The upper band of blue is the sky, the place of the forming of the waters. Then comes the black, jagged rain cloud, stepped off into terraces, because that is the way the clouds are seen against the sharp, square steps of the mesa. Then come the straight, down-pouring lines of the rain in red and below the green of the grass springing up to meet it. That figure may be repeated hundreds of times by the artist in the course of his painting, but it will never be varied.

"Then in the hand of the youth who presents spring time you see the white flute, the symbol of the white mists in the valleys that he is called to dispel like the white breath of man on a cold frosty morning. On the flute in black you see the sign of the tadpole or pollywog, the symbol of spring, and the dragon fly, the symbol of summer. The brother of this youth is the fall of the year. He comes into the pueblo wearing a black mask with a crooked nose, signifying the waving of the corn fields under his touch, and he whistles and dances and curvets about like the dry leaves under the autumn wind, touching the corn with its red tipped wand and turning it brown like the breath of the frost.

"It is, indeed, the most picturesque mythology, and I look back on my life among the Pueblos as a thing that can never be repeated, and that I would not forego for all the misery that went with it, for it was life in a new atmosphere, the dawn of humanity."

The workmen have already been turned into the section of the museum that is to be the hall of the Pueblos, and are moving and arranging cases, cabinets, and models in preparation for the general rearrangement of what will be, when completed, one of the most perfect and curious ethnological exhibits in the world.

A Visual Interlude

Popular Images of Anthropology and Its Subjects at the Fair

CURTIS M. HINSLEY

The Chicago Fair produced a flood of printed materials that anticipated, accompanied, and memorialized this major cultural event of America's high Gilded Age. Historian Neil Harris noted that the Smithsonian Library's list of Chicago Fair publications numbers more than three hundred; and that the great majority of them appeared in 1893 and 1894.[1] In many of these works, images of anthropological subjects served as mere decoration, largely unrelated to accompanying texts; in others, though, "exotic" peoples of the Midway or the fairgrounds proper served as the purpose and focus. For the 27 million people who attended the Chicago Fair such imagery may have served as visual recall of powerful, immediate experiences; for those who only heard or read of the Fair from a distance, published images—photographs, paintings, engravings, newspaper line drawings, cartoons—raised suggestive questions about human global variety and relations. Here we pause to present a sampling of imagery from a variety of publications about the Fair.

World's Fair Puck (figs. 24–26). Founded by Joseph F. Keppler in St. Louis, *Puck* (1871–1918) was a weekly magazine of irreverent humor through cartoon, caricature, and editorial; the magazine moved to New York in 1877. In 1893 Keppler temporarily established editorial and printing operations on the grounds of the Chicago Fair, where his gingerbread-style printing office became itself a point of interest for visitors. The *World's Fair Puck,* a smaller-format, twelve-page version of the thirty-two-page parent publication, appeared weekly (twenty-six issues) for the Fair's duration and could be bought by visitors on the spot.

For most of his publishing career Keppler (who died shortly after the Fair) focused his political satire on the Catholic Church's political influence and political corruption. But in Chicago the spotlight of *Puck's* humor was ambivalently turned on three objects: the anthropological cacophony of the Midway; the befuddlement of midwestern "hayseeds" coming to the big city (a surprisingly common theme); and the ongoing rivalry between Chicago and the urbanites of the East Coast. Ambivalence about anthropological encounters arose from the dilemma that the presence of exotic peoples posed to American visitors: where the gaze of the onlooker can be immediately and directly returned, curiosity and distance must be balanced, lines and distinctions must be drawn (fences, barriers, cameras). The verbal and visual humor that emerged directly from this unprecedented experience was nervous and uncertain, curious but hesitant. Familiarity may yield contempt—or intimacy. The full-color *Puck* cartoons express in various ways these concerns about physical and psychological distance. The identity of the cartoonist is unknown.

Chicago Sunday Herald (figs. 27–31). The Chicago newspapers enthusiastically promoted and supported the Columbian Exposition from the beginning, and the celebration of American (and midwestern) business, technology and "industry" that dominated the Fair received wide and easy acclamation from a compliant press (see Essay 1). Anthropology, on the other hand, seemed a mysterious and vaguely suspect enterprise, and the uncertainty again yielded a specific type of humor. On September 17, 1893, the *Chicago Sunday Herald* ran a major piece on anthropology at the Fair, and Putnam's Anthropology Building in particular. The title gave away the tone: "Long Words the Rule: They Reveled in Anthropology." The anonymous author held his tongue firmly in cheek throughout an unsparing review:

> Be it known in the first place that the Anthropological Building is the most serious place on the face of the earth. The man who enters there leaves fun behind. The man who has studied its mysteries, like King Henry of the song, never smiles again. Before you study anthropology you must have learned all about history, physiology, geology, zoology, and all the other topics ending in y. Your hair must grow long and your tongue must caress with the familiarity of an old love words of fifteen

syllables. You must know at a glance the touching history of a piece of flint, and you must become enraptured with the tales expressed by a long buried image.

The line drawings (by "Denslow") that accompanied "Long Words the Rule" indirectly posed the central questions: What *is* anthropology, anyway? And what kind of strange "ducks" would pursue it? What can it tell us that commonsense will not? The language of text and drawing verged on the facetious, but with an underlying curiosity, perhaps even a benign tolerance. Thus, for instance, the Mesoamerican Chac Mool figure became a cramped commuter (fig. 28). The suggestion seemed to be that the "exotic" might contain after all a certain human familiarity—children, families, daily needs and responsibilities. Because it contained exhibits of history and natural history as well as anthropology and archaeology, Putnam's Anthropology Building seemed especially confusing to visitors. Still, despite the anti-intellectual stance, both author and artist seemed to suggest at least the possibility of some use for anthropological understanding.

Portrait Types of the Midway Plaisance (figs. 32–35). These began during the Fair as a series of pamphlets, for sale on the fairgrounds, of individual and small group studio photos of people considered sufficiently exotic—northern and southern Europeans, Native Americans, North Africans, Asians and Pacific Islanders—to be of interest to American fairgoers. The paperbound portrait pamphlets were then bound together in a published volume of 1894 with an introduction by Putnam—one of several post-Fair publications to which he contributed his prestige. There were several distinctive qualities to this genre of quasi-anthropological presentation. First, with few exceptions the studio photography is formal, drawing on a tradition of frontal, well-clothed portraiture that evinces respect for the sitter. Second, the clothing is intended as ethnographic information, not mere objects of curiosity, and some portraits (e.g., Monahan Levi and friends, fig. 35) display additional material culture that would have been seen on the Midway or elsewhere on the fairgrounds. Third, the subjects include not only people on display but foreign impresarios, sponsors, and handlers of the human exhibits, providing personal insights into the businessmen and investors behind the scenes (generally presented as astute international bankers and businessmen who knew the value of a dollar).

Importantly, the substantive, often informative texts that served as captions beneath the portraits (and accompanying our presentation of the photos here) were intended as an essential interpretive element, gently instructing the reader as to *how* to understand these human subjects and their worlds. The subjects, in short, were to be verbally and visually read. We do not know who wrote these descriptions (there is no evidence of Putnam's involvement beyond the introduction in this or other similar publications), but their distinctive tone is one of mediated distance; that is, the observer or reader is encouraged both to approach the subject figures in a spirit of commonality and tolerant openmindedness, and yet to maintain a distance that preserves the proper hierarchy of cultural superiority. Inclusion, sympathy, and understanding are not to be confused with equality. Frequently, too, there is an attempt to suggest "further reading" by reference to recent works on the subject peoples, their cultural geography, and recent explorations.

Vistas of the Fair: A Portfolio of Familiar Views (figs. 36–38). Published in Chicago in 1894, this compilation offered a series of watercolor renditions of scenes from the recent Fair—one of dozens of such commercial collections intended to capitalize on the desire to preserve memories of the fleeting Fair experience. The artist has remained anonymous. The volume appeared in at least two forms, the smaller of which included a preface by Moses P. Handy, chief of the Department of Publicity and Promotion at the Fair—thus loaning the publication a quasi-official status. Most of the views focused on buildings and promenades of the White City, but several of the imagined scenes added a striking feature: the artist introduced modern-day Mexicans in sombreros (and a Victorian woman with parasol) around the manicured lawns beneath Labná and Uxmal, linking ancient Maya with modernity; Africans strolled pleasantly on the Wooded Isle; a mix of races occupied the steps below the Statue of Industry in the Court of Honor. With such strokes the artist projected a cosmopolitan future of peaceful ease in which cross-cultural conversing and strolling enacted a new level of human exchange and understanding—under perennially blue skies.

Humors of the Fair (fig. 39). A fascinating group of contemporary journalists and observers went to Chicago to report on the Fair, from William Dean Howells to Kate Field to Julian Hawthorne, son of the famous novelist.[2] Hawthorne teamed up with popular Chicago artist Will Chapin to create *Humors of the Fair*, which leaned heavily on the stereotypes of the hayseed, the ingénue, and exotic Others thrown together in Fair-generated proximity. The cover of Hawthorne and Chapin's 1894 review sets a tone of lighthearted mockery (fig. 39).

Harper's Monthly (fig. 40). A magazine that expended a great deal of paper and ink, and the time of its star reporter Julian Ralph, on the Chicago Fair was *Harper's*. A double-page engraving (in itself an unusual feature) in the October, 1893, issue portrayed a young American couple strolling at night down the illuminated Midway toward the Ferris Wheel, faced and surrounded by a cosmopolitan crowd from every corner of the world, mixing with their American hosts. While we cannot see their faces, the young Americans must have realized that they were facing a diverse and dizzying global future.

Notes

1. Neil Harris, "Memory and the White City," in Harris et al., *Grand Illusions*, 14.
2. Not all were Americans. See, e.g., Madame Léon Grandin's *A Parisienne in Chicago*.

Fig. 24. "In the Cairo street," from *World's Fair Puck* (June 5, 1893).

FIG. 25. "A privileged race," from *World's Fair Puck* (October 23, 1893).

Fig. 26. "Travels on the Midway: A Trip to Egypt," from *World's Fair Puck* (1893).

A PRE-COLUMBIAN SHELL GAME FROM PERU.

FIG. 27. "A pre-Columbian shell game from Peru," from the *Sunday Chicago Herald* (September 17, 1893).

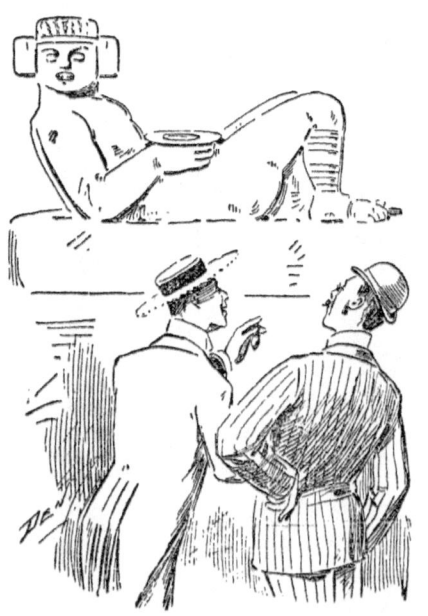

A VICTIM OF LONG AND CONTINUED RIDING IN SUBURBAN TRAINS.

FIG. 28. "A victim of long and continued riding in suburban trains" (a Mesoamerican sculpture of the god Chac Mool), from the *Sunday Chicago Herald* (September 17, 1893).

FIG. 29. The Anthropology Building, from the *Sunday Chicago Herald* (September 17, 1893).

FIG. 30. "I'm not crazy yet," from the *Sunday Chicago Herald* (September 17, 1893).

FIG. 31. "Great excitement—Indian lady throwing out dishwater," from the *Sunday Chicago Herald* (September 17, 1893).

Fig. 32. Mary Dookshoode Annanuck (Eskimo). "The Eskimo are the widest spread aboriginal people in the world, occupying the whole Arctic coast of America and a small portion of the Asiatic shore of Behring [sic] Strait, thus stretching a distance of three thousand two hundred miles. They are short in stature and their skin is of so light a brown that, when clean, red shows in the cheeks of children and young women. In summer they live in conical skin tents and in winter, at times in snow houses, but usually in half-underground huts built of stone, earth and bones, and entered on all-fours by a long tunnel-like passage. They live by hunting and fishing and are enormous eaters. In intelligence, they rank well among barbarous races, have considerable humor and are notable mimics. Their language is peculiar; they have an extensive folk-lore and some published literature. Full accounts of this curious people may be found in the narratives of Parry [sic], Kane, Hayes and other Arctic explorers. This woman, who is a vigorous type of the race, is the wife of Yoo-Ka-Lucke, just described. Brought up in Northern Labrador, until grown, she had never seen a green leaf or a blade of grass. She now lives in Southern Labrador where, during the short summer season, grass and budding trees are to be seen."—From *Portrait Types of the Midway Plaisance* (Anon. 1894d, unpaginated).

FIG. 33. Antonio (Apache Indian). "The Apaches of Arizona are, without question, the most intellectual of the American Indians. They are, at the same time, the most warlike and cunning of the aborigines; and ever since the days of the Spanish conquest, until very recently, they have maintained uninterrupted war against Spaniard, Mexican and American alike. This young man was captured when a child by the late General George Crook, and, with fifteen other children, was sent to Fortress Monroe. He was afterwards educated in Boston, learned the trade of a leather worker, and in 1892 was sent to the Southwest by Prof. Putnam, of Harvard University, to procure ethnological material for the Fair. He is a Chirachaua [sic] Apache by birth and a grandson of Chief Couchise [sic]. He speaks Spanish, Apache and English with equal ease. He was very successful in his mission. The best works on the Apaches are "On the Border with Crook" and "An Apache Campaign," by John G. Bourke, Captain Third Cavalry. Captain Bourke was the army officer in charge of the troops guarding the Columbian relics at the Convent of La Rabida on the lake shore [at the Chicago Fair]."—From *Portrait Types of the Midway Plaisance* (Anon. 1894d, unpaginated).

FIG. 34. William (Samoan). "This athletic specimen of manhood from Samoa declined to use his native name in Chicago and chose the cognomen of William during his stay at the Fair. His fantastic headgear and dress, ornamented with grasses and sea shells, give an idea of the finery in which these people delight. The Samoans belong to the brown Polynesian race and are akin to the New Zealand Maoris. They are, perhaps, the lightest in color of all the Pacific islanders. Their number is decreasing, and the population is now said to be about 35,000. The islands were visited by Bougainville in 1768, and from him they received the name of Iles des Navigateurs as a tribute to the skill of the native boatmen. The Christian religion was introduced in 1830, and the Samoans are now nearly all Christians. June 14th, 1889, representatives of Germany, Great Britain and the United States signed an act, at Berlin, under which the three powers recognized the independence of the Samoan government and the free right of the natives to elect their chief, or king, and choose their form of government according to their own laws and customs."—From *Portrait Types of the Midway Plaisance* (Anon. 1894d, unpaginated).

Fig. 35. Monahan Levi, Isaac Cohn, and H. Hondon (Turkish Jews). "The Turkish village, like many another village on the Midway which was primarily intended to depict certain national characteristics and peculiarities, contained within its walls a good many things which were by no means Turkish, and which are seldom if ever found in a genuine Turkish village but may be seen in Constantinople, which is one of the most cosmopolitan cities of the world. Here might be found at times Egyptians, Turks, Jews, Greeks, Syrians, Armenians and representatives of nearly all the nations bordering on the Mediterranean and of the countries east thereof. Mr. R. Levi, a Jew, was the holder of the concession for the Turkish village, and Mr. Monahan Levi, whose portrait appears above and whose first name has a somewhat Celtic twang to it, is his brother. Mr. Isaac Cohn and Mr. H. Hondon, the other figures in the picture, are also Jews and all were born in Constantinople and claim to be descendants of the Jews expelled from Spain by Isabella the Catholic. They were occupied at the Fair as salesmen in the Bazaars of the Turkish village, and are represented in the picture as smoking the Nahrgeela or water pipe and drinking Turkish coffee."—From *Portrait Types of the Midway Plaisance* (Anon. 1894d, unpaginated).

FIG. 36. Northward from center of Wooded Isle. From *Vistas of the Fair in Color: A Portfolio of Familiar Views* (Anon. n.d., unpaginated), © The Field Museum. #GN85651C.

FIG. 37. Totem poles and Kwakiutl Indians portrayed in their "village." From *Vistas of the Fair in Color: A Portfolio of Familiar Views* (Anon. n.d., unpaginated), © The Field Museum. #GN85650c.

FIG. 38. Statue of Industry, Court of Honor with men and women. From *Vistas of the Fair in Color: A Portfolio of Familiar Views* (Anon. n.d., unpaginated), © The Field Museum. #85649c.

FIG. 39. *Humors of the Fair* by Julian Hawthorne (1894). Illustration by Will Chapin. Courtesy of the Bancroft Library, University of California, Berkeley. PS 1847 H76 1893.

FIG. 40. The cosmopolitan future: Strolling on the illuminated Midway at night. Engraving, Thur de Thulestrup, *Harper's Monthly*, 1893. From author's collection.

ESSAY FOUR

Refracting Images

Anthropological Display at the Chicago World's Fair, 1893

IRA JACKNIS

> When you look down at the water tolerably near you, you can
> see into it, but the things going down into it appear to be bent,
> to change their direction just at the edge of the water.
> This property is called refraction.
>
> —Thomas Eakins, ca. 1887

With a display of ten canvases, Thomas Eakins was one of the most prominent American painters represented at the World's Columbian Exposition of 1893. Two years later, the Philadelphia-based artist created an important portrait of Frank Hamilton Cushing. He would go on to depict another anthropologist active at the Fair, Stewart Culin (1899); Culin's mentor, Daniel G. Brinton (1900); and several collectors and patrons of the local anthropology museum.[1]

Today Eakins is remembered as the great American realist. Like many painters and sculptors of his day, he was an avid maker of photographs, which he used as sources in the composition of his artwork. In many ways Eakins's efforts paralleled those of anthropologists and museum preparators attempting to represent Native cultures. Despite their stated goals of naturalism and realism, however, many of their images were refracted rather than directly reflected. In this, they resembled many of the paintings of the Exposition itself, which, according to art historian Margaretta Lovell, were more a commentary than a transcription, due to their "selection, omission, reiteration, framing, and point of view" (1996, 40).

As Eakins suggested in his drawing manual (Eakins 2005, 85), quoted in the epigraph, refraction is a bending or a change in content caused by a change in the supporting medium (air to water). Each time there is such a shift in location or medium, there is an opportunity for the content to change—yielding a play of alternate versions.

This essay seeks to explore the visual mode of the cultural representations at the World's Columbian Exposition.[2] Given the vast scope of such a topic, for this limited essay I have chosen to focus on forms of refraction—issues of re-presentation and multiple visual versions. Specifically, I examine models of two principal subjects: architectural structures (buildings, villages, and ruins) and costumed mannequins. Whether illustrated in photographs or plaster casts, these are museum-made surrogates and not the unique displays of living peoples and original objects that have been considered in preceding essays. In that sense, what are considered here are creations of the dominant Euroamerican society.

Almost by definition, while the Native-made objects are unique and can be only in one place at one time, the re-presentations are multiple and endlessly repeatable. This was because most of them—such as photographs and plaster casts—were created by a negative/positive process. This mode, so fundamental to the Victorian age, actually marks one important strand in the creation of our contemporary world: as the analog anticipation of a virtual world of digital surrogates.

In this essay I explore the Exposition's exhibits as models of and for cultural action, invoking Clifford Geertz's useful formulation (1973, 93). Where he used it to describe the relation of symbols to social action, here I mean it literally, in relation to the construction of an actual object. Models for this were events and objects leading up to the Fair in the summer of 1893, while models of this followed in its wake.

Historical and Cultural Contexts

The World's Columbian Exposition was the largest fair of the 1890s, a decade that may be regarded as marking the inception of American modernism (Trachtenberg 1982; Evans 2005). The Exposition coincided with the introduction of several critical modern recording media: half-tone reproduction of photographs, the phonograph, and film. At the same time, with the new decade came the official closing of the western North American frontier, followed by an ensuing romantic appreciation of the American Indian.

Like London's Crystal Palace Exposition of 1851, which George Stocking has characterized as "a precipice in time" (1987, 1), Chicago's exposition of 1893 was a temporal fulcrum: picking up earlier ideas and developments, pushing them to new levels, and then projecting them outward into the future. In many ways, too, the Fair marked the effective point of professionalization of American museum anthropology.[3] For the ideas and approaches introduced in Chicago became the dominant paradigm in museum anthropology until their collapse, around 1930, with the beginning of functionalism and the school of culture and personality.

The specific displays and buildings for anthropology must be juxtaposed to everything else at the Fair—the landscape, buildings, and goods on display. In fact, some of these items could also be touched, as they were for sale. Scholars of the period (Bronner 1989; Harris 1990) have long noted the resemblance of contemporary museum exhibits to the period's innovative styles of department store display. This was most apparent, of course, in the use of mannequins to present clothing (Munro 2014).

While the Chicago Exposition may have been modernist in many ways, one critical mode in which it was not was its focus on objects, materialism, and realism—all principal concerns of the nineteenth century (Brown 2003). Moreover, high Victorianism espoused a "culture of imitation." New technologies of mechanical reproduction generated multitudes of inevitably refracted versions. In fact, as Miles Orvell argues, "the climax of this aesthetic of replication" was "the whole of the Chicago Exposition of 1893" (1989, 34). As an exercise in visual culture (Schwartz and Przyblyski 2004), I attempt to reconstruct one component of the contemporary "period eye" (Baxandall 1972).

Disciplinary Contexts

The Chicago Fair arrived at a pregnant moment for American anthropology in general as well as for its institutionalization in museums in particular (Darnell 1998; Stocking 1985). The oldest dedicated anthropology museum in America, Harvard's Peabody Museum (founded in 1866), was represented, of course, by Frederic W. Putnam, who was supervising the Fair's separate anthropology department. Although the Smithsonian Institution had been founded in 1846, it did not come of age as a museum until 1881, with the establishment of the U.S. National Museum, shortly after the start of the Bureau of American Ethnology (BAE) in 1879. Following from the 1876 Philadelphia Centennial fair, and several subsequent expositions, the U.S. National Museum was able to arrange a major anthropology display at Chicago. It is perhaps no coincidence that Cambridge and Washington, as the two centers of the nation's anthropology, between them dominated and divided the presentation of the discipline at the Exposition—each with its own building and displays. Anthropology at the University of Pennsylvania, which had just started in 1889, was well represented but on a smaller scale—principally by assistant director Stewart Culin and Egyptologist Sara Yorke Stevenson.

Three other important anthropology museums around 1900 can be considered as outgrowths of the Fair. Anthropology at the new Field Columbian Museum (1894) was a direct result of the collections gathered for the Exposition. The American Museum of Natural History had no presence there, but its anthropology department would be revitalized in 1894 under the direction of Putnam and Boas, when things did not work out for them at Chicago. And the anthropology museum at the University of California was founded in 1901 by Phoebe A. Hearst, starting with contacts she made at the Fair as well as her first anthropological patronage (her 1895 purchase of the Cliff Dwellers collection for the Philadelphia museum). So in one way or another, the Fair was central to all the American anthropology museums of the 1890s.

The Exposition also came at a pivotal moment for the institutionalization of American anthropology: just before the discipline moved substantively into universities. Putnam had just started his formal graduate teaching at Harvard in 1890; Boas would not begin teaching at Columbia until 1896; and despite the 1886 appointment of Brinton at Pennsylvania, the effective start of instruction there would have to await the hiring of Frank Speck in 1911. In the absence or underdevelopment of academic anthropology, the display work at the Fair thus constituted a dominant mode of anthropological expression.

While it has been natural to regard American museums as a permanent medium and expositions as more ephemeral and performative (Conn 1998), there was in fact a tight back and forth relationship between the two (Rydell 2006). Most profoundly, they shared a fundamental reliance on the visual perception of exhibitions (Jacknis 1985; Jenkins 1994).[4] Before anthropology moved to the academy in the next century, displays like the Chicago Exposition were central to the discipline.

Expositionary Contexts

Like the larger exposition of which they were a part, the anthropological exhibits at Chicago had been anticipated by a succession of previous displays (Rydell 1984). The first important precursor for the 1893 presentation was the Philadelphia Centennial of 1876 in several respects: a prominent role for the Smithsonian, the vast quantities of important artifacts collected (including oversized houses, totem poles, and boats), and the use of what were then innovative visual techniques, such as architectural models, photo transparencies, and life groups. Absent only were living peoples (Giberti 2002). Thus the Chicago fair took media and modes that had appeared previously and presented them on a vastly larger and more influential scale.

Smithsonian anthropologists Otis T. Mason, William H. Holmes, and Frank H. Cushing—who had all worked at the Philadelphia Exposition—honed their presentational skills at a series of successive expositions, followed by installations back at the U.S. National Museum. For many Smithsonian anthropologists, however, a radical shift to another plane seems to have been the experience of living ethnic displays and life groups at the Paris exposition of 1889 (Mason 1890; Wilson 1891).

As they began to absorb the lessons of Paris, Smithsonian curators experimented in a trial run for Chicago with their display at the Madrid Columbian Historical Exposition of 1892. For instance, it was here that the government first displayed the recently published Powell language map (Fagin 1984, 252–53). Much of the display consisted of comparative ethnology, arranged by cultural domains such as warfare, weaving, and body ornamentation. Yet the Madrid Exposition also included regional contextual displays in the form of several groups of mannequins, later presented in Chicago.

Anthropological Professions and Experience

Before turning to a detailed analysis of the Fair's exhibits, we must consider the personal and professional backgrounds of the anthropologists who created them. As Hinsley and Wilcox suggest in their introduction to this volume, the production of the anthropological exhibits in Chicago represented a shift in professional generations. On the one hand, there were the "fathers," born in the 1830s and 1840s: John W. Powell (1834–1902), Otis T. Mason (1838–1908), Frederic W. Putnam (1839–1919), William H. Holmes (1846–1933), and Walter J. Hoffman (1846–99). All except Putnam represented the Smithsonian.

The actual implementation of the exhibits, and particularly the underlying fieldwork, was carried out by those born in following decades: George B. Goode (1851–96), Frank H. Cushing (1857–1900), Walter Hough (1859–1935), James A. Mooney (1861–1921), all of the Smithsonian, as well as Franz Boas (1858–1942) and Stewart Culin (1858–1929).[5] The men of this latter generation were roughly in their middle-aged adulthood in 1893. There are some elders here, but the most active crew, from Holmes through Mooney, were in their mid-thirties to early forties.

Furthermore, the personnel at Chicago represented a transition in anthropological culture theory. The older generation, such as Mason and Holmes, were resolute evolutionists. Cushing was somewhat intermediary, combining a comparative evolutionism with localized ethnography. Mooney and Boas represented a more progressive cultural relativism.

Extending an anthropological tradition of the nineteenth century, the Fair embodied an interplay between urban curators, such as Mason, and field agents or ethnographers, such as Cushing and Mooney. Some, such as Holmes and Boas, served as liaisons between the two kinds of practice.

The visual mode embodied in the exhibits was only one of several forms of professional labor. With the notable exception of Cushing, every one of the participating anthropologists had another occupation before turning to anthropology: Mooney as a journalist, Culin as a merchant, Mason as a school teacher, Boas as a physicist and geographer, Holmes as an artist. Cushing was so young when he began to work at the Smithsonian that museum work and ethnography were his first job, growing from his earlier avocation with crafts.

Of these, Holmes and Cushing were by far the great visualists. Most of the others did not have visual skills but came to make use of them in their professional work. Mason and Holmes probably had the most museum experience, but everybody would have been working with preparators. The multi-talented Cushing did his own manual labor, in addition to relying on his ethnographic knowledge. Mooney was perhaps the great surprise: a writer who came to focus on the visual mode in both his ethnography and professional activity. He developed an interest in artifact collecting and photography as ethnographic modes (Jacknis 1990) and in Native forms of visual expression, such as the Kiowa calendar and Plains "heraldic designs" on shields and tipi coverings (Mooney 2013).

Exhibit Labor and Authority

In order to understand how and why these exhibits came to be, it is necessary to understand them as the product of collaboration. Like other elaborate works of art, such as films or buildings, exhibits are created by patrons, administrators, curators, preparators, and field agents, each playing a distinctive role (Becker 1982). While there may be a director or leader, he or she does not do all the work alone.

There was little coordination between the two main anthropological venues—Putnam's Anthropology Building and the Smithsonian exhibits in the Government Building—although both featured the aboriginal peoples of the New World. Besides communicating with the higher Exposition authorities, Harvard's Putnam supervised the exhibitions illustrating the Peabody Museum's research, such as the Ohio mounds and the Yucatec Mayan ruins. His staff of almost one hundred assistants consisted of field agents—many of them Harvard students—and museum preparators (Dexter 1966c; Essay 1, this volume). Putnam, of course, was also responsible for the entire disciplinary display devoted to anthropology, but much of the labor in this larger effort was carried out, fairly independently, by his second-in-command, Boas. Unlike for Putnam, who already wore many hats, Boas's work on the Columbian Exposition was his only job after he left Clark University in June 1892.

In addition to his general work, Boas focused on his own interests of physical anthropology and Northwest Coast ethnology.

As in earlier expositions, the Smithsonian anthropology display in the Government Building combined the resources of the Bureau of American Ethnology, chiefly concerned with fieldwork, and the U.S. National Museum, long responsible for maintaining and studying the resultant artifact collections. This led to a complex interplay between Mason and Holmes (U.S. National Museum curators), on one hand, and Cushing and Mooney (Bureau of Ethnology ethnographers), on the other. In truth, Holmes bridged the two worlds, as he moved repeatedly in his career between the museum (1882–89, 1897–1902, 1909–20) and the bureau (1889–94, 1902–9).

Bureau director Powell delegated the initial supervision to Henry W. Henshaw, but when the latter became ill in 1892, this role was handed over to Holmes.[6] Given his proven abilities with museum display, Mason soon became the leading partner in the collaboration. It was he, for instance, who had the idea of trying to illustrate the regional distribution of Native American cultures as shown in the Powell linguistic map.[7] Mason spent three years in its preparation, mainly in label research and writing.

In addition to supervising several primarily archaeological life groups himself, Holmes was largely responsible for the groups based on existing collections.[8] In turn, he delegated much of the rest of the actual exhibit preparation to Cushing, who was in Chicago from late June to early September 1893, installing the displays (Document E, this volume). The team was also able to draw on new fieldwork by bureau researchers Mooney and Hoffman.

Despite the critical roles of Mason and Holmes, it can be argued that Cushing was the dominant figure on the Smithsonian team. He seems to have started with Mason's idea of life groups, taken from the Paris exposition, and applied it to the Powell linguistic map. Cushing was the supreme mediator, interacting with Holmes, a curator working for the bureau, and with the bureau's field agents, such as Mooney.

Refracting Venues for "Anthropological" Display

The Chicago Fair was a riot of refraction—almost everything existed in multiple versions. First, the discipline of anthropology was illustrated in two principal displays: the Anthropology Building and the Smithsonian displays in the Government Building (Boas 1893; Starr 1893).[9] According to Nancy Fagin, with little organizational effort at the Fair "the result was repetition and duplication" of the displays (1984, 249). She contrasts the Anthropology Building displays, the result of "open appeals," with the Smithsonian's "closed-collection approach" (1984, 250). Boas explained the contrast as the difference between the "exposition method" of competitive exhibits and the "museum method," "arranged with a view of giving a systematic series of exhibits covering a certain field" (Boas 1893, 607). As Boas's review (Document A, this volume) demonstrates, however, while Putnam's Department M (Ethnology) in the Anthropology Building was open to individually sponsored exhibits, it actually sponsored many of its own. In addition to Boas's own interests on the Northwest Coast and a physical anthropology survey, he noted the systematic presentation of four subjects of American archaeology: "the age of man in America; the cultures of the mound-builders; the archaeology of Central America; and the ancient cultures of Peru."

As indicated by the now well-known 1887 debate between Mason and Boas in the pages of *Science*, issues of cultural classification—comprehending the relations among race, language, and culture—were generated by a discussion of museum display and arrangement (Jacknis 1985, 77–80; cf. Stocking 1968). In the logic of metonymic juxtaposition, Mason advocated an evolutionary typology, while Boas called for a regional approach.[10] Just a few years later, however, when Mason came to arrange the Smithsonian's display, he employed a regional approach, at least partially:

> The plan was to set apart a definite space or alcove for each linguistic family or stock, to place in the center of each a group of lay figures of men and women or children, dressed in proper costume and engaged in typical occupations. About this group, in wall cases and screens, would be assembled as many examples of the handiwork of that people as possible. Especial attention was given to selecting such arts as were quite characteristic and distinctive in each case. (Mason 1895, 129)[11]

In addition to this regional ethnography, the Smithsonian presented "a sample exhibit of the arts of the principal tribes, arranged to show

FIG. 41. Smithsonian Institution display, U.S. Government Building, World's Columbian Exposition, Chicago, 1893: (*left to right*) life groups of a Hupa family, Apache couple, and Navajo weavers. Smithsonian Institution Archives. Image MNH-12273.

their evolution and geographic distribution" (the customary evolutionary series of technology, with raw materials, tools, and processes), and a series of casts and models illustrating the archaeological work of Holmes in the eastern quarries and of the BAE in the Southwest. Everything was to be meticulously labeled, with striking, oversized objects placed above the wall cases.[12]

In contrast to the tightly organized Smithsonian display, Putnam's Anthropology Building included 314 relevant exhibits from foreign countries, state boards, private individuals, and collections gathered by Putnam's own department (Handy 1893). According to the official history:

> The exhibits from foreign countries were arranged in booths or courts, inclosed by partitions or railings and having ornamental entrances. The state, society, individual, and department exhibits were geograph-

FIG. 42. Anthropology Building general view, World's Columbian Exposition, Chicago, 1893. American Museum of Natural History Library. Image #337268.

ically grouped and arranged into table and upright museum cases. The ethnological material was arranged by tribes, and the archaeological exhibits were placed by localities, except in three or four instances where a large mixed collection was owned by an exhibitor who objected to having it separated. The natural-history exhibits were arranged in appropriate glass cases, with backgrounds and surrounds representing natural scenery. (Johnson 1897–98, 3:343)

The apparent disorder of the final display was due partly to the lack of dedicated funding. Unlike the Smithsonian's multi-year budget, Putnam was forced to rely upon open donations of collections, leaving him vulnerable to exigencies arising (Essay 1, this volume). Also beyond his control were the interminable delays in the completion of his facilities (the building did not fully open to the public until July 4), which sabotaged his ability to construct a clear and coherent display. This is the reason that so many of the items—baskets, pots, and nets—were hanging from the ceiling or scattered around the tops of glass cases. As the Fair was a temporary exhibition, there was little time to correct any faults. For a permanent display, the objects would have been in cases, if only for security. Haste also explains the relative lack of labels.

One must note, however, that while Putnam's Department of Ethnology was beset by innumerable practical problems, the Smithsonian exhibit also was not all that its creators had hoped to achieve. As Mason noted, "It is much to be regretted that the contracted space allowed in the Government building at Chicago prevented the curator from giving to the idea its fullest expansion" (1895, 129).

There were also related anthropological materials in many of the pavilions of states and territories (e.g., Colorado and New Mexico) and foreign nations (e.g., Canada and Mexico). Then there were other related nonprofessional presentations of ethnic cultures. Some of the exhibits were typological, such as footwear in the Shoe and Leather Building; boats, carts, and other vehicles in the Transportation Building; or a separate display of musical instruments in the U.S. National Museum (Culin 1894, 58). The Fisheries Building included Native American items, arranged by Goode, and Mason curated a comprehensive display of tribal artifacts in the Women's Building (Trump 1998).

Like almost all the Exposition subjects, Native American cultures were spread repeatedly throughout the grounds. As one Chicago reporter remarked, "He [the American Indian] is everywhere" (in Dillon 2008, 102). Several authors (e.g., Fogelson 1991; Dillon 2008) have noted the multiple presentations of Indians at the Fair: as anthropology, assimilated Americans, art and decoration, advertising, entertainment, and as commodities. In addition to the American Southwest, several displays from other key regions of fieldwork were devoted to Mesoamerican antiquities and Northwest Coast ethnology. As Snead points out for the southwestern antiquities (2001, 23, and Essay 5, this volume), because each exhibitor had a differing motive, each presented the material differently. In the Anthropology Building the displays were pitched as an example of a nascent science. In the Government Building, on the other hand, the collections were presented more as American national patrimony. States and territories featured Native artifacts along with their natural resources, while commercial operators displayed objects for entertainment and, ultimately, profit. At first glance this multiplicity seems confusing and redundant, but in fact such refraction may be regarded as a more truthful image of the world.

All four of the now traditional subdisciplines of American anthropology were represented. And although it was not quite considered anthropology at the time, even the applied form of the discipline was present in the model school run by the federal Bureau of Indian Affairs.

Most of the anthropological displays were, in fact, ethnological. Anthropologists were engaged in a form of "domestication," redefining the meanings of Native objects as tokens of a comparative science. Though somewhat smaller in square footage, the archaeology displays were particularly impressive, among them Holmes's series on aboriginal American stone working, models and artifacts from the American Southwest, and the major display from the Maya. Language was presented mainly through the Powellian map.

Due to Boas's interests, physical anthropology received prime illustration at Chicago. Physical anthropology occupied one of three laboratories in the Anthropology Building, along with those for neurology and psychology. Here the visitor could see scientific instruments; skeletons, skulls, and racial models; and charts, diagrams, maps, and photographs illustrating the growth of school children and the physical characteristics of Native Americans (Johnson 1898, 329). One could get measured and have one's sight, perception, and touch tested.

The visual organization of anthropology at the Exposition reflected the diverse tensions in the discipline at large. On the one hand, it was a major accomplishment for Putnam to secure a dedicated building for anthropology. At the same time, though, the field was not his alone. With Boston in competition with Washington as a center for the discipline in America (Stocking 1976, 9–10), each produced its own display. During this time Putnam was attempting to reach out to a national stage, as witnessed by his plans for the Field Museum and then the American Museum of Natural History, while never giving up his base at Harvard. His protégé Boas would succeed and largely supersede him as a disciplinary entrepreneur.

Refracting Visual Modes

At the Fair not only were there multiple presentations of a given subject, but almost every subject was illustrated with multiple media and experienced through alternate sensory modes, and most displays combined these media simultaneously.

One of the principal reasons for multiple versions was the prominent place given at the Fair to positives made from negative impressions. We are most familiar with this mode in photography, but the same process was involved in plaster casting. By definition, all plaster casts are an obverse image of the item being recorded, even if there is the additional stage of working from a paper cast. While both photography and plaster casting were indexical methods, involving some direct contact between the "original" and the representation, by the time that the print or cast positive was presented to the public, there had been plenty of opportunity for the image to become shifted and refracted.

Plaster casts could be used for recording and reproducing both buildings and bodies. The medium grew out of the desire to preserve sculpture and other decorative architectural fragments, especially those that were fixed *in situ* or were otherwise too heavy to transport. Invented in antiquity, plaster casting was revived during the Renaissance to reproduce classical marble sculpture. During the nineteenth century there was a strong popular movement to reproduce works of art in order to improve tastes in arts and manufactures.[13] By the 1860s commercial firms had arisen to supply the need, primarily for art schools and museums.

In most cases, plaster casts of monuments were made from initial paper casts, further lengthening the chain of refractions. First popularized in the 1830s, these so-called paper "squeezes" could be used to document and preserve monuments that were too large or ruined to move. Layers of moistened paper, with a sticky sizing, were applied to the stone surface and beaten down with a brush. The *papier-mâché* cast was then removed and dried (Maudslay 1893). They were especially suitable for capturing the shallow relief of inscriptions. Paper and plaster casting thus joined photography in what Baker (2010) has called a "reproductive continuum," as complementary modes of reproduction in the nineteenth-century museum.

The same positive/negative method was employed for life casts for human mannequins. The Smithsonian featured a display of more than eighty plaster mannequins. While there were no life groups in the Anthropology Building, several isolated mannequins were displayed (from the Peruvian and Bolivian research of George A. Dorsey and

William E. Safford) as well as casts of Greek statuary and sculpture from the Greek government. Zelia Nuttall's Mexican collections were substantially reproductions (Johnson 1898, 324; Starr 1893, 611–12).[14]

Photography was featured even more prominently at the Exposition. There were walls and walls of photos, both in the Anthropology Building and Smithsonian displays (Brown 1994, 40–46, 49–52). In fact, for many of the prominent exhibits—such as the Ohio mounds, the Mayan ruins, or artifacts from the Zuni—the visitor could turn from photographs to three-dimensional models or the real thing. As at the 1876 Philadelphia Centennial, the Smithsonian featured enlarged transparencies. Of the forty-plus images, at least twenty-five were by John K. Hillers, and another six were enlargements of Mooney's shots of the recent Ghost Dance (Fowler 1989, 156).[15] Systematic series of anthropometric views covered the walls in the Physical Anthropology Laboratory (Banta and Hinsley 1986; Edwards 1990).

In an era obsessed with classification and struggling to form a geographical understanding of Native American cultures, the prominence given to maps at the Fair was not surprising. The largest and most important was the Smithsonian's 16 x 12-foot enlargement of the Powell map of North American Indian languages, published in 1891 and first shown at the Madrid Exposition the following year. On its most basic level, a map is a form of visual imagery, but as Regna Darnell has maintained, it was both a central mode of theoretical knowledge and a professional practice in American anthropology (1998, 45–67).

George Brown Goode, director of the National Museum, was famous for his dictum that "an efficient educational museum may be described as a collection of instructive labels, each illustrated by a well-selected specimen" (1888, 306). Yet in an interview about the Exposition, he explained his visual conception of labels: "The label must be a picture. It should not even be restricted to letter printing. If clearness to the understanding is obtained thereby the words ought to be accompanied by actual pictorial representation. For example, if miniature works of the mound builders are shown a map should be hung up alongside with a spot on it in color designating the locality where these works are found."[16] The ultimate aim, he concluded, was "not to disseminate curiosities but to diffuse knowledge."

Buildings

The World's Columbian Exposition is famous in American architectural history for its popularization of the official Beaux-Arts style of the major pavilions, the so-called White City, under the design supervision of Daniel Burnham. But it also featured a diverse lot of traditional and vernacular architectural styles. Perhaps the most notable was the Japanese pavilion, which influenced American architects Charles and Henry Greene and Frank Lloyd Wright. Even more spectacular were the myriad of architectural settings for the ethnic groups living on the Midway Plaisance, almost all of whom were displayed in some kind of structure.

Architecture is a particularly rich source of refracting images at the Fair, since there were so many overlapping versions of Native structures. During the nineteenth century Native American architecture was a subject of avid study by both ethnographers and archaeologists. One clear impetus was the last work of anthropologist Lewis Henry Morgan: *Houses and House-Life of the American Aborigines* (1881). Despite the cultural importance of architecture, it was an obvious challenge to collect such large artifacts. In addition to occasional complete structures, especially for more portable forms such as Plains tipis, and fragments such as house posts, Smithsonian curators advocated the commissioning and collecting of house models (Mason 1875; Holmes and Mason 1902).

The miniature, in all forms, holds a particular fascination for people (Stewart 1984; Mack 2007). In its reduced size one can grasp and understand objects that may otherwise puzzle and overwhelm us.[17] Miniature models of Native architecture seem to have been introduced to the American public at the Philadelphia Centennial Exposition, with the versions of Mesa Verde executed by William H. Holmes and William Henry Jackson (Fernlund 2000, 59–61). It was a special challenge to present ancient life, which, though enduring, often existed as ruins or fragments.

On view at the Fair were a surprising number of more or less full-size actual buildings. Located near the Anthropology Building were the structures of the department's Out-of-Doors section, almost all Native American: skin tents of Labrador and Greenland Eskimo (Inuit),

Kwakiutl (Kwakwa̲ka'wakw) and Haida plank houses from the Northwest Coast, Plains skin tipis, a Winnebago mat house, an Iroquois longhouse, a Penobscot bark wigwam, even a pioneer cabin. Just outside the official fair grounds were tipis for Buffalo Bill's Wild West show. In addition to the real thing, there were several large-scale simulations and architectural allusions. Because of the problem of snow blocks melting in the hot summer sun, Eskimo igloos made an obvious candidate for simulation. But almost all the Midway structures (e.g., the Street in Cairo, the Dahomey Village) were reproductions of some sort.

From British Columbia came two actual Northwest Coast houses (Jacknis 1991a). For the first time in a public display, these were erected in a kind of simulated coastal setting, at the edge of the South Pond, fronted by several totem poles and canoes from diverse tribes. This became the paradigm for all subsequent totem pole parks, despite its somewhat jumbled provenience. From the Kwakiutl of northern Vancouver Island, Boas's assistant George Hunt brought an impressively painted house, measuring 45 feet square. From the Haida, trader and Indian agent James Deans collected an example from the village of Skidegate, Haida Gwaii (Queen Charlotte Islands). Named "House of the Stormy Sea," it measured 29 by 28 feet and was fronted with a forty-foot pole.[18] In fact, House of the Stormy Sea was doubly present in Chicago, for it was included as part of a model of the entire village of Skidegate.

In March 1892 Deans commissioned a team of at least seventeen carvers to produce miniature models of the village as it would have appeared in 1864 (Johnson 1898, 344–55; cf. Wright 2001, 2009, 2014). Among the team were some of the tribe's leading artists, including John Robson and John Cross. This display—twenty-seven houses, two grave houses, all but three with frontal poles; and seventeen freestanding poles—has been called unique, as "no other aboriginal village in Canada or the United States was systematically documented by its own nineteenth century residents."[19]

Miniatures, in wood as well as argillite slate, had long been a medium of Haida art. By the late 1860s they were being produced for sale to visiting whites. Paradoxically, although Native made, house and pole

Refracting Images

models were not an aboriginal object-type but were made only for export. Furthermore, in most cases, the miniatures were somewhat creative: "We know that models of poles made by Haida artists often were not exact 'copies,' but differed from the originals in their proportions and arrangements of figures while remaining true to the identity or essence of the pole" (Wright 2001, 147). We find this to be the case for many of the Chicago models.

One of the more prominent examples was the house of Captain Gold. In reality, this structure was not even part of Skidegate but sat on a beach west of the village (Wright 2009, 71). Despite the fact that the model's carver and the painter of the original frontal design were the same—Zacherias Nicholas—a photographic comparison (figs. 43–45) indicates that the model's façade has been much simplified from the original: especially noticeable in the central eye and mouth designs as well as the omission of all end designs. Another example was John Robson's 1893 model of a house frontal pole that he had originally carved, ca. 1878–84. "Like other models, this one displays Robson's freedom not to copy the original pole exactly" (Wright 2001, 260, cf. 253).[20] An expression of a distinctive Northwest Coast tradition of refraction, such free variations were actually considered to be "the same" in Native culture, as long as the artist or his patron possessed the inherited rights to a particular crest (Jacknis 2002b, 151–57).

Given the nature of their materials, it is understandable that there were no actual buildings from the pueblo Southwest (though the visiting Navajo delegation occupied a hogan along South Pond). Yet as a key field of anthropological interest, the region's architecture was well represented by other media (Trennert 1987a; Essay 5, this volume). Surely, the most spectacular display was that of the so-called Cliffdwellers. Modeled on Battle Rock mountain in southwestern Colorado, it was constructed by the H. Jay Smith Exploring Company as a commercial operation. Its proximity to the facsimile Mayan ruins—also just outside the Anthropology Building—forced visitors to make the connection between imputed stages of cultural development. Despite its location, in general display approach the Cliffdweller Exhibit more resembled the full-scale realism of the Midway exhibits than those of the Anthropology Building or the Smithsonian. In fact, this elaborate exhibit combined multiple display modes.

FIG. 43. Miniature model of the Haida village of Skidegate, Queen Charlotte Islands (Haida Gwaii), British Columbia, Anthropology Building, World's Columbian Exposition, Chicago, 1893. Photograph by Charles D. Arnold. Courtesy of the Peabody Museum of Archaeology and Ethnology, Harvard University. 93-1-10/100266.1.39, digital file #99010058.

From a distance, the massive five-story structure looked like a large mountainside, realistic though completely fake: "It had the appearance of rock and earth, though built of timbers, iron, staff [a casting compound], stone and boards, and paint was used to simulate nature" (Ives 1893, n.p.). All this, noted the official history, was based on careful research: "Surveys, plans, and pictures of several cañons of Colorado and Utah were made by this company in preparing for this exhibit" (Johnson 1898, 335). Yet one wonders at the necessary compromises that appear to have been made in the interests of visitor appeal.

The interior imitated caves and canyon walls: "Several rooms, *estufas*, granaries, and other portions of the cliff houses were reproduced in exact size, showing the material used and the method of construction." Within many of these stony rooms, a visitor could view miniature models of the very kind of structure one was inside: "The first

Refracting Images 279

FIG. 44. Model of Captain Gold's house, First Beach, Queen Charlotte Islands (Haida Gwaii), British Columbia; paintings on both the original house and the model have been attributed to Zacherias Nicholas (Haida), ca. 1892. Field Museum #17819. Photograph by Bill Holm. © The Field Museum. Catalog no. 1893.21.17819.

room represented Mancos Cañon. In the recesses of the sides of the cañon were accurate reproductions, on a scale of one tenth, of several groups of the most noted cliff houses of the cañon. In an artificial underground cave panoramic paintings were arranged to show the cañons and many of the cliff houses and pueblo ruins, with a system of lighting so skillful as to procure the effect of reality" (Johnson 1898, 335).

The imaginative visual effects were innovative: artificial lighting and "mirrors to make the number of niches seem larger" (Flinn 1893b, 43). Along with the contextual simulation was a museum, containing diverse collections assembled by C. D. Hazzard from the Wetherills and others. Here, in displays arranged with the help of Frank Cush-

FIG. 45. Captain Gold's house, First Beach, Queen Charlotte Islands (Haida Gwaii), British Columbia, with painted design attributed to Zacherias Nicholas (Haida). Photograph by Richard Maynard, 1884. Courtesy of Royal BC Museum, BC Archives. Image PN 9059 (AA-00194).

ing, were "many mummified bodies found near the cliff houses, and the large collection of textile fabrics, feather-cloth, skin garments, ornaments, implements, and pottery of the ancient people" (Johnson 1898, 335; Trennert 1987a, 137–38).

On a miniature scale the Smithsonian presented a number of southwestern models: some ancient ruins in the Government Building and the modern pueblos of Taos, Acoma, and Hopi in Anthropology (Fowler 2000, 210). These were largely the work of architects and modelers Victor and Cosmos Mindeleff. Due to Morgan's influence on Powell, in 1881 the BAE had hired the Mindeleff brothers to record Native architecture in the Southwest: in books, photographs, maps, and plans as well as plaster models for display in expositions and museums (Nabokov 1989).

Between 1881 and 1889 the Mindeleffs spent every field season in

Fig. 46. Cosmos and Victor Mindeleff working on models of Peñasco Blanco Pueblo Indian village, U.S. National Museum, Smithsonian Institution, 1885. Smithsonian Institution Archives. Image MNH-6084.

the region. Victor did most of the research, while his younger brother focused on the model construction back at the museum. In preparing their models the brothers produced meticulous records: measurements, field sketches, and photographs (mostly by John Hillers). Using surveying instruments, compasses, and tape measures, they recorded with colors on graph paper and supplemented these with textual notes on architectural features. They also surveyed the local topography in order to set the buildings into their physical surroundings.

In 1883 the brothers began to produce models of prehistoric sites: Canyon de Chelly and the nearby site of Wide Ruins. Archaeological models such as these could be of two types. In Christopher Evans's typology of British archaeological models (2004), they were the "antiquarian" (depicting architectural monuments, a form begun in the late eighteenth century) or the "reconstructive" (offering imaginative recreations of ancient life, a genre created by museums for public display, largely in the twentieth century). Unlike these reconstructions, ethnographic structures could be directly observed; thus their models had the possibility of being a more direct reflection. In their miniature Zuni pueblo (reproduced at one-sixtieth scale, mounted on a wooden board of 11 by 20 feet), the Mindeleffs painted a scene, with miniature sheep corrals, gardens, and the Catholic Church (Nabokov 1989, xvi–xvii).

Clearly, these miniatures could not be direct impressions, unlike other plaster casts displayed at the Fair, such as human busts or casts of the Mayan ruins. Instead, like free-form sculptures, they were originally modeled in clay, guided by a working plan or design, and then cast by means of a paper negative and a plaster positive. As Nabokov explains the process: "First they were molded in clay after the field measurements, then tissue paper and glue produced a papier-mâché cast. Finally emerged the plaster miniature, which was painted, detailed, and carefully mounted for safe transport" (1989, xx).

The models then became embedded in a vast refractory process. Many of the models sent to Chicago were duplicates of originals prepared for the National Museum.[21] Both old and new displays traveled extensively, carted from exposition to exposition and back and forth to the National Museum. The inevitable damage they suffered led to repairs and replacements: "Cosmos was constantly turning out duplicates as old models became chipped or mishandled and upcoming exhibitions demanded fresh material" (Nabokov 1989, xx). So worried was he about their condition that Cosmos recommended hiring a curator of models. He was right to be concerned, since the models suffered much damage over the years; today almost none of them have survived (Longacre 1999, 364).

Perhaps the most impressive architectural miniatures in the Anthropology Building were those devoted to the Ohio mounds. One came from the Ohio State Archaeological and Historical Society, supervised by Dr. Charles L. Metz (Turner Group, Fort Hill, and the Hopewell Group), while the other was prepared by the Peabody Museum, directed by Putnam (Serpent Mound). In fact, however, both illustrated Harvard research, whether Putnam's own work, that of his Ohio collabo-

FIG. 47. Model of Serpent Mound, Ohio, made by Charles Willoughby, Peabody Museum, Harvard University; World's Columbian Exposition, Chicago, 1893. At the left rear, model of "Tegua Pueblo" (First Mesa, Hopi) by William Henry Jackson, Bureau of American Ethnology. Courtesy of the Peabody Museum of Archaeology and Ethnology, Harvard University. 93-1-10/100266.1.3, digital file #99010021.

rators such as Metz and Warren K. Moorehead, or that of his Harvard students such as Marshall Saville (Dexter 1965b; Burns 2008).

The Ohio displays were quite complex representationally, including photographs, drawings, and raised maps (about 6 x 8 feet) as well as plaster or papier-mâché models (Johnson 1898, 326, 328). While some of the miniatures were made expressly for the Exposition, we do know that the Serpent Mound model was a papier-mâché copy of an original at the Peabody Museum (Johnson 1898, 326). According to one contemporary news account: "One look at these beautiful maps shows that no pictures have ever done this subject justice."[22]

These Peabody models were the first devoted to the subject of the Ohio mounds. Yet they were the culmination of decades of archaeo-

FIG. 48. Serpent Mound, Ohio. "Showing three full folds of the Serpent from the neck to the central portion of the body." Photograph by John Cone Kimball, 1887. Courtesy of the Peabody Museum of Archaeology and Ethnology, Harvard University. 2004.29.2256, digital file #160290014.

logical research, effectively initiated in 1848 by the study of Ephraim Squier and Edwin Davis. Like other archaeological sites of the nineteenth century, the mounds were first represented in textual and graphic modes (printed engravings and then photos). Although the State Archaeological Association of Ohio had sent a large and popular display of mound builder objects to the 1876 Centennial, there were no models of the sites themselves (Barnhart 1998, 132–34), only facsimiles of petroglyphs, as well as charts and maps. And just as the Smithsonian had used the Madrid fair as a trial run for its Chicago displays, Putnam had an 1892 preview: he displayed a model of Serpent Mound at the annual meetings of the American Association for the Advancement of Science, held in Rochester in August of that year (Dexter 1965b, 113).

As earthworks—giant human constructions on the land—the mounds could not be directly collected or easily represented at full size. In this they resembled buildings such as Pueblo villages, Anasazi cliff dwellings, or Mayan ruins. Yet while Mayan stelae or objects uncovered from inside the mounds could be collected, the only way to record and represent larger structures were in measured drawings, photographs, and miniature models. Necessarily all these surrogates were interpretations, varying from observer to observer.

The model of the Great Serpent Mound was a particularly fine example of refraction, beginning with the very acts of perception and definition. At a height ranging from two to six feet and a length of 1,348 feet, Serpent Mound could not readily be perceived at the site itself, or at least not viewed in a single glance.[23] As Charles C. Willoughby's later article on the mound makes clear (1919), it was not a straightforward matter to know what this object was, and many of his predecessors had had different views of it (Glotzhober and Lepper 1994).

Furthermore, as Willoughby acknowledged, restoration had soon changed its appearance. "Putnam had reconstructed the site owing to its rapid deterioration. The site was more intact in 1846 when Squier and Davis made their plan than when Willoughby [in 1918] made what is doubtless a more accurate survey" (Barnhart 2005, 211). The Peabody Museum purchased the site in 1886, which allowed it to transform the grounds from a working farm to an archaeological site (excavated over the next three years) and then to a public display, donated to the State of Ohio in 1900.[24] Not only did Putnam clear away the corn field and other heavy vegetation that surrounded the site when he first saw it, but he built up eroded sections to conform to what he believed the original looked like. The miniature model displayed in Chicago depicted the manipulated "Peabody version" of the mound, with both positive and negative refractions.

There was yet another archaeological model presented by the Peabody Museum, but not in the Anthropology Building, where it would have served to illustrate Native culture. Rather, Harvard University presented it in the Liberal Arts Building, along with other exhibits of schools and colleges. In a sophisticated and reflexive display, the miniature depicted the process of excavating the shellmounds of Maine (Willoughby 1898; Browman 2002b, frontispiece, 249). It was constructed by Willoughby to show "Methods of Archaeological Research of the Peabody Museum." Demonstrating the so-called Peabody method, it included miniature stakes set out in a ten-foot grid, stratigraphic faces, and a range of scientific tools such as tape measures and cameras.[25]

This display, illustrating the process of excavation, was an example of what Evans (2004) calls the "demonstrative/presentational" form of archaeological model. In England they were produced primarily in the nineteenth century by archaeologists—most notably by Augustus H. Lane-Fox Pitt Rivers—to accompany professional lectures. In America such professional displays were neglected in favor of models of sites, either in their contemporary state or as reconstructions of ancient life.

Undoubtedly, the largest, most spectacular and significant displays of architectural models at Chicago were those devoted to pre-Columbian Mayan archaeology (Fane 1993, 159–62; R. T. Evans 2004, 152–60). There were full-size facsimiles both inside and outside the Anthropology Building, most produced under the sponsorship of the Peabody Museum (Fash 2004). "This striking exhibit, the first major display of Maya architecture in the United States, convinced millions of fairgoers that New World archaeology could be a source of pride, worthy of attention and perhaps investment" (Banta and Hinsley 1986, 79).

In front of the building were large facsimile models of six monumental temple façades, drawn from the ruins of Uxmal and Labná in Yucatán: "The Portal of Labná, twenty-five feet high, shown in a portion of the wall forty feet long; the Straight Arch of Uxmal, twenty-seven feet high and twenty-two feet wide; the central portion of the famous façade of the Serpent House; the west and central sections (north wing) and the southeast corner (east wing) of the House of the Nuns at Uxmal; and a carved monolith found at Uxmal" (Johnson 1898, 328).

These were the product of explorations conducted by Edward H. Thompson, the U.S. consul in Mérida, Yucatán (Brunhouse 1973, 166–95). Massachusetts banker Charles P. Bowditch had sponsored an earlier expedition to Labná in 1888, marking the beginning of the Peabody's work in the region. In fact, this was the first "archaeological expedition by any national or academic institution to a Maya site" (Graham 2002, 126), earlier work having been individual and informal. Thompson, whom Putnam hired for the Exposition in May 1891, labored for fourteen months with a crew of forty. "By the close of this project, Thompson had reproduced a staggering ten thousand square feet of

FIG. 49. Plaster casts of Mayan ruins from Uxmal (center) and Labná (right), Yucatán; outside the Anthropology Building, World's Columbian Exposition, Chicago, 1893. Published in Shepp and Shepp (1893, 321). Original casts and reproduction by Edward H. Thompson for the Peabody Museum, Harvard University.

the ancient temples—far more, and in a shorter space of time, than either [Augustus] Le Plongeon or [Désiré] Charnay had produced over the course of their careers" (Thompson 1929; cf. R. T. Evans 2004, 155).

Like all the architectural models at the Fair, these were created for purposes of display, not research. Following accepted practice, Thompson had first prepared papier-mâché molds of "typical portions," supplemented with photographs. In the autumn of 1892 he came to Chicago to supervise their reproduction in staff and their erection: the official Exposition history, noting the realism of these "perfect facsimiles of the stately old ruins," concluded: "This work was considered a great achievement in archaeology, as nothing of the kind had been done before on anything like so grand a scale. The student, by means of these reproductions, is afforded a fine opportunity for study without loss of time or risk of life" (Johnson 1898, 328–29).

Great efforts at producing a realistic effect were expended. Though

FIG. 50. Vaulted archway, northwest façade, with adjoining portions of residential group, Labná, Yucatán. Photograph by Henry N. Sweet, as a member of the Edward H. Thompson/Peabody expedition, 1888–91. Courtesy of the Peabody Museum of Archaeology and Ethnology, Harvard University. 2004.29.7087, digital file #99090089.

coming from diverse locales, the models represented sites from a relatively limited region and period. With their plaster surfaces artificially aged, the models were landscaped with tropical vegetation. Despite their stunning impression, however, these "ruins" were substantial refractions of their originals. The models were carefully arranged in a circle, as in a park. Setting aside the shifts that had occurred before Chicago, the scene at the Exposition was a free fantasy: "The works represented small fragments of much larger structures, their placement was arbitrary, and the casts provided no sense of plan, volume, or interior space—to say nothing of the temples' original function" (R. T. Evans 2004, 156).

Models of ruins, both full-size and miniature, were also displayed inside the Anthropology Building. In addition to its models of the Ohio ruins, the Peabody Museum presented examples from ancient

Central America. There were "several casts of sculptured stones, stone heads, and bands of hieroglyphs" from the Thompson collection (Johnson 1898, 328–29). Most, however, were based on fieldwork carried out by Harvard graduate students John G. Owens and Marshall H. Saville. From late 1891 until his untimely death in February 1893, Owens worked in Copán, Honduras. At Copán and for Thompson's work at Labná, Saville (who had also worked in Ohio) assisted with the photography. Back in Cambridge, E. E. Chick superintended the work of making the casts from the molds, while Saville helped arrange and label the casts and photographs (Johnson 1898, 329).

In addition to the Peabody models, the Anthropology Building had displays from two leading Mesoamerican explorers. The French ministry of public instruction sponsored Désiré Charnay's presentation of paper casts and photos of Palenque and Chichén Itzá, and Englishman Alfred Maudslay displayed some of his large-scale photographs.[26]

Charnay and Maudslay were among the pioneers of casting in the Mayan region.[27] Maudslay expressed two motives for making casts: research or preservation, in order to have permanent records that would survive beyond the condition of the originals still exposed to nature; and display, for scientific and educational purposes (Graham 1993, 71). As Diana Fane notes, however, there were important differences between casting classical subjects (where the medium had first been applied) and objects from Mesoamerica (1993, 152). First, since the canon to be reproduced had to be created, it could be idiosyncratic and biased; and second, the *in situ* workplace of the jungle was much more challenging than a studio. Among the environmental problems that Alfred Maudslay noted, casts could not be made when the surfaces were wet (Fane 1993, 152; cf. Thompson 1932, 142).

The models for the larger and more extensive outdoor display were composed of reinforced staff, while plain plaster served for those inside. Plaster was preferable for transportation and durability, but many casts were initially created from papier-mâché molds. The first photographers in Egypt and Mexico had made squeezes (Fane 1993, 150). In 1882 Maudslay learned of the technique from Charnay when he observed him making paper molds in Yaxchilán, Guatemala. It seems that Maudslay used them especially to record inscriptions.[28]

Inside the Anthropology Building, Mayan architecture was also

FIG. 51. Alfred Maudslay's team molding the Great Turtle, Quiriguá, Yucatán. Photograph by Alfred P. Maudslay, 1883. Brooklyn Museum Library. Special Collections. BM image no. F1435_M442_Maudslay_019.

presented photographically. The tradition of making images of ancient Mesoamerican ruins had begun with the pioneering travels and reports in 1839 and 1841 of the American lawyer John Lloyd Stephens and English architect-artist Frederick Catherwood. On his first trip Catherwood used a camera lucida, and on his second he brought a daguerreotype camera, producing some of the first photographs taken of Mesoamerican ruins (Howe 2003, 40). Like many successors, the team also made plaster casts of sculptural elements. According to contemporary practice, these photographs were commonly reproduced as engravings. This was because the images might fail to show the necessary details due to disfiguring shadows and angles. Also, until the invention of the half-tone printing technique around 1890 it was difficult and expensive to reproduce photographs. Catherwood and Stephens's photos and drawings thus became the basis for lithographs and engravings published in 1844. Each version

Refracting Images

FIG. 52. Photographs by Désiré Charney, Alfred Maudslay, and others and plaster casts of Mayan ruins, Anthropology Building, World's Columbian Exposition, Chicago, 1893. Photograph by Charles D. Arnold. Courtesy of the Peabody Museum of Archaeology and Ethnology, Harvard University. 93-1-10/100266.1.2, digital file #99010020.

opened up room for refraction and shift. These pioneers were followed by Charnay, Le Plongeon, Maler, and Maudslay, each inspiring the next (Pillsbury 2012).

Harvard's own Copán expedition was documented with photos taken by Owens and Saville. Of the approximately five hundred photos produced during the first two field seasons, the Peabody chose 162 to display at Chicago (Banta and Hinsley 1986, 79). The sites of Palenque and Chichén Itzá were illustrated twice at Chicago: by Charnay's photos and casts and by 1889 photos taken by Maudslay and Henry N. Sweet, a Boston photographer who had also worked with Thompson the year before. These photos were stacked five deep on the walls, in front of some stone sculptures (Johnson 1898, 327) and adjacent to a life-sized mannequin of a native. Thompson's sites of Labná and Uxmal were also replicated photographically. Thus for much of the

Mesoamerican display, photographs and casts reinforced (or perhaps contradicted) each other.

The photographs of Maudslay and his predecessors were hardly candid snapshots. Instead, they were preceded by painstaking preparation of the site before exposure. Almost always, vegetation had to be cleared first. Catherwood's practice served as a model for most of his followers. When necessary, Maudslay also used brushes to clear away moss and vegetation. Broadly, these acts may be regarded as a metaphor for the European discoverer's role in making known the ruins, but they also marked a more literal act of clearance (Aguirre 2005, 113). Taking a cast served to clean the sculpture, as bits of dirt and moss would come away with the plaster, revealing a smooth surface which could then be documented in a photograph (Graham 1993, 71). At other times Maudslay's practice was even more interventionist. He "ordered stelae moved if the lighting where they were found was inadequate for good photographs, and he coated sculptures with a mixture of whitewash and ash to create an even tonality that would photograph better" (Howe 2003, 48).

As in contemporary science more generally, Maudslay's casts bore a complex relationship to their graphic representation in drawing and photography. They served as models, both before and after the Exposition. Maudslay asked English artist Annie Hunter to produce detailed drawings from his photographs (Graham 2002, 221–23). This formed his third purpose for making casts: "to enable a trained illustrator to prepare accurate drawings under good working conditions, since the controllable lighting that an illustrator needs in order to distinguish faint details in low-relief carving could not have been provided in the jungle. In addition, Maudslay needed to compare each unfinished drawing with the original (or cast) before approving it, or sometimes asking for corrections" (Graham 1993, 71).

Thus, there was never a "final version," only a continuous wave of states.

These versions only multiplied as the negatives were made into prints. In his preparation of prints for the Madrid Exposition, Maudslay was forced to rephotograph the prints in order to make the required enlargements—measuring 30 by 24 inches. Because the photographic paper available at the time was not sensitive to the yellowish light of carbon filament electric lamps, "the only recourse was, first, to make a contact print from the negative, then to photograph that print with a camera using a negative of at least the size required for the enlargement, and finally, to make a contact print from that enlarged negative" (Graham 2002, 195). As these forty-plus prints were destined for the British Museum, Maudslay made a duplicate set for Chicago.[29]

These architectural representations in the studio bore a problematic relationship to inscriptions in the field. For his part, Putnam repeatedly insisted to his assistants on the necessity for well-documented artifacts, supplemented by detailed field notes, drawings, plans, and photographs (Burns 2008, 6). Unlike the casts employed for fragments such as Maya stelae, for mounds and other architectural forms, no direct impressions were made in the field. All of the original inscriptions were merely the starting point for later elaboration in another medium and size. (As representational tropes, they were analogical or metaphorical, rather than indexical). In this regard, the practice of the Mindeleffs in the Southwest and the Peabody in Ohio were essentially the same, and different from the various Maya casts.

Like the Nasca lines in Peru, many mounds needed to be represented in another medium in order to be apprehended. Miniature models and photographs must be seen in relation to one another as well as to earlier representational devices, like mapping. These media were especially suited to spatial extremes: the very large and the very small. In this they differed from the Maya display. What was so impressive about those was that whether they were inside or outside the Anthropology Building, they were large, much bigger than a person. While the mounds themselves were also immense, their displays were very small. Yet neither were the kinds of human-size artifacts contained in most anthropology displays—whether at the Chicago Fair or in museums.

In this section we have considered indigenous architecture along at least six axes of variation: real material vs. simulated medium, three-dimensional (sculpture) vs. two-dimensional (photographs), full-size vs. miniature, ethnographic vs. archaeological, Native vs. Anglo-made, more accurate (the Yucatán display) vs. less accurate (the Cliffdwellers), and a range of regional representation: the Northwest Coast for ethnography and three key case studies of archaeology (ancient Puebloan of the American Southwest, mound builders of Ohio, and ancient

Maya of Yucatán and Guatemala). Because of the inherent problems of representing such large objects outside their natural habitats, almost every instance opened itself up to angles of refraction.

Bodies with Objects

The World's Columbian Exposition was notable as the first display at an American fair of exotic ethnic groups; the intended participation of American Indian groups at the Philadelphia Centennial had fallen through. There were actually two "producers" of living groups: Putnam's Department of Ethnology, with groups living outside its pavilion, and the commercial operations on the Midway Plaisance, which presented the majority of the groups. (Although the U.S. Bureau of Indian Affairs did have a model school, the Smithsonian did not present live groups.)[30] In contrast to the focus on Native Americans by both the Smithsonian and Putnam's Department M (Ethnology), most of the Midway groups were foreign.

For the public, this was a display of objects as well as racial types. The people were costumed and were seen within artifactual settings of buildings and objects that they were making and using. Every visiting group came with some kind of building, either real or simulated. As impressive as the array of live groups on the Midway Plaisance was, they could not have been a precedent or model for the National Museum life groups. Instead, they were a parallel mode, since the dioramas were prepared before and separate from the presentation of the live groups.[31]

Perhaps even more innovative for American anthropological display was the introduction of the "life group." Commonly referred to at the time as "lay figures," the mannequins used by artists, these were a group of figures, typically molded in plaster, dressed in costumes and holding Native artifacts.

In his summary of display techniques, Smithsonian administrator G. Brown Goode identified three museological functions of human figure models: "(1) To show the characteristics of the different races, (2) to display costumes, and (3) to illustrate the methods of use of weapons, instruments, and processes of various arts and crafts" (1895, 52). As he further notes, for the first purpose, greatest accuracy was needed, but this was less important for the others.

FIG. 53. Hopi bread makers life group, U.S. National Museum, ca. 1894. National Anthropological Archives, Smithsonian Institution. [INV] 02231900.

The life group was one of at least three possible kinds of display: objects presented as individual or isolated specimens, juxtaposed with other types of species or varieties in a systematic way, or grouped in a metonymical setting as they are found "in nature." Clearly, life groups were the last kind, a contextual display giving a cultural or social surrounding, which Boas had advocated in his 1887 debate with Mason (Jacknis 1985, 77–83). As such, they were the cultural equivalents of the habitat dioramas of natural history museums (Wonders 1993) and the period rooms of history and art museums (Alexander 1964).[32]

The state of arrested motion represented by the life group was a particular problem in contemporary aesthetic theory. Visual narratives were being explored in the performative genres of theater and dance as well as the visual modes of photography and film. The creation of this kind of instantaneous vision was stimulated by the introduc-

FIG. 54. Hopi bread makers: Betty bakes piki corn bread, while her mother grinds corn flour. Photograph by James A. Mooney, Hano, Arizona, January–March 1893. National Anthropological Archives, Smithsonian Institution. GN 01878b.

tion of smaller, faster, and more portable cameras and film. Photographers such as Eadweard Muybridge experimented with a series of instantaneous and multiple images to capture the movements of people and animals. As an illustration of a given movement in time, these moments were behavioral excerpts. Like the life group, they implied action that came before and action that would come after the scene depicted (Mathews et al. 2005, 8).

Anticipating the soon-to-be-introduced medium of film, the life group was essentially a permanent form of the Victorian craze for *tableaux vivants*, a medium also presented at the Fair. People holding frozen poses, often taken from well-known paintings, were almost an inversion of the practice of posing for paintings. Instead of a human pose translated into a painting, in a *tableau vivant* a painting is retranslated back into a pose. Tableaux dealt with groups and narratives, but a related practice was the "living statue," painted but otherwise nearly nude individuals holding a pose (Mathews et al. 2005, 6). The theatrical reference was especially pertinent to the live ethnic groups.

While still innovative in 1893, the life group had grown out of earlier museum display modes. Built on a tradition of waxworks, by the mid-nineteenth century such displays were common in Europe. Between 1853 and 1866 London's Crystal Palace pavilion presented several groups of strikingly realistic figures, made of painted plaster and set in realistic scenes of vegetation (Qureshi 2011, 195–97).[33] Smithsonian anthropologists would have been familiar with the dramatic groups of Swedish peasant life presented by Artur Hazelius at the Philadelphia Centennial or at the 1889 Paris Exposition. By 1893 Swedish museums had been using elaborate mannequin groups for well over a decade (Sandberg 2003).

The style took longer to become rooted in America. By the early 1870s the Smithsonian was displaying costumed wax figures representing Arctic explorer Elisha Kent Kane with an Eskimo couple (Ewers 1959, 519). In 1875 the museum imported four Japanese figures, and the following year they displayed costumed figures at the Centennial Exposition. With the exception of two groups depicting the Zuni and Paiute, the Smithsonian displays were restricted to individual costumed figures (Kavanagh 1990).[34]

At Chicago in 1893 the Smithsonian presented about eighty costumed mannequins, forty-seven of which were arranged into fifteen multi-figured groups (Bergmann 1893).[35] In addition there were some isolated mannequins in the Anthropology Building.[36] One journalist, writing a few months before the Fair's opening, offered a good overview of the number and technique of the groups:

> These figures, which have been made by the sculptors employed by the Smithsonian Institution of Washington, are so perfect as to deceive even the most expert at a little distance. The work was done under the supervision of Prof. Otis T. Mason, the curator of the department of ethnology in the Smithsonian. A special appropriation was made by Congress for this exhibit, and it promises well to be one of the most interesting at the great show. The groups are made in most

lifelike form and show the peoples they are intended to represent in some natural and characteristic positions. Thus, for example, there is one group that shows a number of Zuni Indians at work manufacturing pottery and another representing them as engaged in a religious ceremony. The figures are all dressed in genuine garments that were secured from the Indians by the head agents of the ethnological bureau and in other ways. In all there will be upward of seventy figures in the different groups, all life size and thoroughly realistic.[37]

Like all museum display, production of the life groups depended on a complex and close collaboration among a team with various skills: from administrators to museum designers, and from field ethnographers to the actual preparators. Holmes has long been credited with introducing the life group to America at the Chicago Fair (Ewers 1959, 519), but in fact the parentage for the technique was more communal.

While historical records are not explicit, it appears that between them Cushing and Holmes supervised the design and construction of the groups. Thus they would have drawn on personal knowledge of their own fieldwork for the Zuni and archaeology (a series on aboriginal stone workers), respectively, but had also to interpret the ethnography and collections of field agents Mooney and Hoffman.[38] For all the other groups, Cushing and Holmes seem to have relied on existing Smithsonian sources.

Many of the preparators who produced these displays were sculptors working in Washington, often on federal commissions. For the Chicago Exposition, Theodore A. Mills and U. S. J. Dunbar modeled and cast the bodies, heads, and limbs of the group figures; Carl Bergmann was responsible for their mounting and costuming; and Thomas W. Sweeney arranged and labeled the cases containing the comparative collections (Mason 1895, 127–29).

Among the popular materials for mannequins were wood, wax, papier-mâché, and plaster. Although commonly referred to as "plaster casts," it seems that the figures at Chicago were made of much the same material as the Fair's buildings and statuary: the composite substance called staff. The forms were built up of excelsior (fine wood shavings), mixed with a preparation of glue, and covered with a layer of plaster (Mason 1895, 127–29). The usual practice was to cast only the extremities—the heads, arms, and legs—which would be seen extending beyond the costume. Partly this was done for expediency, but a more critical reason was to facilitate placing the costumes over the figures.

Following the sculptural conventions of the time, there were two ways to derive a portrait from a subject: direct life casts or free modeling in clay. In the former, one first applied a plaster coating over the body, while in the latter one first created a clay model of a face or body (Hough 1922, 613). In both cases the final plaster mannequin, a positive, had to be cast against a negative cast. With the clay model, however, there was an intermediate step of coating the clay with plaster to produce the negative.[39] The Smithsonian seems to have employed few actual life casts for its life group mannequins. Its collection of casts, made primarily from Indians visiting the capital and not in the field, was produced mostly after the Fair. Furthermore, Holmes thought that they often yielded a distorted representation of facial features (1903, 201). Paradoxically, the artistic "lie" was felt to be truer to reality than the actual impression.

A special challenge was the reproduction of skin, hair, and eyes. While they could be (and often were) made of painted plaster, their contrast to real costumes and objects encouraged a greater realism. For the Chicago Fair, preparators used wigs of real human hair, ordered from local shops. Some museums used glass eyes, but the Smithsonian team seems to have merely painted the plaster.

Although partially composed of plaster mannequins, unlike the case of architectural ruins, life groups went beyond mere reproduction, for they incorporated actual museum artifacts. Realism came from the objects: the costumes on the figures and the objects held in their hands. There was, however, a mutually reinforcing verisimilitude here: the groups created a context for the artifacts, while the real artifacts served as props in creating an impressive scene (Sandberg 2003, 198).

As intended, there was a wide regional coverage in the life groups, although not as diverse as in the complete roster of mannequins: Arctic (Labrador and Anderson River Eskimo), Subarctic (an intertribal group from Fort Yukon, Alaska), California (Hupa), Plains (Kiowa, Sioux, Comanche), and Southwest (Hopi, Zuni, Navajo, Apache).[40]

Visual analysis of the life groups reveals that the innovation of the

Chicago Fair was the expansion of mannequin display from single figures to groups of interrelating figures. The display now became a composition, going beyond the relatively simple issue of re-presenting visible surfaces. Whenever possible, the figures seem to be visually balanced. When pairs are presented, usually one will be standing and the other sitting, or one faces outward while the other has its back turned. Often one figure gazes into the eyes of the other. Since most are making something, they usually peer down at the object in their hands. All these methods help create a realistic effect.

Among the more complex groups were Mooney's Hopi bread makers and Navajo silversmiths. In the latter, for example, one figure, dressed in white, stands and pumps the bellows; his partner at the opposite end, darkly costumed, crouches as he tends the fire. Opposite the fire tender is a sitting figure pounding silver into a mold, his arched back echoing the curve of the standing men. Thus the visitor's eye is drawn into the life group, following the echoing forms around from figure to figure.[41] Holmes was a special master at such compositions, as he later demonstrated in his expanded groups for the 1901 Buffalo Exposition.

While from one perspective these grouped figures are a kind of complex form, on another level they also convey content, introducing the aspect of narrative and drama (Brown 2003, 92–99). Such innovations were clearly intended by the curators. As Goode noted, the figures at Chicago were "no longer pieces of sculpture but pictures from life" (1895b, 54). To an interviewer, Holmes explained: "The groups . . . are composed of life-sized and lifelike figures, for the most part of Indians, and show the red men at work and at play. They are making baskets, molding pottery, drawing pictures on skins, and in ways like that present vivid pictures of life and customs that will become even more valuable as time passes on and the Indian passes away with it."[42]

The Chicago groups were isolated figures, without painted and sculpted environmental backgrounds (similar to the semi-habitat diorama of the natural history museum; cf. Parr 1959, 107).[43] Usually, however, they did include foregrounds, simulating the ground and vegetation. There could be no backgrounds because most of the groups were set in four-sided glass cases, meant to be seen from all angles. The backgrounds that we know of—such as for the Hopi bread

FIG. 55. Navajo silversmith life group, World's Columbian Exposition, Chicago, 1893. Smithsonian Institution Archives. Image MNH-12279.

makers and the Kwakiutl *hamatsa* initiate—were added later when the groups were put on display in Washington, where the preferred viewing angle was from directly in front.

The innovation of the Fair's mannequins was that they simulated narrative action. What, then, was their dramatic content—what were these people doing? In other words, how are they telling stories? In terms of social categories we can consider their sociality, gender, age, and the nature of their labor. All these modes were in implicit contrast to the dominant Anglo-American society as well as to that of the masses of newly arrived immigrants. And all spoke to preoccupations and worries of the larger society.

About half of the Chicago mannequins were arranged in social groups. They ranged in size from two (husband and wife, mother and child, Sioux hide dressers, Zuni potters), three (Hupa mother and children, Navajo weavers), or four (Zuni priests, Hopi bread makers,

FIG. 56. Navajo silversmith Peshlakai (Pesh-'lákai-ilhini) with two of his children and forge. Photograph by James A. Mooney, near Ganado, Arizona, December 1892. National Anthropological Archives, Smithsonian Institution. [Neg] 2427.

Navajo silversmiths, Alaskan intertribal group) to five (Sioux mother and children, Kiowa children at play).

Curators preferred groups that were mixed in gender and age, presenting the Victorian ideal "nuclear family"—husband, wife, and children. Beyond any moral values, there was also a didactic component in these natural history dioramas: depicting in a condensed form the range of variation found in the species or culture at hand (Holmes 1903, 258). In fact, however, of the fifteen groups at Chicago, there was only one husband and wife pair (Apache) and none with a father and children. The other groupings consisted of mothers and children (Labrador Eskimo, Anderson River Eskimo, Hupa, Kiowa, Sioux), all women (Hopi bread makers, Zuni potters, Navajo weavers, Sioux hide dressers), all men (Zuni priests, Navajo silversmiths), all children (Kiowa, Comanche), and one mixed tribal and gender grouping (Fort Yukon, Alaska).

Narrative, in the sense of linked action sequences, was directly implicated in the Powhatan quarry group. Literally, it consisted of a set of three different figures, illustrating three actions: prying up boulders with a pike, breaking up the stones, and roughing out the tool forms. Seen from another perspective, it illustrated the successive action sequences that would have been executed by a single individual in his construction of a stone tool (Meltzer 2010: 174–75).[44] This kind of "freeze frame" series was just the kind of visual experiment being carried out by photographer Eadweard Muybridge and painter Thomas Eakins.

A fascinating example of refraction concerns the illustration of homosexuality. The models for two of the figures, the Zuni belt weaver and the Navajo blanket weaver, were modeled on *berdache*, transvestite men: We'wha and Hosteen Klah, respectively.[45] When the time came to create the mannequins, their gender was rendered as female, to conform better with accepted cultural expectations.

The images of weaver Klah and silversmith Peshlakai, the two principal subjects for Mooney's Navajo field photography, were ironically refracted at the Exposition. Both ended up visiting Chicago, where they could have stood in front of their own mannequins in the Smithsonian display. Klah, who demonstrated weaving at the New Mexico Territorial pavilion, completed his first blanket over the summer (Newcomb 1964, 113).[46] Sponsored by the State of Colorado, Peshlakai demonstrated and sold his jewelry out on the Midway. The invaluable experience he gained supported his later career as both a maker and a merchandizer of silverwork, including another stint at the St. Louis fair in 1904 (Greenberg and Greenberg 1984, 8; Essay 1, this volume; Parezo and Fowler 2007: 120–24, 406).

In terms of social action, by far the principal theme was domestic labor: people engaged in productive work, especially making artifacts. Among the specific crafts on display were Sioux hide dressing, Hopi bread making, Zuni pottery, Navajo weaving, and Navajo silversmithing. The industrialization of American work during the nineteenth century produced an anti-modernist counter-action: the Arts and Crafts movement. Prizing the fruits of hand labor, the movement valorized the artifacts of the Native American (Dilworth 1996, 125–72; Hinsley and Wilcox 1996, 196–205; cf. Shapiro 2008). Some of the crafts represented at the Exposition, such as Navajo silverwork, were actually quite innovative at the time; while others, such as food production by the Hopi bread makers or the stone work of the Powhatan quarry men, were more ancient.

In addition to groups depicting the domestic crafts of pottery, weaving, and silver and hide working, there were two displays devoted to "artistic" labor, both supervised by Walter Hoffman: a Crow hide painter and an Ojibwa (Chippewa) birch-bark scribe (who interestingly was glossed as a writer rather than as a priest involved in the sacred).[47] Another subject was even rarer: the political representation of chiefs and other non-religious leaders. Only one figure was so identified at Chicago—a Comanche chief.

One theme was not as well-represented, despite its importance: the sacred or ceremonial, a theme resonant in American culture at the time. Concerned with a general loss of faith—what sociologist Max Weber referred to as the disenchantment of the world—many looked to the "vanishing Indian" as a source of spiritual wisdom (Lears 1981). One reason for the domestic focus, in fact, was Native religious tenacity in the face of government and missionary pressure to the contrary. Mooney was forced to focus on the crafts of bread making, weaving, and silverwork because the Hopi refused to sell him any sacred items (an indication that the Indian was not so vanishing after all). Tellingly, Cushing had no such problems, and indeed his Zuni kiva ceremony ("ritual of creation") was the only life group devoted to the sacred. This was possible for two reasons: because he had been initiated as a Zuni bow priest and was able to reconstruct these scenes from his personal knowledge, and because he and Matilda and James Stevenson had collected much relevant material over an extended period.

For most of the cultures represented, only a single group was constructed. Among those with multiple displays were the Eskimo, Sioux, Kiowa, Zuni, and Navajo. They were undoubtedly chosen because of their larger collections at the Smithsonian, which in the case of the Kiowa and Navajo had involved dedicated field collecting. In selecting one or a limited number of scenes from a full cultural panoply, curators were creating ethnic stereotypes (Babcock 1990). Why are Hopi millers, Navajo silversmiths and weavers, and Plains warriors chosen to represent those cultures? For example, bread making was already an enduring trope for the representation of Pueblo peoples (Hinsley

1996b, 200–2), as rehearsed in photos by Jack Hillers and engravings by Willard L. Metcalf and Henry F. Farny, some produced to illustrate Cushing's articles on Zuni bread (1920, pl. 22). Bread making was seen as a pre-modern form of domesticity. This village-based agriculture resonated with the trope of the Pueblos as cultural analogs of the ancient Middle Eastern desert dwellers.

Although the Smithsonian's label texts apparently have not survived, scattered evidence supports a stereotypic approach in the titles. General cases were headed as, for example: "The Textile Art," with a subsection called: "Textiles of the Zuni." The life group for the Sioux hide dressers was not identified by tribe in the title but as "Women Dressing Hides." And the mannequin of the Ojibwa birch-bark writer was given quite a grand title: "The Primitive Scribe."[48]

The Smithsonian had three principal sources for the displayed items: existing museum collections (most of the displays), specially commissioned field collecting, and occasionally reproductions or models fabricated in museum studios.

When drawing from existing museum collections, sometimes the curators selected from a limited provenience (items collected by one collector at one time and place), but more often they needed to combine sources to complete a display. For example, the Zuni were illustrated with artifacts gathered by Cushing, the Stevensons, Powell, Mooney, Edward Palmer, and Frederick Hodge—all gathered since the first expedition in 1879.

Some objects were fabricated at the museum or the Exposition itself. Displaying his craft skills, Cushing made most of them. We would expect those from Zuni, where he had conducted fieldwork: an unfinished pot for the potter; imitation beads and a ceremonial lance for the warrior; a shirt and salt bag for the priest, and unfinished pots for the Hopi potter. But he also made a headdress and a headband for an Apache couple, an arm bracelet for a Yuma man, and a beater for the Sioux hide dresser. Among those not by Cushing were a breechcloth for the Zuni driller; the Sioux travois; and the mat, frame, and pole for the Ojibwa medicine man.

Documentary sources employed in the construction of the life groups varied greatly. Some were minimal, drawing almost solely from existing museum collections, supplemented by only the barest information from photographs and publications. Sources for the prehistoric group of the Powhatan quarriers were obviously a special problem. Holmes could rely on his own excavations in the area, documented in his sketches and notes, as well as the advice of the flint knapper Cushing, who was photographed demonstrating one of the poses.[49] Historic paintings were another source. For the Sioux groups, early paintings by George Catlin served as a reference for the costumes.[50] The quarry group was based partly on the watercolors of Englishman John White in North Carolina painted between 1584 and 1590.[51] Although this group was a reconstruction, intended to depict pre-contact culture, it ironically proved a marked contrast with contemporary Algonquian cultures.[52] Nevertheless, it marked one of the earliest anthropological uses of ethnohistorical visual sources, an innovation undoubtedly due to Holmes's artistic training (Fernlund 2000, 138).

The curators varied in the degree of their personal knowledge and whether their fieldwork had been conducted specifically for the Fair. Although Cushing's fieldwork came years before the Fair, it was extensive and spanned several years: Zuni (1879–84) and Hopi (1879, 1881, 1882). Some of the groups, however, were based on collecting and fieldwork specially undertaken for the Exposition. On several trips during 1891–92 Hoffman returned to the reservations of the Menominee (Wisconsin), Ojibwa (Minnesota), and Crow (Montana), the scenes of his earlier fieldwork. For much of 1892–93 the Bureau of Ethnology's Henry W. Henshaw collected in New Mexico and California, but subsequent ill health prevented him from fully working up the material.

Mooney's fieldwork among the Kiowa, Hopi, and Navajo was the most extensive carried out expressly for the Fair. Among the Kiowa of Oklahoma, Mooney spent three months in the spring of 1891, marking the beginning of his ethnography among these people. He collected six complete outfits, including camp accouterments, toys and games, ceremonial and war paraphernalia, and house models (Colby 1977, 276–77). In Chicago these were transformed into two life groups—a mother and child and five children playing games, the largest and most elaborate group at the Fair—in addition to several single mannequins. As Mooney later recounted:

> Having studied the Kiowas for some time I selected that tribe from which to make a collection under a commission from the World's Fair. My purpose was to make one complete tribal collection—something which until then we had not in the Museum—to include everything used by the tribe for any purpose whatever, dress, domestic or ceremonial. This idea was practically carried out and the result is now in the National Museum. Only one thing of each kind was procured, however, except where several costumes had to be obtained for dressing life figures. All this is only a small part of what can and should be done to give a complete museum exposition of the home life of a typical prairie tribe. (Mooney 1894, 4)

On the other hand, Mooney had little interest in or familiarity with the Hopi and Navajo, as he complained to his superiors. Spending four months over the winter of 1892–93, he collected among the Hopi and Navajo of New Mexico and Arizona. Among his consultants were bureau ethnologist Washington Matthews and traders Thomas V. Keam and Alexander M. Stephen.

Finding that no Hopi would sell kachina masks and costumes, Mooney decided to concentrate on crafts. Keam helped him buy crafts, food items, and tools for their preparation. In the Hopi villages Mooney and Keam spent several days watching women grind corn flour and prepare foods (Colby 1977, 282–83). Mooney arranged for two Hopi bakers to set up a grinding mill and oven near Keam's trading post. He photographed each stage in the procedure, including pulling corn bread out of the oven, before purchasing the outfit. A former newspaper man, Mooney later wrote an informative article about his experiences:

> I spent several days at the nearest village, watching the women at work grinding flour and making bread, noting all the arrangements for milling and baking, learning the different kinds of corn and flour, and finding out for myself how they tasted. The women were very good-natured in explaining everything. . . . We arranged with two of the women to come down to the trading post and set up a flour mill and furnace like those in the houses and grind corn and make breads so that I could photograph them at work and afterward buy the outfit and send it on to Washington. . . . After the photographs were made

the mill and the furnace were taken to pieces and boxed up, together with complete costumes sufficient to dress figures to show all the different steps of the process, and specimens of corn, flour, bread, and all sent on to Washington where a group of bread-makers has been prepared and forwarded to Chicago.[53]

Keam accompanied him to Navajo hogans, where he observed and photographed weaving and silverwork, purchasing silver-making tools and a woman's loom with a partially woven blanket.

For purposes of composing a life group, photography was the most useful source, beyond a collection of actual artifacts. These images helped with general poses, depicting how an object would have been held or used. And their documentation helped greatly with the bodies themselves—particularly the faces—since the Smithsonian had few life casts at the time (Scherer 2014, 226–27).

As a form of visual note taking, photos could be later worked up in the studio, like painters' sketch drawings, into something more considered and permanent. Yet this process also involved a dimensional shift. While there was a transition from three-dimensional to two-dimensional formats in paintings, for life groups these photo-notes went from two to three dimensions. In this they resembled more closely the movement from an architectural plan to a finished building. Within this space, there was plenty of room for museological refraction.

Most of the anthropologists supervising these life groups used photography in the field, as a form of ethnographic documentation, and their images did serve as visual notes for the model makers.[54] For the Fair groups, we know of a few such examples: Cushing used Zuni pictures taken by John Hillers, and the preparators worked from Mooney's field pictures for the Hopi, Navajo, and Kiowa groups.

Even if taken in the field, however, these photos were not casually snapped records of ongoing behavior. If only because the film at the time was so slow, before taking the picture there was scenic recreation, as in theater or film. The best example of this approach is Mooney's careful posing of the Hopi millers. Because it was so dark inside the home, with the actual grinding bins and hearth, Mooney set up his bread makers outdoors. This shifted the spatial relations of the figures and simplified the related artifactual array. In fact, in almost every case we find that the preparators relied on the photos more for content and were not bound by the photographer's original composition. As they worked under the guidance of curators such as Cushing or Holmes, the preparators departed from the photos in other, more critical ways. For instance, the standing male figure in Mooney's Hopi photo was removed entirely, the single grinder and baker were each made into a pair, and the unmarried baker (as indicated by her hair whorls) was changed into a married woman (with straight hair). Similar shifts occurred with Mooney's Navajo weavers and silversmith (Jacknis 1990, 182–83).

Undoubtedly for practical reasons, no field photos seem to have been used in the development of mannequins prepared by Hoffman (Ojibwa, Crow) or Holmes (e.g., Powhatan, Sioux, Hupa, or Kutchin), although Hoffman would have had the opportunity to do so, given his dedicated field trip.[55]

Compensating in some cases for the lack of field documents were photographs produced in museum studios of anthropologists posing as models. "Playing Indian," as Philip Deloria refers to it (1998, 119), these white men sometimes donned Native costumes, at other times dressing in normal business attire and in yet other sessions appeared nearly naked.[56] Today many of these sensational images have become famous and widely reproduced, but we must remember that none of them were meant for public display. For the Chicago groups we have surviving images of Cushing as a Comanche mounted chief (in several poses: in a loincloth, on a sawhorse—see figs. 57 and 58), taking the poses of several of Zuni ritual dancers (kachina and mudhead), and chipping stone tools (evidently for the Powhatan quarry group); and of Hoffman as an Ojibwa scribe (figs. 59, 60), a Crow painter, and a Hupa fire-driller (not at the Fair, but probably installed in 1901). And the Smithsonian curators were not the only ones engaged in this practice. Following his first field trip, to Baffin Island in 1883–84, Boas was photographed in Berlin posing as an Eskimo hunter.[57] Shortly after the Fair, he demonstrated poses for several of the figures of a Kwakiutl diorama (Hinsley and Holm 1976).

To some extent, and especially for those curators with field and photographic experience, their own poses were a necessary stopgap

FIG. 57. Mannequin of Comanche mounted chief, World's Columbian Exposition, Chicago, 1893. Smithsonian Institution Archives. Image MNH-12282.

for the lack of Native models. On the other hand, curators like Cushing and Holmes believed that ethnographers could best understand Native crafts by being able to reenact and replicate them (Hinsley 1981, 104–5; Isaac 2011, 213–15).

Despite the clear innovations of realism, authenticity, and detail in the life groups, not all Smithsonian anthropologists were of the same mind. Cushing and Mooney had pioneered long-term and sen-

Refracting Images

Fig. 58. Frank H. Cushing posing for mannequin of Comanche mounted chief, ca. 1892. National Anthropological Archives, Smithsonian Institution. Image # 8255.

sitive participant observation methods of ethnography, yet they disagreed over its importance in guiding public presentations (Colby 1977, 283). Evidently Mooney was meticulous in his labeling and in trying to get right the details of the display; he strove for accuracy, comprehensiveness, and detail. Cushing did not feel that all the minute labeling was necessary. The two had argued after Cushing corrected

FIG. 59. Mannequin of Ojibwa scribe, World's Columbian Exposition, Chicago, 1893. Smithsonian Institution Archives. Image MNH-12269.

and deleted much of Mooney's label text, ordering additional artifacts from other tribes to be included in the Navajo and Hopi exhibits. In another instance, Mooney objected to putting a costume from one tribe on the figure of another: "The hands and arms of that figure never belonged to the tribe that wore this blanket. The exhibit is to educate, not mislead the people" (Moses 1984, 80).

From surviving archival evidence (Bergmann 1893), we have clear documentation that many of the life groups—not just Mooney's—freely combined objects from diverse tribes. In some cases, these might be from neighboring groups, such as a Hopi with a Zuni object, but in other cases, they were virtually impossible combinations, such as an Alaskan boy with a Missouri River knife or a Hupa woman with a Costa Rican armlet.[58] One odd group seems to have combined a Zuni potter with one from Hopi, although they are working on Zuni-style pots (made by Cushing!).

Refracting Images

FIG. 60. Walter J. Hoffman posing for mannequin of Ojibwa scribe, ca. 1892. National Anthropological Archives, Smithsonian Institution. Image # 6898.

Ironically, most of Mooney's displays were "tribally pure," since they drew on his dedicated field trips. All the changes in his groups were the presence of Pueblo items in the Navajo groups (a Hopi distaff and a Zuni loom in the weavers and Hopi raw materials, blowpipe, and moccasins in the silversmiths).[59] Holmes supported Cushing's more liberal position:

> Go ahead; you are doing nobly; dont antagonize Mooney more than necessary, but see that the work goes on. I have no doubt you are get-

ting good results.... You can start the silver if you feel like designing it. I wish Mooney would go ahead with some of these groups. He has taken an unfortunate position. It matters little for our purposes here about strict scientific accuracy; when the groups are finally set up in the Museum every feature must be scrutinized. Here show is the main issue. Our warrior is in place and is superb with all his faults—He is the finest thing of his class in the Government Building. The squaw and family group is not here yet but will also make a fine show.[60]

Writing to Cushing a few weeks later, from Chicago, Mason seconded Holmes's desire for public effect, as well as the great popular success of the life groups:

The groups look splendid. Everybody has done his best.... Nothing draws the crowd like the groups. When the Bread Makers and Basket Makers and Silversmiths and, magnificintissimum opus, the religious group shall arrive, the world will stop to admire. No part of the Exposition is more frequented. A few days' experience teaches one that the coup d'oeil [glimpse or glance] is the thing, both in the label and in the group. Don't attempt too much in the Chicago labels. The crowd shove one another along just reading the head lines.[61]

Although both Cushing and Mooney were advocating the relatively innovative geographical/cultural approach, as opposed to the evolutionary typological one, they clearly differed on strictness of detail. Cushing, with his profound interest in comparative cultures, thought that culture could be shown in regional complexes, while Mooney, with his years of detailed fieldwork and journalistic background, insisted on the presentation of a single culture.[62] In the end Cushing was more of a showman, interested in the final effect, which was what made him such a charismatic yet controversial figure.

Such inaccuracies in the interests of exhibitional drama were something of an established Smithsonian tradition by 1893 (cf. Scherer 1975, 74–75; Fitzhugh 1997, 244). A decade later, this problem with life groups was raised again by George Dorsey in an exchange with Boas (Dorsey 1907b, 587). In fact, the question of intertribal combinations still poses a curatorial conundrum about cultural hybridity. One could argue that no tribe is culturally pure and that it is more realistic to depict the cultural borrowings that go on in real life. On the other hand, without clear labeling, the average visitor is bound to be confused. Some ethnologists at the time—among them Mooney, Dorsey and Boas—were lining up against the freer refractions of curators like Holmes and Cushing.

Representational Legacies of the Chicago Fair

Just as we have considered these miniature buildings and life groups as models *of* a cultural reality, we can also treat the Exposition's representations as models *for* a subsequent reality—in this case, further museum practice.

At the Peabody Museum the Fair offered a great opportunity for young scholars such as Charles C. Willoughby (1857–1943), Warren K. Moorehead (1866–1939), Marshall H. Saville (1867–1935), George A. Dorsey (1868–1931), and Harlan I. Smith (1872–1940), who went on to important careers as anthropology curators. For the Peabody, Chicago marked an effective culmination of its Ohio mound research but just the beginning of its program in Central America. At Copán, George Byron Gordon continued Owens's work with the assistance of Alfred Maudslay during the 1893–94 season. In Philadelphia, Culin was transformed through the friendship that he had established with Cushing at Chicago (see Essay 3, this volume). For Boas, the Fair served as entrée to his permanent setting in New York, though not Chicago as he and Putnam had hoped.

For the Smithsonian, the decade following the World's Columbian Exposition was a critical period of innovation, both for exhibition and in the formulation of general theories of museum anthropology. Chicago actually represented the high point of Cushing's specifically museological career, for he was not able to realize his ambitious 1887 plan for anthropology museums, neither with Mary Hemenway nor at the National Museum.[63] Instead, he began an innovative research program in Florida, sponsored jointly with the University of Pennsylvania Museum, and further developed his unified approach to archaeology and ethnology.

Mooney's orientation to museums and material cultures substantially expanded, largely as a result of his experience for the Fair. In November 1894 he outlined an ideal plan for museum display to U.S.

National Museum Director Goode. In his comprehensive scheme, Mooney advocated a multi-media approach, complete with photos and wax cylinders. Desiring a monographic concentration, he proposed one room dedicated to the Kiowa, one of the foci of his ethnography. "This plan should be so broad and systematic that any one entering the room would feel for the moment that he was in the camp of a prairie tribe, and so genuine and exact in detail that a Kiowa Indian would be satisfied with it" (Mooney 1894, 8). Implementing a format clearly inspired by the Exposition, he also wanted to set up in Rock Creek Park a series of aboriginal houses, where Natives could demonstrate their crafts (1894, 8–9). While neither of these plans came to pass, Mooney was able to commission from Native artists a series of miniature Plains tipis. Their initial display at the Nashville fair of 1897 marked the beginning of his extensive research into Plains "heraldry" (Ewers 1978; Mooney 2013).[64]

The Fair's most important effect for the Smithsonian was in its exhibit program. Somewhat surprisingly, after Mason's 1887 debate with Boas the staff began to implement a geographical arrangement, what came to be known as "culture areas." Ironically, Putnam and Boas had employed a generally geographical approach in the Anthropology Building, though the arrangement was hard to perceive among all the confusion. But in the Government Building, the regional approach stood out clearly: tightly ordered alcoves marked with dramatic mannequins, all beneath the giant Powell map.

It was Mason who codified the culture area both in the galleries and in publications. Undoubtedly thinking of his recent debate with Boas, Mason characterized his Chicago exhibit: "So far as possible, I have arranged the costumes and art productions of these families in separate alcoves, so that the student taking his position in one of them may have before his eye practical solution of some of the theoretical questions which have recently arisen concerning the connection between race and language and industries and philosophies." Still, as he had maintained in the debate, for Mason cultural areas were not the only relevant schema: "In order to afford the student another point of view from which to look at the same set of phenomena, a few alcoves have been arranged upon another plan, in which a typical industry is made the primary classific concept, tribe or nation-

Refracting Images

ality the second concept, and linguistic affinities the third concept" (Mason 1894, 211).

As I have noted elsewhere (Jacknis 1985), the exhibits of Mason and Boas ended up looking somewhat alike but for different reasons. Boas had famously insisted that like objects can have different causes; while Mason continued to conceive of culture areas as generated by material and environmental factors: "The earth, with its climate and natural resources, has much to say about the material and form of human industries. Blood and language and social life and religion have their say also in the arts of life, but their influence is superadded, and not fundamental" (Mason 1895, 129). For Boas, on the other hand, artifacts were the result of essentially historical and cultural developments. In a kind of refractory pun, the same surface structures could share different deep structures, invoking two frames of reference.

At the National Museum, culture areas were incorporated slowly and implemented fully only in 1911, with the opening of the new Natural History Museum. Before this, however, the museum was able to expand vastly its program of life groups, which were then arranged geographically. Holmes spent much of the decade following the Fair in codifying his theories and practices of museum display (1898, 1902). The turning point in his own development of life groups came at the 1901 Buffalo Exposition (Holmes 1903). In Chicago many of the mannequins were still single figures or couples, but in Buffalo most of the dioramas consisted of multiple figures interacting with one another in a social drama. For Holmes this was a flowering of his work at Chicago, which he had joined relatively late. As he concluded, the life group format was "of much importance in object-teaching and museum arrangement" (Holmes 1893, 432).

The actual life groups displayed in Chicago had their own later life, in many cases amazingly long-lasting. Following what had become Smithsonian practice, the displays were presented at subsequent expositions—Atlanta (1895), Nashville (1897), Omaha (1898), Buffalo (1901), and St. Louis (1904)—before their permanent installation in the museum. And as they made their way from place to place, many were transformed. In most cases they were expanded by addition of more figures, but as Holmes had always intended, they were also revised with the substitution of new and different artifacts (Hough 1922; Kavanagh 1990). In fact, many of them were included in the 1955–57 renovation of the North American Hall and were only removed with the closure of the hall in 2004—a run of more than a century (Walker 2008; Fitzhugh 1997).[65]

Of all the "second lives" of the Exposition's life groups, the two most interesting were Holmes's Powhatan quarrymen and Boas's group of a Kwakiutl hamatsa ceremony. Both involved photographic reproduction as they were diffused and replicated through publications. Shortly after the Fair, Holmes arranged for the figures of the Powhatan quarry group to be erected in their "natural habitat" on Piney Branch in Rock Creek Park in Washington—at the very spot where Holmes had first discovered evidence of stone workers in 1889 (see figs. 61 and 62). In Holmes's absence Cushing and bureau assistant William Dinwiddie carried out the work, but with dramatic changes: substituting one of the figures and adding a house and a wide array of domestic artifacts. Holmes then used the photographs to illustrate his monograph on *Stone Implements of the Potomac-Chesapeake Tidewater Province* (1897b, 150–51, frontispiece, pl. 102), ostensibly devoted to prehistoric cultures. The group was erected at the site merely for purposes of the photography, a practice much like a film shoot (though anticipating Mooney's own desire for similar groups in the park).[66] For his later installation of the group in the Natural History Building, Holmes took the opportunity of completing the set with figures illustrating the final two stages (trimming away flakes and finishing the blade). As he noted, however, these final steps would not typically have been executed in the single site of the quarry (Holmes 1897b, 150). And although it did not come to fruition, Holmes had planned a still further iteration of the quarriers group: he was campaigning in 1925 for a bronze version to be erected at the site as a memorial to the local indigenous inhabitants (Fernlund 2000, 140–41).[67]

Although it was not quite on display at the Chicago Fair, the history of Boas's Kwakiutl group, a direct outcome of the Exposition, is even more curious. Boas first saw the Kwakiutl hamatsa ceremony not on the Northwest Coast but in the displaced tourist setting of the hot Chicago summer of 1893 (Jacknis 1991a). During his next field trip to British Columbia, in the fall of 1894, he was able to observe this ritual for the first time *in situ*, in Fort Rupert, Vancouver Island. Draw-

Refracting Images

FIG. 61. Powhatan quarry life group, World's Columbian Exposition, 1893. Smithsonian Institution Archives. Image MNH-12906.

ing upon both experiences, Boas was able to pose authoritatively for photographers at the National Museum in December 1894–January 1895. Just as Cushing and Hoffman had done before him, he posed as a model for the several figures that would comprise the life group (Hinsley and Holm 1976). The diorama premiered at the Atlanta Exposition of 1895, before being installed in the National Museum.

This diorama was then multiply refracted through photography. Using the illustration of the hamatsa diorama in Boas's 1897 *The Social Organization and the Secret Societies of the Kwakiutl Indians*, Field Columbian Museum curator George Dorsey explicitly set out to replicate the exhibit, instructing his field agent Charles F. Newcombe to acquire similar artifacts for a display in Chicago. This was completed in 1903. The image continued to resonate in museums, replicated (in miniature) by Samuel A. Barrett at the Milwaukee Public Museum in 1927 (Jacknis 2002b, 100–2; cf. Glass 2009).[68]

FIG. 62. Powhatan quarry life group, Piney Branch, Rock Creek Park, Washington DC, ca. 1895. Uncropped version published in Holmes (1897b, pl. 102). National Anthropological Archives, Smithsonian Institution, 08708300.

Architectural models also proliferated after Chicago. For the Southwest, pueblo models—both full-size and miniature—were displayed at many later fairs, at least through St. Louis in 1904 and San Diego in 1915 (Trennert 1987a). For Mesoamerica the heyday of temple and stelae models was just beginning, filling the galleries of the Peabody, American Museum of Natural History, and the Brooklyn Museum (Fane 1993; Fash 2004). An important series of miniature house and totem pole models of the Northwest Coast was commissioned by John Swanton at the American Museum of Natural History, some from the same carvers represented at Chicago and some even of the same houses (Jonaitis 1992).

In the initial planning for the Chicago Fair, Powell "insisted that their ethnology exhibits at the World's Fair be realistic and provocative."[69] In this he must have succeeded, for some visitors preferred the curatorial vision over the living experience. In 1894, when the life

FIG. 63. Powhatan quarry life group, expanded version, U.S. National Museum, Smithsonian Institution, ca. 1920. Published in Hough (1922, pl. 17). Smithsonian Institution Archives. Image MNH-28540.

groups came back to the Smithsonian, one journalist noted that this comprehensive exhibit "is such a plan as has never been attempted, even at any of the great expositions of the world, the nearest approach being in the various tribal villages of the Midway Plaisance, the only difference in the present instance being that the villagers will be perfect models instead of live subjects of doubtful nationality."[70]

Despite the overwhelming experience that the Fair was a reflection of some exotic cultural reality located far away from Chicago, in many important ways the Exposition itself was an ethnographic site. Just as Native cultures had been displaced and re-presented, much of what was presented at Chicago became re-presented. A wide range of media were employed. Boas spent a great deal of time at the Fair with his Kwakiutl assistant George Hunt, recording ethnographic "field notes" and teaching Hunt a Kwakwala orthography with which to record his own language.

Actually visiting the Fair was not the only way that people could experience it. The exposition was widely disseminated in both words and images in a virtual mountain of books, magazines, and newspapers. At the Exposition itself one could purchase a range of souvenir guidebooks. Soon thereafter one could buy more substantial records, such as the especially popular photo albums illustrating the visiting ethnics on the Midway (Brown 1994, 83; see also Visual Interlude, this volume).

The Chicago World's Fair of 1893 was surely the most photographed exposition of the nineteenth century. At the (commercial) Cliffdwellers display one could buy—in prints or publications—souvenir photos of exterior views, the exhibits, and even reproductions of the photographs taken during the original survey of the site, which in turn became the basis for the model's reconstruction (Brown 1994, 84). Boas commissioned frontier photographer John H. Grabill to document his visiting Kwakiutl troupe; he then distributed the images to the party when he visited them the following year (Jacknis 1984, 6). In turn, many of these photographs were propagated through half-tone prints. The Fair opened just a few years after the widespread introduction in America of half-tone technology, allowing photographs to be cheaply and easily reproduced through a system of inked dots, anticipating our current digital technology.

Anthropologists also gave permanent expression to the Fair in book form, though it was often disguised. In subsequent years, the BAE illustrated several of its annual reports with photos of the Fair's life groups. Even more anachronistically than the pictures in Holmes's Potomac report, several of the southwestern groups illustrated a historical work on the Coronado Expedition of 1540–42, accompanying a translation of Pedro de Castañeda's narrative (Winship 1896).[71] For this volume, the temporal confusion of the "ethnographic present" could not have been better demonstrated. (At least for the Holmes report, one might argue that his models and their photos were imaginative— and acknowledged—attempts at archaeological re-creation.) Further complicating the situation, the pair of a Navajo spinner and weaver was labeled as "Pueblo" (pl. 67).

Again, the visual refraction concerning Boas's hamatsa life group was even more dramatic. His 1897 monograph had included several photos of the Kwakiutl at the Chicago Fair, along with the illustration of his subsequent National Museum diorama, in addition to a long series taken in Fort Rupert in the fall of 1894. While this volume may have been one of the first ethnographies to be illustrated by half-tone photographs, all the photos taken in Chicago were retouched. The Leather and Shoe Trades pavilion in the background of the dancers was removed, leaving the impression that the photos had been taken in British Columbia (Jacknis 1984, 36–39; 1991, 107). Most likely it was the Smithsonian editors and not the author who asked for the masking out, but the action clearly shows that anthropologists—especially curators dedicated to popularization—were uncomfortable with revealing too much of the "backstage" pragmatics of their ethnography.

The visual modes employed at the Fair were only one strand out of a multi-sensory array of representational modes in ethnography (Jacknis 1996). All, one must note, were overshadowed by the dominant medium of writing.[72] The anthropologists at the Exposition were challenged to express their ideas visually. Some of them (such as Cushing, Mooney, and Boas) had important participant-observation fieldwork experience, a relatively innovative approach in American anthropology. Scholars like George Stocking and Curtis Hinsley have considered the adoption of the ethnographic mode as a theoretical concern, which it was, but it also must be seen as an issue of visual expression. For these ethnographers drew upon their visual memories (along with sketches, artifact collections, and photos) to create visual surrogates of Native cultures, by posing for dioramas, for example. For the most part this combination of experiential and conceptual knowledge was unprecedented in American anthropology. While this was happening for its own disciplinary reasons, it was the Chicago Exposition that helped call it forth.

Along with the visual media of photography and plaster casting, emphasized here, the Exposition arrived on the cusp of new representational forms: the time-based media (as archivists refer to them) of sound recording and film. While no prerecorded Native sounds were played back at the Fair, an important series of wax cylinders was recorded. Boas and musicologist John C. Fillmore used the phonograph to capture Kwakiutl music; another more multi-cultural session was conducted by Harvard psychologist and museum official Benjamin I. Gilman, sponsored by Mary Hemenway and the Peabody Museum (Brady 1999). In keeping with contemporary attitudes toward sound recording, these cylinders became the basis for subsequent transcription and analysis but were not reproduced so that a larger audience—professional or popular—could experience them directly.

Neither were any anthropological films made or shown, despite the presence of the new medium in the exhibits of Thomas Edison and Eadweard J. Muybridge. Instead, the life groups served as a privileged moment in the development of modern visual culture, transforming the expressive genres of theater, live ethnic display, and tableaux vivants into the new displays of dioramas and cinema (Griffiths 2002; Sandberg 2003; Mathews et al. 2005; Ames 2008, 198–229). Some anthropologists active in Chicago, such as Mooney and Boas, would go on to play a role in the early development of anthropological cinema.

In the end, despite the best intentions of both Putnam and the Smithsonian anthropologists, visitors often left with the same prejudices they had brought with them (Dexter 1966c; Essay 1, this volume). To offer just a single example, one journalist thought the Haida house models were "decorated in front with the curiously and hideously carved and painted totem poles peculiar to the Heidah tribe. . . . One peculiarity of the ornamentation is the frightful carvings of dragon heads protruding from the eaves." Another felt that "the frame buildings of the Haidas would probably attract but little attention were it not for the hideous decorations and the intensely crude and ugly carvings of their totem poles." Similar comments had been expressed at the 1876 Philadelphia Centennial.[73]

On the other hand, some impressionable young people were clearly inspired. We know that the visits by two future archaeologists of the Southwest, Byron Cummings and Kenneth Chapman, inspired their careers (Bostwick 2006, 23; Chapman and Barrie 2008, 19–21); this also applied to the careers of two of the leading ethnomusicologists of their generation, Frances Densmore and Natalie Burlin Curtis (Hofmann 1968, 2; Patterson 2010, 110).

Epilogue

Returning to the work of Thomas Eakins, we are now in a position to see the profound resonance of his work with that of contemporary anthropologists, which went far beyond the subjects of his portraiture (Braddock 2009, 171–212). Like the scientists of his day, Eakins was a careful student of visual facts, which he recorded in several kinds of "sketches." In turn, these would be used as the basis for his finished art.

Although he kept it somewhat hidden at the time, Eakins was passionately committed to photography, both as an independent mode of expression and as a precursor for his paintings (Sewell et al. 2001, 225–38). And as still photography developed into the moving image, he followed along. Inspired by his friendship with Eadweard Muybridge, Eakins produced his own sets of sequential photos of human and animal locomotion.[74] Eakins was clearly thinking of the issue of arrested motion, as represented in the life groups.

Eakins also went to great lengths in the "research" for his paintings. On an 1887 trip to North Dakota, reminiscent of Teddy Roosevelt's sojourn in the same decade, the artist took a "camp cure" at a ranch (Sewell et al. 2001, 117). In a kind of participant observation, he worked alongside the cowboys, documenting the experience in photography and paint, and returned home with a collection of souvenirs—a buckskin outfit, lariat, and saddle, guns, even two horses. He drew upon these "field notes" for a series of cowboy paintings around 1891—including one exhibited at the Chicago Fair.

Eakins brought the same passion for objective investigation to his 1895 portrait of Frank H. Cushing. In this life-size image Cushing is portrayed in his personal costume of a Zuni bow priest (Treuttner 1985). In preparation for the work Eakins had set up a model Zuni "kiva" in his Philadelphia studio earlier in the year. He recorded this elaborate pose in several preliminary photos and one preparatory sketch (Sewell et al. 2001, 290–91). According to one of Eakins's students, a fire was lit in the studio to produce the smoky haze visible in the canvas (Sewell et al. 2001, 261–63).

Despite these painstaking efforts at realism, there was a good bit of refraction. Cushing's costume itself was a personal composite of Native and Anglo garb, not the Zuni costume it appears to be. Eakins then continued the shift, leaving out and changing aspects that were documented in his studio photos. For instance, in the painting Cushing's hair is longer and he wears earrings.

While there is no evidence of who suggested this mimetic scene, clearly both Eakins and Cushing would have been comfortable with such recreations. Undoubtedly Cushing was acting, as he had in Chicago, as a set designer and preparator. For his part, Eakins had previously behaved as a kind of a museum preparator—in making, for instance, miniature wax models in order to work out a complex scene of a carriage and horses (Mathews et al. 2005, 18).

Writing of Eakins's adoption of a contemporary anthropological stance, art historian Alan Braddock comments: "The point I wish to make is not that Eakins became a professional ethnographer—he did not—but rather that he adapted aspects of ethnographic vision to his artistic practice, analogous to the manner in which he used anatomical knowledge borrowed from the field of medicine" (Braddock 1998, 137). On the other hand, commenting on the deceptive realism of Eakins's paintings, which have long been taken as mirrors or "windows onto the world," Braddock reminds us of the necessity of considering them as the creative works they are, with their own agendas and their own refractions (1998, 136).

In many ways, then, Eakins's creation of the Cushing portrait resembled the work of the Smithsonian curators. Both used photos as a rehearsal for a later product. Cushing, in Philadelphia as well as Washington, posed for photos that were intended to be seen only by artists, by Eakins and the in-house sculptor-preparators, respectively. But in another way, Eakins's practice is the reverse of museum procedures, since it starts with the three-dimensional state of Cushing and the re-created altar in his studio and then "reduces" it to two-dimensional forms: first a photograph, then an oil painting.

Eakins's art also resonated with much of the Exposition itself. For despite the overwhelming presentness of the Fair for its visitors, things were not quite what they seemed (cf. Leja 2004)—literally, since the apparently marble buildings were in fact made of a plaster-fiber composition called staff. From a broader perspective, almost everything at the Fair was displaced. This applied especially for anthropology, which was concerned with Native worlds elsewhere and not in Chicago. Certainly this applied to the representations of photographs and life groups, but it was largely true even for the visiting Native peoples and the artifacts. While both were real in their way, they were not in their natural, original habitats or contexts.

Considered as symbolic tropes, the dioramas were metaphoric, analogizing Native life, while the artifacts and visiting people were metonymic, parts standing for the whole. For both, reality was neither given nor obvious; both could be false or misrepresentational. One needs to consider the question of selection and sampling. In fact there was a complex relationship between metaphoric and metonymic representations, as one was modeled on the other. Casts and photographs are both indexical and both produced as negatives and positives. Hence, while the artifacts and people were three-dimensional and not re-presented, they were still out-of-place and away from their home (Kirshenblatt-Gimblett 1998, 19–21).

Refraction is thus inevitable for reproductive media such as the photograph and the plaster cast, both producing a positive impression from a negative. The photograph almost always exists as a multiple; while plaster casts could conceivably take the same form, they usually exist in smaller editions.

Like the paintings of the Fair (Lovell 1996, 53–54), the Columbian Exposition traded heavily on illusion and façade. The White City, as discussed so well in the literature, presented neoclassical buildings composed not of the apparent marble but of plaster on iron frames. The White City marginalized race while it occluded its own infrastructure, not to mention the urbanity of the surrounding city.

My account has revealed many instances in which anthropologists shifted or transposed a given state of cultural reality. Although one may be tempted to regard one of these states as the true and authentic version of Native culture—and to that extent more scientific or objective—in fact this is a false issue. For all we have in culture and in cultural representation are acts of interpretation. Indeed, different cultures and the same one at different times maintain different conceptions and valuations of originals and copies (Isaac 2011, 212).

In our contemporary age of digitization and virtual worlds, issues of multiplicity have been given a new urgency. While the Chicago

World's Fair of 1893 may have been modern in many ways, in others it was arguably postmodern, with an endless profusion of versions and simulacra (Cantwell 2009). Anthropologists are still living with its refractions.

Notes

1. Eakins painted the canvas of Daniel Brinton, now at the American Philosophical Society, in 1900 from a photo. He also produced portraits of Daniel's uncle, surgeon John H. Brinton (1876), and his wife, Sarah Ward Brinton (1878). Unfortunately the portrait of Culin, titled "The Archaeologist," was stolen and is still missing (Foster et al., 1997, 210–12). Cushing's portrait, obtained by Culin for the Brooklyn Museum, was sold in 1947 to the Gilcrease Museum in Tulsa. In addition to these scholars, Eakins painted a full-size portrait of Sarah S. Frishmuth (1900), patron and collector of musical instruments for the University of Pennsylvania's anthropology museum, and began another of Lucy Wharton Drexel, donor of a collection of fans. For a time both the Cushing and Frishmuth portraits were on display in the museum (cf. Braddock 2009, 171–212).

2. This essay is a more detailed and focused treatment of issues I first explored in my essay on the exhibits of Franz Boas (Jacknis 1985, 80–83). Like that one, it adopts a comprehensive model of exhibit analysis, first considering "political" concerns of institutional authority and funding before turning to more "poetic" issues of medium, representation, and realism. Regionally, I examined the Northwest Coast displays in Jacknis 1991a (cf. Jacknis 2002b).

3. While the Fair's general significance for anthropology has been noted before (e.g., Darnell 1998, 133–35), there has been surprisingly little attention to its importance as visual representation (cf. Fagin 1984; Jacknis 1991a; Jenkins 1994, 258–60; Griffiths 2002, 46–85).

4. As a case study of visual modes in the discipline, this essay is a contribution to the larger history of visual anthropology (cf. Banks and Ruby 2011).

5. Although the Bureau's Henry W. Henshaw (1850–1930) was involved in some of the preparatory fieldwork, because his health failed around 1893, he did not have much to do with the final exhibits.

6. In fact, due to Henshaw's illness in late 1891, Mason recommended that Holmes be authorized to arrange a series of models on Aboriginal stone work, a request that was granted. Otis T. Mason to George Brown Goode, November 27, 1891, RU 70, box 39, folder 3, Smithsonian Institution Archives (hereafter cited as SIA).

7. Otis T. Mason to George Brown Goode, April 17, 1891; November 14, 1892, RU 70, box 39, folder 3, SIA.

8. In reviewing the staff contributions, Mason wrote that Holmes helped "not only in preparing illustrations of his own remarkable investigations, but in advising and directing the preparators in arranging groups of costumed figures, etc. In this work Mr. Frank Hamilton Cushing, through his familiarity with the customs and

arts of the Pueblo people, rendered also most valuable services. Mr. James Mooney also participated, and the group of Kiowa children, prepared under his direction, was among the most attractive of them all. But for his absence in the field, collecting material, he would have been able to devise others of similar excellence. Dr. W. J. Hoffman superintended the preparation of groups of Northern Indians" (Mason 1895, 127).

9. This kind of apparent redundancy in museum presentation has continued to characterize the Smithsonian, with, for example, a Museum of African Art and an African anthropology hall in the Natural History Museum (cf. Jacknis 2008, 22–23).

10. Stewart Culin's exhibit on folklore and games, in the Anthropology Building, was also built on a comparative approach (Culin 1894).

11. This Smithsonian plan to illustrate the Powell map with regional life groups was adopted at a meeting in April 1891; Otis T. Mason to George Brown Goode, April 17, 1891, RU 70, box 39, folder 3, SIA.

12. Otis T. Mason to George Brown Goode, November 14, 1892, RU 70, box 39, folder 3, SIA.

13. According to Graham's summary, "Although the technique of employing piece molds for casting sculpture in the round dates from the sixteenth century, the first planned campaign of making casts in this way was seen in the 1830s, when casts of medieval sculpture were assembled in Nuremberg for the purpose of illustrating outstanding German achievements in architecture and sculpture, the undeclared motive of which was . . . to engender the sense of German national consciousness" (1993, 70).

14. Some of this cast work was done at the Fair. In January 1893 Anthropology took over an annex building, which was "used for making plaster casts from molds made by assistants in the field," taking "the place of a similar workshop in the Forestry Building, which had been occupied by the department for several months" (Johnson 1898, 3:316).

15. "Snapshots at Ghost Dancers," [Richmond, Indiana] *Daily Palladium*, April 26, 1892 [1893?], folder 733, newspaper clippings–Chicago World Exhibition, Frank Hamilton Cushing Collection, Braun Research Library, Southwest Museum (hereafter cited as SWM).

16. "What a Museum Does," *Washington Evening Star*, November 9, 1890, U.S. National Museum ms. and pamphlet file, box 47, folder 660, National Anthropological Archives (hereafter cited as NAA).

17. In addition to those discussed here, other miniature models represented the necropolis at Ancon, Peru (from the Peabody Museum), "an entire model of a mesa village" (from the territory of New Mexico, cf. Fagin 1984, 256), and St. Peter's basilica, made of "carved wood, coated with a substance that closely resembled marble" (Johnson 1898, 3:342–43).

18. House of the Stormy Sea, the home of chief *tl'aajaang quuna* ("Great Splashing of Waves"), arrived in Chicago by November 1892. Although it was apparently destroyed after the Fair, its frontal pole was preserved and is now on display in the great hall of the Field Museum. "James Deans and his Company of Indians," 1893,

American Antiquarian and Oriental Journal, 15, 185–86; Johnson (1897, 2:429); MacDonald (1983, 46); Wright (2001, 112, 266).

19. According to Robin Wright, who is researching the Skidegate village, "Ten of these house models and 22 poles have survived in the collection of the Field Museum of Natural History; 19 house models and 21 model poles were exchanged or given away, and of those, 13 houses and 13 poles have been lost," ("Skidegate Haida Model Houses and Poles," http://www.washington.edu/burkemuseum/bhc/haida_models/index.php).

20. About a decade after the Fair, John Robson made a model of the House of the Stormy Sea, the full-size Haida house erected in Chicago. Commissioned by John Swanton for the American Museum of Natural History, it also differs from the original in many ways (Wright 2001, 270; cf. Jonaitis 1992).

21. *Thirteenth Annual Report of the Bureau of Ethnology, for 1891–92* (1896), xxxvii; *Fourteenth Annual Report of the Bureau of Ethnology, for 1892–93* (1896), xlvii.

22. "In Study of Mankind," *Chicago Tribune*, July 2, 1893, Exposition scrapbook, Stewart Culin papers, Brooklyn Museum Archives.

23. As confirmation of my general point about refraction, almost every source on the Serpent Mound gives a different length and height. Here I use that of Glotzhober and Lepper (1994).

24. This purchase of an archaeological site anticipated Edward H. Thompson's 1894 acquisition of the Yucatán site of Chichén Itzá, also excavated by Harvard.

25. This was not the only model that Harvard displayed in the Liberal Arts Building. Along with the Maine miniature for Anthropology, the Psychology Department presented wax models of brains, eyes, ears, and other organs. There were also two "anthropometric statues" in the Anthropology Building. A pair of plaster figurines representing ideal male and female types, they were based on measurements and a large corpus of photographs of Harvard freshmen (Brown 1994, 45–47).

26. After the Fair, Charnay's plaster casts were accessioned by the Field Museum, where they were subsequently painted (McVicker 2005, 112).

27. The Mayan casts from Anthropology were not the only Mesoamerican examples at the Fair: the Mexican pavilion displayed four "archaeological reconstructions" of Aztec sculptures from Mexico City, from five to ten feet square. The largest was the temple of Huitzilopochtli; another depicted the triumphal entry of Cortez into the city, and two showed the final stages in the capture of Cuauhtemoc (Fane 1993, 160; cf. Tenorio-Trillo 1996).

28. The British Museum has 400 plaster casts from Maudslay (Aguirre 2005, 97). Those from Chichén Itzá were painted to match traces of color still visible on the originals (Graham 2002, 165).

29. In another expression of refraction, two museums lay claim to the Chicago set. According to Graham (2002, 298) and Brown (1994, 42), Putnam sold the set to the Field Museum, while the Brooklyn Museum implies that their set was purchased by curators Stewart Culin and William Henry Goodyear from the prints exhibited at the Exposition. It is possible, however, that even though the two

had seen Maudslay's prints in Chicago, the ones that they received were another printing from the original negatives, as was the earlier set, which went to the British Museum (http://www.brooklynmuseum.org/opencollection/archives/set/72/collection_of_photographs_by_alfred_p._maudslay_1883-1890./copy/history).

30. These living groups have attracted a great deal of scholarly attention (e.g., Rydell 1984; Hinsley 1991; Griffiths 2002; Bank 2002).

31. Living ethnic groups and life group dioramas were separate at least as far the Chicago presentation was concerned. As we know from Mason's testimony, his use of the dioramas in America had been stimulated by seeing the live groups at the 1889 Paris exposition (Mason 1890; cf. Kohlstedt 2008, 185, 194–96). At the end of his tour, he visited museums in Scandinavia, where he undoubtedly was exposed to the dioramas in the folk museums (Kohlstedt 2008, 200–1).

32. In fact, another clear model for the Smithsonian's development of cultural life groups was William T. Hornaday's American bison group, constructed at the U.S. National Museum in 1888 (Wonders 1993, 120–23).

33. Two of them were modeled on body casts of Zulu and San "Bushmen" brought to London for ethnic shows.

34. While Kavanagh's unpublished review of Smithsonian mannequins and life groups (1990) is extremely useful, it does contain errors, especially in regard to admittedly difficult dating.

35. During the years of preparation, plans were repeatedly changed—some at the last minute—but the most complete and authoritative listing of the mannequins and life groups at Chicago seems to be the one compiled by preparator Carl Bergmann (1893). A treasure trove for analysts, it lists the subject of each group—number of figures, gender, age, occupation—in addition to giving a complete list of the museum specimens (with catalog numbers).

36. A news article claimed that Putnam would be displaying some figures made by the Smithsonian near the center of his building: "Doings at the Fair," *Fort Wayne Sentinel*, April 1893, World's Columbian Exposition (WCE) Scrapbook 2, F. W. Putnam Papers, Harvard University Archives (hereafter cited as FWPP).

37. "Doings at the Fair," WCE Scrapbook 2, FWPP.

38. Despite some confusion and lack of funding, especially in Putnam's displays, Fagin's conclusion (1984, 263) about the impact of the fair is grossly inaccurate. First, she claims: "Most of the exhibits came from Washington. Apparently, few pieces were collected specifically for the Exposition; all artifacts came from the permanent collections of one of the participating institutions or from active field researchers." As we have seen, in several instances for the Smithsonian (Mooney among the Hopi, Navajo, and Kiowa, and Hoffman among the Ojibwa), not to mention in the Anthropology Building, many of the displays were specifically collected for the Fair. Even less accurate is her conclusion that "the exhibit, for all its planning and artistry, made only a small impact on museum history, however."

39. In the 1840s the father of preparator Theodore A. Mills had developed a method of using life casts from his sitters to simplify the production of portrait

busts; Mills and his father had produced one of Lincoln just two months before the president's death.

40. The eighty costumed mannequins revealed an even wider tribal range: Arctic (Eskimos from Greenland, Hudson's Bay, Cumberland Gulf, Labrador, Anderson River, Alaska, Point Barrow), Subarctic (Fort Yukon, Interior Alaska, Naskapi), Northwest Coast (Klallam, Tlingit), Plateau (Nez Perce), California (Hupa), Great Basin (Paiute, Ute), Southwest (Zuni, Hopi, Navajo, Apache, Yuma), Plains (Sioux, Crow, Kiowa, Comanche), and Eastern Woodlands (Ojibwa). Despite the Exposition's focus on Native America, there were a few groups devoted to Historic America (a cowboy and turkey hunter) as well as a few foreign countries: Peru, Morocco, and Italy.

41. Photograph neg. no. 12279, SIA.

42. "The National Museum: How It Will Be a Gainer through the World's Fair," *Washington Evening Star*, July 26, 1893, FWPP.

43. In fact, semi-habitat dioramas remained the most popular kinds of life groups in anthropology; very few included illusionistic painted backgrounds. Important exceptions were those in the Southwest Hall at the American Museum of Natural History (Jacknis 2015).

44. William H. Holmes, 1911, exhibit label, "The Manufacture of Stone Implements by the American Aborigines," in his "Random Records of a Lifetime, 1846–1931" (Holmes n.d., vol. 6).

45. The documentation of the mannequin of the Zuni belt weaver is somewhat contradictory. It is missing from Bergmann's listing and installation photos at the Smithsonian Institution Archives (RU 95, Photographic Collections, series 7, Expositions, 1851–1893, World's Columbian Exposition, box 61, folder 11-A). On the other hand, Cushing (1893b) clearly refers to it as installed in Chicago. Kavanagh (1990), who illustrates several versions, also lists it as being at the Fair.

46. During the six months in 1886 that We'wha spent with Matilda Coxe Stevenson in Washington, he was photographed at the National Museum demonstrating weaving (Roscoe 1988; 1991, 61–62, 87–89; Isaac 2013). The identification of We'wha comes principally from a visual comparison of these images with the final mannequin (e.g., Hough 1922, pl. 38). That of Klah comes from a manuscript report by Frank Cushing (1893b, footnote; cf. Fowler 2000, 210): "While costumed as a *woman*, this figure really represents a man belonging to a peculiar class of '*women-men*' who, when they do woman's work such as weaving and cooking, herding, etc., are dressed, and are spoken of, as 'women.'" Although Cushing does not give his name, Hosteen Klah was probably the person. Interestingly enough, while Klah is not identified as a subject in Smithsonian photo documentation, the weaver, a male, is called "Charley" (Fleming and Luskey 1986, 168).

47. Undoubtedly this focus stemmed from Hoffman's own scholarly interests. As his obituary noted, "Dr. Hoffman's special studies were largely concerned with sign language, pictography, secret societies, primitive ritual and primitive art" (Chamberlain 1900, 44).

48. Titles visible in photographs in the Smithsonian Institution Archives: Zuni creation group (neg. no. 12265), Sioux hide dressers (neg. no. 12257), Ojibwa scribe (neg. no. 12269).

49. See photograph neg. no. 56,322, in NAA; cf. Brown 1994, 142.

50. William H. Holmes, undated, notes for a Sioux life group, pamphlet file Museums: installations and scenarios, folder 666, NAA.

51. Frank H. Cushing to Stewart Culin, October 3, 1894, University of Pennsylvania Museum Archives (Cushing 1893–98).

52. A few years after Chicago (1899 and 1901), James Mooney and Bureau photographer DeLancy Gill found an almost complete visual acculturation among the surviving Algonquians (Pamunkey, Mattaponie) of King William County, Virginia (Colby 1977, 137–40; cf. Jacknis 1990, 187).

53. James Mooney, "Some Primitive Bread," *Baltimore News*, May 28, 1893, folder 733, newspaper clippings–Chicago World Exhibition, Frank Hamilton Cushing Collection, Braun Research Library, SWM.

54. Ironically, Mooney was the only one of the participating anthropologists to exhibit any of his field photographs at the Fair, and then there were only six of his Ghost Dance pictures.

55. Two years after the Fair, Boas employed pictures taken by Oregon C. Hastings in Fort Rupert for re-creating his group of Kwakiutl cedar crafts at the American Museum of Natural History (Jacknis 1984, 33–36).

56. Deloria is mistaken in regard to the place and date of a famous image of Cushing in his Zuni costume; it was not taken in his New York apartment, ca. 1900, but by Jack Hillers in Zuni, ca. 1881 (Truettner 1985, 48).

57. Boas posed again as an Eskimo hunter about fifteen years later for the American Museum of Natural History (cf. Lesser 2004, 1).

58. According to Bergmann's listing (1893), of the eighty WCE mannequins, the following contained artifacts from foreign tribes: Alaskan group (Blackfoot knife), Fort Yukon boy (with Missouri River knife and Northwest Coast arrow), Klallam chief (Haida headdress), Hupa woman (Wintu cap and moccasins, Costa Rica armlet), Hupa child (Wintu cap), Paiute woman (Kiowa cradle), Ute burden bearer (Kiowa belt), Apache man (Zuni bow, Navajo bow/arrow/quiver, Navajo bracelet, Hopi shirt and hat), Zuni warrior (Paiute or Navajo leggings), Crow hide painter (Cheyenne moccasins), Sioux woman (Cheyenne bridle and knife, Piegan shirt, Kiowa lance and war bonnet), Sioux woman (Mexican bridle), Sioux baby (Crow bonnet), Sioux child (Crow jacket, Ute shirt), Sioux child (Crow parfleche), Sioux hide scraper (Kiowa scraper), Ojibwa medicine man (Sioux beaded braid, skins), Anglo cowboy (Pueblo hat, Mexican spurs, Comanche whip), Anglo turkey hunter (Zuni belt and pouch).

59. Another related problem of tribal identifications may be the result of curatorial confusion about just what tribe was being represented. For instance, many of the life group photographs at the Smithsonian are tribally misidentified, some of which were then published (e.g., Goode 1895b, 54, where many of the Hopi groups were listed as Zuni; cf. Brown 2003, 97, repeating the error). The bread makers diorama

clearly depicted the Hopi, as attested to by Mooney's field collection and photography in Hopi and the identification in Bergmann's 1893 listings (figures no. 69, 70, 71, 75). While one would normally pay little attention to such slips, in this case it may indicate a more fundamental confusion in contemporary Smithsonian ethnic identifications of the life groups, where artifacts were mixed and matched to represent diverse groups. In fact, this was precisely the point of the Mooney-Cushing dispute.

60. William H. Holmes to Frank H. Cushing, April 29, 1893, Frank Hamilton Cushing Collection, Braun Research Library, SWM.

61. Otis T. Mason to Frank H. Cushing, May 14, 1893, Frank Hamilton Cushing Collection, Braun Research Library, SWM.

62. Mooney was able to expound his philosophy of cultural holism in his "Outline Plan for Ethnology Museum Collections" of 1894. His multi-media approach to museum exhibits was intended to capture the inter-relations of cultural domains, a position quite close to Boas's own (cf. Jacknis 1996).

63. Cushing outlined his dreams for a "Museum Institution of Ethnology," based on the results of the Hemenway Expedition, in a long letter to Sylvester Baxter, 2 August 1887, Letterbooks, Hemenway Southwestern Archaeological Expedition Papers, Division of Rare and Manuscript Collections, Cornell University Library.

64. In the summer of 1891 Mooney commissioned six Kiowa model tipis and summer houses (Colby 1977, 275). The following year he had the idea of recreating miniature versions of shields. According to Fagin (1988, 262), Mooney commissioned the Kiowa or Kiowa Apache to construct thirty-one tipi and shield models to be exhibited at the WCE, representing a camp circle of the 1867 Kiowa Sun Dance, but there is no evidence that they were ever made.

65. Among the mannequins first presented in 1893 that were still on view when the hall closed in 2004 were the Eskimo in a kayak, Kutchin family, Tlingit chief, Hupa family, Kiowa family, Crow painter, Sioux hide dressers, Apache family, Hopi bread makers, Zuni potters, Zuni belt weaver, Navajo weavers and silversmiths, and Jivaro man; and there were probably a few others.

66. Frank Cushing to Stewart Culin, September 24, October 3, 1894 (Cushing 1893-98). Holmes reports (1897b, 151) that a copy of his quarry life group was set up at the Field Museum, as was done with the Kwakiutl hamatsa ceremonial.

67. Original documentation on Holmes's 1925 proposals for Piney Branch memorial are contained in his "Random Records of a Lifetime, 1846–1931" (Holmes n.d., vol. 6, sections 4 and 5).

68. On the same field trip Boas gathered material for a second life group at the American Museum of Natural History, illustrating the uses of cedar. Unlike Dorsey, however, Putnam in New York was consciously trying to avoid duplication (Jacknis 2002b, 100).

69. Walter Hough, "Historical Sketch of the Division of Ethnology," handwritten ms., 1906, file no. 4787, NAA.

70. "The Pueblos at Home," *Washington Post*, September 4, 1894 (Document G, this volume).

71. Hopi bread makers (pl. 64); Hopi basket maker (pl. 65); Zuni potters (pl. 66); and Navajo weavers (pl. 67).

72. For the ethnographic imagination in literature, see Evans 2005.

73. Respectively, *Chicago Tribune*, July 2, 1893, scrapbook, newspaper clippings, 1887–94, Stewart Culin papers, Brooklyn Museum Archives; *Baltimore American*, August 27, 1893, clipping in WCE Scrapbook 3, p. 68, FWPP.

74. One of the supporters of Muybridge's work at the University of Pennsylvania was Dr. William Pepper, provost of the university and founder of its anthropology museum—a sign of the relatively small world of Philadelphia intelligentsia among whom Eakins moved.

ESSAY FIVE

Relic Hunters in the White City

Artifacts, Authority, and Ambition at the World's Columbian Exposition

JAMES E. SNEAD

Among the many anthropological treasures on display at the World's Columbian Exposition were hundreds of newly excavated artifacts from Pueblo ruins in the American Southwest. Exhibited at many different venues, the highly visible southwestern antiquities marked a new emphasis in American archaeology. Fourteen years earlier Frederic Ward Putnam, curator of the Peabody Museum of Archaeology and Ethnology at Harvard, had predicted that only properly equipped expeditions and years of fieldwork would provide answers to questions about ancient peoples of the western states and territories (Putnam 1879, 318; Essay 1, this volume). The wealth of archaeological evidence on display in Chicago—and Putnam's eminence as chief of the Department of Ethnology at the Exposition—might have implied that his vision for a comprehensive research program had been realized.

Yet rather than represent a new scientific paradigm, displays of the pre-Columbian Southwest at the Fair signified a chaotic market for American antiquities. American archaeology in the 1890s was a competitive arena, one in which the emergent class of professional archaeologists in eastern institutions collaborated and competed with "relic hunters" working on behalf of patrons who provided the capital for acquisitions. The ambitions of such different interest groups often led to clashes over excavation rights and interpretations of the past. Individuals often straddled these conceptual boundaries, maneuvering for funding and prestige (Hinsley 1991). Grand public events such as the Chicago Fair created common ground for alliances and relationships of convenience associated with such antiquarian "capital," not unlike circumstances documented by other historians of field sciences, such as Simon Knell (2000). Chicago's focus on the Columbian encounter, and thus the high visibility of Native Americans as performers and "living exhibits"—as well as producers of material culture—created a unique convergence of individuals and institutions associated with this heritage (Fogelson 1991; Raibmon 2005).

The networks of patronage and fieldwork that were forged at the Exposition ultimately created conditions within which "professional" archaeologists gained ascendance over their competition (Snead 1999). The success of individuals within these matrices was quite variable, however, with some ultimately driven out of the emerging discipline even while former compatriots were lionized as elders of the discipline. Their experiences as relic hunters in the western landscape and in the White City—distinct from those provided by the intellectual gatherings that also took place at the fair—provide an important illustration of a "community of inquiry" in transition.

Relic Hunters

The expansion of Anglo-American settlement into the West brought new immigrants into regular contact with ancient monuments (Fowler 2000; Hinsley 1981; Martinko 2009; Snead 2001 and n.d.). The federal survey parties that documented ruins in the post–Civil War Southwest were often guided by settlers who had first discovered them while building homesteads and hunting for cattle. Thus by the time news of these antiquities reached the scientific community and the eastern public, some had been investigated by local inhabitants for decades (Hardacre 1878; Holmes 1878).

The dominant utilitarian ethos on the frontier quickly led to the emergence of local markets for antiquities. In most cases residents supplemented their income by relic hunting in their spare time, selling artifacts to schoolteachers and other interested parties. The rise of the tourist trade allowed for modest expansion of the relic hunting economy (Batkin 1998; Wade 1985). Demand for artifacts to display in eastern institutions such as the U.S. National Museum was ultimately more influential, since the collections were larger and the potential payoff greater (Parezo 1987; Stevenson 1883). Even this market was easily saturated, however, and relic hunting remained just one of many sources of income for western traders and entrepreneurs.

The relic hunting economy was intertwined with cultural interests in ruins and the associated desire on the part of rural Americans to participate in their exploration (Hinsley 1996a; Snead 2001). Consistently, many of these "discoverers" saw their finds as means to enter the still small world of American anthropology. Local knowledge and access to artifacts were perceived as assets that would allow them to overcome the potential barriers of class, region, and education to join the evolving professional ranks. This perception was not necessarily shared by either patrons or those already occupying positions of disciplinary authority, however. The tension thus generated between those who wanted more than money for their artifacts and the consumers who saw the arrangement strictly in economic terms was endemic in the relic trade.

Opportunities for relic hunters expanded considerably in the run-up to the Chicago Fair. Under Putnam's auspices events had been scheduled to highlight scholarly achievements—in particular, the International Congress of Anthropology that began in late August (Essay 2, this volume; Rydell 1984, 58)—but he was also committed to extensive public programming. Exhibits were the centerpiece of this effort, and the lion's share of material to be placed on display had to be newly acquired.

The demand for collections and exhibitions placed enormous strain on the existing structure of American anthropology, particularly since most of the institutions involved focused on their own contributions to the Fair. Because Putnam invited private collectors to exhibit their antiquities in the Anthropology Building, displays sponsored by "official" organizations were mounted adjacent to those of individual entrepreneurs and enthusiasts of all stripes (Essay 4, this volume; Lange 1998).

These circumstances fueled the relic hunting economy. Putnam had a substantial budget for acquisitions, and in his zeal to acquire representative material he corresponded with individuals, agents, and dealers (e.g., Frazar 1891). Control over the collecting process was desirable, however, and over the course of the Fair he hired as many as seventy-five "assistants" to obtain artifacts (Putnam 1896; McVicker

2003; and Essays 1 and 3, this volume). There were very few advanced students available, and these had limited field experience. The expertise required to locate and obtain museum-quality collections resided largely in the existing network of relic hunters, some of whom had worked with Putnam for years.

Necessity brought opportunity, particularly for those who harbored ambitions to participate in American archaeology at a higher level. To these men—women could participate only obliquely—the World's Columbian Exposition represented a foothold to reach the broader market directly and perhaps to establish more secure positions. Among those who attempted to seize this moment were two who would go on to build very different reputations in American archaeology: Richard Wetherill and Warren King Moorehead. Their intertwined experiences illustrate the complexities of the era and provide a more nuanced picture of the development of professional anthropology.

Richard Wetherill

The complex motivations behind relic hunting were fully expressed in the career of Richard Wetherill. The Wetherill family was based at the Alamo Ranch, near Mancos, Colorado, at the foot of Mesa Verde, with which their legacy is intimately associated. The archaeological reputation of the Wetherill family has grown in recent decades, and related studies and accounts are numerous (Atkins 1993; Blackburn 2006; Blackburn and Williamson 1997; Brugge 1980; Fletcher 1977; Gabriel 1992; Gillmor and Wetherill 1934; Harrell 1987, 1992; Lister and Lister 1985; McNitt 1966; Smith 1988; Snead 2001).

Excavations in the Mesa Verde ruins began in the 1860s, but no consistent market emerged for artifacts unearthed during these decades (Blackburn 2006). The Wetherills' own exploration proceeded as opportunity allowed and was closely tied to the tourism business that developed at their Alamo Ranch. The rugged appeal of the vicinity was enhanced by trips to ruins, and by the late 1880s a regular flow of visitors passed through in the summer months.

The relic hunting economy of southwestern Colorado became more firmly established in 1889, when the collections excavated from Cliff Palace and nearby sites by the Wetherill brothers and local miner Charles McLoyd were purchased by the Colorado State Historical Soci-

FIG. 64. Richard Wetherill at Round Tower, Mesa Verde. By Nordenskiold, Image MEVE 111110/588. Courtesy of Mesa Verde National Park.

ety (Phillips 1993, 104). McLoyd seems to have been the instigator of this effort, and with the successful sale he moved westward to dig in the Grand Gulch country of southeastern Utah with Charles Carey Graham (Daniels 1976). Others followed (Blackburn and Atkins 1993). The Wetherills participated in this artifact rush only obliquely, but as their tourism business prospered it is probable that many small collections were produced for these clients.

The patronage network nurtured at the Alamo Ranch proved critical to the Wetherills' sustained participation in archaeological work, because it created durable personal relationships (Snead 2001, 21). Particularly influential was the Swedish aristocrat Gustav Nordenskiold, who excavated at Mesa Verde with the Wetherill brothers in 1891 and is credited with introducing them to current archaeological methodology (see Diamond and Olson 1991). Another was T. Mitchell Prudden, a New York doctor who began making annual trips to the Southwest in 1892 and became what he called "a poacher on archaeological preserves" (Anon. 1927, 128).

Relationships forged on the trails to Cliff Palace resulted in popular books and publications that raised public awareness about the Colorado ruins (e.g., Chapin 1892; Prudden 1906). Such affiliations, however, were only partially successful in advancing the Wetherills' desire for greater influence in the study of southwestern antiquity. Prudden, Nordenskiold and the others, like the Wetherills, were on the margins of American anthropology and were of little assistance in helping attract institutional sponsors more central to the rapidly evolving profession.[1]

Thus when it became clear that the World's Columbian Exposition would require new collections, the Wetherill brothers seized the opportunity to pursue their own archaeological ambitions as well as to generate needed income. The field, however, was already crowded. McLoyd and Graham's first Grand Gulch collection was sold to the Rev. C. H. Green, a Durango pastor, who sponsored a subsequent expedition of his own and took the combined set of artifacts to Chicago for sale (Blackburn and Atkins 1993; Hayes 1993). C. D. Hazzard, an entrepreneur with deeper pockets than Green, purchased another McLoyd and Graham Grand Gulch collection that had been exhibited in Durango in the spring of 1892. Later that year he staked another expedition, led by H. Jay Smith (Phillips 1993, 107).[2]

The Wetherill brothers served as guides for Smith and, after the completion of that project, were engaged to obtain yet another collection destined for the Exposition, this one sponsored by the State of Colorado, under the general direction of A. F. Willmarth (Phillips

1993, 108). This effort was supervised by Richard Wetherill, who had begun to take the leading role in his family's archaeological efforts, and he was ultimately dispatched with Willmarth to Chicago to install the collection. Like many other relic hunters of the day, Wetherill took the opportunity to travel east to participate in the Fair and to see what could be stirred up for future work.

Warren King Moorehead

Another relic hunter who haunted the Midway was Warren King Moorehead. Moorehead was born in 1866 and grew up in Xenia, Ohio (Byers 1939; Christenson 2011; Moorehead 1903–4).[3] Popular interest in Ohio archaeology was high during Moorehead's youth, with an extensive community of interest built around the collection and display of artifacts (Barnhart 1998; Hinsley 1996a). Moorehead credits his early interest to a doctor in Muskingum County, Ohio, who had "opened a small mound. On visiting the spot a short time afterward, my cousin and myself found broken bones scattered about the surface. None of them were large but I secured the head of a femur and have since religiously preserved it as a most treasured possession" (Moorehead 1903–4, 2). Moorehead's very first article, published in the *Young Mineralogist and Antiquarian,* demonstrated the precocity of his interest (Moorehead 1884).

Moorehead attended Denison University for two years in the mid-1880s and there crossed paths with George Dorsey, who went on to become one of Putnam's first doctoral students at Harvard.[4] His own career took a different path. As a youthful exhibitor at the Centennial Exposition of the Ohio in Cincinnati in 1888—where he displayed roughly four thousand objects from his own collection (Moorehead 1903–4, 2)—Moorehead met Thomas Wilson of the U.S. National Museum and was invited to Washington. This experience whetted his appetite but did not translate into substantive employment. Fortunately, his maternal relations, the King family, ran a prosperous milling business, and this personal network provided some financial support at critical intervals.

Efforts to enter anthropology on his own terms took Moorehead in various directions. He pursued independent fieldwork in Ohio, building on his close relationships with collectors and local organizations

FIG. 65. Warren K. Moorehead (with cigar) and workers at Fort Ancient. © Robert S. Peabody Museum of Archaeology, Phillips Academy, Andover, Massachusetts. All Rights Reserved.

such as the Ohio State Archaeological and Historical Society and the Ohio State Academy of Sciences (Barnhart 1998; Dexter 1966b). He also became a freelance writer on archaeological and anthropological subjects, traveling to the Dakotas in 1890 to write a series of articles on the Sioux that appeared in *American Illustrated Magazine*. But the young Moorehead had difficulty satisfying the magazine's editor, Maurice K. Minton. "You are writing as an ordinary correspondent not as a student of Indian matters," Minton wrote, "as you claimed yourself to be–that is–one who had made the Indian question a study" (Minton 1890). His major publication from this era, a novel entitled *Wanneta, the Sioux* (Moorehead 1890), reflects this journalistic approach.

Putnam knew of Moorehead—either through Dorsey or Wilson or perhaps because of his personal involvement with Ohio archaeology—and in March 1891 contacted him regarding "Fort Ancient and the importance of representing that very interesting site of early habitation in the Ohio Valley, in a proper manner, at the Exposition of 1893." Putnam requested that he "take the field as soon as practicable," and Moorehead soon joined the corps of assistants (Putnam 1891a). The work at Fort Ancient was productive, and by the fall of that year he shifted to the Hopewell site, where additional significant discoveries were made. During his field season Moorehead hosted several prominent visitors, including Wilson and Putnam's student Hilborne T. Cresson (Burns 2008, 15). It must have seemed an auspicious step in his developing career (Moorehead 1891, 1922).

In early 1892, however, Moorehead came forward with a new proposal: to lead an expedition to the Southwest. He was clearly aware of the interest generated by "cliff dweller" discoveries and apparently saw participation in this work as a way to gain professional prestige. Putnam, desiring a more direct role in the region's booming relic hunter economy, approved. Moorehead resuscitated his relationship with Minton at *American Illustrated*, offering publication rights in exchange for financial backing. By March 16 a camp had been set up at Aztec Ruin in New Mexico, and the project was under way (Moorehead 1892a).

The articles published under the auspices of the "*American Illustrated* Exploring Expedition" provide a unique picture of archaeological reconnaissance in the 1890s (Knipmeyer 2006). The endeavor itself, however, was doomed. Moorehead failed to inform Putnam about his relationship with the magazine, creating at least the appearance of bad faith. The Peabody curator may already have had a poor opinion of Minton, who had tried to involve him in an expedition to the Congo (Minton 1891). The timing was also unfortunate since Moorehead had recently made damaging allegations against Putnam's student Cresson (Wilson 1894). Whether Putnam was concerned about the appearance of impropriety, thought Moorehead was out of line, or simply felt that he should have been informed earlier, the relationship between director and field assistant cooled.[5]

To aggravate the situation further, Moorehead antagonized his other patron by requesting more money. "This telegram of yours surprises me," Minton wrote, even before exploration began, "as you distinctly told me that the $500. I gave you would be sufficient for all purposes" (Minton 1892). Since Putnam had only offered to cover the costs of shipping the collection, funding quickly became scarce. Moorehead drew from his own savings and tapped his relatives, assuming considerable debt. Spring snow in Colorado also made fieldwork difficult. "We will make it a success or leave our bones in the San Juan country," he declared in his journal (Moorehead 1892b). Better weather arrived in late spring of 1892, but while the field team continued with fieldwork Moorehead spent most of his time at the Strater Hotel in Durango, writing another novel based on his Sioux notes and touring Charles McLoyd's 1892 Grand Gulch collection, on exhibit nearby.

This was at the height of the relic hunter boom prior to the Fair, and Moorehead began making plans with McLoyd (Moorehead 1892c). The two men worked out a complex scheme to attract patronage, in which a graded scale of "memberships" in an archaeological society would be advertised in magazines throughout the United States, with the goal of generating nearly $150,000 for a ten-year plan of fieldwork at the national level. "Heavens, what we could accomplish!" Moorehead wrote in his diary (1892d).[6]

Despite the commotion, Moorehead managed to keep in regular contact with his various patrons, bombarding them with updates and suggestions for future projects. In these proposals he worked to distinguish his own work from those of other relic hunters in the field even as he collaborated with them as well. Writing to Putnam, he promoted new collecting initiatives:

> It would certainly pay to send a survey among the ruined pueblos south of this place. . . . I never saw an extent of country on the surface of which were scattered more implements or utensils. We could fill several wagons with valuable objects for you could your department make us an allowance of $440.
>
> The opportunity is yours. If you do not take advantage of it, the relic hunters–who, by the way, are fast despoiling these sacred ruins, will carry off all the treasures. They will fall into the hands of Tom, Dick, and Harry (Moorehead 1892e).

Putnam was, of course, quite familiar with "Tom, Dick, and Harry," since he had already hired another relic hunter to obtain precisely the sort of collection that Moorehead sought. Conrad Viets, a farmer in southwestern Colorado, had recently made a collection from the region for the Peabody Museum, and Putnam sent a query asking if he was "ready to spend the rest of the year in exploring mounds [sic] cliff-houses, caves etc." (Phillips 1993; Snead 2001, 3; Putnam 1891b). Viets reported "several parties out around here collecting now" (Viets 1891) and had largely ceased his own work by the time of Moorehead's arrival. Their parallel efforts, along with those of McLoyd, Wetherill, and others, indicate the complexity of the collecting situation on the ground. Over time these relationships grew even more convoluted: when Putnam was consulted by the State of Colorado regarding a collection to be housed in the Anthropology Building—the collection ultimately made by Richard Wetherill—he cabled Moorehead and asked him to assist the effort (Putnam 1892h).

By the time this telegram reached Durango, however, Moorehead's schemes and the *American Illustrated*'s expedition had come to an abrupt end. Details of the project's demise are unclear: Moorehead later noted that the magazine failed. Minton vanished from the pages of his diaries, and by May 3 Moorehead was on the train en route back to New York (Moorehead 1892f). After getting married in November 1892, Moorehead proceeded to Chicago, where he joined the cadre of Putnam's assistants in preparing the exhibitions.

Relic Hunters in Chicago

The Columbian Exposition was to open on May 1, 1893, but organizing the anthropological exhibits had begun long before. Throughout that spring southwestern collections were shipped to Chicago to be put on display in various venues. Exhibits from the U.S. National Museum were placed in the Government Building, along with artifacts contributed by entrepreneurs, such as Reverend Green and Gustav Nordenskiold. The collections made by Viets and Moorehead, with their relatively official imprimatur, were joined by some state exhibits— including Colorado's Wilmarth collection, a cliff dweller display in the Utah pavilion, and a New Mexico contribution at the "Joint Territories Building" (Phillips 1993, 109; World's Columbian Exposition 1898, 183–85, 208). The Anthropology Building itself was not completed until early July (Essay 1, this volume). Many of the individual collections targeted for this space failed to arrive, adding to the confusion.[7]

Some of the relic hunters developed independent exhibits. The most dramatic installation of southwestern artifacts was set up to the south of the Anthropology Building, where H. Jay Smith exhibited the Hazzard collection in a lath-and-plaster replica of a Colorado butte, complete with artificial vegetation, climbing trails, burros, and sheep. The interior featured scale models of the cliff palace and balcony house, made by expedition artist Alex Fournier, along with artifacts and a female "mummy" named "She," after the H. Rider Haggard character (H. Jay Smith Exploring Company 1893). The exhibit attracted a considerable crowd. Frank Hamilton Cushing wrote that it "was the finest I ever saw" (Cushing Diary, June 30, 1893, Document E, this volume). Souvenirs, particularly photos, were available, and Smith's employees were famously aggressive in their sales tactics (Essay 3, this volume). Gross receipts of the attraction were later reported to have been $87,366.28 (World's Columbian Exposition 1898, 483).

The H. Jay Smith Colorado Cliffdweller Exhibit attracted archaeologists, relic hunters, and the general public, providing an informal gathering place for diverse transactions. H. Jay Smith had his own tent camp nearby and entertained various colleagues. Cushing was a frequent visitor, as were Stewart Culin, Washington Matthews, and Antonio Apache. C. D. Hazzard spent time in Chicago as well and discussed possible future expeditions with Cushing and others (Cushing Diary, September 7, 1893, Document E, this volume). A fragment of Colorado had come to Chicago, and the gigantic replica came to represent common ground for the different groups of archaeological practitioners.

Richard Wetherill probably visited the Cliffdweller Exhibit, but he left no firsthand account. Whatever duties he had following the installation of the Wilmarth collection were probably minor, and he may not have stayed a particularly long time. He went unmentioned in the journals kept by various archaeologists at the Fair, and his impression of the event—and of the fate of various collections with which he had been involved—apparently remained unrecorded.

Wetherill did, however, have one significant encounter in Chicago, and it provided an opportunity for him to participate more directly in southwestern archaeology over the next decade. In 1892 the Alamo Ranch had hosted a trio of wealthy New Yorkers—Frederick Hyde and his sons, Talbot and Frederick—en route west on a world tour. Their

FIG. 66. The "Cliff Dwelling," World's Columbian Exposition, Chicago, 1893. H. H. Bancroft, *The Book of the Fair* (Chicago, 1893, 643).

brief visit to Mesa Verde, however, left as strong an impression in their minds as did those of the more exotic locales they visited before returning home. When the Hyde Brothers ran into Richard Wetherill in Chicago, in an atmosphere redolent with the relic hunting scene of the Southwest, they arranged to sponsor a new expedition under his leadership (Snead 2001).

In contrast to Wetherill's lack of a paper trail, Moorehead's diary provides much greater detail about his experiences at the Exposition. The Ohio collection was fully mounted in time for the delayed opening of the Anthropology Building on July 4. Thereafter Moorehead sold copies of his books and circulars to visitors and aggressively sought out future patrons, contacting, among others, "Prince [Roland] Bonaparte, the French Archaeologist," the president of Denison University, a "Mr. Parker of Omaha," the German ambassador, and representatives of a new museum being established in Dayton, Ohio. His efforts were facilitated by colleagues among the older generation of museum anthropologists, particularly those whom he had met in Washington. Thomas Wilson tipped Moorehead off about Bonaparte, while Otis Mason put him touch with a "Mrs. Stanford who desires to buy some collections for her husband's museum" (Moorehead 1893a).[8]

Some modest artifact sales took place, but no longer-term relationships developed. Moorehead also brokered the sale of some of the Exposition's other private collections for a percentage of the purchase price. One of these was apparently the McLoyd and Graham collection that he had seen in Durango, but his hope for a thousand-dollar commission was not realized. In the meantime he visited colleagues who attended the Exposition, including Gerard Fowke, another archaeologist working outside the central networks of the discipline. Fowke came to Chicago nursing grievances against former patrons, particularly those at the Smithsonian. Moorehead described him as "very bitter against the Major [Powell] and the other gentlemen of the Bureau" (1893b).

Instead of anthropology, the dominant force that shaped Moorehead's experience at the Exposition was the threat of financial ruin. Legal action had extracted a token settlement from Minton, but Moorehead still took a considerable loss (Phillips 1993, 110–11). He had also lost heavily in the collapse of the bond market in the 1893 panic, and the hard work to salvage the situation embittered Moorehead toward the people of Chicago. "I saw them today eating in the Grand Pacific Hotel," he wrote in his journal, "several hundred men around the lunch counter standing up. One would think there was a prize up for the one who first devoured his pie, sandwich and coffee" (Moorhead 1893c). Under these circumstances Moorehead—like Gerard Fowke—began to see the anthropological establishment as an obstacle to his success. "I guessed Putnam had it in for us," he wrote (Moorehead 1893d).

Animosity between patron and client pertained to control of the collections. Moorehead was convinced that the Southwest material, at least, was his to dispose of, but the tangled communications regarding the *American Illustrated* expedition left ownership unresolved. Moorehead's Ohio collection in the Anthropology Building won a prize (Thatcher 1894), but the destiny of these artifacts was uncertain as well. In his financially distressed situation Moorehead hoped to sell artifacts as a way to recoup some of the costs he had incurred in obtaining them, but his subordinate role in the process made this difficult. His original perception of the Exposition as a setting for professional opportunity gave way to feelings of betrayal and loss.

After the Fair: Patrons and Pitfalls

As the curtain came down on the Exposition at the end of October 1893, all those concerned with the Southwest relic trade sought to capitalize on the favorable publicity. For the various entrepreneurs and middlemen, this meant negotiating rapid sales. C. D. Hazzard, for instance, embarked on a prolonged series of negotiations that consolidated some of the collections and resulted in their purchase by Phoebe Hearst on behalf of the University Museum in Philadelphia and the University of California (Allen 1990; cf. Essay 3 and Document H, this volume).

A different approach was adopted by Reverend Green, who allied himself with Selim Peabody, an officer of the Fair and friend of Putnam's, to establish the "Society of Cliff-Dweller Archaeology of America." Although the organization's letterhead announced a goal of exploration, "with the view of ascertaining the antiquity, as well as tracing the progress of man upon this continent" (Green 1892), its primary function was the disposal of Green's collections. Their preferred customer was the newly planned Columbian Museum (Wilcox 2003a), and Putnam gave them some encouragement in that direction. He corresponded with Boas, then briefly associated with the Columbian, half-heartedly noting that "the price might be considered a fair one, although for the same amount of money used in sending a man into the field you could probably secure a similar collection of thorough scientific importance" (Putnam 1893p, 1894b). The sale ultimately went through, although at a substantially lower price than the "stockholders" of the society would have preferred (Hayes 1993, 126).

Richard Wetherill may have reaped little financial reward in Chicago, but his successful quest for patronage at the Exposition placed him in a good position to provide collections and expertise to the archaeological community. By the end of 1893, even as the Exposition was shutting down, the Hyde Exploring Expedition was making discoveries in the Grand Gulch country (Phillips 1993, 112). "I am receiving inquiries almost daily," Wetherill wrote to Talbot Hyde, "for such relics as we have" (Wetherill 1893a). The promise of these discoveries and his relationship to the Hydes must have seemed to validate his strategy of building strong personal relationships with his clients, and Wetherill's letters, some addressed to "friend Hyde," reflect this ethic.

In contrast, the Fair meant neither financial gain nor patronage for Moorehead, and for him the years immediately following the Exposition were filled with recrimination. His failed investments left him desperate for stable employment. He took up a low-paying position at Ohio State University, but attempts to gain a foothold at more prestigious institutions were rebuffed (Winser 1893). Thomas Wilson pointed out that "one of Putnam's objections to you [was] 'that you sometimes went off half-cocked'" (Wilson 1897), an impression confirmed by the debacle of the *American Illustrated* expedition. Earlier Moorehead had expressed the hope that his cultivation of Putnam would help him rise above the competition represented by the Harvard students, such as George Dorsey and Marshall Saville—"they can be either outwitted or handled, without gloves" (1892g)—but his confidence was misplaced. Dorsey joined the Field Columbian Museum, while Saville took a position at the American Museum of Natural History. Moorehead assumed the editorship of a popular journal called *The Archaeologist* (Milanich 2001), brokered sales of artifacts, and launched various writing projects, none of which proved particularly lucrative.[9]

In this context the dispute with Putnam regarding control over collections became overtly hostile. Moorehead was only one of many who felt aggrieved at the outcome of the Exposition—a list ranging from individual collectors to Putnam himself (Putnam 1893q; Dexter 1966c; Essay 1, this volume). A month after the Fair closed, Moorehead appealed to the legal office of the Columbian Exposition, making his case for ownership of the Southwest collection by stating that it was "worth at the most only about $100. It can be of little benefit to the Columbian Museum as it does not represent to any great extent the arts, industries and customs of primitive people of the South-west" (Moorehead 1893e).[10]

It is difficult to see how Moorehead could have benefitted from such personal attacks, and the affair served largely to roil the community of American anthropologists. In 1896 Boas—always ready to stir the pot—wrote to tell Putnam that Moorehead had come to New York collecting information to "get even" and possibly be rewarded by the Field Columbian directors (Boas 1896a). Moorehead's own correspondence suggests that authorities in Chicago indeed took an interest in the matter, and Putnam eventually felt compelled to respond

(Putnam 1896). When the broader controversy was finally resolved, however, there is no hint that Moorehead's interests were advanced (Higinbotham 1896).

Wetherill, Moorehead, and Pueblo Bonito

Given what appeared to be the divergent fortunes of Richard Wetherill and Warren King Moorehead at the close of the Fair, there is irony in the ultimate resolution of their roles within American anthropology. That this transformation began in the Southwest—to which Moorehead had preferred not to return—could also not have been predicted.

Wetherill's initial position with the Hyde Expedition was based on his skill at locating and excavating archaeological collections in the southwestern terrain, which no outsiders could equal. He remained cognizant of the structure of authority in the field, however, and understood that institutional connections would bring greater stability to the project and for himself. He would have seen such relationships in operation in Chicago and witnessed the marginal status of relic hunters working outside the professional networks. Thus Wetherill continued to correspond with Putnam, announcing discoveries and offering his future services (Wetherill 1893b).

By 1894 Putnam indeed began to take an interest in the Hyde Expedition, stimulated both by Wetherill's letters (Wetherill 1894) and by personal contact with Frederick Hyde Jr., who was taking classes at Harvard. Putnam's attraction to the work stemmed in part from his new position as curator of anthropology at the American Museum of Natural History, which he maintained simultaneously with his existing post at the Peabody. Building relationships with New York patrons was essential, and the Hyde brothers provided entrée into that community. Their continued support also represented the opportunity that Putnam had long sought to integrate "professional" fieldwork with the acquisition of collections in an institutional setting (Snead 2001).

The results of these evolving interactions were the depositing of Hyde collections at the American Museum and museum sponsorship of the ongoing Hyde Exploring Expedition. Their next target was Chaco Canyon, which Wetherill had identified as an optimal setting for new excavations. They began work at Pueblo Bonito in the summer of 1896, and—despite efforts to limit publicity—word of important discoveries began to circulate immediately (Snead 2001).

News of these finds reached Moorehead, who kept well informed about archaeological developments despite antagonistic relationships with many in the professional community. When diagnosed with tuberculosis in March 1897, he immediately headed westward in hope that the "rare, dry atmosphere" would arrest the condition (Moorehead 1897a, 1898)—but also to follow the trail of the Hyde Expedition. He reached Chaco Canyon in April, before Wetherill and other members of his team arrived for their summer season, and began his own excavations at Pueblo Bonito. Working in his usual mode, Moorehead petitioned various patrons, such as the Columbian Museum and Thomas Wilson of the U.S. National Museum, for support (Wilson 1897).[11]

Moorehead's few weeks at Pueblo Bonito—where he investigated the older, interior rooms of the complex—produced thousands of artifacts. In this "catacomb"-like environment he made several important discoveries, including a burial with a feather robe (Moorehead 1906a, 34, 38). As before, however, he found the southwestern landscape difficult. "Truly it is a peculiar—a lonely country, yet like the ocean—a grey and melancholy waste—men learn to love it.... For my own part, I do not like to be shut off from the society of men" (Moorehead 1897a).

Of most profound importance to Moorehead's future, however, was his nascent relationship with Robert Singleton Peabody, which evolved while the work at Bonito was in progress. Peabody was a wealthy philanthropist and nephew of transatlantic dry goods merchant George Peabody, who had endowed museums at Harvard, Yale, and in his hometown of Salem, Massachusetts. The younger Peabody had been raised in Ohio, and like Moorehead's, his early life in the mound country had stoked an interest in archaeology (Moorehead 1906b, 26). In the winter of 1897 Peabody purchased one of Moorehead's collections of Ohio artifacts and, in the course of correspondence, learned about both the archaeologist's illness and his new southwestern plans. Moorehead described Chaco Canyon as "one of the greatest—if not the greatest—place I ever examined," he wrote. "If you would like a good collection from here with full descriptions I will be glad to reserve what I find at my own expense now, until I can hear from you" (Moorehead 1897a).[12]

Peabody's response was highly positive, both to the artifacts initially received and to the offer of providing a collection from Pueblo Bonito. "It will give me *more* than ordinary pleasure, if you find that you *can* do so," he wrote, "*Always* with *every* regard to your own health convenience & interests" (Peabody 1897, emphasis in original). Funds wired by Peabody helped Moorehead ship the material east, pay off his crew, and make up for some of his initial outlay (Moorehead 1897b). "This with what collection you already have will give a complete cabinet on ancient life in America," he wrote from Ohio, whence he had returned in the summer, convinced that his health had recovered (Moorehead 1897c).

Even by the indefinite protocols of the day Moorehead's raid on Pueblo Bonito during the Hyde Expedition's off-season had been ethically questionable. Wetherill returned to Chaco early in the summer to find various tokens of the interlopers. He took some satisfaction that they had been careless in their haste. Writing to Hyde, Wetherill referred to a "find of Turquoise overlooked by Morehead [sic]," but no more formal recourse was possible (Wetherill 1897a). Moorehead may have seen his Chaco incursion as a slap at Putnam, who had yet to visit the locale but was technically the director of the Hyde Expedition's fieldwork.

By the summer of 1897 Wetherill had more pressing problems than those presented by Moorehead. Although theoretically he was the authority on the ground at Chaco, the structure of the project had evolved in ways that began to marginalize his contributions. When Putnam was brought in as director he nominated his own candidate, George Pepper, to supervise the fieldwork. Pepper had archaeological experience in the Northeast and had spent a little time with Putnam at Cambridge, but had never previously been in the West, nor had he run a project of this sort. The Hyde brothers acquiesced to this shift, and Talbot Hyde in particular came to look on Pepper as a protégé (Snead 2001, 39). How Pepper exercised his "supervisory" role is not clear, but the intervention of such a neophyte must have been galling to Wetherill.

The Wetherill family worked hard to sustain their side of the relationship—going so far as to name the post office at Pueblo Bonito "Putnam"—but their own roles stagnated into those of guides and roustabouts. Despite superficially cordial interaction, it must have been clear that the eastern archaeologists preferred to work with their own, and that the "relic hunter" label was not easy to shed. Thus while the Pueblo Bonito excavations did indeed become a prototype for future archaeological expeditions to the Southwest, the hoped-for opportunities for local collaborators did not emerge.

Under these conditions, securing a stable income again became a concern for Richard Wetherill, particularly after the collapse of the Alamo Ranch in the late 1890s. While the Chaco excavations continued, he spent the off-season roaming the Southwest, working in Tsegi Canyon and elsewhere (McNitt 1966). He again found himself struggling for patrons, and he faced a stark shift from the prestigious connection with the American Museum to smaller endeavors—a failed plan to collect for the "Academy of Sciences of San Francisco," for instance, and the "Bowles Expedition," a fiasco sponsored by a Harvard undergraduate and his tutor (Wetherill 1896, 1897a). He also continued to sell artifacts from his own collection, such as a pottery "bell" found during the Tsegi Canyon work "now owned by Mrs. Posey of California" (Wetherill 1897c). These new efforts did not live up to the standards he had set for himself a few years earlier; rather, they represented a return to the relic hunting practices that he had hoped to leave behind.

In 1900 Wetherill made a final attempt to reinvigorate the Chaco Canyon work and, in the process, provide another professional opportunity. One of the visitors to the Hyde headquarters was Richard E. Dodge, a geologist at Columbia Teacher's College and an officer of the New York Academy of Science. Dodge was interested in desert climate and human-environment interaction, and he found New Mexico to be an ideal setting for research. His comparatively scientific approach must have appealed to Wetherill, and it is not difficult to imagine that the relationship between the two men resembled that between Wetherill and Nordenskiold or Prudden a decade earlier. They developed a plan for coordinated archaeological fieldwork at Chaco Canyon, which among other things suggested making a baseline for the proper mapping of ruins, for photographs and three-dimensional measurements of each room, and for standardizing the note-taking procedures (Dodge 1900).

This comparatively sophisticated program required financial support, and the proposal was submitted to Talbot Hyde; but there is no evidence that he took any action. Dodge never published about the work in Chaco Canyon, despite indicating in later correspondence that they had recorded 170 archaeological sites there (Dodge 1922). By 1903 he had faded into the background, one of many scholars attracted to Chaco by the promise of the Hyde Expedition, only to return comparatively empty-handed.

More than disappointment was in store for Richard Wetherill. The Dodge plan was his last formal effort to transcend relic hunter status and put his archaeological ambitions on a more professional footing. Exploration continued, and Putnam himself visited Chaco Canyon twice in the process, but fieldwork gradually ground to a halt. The Hyde brothers were distracted by other schemes, such as establishing a trading post system and staking a homestead claim to Pueblo Bonito. Since Wetherill depended on their support, he was drawn into these efforts as well. Not only did this make it impossible for him to maintain any momentum on archaeological projects, but his old patronage network also withered. Friends like T. Mitchell Prudden continued to stay in touch, but further amelioration of the situation proved impossible.

Conclusion: Ambition, Authority, and the Columbian Exposition

The World's Columbian Exposition provided an arena in which complex interactions over artifacts and collections grew particularly sharp and clear. The reality of the various displays, their creators, and their ultimate fates depicted archaeology in ways that exposed gaps between professional ideology and circumstances on the ground. Far more was at stake than simply presenting a story to the public.

The intertwined fates of Richard Wetherill and Warren K. Moorehead reflect both the complex structure of American archaeology in the late nineteenth century and the role of the Columbian Exposition in shaping these complexities at a critical moment. All those who participated in bringing southwestern artifacts before a public audience in Chicago—professionals, collectors, relic hunters, middlemen—sought the prestige that came with popular approbation. Status, financial gain, and opportunities for further work were all at stake. Artifacts from the cliff dwellings represented the capital through which such ambitions could be achieved, but they were of themselves insufficient to guarantee success. Ultimately it would be networks of association and patronage that made the difference, and the ability to establish such relationships was shaped by class, economic, and regional boundaries that proved impossible for some to transcend.

What began for Moorehead and Peabody as a typical patron-client transaction grew over the next few years into something far more substantial. The two men quickly established a close bond, in part because when Moorehead's health began to deteriorate once more, Peabody arranged for him to take the "cure" at Saranac Lake, New York, where Peabody himself spent his summers. Moorehead recovered, and during the lengthy convalescence he spent considerable time in conversation about archaeological topics with his patron (Moorehead 1904–5). Peabody had been developing a plan to found an archaeological institution at his prep school alma mater, Phillips Andover, but did not apparently have an individual in mind to direct the effort. Within a short period Moorehead had been tapped as curator of the new Department of Archaeology. He held the position until his death, in 1939, by which point he was described by some as the "dean of American archaeology."

Wetherill's fortunes moved in precisely the opposite direction. Ironically, when agitation in favor of "locally based" scholarship began in the Southwest after the turn of the century, the westerners who had taken the most direct interest in antiquities—relic hunters—were instead targets of calumny (Snead 2002a). Archaeologists such as Edgar Lee Hewett sought to establish their authority on the ground, designing a regionally based professional structure that they could control. Relic hunters continued to provide collections to buyers, but their subordinate position was by this time institutionalized. By the time he was killed in 1910 Richard Wetherill was essentially a Chaco Canyon rancher, his archaeological ambitions a closed chapter (McNitt 1966).

There is no written evidence that Moorehead and Wetherill ever met. That their paths crossed so many times—in the Southwest and in Chicago—without any evident interaction is curious. Wetherill's wry reference to Moorehead's incursion at Pueblo Bonito is the only place in his currently available correspondence where the name is mentioned (Wetherill 1897c). Moorehead was undoubtedly aware of Wetherill's 1897 letter in the *Antiquarian* regarding an enigmatic artifact type called a "sandal last" (1897d)—since Moorhead himself published pieces in that journal—but he made no mention of it a few years later, when presenting his own thoughts about the subject (Moorehead 1906a, 38). The pattern suggests either some personal antipathy or, more likely, a rejection of his own relic hunter roots. In fact, once established, Moorehead assiduously rebuilt professional bridges long burned. In a particular bit of irony, he heaped praise on the Hyde Expedition's leaders only a decade after scooping their discoveries at Chaco Canyon. "Archaeologists will rejoice," he wrote, "if Dr. Pepper is able to resume the explorations of this remarkable place and bring them to a successful termination" (Moorehead 1906a, 53).[13]

Putnam's ambitions for a scientific discipline had very little to do with the actual structure of the field, and his resolute characterization of the "professional" approach should not blind historians to the more complex reality it masked. Some years after the conclusion of the Exposition he responded to a query about the public-professional divide in the field with a statement that captured this ambiguity. "I am perfectly willing that you should mention in your circular that the Peabody Museum of Harvard University and the Department of Anthropology of the University of California are among your customers and you can refer to Professor Putnam for your reliability," he wrote to a nephew in the curio business. "Of course you must do this in such a way that it does not savor of commercialism. I try to keep all scientific matters clear of a commercial basis" (Putnam 1907).

Notes

With apologies to Ray Fogelson (1991).

1. The most famous attempt by the Wetherills to attract the attention of the archaeological "establishment" was a frequently cited letter to W. H. Holmes at the U.S. National Museum (see Harrell 1987; Blackburn 2006). Much of the discussion of this issue centers on negative evidence—whether letters were sent or received, a perceived "coldness" of tone on the part of W. H. Holmes in his response to the communique, etc.—all of which are largely hypothetical.

2. The most reliable summary is in Blackburn 2006, 187–88. Drawing from similar sources—principally a 1930s interview with John Wetherill arranged by Jesse Nusbaum now in the archives at the Laboratory of Anthropology in Santa Fe (file

89L A3.023.2)—I previously suggested that the 1886 sale of a collection to Helen Chain in Denver marked the Wetherills' first substantive foray into the antiquities market (Snead 2001, 19). Such recollections, written decades after the events described, are often only accurate in a general sense, and the sale described in John Wetherill's interview may actually have been that of the McLoyd-Wetherill collection in 1889.

3. There are only a few sources of biographical material on Moorehead's early life, in particular his obituary in *American Anthropologist* (Byers 1939). Moorehead's autobiographical account of his activities prior to 1902 is replete with detail but has been somewhat sanitized. A few more specialized studies of Moorehead's career exist, and more are in process (Christenson 2013; Milanich 2001).

4. According to Moorehead (1903–4, 2), Dorsey was not interested in archaeology when they first met, a circumstance that (if accurately reported) undoubtedly rankled as Dorsey became close to Putnam.

5. The Cresson affair remains obscure. "I laid the matter before Professor Putnam," reads Moorehead's account of the matter, glossing over the details (1903–4, 30). Cresson had a knack for attracting controversy. Shortly afterwards he faced allegations of artifact fraud and in 1894 committed suicide in New York's Central Park (Saville 1894; cf. Griffin et al. 1988). Thomas Wilson's letter to Moorehead about the death is revealing: "Cresson had many good qualities, had large experience and great preparation, but there was a screw loose, a wheel misplaced, cogs broken out, or something broke in his intellectual or his moral nature which incapacitated him from success in this life" (Wilson 1894).

6. Moorehead's outline of the scheme was based on his assessment of American archaeology and cost estimates from his earlier work: "The work carried on at Hopewell's cost 3000—in round figures. There are not more than twenty groups of that size in the United States. The smaller ones could be examined for 1000—per group. Say $75,000 of the money be spent on groups. That would open forty of both classes (15 and 30) the single mounds average 13.60. We could explore two thousand village sites, gravel banks and fortifications would use the remainder. It would give the men conducting the work a lasting reputation. Can it be done? Possibly it can!" (Moorehead 1892e).

7. Wilmarth ended up causing Putnam considerable trouble. He had arranged for hogans to be erected on the grounds near the Anthropology Building but apparently failed to pay the Navajos who built them (Putnam 1893r, s). Nordenskiold's exhibit ultimately traveled on, appearing in the Madrid Exposition of 1894. The figure 64 photograph was originally exhibited at Madrid.

8. Accounts of other "professional" encounters and events are sparse in Moorehead's journal. Cushing's diary for July 17 mentions meeting Moorehead in the Anthropology Building, for instance, but Moorehead made no corresponding entry for that date.

9. Dissatisfaction with Moorehead himself was expressed by various individuals in the archaeological community. Stephen Peet, who published the *American*

Antiquarian, wrote to Putnam that "Moorehead was very careless in his exploration, and very indefinite in his published reports" (Peet 1896).

10. Putnam's hopes of playing a substantial role in the creation of the Columbian Museum at the end of the Fair were thwarted by local interests, and he spent years fighting personal and professional slights as a result (Essay 1, this volume). The Moorehead affair was only one of these, which also included minor but embarrassing rumors, such as the tale that he had been bombarded by tomato sauce at a meeting of the chiefs of department at the Exposition (Peabody 1896). Putnam's interaction with Moorehead regarding the collection is obscure. There is limited direct correspondence in his files for this period, but a letter indicating that such material was forwarded to the attorney for the World's Columbian Exposition indicates that he took it very seriously (Baldwin 1893).

11. Other archaeologists made the journey west to fight tuberculosis in the same era. Frank Russell, who had just begun a promising career at Harvard, went to Tucson in 1901 after a similar diagnosis. He returned to Cambridge in 1902, but the disease returned and he died in Arizona in 1903 (Frank Russell 1901; Teresa Russell 1903).

12. Moorehead's published account of these events (1906b, 33) makes it appear as if the Chaco work was begun under Peabody's patronage from the beginning, but—despite my previous acceptance of this position (Snead 2001, 49)—this is not borne out by the correspondence. Even Moorehead's journals are circumspect about the matter, since they were drafted a year after the expedition had concluded, when his relationship with Robert Peabody was more firmly established.

13. A letter from Neil Judd suggests that a publication on Pueblo Bonito coauthored by Moorehead and Pepper had been discussed (Judd 1920). Pepper's own career makes an interesting study in patron-client relationships. When Talbot Hyde's finances deteriorated, his protégé adroitly transferred his allegiances to the collector George Gustav Heye, for whom he worked in the field and at the Museum of the American Indian until his death in 1924 (Snead 1999).

DOCUMENT H

Cushing's Analysis of the Hazzard Cliff Dweller Collection, 1895

29th October, 1895

My Very Dear Culin:

I find, this morning, that it will not be possible for me to leave here for Philadelphia until next week Monday or Tuesday at earliest. I am therefore making some rough pencil notes for you on special divisions of the Hazzard collection. I cannot undertake, away from the collections, to give form to these notes as general labels. Even were I able to do so I would question the advantage of it; for I think you have special abilities in that direction and that you can, with my notes, make better [labels] than I could. Therefore I am not specifying objects, to any great extent, but giving general characteristics and values. I will send you at once what I have written of the basketry and textiles and if these meet your needs I will write and send you similar notes relative to stone work, wood work, etc.

I am glad you are progressing so finely, and very sorry to miss the visit—or part of the visit I had anticipated having with you.

But what can Church mice do?

With love to you and Mrs. Culin and with hope that she continues better

Ever truly Your Friend

[signed] Frank Hamilton Cushing

Frank H. Cushing letter and notes, University Museum, University of Pennsylvania, transcribed by David R. Wilcox

Cliff Dwellers

Given a people who were as were the Cliff Dwellers, isolated alike by the nature of their country and by their defensive ~~position~~ condition and we have exemplified in their art-objects or—remains, examples of pure natural, unaffected development in abundance. When we see that many of these examples of arts and devices [s]how pecul[i]arly close relation to the necessities of the special condition of life and to the environment of this people we may feel doubly assured that these articles have been produced by a kind of slow spontaneous generation that they represent chapters in the history of this particular people's struggle with one or another of the difficulties with which their way of life was beset. And where the number of such developments is great behold, we have exemplified with an exactitude not to be questioned or distrusted the way in which similar things have been evolved in far remoter periods of the world's history and in lands ~~of~~ so far removed that we know there could have been no means of borrowing ~~or of m~~ and no memory from one to the other. Thus where as over and over again in this collection, we can trace from its beginning in something else, an art through all the stages of its development,— can clearly perceive what it was that ushered in each of these stages too—up to its maturity and its marriage with other arts, and its productively of yet newer arts themselves to be studied as this [sic] parent ones were then we have a grand opportunity for studying like origins where ever they have occurred.

Such is the opportunity this collection gives the student of *man*— gives more abundantly than ~~eve~~ any other collection has ever yet given, as I might illustrate over and over again were time sufficient. But only one or two examples can be allowed.

When I see in the China shops of our every day streets pitchers with double handles, along side of pitchers ~~of~~ with very different handles, I can safely infer that these two kinds of pitchers had different origins or that at least they had origins in very different periods. I can go farther and find far richer entertainment nearing my journey's end. I can see that once upon a time, far beyond the period of written history my ancestors, or some of them, or some from whom they inherited[,] lived in a rugged and broken country dry and scantly supplied with food and drink. That wandering from spring to spring it was ever needful for them to carry water in a vessel so light that it could have been made only in wicker or gourd; that it had a slender neck to keep the precious water from spilling as it was borne, a large globular body that enough water might be carried and that the vessel might hang the more readily upright and that attached to the side or neck of the bottle just above this weightier portion was a handle consisting of two loops, one close together that they might be used together when the vessel was lifted or set down, yet double that one might receive one end, and the other the other end of a burden strap when it was being carried, and thus keeping the vessel from swaying as it was borne along on back, at side, [or] on shoulder. That some day these ancients came to rest and learned to mold mould clay in to a form like this, and that they faithfully carried out the notion of the double handle by making handles of on each of these new sorts of vessel of two strips of clay—still believing that half a handle made from a single strip of clay, no matter how big, would defraud the sentiment and beneficent vessel of its perfection would after all be only half a handle. And for long ages they would continue the double lobed handle—even after the ease of making single ones lead and the introduction of modifying led them to make it single in form but still to divide it with a little line and at last even with a mere and gradually fading streak of paint.

Such an original wicker bottle with its little carrying loops [lingered] along with the cliff-dwellers for ages alongside beside the earthen pitcher made in its pattern, and with the latter in turn alongside its degenerate descendant at last the flat single flat handled mug, made flat and with olden line obliterated by added symbolic marks dating from newer uses which brough[t] with them newer conceptions and freedom after ages and ages from bondage to the old. In such examples through out well nigh the whole range or art these collections abound. They offer a striking epitome of the origins or beginnings of all arts like them no matter where found in the world, and whither in their native lands or in far off regions wither by barter or borrowing they may have been transported.

Thus this obscure Cliff collection connects with the History of the world. Verily it is a Chapter of Universal Ancient History, seeming dead and lost for ages ~~revivified~~ come alive in our midst reenacting its part in [sic] with faithful detail and with flawless memory of incident.

Basketry, Pottery, Textiles
General Significance

In the Basketry of the Hazzard Collection is Epitomized the History of the Oldest distinctive art of the Cliff Dwellers, and in it as in no other ~~like~~ existing collection are illustrated the origins of ~~their~~ both the textile and the pottery arts.

There were two great periods in the existence of this people previously to that of their occupancy of the cliffs. During the first of these periods they were few, and new-comers into the Desert. They were compelled to wander almost ceaselessly from watering place to watering place, and thus to transport over the dry wastes they traversed, every thing, even water, in light and durable ~~and water tight~~ receptacles. Thus their development of the Basketry art which alone met these requirements was carried to the highest point of perfection, and during this their earliest period they discovered every possible stitch and device in plaitted and interwoven work,—including the spirally built and closely twine-stitched vessels in which they both transported, and cooked, (by consequent necessity[)] which arose, for their cultivation of the soil and their more or less permanent occupation in scattered bands, of the scant watering places of their arid habitat they developed out of their coiled water tight basketry art, the art of making coiled boiling baskets or vessels of clay and thus began their development of the potters art,—still as a basketry art, but in the materials of earthen ware. This, their earliest pottery was, however, used almost exclusively in the preparation and serving of food, and hence the Basketry art which had given birth to it continued to flourish; ~~and~~ for as yet these peoples were ever shifting their abodes[,] not constantly as before, but from season to season, and had but begun to learn the arts of agriculture and of the beginning of culture which the Desert forced them to and in turn taught them. Thus in their arts and handicrafts no less than in their development of the agricultural and the settled and organized mode of life which this fostered and increasingly demanded, they were the product of life in the desert and in their basketry first and their other remains ~~illustrate~~ later, are illustrated the part the desert has played in the beginnings of civilization the world over.

Toward the close of their second period, however, their prosperity, their possession of stores and provisions drew down upon them anew from the north and from the mountains around them lingering bands of the foes who had first driven them into the desert, and thus they were compelled to move again and ultimately to fortify themselves in the caves and buttes of their cañon broken land. Thus their third ~~and~~ period of development began.

Still, the equal necessity for transportation of both food and water ~~fr~~ to and from their fields, far below and sometimes far away, kept equally active their practice of the older art of Basketry.

Owing to this long period of its development, the basketry art of the cliff dwellers was, ~~the~~ although still comparatively plain and utilitarian—the finest and most highly perfected of the western hemisphere, and in it occur examples of every kind or type of basket work devised by the natives of America, North or South.

The Pottery of the collections although resulting from a period of many centuries of development out of the first crude coiled and stitch pinched baskets of clay in which it began, still retains even in the latest painted and finely moulded forms, the traces of its basketry origin. For these primitive people believed that the use (or "life power") of each special kind of basket was conditioned by its form and the relation of its parts. Hence, in the coiled cooking pots of the collection the shapes of the original boiling baskets they were made to reproduce, the stitches of their coils, the very loops by which they ~~were~~ the baskets had been handled were faithfully reproduced that these new kind of boilers might have the same kind of (magical) efficacy ~~that~~ the original kinds had possessed.

Thus too, the ornaments in paint line and even added figure device for symbolic purpose on the latest food jars and water vases retain much of the art character to be found in the oldest basketry and textile designs. The double handles on the older pitchers of the collection illustrate in a remarkable degree these characteristics for the original basketry water-bottle was provided with two hair or fibre loops, for use singly or together as handle when the vessel was ~~in use~~ taken up or set down, and for use apart [for] stringing to the two ends of a burden strap when it was transported full of water, from place to place; and this ~~in turn illustrates~~ again demonstrates the isolation of development, of the Cliff Dweller cultus, the purely native ~~production~~ American origin of this handled pitcher so much resembling our own and in turn illustrates how, in all probability[,] our own was developed.

The people of the cliffs were often beleagured in their ~~cliff~~ secure retreats; were forced to remain within easy distance of them for such long periods of time that their supplies of large skins and robes the product of distant and long continued hunts were now and then utterly exhausted. This had a profound influence on their textile art. It led to the employment of the ~~skins~~ fur of small animals ~~cut in strips and wound upon strands of yucca~~ easily captured near at hand (like the rabbit[,] the prairie dog and the coyote or wild cat), and the skins of birds, which pelts and skins were cut into strips and wound around strands of yucca fibre, and these in turn were plaitted, wattled or twined together precisely as the basketry mats were, to form mantles and robes,—superb examples of which occur in the collections. Thus gradually hand woven fur and feather work, then frame woven textiles of yucca and bark fibre, cotton and cottonwood down as well as bison hair and mountain sheeps hair, eagle and turkey down and plumules, took the place of garments of skin and finally this frame weaving from the ever increasing need this change entailed was developed into the better and more rapid, but strictly analogous modes of pole loom weaving with warp sticks and healding rods ~~in place~~ with loop harness in place of finger plying, and with batten blade in place of bodkin pressers for the strands of woof. With use of such looms, well nigh all the possibilities of the weaver's art were discovered and applied as exemplified by the plain two ply, the ingrain, the three ply, and even the four ply or twilled fabrics of the collection. Yet with the continuous need of making robes of furs or peltries and feather stuffs too small for use by themselves, the earliest hand work which had been developed directly from basketry plying, and even the frame work for large pieces which had immediately succeeded this, continued to be kept up, and thus in this single collection the beginnings and the ends of the weavers complex art are both variously and perfectly exemplified.

From the platting of sandals on stone forms ~~of stone of~~ from fibre so tough that it had to be kept wet while working and had to be wrought together by means of small rods or needles of wood was developed, too, the arts of knitting from simple foot hosiery to patterned leggings and girdles, and to crochetted bags and head bands so that this single collection exhibits too what no other collection has hitherto even helped us to see find, the very origin of knitting and the allied arts of hosiery.

Moreover the the beginnings of the Dyer's and fuller's arts are here shown also,—in work produced like the patterns of basketry from the weaving together of differently dyed warp and woofs, to the tapestry treatment of many colored wefts, and finally to the work of parti-dyeing or figure dyeing, as in the remarkable blanket displayed in Case [author's blank]. The regularly recurring dotted square figures in this were produced by folding the fabric into small squares, wrapping the corners of these squares in corn husks—and rendering the latter impervious by coating of wax or gum, then, dipping and [dyeing] the whole piece and finally removing the husk folds from the corners, and boiling away the gum or wax which remained. An examination of the edges of these parti=colored [dyeing] shows that the Cliff Dwellers were not unacquainted with a mordant made principally (as is that of their descendants the Zuñi) from a kind of boracic alum obtained from formations in dried up mineral springs,—a knowledge known in no other portion of America at the time of the discovery save in Old Mexico and Peru. The presence in some of the edges of finished pieces of textile comparatively unworn at the time of their loss or burial indicates the attachment of drawing strings or loops for stretching the fabric during processes of fulling with clay and sand; so that even this art of our own ancestry is here illustrated at its very beginning.

Note

Sources: Cushing Notes with cover letter, 1895, American Section, Collectors and Collections, Hazzard-Hearst Collection, University Museum of Archaeology and Anthropology; transcribed and lightly edited by David R. Wilcox, Museum of Northern Arizona. The exhibition of the Hazzard Collection opened at the University Museum about November 10, 1895. See "Primitive Civilizations: The Great Exhibition at the University of Pennsylvania and Its Wonderful Light on the Past," *Philadelphia Times,* November 10, 1895; "With Western Mummies: A Glimpse of Some of the Wonders of the Cliff Dwellers Relics," *Philadelphia Record*, November 10, 1895; Allen 1990, 61–88.

DOCUMENT I

The Ancient Man

The Anthropological Exhibit at the World's Fair

It will open next month

The Work Which Has Been Done by Professor Putnam

Aside from "Man and Glacial Epoch," by Professor Wright, Ohio's Exhibit is Below the Standard

WARREN KING MOOREHEAD

About the 1st of July Professor Putnam will open his display to the public. There have been many delays both in the erection of the building and in the preparation of exhibits. The professor divides his department into physical anthropology, ethnology, and prehistoric archaeology. Before entering into a description of these three divisions, I will say a few words concerning the general character of the exhibit.

One cannot emphasize too strongly the difference between this exhibit and such as have been made at former expositions in this country. At the Centennial in '76, the government made a creditable display, but outside of its department there was little attempt at a representation of the progress of the science of anthropology. In fact, little attention was paid at that time to this important study. Following the Centennial were many smaller expositions, at which exhibits of collections of relics were made in greater or less profusion. The department at the Columbian Exposition and the government exhibit cannot be said to partake of the nature of former displays. Some of the States have, perhaps, in their displays scarcely realized the dignity and importance of this new science. Visiting anthropologists will be

Special Correspondent of the *Cleveland Leader*, Chicago, June 22, 1893 pleased with what the government and the professor have done. They will realize that America does understand to a considerable extent the importance of this science and that she has made a worthy display of her progress and her researches. Professors Mason and Holmes and Wilson, Mr. Mooney, and others in the government building, have made a most beautiful display. It covers both ethnologic and archaeologic matters, and is especially strong in the points in which Professor Putnam's department is weak. This is especially gratifying, for the visitors would not like to see two displays identical in character. Mr. Holmes shows a number of cases of "rejects" and quarry and workshop specimens, thereby illustrating his views concerning paleolithic man. Mr. Mooney and Professor Mason have illustrated by a series of life-like groups the habitations, the costumes, the sports, and pursuits of many of the Indian tribes. Mr. Wilson has several cases filled with a synopsis of the stone age of America and Europe.

In Professor Putnam's department Dr. Franz Boas has charge of physical anthropology. He is more interested in modern than prehistoric people, and his observations, measurements and statistics of some 50,000 schoolchildren in the United States are very instructive. He has also taken measurements of thousands of Indians and the results will be graphically shown by means of colored charts. These charts will give an idea of the distribution of the various families of the American race, both from a linguistic and physical points of view. It will be well worth noting how closely he follows the able map constructed by Major Powell and his assistant, and also that one made by Dr. Brinton. Dr. Boas has studied the artificial shaping of the human head among savage peoples. This, together with the methods observed in studying anthropology[,] will be shown.

Mr. George A. Dorsey, a graduate of Harvard, spent nearly two years in Peru in the interests of the department. Lieutenant Safford was associated with him and shares the honors. His collection of photographs and utensils, maps, diagrams, etc., completely represents the every-day life, the architecture, arts, and the mortuary customs of the Peruvians. He dips somewhat into ethnology, and shows the characteristics of the more savage tribes at present living in the interior of the country. His work extends further than the limit of Peru and includes portions of Chile, Ecuador, Columbia [sic] and a number of islands. He crossed the Andes a number of times in pursuit of his investigations. Probably no exhibit will be more extensive than that of Mr. Dorsey and Dr. Boas.

A great deal has been written upon the antiquities of Peru and I think it is safe to say that no work approaches in scientific value that done by Mr. Squier and Messrs. Tyschudi, Reiss and Stubel. The two latter are Germans, while M. Tyschudi is French. A great many travelers have attempted to solve the difficult problems connected with the history of the Peruvians; their articles have appealed to the general reader and have no value in the eyes of the student.

The most important feature of Mr. Dorsey's collection is his series of mummies. Most of these come from Ancon on the coast. Not a few are from the Inca capital, Cuzco. The mummies do not in any particular resemble those of Egypt. They are buried (as I suppose is generally known) doubled up with the knees near the chin. With some of them he found wands, silver bracelets, feather cloth, ivory ornaments, beautiful pottery, vases and jars, etc. A long list of several hundred objects could be named, but it is not the purpose of this paper to publish that which properly belongs to the catalogue. These mummies present many varieties of hair-dressing and tattooing. The high degree of art exhibited in the objects accompanying the burial is too well known to be commented upon there. The cloth in which the bodies were wrapped, the ropes with which the bundle was finally bound up, and the remains themselves have been carefully examined for description in the official report of the department.

His collection of cereals and other food products is very considerable. He has thousands of pieces of feather cloth, hides, and linen cloths, garments, tapestries, etc. Quite a number of implements in gold, silver, copper, and bronze, many of them being in effigy and others taking the form of utensils, he found at Titicaca and on the island of La Plata. His pottery is largely from the valley of the Cauca and the Ancon Coast. Some of the more beautiful forms in imitation of human faces and animals are from Cuzco.

His osteological material comprises trepanned crania, perforated and unperforated humeri and many bones which show the marks of disease. His work covers both archaeology and ethnology.

In the department of ethnology several Indian villages will be on exhibition, located on the margin of South Pond. A number of tribes from distant lands are located in the Midway Plaisance. The contrast between the Indians from the Northwest and those in the government school exhibit is very marked. Persons who think the Indian cannot be educated will find food for thought. The Canadian Government will send down some of the northern Crees, who will live in large houses, constructed of rough slabs of wood, before the doors of which stand carved totem poles. In this department are Mr. Stewart Culin and Dr. Joseph Jastrow, both of whom are interested in folk lore and the various beliefs of savages and civilized people. Dr. Jastrow will present the result of his investigations in neurology and psychology.

In the Ohio Valley a great deal of work has been done in archaeology. The result of the explorations carried on by the writer of this article have been presented to the public elsewhere and it is not necessary to mention them here.

Along the Pacific Coast and among the Pueblos of the Southwest Dr. J. W. Fewkes and other gentlemen have made collections and pursued studies. Mr. Fewkes is especially interested in the Zunis. It is very unfortunate that Mr. Frank Cushing could not have prepared an exhibit for the department. His work is much more comprehensive and extends over a greater length of time than that of Dr. Fewkes. Cushing was with the Zunis six or eight years and is the best posted man in this country concerning their tribal life and religious custom.

Mr. Edward Thompson was sent to Yucatan for some time in order that he might excavate, make casts, and take measurements of the more important ruins of the Mayas. He has returned with many papier-mache imprints of idols, statues, gateways, and sculptures. Several of the corners of large buildings, a series of bas-reliefs and numerous hieroglyphs are shown full size in front of the anthropological building. The casts constitute the most remarkable collection ever brought out of Yucatan.

Some collections were made along the Atlantic seaboard, but these are scarcely of sufficient size and importance to be mentioned here. It seems that no one has carried on as extensive work among the shell heaps or village sites of the Atlantic Coast Indians as has the Bureau of Ethnology of the Geological Survey [sic].

In the Miami Valley (Ohio), Dr. Metz and his assistants did some work. Unfortunately, the explorations were limited, as the doctor is a very busy man and can give only a small portion of his time to the science to which he is so devotedly attached. In Southern Warren county he discovered a remarkable embankment which at first was thought to represent a serpent. The discovery was hailed with delight. Those who have visited the structure since claim for it a defensive, rather than a serpentine character.

Space will not permit me to describe the collection from Alaska, the Pacific Coast, New South Wales, Australia, Africa and the foreign museums. Suffice it to say that they will be complete and well arranged.

The states have their respective displays in the professor's department. So far as I am aware nearly all of them will make a creditable showing except Ohio. As I am a Ohio citizen, I feel free to express myself. The commissioners have made a great mistake. Whether they are to blame, or because of the paltry appropriations given them by the Legislature, it is not my purpose to inquire. Suffice it to say that the exhibit is not that which Ohio could make. I say this in all kindness to the commissioners, who are personal friends of mine. The exhibit is largely confined to a collection of specimens from the cabinets of several gentlemen, a series of maps and charts, a large painting representing the first settlement at Marietta, and a number of miscellaneous objects. Some of these maps have done duty at State fairs and small expositions. They are decidedly crude and insignificant. Had the commissioners drawn upon the Cincinnati Art Museum, Cincinnati Society of Natural History, or the Western Reserve Historical Society, they could have made an exhibit which would have been both scientific and important. I hear that some of the maps are from the president of the Western Reserve Society, and if this be true, that part of the exhibit is worthy. If the commissioners had no money, they should not have attempted the display.

No state in the union affords more material for a splendid archaeologic display than Ohio. All the museums of the East are enriched at the State's expense. If the commissioners had constructed some modern models they would have done the State a service and have presented visiting scientists with an important exhibit. The day has passed when a collection of relics (gathered by men ever so careful) will attract any attention on the part of intelligent people, when placed alongside of exhibits of a broader scope and of more dignified appearance. It is very disappointing to those of us who have seen what others have taken from Ohio, to note this meager State exhibit, which savors of a State fair and fails to equal surrounding exhibits. The collection will only hurt the State in the eyes of visiting scientists, and I deeply regret that Ohio in her showing has failed to comprehend the importance of anthropology and the scope of an international exposition.

The only redeeming feature in the Ohio Historical Society display is the "Man and the Glacial Epoch," made by Professor Wright and Judge Baldwin. That is excellent. These two gentlemen are to be congratulated; they have done a good work.

Professor Putnam has models of the serpent mound, Fort Hill, and the Turner group on exhibition. He did not have time to make representations of several of the larger and more important fortifications and mound groups in the Ohio Valley. But as he himself was in the field during the exploration of the three ruins which he has represented, one is not surprised that his preference should be for those with which his name is more intimately connected.

Natural history and history also participate in taking up the space of the building. Already it seems as if there would be more material to be exhibited than there is room.

A library will be formed in the department which will cover all the subjects embraced under the general name of anthropology. All the writers on matters pertaining to this great science have been requested to contribute their various work to this library.

There are indications at present that the collections will be turned over to a new Chicago museum at the end of the fair. It is said by some that this museum is to perpetuate the name of the fair and that the amount of its endowment depends largely upon the success of the exposition. It certainly would be a most commendable project and should receive hearty support.

A great deal of credit is due Professor Putnam in making the department a success. He has frequently laboured under great difficulties. In conclusion I would most strongly urge all persons interested in this science to visit the fair and see his display. But do not come before the 1st of July, as the department is sadly behind time.

ESSAY SIX

Patrons, Popularizers, and Professionals
The Institutional Setting of Late Nineteenth-
Century Anthropology in Chicago

DONALD MCVICKER

By the time of the 1893 World's Columbian Exposition, Chicago was becoming a showcase for midwestern wealth, progress, and determination. Rising from the ashes of the great Chicago fire of 1871, immense fortunes had been made, and the new financial, industrial, and merchant elite intended to rival anything the East Coast could offer. How did these Chicago boosters shape anthropology at the Fair and how did they impact the cultural institutions that they founded? In turn, how did anthropologists respond and adapt to this milieu?

I propose that Chicago's patrons bought into the traditions of philanthropy in the East and then reinterpreted those traditions to fit their historical moment—a moment characterized by the triumph of science. Philanthropists responded by embracing scholarship and science as well as the arts (Horowitz 1976, 25). As a result, by the 1890s Chicago's elite could boast of their Art Institute (founded 1879, present location 1893); symphony orchestra, university, and natural history museum (1890, 1892, 1893); and two privately endowed libraries—for science the Crerar, now located on the campus of the University of Chicago, and for humanities the Newberry (present building occupied 1893; Towner 1985, 11). All seemed to compare favorably to their East Coast counterparts.[1] The Fair itself, a celebration of art, science, and scholarship, and not incidentally commerce and capitalism, attracted the support of Chicago's elite. It confirmed and reinforced their assumption of responsibility for the global standing of their city.

Anthropology was often a puzzle, however, to the cultural philanthropists who sought to support art, science, and scholarship. Where did anthropology belong? Was it truly a science, as Frederic Ward Putnam, chief of the Department of Ethnology at the Fair, and his able assistant Franz Boas insisted? Or was it an arena for collectors and a stadium for the "big show"? In a sense the Fair was a battleground between inclusive popular science as displayed on the Midway—and practiced by Frederick Starr and George Dorsey—and exclusive professional science presented on the Jackson Park fairgrounds by Putnam and Boas.

As Steven Conn (1998, 75–113) has pointed out, the anthropological puzzle was closely related to the tension between art museums and natural history museums over the place of ethnological and archaeological objects. These objects could be classified and displayed as art or as science. Should they be placed with plants, animals, minerals, and fossils as products of "natural man"—as they would be in Chicago—or should they occupy a special space between science and art and be displayed in a separate museum of *kulturgeschichte* (culture history)?

In Cambridge, Harvard's Peabody Museum faced a similar dilemma. Putnam soon found that his scientific focus on early man in North America failed to attract the support of classically educated Boston Brahmins. As Hinsley (1985, 69–72) has perceptively noted, it was not until the museum changed its focus to the aesthetically acceptable (and literate) Maya that a "worthy subject was chosen for the professionally worthy." Indeed, the ambiguous position of Maya culture, between art and ethnography, probably played a role in Field Museum patron Allison V. Armour's decision to support early archaeological work at Chichén Itzá, before switching his patronage to the Classical Mediterranean.

The art vs. ethnography conundrum was further complicated by the winds of change that were sweeping through all sciences during the last decades of the nineteenth century, as tensions increased between popularizers of science and professionalizing scientists. Bernard Lightman (2007) recently analyzed in some detail how this conflict played out in Victorian England. In his preface (vii) he quotes an 1875 *Saturday Review* critic who condemned "sensational science . . . as a counterfeit to stand for it [real science] upon public platforms in order to secure the 'patronage of the vulgar.'" Negative baggage gradually accrued to the term "popularize" during the early twentieth century as the scientific elite succeeded in subjugating the lecturers and authors of popular science.

While today the distinction between a scientific elite who produced genuine and privileged knowledge and popularizers who disseminated simplified accounts of this knowledge for more general consumption may have some validity, this was not true in 1893. The age of "democratic science" had not yet ended, and men like Frederick Starr and George A. Dorsey who were properly credentialed as producers of knowledge could view bringing scientific knowledge to the masses as a legitimate calling.

Popularizers and Professionals

Much has been written concerning Putnam and Boas at the Fair and their exclusion of vulgar popularizers from anthropology as a science. Much less has been written about popularizers at the Fair and their role in educating the populace about the science of man. Starr was one of the greatest popularizers of anthropology in the last decade of the nineteenth century and into the twentieth (Evans 1987). In 1892 he was hired by University of Chicago president William Rainey Harper to establish anthropology at the new university. Starr came to Chicago convinced that he and the university would play a major role in anthropology at the Exposition. In 1892 Boas had already sent him off to measure Cherokees, and Starr thought this would be an entrée to a larger role in anthropometry, Boas's laboratory, and Putnam's ethnographic circle. Starr wrote to Harper: "Can we allow [the planning for the Exposition] to go along without us? Ought not we, at least, to have some connection with it in such a way as to make it helpful to us?" (Starr to Harper, February 27, 1892, Correspondence BXIV, William Rainey Harper Papers, University of Chicago Regenstein Library Special Collections, hereafter cited as Harper Papers).

Unfortunately for Starr, he and Putnam had not gotten along when Starr was in charge of the ethnography collections at the American Museum in New York from 1889 to 1891. When Harper commented on Putnam's position in Chicago, Starr replied: "Please do not call the Harvard archaeologist an anthropologist. There is a difference. He has been growing huffy ever since I went to the [American] Museum. He

FIG. 67. Frederick Starr "at home," in mid-career at the University of Chicago. Photographer unknown. Courtesy of Special Collections Research Center, University of Chicago Library.

lately wrote me a letter which was not polite. . . . Possibly he feels there is not room for two in Chicago" (Starr to Harper, June 26, 1892, Harper Papers). Starr's relationship with Boas was also problematic (McVicker 1989). In effect, Starr was shut out as an active participant in Putnam's Department of Ethnology at the Fair—only the first of Starr's ambitious plans that would fail to be realized in Chicago and at the Fair.

The Folklore/Folk-Lore controversy at the Fair exemplifies the professional/avocational debate that found Starr and Boas on opposite sides (McVicker 1989, 213–214; cf. Zumwalt 1988 and Bendix 1997). Boas was involved with the Boston-based Folk-Lore Society and saw its young (1888) journal as an excellent resource for anthropological publications. At the Fair the local, Chicago-based upstart Folk-Lore Society proposed and tried to control an International Congress of Folk-Lore. The plans of the midwestern Folk-Lore Society, dominated by amateurs and popularizers, were rejected by the East Coast professionals, and Boas led the more broadly based Folk-Lore Society to participate in the International Congress of Anthropology in August; he largely ignored the International Congress of Folk-Lore in July. Starr, of course, supported his new Chicago acquaintances, naval lieutenant Fletcher S. Bassett, his wife Helen Wheeler Bassett, and his colleague, folklorist William J. Knapp, since Starr viewed the Bassetts as potential patrons and supporters of publications (Bassett and Starr 1898). But once again Starr was on the wrong side of the growing professional/popularizer split.

There were two major anthropological exhibits at the Fair: the Department of Ethnology's, under the guidance of Putnam and Boas, and the government's, directed by Powell, Mason, and Holmes (Essays 1 and 4, this volume).

The displays in the Government Building combined the forces of the Smithsonian, U.S. National Museum, and Bureau of American Ethnology to demonstrate the research and results of the bureau's activities.

The government exhibit was thematic and attempted to educate the public about the evolution and diversity of the cultures of North American Indians. Displays were based on the bureau's research and collections rather than on objects gathered for the Fair (Fagin 1984, 262–63). These displays were partially tied together by the bureau's linguistic map of North American Indian tribes. Archaeology was overshadowed by ethnography; an excellent example was Frank Hamilton Cushing's Zuni installation (Essays 3 and 4, this volume).[2]

Powell, like Putnam and Boas, sought to professionalize ethnology. He had made his position regarding amateurs in science crystal clear in the early 1880s when he launched a vendetta against the Davenport (Iowa) Academy of Natural Sciences during the mound builder controversy (Powell 1883, 1890a). At that time the Academy, founded in 1867, was one of the leading local scientific societies in the United States; but it became mired in controversy when prominent members vigorously supported the theory that the mound builders were immigrants from the civilized Near East and not ancestors of the savage Indians encountered by the settlers. Proof, for these supporters, lay in inscribed tablets, elephant pipes, and other artifacts excavated from local mounds—which turned out to be frauds (McKusick 1991). For Powell and his colleagues these were obvious fakes, and the members of the Davenport Academy seemed naïve amateurs. By the time of the 1893 Fair, a decade later, its members had been publicly ridiculed and the society thoroughly discredited by Powell and those he supervised (McVicker 2007).

At the time of the "Davenport Conspiracy," Starr had been a professor at Coe College in Cedar Rapids and had been caught up in the controversy. During his tenure at Coe he had been a strong supporter of the academy and had become close friends with its leading family, the Charles Putnams—who were, ironically, distant relatives of Frederic Putnam. The Davenport Putnams acted as patrons to the young scholar and offered a reputable *Proceedings* for publishing many of Starr's early papers. For these reasons Starr had not been able to support the government position during the mound builder controversy and felt that his relationship with the Bureau of American Ethnology under Powell and his supporters had been permanently damaged. Clearly there would be no role for him to play in government anthropology at the Fair.

Powell's actions to suppress local scientific academies and their avocational members represented a significant change in the mission of government anthropology. The first secretary of the Smithsonian Institution, Joseph Henry, and his assistant secretary (and successor) Spencer Fullerton Baird had championed a "democratic" view of science similar to that prominent among English popularizers during the latter half of the nineteenth century (Lightman 2007, 183; Hinsley 1981, 34–63). Henry and Baird envisioned engaging local citizens in the scientific endeavor. All could contribute as "correspondents," regardless of professional credentials (Goldstein 1994).

In the mid-nineteenth century "the republic of science" tended to blur any distinction between popular and professional science. Louis Agassiz, despite his preeminent position at Harvard, probably did more to engage the American public with science in the pre-Darwinian era than any other national figure. He is quoted as insisting that the observant amateur could discover scientific patterns in nature as readily as the learned scholar: "'Study nature, not books,' he urged his audience, espousing a seductively egalitarian notion of what it takes to master a discipline" (Dobbs 2005, 52).[3]

Starr was not the only popularizer at the Fair. George A. Dorsey, who would become Putnam's first PhD recipient in 1894, was at the time a minor player but would later become a major force in Chicago anthropology. Sponsored by Putnam, he went on a whirlwind tour of South America to collect artifacts for Putnam's exhibition; when he returned to Chicago, Putnam appointed him superintendent for the Exposition's archaeology. After the Fair Dorsey returned briefly to Harvard and received his PhD, but in 1896 he traveled back to Chicago as assistant curator of physical anthropology at the new Field Columbian Museum. After the abrupt departure of Holmes, he advanced first to acting curator and then full curator of anthropology (Almazan and Coleman 2003, 87–88). If anyone was responsible for the reputation of Chicago anthropology as a "big show" run by money and politics, it was Dorsey during his early years as curator and collector. Furthermore, as Douglas Cole (1985, 167) described Dorsey in Tennyson's exceptionally well-turned phrase, he "wore his learning lightly." Surprisingly, though, Starr and Dorsey failed to connect personally or professionally. As Starr wrote at a later point to his mother: "He [Dorsey] is *not* my friend." He confided in his notebook, "I always feel insecure with him" (Frederick Starr Papers B6, Family Correspondence, September 19, 1911, box 15a, folder 2; letter, September 26, 1911, box 6, folder 13; Special Collections and Research Center, University of Chicago Library).

Powell, Putnam, and Boas stood on one side of the approaching

FIG. 68. George A. Dorsey with Patagonian (Tehuelche) "Giant" Colojo at the St. Louis World's Fair, 1904. Charles Carpenter, photographer. © The Field Museum. CSA13257.

watershed between nineteenth-century popularizers (and their personal patrons), on the one hand, and on the other, twentieth-century professionalizers who built institutions and attracted institutional patrons and mentors. While they held advanced degrees, Starr and Dorsey chose to collect, lecture, and write for popular audiences. Dorsey and his many supporters were determined to challenge the collection arrogance of the East Coast museums and to place Chicago in the top rank. Chicago boosters were only too glad to oblige, and Dorsey could always find time to mingle with "Chicago's social elite who could afford to sponsor his various projects" (Welsch 2003, 100).

Starr would appear to have been in an ideal position to challenge Boas in the establishment of anthropology in an academic setting, yet he failed to found a separate department of anthropology at the University of Chicago, let alone a graduate program. As George Stocking (1979, 15) remarked: "By 1910 it was clear even to Starr that his hopes to establish a graduate department of anthropology had been frustrated." Instead, his prodigious energy was directed toward teaching, lectures, and the popular press as well as frequent, extended field expeditions. These trips were increasingly referred to by his critics and the press as touristic travels. Yet they provided him with anecdotes and visual materials for self-promotion.

Starr's ventures were poorly supported by university funding, and Starr was always scrambling for patrons to support his insatiable travel-collection habit—and for buyers of his collections, so that the proceeds could be used to support yet another expedition. He eventually reached a contractual agreement in 1904 with William N. Selig, president of the Selig Polyscope Company. The contract permitted Starr to travel to exotic locales and supply films to be released by the company—in exchange for Selig's financing.

The nineteenth-century patrons that Starr and Dorsey sought were idiosyncratic individuals who carefully chose their clients—who then amassed less-than-systematic collections for them. The patrons often donated the collections to institutions without considering overall development plans. A case in point is Edward E. Ayer's decision when in Cairo to purchase a large collection of Egyptian antiquities and later to convince Dorsey to accept it as a donation to the Field Museum.

Putnam deplored this Chicago pattern. In 1894 he wrote to his

Yucatecan fieldworker E. H. Thompson (W.C.E. #33, Putnam Papers, Field Museum of Natural History Archives, hereafter cited as FMA): "In Chicago all would be drive and rush and largely sensational effects. That is what they are now after, and it is natural in a place which has started out with great hopes and plenty of money and a feeling that money will do anything. By and by they will realize that while money is an important factor in the work, it alone will not make a scientific institution." He went on to note that although Field Museum director Frederick J. V. Skiff was a good administrator, he was "entirely devoid of all scientific knowledge or feeling." On this occasion Putnam concluded by taking the moral high ground: "All political methods I sincerely detest and one side seems to be just as bad as the other in such affairs; and when these methods come into science they are so thoroughly disgusting and contemptible as to make one wish for a radical change in things. One thing is evident[:] that no purely scientific men will ever condescend to them."

The failure of professional anthropology to take root in Chicago (unlike in Cambridge and New York) must be understood in terms of the difficulty that popularizers like Starr and Dorsey confronted in building institutions. The Fair's appeal to the masses opened the doors for collectors and promoters of popular anthropology (Essays 1 and 5, this volume). Searching for funding from wealthy patrons became the goal of those anthropologists, and collections were the bait. The solidification and expansion of departments, whether based in museum or university, and the education of the next generation of professionals were not their primary goals. Instead, bringing anthropology to the public by attracting them to vivid displays or entertaining lectures became the chief mission. In a sense they were "free spirits" who left little legacy of academic discipline or organizational structure. Furthermore, unlike Putnam, Boas, or Powell, they could never become organization men. In Chicago they were seduced, it seems, by the hot footlights and applause of the Midway Plaisance, not the cold perfection of the White City.

Patrons and Philanthropists

As Chicago's elite "sought to redirect their city's values and preoccupations, to lift Chicago from materialism to the realm of spirit"

(Horowitz 1976, 69), they faced two problems. The first was shared with cultural institutions across the nation: How could the elite raise up the masses through exposing them to the finer things of life, and at the same time protect themselves from vulgarity and the big show that the masses desired? As Palma di Cesnola, the first paid director of the Metropolitan Museum of Art, stated after a plumber wearing overalls had been denied admission to the museum: "We do not want, nor will we permit a person who has been digging in a filthy sewer or working among grease and oil to come in here" (quoted in Tomkins 1970, 84). The parallel with the exclusions by the growing scientific elite of the benighted amateurs is all too obvious.

At the Fair some thought the problem of controlling the masses could be solved by dividing the uplifting White City from the carnival Midway Plaisance; scientific anthropology could be separated from the "faux ethnology" promoted by exploiters of the exotic (Meltzer 2010; Essay 1, this volume). However, a Fair run by businessmen, no matter how philanthropic, still demanded attendance and return on investment; the purity of the White City was to be sullied by the necessity of popular events. Even Boas brought in the crowds by having his Kwakiutls perform a "cannibal ceremony" for the fainting ladies of the Midwest. At least this was "real ethnology," unlike the scandalous dance performances of "Little Egypt," the most talked about act on the Midway.

The second problem faced by Chicago businessmen involved the form that philanthropy should take. Clearly the European model of princes and merchants supporting individual artists did not fit the democratic ideals of midwestern capitalists or of their eastern counterparts (cf. Tomkins 1970). The solution was to patronize institutions and associations that would reshape public taste and elevate the masses (Horowitz 1976, 91). However, the desire to be recognized and play a direct role in collecting edifying objects was not easy to suppress. In New York, Cesnola complained, "[millionaires] will give money for buying collections, and for building purposes, because both remain visible monuments of their generosity . . . while endowment funds are invisible and remain unknown to the general public" (quoted in Tomkins 1970, 89).

The contrast between personal and impersonal giving can be highlighted by distinguishing three types of philanthropists. The first is the familiar wealthy individual who personally supports an anthropologist or archaeologist in pursuing professional activities. Here the emphasis is on collecting spectacular objects, forming notable collections, and establishing "patron-client" relationships. A notable example is the relationship established at the Fair between Allison V. Armour, the scion of one of the wealthiest men in Chicago, and Edward H. Thompson. Armour's encounter at the Fair with Thompson's casts of Mayan temples led to his fascination with the ancient civilization. Later a similar though briefer relationship would be established between Armour and Holmes, the Field Columbian Museum's first curator of anthropology (Meltzer 2010).

The second type of patronage focuses on the institution rather than the individual. Here the intent is to support the mission of the museum, library, or university through donations of money or objects. Sometimes, intentionally or not, the philanthropist defines these missions. As Horowitz (1976, 93) remarks, " the nature of cultural institutions in the nineteenth century was such that the men who served them as trustees were . . . able to exert control over policy"—but not necessarily over the scientists at the Field Columbian Museum or the librarians of the Newberry Library. This issue of the benefactor's control over the scientific curators shaped anthropology at Field Museum, as it also did at the American Museum in New York. Exemplifying such institutional patronage was Edward E. Ayer, the self-made lumber baron, a prime mover in the foundation and continuation of both the Newberry Library and the Field Museum.

A third type of patronage might be labeled "professional" and is more akin to mentorship than philanthropy. Here, although the relationship is personal, its ends are impersonal—in the interests of science. The relationship solidified at the Fair between Putnam and Boas is a classic example. In the case of Holmes at the Bureau of Ethnology it could be argued that the government was his patron (Meltzer 2010).

Putnam and Boas recognized that the frequently conflicting aims and perceptions of collectors, patrons, and philanthropists posed a danger for the future of scientific anthropology in Chicago. They feared that museum dependence on patronage and the demand for crowd-pleasing exhibits would keep anthropology tied to a nineteenth-century collecting mentality. Later in New York, Boas's fears were realized at the American Museum, and he concluded that the future of anthropology as a science lay in the academy (Freed et al. 1988b, 2).

Unfortunately, in Chicago in the 1890s there would be no Boas to lead anthropology into the academy. Although most academic disciplines at the University of Chicago were well supported by all three types of patrons, anthropology under Frederick Starr was an exception. Starr failed to attract sufficient patronage in Chicago to advance his research agenda—although, as already recounted, he later included motion pictures in his field agenda so that Selig films would pay for his travel in exchange for the rights to the films.

Perhaps Starr's choice of the Indians of southern Mexico as a focus for his fieldwork from 1894 to 1904 failed to ignite the enthusiasm among collectors that Putnam's switch to the ancient Maya had at the Peabody (Hinsley 1985). Further, Starr's focus on anthropometry and physical abnormality lacked the popular appeal of artifacts as art. In addition, Starr's interest in attracting public attention to the "science of man" often led to controversy and contemptuous responses. He was a prominent anti-imperialist and took an unpopular stance against the U.S. occupation of the Philippines at the turn of the century. Yet after spending a year in the Congo Free State, he published *The Truth about the Congo*, in which he supported King Leopold's internationally condemned policies in "his" colony. The book earned him few friends in high places outside Belgium (McVicker 2012).

Starr also failed to catch the ear of highly placed administrators at the University of Chicago in support of his agendas. Only George C. Walker's donations for the building of the Walker Museum on campus, after the University failed to "take over" the Columbian Museum, provided an institutional setting for the lone academic anthropologist (McVicker 1986, 1999; Meltzer 2010). Unfortunately for Starr, the university museum was to become a general museum serving the needs of many scientific academic disciplines. Starr was restricted to a single floor and was constantly pressured by the expansion of geology and geography. His position as "anthropology curator" was further undermined by the Field Museum and its voracious collector-curator George Dorsey. Starr's portion of the Walker Museum soon became oriented to teaching undergraduates and failed to attract collections suitable for research. Ironically, when he had completed his Mexican researches and was seeking money to go to the Congo to study pygmies and buy African objects, Starr wound up selling his extensive Mexican collections to Field Museum. Backed by Chicago philanthropist and art collector Martin A. Ryerson, Dorsey bought the results of Starr's ten years of expeditioning and collecting in Mexico. The Starr collection still forms the irreplaceable nucleus of the Field Museum's Mesoamerican collection in both archaeology and ethnology (McVicker 1986, 1992b).

Preparing for the Fair

Putnam had a vision of a great museum for Chicago based on the extraordinary exhibits planned for the Exposition (Essay 1, this volume). To help realize his vision he found funding for international expeditions to supply objects, first for his own anthropology displays and later for those of the new museum. Among the most successful achievements of his sponsored expeditions were Edward Thompson's full-size casts of Maya buildings from Uxmal and Labná (Essay 4, this volume) and George Dorsey's grand exhibit displaying the results of his collecting in Peru. The ethnography exhibits were equally popular. Here Putnam had to balance carefully the crowd-pleasing performances with his devotion to science. However, as Hinsley remarked in the film biography *Franz Boas: 1858–1942* (Timreck 1980), when Boas set up a modern laboratory of physical anthropology to gather statistical data, the public mainly wanted to have their heads measured.

Obtaining funds for these expeditions and exhibits was a challenge. While Congress served as an institutional patron for Powell, Holmes, and their associates, Putnam had to balance his departmental budget at the Fair with access to private funds through Harvard's Peabody Museum. Dorsey's fourteen-month collecting trip to South America illustrates the critical division of funds and its implications. According to Putnam, the Peabody and he personally paid out between $1,800 and $1,900 for the expedition, while the Fair's Department of Ethnology paid out $3,500, about $700 of which went to cover Dorsey's personal expenses in the form of a salary. Putnam observed: "It will thus be seen that the material he [Dorsey] sent up should have been about equally divided, allowing for Mr. Dorsey's time, whereas more than three-fourths of it was turned over to the Columbian Museum" (Putnam to Higinbotham, August 7, 1895, Putnam Papers, FMA). Although Putnam's mathematics is not too clear, his concern with achieving equity in the division of expenses and collections is undeniable.

As a scientist, Putnam never felt comfortable putting values on scientific collections (McVicker 2004). The trustees in Chicago felt no such compunction. Replying to Skiff, Putnam stated: "You ask about the money value of the objects. To me all archaeological objects have only a scientific value. The money value is what it cost to get them, and not what the collector would pay for them. A collector would often pay a very large sum for some large or showy object which he did not have in his collection, while a mere fragment of some other object would be scientifically a hundred times its value. I therefore have never debased my science by putting money value upon anything which has been collected either by me or under my direction" (Putnam to Skiff, June 2, 1894, Putnam Papers, FMA). A stronger contrast with Starr's buying and selling of artifacts and specimens is hard to imagine.

Putnam's convictions would hardly endear him to Ayer or other major patrons and collectors the museum was trying to attract. However, taking the high moral ground was a necessity in 1894 since Putnam had been accused of shipping to the Peabody large numbers of specimens from the Fair that should have gone to the new Field Columbian Museum. These accusations may have affected the decision of the Field not to offer Putnam a high administrative position.

Everybody Comes to the Fair (or Do They?)

Cushing's diaries covering his three weeks at the Fair and the International Congress of Anthropology give immediacy and insight into interactions at the Fair (Essay 3, Document E, this volume). It seems clear that although a certain amount of camaraderie developed among those engaged in the anthropological endeavor, the circles of Washington and the Peabody rarely intersected socially; professional interaction may have been problematic as well. Although Holmes did visit Boas and inquire about his availability for a position in Washington (Meltzer 2010), Cushing rarely mentions Boas or Putnam despite frequent visits to the Anthropology Building for his own inspection and for the entertainment of his many visitors. At this point "good old

Holmes" appears to be his professional mentor. On one visit (June 30) Cushing remarks, on examining Thompson's full-size molds of the Yucatán ruins, that "they are remarkably realistic, but not so impressive as might have been made." Unfortunately Cushing does not apprise the reader of what could have been done to improve the generally praised casts. Among those professionals not mentioned by Cushing is Frederick Starr.

One person who did not intend to go to the Chicago World's Columbian Exposition was one of the wealthiest and most noted of all Chicago merchants, Marshall Field. In a familiar anecdote of Chicago cultural history, Edward Ayer persuaded him to go and convinced him that immortality was not the province of merchants but of philanthropists (Edward E. Ayer Papers, box 4, folder 50, Newberry Library Archives, hereafter cited as NLA; Ayer 2003). So persuasive was Ayer that Field wrote a check for one million dollars, thereby assuring that Chicago would have its great museum. Recently the veracity of Ayer's self-congratulatory account has been questioned, as has the self-effacing modesty of Field's philanthropy (Wilcox 2003a).

The Aftermath: Founding the Columbian Museum

When the Field Columbian Museum was founded, there was an initial discussion that it be incorporated under the charter of the Academy of Sciences of Chicago. Harlow N. Higinbotham, president of the Fair and prospective chairman of the board of the new museum, stood firmly against this plan and argued successfully for "a new and strong organization, independent of educational institutions, locality, creed or calling, strong enough to stand alone, and large enough to take in everything" (Lockwood 1929, 186). When the Fair closed at the end of October the new institution indeed "took in everything," as the Herculean task of moving exhibits into the former Fine Arts Building began. It was not until nearly a decade later that industrial and historical materials were returned to donors, and the museum defined itself as a "repository of science, not of industrial achievements" (Field Museum of Natural History Report Series 1 [1899–1900], 433; cf. Horowitz 1976, 100). Putnam and Boas were responsible for gathering in the anthropological collections, and Boas would conduct their classification and arrangement. Their assignment was particu-

FIG. 69. Edward Everett Ayer, portrait by Elbridge Ayer Burbank, 1897. Oil on canvas, 32 x 25 in. Courtesy of the Newberry Library, Chicago. Call #NL Paintings 012.

larly significant because, at least from Ayer's perspective, "the largest single subject practically of natural history would be anthropology" (Ayer Papers, box 4, folder 50, NLA).

Among the first tasks faced by the new museum was to establish its corporate structure. The new board was dominated by wealthy businessmen, with Higinbotham as chair and Ayer as president. To no one's surprise the board included both the meat-packing Armour (Philip D.) and the socialite Armour (Allison V.). Frederick J. V. Skiff was then appointed as director of the museum. Ayer records (Ayer Papers, box 3, folder 41, NLA) that Skiff was chosen because his Colorado exhibit was the best, cleanest, and most organized collection at the Fair: "We thought that any man that could keep a collection in that condition and maintain it in the condition at the time of exhibit would make a good Director" (Ayer Papers, box 3, folder 41, NLA).

FIG. 70. Harlow N. Higinbotham. Date and photographer unknown. © The Field Museum. GN78499.

FIG. 71. Marshall Field (1834–1906). From Thomas W. Goodspeed, *The University of Chicago Biographical Sketches* (Chicago: University of Chicago Press, 1922): 1:1.

By the second year of operation, A. V. Armour was honored with the title of "patron." With the philanthropists in place, the next task was to appoint the scientific staff.

Staffing the Field Columbian Museum

There is reason to believe that Putnam assumed he would be head of the scientific division and that Boas would become chairman of anthropology. In a move that would have long-standing consequences, Putnam was passed over and Boas was ousted (McVicker 1999; cf. Meltzer 2010). Both men returned to the East extremely bitter about Chicago and its business-dominated new museum. Although Putnam's differences were resolved by 1898 and he was honored by being elected a patron (#34 [1893–1907], Putnam Papers, FMA), Boas remained at odds with Chicago and the museum until one of his colleagues, Berthold Laufer, became curator nearly two decades later.

The Boas affair was the result of a decision by the board to buy the best curator they could. The choice fell on Holmes, one of the most prominent younger anthropologists with the Bureau of Ethnology and well connected in Washington. The appointment of Holmes was also part of a labyrinthine "conspiracy," led by Thomas C. Chamberlin, noted geologist and head of the new department at the University of Chicago. Chamberlin and others at the university plotted to pack the staff at the museum with sympathetic scientists and thereby indirectly control it. While only partly successful with the larger scheme, they managed to bring Holmes to Chicago (McVicker 1999; Meltzer 2010).

Although Putnam and Boas had failed to impress Higinbotham and others, it is clear that Holmes was well liked and noncontroversial. "Good old Holmes" was also viewed as a curator who would attract philanthropic donors. His WASPish credentials were in order, and he was a "scientist" without the rhetoric of Putnam or the rough edges of Boas. In addition, his background in drawing and illustration attuned him to the aesthetics of artifacts.

Stuffing the Field Columbian Museum

On arrival in 1894 Holmes was immediately caught up by patron A. V. Armour, who invited Holmes and chair of botany Charles Millspaugh on a three-month scientific cruise aboard his yacht the *Ituña*.

The itinerary called for explorations in the Yucatán and then travels through Palenque and on to the Valley of Mexico (Holmes 1895, 1897a). When they docked at Progreso their guide was none other than Allison Armour's old friend Edward Thompson. Despite Putnam's warnings, Thompson had been caught up by the money and opportunities offered by the museum and its patrons. With Armour's influence he was supported by the museum for his work at Xkichmook and most spectacularly at Chichén Itzá. Not only did Armour purchase the results of Thompson's excavations, but he also supplied the funds to purchase for Thompson the hacienda on which Chichén was located (McVicker 2003).

A. V. Armour exemplified the personal patron, taking his lead from the East, where patrons like the Duc de Loubat and, later, George Heye would run the show for men of science such as Marshall Saville and George Pepper (McVicker 1992, 2004; Snead 1999). Similarly, Boas's early days at the American Museum were strongly affected by museum president Morris K. Jesup and his sponsorship of the expedition that bears his name (Freed et al. 1988b; Freed 2012).

Armour (1863–1941) was the son of the extraordinarily wealthy Chicagoan and Scottish immigrant George Armour, whose fortunes were based on control of grain elevators. The elder Armour was a financier and astute investor as well. He saw to it that his sons went to the best schools, with A. V. Armour graduating from Yale in 1884. When he returned to Chicago (his father having died in 1881), he took up the life of a wealthy young socialite and yachtsman. As a member of the Chicago elite Armour had purchased stock in the Fair and was prepared to enjoy all of its pleasures. In the A.V. Armour collection at Chicago Historical Society is an invitation dated August 3, 1893, to the "queen of Chicago society," Mrs. Potter Palmer, to go with him "on the little yacht this afternoon, dine at the German Village, view the illuminations and return during the evening." When this invitation was given to the Historical Society by Cornelia Conger in 1959, she described it as a "memento of a vanished world." She noted, too, that A. V. Armour and his brother George were not related in any way to the [meat-packing] Armours, and concluded that "in those far-off days [the brothers] fancied themselves as infinitely more chic!"

Infinitely less "chic" or not, Philip D. Armour of meat-packing fame was equally involved in cultural philanthropy, but only as a donor of funds to institutions and as a board member of museums, including the Field Museum. He also made a distinction between those actively engaged in cultural activities and those who lent financial support. When asked about his cultural philanthropy P. D. Armour reputedly replied, "My culture is mostly in my wife's name" (quoted in Horowitz 1976, 55).

Allison Armour was not only a socialite and civic-minded citizen but was also filled with the Chicago spirit of cultural philanthropy. He served on the board of the Field Museum (donating both World's Columbian Exposition stock and cash) as well as the boards of the Chicago Symphony and Art Institute. However, it was his interest in science and his approach to patronage that set him apart from many others of his time and social class. The Fair and the founding of the museum had a profound effect on Armour, for it was there that he encountered Edward Thompson and the ruins of Mexico and was impressed enough to support him as an employee of the Field Columbian Museum.

Following his return from the Armour yachting expedition to Mexico, Holmes wrote to Skiff on May 3, 1897 (Director's General Correspondence, FMA), praising Thompson's work among the ruins of Chichén Itzá for the previous year and declaring that he did "most earnestly recommend the renewal of the contract with Mr. Thompson for the year ending April 30th 1898." Holmes's recommendation was based not only on Thompson's "detailed reports" and contributions to the museum but also on "considering especially the obligations we are under to Mr. Armour, under whose patronage our work in Mexico has been largely carried on." Several weeks later, writing to Armour, Higinbotham expressed the extent of the debt. Armour was to pick up Thompson's salary and "the members of the Committee, and Mr. Field as well, desire an arrangement that will be entirely to your satisfaction, as we appreciate very fully your efforts on behalf of the Museum, and we do not wish to conclude an arrangement that will not be perfectly satisfactory to you" (Higinbotham to Armour, May 15, 1897, Director's General Correspondence, FMA).

Holmes and the museum were also indebted to Armour for publication of the results of the maritime archaeological expedition, including (because of high demand) a special edition of *Archaeological Studies among the Ancient Cities of Mexico* (Holmes 1895, 1897a; #67, November 4, 1895, Executive Committee, FMA). Armour was equally interested in botany and, as noted earlier, included the new curator of botany, Charles Millspaugh, on the *Ituña* cruise to Mexico. There is no evidence that Holmes's departure from the museum affected Armour's patronage of that institution. He continued to support Field Museum botanical expeditions, particularly to the West Indies.

Unfortunately for Chicago, Armour moved to New York and Miami at the turn of the century. However, once he relocated, he continued his patronage of archaeological expeditions, shifting his interests to the Mediterranean. As late as the mid-1920s he sponsored government botanist David Fairchild on a three-year global plant collecting expedition aboard the yacht *Utowana,* his 230 x 33-foot, 1,315-ton floating laboratory (Fairchild 1931). Fairchild (1931, 235) recalled that Armour conducted an archaeological survey of Crete and the eastern Mediterranean for the School of Classical Studies in Rome and assisted at the excavations undertaken by the Archaeological Institute of America on the site of Ancient Cyrene in Tripoli. This later excavation yielded the world famous "Venus of Cyrene," now in Rome.

Armour's continuing interest in botany and classical archaeology reflects the focus of philanthropy on science and art. Although in his younger and more adventurous days in Chicago he was caught up in Mexican archaeology, this was soon dropped in favor of more traditional patronage.

Contrast between Armour's personal patronage and Chicago's cultural philanthropy is exemplified by the career of lumber baron Edward Ayer (Lockwood 1929; Webber 1984). He grew up in rural Illinois just south of the Wisconsin border. At age eighteen he "caught the wanderlust" and in 1860 set out for California. There he labored until the Civil War broke out and he enlisted in a California cavalry company. No East Coast education for Edward Ayer! He was serving as a soldier on the Mexican frontier in 1862, protecting the Cerro Colorado mine, when he discovered William H. Prescott's *Conquest of Mexico.* Reading that book changed his life and turned him toward books and collecting. The history of the American West and the Indians of the New World became his first love (Lockwood 1929, 47–48; "Why I Love Prescott's 'Conquest of Mexico,'" Ayer Papers, box 4, folder 60, NLA).

When the young soldier returned home he went into the lumber business and used his first dollars to purchase his own copy of Prescott. By 1871, at the age of thirty, he was selling almost a million railroad ties a year. His growing fortune allowed him to become a major collector of Indian "relics." He stepped forward as a benefactor of the Fair and loaned his large anthropological collection to the Department of Ethnology. When the Field Columbian Museum was founded, Ayer accepted the presidency of the museum's Board of Directors and donated the collection that had been on display at the Fair.

Ayer's avid collecting did not falter following the Fair; he frequently purchased new collections and donated additional funds. As mentioned, the remarkable series of Egyptian items Ayer presented to the museum is an example of how the patron as collector (and board member) can leave a stamp on a museum collection. According to Webber (1984), Dorsey did not at first welcome the material, for "he had no interest in building an Egyptian collection." Ayer thought differently and apparently "converted" Dorsey. As Webber (184) comments, "trustees of the Field merged their own acquisitiveness and love of the chase with the desire of the museum to add to its collections."

Ayer was equally generous with his time, collections, and capital at the Newberry Library. Of even higher value to him than his archaeological and ethnological specimens were his books. He donated his library to the Newberry and ultimately endowed the collection so that it could continue to grow. Today the underused collection contains colonial documents and collections of photographs, paintings, and sketches that are invaluable to archaeological research. Ayer was also an admirer of Holmes, whom Lockwood (1929, 269) records as being received with "reverence and pride" as an artist, sociologist, and anthropologist. Among the items in Ayer's Newberry collection are the original drawings from Holmes's Armour-sponsored research. Ayer probably purchased them from his friend.

As a part of Chicago's philanthropic network, Ayer also became a benefactor of the institutions his friends supported. He made major gifts to the University of Chicago in honor of wealthy industrialist and University of Chicago trustee Martin A. Ryerson. In turn Ryerson provided the funds for the purchase of the Abadiano collection of Mexican antiquities, which Starr desired for his Walker Museum collections; this collection, with Ryerson's blessing, was later transferred to the Field Museum. Ayer also gave to the Art Institute in honor of its president Charles L. Hutchinson, a banker and major figure of the Chicago cultural scene (Webber 1984). One of the first trustees of the University of Chicago and well acquainted with Starr, too, Hutchinson served as the director and chairman of the Fine Arts Committee of the World's Columbian Exposition and was the first president of the Chicago Art Institute.

Things Fall Apart

The generosity of Armour, Ayer, and others did not resolve the issue of anthropology as science or entertainment. It took Holmes only two years to feel the impact of the same forces that Putnam had recognized as detrimental to science (Meltzer 2010). As soon as he could get a job back in Washington, he resigned. In his unpublished "Random Records of a Lifetime" (Holmes n.d.) he encloses a copy of a letter received in April 1894 from his friend John M. Coulter, then president of Lake Forest College and two years later chair of the Botany Department of the University of Chicago. After expressing his pleasure at Holmes's acceptance of the offer from the "Columbian Museum" because it "indicates that we are to have some genuine scientific work there," Coulter warned Holmes: "The danger has been the common danger of Chicago, namely, to make the Columbian Museum a big show instead of a center for scientific collections, for study and work." Following his resignation in 1897 Holmes placed the blame on director Skiff, who was "acting consistently with his innate cunning." He recollected how the scientific staff was in a state of rebellion against Skiff but that Higinbotham stood by his protégé.

Meltzer (2010) rightly questions the veracity of Holmes's "Random Records." As he points out, up until the time of Holmes's resignation there was little evidence of disillusionment. Curiously, Holmes's complaints about Skiff and his interaction with the scientific staff parallel Boas's own excuse for his "forced" resignation (McVicker 1999). Further, as Meltzer notes, none of the other members of the scientific staff chose to leave. In fact, botanist Millspaugh, Holmes's companion on the Armour expedition, continued as curator for decades until his death at age seventy.

An anonymous editorial in *American Naturalist* in September 1895 (vol. 29, p. 827; in Works about Edward E. Ayer, NLA) sums up well the challenges to science in Chicago after its Exposition. The editorialist comments that the hopes for benefits to science at the Field Museum had not been realized. Noting that nearly all scientific men who obtained positions had left with expressions of dissatisfaction, the author blames it on the fact that "the most active member of the management was a successful lumber merchant [Ayer] and the appointee as director [Skiff] was of an equally impossible stamp." The author argues that the reason European museums focusing on the western hemisphere are superior is because competent scientific men manage them. He concludes that in the United States the sole exceptions are a museum connected with a university [Harvard] and one in New York [the American Museum of Natural History], "where exceptional sagacity holds the reins." Given various letters and comments by Putnam at this time, it is possible that he or Boas was behind this editorial.

After Holmes abruptly returned to Washington in 1897, assistant curator George Dorsey took charge of anthropology at the Field Museum. As we have seen, Dorsey had gained prominence (and some notoriety) for his collection of Peruvian mummies and artifacts for Putnam's department at the Fair. Ironically, Putnam's first PhD graduate at Harvard turned his back on his mentor's science and, caught up in Chicago's drive to become a world-class center of art and science, turned out to be one of the most avid collectors and patronage seekers that anthropology at the museum had ever experienced.

Anthropology in the new natural history museum was particularly subject to scrutiny by patrons wishing to target their support. For example, director Skiff declared that the mission of the museum was the diffusion of existing knowledge, in contrast to the university, which produced it (cf. Horowitz 1976, 106). However, when Dorsey took over the curatorship of anthropology he attempted to broaden Skiff's mission statement. Dorsey (1907a) proclaimed that the mission was to be the *discovery* of knowledge. Still, for Dorsey the discovery of knowledge and the collection of objects merged. As a result, his anthropological collections fell far short of art and were questionable science.

Dorsey's curatorship was harshly criticized by his successor, Boas's colleague Berthold Laufer. In a 1908 letter to Boas (Cole 1985, 340)

Laufer comments: "According to the Dorsey method, . . . it is possible for every ethnologist to work in any territory; he photographs a little bit, buys indiscriminately everything he can get his hands on, has a good time with the people, and that settles the matter." This arrogant and ungracious response was written shortly after Laufer had been hired by Dorsey to lead a three-year expedition to Tibet funded by Chicago patron Mrs. Timothy B. Blackstone. Laufer also commented on Dorsey's "downright shocking superficiality" (Bronson 2003, 125). The view from Chicago was different, and in Dorsey's obituary Fay-Cooper Cole (1931) noted that "no one of our generation has done more toward popularizing science." From Laufer's view this was one of Dorsey's greatest sins, although he also sarcastically commented in 1908 that he envied Dorsey's "enthusiasm and childish joy in all things." Laufer considered popularizers little better than dilettantes. In reviewing Starr's *Korean Buddhism: Three Lectures* (Laufer 1919, 84), Laufer damned the publication with faint praise: "His lectures make a pleasant *causerie*, and when the author recites his adventures and impressions, he is always entertaining, but, not having access to original sources he sometimes treads on unsafe ground as soon as historical questions or Buddhist philosophy come to the fore."

Fay-Cooper Cole, Starr's successor at the University of Chicago, was a remarkably adept organizer, administrator, and teacher (Stocking 1979, 17). He was able to break his museum ties and by 1929 (six years after Starr retired) had achieved his goal of establishing a separate anthropology department. Cole also recognized the value of archaeological fieldwork in attracting both students and funding, and he soon established a tradition in United States archaeology, the summer field school (Stocking 1979, 17).

Dorsey's program of discovery through collection matched well with the visions of Ayer, Higinbotham, and Skiff. Over time Dorsey shifted his focus from archaeology to ethnography and from South America to the American West. It is not surprising that a delighted Ayer continued his munificent support of Chicago's anthropology. Ayer resigned as president of the museum Board of Directors in 1899. In his letter of resignation, he only states: "Differing in policy with one of my fellow trustees, I believe the best interest of the Museum will be promoted by my resigning the Presidency." However, he promised to continue to be a faithful and interested friend (and kept his promise). He concluded his letter with a statement that echoes the argument he had used only six years earlier to sway Marshall Field:

> Individuals and their acts are unimportant. The museum is one of the very great ones of the world, and is here to stay. For years to come it will be the great educational center for the Mississippi Valley. More than that it will immortalize its founder and all who have helped to further its interests. We are all reasonably intelligent, hard-headed business men, and as such, none of us will be remembered in the business world over five years, but in the intellectual world, every man who has honestly put his shoulder to the wheel in an effort to leave the world better than he found it, will live forever. (Ayer Papers, box 3, folder 41, NLA)

Conclusion

Libraries, museums, and universities all had diverse missions and were differently shaped by the World's Columbian Exposition, as were the anthropologists who staffed them. Similarly, patrons had different goals and their legacies took various forms. Although often unacknowledged today, all these men left their imprint on anthropology in Chicago. Certainly Edward Ayer's contributions to the Newberry remain best known in library circles. At the Field Museum he is primarily immortalized for his "selling" Marshall Field on the idea of a great Chicago museum; his philanthropic patronage is little remembered outside the museum. As Webber (1984) remarks: "There are also those who don't leave their name on an institution, but in some respects have had a more profound effect on the city than some whose names have been institutionally perpetuated."

Allison V. Armour's contributions to the Field Museum and other cultural institutions in Chicago also remain little recognized. While everyone remembers Philip D. Armour, the fabulously rich butcher baron, little is found in Chicago history regarding A. V. Armour, nor is he listed in compilations of the city's prominent figures (Bishop and Gilbert 1932; Gilbert and Bryson 1929).

Beyond the museum and library, the Fair and its patrons had only a small direct impact on anthropology at the university. Starr felt put off by Putnam and Boas, had little to do with Holmes, and distrusted

Dorsey. Although Laufer did spend most of his time collecting and conducting historical research in the Orient after he joined the Field Museum, Starr virtually ignored him. The professional reputations of Starr and Dorsey were gradually eclipsed by the rising prominence of Boas and his students. Of the anthropologists involved in the Exposition the most prominent were Putnam, Boas, and Holmes, all of whom ended up as outsiders in Chicago. Since they virtually defined what anthropology would be in the twentieth century, it is not surprising that anthropological insiders, popularizers Starr and Dorsey in Chicago, are judged as outsiders from a broader scientific or disciplinary perspective.

Robert Rydell (1984) suggested that men of science did not understand the purpose of the Fair. The Fair was commercial, was popular, and presented an image of American triumphs in business and industry. Since the Chicago World's Fair was defined by the merchants and captains of industry who invested in it, who in turn gave shape to the anthropology that emerged from it, is it surprising that those "men of science" who remained in or returned to Chicago carried on a "big show"?

Notes

When Curtis Hinsley and David Wilcox invited me to join the symposium they were organizing for the Chicago Meetings of the Society for American Archaeology I was unsure as to the contribution I could make. I had completed research on Holmes in Chicago, and the article "Buying a Curator" was in press (McVicker 1999). My previous work on Frederick Starr at the University of Chicago had covered much of the same ground. However, when I heard that David Meltzer was to take a different perspective on Holmes, I was encouraged to focus more on the role of institutions, rather than individuals, and on patrons and popularizers, rather than professionals. I hope all participants are pleased with the results of their encouragement.

A Smithsonian Institution summer research fellowship in 1988 provided the opportunity to begin archival research on the career of William Henry Holmes. Various other archival resources were made available during research for this chapter. Permission to quote from these materials was granted by the Chicago History Museum, Field Museum of Natural History, National Anthropological Archives, Newberry Library, and University of Chicago Special Collections. All support is gratefully acknowledged.

1. The Chicago Academy of Sciences (1857, chartered 1865) was very much a presence at this time and still plays an active role in science education in the Chicago

area. Its museum collections were sought after by both the Field Museum and the University of Chicago's Walker Museum. Unfortunately for these competing institutions the CAS decided to construct its own museum on the north side of Chicago. However, it was to suffer the fate of academies of sciences throughout the United States as professionalization took the field in museums and universities. Consequently organizations that promoted engagement in scientific activities for all citizens by keeping their membership open to uncredentialed amateurs were marginalized.

2. Cushing remains one of the great enigmas in any attempt to polarize popularizers and professionals. He was one of the romantics in the history of anthropology and was a public attention grabber. Yet, unlike Starr and Dorsey, he neither lectured widely nor wrote frequently for the general public. As Darnell (2003, 765) expresses it in her review of *The Lost Itinerary of Frank Hamilton Cushing* (Hinsley and Wilcox, ed. 2002), "The editors suggest (2002, xvii) that Cushing was seeking 'a scientific poetics,' a language that would capture both the adventure of the search and the meaning of the emerging archaeological record. The narrative genre emphasized eyewitness accounts of travel and exploration." As Cushing told his patron Mrs. Mary Hemenway in a letter dated June 1, 1888, "It is not the 'science,' it is the poetry, about my dear subject which makes me love it,—far better than life, and far better than fame" (quoted in Wilcox 2003b, 105, note 2).

3. At the same time in England John George Wood, who died in 1889, was to be eulogized by the *London Times* as the writer who "did more to popularize the study of natural history than any writer of the present age." Wood made a point of inviting readers to participate in the making of science. He wrote that some of the most valuable original observations were made by an "old lady in her daily perambulation of a little scrap of back yard in suburban London barely twelve yards long" (Lightman 2007, 183).

DOCUMENT J

Heir of the Big Fair
Field Columbian Museum Opened

Thousands of Persons Witness the Formal Dedication of the Institution—Magnificent Collection of Wonders of Science, Art and Nature.

No bands played. No words were wasted in meaningless oratory. No time was allotted for ostentatious exaltation of individuals. The ceremonies were simple, sober, dignified, alike befitting the institution and the character of the man who made it possible. One single prayer of thankfulness was uttered. The history of the institution was told in language stripped of extravagance. Its character, its purpose, its place in the world was interpreted by one who spoke with full knowledge of his subject. Ten thousand throats answered in cheers.

The Field Columbian Museum was a fact—organized, installed, opened, dedicated to its mission as a monument to the greatest achievement of the Chicago of to-day and as a finger-board to the Chicago of tomorrow.

The museum dedicated yesterday is the crystallization of an idea conceived before the magic city it commemorates had begun to rise beside the waters of the lake.

"We have undertaken and will achieve a wondrous work," said the white city builders, "but all its greatness is destined to fade in a day. Treasures gathered from the ends of the earth will be spread before the eyes of men and will be scattered again, leaving nothing but memories. This should not be so. Let us, then, raise on the ruins of this

Chicago Sunday Herald, June 3, 1894

great work an institution which shall stand, at once a monument to its greatness and a teacher of its best lessons."

The white city rose and was peopled. Within the walls of its palaces the fruits of a world's progress were gathered. A world's men and women thronged its streets, gazed upon its wondrous beauty, drank from its gushing fountains the essence of man's evolution and ascension through countless ages, and went away bewildered, thankful for having seen, but carrying away with them oftentimes nothing more than the vague shadow of an Elysian dream.

Birth of the Field Museum

The white city and all its wonders died and of its death the Field Columbian Museum was born, brought into the world to preserve the memory and perpetuate the work of what had passed away.

It was a noble and complete monument, as it stood yesterday under the blazing sunshine. As the museum itself stands for what was best of the fair's interior, so its home stands for what was best of the fair's exterior.

Jackson Park was beautiful, but its beauty lay not in what it was, but in what it called back to the memory. The beauty of the Fair—that matchless beauty which won for it the name of "Magic City"—had been swept away. The stately palace of art alone remained of all that sublime city of palaces. And it was eloquent of the past. All around it were half demolished buildings, piles of stone, heaps of rubbish, shapeless holes in the earth, ruin and desolation. The storms of winter had dealt kindly with its outlines and wherever the hand of destruction had fallen upon it the injury had been repaired. Its majestic walls were not quite so brilliantly, dazzlingly white as a year ago, but the mellower tones seemed to give it an added dignity. From every side it looked greater and grander than ever. When Jackson Park was filled last summer with great palaces, each a titan of its class, and the broad avenues were filled with thousands, in an ever moving throng, the imposing greatness of the parts was lost in the immensity of the whole. Yesterday the art palace looked a whole city under one roof. Probably not one of the thousands who saw it yesterday ever before appreciated all that the fair had been in its great perspectives, its balanced proportions and its sublimity as a whole. Undwarfed by magnificent surroundings, isolated by its preservation, the Art Palace stood alone in its immensity, its perfect symmetry, its grandeur as the one remaining feature of the most sublime architectural panorama the eye of man ever saw.

Really a Permanent Exposition

And inside the great building one found the other monument to the other side of the fair. Every line along which human endeavor is expended was represented by its achievements in one of the great departments of the fair. Each one of those great departments is represented by its best in the Field Columbian Museum. And the representation is not only complete but unique. Almost in a day, one might say, the builders of the fair—the United States and particularly Chicago—accomplished what no other nation had ever done even after years of effort. And when their work was done there was in it no trace of circumscription to section, nation or continent: it represented the whole world and the highest results of ages of time. The great museums of the world have grown by the slow accretions from successive expositions, covering years, generations, even centuries. The Field Columbian Museum has grown from a single exposition and at a single bound; within little more than a half-year of its birth has taken its place as a great museum.

In another way this museum dedicated yesterday is unique and typical of the fair that gave it birth and the city in which it stands. It is not a curiosity shop. It is called a museum, but it is in effect an exposition. It speaks not alone of a musty past buried beneath the weight of ages; its treasures are not for the delectation of the savant burrowing for the forgotten, useless secrets of other days. This museum does epitomize all that is worth learning and knowing of the ages gone before and it does more. It speaks of the hot, pulsating world of to-day and its work in which every man is interested and which every man can understand. It tells the stories of the land and the sea, of the rocks and the valleys and the mountains. Its shelves and cabinets contain the history of the nations that have come and gone on the earth and the history of their achievements told in their handiwork. More than all, it speaks to the mind of to-day of the things done to-day in every part of this world from pole to pole, from orient to occident and back again. It contains the annals of men for all men.

All Classes of People Represented

This was the museum 10,000 people went to Jackson Park yesterday to see opened and dedicated to its great work. As they understood its message to be for all men, so they came from the walks of all men. The scholar was there, with spectacles on nose, eager for a peep at the secrets denied to all but such as he who spend their lives in study. Next to him stood the man of leisure who travels, reads books, explores the unknown land, dives into the bowels of the earth and walks through galleries and museums because he wants occupation for a mind averse to idleness. The man of science came, too, looking for that which would be of service to him in his research and experimentation; also the mechanic with his ambition to become the inspiration of mechanics. And besides these there were those representatives of the greatest class of all, the class that wants to see and to know what everybody else sees and knows and does. They came on foot, in street cars, on trains, in carriages with liveried footmen. They came and stood patiently around the great doors waiting for the dedication and the opening.

Within the building the curators visited every department, directing their assistants and taking a last look to see that everything was ready for the supreme moment when their work would be exposed to eager eyes. The men who had borne the burden of organizing, collecting and installing for the museum were there, too, proud of the part they had taken and feeling repaid for all their care by the completeness of their work and the manifest interest of the public, for whom that work had been done. Last came the men whose generosity had made this museum possible, and among these one stood above all the rest.

Marshall Field Well Pleased

Marshall Field came to assist in the dedication of the work which will immortalize his name, but he came with misgiving. Mr. Field had been averse to opening the museum so soon. He feared it was not so complete as it should be; not so complete as he intended it should be when he drew the check for $1,000,000 and insured to Chicago the possession of a monument to her wonderful achievement and an educator for her people. He was shown the museum before the doors were thrown open and he was satisfied. He said so. A few minutes later in the director's room, when the curators of the various departments were presented to Mr. Field, he complimented each upon his part in the preparation for the opening day.

All this time the crowd was growing and beating against the doors, anxious to get in but patient to wait for the word. An inclosure for the invited guests had been roped off in front of the north door of the building. It was not half large enough. The crowd spread out on each side and back into the avenue that used to lead past a row of state buildings. It waited in the hot sun and looked in pity upon the great statue of Caesar Augustus, whose glorious reign in the golden age of Rome never saw anything to compare with that vision of a year ago, brought back so clearly by the programme of yesterday. Even the Columbian guard was there answering questions and trying to keep the crowd within prescribed limits. But he was tamer and milder and better in every way than he had ever been in the days of his uncrowned kingship, for the chastened spirit of last year rebuked him.

Promptly at 2:30 o'clock President Ayer, of the museum's board of trustees, led the way to the platform reserved for the museum directors, the contributors to the fund that made it and Chicagoans entitled by their position and prominence in connection with the fair to special distinction.

Beginning of the Exercises

The crowd uncovered while Dr. Gunsaulus prayed in thankfulness for all that had gone before and prepared the way for this museum and asked the divine blessing upon its future. President Ayer congratulated his hearers on being permitted to assemble to dedicate the Field Columbian Museum. They would want to know something of its inception, how the preliminary work was done and what had been accomplished. He introduced as the man best qualified to tell the story of the museum's birth F. J. V. Skiff, who was an active promoter of the museum from the first, and who is now its managing director.

Mr. Skiff told this story in all its completeness without dwelling on individual efforts. His address was a straightforward history of the museum idea and the museum actuality. It was too hot under the blistering sun for the expenditure of energy in applause, but at the mention of the name of Marshall Field, the heat was forgotten. The cheer that greeted his name was as hardy as it was spontaneous, and the modest merchant prince blushed.

Edward G. Mason, president of the Chicago Historical Society, interpreted the message of the museum to Chicago and the world. He spoke of its completeness, of its greatness as a museum, of its perfect representation of the wonderful work of which it was born, of its place in the future of Chicago. He spoke eloquently and his eloquence found an echo in his audience.

But all this had been merely preparatory. The museum had not yet been opened. President Ayer rose and warned those in the rear to refrain from crowding in the rush for the doors, lest anyone be injured. Then he raised his gavel and said: "I now declare the Field Columbian Museum open."

The gavel fell and a cheer arose. At the same instant a man away up on the roof pulled a halyard. A handsome banner fourteen feet wide and thirty-two feet long was loosed from its stops at the tip of the fifty-foot staff. The wind caught its folds and the great white flag bearing the name of the museum in big black letters floated out for all to see.

Crowd Wanted Mr. Field to Speak

The museum had been dedicated and opened, but the crowd was not satisfied. Cries of "Field! Field!" rose on every side. The crowd wanted to hear, at least to see, the father of the museum. But Mr. Field would not. At the first shout of his name he rose to escape into the building. Thomas B. Bryan, his face aglow with youthful enthusiasm, sought to drag Mr. Field to the front of the platform, but the modest merchant would take no part. Without ostentation he had made the museum possible and he would not pose in the public eye now that it had become a fact. He broke from the restraining hand and mounted the steps. Mr. Bryan would not be balked. He sprang to the front of the platform, hat in hand, and called:

"Three cheers for Mr. Field."

They came heartily and saluted the ears of him for whom they were given before he could escape within the building.

Then the doors were opened and the crowd thronged inside, to be swallowed up by the broad corridors and deep chambers. Around the north door the crush had been greatest and in the hottest sun. No seats were there, and frail women almost fainted, but the coolness inside soon revived them.

The hand of Jimmy Hunt—another relic from the fair—had made the interior of the museum gay with the flags of all nations and a great American flag waved lazily in the main corridor.

Inspecting the Exhibits

Every corridor and every chamber of the building was explored and a glance bestowed upon every exhibit. But yesterday was no day for studying the exposition. It was a day of introductions merely. The study will come later and the number of catalogues bought yesterday indicates that the Field Columbian Museum will not want for students.

The museum was closed at 6 o'clock. Slowly, regretfully the visitors streamed out and down its broad approaches. They looked around once more upon the wreck of magnificence accomplished since last November, then turned their eyes back upon the stately palace beside the lagoon. It rose before them, glowing softly in the mellow evening light, greater, grander, more majestically beautiful than ever before, and those dreamy nights of a year ago, filled with the intoxication of radiant beauty and sublimity merged, all came back to them. They were thankful this much had been spared. They looked again and went home thinking.

The Field Columbian Museum had been dedicated, opened and approved. The crowning glory of Chicago and the century had been commemorated.

ESSAY SEVEN

Going National

American Anthropology Successfully Redefines Itself as an Accepted Academic Domain

DAVID R. WILCOX

*C*oming of Age in Chicago by the young science of anthropology is a story about both increasing maturity or professionalization, and the dynamics of interaction with audiences that included interested amateurs or avocationalists. Some sought to make their own contributions to knowledge, while others wanted entertainment more than enlightenment. The Chicago World's Fair, or World's Columbian Exposition, was pivotal in this process, marking the transition from an older generation to those who would begin to take American anthropology in different if not entirely new directions. By examining the journey of American anthropology before, during, and after the Fair, we have attempted to chart that trajectory and explain both successes and dead ends. In this essay, after briefly reviewing what came before and during the Fair, echoing points made previously, the main focus becomes what happened later, as American anthropology "went national" and succeeded in becoming established as an accepted academic domain of inquiry and debate.

Professionalization is a process, not simply an event, but events can be significant structural episodes that transform both possibilities and constraints on behavior—"raising the bar," as it were, for what is judged to be "good work." Fernand Braudel (1980) called the analysis of such "structural moments" the history of conjunctions. For example, the formation in 1879 in Boston of the Archaeological Institute of America (AIA; Allen 2002) and in Washington of both the Bureau of Ethnology and the Anthropological Society of Washington (ASW; Flack 1975; Hinsley 1981) constituted a conjunction of more or less independent events. Together they created forums where new contributions could be critically discussed and evaluated. Or consider the year 1888, when the beginning of the *American Anthropologist* (AA) as the publication organ of the ASW created a new outlet for contributions, many of which were first read as papers at ASW meetings (Lamb 1906). The same year in Cambridge, Massachusetts, the American Folk-Lore Society (AFS) appeared; the close alliance between its editor, William Wells Newell, and Franz Boas made it a second anthropological instrument, what we see as a kind of "second trumpet"—or fifth wheel (cf. Zumwalt 1988). Again in 1888, the Peabody Museum at Harvard began publishing its archaeological series (Bernal 1980, 154).[1]

The Chicago Fair was similarly a significant "structural moment" that effectively began to redesign the "playing field" in subsequent years for anthropology. In the first place, the Fair marked a consensus point for Americanists, an agreement about the bounds of anthropology that found expression in the diverse presentations there—the Midway, the Government Building, the Anthropology Building and village—and that justifies Boas's later characterization of Powell, Brinton, and Putnam as the "three fathers" of the field. Second, the number of participants was growing, partly due to their Chicago opportunities. As we have seen, Frank Cushing was there much of the time, constantly networking with many of the principal figures in American anthropology. Powell (1890) had noted only a few years earlier that there were literally only a handful of archaeologists practicing in the United States. But in preparation for the 1893 Exposition Putnam was able to put at least fifty-five workers in the field collecting archaeological and ethnographic materials (Dexter 1966c; Johnson 1897–98). And many would soon get jobs in newly founded institutions. One was the Field Columbian Museum itself, which aimed to garner the anthropological treasures of the world from the Fair (Dexter 1970; Nash and Feinman 2003; Meltzer 2010; McVicker 2012). Philadelphia had already joined the competition in 1889 with the formation of the Free Museum of Science and Art (later the University Museum) at the University of Pennsylvania (Fowler and Wilcox 2003); a year later the Brooklyn Institute of Arts and Sciences was organized by Franklin William Hooper; and in 1894 the American Museum of Natural History (AMNH) in New York invited Putnam to restructure its anthropology department. He soon brought Boas to help him (Cole 1999; Freed 2012). Options were rapidly growing and changing.

After the Chicago Fair a stunning succession of structural changes in anthropology occurred—as it happens, about every five years. These events provide a rational, albeit heuristic, basis for a periodization scheme for the early disciplinary history of American anthropology: 1894–98, 1899–1903, 1904–9, 1910–15, 1916–20, and 1921–25.² The beginning and end of each period can be viewed in retrospect as "structural moments"—or what Rosenberg describes as "significant points in time, moments [that] inevitably present particular configurations of social possibility" (1996, 13). These points chart mileposts in the journey of American anthropology as it struggled to shape an identity within larger cultural perturbations.

My approach in formulating this structural scheme has been first to assemble data on individuals from the membership lists of the American Anthropological Association (AAA) and authors in the *American Anthropologist* (AA) and, having organized them into sets defined by period, then to examine the spatial and institutional patterns of these grouped data in order to trace the shifting power centers within American anthropology. The goal is to track anthropology as it became an increasingly professional organization with a growing national audience. Crucial in the overall period (1894–1925) were the establishment of departmental structures in museums or universities and of support groups that often also provided publication outlets. In this way local anthropological "communities" formed and were linked together into a national confraternity network by the AAA and the AFS, even as they gradually reached outside the United States into Latin America and Europe.

In particular, analysis of the membership of the AAA between 1904 and 1915 demonstrates how the new national organization fared in the decade before World War I. Needless to say, it was a period of profound, complex change in the United States. The fading Victorian age of these years was challenged by new imperial responsibilities and aspirations (Kennedy 1987; Kagan 2007) and by a vigorous *avant-garde* movement (May 1994 [1959])—in which Elsie Clews Parsons, among others, was a prominent figure (Deacon 1997). In other words, the larger cultural context was a maelstrom of new philosophies and changes in basic understandings about the very nature of reality, changes that came to be called Modernism (Everdell 1997; Gay 2008; see also Singh 2004).

The immediate postwar years were, if anything, even more tortured. In the profound economic transformations wrought by World War I, during which New York replaced London as the banking capital of the world (Zimmerman 2002; Kessner 2003; Morris 2005), the coming of the Jazz Age marked a further change in the moral compass of popular culture in America, as indigenous and immigrant cultural experiences more openly affected what it meant to be an American (Gioia 1997; Lewis 1997). Developments in the philosophy of science, psychology, and history directly influenced anthropology (Lowie 1956). Historian Louis Barkan (1992, 128, n. 134) insightfully notes, however, that "the choice of anthropology [by students at that time] was mildly conservative. [Margaret] Mead [1972, 105, 107] described her friends in college as radicals 'in terms of our sentiments rather than our adherence to any radical ideology.' This explains why conservatives could be part of the group, but more importantly reflects on radicalism as a political expression where substance was secondary to appearance."

Any explanation of the success of American anthropology in the periods on either side of World War I, then, must seek out its relationships to larger social realities such as these, which affected the intellectual interests of the individuals drawn to it, both professionals and nonprofessionals (see Stocking 1976; Barkan 1992; Black 2003; Spiro 2009). The principal conclusion we draw from the data presented is that American anthropology by 1915, and even more so by 1925, achieved a new level of system equilibrium as an established domain of scientific and humanistic inquiry in American institutions, especially in museums and academia, and in the imagination of a broader public both in this country and abroad. Four indices provide a calculus for measuring this process of professionalization:

> 1. the status of competing intellectual paradigms or research agendas that define the problem domains to be studied and how to study them within a shared conception of a larger whole;

2. the emergence of institutional structures that provide employment, training, and a framework for competition and debate about the discipline's agendas;

3. a cadre of like-minded individuals whose roots, motivations, expectations, and training bring about a shared long-term commitment to the discipline's agendas, which they may also modify and debate;

4. professional organizations, regular meetings, and publication outlets that serve to define who the "professionals" are, to legitimate their contributions to knowledge, and to provide a variety of forums to critique work regarded as substandard (cf. Kuhn 1970; Lakatos and Musgrave 1970; Reingold 1991 [1976]; Rosenberg 1997 [1976]).

Taken together, the emergence of these four indices in a systemic structural nexus arguably marks the time when a professional organization has achieved a state of equilibrium.

Certainly not all these developments are traceable to Chicago in 1893. But at the Fair most of the anthropological players active at the time came together and collectively, in their various activities, put on display what they thought American anthropology was all about. Soon afterward Brinton became president of the American Association for the Advancement of Science (AAAS), and in his presidential address (Document K) he set forth his conception of the domains of study in anthropology. Almost immediately Boas, more securely situated in New York, challenged and discredited the methods advocated by Brinton (Document L). And yet more than a decade later he was able to toast Brinton as one of the "three fathers" of American anthropology (Boas 1909). Why? He did so because he agreed with Brinton about the domain of study, what later became known as the "four-field" approach to anthropology (plus folklore)—a conception that allegedly set American anthropology apart from the practice of anthropology in other parts of the world (Cole 1976; Stocking 1988; but see Kuklick 1993; Hicks 2013). Putnam accepted this wide conception as well, and it is reflected in his presentation of American anthropology at the Fair.[3] The Fair was the structural moment when that consensus fully coalesced, opening the door to institutional developments where the dynamic interplay of answers to this peculiar set of anthropological questions could be debated.

This first generation of "professional" American anthropology (the "three fathers") and even the second generation of Boas and McGee, Holmes, Hodge, and Fewkes, were largely superseded by the generation of successful students of Boas and Putnam.[4] This third generation, coming themselves of age with the new century, defined their own research agendas and created new institutional nexuses to replicate further their vision of what the field should be. In other scientific disciplines "theory groups" formed that dominated the replication process (Mullins 1973); but in anthropology this was a process in which individuals had much more opportunity to chart their own courses (Rowe 1962; Barkan 1992, 315; Woodbury and Woodbury 1999; cf. Darnell 2001; Darnell and Gleach 2002, 421); and it remains true to this day. Partly this may be due to "the independent and entrepreneurial spirit so valued in graduates of American colleges," where doctoral programs centered in departments have been closely tied to undergraduate teaching (Kohler 1996 [1990]). Perhaps because of this, the European model more familiar to Boas had to be modified, bringing about a certain reconciliation between the objectives of professionalization and popularization (Boas 1911, 1928; see McVicker 2012). Later in this essay I offer a general explanation for why American anthropology, beginning at the 1893 Fair, succeeded so well in capturing the attention of the American public in the subsequent century.

A Proposal of Structural Moments Following the Fair, 1894 to 1925

1894–1898

Increasingly prominent on the diplomatic world stage, in 1893 the United States changed the title of its representatives to important foreign governments from minister to ambassador (see Collin 1985, 156; Zwerdling 1998, 192), signaling less deference and greater assertion. In Washington, at the ASW, anatomist Frank Baker, head of the National Zoo, in 1894 replaced Henshaw as editor of the *American Anthropologist*, reflecting a largely avocational editorial committee. Mary Tileston Hemenway died that year, leaving funding at the Peabody Museum for a fellowship in archaeology (initiated in 1891). Harvard also began offering the first regular course in general anthropology for graduate students and selected undergraduates (Dixon 1930, 211) and graduated its first PhD in anthropology, George Dorsey. In 1894 the name of the Bureau of Ethnology was changed to the Bureau of *American* Ethnology (BAE). While retaining his positions in Cambridge, Putnam became curator at the American Museum of Natural History in New York City, after Holmes turned down that job to go to the Field Museum in Chicago (Cole 1999; Meltzer 2010; Freed 2012). Putnam was soon (1896) able to hire Boas, his assistant from the Fair; in turn, Boas soon became associated with Columbia University, where he began to train students. After Holmes left the Field Museum to return to the BAE, Dorsey (1868–1931) became curator at the Field in 1897.[5]

Charles P. Bowditch (1840–1911) in 1894 became a trustee of the Peabody and established a chaired position (as well as a fellowship) at Harvard in Central American archaeology. He was among a group of wealthy patrons drawn to anthropology at this time, partly as a result of the Fair: Phoebe Apperson Hearst (1842–1919), who sponsored Max Uhle in South America and Frank Cushing in Florida for the museum at the University of Pennsylvania in Philadelphia; Allison Vincent Armour (1863–1941) in Chicago, who sponsored Holmes in Mexico for the Field (Meltzer 2010); and Henry Villard (1835–1900) of New York, who sponsored Bandelier in South America for AMNH. In 1894 banker Morris K. Jesup (1830–1908), president of the Board of Trustees of the AMNH, decided that anthropology and paleontology were the two fields of study the museum should most support; excited by Boas's program for examining Asian–New World contacts, he sponsored the Jesup North Pacific expedition from 1896 to 1902 (Cole 1999; Freed 2012), thus addressing a key controversy that had been discussed at the International Congress of Anthropology in Chicago (Document D). A fascinating New Yorker (and a papal duke), Joseph Florimond M. le Duc de Loubat (1831–1927), began sponsoring prizes for the best work in anthropology in the previous year. In 1898 the Loubat Prize went to Holmes. Finally, brothers Fred and Talbot Hyde reconstituted the Hyde Exploring Expedition to the Southwest by initiating excavations at Chaco Canyon in the spring of 1896—beginning a long relationship with Putnam and the American Museum (Snead 2001).

Otis Tufton Mason, one of the leading figures in the ASW, suffered a serious stroke in 1898 (Hinsley 1981, 113; Lacey 1979, 76), greatly curtailing his ability to contribute—but his predominance as a contributor to the *Anthropologist* in the 1899–1903 period continued (see later discussion). In 1898, too, the ASW joined twelve other societies in the capital to form the Washington Academy of Sciences (Flack 1975; Lacey 1979, 112).

The period ends in the year of the Spanish-American War, in which the United States took over Puerto Rico and the Philippines, beginning its modern venture in American imperialism (Karp 2003 [1979]; Kagan 2007). The year before a decision was made to reorganize the *American Anthropologist*, with W. J. McGee and Franz Boas playing the leading roles (Stocking 1960), so that it could "more fully represent the field of anthropology in America than any magazine which the Anthropological Society, with the comparatively limited funds at its disposal, could alone guarantee" (AA, old series 11, 389). Hodge became editor, with a new editorial board with representation from Boston, New York, Chicago, Philadelphia, and Washington. Only Charles Mercer Dawson, the director of the Geological Survey of Canada and friend of both Boas and McGee, came from outside the country (McGee in AA 3, 159–63; Flack 1975, 127).[6]

1899–1903

Primary sponsorship of the *Anthropologist* now shifted from Washington to the Anthropology Section of the AAAS, a national organization (Flack 1975, 126). Boas and McGee became co-owners of the journal, with Boas and Dorsey actively soliciting funds from wealthy patrons to support it. Boas also put in a good deal of his own money; even so, by 1902 when the American Anthropological Association took it over, a deficit of $1,370 remained (Cole 1999, 211; Guthrie and Lathrop 2002; Hinsley 2002).

Brinton died in 1899 and was replaced on the AA editorial board by Stewart Culin, who moved to the Brooklyn Institute in 1903 (Darnell 1970). The Free Museum of Science and Art at the University of Pennsylvania opened in 1899. However, Phoebe Hearst transferred her philanthropic interests to the University of California at Berkeley in 1901, taking Max Uhle with her and supporting the work of George Andrew

Reisner (1867–1942) in Egypt. On behalf of the Field Museum Stanley McCormick (1874–1947) sponsored a Southwestern Expedition that also led to Hermann Voth's controversial installation of Hopi exhibits in the museum. Jacob Henry Schiff (1847–1920) bankrolled Berthold Laufer's AMNH expedition to China (1901–4). In 1903 the Carnegie Institution of Washington was incorporated, and in 1902 the departments of anthropology and psychology at Columbia University separated, lending in both cases added support to anthropological research.

Quick to sense the possibilities in change, McGee insisted that a national organization of anthropology be formed, and he had his way in 1902, becoming the first president of the AAA. While Boas had wanted an all-professional organization, McGee preferred to include people with avocational interests (as had long been true in the ASW and AAAS), and he outmaneuvered Boas (Stocking 1960). McGee was also the acting president of the National Geographic Society in 1902 (Flack 1975, 163). For a brief shining moment, it seemed he would be the new leader of American anthropology.

Hodge continued as editor, a position he would hold until 1915, when he became AAA president. Through editorial competence, institutional neutrality, and effective negotiating skills he added greatly to the stability of the emerging profession.[7] The cordiality engendered in New York during the 1901 International Congress of Americanists led to invitations to many people from Latin America to serve on the *Anthropologist*'s editorial board, making it truly Americanist in scope for the first time, and perhaps reflecting a certain American assertiveness in the Americas. These men included Juan Bautista Ambrosetti from Argentina[8]; David Boyle from Canada (replacing Dawson)[9]; Alfredo Chavero from Mexico[10]; Hermann von Ihering from Brazil[11]; and Rodolfo Lenz from Chile.[12] Chavero was briefly replaced by Antonio Peñafiel in 1907,[13] and then by Nicolás León in 1909.[14]

American anthropology was clearly becoming more international in its impact and in its audience. As a consequence of the Spanish-American War, several *Anthropologist* contributors or AAA members filled key roles in the Philippines, from secretary of the interior (Dean Conant Worcester, 1901–13) to lieutenant governor of the Philippines Civil Service (Daniel Folkmar, 1903–7), chief of the non-Christian tribes (David Prescott Barrows, 1901–3, who later headed the education system, 1903-9), and chief of the Ethnological Survey (Albert Ernest Jenks, 1903-5).

1904-1909

Robert Singleton Peabody died in 1904, leaving to the Phillips Academy of Andover, Massachusetts, an endowment for archaeology, which his son Charles and his friend Warren King Moorehead were the first to employ. The University Museum in Philadelphia began work in Mexico in 1904 (Bernal 1980, 154). McGee abruptly left the BAE in 1903 after Holmes was appointed to replace Powell. He then took charge of the anthropology exhibits at the St. Louis Exposition in 1904, briefly becoming director of the St. Louis Public Museum the following year (Parezo and Fowler 2007). But this institution failed to become another Field Museum; McGee left anthropology for the national conservation movement (Hays 1959). Importantly, McGee's withdrawal left the field wide open for Boas to assume leadership.

Holmes, another Boas competitor, moved from the BAE to the U.S. National Museum in 1909, the same year he served as president of the AAA. Hodge then became the ethnologist in charge of the BAE (Woodbury and Woodbury 1999, 290). Boas became editor of the *Journal of American Folk-Lore* in 1908, a position he held until 1924—giving him a publishing outlet independent of the *Anthropologist.* Interestingly, in 1908 Kroeber withdrew from folklore in favor of archaeology and California linguistics (Thoresen 1973, 42; Zumwalt 1988, 80). When Putnam retired in 1909, Boas edited the festschrift volume in his honor—a symbol of his increasing prominence.

In these years the American Southwest and the ripe fields of Mexican studies became an arena of intense jockeying for access and institutional dominance—especially between East Coast groups and Edgar Lee Hewett and his AIA allies in New Mexico. One of those allies, the inveterate popularize Charles F. Lummis, founded first the Southwest Society of the AIA and, in 1906, the Southwest Museum in Los Angeles (Thompson 2001). Clark Wissler in 1909 persuaded a new trustee of the AMNH, Archer Milton Huntington (1870-1955), to sponsor a survey of the American Southwest (Fowler 2000; Wilcox and Fowler 2002). Hewett became the first director of the new Museum of New Mexico (Chauvenet 1983; Hinsley 1986; Fowler 1999; Munson 2007), and in the same year the AIA, with lobbying by Alice Fletcher (Mark 1988), established a School of American Archaeology in Santa Fe, also under the direction of Hewett. He quickly began a program of research in Mexico headed by Sylvanus Griswold Morley (Snead 2001; Wilcox and Fowler 2002). In Mexico the Museo Nacional de Arqueología, Historia y Etnografía became a separate institution in 1909, and that same year the Escuela Internacional de Arqueología y Etnología was approved, beginning its work in 1911. Eduard Seler, Boas, Alfred Tozzer, G. C. [Jorge] Engerrand, and Manuel Gamio followed in annual sequence as director (Godoy 1977; Bernal 1980).

Meanwhile, at Oxford University in England, Edward Burnett Tylor retired in 1909 (AA 11, 817), while in the United States the National Association for the Advancement of Colored People was founded to combat racism against blacks (Recchiuti 2007). Also of note, Sigmund Freud and Carl Jung visited the United States in 1909 to help celebrate the twenty-fifth anniversary of Clark University, stimulating American interest in psychoanalysis. More ominously, in December 1909, the American Breeders Association, the president of which was James Wilson, U.S. secretary of agriculture, was persuaded by the biologist (and AAA member) Charles Benedict Davenport (aided by Alexander Graham Bell) to found the Eugenics Record Office. Davenport soon lined up significant funding from Mrs. E. H. Harriman, whose husband had died in 1909, leaving her one of the great American fortunes. Their objective was "the physical and social regeneration of our beloved country" through a program of sterilization or segregation of the "unfit." California became the third state to adopt forced sterilization in 1909, behind Indiana in 1907 and Illinois in 1909 (Kevles 1995; Baker 1998; Black 2003; Spiro 2009). It was against the powerful pretensions of this pseudo-scientific movement that Boas (1916) and Kroeber (1916, 1923) would promote the discipline of anthropology as a more scientific and humane alternative (see later discussion).[15]

1910–1915

In 1910 Hodge finished editing the second volume of *Handbook of North American Indians*, completing a major item on the agenda of nineteenth-century government anthropology (Fowler and Wilcox 1999). In Mexico the work of the Escuela Internacional de Arqueología y Etnología inaugurated the European method of stratigraphic analysis to the study of American archaeology (Bernal 1980). In the American Southwest similar researches for the Huntington Survey by the AMNH based on stratigraphy and "time relations" led Wissler (1917) to proclaim a "New Archaeology." Nels Nelson was initiating this revolution in the Galisteo Basin in 1912, and soon Kroeber (1916) and Spier (1917) added to the momentum with "seriation" studies of ceramic variability. Spier had already (1913) shown how the new methods could revisit the nineteenth-century controversy of the Trenton gravels and their relevance to the question of the antiquity of human presence in the New World, something that Holmes had addressed with devastating logic in the late 1890s (see McGee in AA o.s. 10, 317–45; Meltzer and Dunnell 1992). Kidder's work at Pecos Pueblo for the Phillips Academy, begun in 1915, was based on similar methods, and his 1914 Harvard dissertation advanced the study of potsherds to primary importance. Independently of these developments, Parsons began her epic work in the American Southwest in 1915 (Hieb 1993; Deacon 1997; Fowler 2000). According to Willey and Sabloff (1974, 72), by 1914 "a new age in Mesoamerican archaeology was definitely dawning." They point particularly to *Mexican Archaeology* by Thomas A. Joyce (1914) and Herbert J. Spinden's *A Study of Maya Art* (1913). One could also cite Morley's new allegiance to the Carnegie Institution of Washington at the same moment.

Hodge continued for more than a decade as editor of the *Anthropologist* with largely the same board, but that situation changed significantly in 1915 when Pliny Earle Goddard succeeded him. The international members were dropped, except that Edward Sapir (an American and a Boas student) represented the Geological Survey of Canada. Robert H. Lowie and John R. Swanton, both Columbia graduates, became associate editors. These changes seemed to signal Boas's growing power in the association. Although not a Boas student, "Goddard formed a close intellectual alliance with Boas and became a forceful proponent of Boas's views in anthropology and linguistics, in particular Boas's conservative view of linguistic relationships" (*International Dictionary of Anthropology*, 241–42). It should be added that in 1915 Goddard also became president of the Boas-oriented American Folk-Lore Society.

Dorsey resigned from the Field Museum in 1915 (Stocking 1979; Wilcox 2003a), and by that year at the University of Pennsylvania another popularizer, George Byron Gordon, was excluded from the department of anthropology chaired by Frank G. Speck, a Boas student (Darnell 1970). Dorsey and Gordon had both studied with Putnam in the 1890s. Berthold Laufer, a Boas protégé, replaced Dorsey as curator at the Field Museum, having returned from his expedition to Tibet and China (AA 13, 168). At the instigation of Kroeber, Sapir published an influential study on *Time Perspective in Aboriginal American Culture: a Study of Method* (1916), which implicitly challenged some of the foundations of Boas's methodology (Darnell 2001, 51–67). Bandelier died in 1914, and in 1915 Fletcher, the first American woman to make major contributions to anthropology (Mark 1988), published her last book, *Indian Games and Dances*. Finally, as the country debated the war in Europe and relationships beyond the seas, Putnam himself, the last survivor among the "three fathers" and the chief architect of anthropology at the Chicago Fair, passed on in 1915. A generation passed with him; a new era was beginning.

Boas's hesitation in 1902 to endorse the formation of the AAA, feeling the timing was premature—given his preference for a purely professional organization—was no longer necessary a decade or more later (but see Darnell 1969). By 1915 the association had become a much more professional organization, with the *Anthropologist* as its professional organ (although the journal still also represented the ASW and the American Ethnological Society); and the association continued to accept avocationalists as members. Enduring methodologies in ethnology, linguistics, and archaeology were in place. Anthropology had now "appropriated a systematized, esoteric body of knowledge," signaling "its arrival among the scientific professions," with "the integrity and authority to legitimize, to set and judge qualifications for practice, to certify, and to sanction a code of guild procedures" (quoting Flack 1975, 119, but applying the criteria to the state of affairs in American anthropology in 1915). The modern era of professional *American* anthropology arguably had begun—even though other historians of the field are more cautious (see later discussion).

1916–1920

The war years of 1916–19 saw the beginnings of renewed debate over race in the United States, often in the framework of eugenics. Boas

(1916, 1917) and Kroeber (1916, 1918) were among the first scientists to attack the premises of the growing eugenics movement in America (Spencer 1997; Black 2003; Spiro 2009). Madison Grant's *The Passing of the Great Race: The Racial Basis of European History* (1916) received far more public acclaim, however. The period ends when Goddard stepped down as editor of the *Anthropologist* and Boas (1920) publicly broke with Sapir (1917) about the interpretation of language. Boas and Goddard founded and co-edited the *International Journal of American Linguistics* in 1917. The famous censure of Boas (Darnell 1969, 476–83; Stocking 1968, 270–308; 1976) occurred in 1919. Three of the unnamed men he had criticized for spying (Morley, Spinden, and Lothrop: see Harris and Sadler 2003), although they had clear conflicts of interest, voted for censure (Darnell 1969, 483). Boas was forced to step down from the AA Council, and from the National Resources Council as well, but in the latter case the *Anthropologist* editorialized that this occurred "with regret that the Division must lose the services of the most eminent anthropologist in America and a man of unimpeachable devotion to his ideals" (AA 21, 98). In 1920 Lowie published *Primitive Society*, perhaps his most influential book (Murphy 1972). It systematically took issue with Lewis Henry Morgan's theory of *Ancient Society* (Morgan 1877) and the revival of Morgan's ideas by English anthropologist W. H. R. Rivers (1914; see also Kroeber 1909). Elman Service (1985) argues that from this baseline modern American anthropology in the twentieth century was erected.

1921–1925

Lowie was permanently appointed in 1921 to the University of California in Berkeley, marking the beginning of serious graduate training there. Julian Steward summarized the results: "Prior to 1926, California had given only two PhD's in anthropology. [By 1925, when Julian Steward entered the department,] William Duncan Strong, Forest Clements, Anna Grayton, Theodora Krakow Brown [who became Kroeber's second wife], and Lloyd Warner were well into graduate work. Ralph Beals, Ronald Olsen, Lila O'Neale, and [Steward] were starting, and W. W. Hill, Isabel Kelley, Theodore McCown and others were interested seniors" (Steward 1961, 1046–47). Fay-Cooper Cole moved from the Field Museum to the University of Chicago in 1924, replacing Frederick Starr, and the growth of that department finally began (Stocking 1979; McVicker 1986, 2012). In general, anthropology departments in the United States were rapidly becoming a more common feature of university training at several institutions by this period (Stocking 1976).

Many data confirm that in the early 1920s Kroeber became one of the principals in American anthropology. From 1910 to 1925 he was first among the primary contributors of articles or book reviews to the *Anthropologist* (see appendix to this essay). His textbook, *Anthropology*, appeared in 1923. In this seminal work Kroeber makes clear at the outset that he—like the fabled Ulysses, we might say—was launching the craft of anthropology to sail between the dangerous pseudo-scientific forces of eugenics: a seemingly beautiful maiden become a snaky monster, Scylla, and the Charybdis whirlpool of environmental determinism. His student Waldo Wedel (1977, 6) recalled Kroeber's advice to him: "he observed tersely that I was on the wrong track in seeking an environmental explanation for what we'd seen, that I should keep in mind the fact that 'the causes of cultural phenomena are other cultural phenomena,' and finally, that I shouldn't be another Ellsworth Huntington—a dirty name around Berkeley in the 1930s!"[16] Huntington was a Yale professor known for his environmental determinism (Huntington 1914) and later eugenics views (Martin 1973).[17] Kroeber's synthesis of California anthropology, the *Handbook of the Indians of California* (1925a), appeared in the mid-1920s, and he immediately began to expand beyond California in important studies of the Archaic sequence in the Valley of Mexico (1925b) and Peruvian pottery (1926).

The aging Holmes, who had been one of Boas's chief adversaries, left anthropology in 1920 to become the head of the National Gallery of Art, while retaining his AAA membership to 1927.[18] Boas himself, aged sixty-one in 1919, returned to the field, accompanying his friend Elsie Parsons to Laguna Pueblo; she then went on to Zuni Pueblo, where Cushing had worked forty years earlier (Deacon 1997). Whereas in 1901 Boas had written to Phoebe Hearst via her friend Zelia Nuttall that the way to upgrade the field of anthropology was to train "a small number of young men" (cited in Rossiter 1996 [1980], 131), now he wrote to Laufer in 1920 that "all my best students are women" (cited in Deacon 1997, 255). By embracing the training of women to become anthropologists, Boas and Parsons together added an important dimension to the diversity that was becoming the hallmark of American anthropology (but see also Parezo 1993; Deacon 1997, 255–72; Browman 2013). Stepping down in 1924 as editor of the *Journal of American Folk-Lore*, Boas passed the baton to Ruth Benedict (Modell 1983), the first woman to teach beside him in the department of anthropology at Columbia. She was editor for fourteen years (Zumwalt 1988, 31) and gave considerable opportunity to women to publish both articles and book reviews.

The American eugenicists in 1924 succeeded fundamentally in affecting public policy with the passage of the National Origins Act, which used the U.S. Census of 1890 to regulate immigration to the United States. Its principal author, Representative Albert Johnson, chairman of the House Committee on Naturalization and Immigration from 1919 to 1921, was also a regent of the Smithsonian Institution, 1922–34. John C. Merriam, head of the Carnegie Institution of Washington (1920–38), supported this effort, as did numerous trustees of the American Museum of Natural History, including its president, Henry Fairfield Osborn, and Madison Grant, Frederick Osborn, and John Bond Trevor Jr. (Spiro 2009).[19] Facing such strong political headwinds, anthropologists had a long way to go to turn around public opinion about this virulent pseudo-science (see also Barkan 1992; Recchiuti 2007). But now they had a new rudder: prior to Kroeber's 1923 textbook, notes historian Robert Nisbet, "the whole field [of anthropology] was notoriously formless, without the structure that a science should have. Kroeber, master of every specialty in anthropology, made it possible for the first time to teach, that is, really teach in a course called Anthropology 1A-B" (1992, 115–116; see also Deacon 1997).[20]

Applying the sociological theory of Nicholas Mullins (1973) to these developments, we can see that the concentration at Berkeley of Kroeber, Lowie, and Gifford (who became curator of the museum in 1925) should indicate the beginning of a "cluster" phase in the development of a distinctive theory group in anthropology, whose methodology Boas began to attack a few years later.[21] However, both Kroeber and Lowie disavowed the creation of "acolytes" and emphasized instead sound empirical work and independent thought by their students (Lowie

1959; Rowe 1960; Steward 1961; Hymes 1962; Murphy 1972). While they both were students of Boas, and were in some sense "Boasians," there arguably was no Boas "school" (Stocking 1976, 7; Jacknis 2002a, 529); his students were too polythetic in their interests and experiences for that. Both Kroeber and Lowie sought to speak with their own voices, and did not simply repeat what they had learned from their mentor, who it should be noted never published a narrative textbook (but see Boas 1911, 1928, 1938). It seems that a different sociological explanation than Mullins's is needed to account for the successful rise of American anthropology as an accepted scientific domain of inquiry.[22]

What is more certain is that several students of the history of American anthropology have preferred to pick 1920 as the date for the end of the first major era in its history, rather than 1915 (De Laguna 1960; Darnell 1969, 1988; Stocking 1976; Service 1985). One could just as well argue for 1925 as the moment when American anthropology emerged into a recognizably modern form. Following Boas's 1919 censure (Darnell 1969), Goddard stepped down as editor of the AA in 1920. John R. Swanton (at the BAE) then moved into the editor's chair, while Lowie remained as associate editor, and Speck, in Philadelphia, became the second associate editor. An "Advisory Sub-Committee" composed of Hodge, Fewkes, and Laufer was also instituted, and this arrangement continued to 1925. Hodge, working in New York at the Heye Foundation, and Fewkes, chief of the BAE, clearly represent the old guard, while Laufer, curator at the Field Museum and Boas supporter, presumably provided balance. A publication committee further broadened representation of many institutional interest groups. W. C. Farabee (at the University Museum in Philadelphia) was chairman ex-officio of this group from 1921 to 1922 and then was replaced in that role by Walter Hough (of the BAE). In 1924 Lowie replaced Swanton as editor, and a second person from the University of California, E. W. Gifford, became the second associate editor; this team remained in place until the end of 1933. Speck at the University of Pennsylvania continued as an associate editor; he became chair of his department in 1925 and professor in 1926 (Darnell 1970). By 1925 both the advisory subcommittee and the publications committee were dropped from the title page, apparently leaving the editor with unprecedented autonomy (see Lowie 1933).

By the mid-twenties, then, power once concentrated on the East Coast in New York, Boston, and Washington had become more evenly distributed, with new concentrations in Berkeley, Chicago, and Philadelphia. Although control of the *Anthropologist* had moved to the West Coast, Boas's "second trumpet" of anthropology, the *Journal of American Folk-Lore* remained in New York, where the greatest numbers of members of the AAA still resided (see later discussion). More generally, the triumph of "Boasians" was complete: both Lowie and Speck had voted against Boas's censure (Darnell 1969, 483; Pinsky 1992, 181), and the second-trumpet's editor, Ruth Benedict, would also have voted against it, had she been allowed that privilege. Most apparent is the profound diversification of American anthropology that had crystallized by 1925, with the principal new challengers to its family of methodologies already on stage and beginning their assaults (Malinowski 1922; Radcliffe-Brown 1923). Kroeber's (1923) textbook was also in place, however, and it was used successfully to train new anthropology college students in America for decades to come (Steward 1961).

Spatial and Institutional Analysis of American Anthropology, 1888–1925

The chronology of the structural moments identified so far in this essay, and the periods they form, can be used heuristically for delineating the roles played by various people in the growth of anthropological knowledge and debate about it. Who commanded the "attention space" (Collins 1998) of the AAA membership in each period? By simply counting the number of articles and book reviews each person published in the AA for each period, each author can be classified into primary, regular, occasional, or one-time contributor, and an overall ranking can be established. How the rankings changed through time can then be charted (see appendix to this essay). This analysis reveals that the chief primary contributors to the *Anthropologist* in the seven five-year periods defined here from 1888 to 1925 were, successively, Holmes (BAE), Fewkes (BAE), Mason (BAE), Alexander Francis Chamberlain (Boas's first PhD student), George Grant MacCurdy (the Yale archaeologist [Bricker 2002]), Kroeber, and Kroeber again. Interestingly, Boas, though a persistent contributor, was only a low-ranked primary contributor in two of these periods, which should make us cautious about the full meaning of these findings.[23] That there was only one woman (Parsons) as a low-ranked primary contributor is also significant (cf. Parezo 1993; Deacon 1997).

Table 1 presents the totals of membership in the ASW for 1888 and 1894 (new members) and for the AAA during five periods from 1902 to 1925, broken down by geographical areas. The relative ranking of each area is also given, and four "equivalence classes" for the largest membership sets are also indicated. The most striking pattern documented in this table is the large size of the Washington anthropological community in the late nineteenth century compared to those in other places. In 1888 other regions of America were represented in the ASW only to a token extent.[24] Only about a fifth of the 1888 membership of 150 people became members of the AAA in 1902, and only 12 percent of the new members of the ASW in 1894 ultimately joined the AAA. Second, the European honorary or corresponding membership in 1888 is strikingly larger than it became in subsequent periods up to 1925. Clearly, the ASW at the time the *Anthropologist* was launched was oriented toward the European anthropological community far more explicitly than is apparent on the part of the AAA—although European membership in the latter did gradually increase again after 1908.

At the time that the AAA was formed in 1902, the AAA membership list (published in 1903) included 178 members, of which one (Powell) was deceased. Washington initially maintained its leadership position, but its membership was equivalent to that of greater New York. Pennsylvania, Massachusetts, and California—in that order—each had small anthropological "communities" that were centered on Philadelphia, Boston, and Berkeley, respectively, where there were already departments of anthropology and museums (Darnell 1970; Hinsley 1992; Thoresen 1975). Washington lacked a strong department of anthropology in a university. In contrast there were already functional departments at Harvard, Phillips Academy, Yale, Columbia, Clark, the Wistar Institute (in Philadelphia), Bryn Mawr, and Berkeley. Although an effort was made to attract the interest of the Latin American anthropologists working in newly established anthropological institutions in those countries, only modest success was realized.

In the next period, 1904–9, New York surged to nearly twice as many members as any other region, and that predominance continued to grow in subsequent periods. Surprisingly, California was second,

Table 1. Comparison of membership levels in the Anthropological Society of Washington and the American Anthropological Association for selected periods and places

Place	ASW 1888	ASW 1894 new	AAA 1902–1903	AAA 1904–1909	AAA 1910–1915	AAA 1915–1920	AAA 1921–1925
Washington DC	150 (1)	115	29 (1) I III	31 (3) III	28 (4) III	23 (4) IV	25 (5) IV
European	35H, 36C		3	10^a	16	22 (5) IV	24^b IV
NY and NJ	1C	11	26 (2) I	67^c (1) I	69 (1) I	82 (1) I	112^d (1) I
PA	4C	1	11 (4) II	25 (5) IV	31 (3) III	34^e (2) II	52^f (2) II
CA	1C	2	9 (5) III	36^g (2) II	26^h (4) IV	13	26^i (4) IV
Boston MA	5C	1	14 (3) II	28 (4) III	35 (2) II	28 (3) III	35 (3) III
Latin America	1H, 5C		4	15^j	20 (5)	20 IV	24^k IV
St. Louis	3C		5 IV	20^l	17^m	7	11^n
MI, WI, MN	3C	2	4	13	12	10	18°
South	1C		5	17	12	11	17
IL	2C	2	6 III	10	13	12	15^p
OH and IN	2C	4	7 III	10	10	10	12
IA, KS, NE	1C		1	9	6	4	9

Bold indicates the time of largest membership; brackets indicate the relative rankings, and Roman numerals show relative rankings by the top four equivalence size classes (those within four members of the highest in this class being grouped together). *Key*: H = Honorary members; C = Corresponding members. Data assembled by David R. Wilcox, Museum of Northern Arizona.

a. Five of these were members only in 1909.
b. Eight of these were members only in 1921 and three joined in 1925.
c. Four of these were members for one year only; five others only in 1910 and three only in 1909.
d. Nine of these were members only in 1921; 12 joined in 1925.
e. Twelve of these were members only in 1920 in this period.

f. Five of these joined in 1925 and four were members for only one year.
g. Nine of these were members for only one year.
h. Six of these were members only in 1910.
i. Eleven of these joined in 1925.
j. Four of these were members only in 1910.
k. Five of these joined in 1925.
l. Three of these were members for only one year and three only in 1909 in this period.
m. Four of these were members only in 1910.
n. Three of these joined in 1925.
o. Nine of these joined in 1925.
p. Six of these joined in 1925.

but nine of these members joined for only one year (most in 1906); if we reduce the California membership by nine, we get twenty-five members, the same as for Pennsylvania. Washington would then be ranked second, with Boston in the same equivalence class, Pennsylvania and California being third, and St. Louis fourth. Interestingly, in this period the AAA membership in St. Louis reached its peak, following the St. Louis Exposition of 1904 (Parezo and Fowler 2007). The failure to establish a public museum in St. Louis to take the collections of the Exposition, which McGee tried to do, probably accounts for the subsequent decline of the St. Louis anthropological "community" apparent in table 1.[25] However, a St. Louis chapter of the Archaeological Institute of America was founded in 1906, which began local archaeological investigations (Fowke 1910; Browman 1978) and allied itself to the newly formed St. Louis art museum; in 1910 it supported Hewett's AIA expedition to Guatemala.[26]

By 1910–15, Massachusetts was in second place, with Washington and Pennsylvania equivalent in third and California a close fourth. Latin America had gained strength in the size of its AAA membership, and European representation was more apparent as well. World War I is the underlying factor in the next period, 1915–20; by this time the Washington intellectual community in general had significantly declined (Flack 1975; Lacey 1979), slipping to fourth place in the anthropological membership rankings. Pennsylvania now achieved second place, and this continued even more strongly into the next period. The Boston region slipped to third place, which it maintained into the following period as well. AAA membership in California declined in this period, perhaps due to the preoccupation of Kroeber's work for the AMNH in the American Southwest and to Berkeley's emphasis on undergraduate training (Nisbet 1992). Both Latin American and European representation declined.

By 1915, in addition to the eight teaching departments around 1903, there now were new departments of anthropology or archaeology at the University of Arizona (Wilcox 2005), the University of Minnesota, University of Texas (Davis 1992), University of Pennsylvania (Darnell 1970), University of Washington, University of Nebraska, and Smith College. Soon there would also be programs at Beloit College, the University of Michigan, New School of Social Research in New York, University of Denver, and Washington University in St. Louis. Certification in the form of a PhD degree, however, was more limited. While the University of Arizona, for example, began issuing MA degrees in 1928, it was only in 1953 that the first PhD degrees were granted (Thompson 2005). This is why the new program at Berkeley was so important, adding a graduate program to what had long been an undergraduate track (Nisbet 1992). The fact that Lowie as editor of the *Anthropologist* asked the popularizer Dorsey (1925) to review Kroeber's new textbook also suggests that a certain reconciliation between graduate training and popularization (teaching undergraduates) was brought about, encouraging Dorsey to become an AAA member again.

By 1925 the anthropological communities in all but one region were strengthened, often exhibiting their highest numbers to date. Indeed, in California, there was a surge in membership in that year, nearly doubling its total. In Latin America, the upper Midwest (Michigan, Wisconsin, and Minnesota), Illinois, and the western Midwest (Iowa, Kansas, and Nebraska) there were also relatively substantial increases in membership in 1925. Only among Europeans, where eight people were members (and only in 1921), was there a decline in relative position. The AAA was in good shape by 1925.

Analysis of Membership of the AAA, 1902–1915

Drilling down and looking closely at the membership of the ASW and AAA for the period 1888 to 1915, we can achieve a more nuanced and finely textured understanding of the growth of interest in American

Table 2. Members of the AAA, 1902–1915, by category of interest

Category	1902–1903 N %	1904–1915 N %	Total N %
Practicing	83 (47%)	103 (28%)	186 (34%)
Interested	74 (42%)	171 (47%)	245 (45%)
Fleeting	21 (12%)	91 (25%)	112 (21%)
Total	178	367	545

anthropology. The people who joined the American Anthropological Association initially in 1902 and 1903, and those who subsequently joined up to 1915, can be classified into three groups: (1) practicing anthropologists; (2) interested in anthropology; and (3) fleetingly interested, for only 1–2 years (table 2). One can certainly quibble about who counts as a "practicing anthropologist" at this early period. George Kunz and W. W. Newell, for example, are accepted here (and at the International Congress of Anthropology: see Essay 2 and its appendix) as "practicing anthropologists"—but they remained members of the AAA only for one to two years, thus clearly not self-identifying as anthropologists. Like others discussed later, they are interesting "borderline" cases that can help us to understand what American anthropology was and was not in this early period. As seen in Essay 1, just what counted as American anthropology in the late nineteenth century was still in flux; and we argue here that it did not begin to stabilize until about the time America entered World War I or even a decade later. Already by 1898, however, it had begun to reach for a national status, which the creation of the association in 1902 further expressed (Stocking 1960).

As a baseline for these analyses, we note first that of the 150 active members of the ASW in 1888, only 29 (19%) can be classified as practicing anthropologists. In the 1894 membership list (available online) we find only 9 more out of the 115 new members (8%) were practicing anthropologists. Looking over the membership of the ASW, most of whom worked in government offices and many of whom also belonged to other organizations that collectively made up the Washington intellectual community (Flack 1975), it appears that most of them were what Nathan Reingold (1991 [1976]) called "cultivators," as contrasted with "practitioners" or "researchers." He defined cultivators as not professional scientists but people "who had a sincere interest in the knowledge of science, and who somehow or other participated meaningfully in the scientific endeavor." The difference he suggested between "researchers" and "practitioners" is qualitative, and we have lumped both together under the rubric "practicing anthropologists," while calling his "researchers" ("the leaders of the emerging scientific community") professionals.

Of the original 83 practicing anthropologists in the 1902–3 AAA list accepted here, 46 (54.88 %) remained members until their deaths, or 1–2 years before death. Another 16 (19.5%) remained members for more than 20 years and several for as long as 34 years. Only six (7.3%) remained members for only 1–4 years, and three of those later rejoined the association (but not Kunz or Newell).[27] As for the 103 practicing anthropologists who joined between 1904 and 1915, 53 (51%) continued as members to their deaths or 1–2 years before. Another 14 (13%) were members for 20 years or more and six of them for more than 30 years. Only 13 (13%) remained members for only 1–4 years, and two of them later rejoined. Compared to the 83 practicing anthropologists in 1902–3, there were still only 87 in the 1914–15 period, and 12 of them dropped out after 1915. However, in 1916 or 1917, 28 new practicing anthropologists joined the association, suggesting that prior to the United States entry into World War I American anthropology was a fairly stable but small domain of professional inquiry that was perhaps beginning to thrive.

Based on their loyalty to the AAA, we identify 13 members in the 1902–3 group and 15 in the 1904–15 set who are "borderline" cases of practicing anthropologists. Only six of these 29 cases (21%) can be called professionals (George Dorsey, Livingston Farrand, Alexander Goldenweiser, John Alden Mason, Paul Radin, and T. T. Waterman). The archaeologists Henry Mason Baum (editor of *Records of the Past*), Charles E. Brown (of the Wisconsin Archaeological Society), Dorsey, Mason, Charles Owen (of the Field Museum), and eventually Edgar Lee Hewett and Charles Peabody all dropped out, although Brown, Dorsey, Mason, and Owen later rejoined. Ethnologists Constance Goddard DuBois (Laylander 2004), Farrand, J. N. B. Hewitt, George

Wharton James, Stephen Chapman Simms, and George Rochford Stetson similarly dropped out early, with Hewitt and Stetson eventually rejoining. Simms later became director of the Field Museum, 1928–1937 (Wilcox 2003a).

For the 1904–15 period, three archaeologists and an explorer (Henry M. Ami, Oric Bates, Frederick Monsen, and George Arbor West) dropped out early, as did two physical anthropologists (William Hastings and Frances Howe Seymour Knowles) and six ethnologists/linguists/sociologists (Paul-Louis Faye, John Fryer, Goldenweiser, James Murie, Radin, and Waterman), although four of them later rejoined. For Dorsey, Goldenweiser, Mason, Radin, and Waterman, all of whom were professional anthropologists, their individual life trajectories evidently account for their coming and going from the association. Farrand went on to a career as a university president, first in Colorado and then at Cornell University, 1921–37.

Members of the association who were not practicing anthropologists but were enduringly interested in AAA activities or its publications provide further insight into the early support for anthropology in America. At least 15 of these people were philanthropists: from New York City, Edward Dean Adams (1846–1931), Hermann Henry Cammann (1845–1930), James Bishop Ford (1845–1928), Mrs. [Henry] Esther Herrman (1823–1911), Archer Milton Huntington (1870–1955), and Benjamin Talbot Babbitt Hyde (1872–1933); from Chicago, Edward Everett Ayer (1841–1927) and Stanley McCormick (1874–1947); from Paris, Joseph Florimond M. le Duc de Loubat (1831–1927) and Prince Roland Bonaparte (1858–1924); and one each from five more U.S. cities, William Keeney Bixby (1857–1931) of St. Louis, Charles Pickering Bowditch (1840–1911) of Boston, Peter Goddard Gates (1855–1925) of Los Angeles, Phoebe Apperson Hearst (1842–1919) of San Francisco, and Benjamin Thaw (1859–1933) of Pittsburgh.

Aside from the philanthropists, in the 1902–3 list 68 other interested people were members, 18 (26.87%) until within 1–2 years of their deaths. Given that death dates are not presently known (to me) for 14 of them, 18 out of 53 = 33%. For the 1904–15 period, 13 were members to within 1–2 years of their deaths; death dates are presently unknown for 65 out of 159; so 13 out of 95 = 14%. However, 48 continued as members for at least 10 years, or 48 out of 159 = 30%.

Some "Interested Members," 1902–1903

The 245 people seriously interested in anthropology clearly cannot be discussed in any detail here, even if we delete the 21 about whom little or nothing could be learned. Their diversity is rather astonishing, although a few prominent subsets are evident. Seventeen were curio dealers or artifact collectors, of whom one, J. F. Huckel, worked for the Fred Harvey Company and another was John Lorenzo Hubbell, the Navajo trader. Fifteen were businessmen (as were 10 of the collectors). Another 29 members were in the medical profession. Seven were librarians, book dealers or bibliophiles. Nineteen were clergymen, a rabbi, or priests. Six were lawyers. Seven were geologists, seven biologists, three sociologists, and four professors of philosophy. Most of these people were highly educated and it seems the subject matter of anthropology was simply part of their general intellectual interest. Clearly, however, there were vastly more physicians, lawyers, businessmen, clerics, and even geologists, biologists, bibliophiles, sociologists, and professors of philosophy in America who did *not* become members of the AAA. In order to shed more light on why at least a few did join the AAA, following are biographical notes about them, in alphabetical sequence (detail not otherwise sourced was gathered through Google and WorldCat searches).

Among the original 1902–3 members was James W. Benham (1866–1914), a curio dealer in Phoenix, Arizona Territory, who in 1903 published Herbert Patrick's study of Hohokam irrigation systems in the Salt River Valley. He operated The Curio Store from 1895 to 1908, bought out the Hyde Exploring Expedition (Snead 2001), and participated in the 1904 St. Louis Exposition (Parezo and Fowler 2007). In 1901 he was also a member of the American Ethnological Society (AA 4, 367).

Henry Grier Bryant (1859–1932) was secretary of the Edison Electric Company from 1889; he helped bring back the Perry Expedition and off-and-on from 1894 to 1928 was president of the Geographical Society of Philadelphia; in 1913 he was president of the American Association of Geographers (*National Cyclopedia of American Biography* 25:359, hereafter NCAB; *American Men of Science* 1921:96, hereafter AMS). In contrast, Mrs. Egbert Frank Bullene, nee Emma Jay (1829–1915), was the author of *The Psychic History of the Cliff Dwellers, Their*

Origin and Destruction (Denver: Reed, 1905; Southwest Museum); and an ornithologist, Amos William Butler (1860–1937), was secretary for the Indiana Board of State Charities, 1897–1923 (*Who Was Who in America* 1:176, hereafter WWWA; *New York Times*, August 7, 1937, p. 15, col. 6).

The artist Frederick Samuel Dellenbaugh (1853–1935) had accompanied Powell on his second expedition down the Colorado River and was on the E. H. Harriman Expedition to Alaska in 1901; from 1909 to 1911 he was librarian of the American Geographic Society and editor of its *Bulletin* (NCAB 32:441–42). George Edward Dimock (1852–1919) retired from banking in 1908 and became a classicist and the father of a professional classicist of the same name; he was also a trustee of Vassar College, 1914–19.

The wife of the civil engineer John Hays Hammond, Natalie Harris Hammond (1861–1931), in 1908 was a member of the managing committee of the School of American Archaeology (AA 10, 354); in 1911 she founded and was national chair of the woman's welfare department of the National Civic Federation; she was also the author of *Woman's Place in Civic Life*, 1911. Elizabeth Mead Hyde Brace was the aunt of the organizers of the Hyde Exploring Expedition (Snead 2001) and the wife of Robert Neill Brace, the younger son of Charles Loring Brace, founder of the Children's Aid Society in New York City.

Horace Fort Jayne (1859–1913) was the director of the Wistar Institute of Anatomy, Philadelphia, 1894–1905 (NCAB 13:299). David Starr Jordan (1851–1931) was president of Stanford University, 1891–1913, and later a prominent eugenicist (NCAB 22:68–70). His successor as Stanford president, geologist John Casper Branner (1850–1922), was also an enduring member. The San Francisco civil engineer Eusebio Joseph Molera (1846–1932) was active in the California Academy of Science and had been a close friend of Frank and Emma Cushing. Mary Alicia Owen (1858–1935) was a graduate of Vassar College who "made a special study of the myths and legends of the Mississippi Valley, and of the Sac Indians, who adopted her as an honorary member of their tribe"; she wrote under the pseudonym of Julia Scott (NCAB 13:188). She was a life member of the American Folk-Lore Society as early as 1896. Her books included *Old Rabbitt, the Voodoo, and Other Sorcerers*, 1893; *Old Rabbitt's Plantation Stories, as Told among the Negroes of the Southwest*, 1898; and *Folk-lore of the Musquakie Indians of North America*, 1904. Lucy Evelyn Peabody (b. 1865), who had been a secretarial assistant in the BAE for nine years, led the fight to preserve the Mesa Verde Park (WWWA 4:739; Smith 2005).

With a PhD from Johns Hopkins University, John Dyneley Prince (1868–1945) went to Babylonia with a University of Pennsylvania expedition, 1888–89; from 1895 to 1902 he was dean of the graduate school of New York University, moving to Columbia (1902–15) as professor of Semitic languages (Smyk 2012); in 1906 and 1908 he was elected to the New Jersey Assembly (speaker, 1909); to the New Jersey Senate, 1910–13 (leader, 1911, and president, 1912), and later was acting New Jersey governor in 1912 while Woodrow Wilson campaigned for the U.S. presidency; he was then U.S. minister to Denmark, 1921–26, and minister to Yugoslavia, 1926–33 (NCAB 43:74–75). Another American Ethnological Society and AAA member who went far, James Wickersham (1857–1939), was a U.S. district judge in Alaska, 1900–8, and later served in the U.S. Congress, where he helped to pass the Alaska Organic Act.

Interested members in the 1904–15 period included life member Charles Custus Harrison (1844–1929), the provost of the University of Pennsylvania, 1895–1911, and President of the University Museum (WWWA 1:526). Mrs. Thomas Bringham Bishop, the daughter of the New York geologist James Hall, was a world traveler who had her own private museum in her San Francisco home (*San Francisco Chronicle*, February 8, 1906, p. 16, col. 3).

Alvin Hiram Dewey (1859–1928) ran a drugstore in Rochester, New York, 885–1900, and was vice president and general manager, Rochester and Lake Ontario Water Company, 1910–23, and president, 1923–27; in 1908 he began local archaeological researches, being awarded the Cornplanter medal in 1918: "He was president of the [Rochester] Municipal Museum commission from its formation in 1925 until his death" (NCAB 22:353–54).

Dr. Henry Herbert Donaldson (1852–1938), a close personal friend of Boas (Cole 1999), from 1906 was professor of neurology, Wistar Institute of Anatomy and Biology (WWWA 3:331). The Presbyterian minister George Patterson Donehoo did special historical work and archaeology, 1903–11; he was pastor at Condersport, Pennsylvania, 1911–21;

and then state librarian of Pennsylvania, 1921-24; and director of the Bureau of War History, Department of Military Affairs Pennsylvania, 1927-31 (WWWA 1:331). In 1922 he was secretary of the Pennsylvania Historical Commission and in that year was appointed director of the Pennsylvania State Museum (AA 24, 251).

George Thornton Emmons graduated from the U.S. Naval Academy in 1874. He was stationed in 1882 on the *Pinta* in Alaska and stayed through the 1880s and 1890s. He became interested in Alaskan natives, especially the Tlingit and Tahltan, and was assigned to the World's Columbian Exposition, 1891-93. He retired in 1899 but took on special government assignments in Alaska. The AMNH purchased his first two collections, and in 1902 the Field Museum purchased another large one. He was the author of *Ethnological Report on the Native Tribes of Southeast Alaska*; an unfinished report he long worked on was completed by Fredericka de Laguna in 1991 as *The Tlingit Indians* (Cole 1985).

William Henry Furness III from 1895 to 1903 traveled extensively in Asia and the Pacific, making ethnological and zoological collections for the University of Pennsylvania; he was an associate of the Free Museum of Science and Art as curator of general ethnology and secretary of the Board of Managers, 1903-5—replacing Stewart Culin (Adria H. Katz in *International Dictionary of Anthropology* 222-23; AMS 1921:244). Mrs. Henry Hunter Smith Handy (b. 1880?) was the mother of anthropologist Edward Craighill Smith Handy. Mrs. Ralph Chandler Harrison (d. 1922), the niece of the New York journalist Whitelaw Reid, left a bequest for a library named for her husband that was designed by Bernard Maybeck and opened in 1928 at Carmel-by-the-Sea.

William Jacob Holland (1848-1932) was chancellor of the Western University of Pennsylvania (now the University of Pittsburgh) 1891-1901, and director of the Carnegie Institution, Pittsburgh, 1898-1922 (WWWA 1:345); interested in zoology, languages, and local history, Holland edited the *Annals and Memoirs of the Carnegie Museum*, was a trustee of the Carnegie Fine Arts and Museum Fund of Pittsburgh, and the author of an "act creating the college and university council of the state of Pennsylvania" (NCAB 13:141-42; AMS 1921:324). A businessman, the lumberman Louis J. Hopkins (d. 1942) of Winnetka, Wisconsin, having harvested about a billion board-feet, sold out in 1921 and soon moved to Pasadena, California, but continued as an AAA member. Dr. Henry Mills Hurd (1843–1927) was professor of psychiatry at Johns Hopkins University, 1889–1906; the superintendent of the Johns Hopkins Hospital, 1889–1911; and editor of the *Johns Hopkins Hospital Bulletin* and *Hospital Reports*, 1890–1911 (WWWA 1:365); from 1897 to 1920 he was the editor of *The American Journal of Insanity*; he also co-authored two popular reports on hospitals with John Shaw Billings, an ASW member who did not join the AAA (NCAB 12:112; *New York Times*, July 20, 1927).

Alice Hooker Day Jackson (1872–1926) was a social science graduate student at Columbia University, a close friend of Mark Twain's wife, and in 1918 the vice president of the National League; her husband Percy Jackson was a member of the executive committee of the School of American Research, Santa Fe, New Mexico (WWWA 1:624). The physician Abraham Jacobi (1830–1919) was Franz Boas's uncle by marriage and a close friend of Carl Schurtz (Cole 1999); his second wife, Mary Corina Putnam (1842–1906), daughter of publisher George Palmer Putnam (1814–72), was among the first women physicians in New York City (Bittel 2009). The Philadelphia physician Milo George Miller assisted Clarence Bloomfield Moore on many of his archaeological expeditions as companion and osteologist.

William Barri Kirkham (1882–1969) received a doctorate in biology from Yale and then conducted an archaeological trip around the world, 1907–8. He was an instructor in biology and Sheffield Scientific School, Yale, 1908–16; assistant professor there 1916–20; and professor of biology at the International YMCA College in Springfield, Massachusetts, 1921–30. He was also dean of freshmen to 1930; construction director of the Museum of Natural History in Springfield from 1930; and vice president of the Springfield Library and Museum Association, 1934–41, and its president, 1941–59 (WWWA 5:399).

The Rev. James Buchanan Nies (1856–1922), who had the Church of Epiphany, Brooklyn, from 1893 to 1898, spent the "remainder of his career . . . largely . . . in travel and archaeological researches abroad, except for a brief period (1905–07) when he was rector of Christ Church, Sharon, Conn"; he "explored ruins in southern Italy, Greece, Egypt and Palestine [and] in one year . . . discovered more than 200 mounds of ruins in the Holy Land." In 1901 he became field director for the

American School of Oriental Study at Jerusalem. He was a president of the American Oriental Society, and in 1920 he authored a monograph on *Ur Dynasty Tablets*. "He bequeathed gifts valued at $24,867 to the American School at Jerusalem and his Babylonian tablets to Yale University with $50,000 for enlarging the collection" (NCAB 20:256-57; WWWA 1:899). He is listed in 1915 as a contributor to the publication fund of the American Folk-Lore Society and in 1911 he was a member of ASW (ASW 4821, Records of Treasurer, box 13, National Anthropological Archives).

Grace A. Nicholson opened a shop in Pasadena, California, in 1924 and became a premier collector of Indian baskets and a photographer of Indian life and artifacts in association with Emery Kopta; she later opened a museum of oriental art that was taken over by the city after her death (bio file, Southwest Museum).

Edward Kirby Putnam (1868-1939) was an instructor at Stanford University, 1901-6; acting director of Davenport Academy of Science, 1906-28; and then director from 1928 (WWWA 1:1002). He was president of the Iowa Anthropological Association (AA 9; AMS 1921:556). His sister Elizabeth Duncan Putnam (1867-1928) was also a long-term member.

Rev. John Ogle Warfield (1871-1950) was the curate at St. Paul's Episcopal Church, Chestnut Hill, Pennsylvania, 1901-14; in 1910 he made a trip to the Pamunkey and Mattopony reservations (AA 12, 480); he was connected to the University of Pennsylvania and was interested in the Algonquian Indians of Virginia (AA 14, 711).

Dr. Henry Milton Whelpley (1861-1926) was a professor of practical pharmacognosy, 1884-1922, professor after 1922, and dean after 1924, at the St. Louis College of Pharmacy. He was also professor of physiology, histology, and microscopy and director of the Biology Laboratory, 1890-1900, Missouri Medical College; and the same at St. Louis Post-Graduate School of Medicine, 1890-98. He was professor of materia medica and pharmacy, Medical Department, Washington University, 1900-11; the same at Missouri Dental College, 1900-3; and was editor of the *National Druggist*, 1884-87, and of *Meyer Bros. Druggist*, 1888-; a collaborator of *Medical Fortnightly*, 1893-1907; and the same for *Pacific Pharmacist*, 1911-20 (WWWA 1:1320). In 1914 he became the first president of the Cahokia Mound Association (AA 16, 146). He was one of the largest artifact collectors in the St. Louis area at the time of the 1904 St. Louis Exposition; his collection was donated posthumously in 1943 to the Academy of Science of St. Louis; his papers are at the Ebling Library, University of Wisconsin. In 1909–10 he was on the Council of the AIA.

Some "Fleeting Members," 1902–1903, 1904–1915

Finally, we consider those members who had only a fleeting interest in the AAA. In 1902–03 there were 21 such people (12%), and in 1904–15 there were 92 (25%), or relatively twice as many. No doubt their membership dues helped to keep the AAA solvent during those early years. Only nine of them were clearly members to within a year or two of their deaths. What we know about their primary interests does not vary much from what we know about the people who stuck with the association for longer periods. It thus seems that the decisions to maintain membership or not were personal or individual ones. A few examples again shed a little more light on what attracted some of these people, or why they got away.

Among the 1902–3 fleeting members was Frank Wilson Blackmar (1854–1931), who was dean of the Graduate School, University of Kansas, 1896–1922; he was interested in the Spanish institutions in the American Southwest (NCAB 9:495). William Earl Dodge Jr. (1832–1902) became a partner in the Phelps-Dodge Company in 1864 and was a vice president of the AMNH, chairman of the Executive Committee of the Metropolitan Museum of Art, a member of the Executive Committee New York Botanic Garden, and a trustee of the Carnegie Institution (WWWA 1:329). Franklin William Hooper (1851–1914) organized the Brooklyn Museum of Arts and Sciences and was its president from 1890 (NCAB 13:46–47). Lindley Miller Keasby (1867–1946) was a professor of political science at Bryn Mawr, 1894–1905; his anthropological collection was exhibited at the Louisiana Purchase Exposition, St. Louis, in 1904, and "was awarded a 1st prize" (NCAB 38:230–31).

The 1904–15 fleeting members included Benjamin Walworth Arnold (1865–1932), who joined his father's lumber business in Albany, New York; he "possessed an alert scientific mind and made valuable collections in archaeology and geology"; was a local civic leader in Albany and a president and trustee of the Dudley Observatory; and he was at one time a member of the New York State Board of Charities and the New York State Hospital Development Commission (NCAB 25:111). David Ives Bushnell Sr. (1846–1921) was a Missouri businessman who was president of the St. Louis Archaeological Society and a trustee of the Missouri Historical Society, 1894–1912; his son of the same name became a well-known professional archaeologist—but not an AAA member (AA 44, 104). Edwin Willard Deming (1860–1942) was a painter of western "Indian and animal subjects (folk-lore, domestic, hunting and war)"; after studying in New York and Paris, in 1887 he visited the Apache, Umatilla, and Pueblo tribes, and he was a friend of the anthropologist William Jones in his New York years.

Reamer Ling (1861–1933) was a local editor and judge in St. Johns, Arizona, who looted many sites and advertised the collections in Charles Lummis's *Land of Sunshine*; in 1905 he was accepted as a member of the AIA's Southwest Society, providing payment in artifacts (Lummis correspondence with Ling, 1902–1913,Southwest Museum; see WWW Arizona 1913). Dudley Allen Sargent (1849–1924) was the director of the Hemenway Gymnasium, Harvard University, 1879–1919 (WWWA 1:1079; NCAB 7:97–98, *Anthropology News Bulletin; Dictionary of American Biography*); he had been a member of the New York Academy of Anthropology.

Among the most interesting persons who fled the AAA after being a member in 1909 and 1910 was Mitchell Alexander Carroll (1870–1925), professor of archaeology and history of art at George Washington University, 1910–25. "As a scholar, writer, organizer and teacher of classical archaeology he exercised a great influence in popularizing and developing this field of study in the United States." In 1902 he founded the Archaeological Society of Washington and was its secretary to 1925; the society inaugurated "important archaeological researches abroad, especially in the prehistoric field in southern France and at Carthage." "In 1914 the monthly magazine *"Art and Archaeology"* [sponsored by the AIA] was established, under Carroll's leadership, and he was its first managing editor, occupying after 1918 until his death the position of director and editor." He was associate secretary of the AIA in 1904 and general secretary, 1907–17. In 1913 he established the Art and Archaeology League, serving as president. In 1919 he established the Greece-America Society, serving as chairman of the executive committee. He was also on the board of managers of the School of American Research and State Museum, Santa Fe; E. L. Hewett, who dropped out of the AAA after 1916, published frequently in *Art and Archaeology*, as did his colleague Byron Cummings, the director of the Arizona State Museum and head of the Department of Archaeology, University of Arizona (Wilcox 2005). When Hewett founded a department at the University of New Mexico in 1928, it was a Department of Archaeology. "[Carroll's] versatile scholarship and the charm of his personality made him a prominent figure in Washington cultural circles"; he was "a member of the group of scholars and notables who met at the home of Alexander Graham Bell" (NCAB 24:76–77; WWWA 1:198; AMS 1921:115).[28] His wife (1868–1952) carried on after him at George Washington University as lecturer to 1932 (Boyd 1952).

Discussion

In Chicago in 1893, F. W. Putnam assembled more than fifty workers with various experience to make collections and exhibit them at the fair in the Anthropology Building, just outside it, or on the Midway Plaisance. J. W. Powell appointed W. H. Holmes (Meltzer 2010) to collaborate with Otis Mason at the National Museum, with F. H. Cushing as assistant, to prepare exhibits for the Government Building. D. G. Brinton (Darnell 1988) acted as chairman for an anthropology congress held at the fair that attracted more than forty practicing anthropologists and more than two hundred others interested in cultivating the garden of their knowledge about anthropology. Unknown thousands saw the exhibits, and many of them, we may judge, went home eager to learn more about American anthropology. A national audience was born.

Further forward movement was slow in the 1890s in the wake of a national depression. The *American Anthropologist*, the organ of Powell's Anthropological Society of Washington, struggled to pay its bills. But then McGee and Boas took it over and repositioned it as the organ of a national organization, Section H of the AAAS. In 1902 they again collaborated to found the AAA, a national organization with many local affiliates, including the ASW in Washington, Boas's revived American Ethnological Society in New York, the University Museum in Philadelphia, and the Field Museum in Chicago—which had taken in many of the World's Columbian Exposition exhibits. By then both Brinton and Powell (and Cushing) were gone, but Putnam remained vigorous and succeeded in establishing strong anthropology departments at the American Museum of Natural History in New York and at the University of California at Berkeley. Now American anthropology was truly national in scope with an enduring network of local "communities of interest," the seedbeds for further expansion (Darnell 1969, 2001).

By 1909, when Putnam retired from Harvard and the Peabody Museum, Boas (1909) was celebrating Putnam, Powell, and Brinton as the "three fathers" of American anthropology, all the while gaining strength as the new leader of that discipline (Laufer 1906). McGee's star had burned out, but now that Boas was established at Columbia University, he could train graduate students to engage in his vision of what American anthropology should be. Those students were a feisty lot, however, and all soon began to speak with their own voices, producing a broadcast with harmonies close enough to recognize something "Boasian" about their messages but also distinct in their individual agendas, which sometimes seemed to conflict with Boas's own philosophical conclusions. But then controversy is the life blood of science.[29]

In the lead-up to the entry of the United States into World War I, the intellectual ferment of the *avant-garde* movement, especially in New York City, the introduction of modernist art to America at the Armory Show in 1913, impassioned anti-war rhetoric, and the beginnings of the eugenics movement created a fundamentally new cultural challenge to the genteel Victorian sensibilities still evident in late nineteenth-century America at the World's Columbian Exposition. There the "White City" had been a statement that urban life could be lived well, but it was a vision that did not embrace the cultural diversity of such places as those situated outside along the Midway Plaisance or, for that matter, elsewhere in Chicago. Whereas the eugenics movement was a conservative reaction against such diversity by those in power who felt threatened by it (Spiro 2009), Boas and his student A. L. Kroeber, among others, embraced that diversity and sought to show how one could live with it. When Boas went further, however, and after the war condemned the use of anthropological credentials as a cover for spying for the U.S. government, old-line forces within anthropology stood up against him. Strikingly, most of his critics were archaeologists, museum men, and Harvard graduates (Pinsky 1992).

What anthropology would become in America by 1925 and beyond was probably unimaginable in 1893. But what had already been achieved—in the linguistic work of Powell and his colleagues, and by Brinton; in archaeology by Putnam and others at Harvard University and the Peabody Museum (Browman and Williams 2013); and in physical anthropology by Boas and others—was enough in Chicago at the Exposition to attract a national audience that was excited to learn the meaning of the joining together of Old and New Worlds inadvertently brought about by Columbus's exploits. America was becoming urban and more and more ethnically diverse. Anthropology in America at the 1893 Fair reached for the ring to be the domain of inquiry that could make that diversity and its urban realities civically understandable and morally acceptable. Its future journey was already well under way.

Notes

First thanks go to Curtis Hinsley for his friendship and advice, and for his criticism. Thanks also go to the Christine Callen Trust for support to make four research trips that aided in the development of this essay. I particularly want to thank Alice Kehoe for calling my attention to the Wedel (1977) essay. The Museum of Northern Arizona allowed me the freedom to pursue these studies. Thanks also go to Jim Collette and Keith Greiner for reading the text and providing comments and to the three reviewers for the University of Nebraska Press for their comments and criticisms. For any errors or misleading views that remain, I alone am responsible.

1. Other key events in 1888 can also be cited: in New York City in June 1888, for example, at Columbia College, a newly formed (but short-lived) group, the New York Academy of Anthropology, sponsored an International Congress of Anthropology. Members of the academy seem primarily to have been interested in what was beginning to be called "criminal anthropology": the study of "aberrant" human behavior and the intersection of law and medicine. Meanwhile, at Marietta, Ohio, the centennial of the founding of Ohio and the Northwest Territories under the Northwest Ordinance of 1787 was celebrated in 1888. After one hundred years of expansion, with the frontier about to close—as Frederick Jackson Turner would declare at a WCE Congress in 1893—following the suppression of serious Indian resistance—the time had come to focus the nation's attention on who the Indians were, and what other peoples existed in the larger world where American economic expansion was rapidly contending with other world powers for dominance (Zimmerman 2002; Wilcox and Fowler 2002; Kagan 2007).

Interestingly, also in 1888, in Washington, the National Geographical Society was founded by Alexander Graham Bell and his father-in-law Gardiner Greene Hubbard (Lacey 1979, 88). While its journal certainly increased public awareness of human diversity, it was a skewed awareness (Lutz and Collins 1993; Poole 2004), and rather than becoming a strong ally of American anthropology, the journal helped to define the boundary between anthropology and geography.

2. Studies have been undertaken by the author (Wilcox 2010) of the membership of the ASW for 1888 and 1894; the registrants of the Anthropological Congress at the 1893 WCE (see Essay 2 and its appendix, this volume); all those who contributed articles or book reviews to the AA from 1888 to 1938; and all members of the AAA from 1902 to 1944. In the age of Google, WorldCat, and the Biographical and Genealogical Master Index, it has been possible to look up those names and often to discover their birth and death dates, and to write endnotes about most of them that capture their place of birth, education, and career trajectories. These sources have been supplemented by looking in the historic *Washington Post* online (though a membership in the Martin Luther King Library in Washington DC) and in other research in local libraries, especially in Washington DC, St. Louis MO, and in several California libraries. The data tables thus assembled have been drawn upon to write the present essay. They provide a "bottom up" empirical basis for constructing a fresh inductive analysis of the early history of American anthropology.

3. It would be interesting to compare the formation of American anthropology to that of other scientific domains of inquiry. Pauly (1994; 2000, 158–59), for example, shows that American biology was a concept "difficult, if not impossible to define" that became coherent as the result of an attitude formed at the summer resort of Woods Hole, where numerous practitioners of various biological disciplines came to a consensus that their specialities ("disciplines") were all part of a semantic domain they called "biology." Pauly (2000, 133) also argues that the interaction between university presidents and key biologists about their vision for graduate universities affected what was included in or excluded from biology—an explanatory nexus it would be fascinating to examine in the case of American anthropology.

4. For an informed and helpful analysis of who were professional American archaeologists in 1900, which takes a somewhat different approach to the one discussed here, see Christenson 2011. Taking yet another perspective, on the "co-production of archaeological knowledge by amateurs and professionals," Christenson (2013) argues that there has been a continuing and fruitful interaction among them to the benefit of scientific archaeology, a finding that certainly matches my experience over the last fifty years as a practicing professional American anthropological archaeologist.

5. Born in Hebron OH, Dorsey graduated from Denison College in 1888 and received a PhD from Harvard under F. W. Putnam in 1894 with a dissertation on the Necropolis of Ancon (Darnell 1969, 468). He became a fellow of Section H of the American Association for the Advancement of Science in 1892. He joined the Field Museum in 1896 and became curator in 1898 after the departure of W. H. Holmes. Dorsey was associate professor of anthropology at the University of Chicago, 1909–

15. He left the Field Museum in 1915 and later wrote a popular book about anthropology, *Why We Behave Like Human Beings*. Fay-Cooper Cole said of him that "none in our generation has done more toward popularizing science" (1931, 413–14). He was president of the American Folk-Lore Society in 1902 (see also ABW Minnesota State University; *American Men of Science* 1921: 184). In 1911 he was a member of ASW, having been elected in 1901 (AA 3: 598; ASW 4821, Records of Treasurer, box 13, National Anthropological Archives).

6. Born in Nova Scotia, Canada, Dawson (1849–1901) was the son of John William Dawson, a systematic anti-Darwinian who was the principal of McGill University, 1855–93. The son was the director of the Geological Survey of Canada, 1895–1901, and head of the Ethnological Survey of Canada, 1896–1901; Dawson City, Yukon, was named for him. He published extensive studies of the ethnology of the Northwest Coast (*Cambridge Biographical Dictionary* 395; W. J. McGee in AA 3: 158–63).

7. One may well wonder how much the biases and personal networks of the editor affected his eliciting of particular articles and assigning book reviews. Regrettably, this fascinating issue is largely beyond the scope of this essay. Robert Lowie's practice as editor, however, admittedly resulted in some such biases, especially in assigning book reviews to himself or to colleagues in the western United States (Lowie 1933). Ironically, when this approach was changed under the next editor, Lowie retained his record as the top contributor to the AA! The extent to which such bias affects the statistics presented later in the appendix to this essay cannot be fully evaluated here. Nevertheless, the people singled out by my analysis—however they came to do it—received the privilege of more "attention space" (Collins 1998) than other colleagues.

8. Ambrosetti (1865–1917), director of the Ethnographic Museum of the Faculty of Philosophy and Letters, University of Argentina in Buenos Aires, built the collections of the museum through his own expeditions, which he financed himself. His most valuable contributions were from the Calchaqui region of Argentina (C. W. Mead AA 19:533–541). At Pampa Grande he defined a grave sequence (Willey and Sabloff 1974:80).

9. Boyle (1842–1911) came to Canada from Scotland in 1856 and was a teacher in Elora, Ontario, circa 1865–75. His interests in archaeology and geology led to the accumulation of a large collection, which he presented to the Canadian Institute (later the Provincial Museum). He became curator of the museum in 1885 and issued twelve annual archaeological reports. For the WCE he prepared the mineral exhibit of the Province of Ontario and had charge of the archaeological collection representing the Provincial Museum (Alexander Chamberlain in AA 15:159–164). In 1908 he was awarded the third Cornplanter Medal for his researches on the Canadian Iroquois (AA 10:358).

10. At the time of his death, Chavero (1841–1906) was the director of the Museo Nacional and was acknowledged as the dean of Mexican archaeology. He was also a lawyer of eminence, an active politician, a man of affairs, a brilliant orator, and a successful writer, and it was due to him that the works of Duran, Ixtilxochitl, and Camargo were published. He had been a member of the Mexican Congress since

1869 and became a senator in 1886; he once served as sub-secretary to the Minister of Foreign Affairs, governor of the Federal District (in 1870). His archaeological work centered on a careful comparative study of the Mexican calendar system (Frederick Webb Hodge in AA, 1903; Marshall H. Saville in AA 8:701–702; WorldCat). Chavero proposed the hypothesis that the Aztlán of the Aztecs was in Nayarit. With Vicente Palacios, he was the author of the classic *Mexico A Travez de los siglos*; also *Histori antiqua y de la conquista*, 1883; and *Lienzo de Tlaxcala*, 1892, the first significant analysis of this important document (Phil Weigand, personal communication, 2005).

11. Von Ihering (1850–1930) was a Brazilian anthropologist and naturalist and the director of the Museo Paulista in São Paulo (AA 9:452; Spencer 1997:208, 406).

12. Lenz (1863–1938) was a German-Chilean linguist and folklorist.

13. Peñafiel (1831–1922) tried to bring order to the collections of the Museo Nacional, Mexico City, and argued that the Maya and Mexica cultures were completely independent. He also planned a building for the Paris Exposition of 1889 in an "Aztec" style, though one "which would probably have horrified Moctezuma" (Bernal 1980:153–54).

14. León (1859–1929) was a Mexican archaeologist who lived in Mexico City. In 1902 he published a linguistic map of Mexico through the Museo Nacional. In 1911 León was named professor of anthropology at the Museo Nacional, Mexico (AA 13:344). He was the founder of the Museo de Estado de Michocán (in Morelia) and the Anales del Museo de Michocán. His groundbreaking study, *Los Tarascos* in 1904 was the first truly anthropological study of them and their archaeology (Phil Weigand, personal communication, 2005).

15. In the first excitement after the rediscovery of Gregor Mendel's work in 1900, assumptions were made by some scientists about how genetics worked that proved false once the detailed work on the genetics of drosophila flies was undertaken, which showed that the correlation between genes and behavior was much more complicated than many first thought. The embrace by Boas and Kroeber of methodological fallibility—accepting uncertainty and refusing to jump to conclusions—proved to be much more scientifically sound and would win the day by about 1930 (Kim 1994; Kohler 1994; Schwartz 2008).

16. Having witnessed the dust bowl, however, Wedel (1977) chose to adopt UC Berkeley geographer Carl Sauer as his mentor and would later show that Kroeber's interpretations of Plains culture were mistaken. The point of his bravura performance of this talk at a dinner of Plains archaeologists was to show to the rebellious young people of that time that he was one of them!

17. There is a deeper history to the opposition to the philosophical convictions seen in the eugenics and environmental determinist views that needs more attention in the history of anthropology. John Locke (Strathern 1999), for example, opposed the notion of innate ideas. William Lloyd Garrison (Mayer 1998) already in 1831, based on moral convictions and personal knowledge, firmly believed that the claim made in the Declaration of Independence that "all men are created equal" was literally true, that slavery was a sin that should be immediately abolished, and that there was no

reason to fear that whites could not live compatibly with blacks. Interestingly, one of the papers delivered at the 1888 International Congress of Anthropology (https://books.google.com/books?id=OKdXAAAAMAAJ&lpg=PA304&ots=0xXxqTjEW2&dq=Lucy%20M.%20Hall%2C%20Anthropology&pg=PA304#v=onepage&q=Lucy%20M.%20Hall,%20Anthropology&f=false) by a woman named Lucy M. Hall of Brooklyn, argued against the presumptions of the emerging criminal anthropologists along similar lines. Now, however, this deep-seated philosophical debate had shifted to questions of science, not only morals. It would take another several generations before "scientific" racism would decline—only to be revived again in the debates about sociobiology in our own time (Barkan 1992).

18. Holmes in 1920 was also the editor of Mitchell Carroll's insurgent *Art and Archaeology*, in which Hewett also played a prominent role, and his principal supporter, Frank Springer, was chairman of the board (see *Art and Archaeology* front matter). Carroll's insurgency directly challenged the AIA, but with his death in 1925 and the coming of the Great Depression, this interesting initiative died too (see Dyson 2002).

19. Spiro (2009:329) also finds, however, that passage of the 1924 National Origins Act was the high-water mark of the American eugenics movement. Barkan (1992:95, 268–69), too, finds that the tide had begun to turn in Boas's favor by the mid-1920s. The election of Boas in 1931 as president of the AAAS probably can be seen as confirmation of that change (although Barkan [1992:310–40] shows that within the AAA, Boas's influence remained problematic, but that did not deter him at all [see Boas 1945]).

20. In 1924 it is also worth noting that A. V. Kidder published his synthesis of southwestern archaeology, *An Introduction to the Study of Southwestern Archaeology*, a watershed event. The first Pecos Conference in 1927 soon followed, which established a consensus about and a nexus for continuing discussion of southwestern archaeology that soon influenced other regions of America (Woodbury 1993; Wilcox 2004). In linguistics, Edward Sapir (1925) published his paper defining the phoneme, and in that same year the Linguistic Society of America was founded and its journal *Language* was launched (Darnell 2001:65–66). And in ethnology we can point to the publication by Ruth Benedict (1922) of "Plains vision quest" as a prelude to her *Patterns of Culture* (Benedict 1934) and the "culture and personality" movement that was soon joined by Margaret Mead with the friendly support of Boas (see Darnell 2001).

21. His criticisms of Kroeber led the latter to publish his famous and deeply puzzling essay "History and Science in Anthropology" (1935), which can also be contrasted with Radcliffe-Brown's (1923) notions of ethnology versus social anthropology. Boas (1936) immediately replied, expressing his "complete disagreement" with Kroeber's analysis. Another of Boas's responses to these views (though I do not know if this was deliberately done with either Kroeber or Radcliffe-Brown in mind) was to publish the facts about the positions he had taken during his life on

both history and science and on the several branches of American anthropology (Boas 1940).

22. Nevertheless, a good case has been made that a true theory group independent of Boas did form around Sapir—although he was also a student of Boas. Sapir moved from Ottawa to begin teaching at the University of Chicago in 1925 (Murphey 1993; Darnell 2001:66). Untangling the complexities of these new theory groups is, however, beyond the scope of the present inquiry (but see Stocking 1976; Murphey 1993; Darnell 2001).

23. Indeed, in *Race, Language and Culture* (Boas 1940), only nine out of sixty-three (less than 15 percent) of his selected essays were first published in the AA.

24. The existence of the New York Academy of Anthropology, however, which apparently existed from 1888 to the mid-1890s (https://archive.org/details/bulletin-newyork00anthgoog), shows that a fairly large anthropological "community" already existed in New York and Brooklyn distinct (except most of its honorary members) from the ASW. It seems to disappear concurrent with Boas's move to New York and was in some sense replaced by the regeneration of the American Ethnological Society there; although there were few crossover members, and few Academy members became members of the AAA later. Criminal anthropology, however, continued to be a central focus for A. E. Hooton, but to little effect (Barkan 1992).

25. The formation of the Cahokia Mound Association in 1914 and the Anthropological Society of St. Louis circa 1920, both with a professor at the Washington University Medical School, Robert James Terry (1956; O'Brien and Lyman 2001), as a key player should be noted. However, only after the formation of the Missouri Archaeological Society in 1934–35 and after Carl Chapman completed his anthropological training (at the University of New Mexico) and began working at the University of Missouri, Columbia, after World War II was an enduring anthropological program begun in that state (O'Brien 1996).

26. Of related interest is that five St. Louis people were subscribers to the *Holmes Anniversary Volume* (Hodge 1916): William Bixby, Robert Brookings, David Bushnell Sr., George Mepham, and H. M. Whelpley—but not Robert Terry whose father had been a supporter of McGee's efforts to build a public (anthropological) museum in St. Louis. McGee's principal backer was James A. Reardon, a public-spirited businessman and bibliophile who "almost wrecked his fortune, attempting to establish the Public Museum, at the close of the Fair [of 1904]" (Reedy's *Mirror*, 1914, p. 120). What McGee lacked was the support of the local archaeological community.

27. Kunz and Newell, however, were either subscribers or contributors to the *Boas Anniversary Volume* (Laufer 1906:iv–v). Kunz had been a member of the New York Academy of Anthropology.

28. Citing Conn (1998), McVicker (Essay 6) makes an important distinction between art museums and natural history museums as a locus for archaeological collections and the curators who study them. Mitchell Carroll's interest in art and archaeology, Holmes's shift to become curator at the National Gallery, the close

alliance between the AIA and an art museum in St. Louis, the university museum's alienation from the Department of Anthropology at Philadelphia (until later) all point to deeper processes in play for how American anthropology should be constituted. More research on this "puzzle" is needed.

29. For several different interpretations of the "Boasians" as a sociological construct, see Stocking (1974:1–21; 1976:7–9), Barkan (1992:90–95), and Darnell (1998, 2001). In contrast, I stress their individuality as scholars.

Appendix

Comparison of Primary Contributors to the *American Anthropologist*, 1888–1925

DAVID R. WILCOX

Key: P = Primary contributor no. 1; p2–4 = primary contributors 2–4; p = other primary contributors; r = regular contributors; oc = occasional contributor; one = one-time contributor; AAo = death notice in *American Anthropologist*; * = president of American Anthropological Association (AAA); W = Washington anthropologist (18 of 40 = 45%).

a. Henshaw was a member of the Anthropological Society of Washington but not of the AAA.
b. Thomas was not a member of the AAA.
c. Bushnell Jr. was not a member of the AAA.
d. Bandelier was not a member of the AAA.

Name	1888–1893	1894–1898	1899–1903	1904–1909	1910–1915	1915–1920	1921–1925
*W. H. [William Henry] Holmes —AAo/d. 1933/W	P	one	p2	p	r	oc	
*J. [Jesse] Walter Fewkes —AAo/d. 1930/W	r	P	p4	p	p	oc	r
O. T. [Otis Tufton] Mason —AAo/d. 1908/W	p4	p3	P	p			
Alexander Francis Chamberlain —AAo/d. 1914	r	one	p3	P	p2		
*George Grant MacCurdy —AAo/d. 1947			r	p3	P	r	p

Name	1888–1893	1894–1898	1899–1903	1904–1909	1910–1915	1915–1920	1921–1925
*A. L. [Alfred Louis] Kroeber —AAo/d. 1960			r	p	p	P	P
Washington Matthews —AAo/d. 1905/W	p2	one	p				
James Mooney —AAo/d. 1921/W	p3	p	p	p	one		
*W. J. McGee —AAo/d. 1913/W	r	p2	p				
Albert S. [Samuel] Gatschet —AAo/d. 1907/W	p	p					
Robert Fletcher —AAo/d. 1912/W	p	r					
J. [James] Owen Dorsey —AAo/d. 1895/W	p	one					
W. J. [Walter James] Hoffman —AAo/d. 1899/W	p	one					
Henry Weatherbee Henshaw —AAo/d. 1930/W[a]	p						
*F. [Frederick] Webb Hodge —AAo/d. 1956/W	r	p4	p	r			
Cyrus Thomas —AAo/d. 1910/W[b]	r	p	p				
*Walter Hough —AAo/d. 1935/W	r	r	p		r	r	r
John Wesley Powell —AAo/d. 1902/W	r	one	p				
*Franz Boaz —AAo/d. 1942	r	one	p	oc	r	p	one

Name	1888–1893	1894–1898	1899–1903	1904–1909	1910–1915	1915–1920	1921–1925
Joseph [Deakins] McGuire —AAo/d. 1916/W	r	r	r	p			
*Ales Hrdlicka —AAo/d. 1943/W		r	p	p	r		one
George Amos Dorsey —AAo/d. 1931		one	p	r			one
*John R. [Reed] Swanton —AAo/d. 1958/W			r	p2	r	p	one
D. I. [David Ives] Bushnell Jr. —AAo/d. 1941ᶜ				p4	r		
Frederick Starr —AAo/d. 1933				p	p3		r
Charles C. [Clark] Willoughby —AAo/d. 1943			oc	p	r	one	one
E. L. [Edgar Lee] Hewett —AAo/d. 1946				p			
*Clark Wissler —AAo/d. 1947				p	r	p4	one
Adolph [Francis Alphonse] Bandelier —AAo/d. 1914ᵈ				p			
*Roland B. [Burrage] Dixon —AAo/d. 1934			r	p	r	r	r
Charles Peabody —AAo/d. 1939					p	one	
Stansbury Hagar—d. 1943		one			p	one	one
Berthold Laufer —AAo/d. 1934					one	p2	one

Essay Seven Appendix

Name	1888–1893	1894–1898	1899–1903	1904–1909	1910–1915	1915–1920	1921–1925
*Robert [Harry] Lowie —AA o/d. 1957					p4	p3	p2
Alanson [B.] Skinner —AA o/d. 1925					p	r	p
A. A. [Alexander Alexandrovich] Goldenweiser —AA o/d. 1940					p	p	
*E. [Edward] Sapir —AA o/d. 1939					p	p	r
Louis R. Sullivan —AA o/d. 1925						p	p3
*E. C. [Elsie Clews] Parsons —AA o/d. 1942					one	p	p4
Willson Dallum Wallis—d. 1970						p	oc

DOCUMENT K

The Aims of Anthropology

DANIEL GARRISON BRINTON

A modern philosopher has advanced the maxim that what is first in thought is last in expression; illustrating it by the rules of grammar, which are present even in unwritten languages, whose speakers have no idea of syntax or parts of speech.[1]

It may be that this is the reason why man, who has ever been the most important creature to himself in existence, has never seriously and to the best of his abilities made a study of his own nature, its wants and its weaknesses, and how best he could satisfy the one and amend the other.

The branch of human learning which undertakes to do this is one of the newest of the sciences; in fact, it has scarcely yet gained admission as a science at all, and is rather looked upon as a dilettante occupation, suited to persons of elegant leisure and retired old gentlemen, and without any very direct or visible practical applications of concern with the daily affairs of life.

It is with the intention of correcting this prevalent impression that I address you today. My endeavor will be to point out both the immediate and remote aims of the science of anthropology, and to illustrate by some examples the bearings they have, or surely soon will have, on the thoughts and acts of civilized communities and intelligent individuals.

It is well at the outset to say that I use the term anthropology in the sense in which it has been adopted by this Association, that is, to include the study of the whole of man, his psychical as well as his phys-

Proceedings of the American Association for the Advancement of Science 44 (1895): 1–17 ical nature, and the products of all his activities, whether in the past or in the present. By some writers, especially on the continent of Europe, the term anthropology is restricted to what we call physical anthropology or somatology, a limitation of the generic term which we cannot but deplore. Others again, and some of worthy note, would exclude from it the realm of history, confining it in time to the research of prehistoric epochs, and in extent to the investigation of savage nations.

I cannot too positively protest against such opinions. Thus 'cabbed, cribbed, confined,' it could never soar to that lofty eminence whence it could survey the whole course of the life of the species, note the development of its inborn tendencies, and mark the lines along which it has been moving since the first syllables of recorded time; for this, and nothing less than this, is the bold ambition toward which aspires the crowning bough of the tree of human knowledge.

You will readily understand from this the magnitude of the material which anthropology includes within its domain. First, it investigates the physical life of man in all its stages and in every direction. While he is still folded in the womb, it watches his embryonic progress through those lower forms, which seem the reminiscences of far-off stages of the evolution of the species, until the child is born unto the world, endowed with the heritage transmitted from innumerable ancestors and already rich in personal experiences from its prenatal life. These combined decide the individual's race and strain, and potently incline, if they do not absolutely coerce, his tastes and ambitions, his fears and hopes, his failure or success.

On the differences thus brought about, and later nourished by the environment, biology, as applied to the human species, is based; and on them, as expressed in aggregates, ethnography, the separation of the species into subspecies and smaller groups, is founded. It has been observed that numerous and persistent, although often slight differences arose in remote times, independently, on each of the great continental areas, sufficient to characterize with accuracy these subspecies. We therefore give to such the terms "races" or "varieties" of man.

All these are the physical traits of man. They are studied by the anatomist, the embryologist, the physician; and the closest attention to them is indispensable, if we would attain a correct understanding of the creature man, and his position in the chain of organic life.

But there is another vast field of study wholly apart from this and even more fruitful in revelations. It illustrates man's mental or psychical nature, his passions and instincts, his emotions and thoughts, his powers of ratiocination, volition and expressions. These are preserved and displayed subjectively in his governments and religions, his laws and his languages, his words and his writings; and, objectively, in his manufactures and structures, in the environment which he himself creates—in other words, in all that which we call the arts, be they "hooked to some useful end," or designed to give pleasure only.

It is not sufficient to study these as we find them in the present. We should learn little by such a procedure. What we are especially seeking is to discover their laws of growth, and this can only be done by tracing these outward expressions of the inward faculties step by step back to their incipiency. This leads us inevitably to that branch of learning which is known as archaeology, "the study of ancient things," and more and more to that part of archaeology called prehistoric, for that concerns itself with the most ancient; and the most ancient is the simplest, and the simplest is the most transparent, and therefore the most instructive.

Prehistoric archaeology is a new science. I can remember when neither its name nor its methods were known to the most learned anthropologists. But it has already taught us by incontrovertible arguments a wonderful truth, a truth opposing and reducing to nought many teachings of the sages and seers of past generations. They imagined that the primal man had fallen from some high estate; that he had forfeited by his own falseness, or been driven by some hard fate, from a pristine Paradise, an Eden garden, an Arcady; that his ancestors were demi-gods and heroes, himself their degenerate descendant.

How has prehistoric archaeology reversed this picture? We know beyond cavil or question that the earliest was also the lowest man, the most ignorant, the most brutish, naked, homeless, half-speechless. But the gloom surrounding this distant background of the race is relieved by rays of glory; for with knowledge not less positive are we assured that through all hither time, through seeming retrogressions and darkened epochs, the advance of the race in the main toward a condition better by every standard has been certain and steady, "ne'er known retiring ebb, but kept due on."

Archaeology, however, is, after all, a dealing with dry bones, a series of inferences from inanimate objects. The color and the warmth of life, it never has. How can we divine the real meaning of the fragments and ruins, the forgotten symbols and the perished gods, it shows us?

The means has been found, and this through a discovery little less than marvelous, the most pregnant of all that anthropology has yet offered, not yet appreciated even by the learned. This discovery is that the psychical unity of man, the parallelism of his development everywhere and in all time; nay, more, the nigh absolute uniformity of his thoughts and actions, his aims and methods, when in the same degree of development, no matter where he is, or in what epoch living. Scarcely anything but his geographical environment using that term in its larger sense, seems to modify the monotonous sameness of his creations.

I shall refer more than once to this discovery; for its full recognition is the cornerstone of true anthropology. In this connection I refer to it for its application to archaeology. It teaches us this: that when we find a living nation of low culture, we are safe in taking its modes of thought and feeling as analogous to those of extinct tribes whose remains show them to have been in about the same stage of culture.

This emphasizes the importance of a prolonged and profound investigation of the few savage tribes who still exist; for although none of them is as rude or as brute-like as primitive man, they stand nearest to his condition, and, moreover, so rapid nowadays is the extension of culture that probably not one of them will remain untouched by its presence another score of years.

Another discovery, also very recent, has enabled us to throw light on the prehistoric or forgotten past. We have found that much of it, thought to be long since dead, is still alive and in our midst, under forms easily enough recognized when our attention is directed to them. This branch of anthropology is known as Folklore. It investigates the stories, the superstitions, the beliefs and customs which prevail among the unlettered, the isolated and the young; for these are nothing less than survivals of the mythologies, the legal usages and the sacred rites of earlier generations. It is surprising to observe how much of the past we have been able to reconstruct from this humble and long neglected material.

From what I have already said, you will understand some of the aims of anthropology, those which I will call its "immediate" aims. They are embraced in the collection of accurate information about man and men, about the individual and the group, as they exist now, and as they have existed at any and all times in the past; here where we are, and on every continent and island of the globe.

We desire to know about a man, his weight and his measure, the shape of his head, the color of his skin and the curl of his hair; we would pry into all his secrets and his habits, discover his deficiencies and debilities, learn his language, and inquire about his politics and his religion, yes, probe those recesses of his body and his soul which he conceals from wife and brother. This we would do with every man and every woman, and, not content with the doing it, we would register all these facts in tables and columns, so that they should become perpetual records, to which we give the name "vital statistics."

The generations of the past escape such personal investigation, but not our pursuit. We rifle their graves, measure their skulls, and analyze their bones; we carry to our museums the utensils and weapons, the gods and jewels, which sad and loving hands laid beside them; we dig up the foundations of their houses and cart off the monuments which their proud kings set up. Nothing is sacred to us; and yet nothing to us is vile or worthless. The broken potsherd, the half-gnawed bone, cast on the refuse heap, conveys a message to us more pregnant with meaning, more indicative of what the people were, than the boastful inscription which their king caused to be ingraved on royal marble.

This gleaning and gathering, this collecting and storing of facts about man from all quarters of the world and all epochs of his existence, is the first and indispensible aim of anthropologic science. It is pressing and urgent beyond all other aims at this period of its existence as a science; for here more than elsewhere we feel the force of the Hippocratic warning, that the time is short and the opportunity fleeting. Every day there perish priceless relics of the past, every year the languages, the habits and the modes of thought of the surviving tribes which represent the earlier condition of the whole species, are increasingly transformed and lost through the extension of civilization. It devolves on the scholars of this generation to be up and doing in these fields of research; for those of the next will find many a chance lost forever, of which we can avail ourselves.

And here let me insert a few much needed words of counsel on this portion of my theme. Why is it that even in scientific circles so little attention is paid to the proper training of observers and collectors in anthropology?

We erect stately museums, we purchase costly specimens, we send out expensive expeditions; but where are the universities, the institutions of higher education, that train young men how to observe, how to explore and collect in this branch? As an eminent ethnologist has remarked, in any other department of science, in that, for instance, which deals with flowers or with butterflies, no institution would dream of sending a collector into the field who lacked all preliminary training in the line, or knowledge of it; but in anthropology the opinion seems universal that such preparation is quite needless.[2] Carlyle used to say that every man feels himself competent to be a gentleman farmer or a crown prince; our institutions seem to think that every man is competent to be an anthropologist and archaeologist; and let a plausible explorer present himself, the last question put to him will be, whether he has any fitness for the job.

Hence our museums are crammed with doubtful specimens, vaguely located, and our volumes of travel with incomplete or wholly incorrect statements, worse than purely fictitious ones, because we know them to be the fruit of honest intentions, and therefore give them credit.

But, you will naturally ask, to what end this accumulating and collecting, this filling of museums with the art-products of savages and the ghastly contents of charnel houses? Why write down their stupid stories and make notes of their obscene rites? When it shall be done, or as good as done, what use can be made of them beyond satisfying a profitless curiosity?

This leads me to explain another branch of anthropology in which I have not yet alluded, one which introduces us to other aims of this science, quite distinct from those I have mentioned. That branch is Ethnology.

Ethnology in its true sense represents the application of the principles of inductive philosophy to the products of man's faculties. You are aware that that philosophy proceeds from observed facts alone; it discards all preconceived opinions concerning these facts; it renounces all allegiance to dogma, or doctrine or intuition; in short, to every form of statement that is not capable of verification. Its method of procedure is by comparison, that is, by the logical equations of similarity and diversity, of identity and difference; and on these it bases those generalizations which range the isolated fact under the general law, of which it is at once the exponent and the proof.

By such comparisons, ethnology aims to define in clear terms the influence which the geographical and other environment exercises on the individual, the social group and the race; and, conversely, how much in each remains unaltered by the external forces, and what residual elements are left, defiant of surroundings, wholly personal, purely human. Thus, rising to wider and wider circles of observation and generalization, it will be able at last to offer a conclusive and exhaustive connotation of what man is—a necessary preliminary, mark you, to that other question, so often and so ignorantly answered in the past, as to what he should be.

Ethnology, however, does not and should not concern itself with this latter inquiry. Its own field is broad enough, and the harvest offered is rich enough. Its materials are drawn from the whole of history and from pre-history. Those writers who limit its scope to the explanation of the phenomena of primitive social life only have so done because these phenomena are simpler in such conditions, not that the methods of ethnology are applicable only to such. On the contrary, they are not merely suitable, they are necessary to all the facts of history, if we would learn their true meaning and import. The time will come, and that soon, when sound historians will adopt as their guide the principles and methods of ethnologic science, because by these alone can they assign to the isolated fact its right place in the vast structure of human development.

In the past, historians have told of little but of kings and their wars; some writers of recent date have remembered there is such a thing as the People, and have essayed to present its humble annals; but how few have even attempted to avail themselves of the myriad side-lights which ethnology can throw on the motives and the manners of a people, its impulses and acquisitions?

It is the constant aim of ethnology to present its results free from bias. It deprecates alike enthusiasm and antipathy. Like Spinoza's God, *nullum amat, nullum odit*. Its aim is to compare dispassionately all the acts and arts of man, his philosophies and religions, his social schemes and personal plans, weighting and analyzing them, separating the local and temporal in them from the permanent and general, explaining the former by the conditions of time and place, referring the latter to the category of qualities which make up the oneness of humanity, the solid ground on which he who hereafter builds, "will build for aye."

This, then, briefly stated, is the aim of that department of anthropology which we call ethnology. In yet fewer words, its mission is "to define the universal in humanity," as distinguished from all those traits which are the products of fluctuating environments.

This universal, however, is to be discovered, not assumed. The fatal flaw in the arguments of most philosophers is that they frame a theory of what man is and what are the laws of his growth, and pile up proofs of these, neglecting the counter-evidence, and passing in silence what contradicts their hypotheses.

Take, for instance, the doctrine of evolution as applied to man. It is not only a dictum but a dogma with many scientists. They look with theological ire on any one who questions it. I have already said that in the long run and the general average it has been true of man. But that we have any certainty that it will continue true is a mistake; or that it has been true of the vast majority of individuals or ethnic groups is another mistake. As the basis for a boastful and confident optimism it is as shaky as sand. Taken at its real value, as the provisional and partial result of our observations, it is a useful guide; but swallowed with unquestioning faith, as final law of the universe, it is not a whit more inspiring than the narrowest dogmas of religious bigotry.

We have no right, indeed, to assume that there is anything universal in humanity until we have proved it. But this has been done. Its demonstration is the last and greatest conquest of ethnology, and it is so complete as to be bewildering. It has been thought about by the careful study of what are called "ethnographic parallels," that is, similarities or identities of laws, games, customs, myths, arts, etc., in primitive tribes located far asunder on the earth's surface. Able students, such as Bastian, Andree, Post, Steinmetz and others have collected so many of these parallels, often of seemingly the most artificial and capricious character, extending into such minute and apparently accidental details, from tribes almost antipodal to each other on the globe, that Dr. Post does not hesitate to say: "Such results leave no room for doubt that the psychical faculties of the individual as soon as they reach outward expression fall under the control of natural laws as fixed as those of inorganic nature."[3]

As the endless variety of arts and events in the culture history of different tribes in different places, or of the same tribe at different epochs, illustrates the variables in anthropologic science, so these independent parallelisms prove beyond cavil the ever-present constant in the problem, to wit, the one and unvarying psychical nature of man, guided by the same reason, swept by the same storms of passion and emotion, directed by the same will towards the same goals, availing itself of the same means when they are within reach, finding its pleasures in the same actions, lulling its fears with the same sedatives.

The anthropologist of today who, like a late distinguished scholar among ourselves, would claim that, because the rather complex social system of the Iroquois had a close parallel among the Munda tribes of the Punjab, therefore the ancestors of such must have come from a common culture center; or, who, like an eminent living English ethnologist, sees a proof of Asiatic relations in American culture because the Aztec game of patolli is like the East Indian game of parchesi—such an ethnologist, I say, may have contributed ably to the science in the past, but he does not know where it stands today. Its true position on this crucial question is thus tersely and admirably stated by Dr. Steinmetz: "the various customs, institutions, thoughts, etc., of different peoples are to be regarded either as the expressions of the different stadia of culture of our common humanity; or, as different reactions of that common humanity under varying conditions and circumstances. The one does not exclude the other. Therefore the concordance of two peoples in a custom, etc., should be explained by borrowing or by derivation from a common source only when there are special, known and controlling reasons indicating this; and when these are absent, the explanation should be either because the two peoples are on the same plane of culture, or because their surroundings are similar."[4]

This is true not only of the articles intended for use, to supply the necessities of existence, as weapons and huts and boats—we might anticipate that they would be something similar, otherwise they would not serve the purpose everywhere in view; but the analogies are, if anything, still more close and striking when we come to compare pure products of the fancy, creations of the imagination or the emotions, such as stories, myths and motives of decorative art.

It has proved very difficult for the comparative mythologist or the folk-lorist of the old school to learn that the same stories, for instance, of the four rivers of Paradise, the flood, the ark and the patriarch, who is saved in it, arose independently in western Asia, in Mexico and in South America, as well as in many intervening places, alike even in details, and yet neither borrowed one from the other, nor yet drawn from a common source. But until he understands this, he has not caught up with the progress of ethnologic science.

So it is also with the motives of primitive art, be they symbolic or merely decorative. How many volumes have been written tracing the migrations and connections of nations by the distribution of some art motive, say the *swastika*, the meander or the cross! And how little of value is left in all such speculations by the rigid analysis of primitive arts that we see in such works as Dr. Grosse's *Anfänge der Kunst*, or Dr. Haddon's attractive monograph on the "Decorative art of British New Guinea," published last year! The latter sums up in these few and decisive words the result of such researches pursued on strictly inductive lines—"The same processes operate on the art of decoration whatever the subject, wherever the country, whenever the age." This is equally true of the myths and the folk-tale, of the symbol and the legend, of the religious ritual and the musical scale.

I have even attempted, I hope not rashly, to show that there are quite a number of important words in languages nowise related by origin or contact, which are phonetically the same or similar, not of the mimetic class, but arising from certain common relations of the physiological function of language; and I have urged that words of this class should not be accounted of value in studying the affiliations of language.[5]

And I have also endeavored to demonstrate that the sacredness which we observe attached to certain numbers, and the same numbers, in so many mythologies and customs the world over, is neither fortuitous, nor borrowed the one from the other; but depends on fixed relations which the human body bears to its surroundings, and the human mind to the laws of its own activity. And, therefore, that all such coincidences and their consequences—and it is surprising how far-reaching these are—do not belong to the similarities which reveal contact, but only to those which testify to psychical unity.[6]

So numerous and so amazing have these examples of culture-identities become of late years that they have led more than one student of ethnology into a denial of the freedom of the human will under any of the definitions of voluntary action. But the aims of ethnology are not so aspiring. It is strictly a natural science, dealing with outward things, to wit, the expressions of man's psychical life, endeavoring to ascertain the conditions of their appearance and disappearance, the organic laws of their birth, growth and decay. These laws must undoubtedly be correlated with certain mental traits, but it is not the business of the ethnologist to pursue them to their last analysis in the realm of metaphysics. For instance, we may trace all forms of punishment back to the individual's passion for revenge; or we may analyze all systems of religion until we find the common source of all to be man's dread of the unknown; and these will be sufficient ethnologic explanations of both these phenomena, but not a final analysis of the emotion of dread or the thirst for vengeance. Ethnology declines to enter these realms of abstractions.

I repeat that to define "the universal in humanity" is the aim of ethnology, that is, the universal soul or *psyche* of humanity.

But let me not be understood as speaking of this as of some entity, like the *ame humaine* of the Comtists. That [was] sophistical word-mongering in the style of ancient scholasticism. There is no such entity as humanity, or race, or people, or nation. There is nothing but the individual man or woman, the "single, separate person," as Walt Whitman says. Hence some of the most advanced ethnologists are ready to give up the ethnos itself as a subject of study. Those terms so popular a few years ago, *Völkerpschologie, Völkergedanken*, racial psychology, ethnic sentiments, and the like, are looked upon with distrust. The external proofs of the psychical unity of the whole species have multiplied so abundantly that some maintain strenuously that it is not ethnic or racial peculiarities, but solely external conditions on the one hand and individual faculties on other, which are the factors of culture-evolution.

While I admit that this question is still *sub judice*, I add that the position just stated seems to be erroneous. All members of the species have common human mental traits; that goes without saying; and in addition it seems to me that each of the great races, each ethnic group, has its own added special powers and special limitations compared with others; and that these ethnic and racial psychic peculiarities attached to all or nearly all members of the group are tremendously potent in deciding the result of its struggle for existence.

I must still deny that all races are equally endowed—or that the position with reference to civilization which the various ethnic groups hold today is one merely of opportunity and externalities. I must still claim that the definition of the *ethnos* is one of the chief aims of ethnology, and that the terms of this definition are not satisfied by geographic explanations. Let me, with utmost brevity, name a few other connotations, prepotent, I believe, in the future fate of nations and races.

None, I maintain, can escape the mental correlations of its physical structure. The black, the brown and red races differ anatomically so much from the white, especially in their splanchnic organs, that even with equal cerebral capacity, they never could rival its results by equal efforts.

Again, there is in some stocks and some smaller ethnic groups a peculiar mental temperament which has become hereditary and general, of a nature to disqualify them for the atmosphere of modern enlightenment. Dr. Von Buschan has recently pointed out this as distinctly and racially pathologic; an inborn morbid tendency, constitutionally recreant to the codes of civilization, and therefore technically criminal.

Once more one cannot but acknowledge that the relations of the emotional to the intellectual nature vary considerably and permanently in different ethnic groups. Nothing is more incorrect than the statement so often repeated by physicians that the modern civilized man has a more sensitive emotional system than the savage. The reverse is the case. Since the Dark Ages, Europe has not witnessed epidemic neuroses so violent as those still prevalent among rude tribes.

These and a number of similar traits separate races and peoples from each other by well marked idiosyncrasies, extending to the vast majority of their members and pregnant with power for weal or woe on their present fortunes and ultimate destinies. The patient and thorough investigations of these peculiarities is, therefore, one of the most apposite aims of modern ethnology.

In this sense we can speak of the *Volksgeist* and *Völkergedanken*, a racial mind, or the temperament of a people, with as much propriety and accuracy as we can of any of the physical traits which distinguish it from other peoples or races.

For the branch of anthropology which has for its field the investigation of these general mental traits, the Germans have proposed the name "Characterology" (Karacterologie). Its aim is to examine the collective mental conditions and expressions of ethnic groups, and to point out wherein they differ from other groups and from humanity at large; also, to find through what causes these peculiarities came about, the genetic laws of their appearance, and the consequences to which they have given rise.

This branch of anthropology is that which offers a positive basis for legislation, politics and education, as applied to a given ethnic group; and it is only through its careful study and application that the best results of these can be attained, and not by the indiscriminate enforcement of general prescriptions, as has hitherto been the custom of governments.

The development of humanity as a whole has arisen from the differences of its component social parts, its races, nations, tribes. Their specific peculiarities have brought about the struggles which in the main have resulted in an advance. These peculiarities, as ascertained by objective investigation, supply the only sure foundation for legislation; not *a priori* notions of the rights of man, nor abstract theories of what should constitute a perfect state, as was the fashion with the older philosophies, and still is with the modern social reformers. The aim of the anthropologist in this practical field is to ascertain in all their details, such as religions, language, social life, notions of right and wrong, etc., wherein lie the idiosyncrasies of a given group, and frame its laws accordingly.

Perhaps what I have said sufficiently explains the aims of ethnology. Some one has pertinently called it "the natural science of social life," because its methods are strictly those of the natural sciences, and its material is supplied by man living in society.

The final arbiter, however, to whom it appeals, is, I repeat, not the ethnos, not the social group, but the individual. I think it was Goethe who, nearly a century ago, uttered the pithy remark: "Man makes genera and species; Nature makes only individuals." Hence, the justification of any result claimed by ethnology must come from the psychology of the individual; in his personal feelings and thoughts will be discovered the final and only complete explanation of the forms of sociology and the events of history. As I have elsewhere urged, man himself, the individual man, is the only final measure of his own activities, in whatever direction they are directed.[7]

On the other hand, the only rational psychology—using that term as a science of the mental processes—must be the outcome of anthropology conducted as a natural science. For thousands of years other plans have been pursued. The philosopher would delve in his "inner consciousness"; the theologian would turn to his revelation; the historian would reason on his undigested facts; but the psychologist of the future, taking nothing for granted, will define the mentality of the race by analyzing each of its lines of action back to the individual feelings which gave them rise.

It is quite likely that some who have heard me thus far, and have agreed with me, are still dissatisfied. On their lips is that question which is so often put to, and which so often puzzles, the student of the sciences, *cui bono*. What practical worth have these analyses and generalizations which have been referred to?

Fortunately, the anthropologist is not puzzled. His science, like others, has its abstract side, seemingly remote from the interests of the workaday world; but it is also preëminently an applied science, one the practicality and immediate pertinence of which to daily affairs render it utilitarian in the highest degree.

Applied anthropology has for its aims to bring to bear on the improvement of the species, regarded on the one hand as groups, and on the other as individuals, the results obtained by ethnography, ethnology and psychology.

Such an improvement is broadly referred to as an increased or higher civilization; and it is the avowed aim of applied anthropology accurately to ascertain what are the criteria of civilization, what individual or social elements have in the past contributed and strengthened, and what new forces, if any, may be called in to hasten the progress. Certainly no aims could be more immediately practical than these.

Here again anthropology sharply opposes its methods to those of the ideologists, the dogmatists, and the deductive philosophers. It refuses to ask, What *should* improve man? But asks only, What *has* improved him in the past? And it is extremely cautious in its decision as to what "improvement" really means. It certainly does not accept the definition which up to the present the philosophies and theologies have offered; any more than it accepts the means by which these claim that our present civilization has been brought about.

This department of anthropology is still in its infancy. We are only beginning to appreciate that, in the future, political economy, like history, will have to be rearranged on lines which this new science dictates. The lessons of the past, their meaning clearly apprehended, will be acknowledged as the sole guides for the future. It may be true, as De Tocqueville said of the United States, that a new world needs a new political science; but the only sure foundation for the new will be the old.

Applied anthropology clearly recognizes that the improvement of humanity depends primarily on the correct adjustment of the group to the individual; and, as in ethnology, its ultimate reference is not to the group, but to the individual. In the words of John Stuart Mill, the first to apply inductive science to social evolution, it is that the individual may become "happier, nobler, wiser," that all social systems have any value.

We may profitably recall what the same profound thinker and logician tells us have been up to the present time the prime movers in human social progress. They are: first, property and its protection; second, knowledge and the opportunity to use it; and third, coöperation, or the application of knowledge and property to the benefit of the many.

But Mill was altogether too acute an observer not to perceive that while these momenta have proved powerful stimulants to the group, they have often reacted injuriously on the individual, developing that morbid and remorseless egotism which is so prevalent in modern civilized communities. Nor should I omit to add that the remedy which he urged and believed adequate for this dangerous symptom is one which every anthropologist and every scientist will fully endorse—the general inculcation of the love of truth, scientific, verifiable truth.

It seems clear therefore that the teachings of anthropology, whether theoretical or practical, lead us back to the individual as the point of departure and also the goal. The state was made for him, not he for the state; any improvement in the group must start by the improvement of its individual members. This may seem a truism, but how constantly it is overlooked in the most modern legislation and schemes of social amelioration! How many even of such a learned audience as this have carefully considered in what respects the individual man has improved since the beginning of historic time? Is he taller, stronger, more beautiful? Are his senses more acute, his love purer, his memory more retentive, his will firmer, his reason stronger? Can you answer me these questions correctly? I doubt it much. Yet if you cannot, what right have you to say that there is any improvement at all?

To be sure, there is less physical suffering, less pain. War and famine and bitter cold are not the sleuthhounds that they once were. The dungeons and flames of brutal laws and bigoted religions have mostly passed away. Life is on the average longer, its days of sickness fewer, justice is more within reach, mercy is more bountifully dispensed, the tender eye of pity is ever unscarfed.

But under what difficulties have these results been secured? What floods of tears and blood, what long walls of woe, sound down the centuries of the past, poured forth by humanity in its desperate struggle for a better life! A struggle which was blind, unconscious of its aims, unknowing of the means by which they should be obtained, groping in darkness for the track leading it knew not whither.

Ignorant of his past, ignorant of his real needs, ignorant of himself, man has blundered and stumbled up the thorny path of progress for tens of thousands of years. Mighty states, millions of individuals, have been hurled to destruction in the perilous ascent, mistaking the way, pursuing false paths. Following blind guides.

Now anthropology steps in, the new Science of Man, offering the knowledge of what he has been and is, the young but wise teacher, revealing the future by the unwavering light of the past, offering itself as man's trusty mentor and friend, ready to conduct him by sure steps upward and onward to the highest summit which his nature is capable of attaining; and who dares set a limit to that?

This is the final aim of anthropology, the lofty ambition which the student of this science deliberately sets before himself. Who will point to a worthier or a nobler one?

Notes

1. Professor James Ferrier, in his *Institutes of Metaphysic*.

2. See the pertinent remarks of Dr. S. R. Steinmetz in the Einleitung to his *Ethnologische Studien zur Ersten Entwicklung der Strafe* (Leiden, 1894). I have urged this point further in a pamphlet entitled *Anthropology; as a Science and as a Branch of University Education in the United States* (Philadelphia, 1892).

3. Dr. A. H. Post, "Ethnologische Gedanken," in *Globus*, Band 59, No. 19.

4. Dr. S. R. Steinmetz, *ubi supra*, Einleitung.

5. "On the Physiological Correlation of Certain Linguistic Radicals." By D. G. Brinton. In the *Proceedings* of the American Oriental Society, March, 1894.

6. "The Origin of Sacred Numbers." By D. G. Brinton. In the *American Anthropologist*, April, 1894. In my *Myths of the New World* (New York, 1868, Chapter III, "The Sacred Number, Its Origin and Applications"), I had shown the prepotency of the number four both in American and Old World mythology, ritual, statecraft, etc.

7. "Man himself is the only final measure of his own activities. To his own force and faculties all other tests are in the end referred. All sciences and arts, all pleasures and pursuits, are assigned their respective ranks in his interest by reference to those physical powers and mental processes which are peculiarly the property of his own species." *Anthropology as a Science*, etc., p. 3.

DOCUMENT L

The Limitations of the Comparative Method of Anthropology

FRANZ BOAS

Modern anthropology has discovered the fact that human society has grown and developed everywhere in such a manner that its forms, its opinions and its actions have many fundamental traits in common. This momentous discovery implies that laws exist which govern the development of society, that they are applicable to our society as well as to those of past times and of distant lands; that their knowledge will be a means of understanding the causes furthering and retarding civilization; and that, guided by this knowledge, we may hope to govern our actions so that the greatest benefit to mankind will accrue from them. Since this discovery has been clearly formulated, anthropology has begun to receive that liberal share of public interest which was withheld from it as long as it was believed that it could do no more than record the curious customs and beliefs of strange peoples; or, at best, trace their relationships, and thus elucidate the early migrations of the races of man and the affinities of peoples.

While early investigations concentrated their attention upon this purely historical problem, the tide has now completely turned, so that there are even anthropologists who declare that such investigations belong to the historian, and that anthropological studies must be confined to researches on the laws that govern the growth of society.

A radical change of method has accompanied this change of views. While formerly identities or similarities of culture were considered incontrovertible proof of historical connection, or even of common

Paper read at the meeting of the American Association for the Advancement of Science at Buffalo; *Science* 4 (1896): 901–8 origin, the new school declines to consider them as such, but interprets them as results of the uniform working of the human mind. The most pronounced adherent to this view in our country is Dr. D. G. Brinton, in Germany the majority of the followers of Bastian, who in this respect go much farther than Bastian himself. Others, while not denying the occurrence of historical connections, regard them as insignificant in results and in theoretical importance as compared to the working of the uniform laws governing the human mind. This is the view of by far the greatest number of living anthropologists.

This modern view is founded on the observation that the same ethnical phenomena occur among the most diverse peoples, or, as Bastian says, on the appalling monotony of the fundamental ideas of mankind all over the globe. The metaphysical notions of man may be reduced to a few types which are of universal distribution; the same is the case in regard to the forms of society, laws and inventions. Furthermore, the most intricate and apparently illogical ideas and the most curious and complex customs appear among a few tribes here and there in such a manner that the assumption of a common historical origin is excluded. When studying the culture of any one tribe, more or less close analoga of single traits such a culture may be found among a great diversity of peoples. Instances of such analoga have been collected to a vast extent by Tylor, Spencer, Bastian, Andree, Post and many others, so that it is not necessary to give here any detailed proof of this fact. The idea of a future life; the one underlying shamanism; inventions such as fire and the bow; certain elementary features of grammatical structure—these will suggest the classes of phenomena to which I refer. It follows from these observations that when we find analogous single traits of culture among distant peoples, the presumption is not that there has been a common historical source, but that they have arisen independently.

But the discovery of these universal ideas is only the beginning of the work of the anthropologist. Scientific inquiry must answer two questions in regard to them: First, what is their origin? And second, how do they assert themselves in various cultures?

The second question is the easier one to answer. The ideas do not exist everywhere in identical form, but they vary. Sufficient material has been accumulated to show that the causes of these variations are either external, that is founded on environment—taking the term environment in its widest sense—or internal, that is founded on psychological conditions. The influence of external and internal factors upon elementary ideas embodies one group of laws governing the growth of culture. Therefore, our endeavors must be directed to showing how such factors modify elementary ideas.

The first method that suggests itself and which has been generally adopted by modern anthropologists is to isolate and classify causes by grouping the variants of certain ethnological phenomena according to external conditions under which the people live, among whom they are found, or to internal causes which influence their minds; or conversely, by grouping these variants according to their similarities. Then the correlated conditions of life may be found.

By this method we begin to recognize even now with imperfect knowledge of the facts what causes may have been at work in shaping the culture of mankind. Friedrich Ratzel and W. J. McGee have investigated the influence of geographical environment on a broader basis of facts than Ritter and Guyot were able to do at their time. Sociologists have made important studies on the effects of the density of population and of other simple social causes. Thus the influence of external factors upon the growth of society is becoming clearer.

The effects of psychical factors are also being studied in the same manner. Stoll has tried to isolate the phenomena of suggestion and of hypnotism and to study the effects of their presence in the cultures of various peoples. Inquiries into the mutual relations of tribes and peoples begin to show that certain cultural elements are easily assimilated while others are rejected, and the time-worn phrases of the imposition of culture by a more highly civilized people upon one of lower culture that has been conquered are giving way to more thorough views on the subject of exchange of cultural achievements. In all these investigations we are using sound, inductive methods in order to isolate the causes of observed phenomena.

The other question in regard to the universal ideas, namely that of their origin, is much more difficult to treat. Many attempts have been made to discover the causes which have led to the formation of ideas "that develop with iron necessity wherever man lives." This is the most difficult problem of anthropology and we may expect that it will baffle our attempts for a long time to come. Bastian denies that it is possible to discover the ultimate sources of inventions, ideas, customs and beliefs which are of universal occurrence. They may be indigenous, they may be imported, they may have arisen from a variety of sources, but they are there. The human mind is so formed that it invents them spontaneously or accepts them whenever they are offered to it. This is the much misunderstood elementary idea of Bastian.

To a certain extent the clear enunciation of the elementary idea gives us the psychological reason for its existence. To exemplify: the fact that the land of the shadows is so often placed in the west suggests the endeavor to localize it at the place where the sun and the stars vanish. The mere statement that primitive man considers animals as gifted with all the qualities of man shows that the analogy between many of the qualities of animals and of human beings has led to the generalization that all the qualities of animals are human. In other cases the causes are not so self-evident. Thus the question why all languages distinguish between the self, the person addressed and the person spoken of, and why most languages do not carry out this sharp, logical distinction in the plural is difficult to answer. The principle when carried out consistently requires that in the plural there should be a distinction between the "we" expressing the self and the person addressed and the "we" expressing the self and the person spoken of, which distinction is found in comparatively few languages only. The lesser liability to misunderstandings in the plural explains this phenomenon partly but hardly adequately. Still more obscure is the psychological basis in other cases, for instance, in that of widely spread marriage customs. Proof of the difficulty of this problem is the multitude of hypotheses that have been invented to explain it in all its varied phases.

In treating this, the most difficult problem of anthropology, the point of view is taken that if an ethnological phenomenon has developed independently in a number of places its development has been the same everywhere; or, expressed in a different form, that the same ethnological phenomena are always due to the same causes. This leads to the still wider generalization that the sameness of ethnological phenomena found in diverse regions is proof that the human mind obeys the same laws everywhere. It is obvious that if different historical developments could lead to the same results, then this generalization would not be tenable. Their existence would present to us an entirely different problem, namely, how it is that the developments of culture so often lead to the same results. It must, therefore, be clearly understood that anthropological research which compares similar cultural phenomena from various parts of the world, in order to discover the uniform history of their development, makes the assumption that the same ethnological phenomenon has everywhere developed in the same manner. Here lies the flaw in the argument of the new method, for no such proof can be given. Even the most cursory review shows that the same phenomenon may develop in a multitude of ways.

I will give a few examples: Primitive tribes are almost universally divided into clans which have totems. There can be no doubt that this form of social organization has arisen independently over and over again. The conclusion is certainly justified that the psychical conditions of man favor the existence of a totemic organization of society, but it does not follow that totemic society has developed everywhere in the same manner. Dr. Washington Matthews believes that the totems of the Navaho have arisen by association of independent clans. Capt. Bourke assumes that similar occurrences gave origin to the Apache clans, and Dr. Fewkes has reached the same conclusion in regard to some of the Pueblo tribes. On the other hand, we have proof that clans may originate by division. I have shown that such events took place among the Indians of the North Pacific coast. Association of small tribes, on the one hand, and disintegration of increasing tribes, on the other, has led to results which appear identical to all intents and purposes.

To give another example: Recent investigations have shown that geometrical designs in primitive art have originated sometimes from naturalistic forms which were gradually conventionalized, sometimes from technical motives, that in still other cases they [are] geometrical by origin or that they were derived from symbols. From all these sources the same forms have developed. Out of designs representing diverse objects grew in course of time frets, meanders, crosses and the like. Therefore the frequent occurrence of these forms proves neither common origin nor that they have always developed according to the same psychical laws. On the contrary, the identical result may have been reached on four different lines of development and from an infinite number of starting points.

Another example may not be amiss: The use of masks is found among a great number of peoples. The origin of the custom of wearing masks is by no means clear in all cases, but a few typical forms of their use may easily be distinguished. They are used for deceiving spirits as to the identity of the wearer. The spirit of a disease who intends to attack the person does not recognize him when he wears a mask, and the mask serves in this manner as a protection. In other cases the mask represents a spirit which is personified by the wearer, who in this shape frightens away other hostile spirits. Still other masks are commemorative. The wearer personifies a deceased person whose memory is to be recalled. Masks are also used in theatrical performances illustrating mythological incidents.[1]

These few data suffice to show that the same ethnical phenomenon may develop from different sources. The simpler the observed fact, the more likely it is that it may have developed from one source here, from another there.

Thus we recognize that the fundamental assumption which is so often made by modern anthropologists cannot be accepted as true in all cases. We cannot say that the occurrence of the same phenomenon is always due to the same causes, and that thus it is proved that the human mind obeys the same laws everywhere. We must demand that the causes from which it developed be investigated and that comparisons be restricted to those phenomena which have been proved to be effects of the same causes. We must insist that this investigation be made a preliminary to all extended comparative studies. In researches on tribal societies those which have developed through association must be treated separately from those that have developed through disintegration. Geometrical designs which have arisen from conventionalized representations of natural objects must be treated separately from those that have arisen from technical motives. In short, before extended comparisons are made, the comparability of the material must be proved.

The comparative studies of which I am speaking here attempt to explain customs and ideas of remarkable similarity which are found here and there. But they pursue also the more ambitious scheme of discovering the laws and the history of the evolution of human society. The fact that many fundamental features of culture are universal, or at least occur in many isolated places, interpreted by the assumption that the same features must always have developed from the same causes, leads to the conclusion that there is one grand system according to which mankind has developed everywhere; that all the occurring variations are no more than minor details in the grand uniform evolution. It is clear that this theory has for its logical basis the assumption that the same phenomena are always due to the same causes. To give an instance: We find many types of structure of family. It can be proved that paternal families have often developed from maternal ones. Therefore, it is said, all paternal families have developed from maternal ones. If we do not make the assumption that the same phenomena have everywhere developed from the same causes, then we may just as well conclude that paternal families have in some cases arisen from maternal institutions; in other cases in other ways. To give another example: Many concepts of the future life have evidently developed from dreams and hallucinations. Consequently, it is said, all notions of this character have had the same origin. This is also true only if no other causes could possibly lead to the same ideas.

We have seen that the facts do not favor at all the assumption of which we are speaking; that they much rather point in the opposite direction. Therefore we must also consider all the ingenious attempts at constructions of a grand system of the evolution of society as of very doubtful value, unless at the same time proof is given that the same phenomena must always have had the same origin. Until this is done, the presumption is always in favor of a variety of courses which historical growth may have taken.

It will be well to relate at this place one of the principal aims of anthropological research. We agreed that certain laws exist which govern the growth of human culture, and it is our endeavor to discover these laws. The object of our investigation is to find the *processes* by which certain stages of culture have developed. The customs and beliefs themselves are not the ultimate objects of research. We desire to learn the reasons why such customs and beliefs exist—in other words, we wish to discover the history of their development. The method which is at present most frequently applied in investigations of this character compares the variations under which the customs or beliefs occur and endeavors to find the common psychological cause that underlies all of them. I have stated that this method is open to very fundamental objection.

We have another method, which in many respects is much safer. A detailed study of customs in their relation to the total culture of the tribe practicing them, in connection with an investigation of their geographical distribution among neighboring tribes, affords us almost always a means of determining with considerable accuracy the historical causes that led to the formation of the customs in question and to the psychological processes that were at work in their development. The results of inquiries conducted by this method may be three-fold. They may reveal the environmental conditions which have created or modified cultural elements; they may clear up psychological factors which are at work in shaping the culture; or they may bring before our eyes the effects that historical connections have had upon the growth of the culture.

We have in this method a means of reconstructing the history of the growth of ideas with much greater accuracy than the generalizations of the comparative method will permit. The latter must always proceed from a hypothetical mode of development, the probability of which may be weighed more or less accurately by means of observed data. But so far I have not yet seen any extended attempt to prove the correctness of a theory by testing it at the hand of developments with whose histories we are familiar. Forcing phenomena into the straitjacket of a theory is opposed to the inductive process by which the actual relations of definite phenomenon may be derived. The latter is no other than the much ridiculed historical method. Its way of proceeding is, of course, no longer that of former times when slight similarities of culture were considered proofs of relationships, but it duly recognizes the results obtained by comparative studies. Its application is based, first of all, on a well-defined, small geographical territory, and its comparisons are not extended beyond the limits of the cultural area that forms the basis of the study. Only when definite results have been obtained in regard to this area is it permissible to extend the horizon beyond its limits, but the greatest care must be taken not to proceed too hastily in this, as otherwise the fundamental proposition which I formulated before might be overlooked, viz: that when we find an analogy of single traits of culture among distant peoples the presumption is not that there has been a common historical source, but that they have arisen independently. Therefore the investigation must always demand continuity of distribution as one of the essential conditions for proving historical connection and the assumption of lost connecting links must be applied most sparingly. This clear distinction between the new and old historical methods is still often overlooked by the passionate defenders of the comparative method. They do not appreciate the difference between the indiscriminate use of similarities of culture for proving historical connection and the careful and slow detailed study of local phenomena. We no longer believe that the slight similarities between the cultures of Central America and of eastern Asia are sufficient and satisfactory proof of a historical connection. On the other hand, no unbiased observer will deny that there are very strong reasons for believing that a limited number of cultural elements found in Alaska and in Siberia have a common origin. The similarities of inventions, customs and beliefs, together with the continuity of their distribution through a limited area, are satisfactory proof of the correctness of this opinion. But it is not possible to extend this area safely beyond the limits of Columbia River in America and northern Japan in Asia. This method of anthropological research is represented in our country by F. W. Putnam and Otis T. Mason; in England by E. B. Tylor; in Germany by Friedrich Ratzel and his followers.

It seems necessary to say a word here in regard to an objection to my arguments that will be raised by investigators who claim that similarity of geographical environment is a sufficient cause for similarity of culture[;] that is to say, that, for instance, the geographical conditions of the plains of the Mississippi basin necessitate the development of a certain culture. Horatio Hale would even go so far as to believe that similarity of form of language may be due to environmental causes. Environment has a certain limited effect upon the culture of man, but I do not see how the view that it is the primary moulder of culture can be supported by any facts. A hasty review of the tribes and peoples of our globe shows that people most diverse in culture and language live under the same geographical conditions, as proof of which may be mentioned the ethnography of East Africa or of New Guinea. In both these regions we find a great diversity of customs in small areas. But much more important is this: Not one observed fact can be brought forward in support of this hypothesis which cannot be much better explained by the well known facts of diffusion of culture; for archaeology as well as ethnography teach us that intercourse between neighboring tribes has always existed and has extended over enormous areas. In the Old World the products of the Baltic found their way to the Mediterranean and the works of art of the eastern Mediterranean reached Sweden. In America the shells of the ocean found their way into the innermost parts of the continent and the obsidians of the West were carried to Ohio. Intermarriages, war, slavery, trade, have been so many sources of constant introduction of foreign cultural elements, so that an assimilation of culture must have taken place over continuous areas. Therefore, it seems to my mind that where among neighboring tribes an intermediate influence of environment cannot be shown to exist, the presumption must always be in favor of historical connections. There has been a time of isolation during which the principal traits of diverse cultures developed according to the previous culture and the environment of the tribes. But the stages of culture representing this period have been covered with so much that is new and that is due to contact with foreign tribes that they cannot be discovered without the most painstaking isolation of foreign elements.

The immediate results of the historical method are, therefore, histories of the cultures of diverse tribes which have been the subject of study. I fully agree with those anthropologists who claim that this is not the ultimate aim of our science, because the general laws, although implied in such a description, cannot be clearly formulated nor their relative value appreciated without a thorough comparison of the manner in which they become manifest in different cultures. But I insist that the application of this method is the indispensable condition of sound progress. The psychological problem is contained in the results of the historical inquiry. When we have cleared up the history of a single culture and understand the effects of environment and the psychological conditions that are reflected in it we have made a step forward, as we can then investigate in how far the same causes or other causes were at work in the development of other cultures. Thus by comparing histories of growth general laws may be found. This method is much safer than the comparative method, as it is usually practiced, because instead of a hypothesis on the mode of development actual history forms the basis of our deductions.

The historical inquiry must be considered the critical test that science must require before admitting facts as evidence. By its means the comparability of the collected material must be tested, and uniformity of processes must be demanded as proof of comparability. Furthermore, when historical connection between two phenomena can be proved, they must not be admitted as independent evidence.

In a few cases the immediate results of this method are of so wide a scope that they rank with the best results that can be attained by comparative studies. Some phenomena have so immense a distribution that the discovery of their occurrence over very large continuous areas proves at once that certain phases of the culture in these areas have sprung from one source. Thus are illuminated vast portions of the early history of mankind. When Edward S. Morse showed that certain methods of arrow release are peculiar to whole continents it became clear at once that the common practice found over a vast area must have had a common origin. When the Polynesians employ a method of fire making consisting in rubbing a stick along a groove, while almost all other peoples use the fire drill, it shows their art of fire making has a single origin. When we notice that the ordeal is found all over Africa in certain peculiar forms, while in those parts of the inhabited world that are remote from Africa it is found not at all or in rudimentary forms only, it shows that the idea as practiced in Africa had one single origin.

The great and important function of the historical method of anthropology is thus seen to lie in its ability to discover the processes which in definite cases led to the development of certain customs. If anthropology desires to establish the laws governing the growth of culture it must not confine itself to comparing the results of the growth alone, but whenever such is feasible it must compare the processes of growth, and these can be discovered by means of studies of the cultures of small geographical areas.

Thus we have seen that the comparative method can hope to reach the results for which it is striving only when it bases its investigations on the historical results of researches which are devoted to laying clear the complex relations of each individual culture. The comparative method and the historical method, if I may use these terms, have been struggling for supremacy for a long time, but we may hope that each will soon find its appropriate place and function. The historical method has reached a sounder basis by abandoning the misleading principle of assuming connections wherever similarities of culture were found. The comparative method, notwithstanding all that has been said and written in its praise, has been remarkably barren of definite results, and I believe it will not become fruitful until we renounce the vain endeavor to construct a uniform systematic history of the evolution of culture, and until we begin to make our comparisons on the broader and sounder basis which I ventured to outline. Up to this time we have too much reveled in more or less ingenious vagaries. The solid work is still all before us.

Note

1. See Richard Andree. *Ethnographische parallelen und Vergleiche*. Neue Folge (Leipzig, 1889), pp. 107 ff.

Afterword

The Ironies of the Fair, the Uncertainties of Anthropology

CURTIS M. HINSLEY

The seventy years between 1870 and 1940 can be properly labeled the Age of Expositions: each decade saw an average of thirty-four regional, national, or international industrial and imperial fairs, overwhelmingly in the transatlantic world. At the height of the phenomenon, between 1890 and 1910, no fewer than seventy-eight celebrations of commerce, industry, science, and art occurred—twenty-two of them in American cities. Seen in this light, the Chicago World's Fair of 1893 constituted only one iteration in a much larger discourse over global and national power relations; and the events of Chicago were followed by a series of American fairs that adopted and expanded upon its anthropological initiatives and premises—notably the Pan-American Exposition in Buffalo (1901), the Louisiana Purchase Exposition in St. Louis in 1904, and the West Coast expositions in Portland, Seattle, San Francisco, and San Diego between 1905 and 1916 (Rydell 1984). In Buffalo—the first exposition after the U.S. war with Spain—the emphasis lay on relations with Central and South America; at the St. Louis fair three years later, anthropologist W. J. McGee featured an indigenous "Igorot Village" from America's newest, troublesome overseas possession: the Philippine Islands (Parezo and Fowler 2007; Brownell 2008). To a degree all these efforts were derivative from Chicago—all, for example, featured a Midway of some sort—but none had the initial and lasting impacts of the 1893 Fair.

More than a century after its gates closed our enduring fascination with the Chicago World's Fair of 1893 lies in the snapshot it provides us of high Gilded Age America, laced with so many illusions and ironies:

celebration and certainty on the edge of economic disaster; a utopian "White City" next door to grinding urban poverty; fairground toasts to the history of Spanish expansion only five years before America's "glorious little war" against the "decrepit" Spanish empire; and not least, an ambitious and energetic yet still strangely provincial American society of immigrants confronting—as Columbus had four hundred years before—a world of unimagined human differences.

Human differences—the growing awareness of them, the study of them, in some corners even the acceptance of them—lay at the heart of the practices of anthropology that came to public attention in Chicago: digging graves in Peru, measuring heads in the indigenous American West, collecting weavings and potteries, molding cliffdwellings and casting stelae, gluing wigs on mannikins, composing life group displays of "primitive" lives, and a thousand other activities. Meanwhile small groups of strange people were camped on the shoreline of South Pond in Jackson Park, while others performed gyrations on the Midway, or juggled, or rode horses, donkeys, and bejangled camels. Who in the world, one wondered, were all these people? What were they doing, and what could it all mean?

This volume has been structured as a dialogue between that past and our present. The Chicago World's Fair above all projected future possibilities: it attracted virtually the entire anthropological and archaeological communities of North America, and each man or woman came with ambitions, expectations, dreams, or plans—but without any certainties for the future. In retrospect the gaps between intentions and eventualities are sobering and humbling. It is poignant today to read Cushing noting, in his diary, of sharing a tent with "dear old Holmes"—who was his senior by twelve years but would outlive Cushing by a third of a century. It is moving to picture him strolling with Brinton and Culin by the Javanese Midway encampment late at night, discovering new friendship and making plans for the future—and then to realize that in six years Brinton would be gone, and likewise Cushing himself only a few months later. Wetherill arrived at the Fair with dreams and a career trajectory that first appeared to rise but then plummeted, while Moorehead's ambitions seemingly flattened but finally ascended with a new century and a new patron. How does one account for the strangely stalled post-Fair Chicago careers of Dorsey and Starr, supported yet confounded by the desires of wealthy patrons and businessmen? And finally, the image comes of Boas seated on a wagon with the tiny coffin of his baby daughter Hedwig on his lap on a cold January day in 1894, riding to a cemetery to which he would return on every visit to Chicago for the rest of his life. He and his wife Marie endured sickness, cold, misery and debt throughout the Fair—always supported by Putnam (who sent another hundred dollars for the funeral). Nobody could have predicted that this sad figure would largely shape the next generation of American anthropology.

Still, the essays in this volume demonstrate that we can draw some conclusions about anthropology at the time of the Fair and its impacts on subsequent developments. By the early 1890s the struggle for definition, terminology, and identities that had swirled through the previous decades was beginning to distill down to a shared set of assumptions about the fields of anthropology. An intellectual coalescence had begun to form that embraced ethnology, linguistics, archaeology, and physical anthropology as related (if unevenly developed) subfields of a larger disciplinary nexus—with folklore studies a vibrant but still vaguely defined outlier. Additionally, certain problems that had for decades preoccupied American antiquarian studies—notably the much hypothesized mound builders controversy and associated notions of earlier, superior civilizations in America—had largely exhausted their interest and outrun habits of backyard collecting, occasional observing, and loose theorizing. Systematic, empirical work in the field—linguistics, body measurement, excavation and recording practices—was becoming the hallmark of professional practice.

Systematic practices in turn presumed the need, possibility, and appropriateness of deliberate instruction and certifiable training—and then judgment. This gradual realization is among the most subtle and fascinating developments of the time, and it accounts for many of the personal traumas, misunderstandings, and ultimately the directions of individual career trajectories. It was a sorting process that required a structure of authority. This was a difficult matter in the context of generational change: from a group of (mostly) men whose biographical *bona fides* lay often in intellectually distant structures—personal friendships, military camaraderie, religious affiliations, literary interests, government service, even business or social reform—to a younger set of men and women with narrower but more focused energies. Until the rise and acceptance of the university department after the turn of the century, it was precisely at the few events like the Chicago Fair that distinctions and judgments would be made on the basis of field results, collections and discussions, and personal suasion.

The shape of the emerging authority structure could be seen in various venues: Putnam's Anthropology Building, the Smithsonian (BAE/USNM) displays, and the Congress of Anthropology that began on August 28. Despite his mild manner Putnam fully intended to assert new directions for anthropology in Chicago. In "Ethnology at the Exposition" (1893) Boas set forth (after the fact), in the form of a guide to the exhibits, the essential issues that he and Putnam felt could be usefully addressed at the time: they identified four issues in archaeology, three ethnographic foci, a small set of folklore and games questions, and a demonstration of apparatus for physical anthropology. To a degree these choices merely reflected strengths or interests of the moment, but the important point is that they indicated a willingness to authorize directions for future study—that is, to suggest research agendas. At the same time, over in the Government Building the Smithsonian displays of Mason, Cushing, Mooney, Hoffman, and Holmes—overseen by Powell's long-awaited linguistic map of indigenous North America—gave clear evidence that a paradigm shift was under way in aesthetics and perception: the typological evolutionism of the previous decade ("Kulturgeschichte" or culture history) was ceding organizational authority and interest to new emphases on actual fieldwork experiences (e.g., Cushing, Mooney, Boas), attention to environmental factors, and emerging recognition of culture areas. Finally, the Congress of Anthropology in late August–early September provided a rare occasion for serious, face-to-face exchanges that not only created new bonds and groupings but indicated new directions for research. For example, the live debate among Brinton, Putnam, Cushing, and others over American indigenous cultures as "watertight compartments" suggested that as evolutionism faded, migration, borrowing, and cultural contact were now coming to the table for discussion. The Jesup Northwest Pacific Expedition could not be far over the horizon (Freed 2012).

Studies of world's fairs have often emphasized that overt racism and expressions of repulsion among fairgoers were commonplace. This has led some to conclude that displays of humans on the Midway or in Putnam's living village were inherently degrading. Public reception of anthropological displays at the Fair was mixed, however, because the reality on the ground was complex. If the side streets of the Midway symbolized the domain of the human past and global peripheries—characterized by sensuality and (constructed) chaos—and the White City with its Court of Honor projected an anesthetized future city-utopia, the main concourse of the Midway provided the physical artery of connection between them: periphery and center, past and future. On the Midway, on the Wooded Isle, and elsewhere in Jackson Park, the documents of the Fair convincingly testify, a great deal of intermingling took place: strolling and promenading, crowded camel riding among the street performers of Cairo, or leaning over fences to watch Dahomeyan, Javanese, or North African dances. The fact is, people got very close to each other at Chicago. James Gilbert, in a revealing study of the concessionaires at the Fair, concluded that visitors spent a great deal of time on the Midway; the experience of the Plaisance, he concluded, "was the street itself": "The Midway, then, was people—Americans and others—mixed into an immense procession observing itself, a crowd looking at itself. It was a world of jumbled exteriors, and largely unknown and imagined interiors" (Gilbert 1993, 9–10). To be sure some visitors, as in Clara Burnham's *Sweet Clover*, found the noise, confusion, and sheer physicality beyond the White City to be frightening—she retreated to the "angels on the Woman's Building" (Burnham 1894, 71); but others, like Julian Hawthorne's American girl, Hildegarde, found themselves drawn to the exotic and erotic of the Midway and its environs (Hawthorne 1893a). From these slender beginnings an audience for the stories told by the professionals in the emerging field of anthropological studies was born.

The Fair gave impulse, too, to individual financial support for anthropology and archaeology. Prior to 1893 patronage for anthropology or archaeology of the western hemisphere was limited to a handful of individuals with specific interests—finding a few hundred dollars to save the Serpent Mound in southern Ohio, for instance, had been a major effort for Putnam in the 1880s (Hinsley 1984; 1985). As McVicker

(Essay 6) and Wilcox (Essay 7) relate, directly and indirectly the Chicago Fair created or rekindled enthusiasms to explore and collect, initiating a complex new set of relationships between wealthy individuals and institutions for training, fieldwork, curating, and display. Each arrangement was unique. Before the Fair, Mary Hemenway had planned and even bought land for a "Pueblo Museum" in her husband's hometown of Salem, Massachusetts, with Cushing to be its first director; while Charles Bowditch (whose enthusiasms were Mayan epigraphy and calendrical puzzles) worked for years to fund the training of a Maya scholar at Harvard. In Chicago, Edward Ayer had a long-standing and eclectic interest in the indigenous and Hispanic Southwest, which he transformed after the Fair into support for the Field Columbian Museum and the Newberry Library. Excited by the Mayan exhibits at the Fair, Allison Armour, as McVicker explains, briefly sponsored explorations on the coasts of Mexico and Central America—but then abruptly turned to other interests. Talbot and Fred Hyde met up with Wetherill at the Fair and, inspired by their own southwestern travels and the Cliffdweller exhibits, planned the Hyde Exploring Expedition to Chaco Canyon—which in turn would become closely linked to the American Museum of Natural History (Snead 2001; Essay 5). Phoebe Hearst's support of American work, which began in 1896, involved the Hazzard Cliffdweller collection from the Fair (Jacknis 1999). While there is no record that he attended the Fair, a few years later George Gustav Heye followed yet another path: he bought and collected omnivorously, at first keeping the collections in his New York apartment but eventually expanding to a private museum and research foundation in Manhattan and the Bronx (Kidwell 1999). In sum, the patronage that began in the decade after the Fair took many forms: private or public collections, student scholarships, field expeditions, prizes, even endowed chairs.

In the quarter century following the Chicago Fair anthropology took off in new directions. The number of centers of university and museum work expanded to include New York, Chicago, Philadelphia, St. Louis, and Berkeley. The eclectic enthusiasms embraced by a wide range of men and women at the time of the International Congress of Anthropology could still be felt at the founding of the American Anthropological Association a decade later (Stocking 1960), but by the time of the First World War a new cadre, trained largely at Columbia and Harvard (or both), had begun to join the ranks of the AAA. In archaeology, regionally based avocational fieldworkers persisted as important contributors—as they still do today—but classroom and field school training were also becoming well established by 1920. For these new generations, the nights on Chicago's Midway could be at best only a distant memory, ultimately part of the folklore of the emerging profession.

ACKNOWLEDGMENTS

Coming of Age in Chicago began as a symposium at the annual meetings of the Society for American Archaeology in March 1999. Fifteen years is an embarrassingly long time to reflect upon in reviewing the trajectory and gradual transformation of an idea. Over time we have, of course, accrued significant debts to individuals and institutions.

Jesse D. Green (1928–2011) was a fine scholar and good friend. His generosity in sharing with us the later diaries of Frank Hamilton Cushing (since deposited at the National Anthropological Archives) made our historical project conceivable in the first place. We will always be thankful to Jesse and regret that he did not live to see this book.

The participants in our original 1999 symposium were Regna D. Darnell, Raymond D. Fogelson, Don D. Fowler, Donald McVicker, David J. Meltzer, Nancy J. Parezo, and James E. Snead. Although not all of their contributions ultimately found their way into this volume, we are deeply appreciative of their insights, encouragement, and professional courtesy throughout the long gestation. At a later date we persuaded Ira Jacknis to join the project; his rare and thorough knowledge of the history of museum anthropology has added a critical dimension to our collective understanding of anthropology at the Chicago Fair. Several anonymous reviewers for the University of Nebraska Press added valuable insights and helped to refine the ideas presented.

In addition to the individuals and institutions acknowledged at the end of the individual essays, we wish to thank the staffs of the following archives and libraries for their unfailing help and good cheer, either in person or online: Boston Public Library; Braun Research Library, Southwest Museum, Autry National Center of the American West; Chicago History Museum; Cornell University Archives; Harvard University Archives; Field Museum of National History Archives, Chicago; Henry L. Huntington Library, San Marino, California; Huntington

Free Library, Bronx, New York; Library of Congress, Washington DC; Martin Luther King Library, Washington DC; National Anthropological Archives, Smithsonian Institution; National Museum of the American Indian, Smithsonian Institution; Newberry Library, Chicago; Peabody Museum Archives and Photoarchives, Harvard University; Phillips Library, Peabody-Essex Museum, Salem, Massachusetts; Robert S. Peabody Museum of Archaeology, Andover, Massachusetts; Swan Library, Albion, New York; University of Chicago Special Collections; and the University of Pennsylvania Museum Archives. We have also benefited from the digital transformations of the past decade by full use of search engines such as Google.

Heartfelt thanks go to the folks at the former IDEA Lab, Bilby Research Center, at Northern Arizona University—particularly Ryan Belnap and Dan Boone—for their professionalism and patience in working with the images for the volume.

For financial aid we are grateful to the Christine Callan Trust in Boston and to related support from Gordon Means and John Hemenway. We also have enjoyed the support, at various times, of the Indigenous Studies Department, the Comparative Cultural Studies Department, and the College of Arts and Letters at Northern Arizona University; and several administrations and staff of the Museum of Northern Arizona. Joe Wilder, director of the Southwest Center at the University of Arizona in Tucson, has provided once again vital moral support and administrative services.

Finally, we once again salute our wives, Susan Louise Wilcox and Victoria Enders Hinsley, for their unwavering support over a very long time.

BIBLIOGRAPHY

Abt, Jeffrey. 2011. *American Egyptologist: The Life of James Henry Breasted and the Creation of His Oriental Institute*. Chicago: University of Chicago Press.
Adams, Henry. 1961. *The Autobiography of Henry Adams*. Boston: Houghton Mifflin.
Adams, Rachel. 2001. *Sideshow U.S.A.: Freaks and the American Cultural Imagination*. Chicago: University of Chicago Press.
Aguirre, Robert D. 2005. *Informal Empire: Mexico and Central America in Victorian Culture*. Minneapolis: University of Minnesota Press.
Alexander, Edward P. 1964. "Artistic and Historical Period Rooms." *Curator* 7: 263–81.
Allen, Rebecca. 1990. "The History of the University Museum's Southwestern Pottery Collection." In *Beauty from the Earth: Pueblo Indian Pottery From the University Museum of Archaeology and Anthropology*, ed. J. J. Brody, 61–88. Philadelphia: University Museum, University of Pennsylvania.
Almazan, Tristan, and Sarah Coleman. 2003. "George A. Dorsey: A Curator and His Comrades." In *Curators, Collections and Contexts: Anthropology at the Field Museum, 1893–2002*, ed. Stephen E. Nash and Gary M. Feinman, 87–97. Fieldiana: Publication no. 1525, Anthropology New Series no. 36. Chicago: Field Museum of Natural History.
American Antiquarian Society. 1885. *Proceedings for 1883–1885*. Worcester, Massachusetts.
———. 1887. *Proceedings for 1885–1887*. Worcester, Massachusetts.
Ames, Michael. 2008. *Carl Hagenbeck's Empire of Entertainments*. Seattle: University of Washington Press.
Anonymous. 1893. *The Illinois Building and Exhibits Therein at the World's Columbian Exposition*. Chicago: John Morris Company.
———. 1894a. "The Pueblos at Home." *Washington Post*, September 4, 7.
———. 1894b. "Older Than Mankind; Prof. Cushing Speaks on Primitive Religions." *Washington Post*, July 30, 8.
———. 1894c. *Photographs of the World's Fair: An Elaborate Collection of Photographs of the Buildings, Grounds and Exhibits of the World's Columbian Exposition, with a Special Description of the Famous Midway Plaisance*. Chicago: Werner Company.
———. 1894d. *Portrait Types of the Midway Plaisance*. F. W. Putnam, intro. St. Louis: N. D. Thompson Publishing Company.

———. 1894e. *Vistas of the Fair in Color: A Portfolio of Familiar Views.* Chicago: Poole Brothers.

———. 1900. "In Memoriam, Frank Hamilton Cushing." *Bulletin of the Free Museum of Science and Art* (Free Museum, Philadelphia), May 2, 4.

———. 1927. *Biographical Sketches and Letters of T. Mitchell Prudden.* New Haven: Yale University Press.

Apache, Antonio. 1892a. Letter to F. W. Putnam, June 17. F. W. Putnam Papers, box 31, Harvard University Archives.

———. 1892b. Letter to F. W. Putnam, July 25. F. W. Putnam Papers, box 31, Harvard University Archives.

———. 1892c. Letter to F. W. Putnam, August 16. F. W. Putnam Papers, box 31, Harvard University Archives.

Applebaum, Stanley. 1980. *The Chicago World's Fair of 1893—A Photographic Record.* New York: Dover.

Atkins, Victoria M., ed. 1993. *Anasazi Basketmaker: Papers from the 1990 Wetherill-Grand Gulch Symposium.* Cultural Resources Series 24. Salt Lake City: United States Department of the Interior, Bureau of Land Management.

Ayer, Edward Everett. 2003. "In Re: Founding of the Field Museum." In *Curators, Collections, and Contexts: Anthropology at the Field Museum, 1893–2002*, ed. Stephen E. Nash and Gary M. Feinman, 49–52. Fieldiana: Publication no. 1525, Anthropology New Series no. 36. Chicago: Field Museum of Natural History.

Aymé, Louis. 1892. "What Mexico Will Show: Castles of the Dark Ages to Be Reproduced at the Exposition." *World's Columbian Exposition Illustrated* (Chicago: James B. Campbell) vol. 2, no. 11 (January): 20–21.

Babcock, Barbara A. 1990. "'A New Mexican Rebecca': Imaging Pueblo Women." *Journal of the Southwest* 32, no. 4: 400–437.

Badger, Reid. 1979. *The Great American Fair: The World's Columbian Exposition and American Culture.* Chicago: Nelson Hall.

Baker, Lee D. 1998. *From Savage to Negro: Anthropology and the Construction of Race, 1896–1954.* Berkeley: University of California Press.

———. 2010. *Anthropology and the Racial Politics of Culture.* Durham: Duke University Press.

Baker, Malcolm. 2010. "The Reproductive Continuum: Plaster Casts, Paper Mosaics and Photographs as Contemporary Modes of Reproduction in the Nineteenth-Century Museum." In *Plaster Casts: Making, Collecting, and Displaying from Classical Antiquity to the Present*, ed. Rune Frederiksen and Eckhart Marchand, 485–500. Berlin: De Gruyter.

Baldwin, Charles H. 1893. Baldwin to Frederic W. Putnam, November 28. Putnam, F. W.—World's Columbian Exposition—Correspondence A–Z. HUG 1717.2.12, Harvard University Archives.

Bancroft, Hubert Howe. 1893. *The Book of the Fair: An Historical and Descriptive Presentation of the Columbian Exposition at Chicago, 1893.* 4 vols. Chicago: Bancroft Company.

Bandelier, Adolph F. 1890–92. *Final Report of Investigations among the Indians of the Southwestern United States, Carried on Mainly in the Years from 1880 to 1885,* Parts I and II. Papers of the Archaeological Institute of America, American Series, III and IV. Cambridge: AIA.

———. 1890. *The Delight Makers: A Novel of Pueblo Indian Life.* New York: Dodd, Mead.

———. 1892. "An Outline of the Documentary History of the Zuni Tribe." *Journal of American Ethnology and Archaeology* 3: 1–115.

Bank, Rosemarie K. 2002. "Representing History: Performing the Columbian Exposition." *Theatre Journal* 54, no. 4: 589–606.

———. 2007. "Representing History: Performing the Columbian Exposition." In *Critical Theory and Performance,* revised edition, ed. Janelle G. Reinelt and Joseph R. Roadh, 223–44. Ann Arbor: University of Michigan Press.

Banks, Marcus, and Jay Ruby, eds. 2011. *Made to Be Seen: Perspectives on the History of Visual Anthropology.* Chicago: University of Chicago Press.

Banta, Melissa, and Curtis M. Hinsley. 1986. *From Site to Sight: Anthropology, Photography, and the Power of Imagery.* Cambridge: Harvard University Press.

Barkan, Elazar. 1992. *The Retreat of Scientific Racism: Changing Concepts of Race in Britain and the United States between the World Wars.* New York: Cambridge University Press.

Barnhart, Terry A. 1998. "In Search of the Mound Builders: The State Archaeological Association of Ohio, 1875–1885." *Ohio History* 107: 125–70.

———. 2005. *Ephraim George Squier and the Development of American Anthropology.* Lincoln: University of Nebraska Press.

Barnes, Sisley. 1977. "George Ferris' Wheel: The Great Attraction of the Midway Plaisance." *Chicago History* 6, no. 3: 177–82.

Bassett, Helen W., and Frederick Starr (comps.). 1898. *International Folk-Lore Congress of the World's Columbian Exposition.* Chicago: Charles H. Segel.

Batkin, Jonathan. 1998. "Some Early Curio Dealers of New Mexico." *American Indian Art* 23, no. 3: 68–81.

Baxandall, Michael. 1972. *Painting and Experience in Fifteenth Century Italy: A Primer in the Social History of Pictorial Style.* Oxford: Clarendon Press.

Bay, Mia. 2009. *To Tell the Truth Freely: The Life of Ida B. Wells.* New York: Hill and Wang.

Becker, Howard S. 1982. *Art Worlds.* 25th anniversary edition, updated and expanded, 2008. Berkeley: University of California Press.

Bender, Thomas. 1993. "The Erosion of Public Culture: Cities, Discourses, and Professional Disciplines." In Bender, *Intellect and Public Life: Essays on the Social History of Academic Intellectuals in the United States,* 30–46. Baltimore: Johns Hopkins University Press.

———. 2002. *The Unfinished City: New York and the Metropolitan Idea.* New York: New Press.

Bendix, Regina. 1997. *In Search of Identity: The Formation of Folklore Studies*. Madison: University of Wisconsin Press.
Benedict, Burton. 1983. *The Anthropology of World's Fairs*. Berkeley: Lowie Museum of Anthropology, Scholar Press.
Benedict, Ruth. 1922. "The Vision Quest in Plains Culture." *American Anthropologist* 24:1–23.
———. 1934. *Patterns of Culture*. Boston: Houghton Mifflin.
Bennett, Tony. 1988. "The Exhibitionary Complex." *New Formations* 4: 73–102.
———. 1995. *The Birth of the Museum: History, Theory, Politics*. New York: Routledge.
Berg, David F. 1976. *Chicago's White City of 1893*. Lexington: University Press of Kentucky.
Bergmann, Carl F. W. 1893. "List of Figures and Costumes for the Exposition at World's Columbian Exposition in Chicago." Manuscript no. 7217. National Anthropological Archives, Smithsonian Institution.
Bernal, Ignacio. 1980. *A History of Mexican Archaeology: The Vanished Civilizations of Middle America*. New York: Thames and Hudson.
Besant, Walter. 1893. "A First Impression." *Cosmopolitan* 15 (September): 533.
———. 1894. "Literary Conferences." *Contemporary Review* 65 (January): 124.
Bickford, F. T. 1893. "The Government Exhibit." *Cosmopolitan* 15 (September): 603–6.
Bidlake, John. 1893a. Report to Frederic W. Putnam, n.d. F. W. Putnam Papers, box 35, Harvard University Archives.
———. 1893b. Report to Frederic W. Putnam for May, 1893. F. W. Putnam Papers, box 35, Harvard University Archives.
———. 1893c. Report to Frederic W. Putnam for June, 1893. F. W. Putnam Papers, box 35, Harvard University Archives.
———. 1893d. *Official Catalogue of Exhibits on the Midway Plaisance, Department M: Ethnology, Isolated Exhibits*. Chicago: W. B. Conkey Company.
Bishop, Glenn A., and Paul T. Gilbert. 1932. *Chicago's Accomplishments and Leaders*. Chicago: Bishop Publishing.
Bittell, Carla. 2009. *Mary Putnam Jacobi and the Politics of Medicine in Nineteenth Century America*. Chapel Hill: University of North Carolina Press.
Black, Edwin. 2003. *War Against the Weak: Eugenics and America's Campaign to Create a Master Race*. New York: Thunder's Mouth Press.
Blackburn, Fred M. 2006. *The Wetherills: Friends of Mesa Verde*. Durango: Durango Herald Small Press.
Blackburn, Fred M., and Ray A. Williamson. 1997. *Cowboys and Cave Dwellers: Basketmaker Archaeology in Utah's Grand Gulch*. Santa Fe: School of American Research Press.
Blackburn, Fred M., and Victoria M. Atkins. 1993. "Handwriting on the Wall: Applying Inscriptions to Reconstruct Historic Archaeological Expeditions." In *Anasazi Basketmaker: Papers from the 1990 Wetherill–Grand Gulch Symposium*, ed. Victoria M. Atkins, 41–100. Cultural Resources Series 24. Salt Lake City: United States Department of the Interior, Bureau of Land Management.

Blackburn, Fred M., and Ray A. Williamson. 1997. *Cowboys and Cave Dwellers: Basketmaker Archaeology in Utah's Grand Gulch*. Santa Fe: School of American Research Press.

Blake, William Phipps. 1899. "Aboriginal Turquoise Mining in Arizona and New Mexico." *American Antiquarian* 21, no. 5: 278–308.

———. 1900a. "Mosaics of Chalchuite." *American Antiquarian* 22, no. 2: 108–10.

Blanchard, Pascal, Nicolas Bancel, Gilles Boëtsch, Eric Deroo, Sandrine Lemaire, and Charles Forsdick, eds. 2008. *Human Zoos: Science and Spectacle in the Age of Colonial Empires*. Liverpool: Liverpool University Press.

Bloembergen, Marieke. 2006. *Colonial Spectacles: The Netherlands and the Dutch East Indies at World Exhibitions, 1883–1931*. Singapore: Singapore University Press.

Bloom, Sol. 1948. *The Autobiography of Sol Bloom*. New York: G. P. Putnam's.

Boas, Franz. 1887. "Museums of Ethnology and Their Classification." *Science* 9: 587–89.

———. 1893. "Ethnology at the Exposition." *A World's Fair, 1893: A Special Issue of Cosmopolitan Magazine*, vol. 15, no. 5: 607–9, www.archive.org/stream/worldsfair 1893worl/worldsfair189300worl_djvu.txt, accessed June 9, 2011.

———. 1894. "Classification of the Languages of the North Pacific Coast." In *Memoirs of the International Congress of Anthropology*, ed. C. Staniland Wake, 339–46. Chicago: Schulte Publishing Company.

———. 1896a. Boas to Putnam, January 19. Putnam, F. W.—General Correspondence, 1851–1947. HUG 1717.2.1, Harvard University Archives.

———. 1896b. "The Limitations of the Comparative Method of Anthropology." *Science*, n. s. 4: 901–8.

———. 1897. *The Social Organization and the Secret Societies of the Kwakiutl Indians*. Appendix to *Annual Report of the U.S. National Museum for 1895*, 311–738. Washington DC: Government Printing Office.

———. 1909. *Putnam Anniversary Volume: Anthropological Essays Presented to Frederic Ward Putnam*. New York: G. E. Stechert.

———. 1910. *Changes in Bodily Form of Descendants of Immigrants*. Reports of the Immigration Commission 39. Washington DC: Government Printing Office.

———. 1911. *The Mind of Primitive Man*. New York: Macmillan.

———. 1916. "Eugenics." *Scientific Monthly* 3: 471–78.

———. 1917. "Review of *The Passing of the Great Race* by Madison Grant." *New Republic* 9: 305–7.

———. 1920. "The Classification of American Indian Languages." *American Anthropologist* 22: 367–76.

———. 1925. "This Nordic Nonsense." *Forum* 74, no. 4: 502–11.

———. 1928. *Anthropology and Modern Life*. New York: W. W. Norton.

———. 1936. "History and Science in Anthropology: A Reply." *American Anthropologist* 38: 137–41.

———. 1938. *General Anthropology*. Boston: D. C. Heath.

———. 1940. *Race, Language and Culture*. New York: Macmillan.

———. 1945. *Race and Democratic Society*. New York: J. J. Augustin.
Boehm, Lisa Krissof. 2004. *Popular Culture and the Enduring Myth of Chicago, 1871–1968*. New York: Routledge.
Boëtsch, Gilles, and Yann Ardagna. 2008. "Human Zoos: The 'Savage' and the Anthropologist." In *Human Zoos: Science and Spectacle in the Age of Colonial Empires*, ed. Pascal Blanchard et al., 114–22. Liverpool: Liverpool University Press.
Boller, Paul F., Jr. 1969. *American Thought in Transition: The Impact of Evolutionary Naturalism, 1865–1900*. Chicago: Rand McNally and Company.
Boomhower, Ray E. 2001. *"But Do I Clamor": May Wright Sewall, A Life, 1844–1920*. Cincinnati: Guild Press of Indiana.
Bostwick, Todd W. 2006. *Byron Cummings: Dean of Southwest Archaeology*. Tucson: University of Arizona Press.
Boyd, E. 1952. "Mrs. Mitchell Carroll, 1868–1952." *El Palacio* 59, no. 12: 390–91.
Braddock, Alan C. 1998. "Eakins, Race, and Ethnographic Ambivalence." *Winterthur Portfolio* 33, nos. 2–3: 135–61.
———. 2009. *Thomas Eakins and the Cultures of Modernity*. Berkeley: University of California Press.
Brady, Erika. 1999. *A Spiral Way: How the Phonograph Changed Ethnography*. Jackson: University Press of Mississippi.
Braudel, Fernand. 1980. *On History*. Chicago: University of Chicago Press.
Breasted, Charles. 1943. *Pioneer to the Past: The Story of James Henry Breasted, Archaeologist*. Chicago: University of Chicago Press.
Brechin, Gray. 2001. *Imperial San Francisco: Urban Power, Earthly Ruin*. Berkeley: University of California Press.
Bricker, Harvey M. 2002. "George Grant MacCurdy: An American Pioneer of Paleoanthropology." In *New Perspectives on the Origins of Americanist Archaeology*, ed. David L. Browman and Stephen Williams, 265–86. Tuscaloosa: University of Alabama Press.
Brinkman, Paul D. 2009. "Frederic Ward Putnam, Chicago's Cultural Philanthropists, and the Founding of the Field Museum." *Museum History Journal* 2, no. 1 (January): 73–100.
Brinton, Daniel G. 1866. "The Mound-Builders of the Mississippi Valley." *Historical Magazine* 11: 33–37.
———. 1890. *Essays of an Americanist*. Philadelphia: David McKay.
———. 1891. *The American Race: A Linguistic Classification and Ethnographic Description of the Native Tribes of North and South America*. New York: N. D. C. Hodges.
———. 1892a. "The Nomenclature and Teaching of Anthropology." *American Anthropologist* o.s. 5: 263–71.
———. 1892b. "Proposed Classification and International Nomenclature of the Anthropological Sciences." *Proceedings of the American Association for the Advancement of Science* 41: 257–58.
———. 1893. Letter to Sara Stevenson, January 30. Director's Office Records, Department of Archaeology and Paleontology, Brinton, American Section, Univer-

sity of Pennsylvania Museum of Archaeology and Anthropology Archives, Philadelphia.

———. 1894a. "The 'Nation' as an Element in Anthropology." In *Memoirs of the International Congress of Anthropology*, ed. C. Staniland Wake, 19–34. Chicago: Schulte Publishing Company.

———. 1894b. "On Various Supposed Relations between the American and Asian Races." In *Memoirs of the International Congress of Anthropology*, ed. C. Staniland Wake, 145–51. Chicago: Schulte Publishing Company.

———. 1894c. "The Present Status of American Linguistics." In *Memoirs of the International Congress of Anthropology*, ed. C. Staniland Wake, 335–38. Chicago: Schulte Publishing Company.

———. 1895a. "The Aims of Anthropology." *Proceedings of the American Association for the Advancement of Science* 44: 1–17.

———. 1895b. "Anthropology." *Psychological Review* 2: 100–101.

———. 1897. "Archaeological Survey of Ohio." *Science* 6 (new series): 763.

Brooks, Van Wyck. 1915. *Coming of Age in America*. New York: B. W. Huebsch.

———. 1952. *The Confident Years, 1885–1915*. New York: E. P. Dutton.

Bronner, Simon J., ed. 1989. *Consuming Visions: Accumulation and Display of Goods in America, 1880–1920*. New York: Norton.

Bronson, Bennet. 2003."Berthold Laufer." In *Curators, Collections and Contexts: Anthropology at the Field Museum, 1893–2002*, ed. Stephen E. Nash and Gary M. Feinman, 117–26. Fieldiana: Publication no. 1525, Anthropology New Series no. 36. Chicago: Field Museum of Natural History.

Browman, David L. 1978. "The 'Knockers': St. Louis Archaeologists from 1904–1921." *Missouri Archeological Society Newsletter* 319.

———. 2002a. "Frederick Ward Putnam: Contributions to the Development of Archaeological Institutions and Encouragement of Women Practitioners." In *New Perspectives on the Origins of Americanist Archaeology*, ed. David L. Browman and Stephen Williams, 209–41. Tuscaloosa: University of Alabama Press.

———. 2002b. "Origins of Stratigraphic Excavation in North America: The Peabody Museum Method and the Chicago Method." In *New Perspectives on the Origins of Americanist Archaeology*, ed. David L. Browman and Stephen Williams, 242–64. Tuscaloosa: University of Alabama Press.

———. 2013. *Cultural Negotiations: The Role of Women in the Founding of Americanist Archaeology*. Lincoln: University of Nebraska Press.

Browman, David L., and Stephen Williams. 2013. *Anthropology at Harvard: A Biographical History, 1790–1940*. Cambridge: Peabody Museum Press.

Brown, Bill. 2003. *A Sense of Things: The Object Matter of American Literature*. Chicago: University of Chicago Press.

Brown, Julie K. 1994. *Contesting Images: Photography and the World's Columbian Exposition*. Tucson: University of Arizona Press.

Brownell, Susan, ed. 2008. *The 1904 Anthropology Days and Olympic Games: Sport, Race, and American Imperialism*. Lincoln: University of Nebraska Press.

Bruce, Robert V. 1987. *The Launching of Modern American Science, 1846–1876*. New York: Knopf.
Brugge, David M. 1980. *A History of the Chaco Navajos*. Reports of the Chaco Center 4. Albuquerque: National Park Service.
Brunhouse, Robert L. 1973. *In Search of the Maya: The First Archaeologists*. Albuquerque: University of New Mexico Press.
Buel, James W. (1894) 1974. *The Magic City: A Massive Portfolio of Original Photographic Views of the Great World's Fair and Its Treasures of Art, including a Vivid Representation of the Famous Midway Plaisance*. Philadelphia: Historical Publishing Company. Reprint, New York: Arno Press.
Burg, David F. 1976. *Chicago's White City of 1893*. Lexington: University Press of Kentucky.
Burnham, Clara Louise. (1894) 1992. *Sweet Clover: A Romance of the White City*. Cambridge MA: Houghton Mifflin. Reprint, Caledonia MI: Bigwater Books.
Burnham, Daniel Hudson. 1895. "The Plan of the Builders." In *The Art of the World Illustrated in the Paintings, Statuary, and Architecture of the World's Columbian Exposition*, ed. Ripley Hitchcock, i–vi. New York: D. Appleton.
———. 1902. "White City and Capital City." *Century Magazine* 63 (February): 619–20.
———. 1989. *The Final Official Report of the Director of Works of the World's Columbian Exposition*. Reprint, New York: Garland.
Burnham, Daniel Hudson, and Francis Davis Millet. 1894. *World's Columbian Exposition: The Book of the Builders*. Springfield OH: Columbia Memorial Publication Society.
Burns, J. Conor. 2008. "Networking Ohio Valley Archaeology in the 1880s: The Social Dynamics of Peabody and Smithsonian Centralization." *Histories of Anthropology* 4: 1–33.
Butterfield, Herbert.1931. *The Whig Interpretation of History*. London: G. Bell and Sons.
Byers, Douglas S. 1939. "Warren King Moorehead." *American Anthropologist* 41, no. 2: 286–94.
Campbell, James B. 1894. *Campbell's Illustrated History of the World's Columbian Exposition*. Chicago: Columbian Guide Company.
Cantwell, Robert. 2009. "White City Elegy: Modern and Postmodern at the World's Fair." In *If Beale Street Could Talk: Music, Community, Culture*, 111–41. Urbana: University of Illinois Press.
Carlton, Donna. 1994. *Looking for Little Egypt*. Bloomington IN: IDD Books.
Casler, Patricia Joanne. 1976. "Personalities, Politics, and Patrons of the Peabody Museum of American Archaeology and Ethnology, 1866–1896." Senior thesis, Department of History, Harvard College.
Cassell, Frank. 1986. "Welcoming the World: Illinois' Role in the World's Columbian Exposition." *Illinois Historical Journal* 72 (Spring): 230–44.
Chamberlain, Alexander F. 1900. "In Memoriam: Walter James Hoffman." *Journal of American Folklore* 13: 44–46.
———. 1907. "William Wells Newell, 1839–1907." *American Anthropologist* 9: 365–76.

Chamberlin, Thomas C. 1894. Letter to William Henry Holmes, January 27. William Henry Holmes, "Random Records of a Lifetime" (20 vols.). Library of the National Collection of Fine Arts, Smithsonian Institution.

Chapin, Frederick H. 1892. *The Land of the Cliff Dwellers*. Boston: W. B. Clarke and Company.

Chapman, Janet, and Karen Barrie. 2008. *Kenneth Milton Chapman: A Life Dedicated to Indian Arts and Artists*. Albuquerque: University of New Mexico Press.

Chauvenet, Beatrice. 1983. *Hewett and Friends: A Biography of Santa Fe's Vibrant Era*. Santa Fe: Museum of New Mexico Press.

Christenson, Andrew L. 2011. "Who Were the Professional American Archaeologists in 1900? Clues from the Work of Warren K. Moorehead." *Bulletin of the History of Archaeology*, http://www.archaeologybulletin.org/article/view/3/3.

———. 2013. "The Co-Production of Archaeological Knowledge: The Essential Relationship of Amateurs and Professionals in 20th Century American Archaeology." *Complutum* (Universidad Complutense de Madrid), *Special Issue: New Perspectives on the History of Archaeology* 24 (2): 63–72.

Cigliano, Jan, and Sarah Bradford Landau, eds. 1994. *The Grand American Avenue, 1850–1920*. San Francisco: Pomegranate Books.

Colby, William M. 1977. Routes to Rainy Mountain: A Biography of James Mooney, Ethnologist. Ph.D. dissertation, University of Wisconsin, Madison.

Cole, Douglas R. 1985. *Captured Heritage: The Scramble for Northwest Coast Artifacts*. UBC Press, Vancouver.

———. 1999. *Franz Boas: The Early Years, 1858–1906*. Seattle: University of Washington Press.

Cole, Fay-Cooper. 1931. "George A. Dorsey." *American Anthropologist* 33: 413–14.

Cole, John. 1976. "Nineteenth Century Fieldwork, Archaeology, and Museum Studies: Their Role in the Four-Field Definition of American Anthropology." In *American Anthropology: The Early Years*, ed. John V. Murra, 111–25. St. Paul: West Publishing.

Colton, Harold S., and Lyndon L. Hargrave. 1937. *Handbook of Northern Arizona Pottery Wares*. Bulletin 11. Flagstaff: Museum of Northern Arizona.

Collier, Donald. 1969. "Chicago Comes of Age: The World's Columbian Exposition and the Birth of the Field Museum." *Bulletin of the Field Museum of Natural History* 40, no. 5: 2–7.

———. 1972. "Men and Their Work." *Field Museum of Natural History Bulletin* 43, no. 8: 7–9.

Collin, Richard H. 1985. *Theodore Roosevelt, Culture, Diplomacy, and Expansion: A New View of American Imperialism*. Baton Rouge: Louisiana State University Press.

Collins, Randall. 1998. *The Sociology of Philosophies: A Global Theory of Intellectual Change*. Cambridge: Belknap Press.

Condit, Carl W. 1973. *Chicago, 1910–1929: Building, Planning, and Urban Technology*. Chicago: University of Chicago Press.

Conkey, W. B. 1893. *Conkey's Complete Guide to the World's Columbian Exposition*. Chicago: W. B. Conkey Company.

Conn, Steven. 1998. *Museums and American Intellectual Life, 1876–1926*. Chicago: University of Chicago Press.

———. 2004. *History's Shadow: Native Americans and Historical Consciousness in the Nineteenth Century*. Chicago: University of Chicago Press.

Crompton, Samuel Willard. 2005. *Emanuel Swedenborg*. Philadelphia: Chelsea House (online).

Cronon, William. 1991. *Nature's Metropolis: Chicago and the Great West*. New York: W. W. Norton.

Culin, Stewart. 1893. "Exhibition of Games at the Columbian Exposition." *Journal of American Folklore* 6: 205–27.

———. 1894. "Retrospect of the Folk-Lore of the Columbian Exposition." *Journal of American Folklore* 7: 51–59.

———. 1898. "American Indian Games." *Journal of American Folk-Lore* 11: 245–52.

———. 1902. "American Indian Games." *American Anthropologist* 5(1): 58–64.

———. (1907) 1975. *Games of the North American Indians*. 24th Annual Report of the Bureau of American Ethnology. Washington DC: Government Printing Office. Reprint, New York: Dover Publications.

Cushing, Frank Hamilton. 1882–83. "My Adventures at Zuñi." *Century Magazine* 25: 191–207, 500–511; 26: 28–47.

———. (1884–85) 1974. *Zuñi Breadstuff: The Millstone*. Indianapolis. Reprint, New York: Museum of the American Indian.

———. 1890a. "Preliminary Notes on the Origins, Working Hypothesis and Primary Researches of the Hemenway South-western Archaeological Exposition." *Proceedings of the International Congress of Americanists* (Berlin, 1888): 151–94.

———. 1890b. Letter to Washington Matthews. CLB7: 10–14. Cornell University Archives, Ithaca.

———. 1893a. Diaries. National Anthropological Archives, Washington DC.

———. 1893b. Monthly Report of Mr. Frank Hamilton Cushing, September, 1893 (inclusive of July and August). Manuscript. Southwest Museum, Frank Hamilton Cushing Collection, Ms. 6, BAE 3.5. Transcribed by David R. Wilcox, Museum of Northern Arizona, 1999.

———. September 3, 1893–December 14, 1898. Letters to Stewart Culin. University of Pennsylvania Museum Archives; and Cushing Correspondence, Culin Archival Collection (6.1.001–005, 1893–1900, n. d.), Brooklyn Museum of Art Library, Brooklyn NY. Transcribed by David R. Wilcox, Museum of Northern Arizona, 1998–2000.

———. 1894. Letter to Stewart Culin, November 27. Culin Archival Collection, Cushing Correspondence, 1.6.002. Brooklyn Museum of Art Library, Brooklyn NY.

———. 1895a. "The Arrow." *American Anthropologist* o.s. 8, no. 4: 307–49.

———. 1895b. Letter to Stewart Culin, February 12. Culin Archival Collection, Cushing Correspondence, 1.6.003. Brooklyn Museum of Art Library, Brooklyn NY.

———. 1896. "Outlines of Zuñi Creation Myths." In *Thirteenth Annual Report of the Bureau of Ethnology, 1891–1892*, 321–447. Washington DC: Government Printing Office.

———. 1897. "Exploration of Ancient Key-Dweller Remains on the Gulf Coast of Florida." *Proceedings of the American Philosophical Society* 35: 153.

———. 1920. *Zuñi Breadstuff*. Indian Notes and Monographs 8. New York: Museum of the American Indian, Heye Foundation.

Cusick, Cornelius C. 1891. Letter to F. W. Putnam, September 27. F. W. Putnam Papers, box 31, Harvard University Archives.

———. 1900. *Military History of Captain C. C. Cusick, U.S. Army*. Chicago: National Archives and Records Administration, Great Lakes Region.

Daniels, Helen S. 1976. *Adventures with the Anasazi of Falls Creek*. Occasional Papers of the Center of Southwest Studies 3. Durango: Fort Lewis College.

Danien, Elin C., and Eleanor M. King. 2003. "Sara Yorke Stevenson and the Development of Archaeology in Philadelphia." In *Philadelphia and the Development of Americanist Archaeology*, ed. Don D. Fowler and David R. Wilcox, 36–47. Tuscaloosa: University of Alabama Press.

Darnell, Regna Diebold. 1969. The Development of American Anthropology, 1879–1920: From the Bureau of American Ethnology to Franz Boas. PhD dissertation, University of Pennsylvania, Philadelphia.

———. 1970. "The Emergence of Academic Anthropology at the University of Pennsylvania." *Journal of the History of Behavioral Sciences* 6: 80–92.

———. 1988. *Daniel Garrison Brinton: The "Fearless Critic" of Philadelphia*. Philadelphia: Department of Anthropology, University of Pennsylvania.

———. 1998. *And Along Came Boas: Continuity and Revolution in Americanist Anthropology*. Philadelphia: John Benjamins Publishing.

———. 2001. *Invisible Genealogies: A History of Americanist Anthropology*. Lincoln: University of Nebraska Press.

———. 2003. "Review: The Lost Itinerary of Frank Hamilton Cushing. Curtis M. Hinsley and David R. Wilcox, eds." *American Anthropologist* 106, no. 4: 764–65.

Darnell, Regna Diebold, and Frederick W. Gleach. 2002. "Introduction." *Special Centennial Issue. American Anthropologist* 104, no. 2: 417–22.

Darrah, William Culp. 1951. *Powell of the Colorado*. Princeton: Princeton University Press.

Davis, E. Mott. 1992. "Effect of Pioneers on Regional Archaeology: The Texas Example." In *Rediscovering Our Past: Essays on the History of American Archaeology*, ed. Jonathan E. Reyman, 203–16. Aldershot, U.K.: Avebury.

Deacon, Desley. 1997. *Elsie Clews Parsons: Inventing Modern Life*. Chicago: University of Chicago Press.

De Laguna, Frederica, ed. 1960. *Selected Papers from the American Anthropologist, 1888–1920*. Washington DC: American Anthropological Association.

Deloria, Philip J. 1998. *Playing Indian*. New Haven: Yale University Press.

de Wit, Wim. 1993. "Building an Illusion: The Design of the World's Columbian Exposition." In *Grand Illusions: Chicago's World's Fair of 1893*, ed. Neil Harris, Wim de Wit, James Gilbert, and Robert W. Rydell, 41–98. Chicago: Chicago Historical Society.

Dexter, Ralph W. 1965a. "The 'Salem Secession' of Agassiz Zoologists." *Essex Institute Historical Collections* 101, no. 1: 27–39.

———. 1965b. "Contributions of Frederic Ward Putnam to Ohio Archaeology." *Ohio Journal of Science* 65, no. 3: 110–17.

———. 1966a. "Frederic Ward Putnam and the Development of Museums of Natural History and Anthropology in the United States." *Curator* 9, no. 2: 151–55.

———. 1966b. "Origin of the Social Science Sections of the Ohio Academy of Science." *Ohio Journal of Science* 66, no. 5: 455–58.

———. 1966c. "Putnam's Problems Popularizing Anthropology." *American Scientist* 54, no. 3: 315–32.

———. 1970. "The Role of F. W. Putnam in Founding the Field Museum." *Curator* 13, no. 1: 21–26.

———. 1977. "Contributions of Cincinnati-Area Physicians to Ohio Archeology in the Nineteenth Century." *Ohio State Medical Journal* 73, no. 6: 409–11.

———. 1978. "Guess Who's Not Coming to Dinner: Frederick Ward Putnam and the Support of Women in Anthropology." *History of Anthropology Newsletter* 5: 1.

———. 1982. "The Putnam-Metz Correspondence on Mound Explorations in Ohio." *Ohio Archaeologist* 32, no. 4: 24–28.

———. 1985. "F. W. Putnam's Naturalists' Directory and Naturalists' Agency." In *The Naturalists' Directory and Almanac (International)*, ed. Ross and Mary Arnett, 1–7. Gainesville FL: Flora and Fauna Publications.

Diamond, Irving L., and Daniel M. Olson, ed. 1991. *Letters of Gustaf Nordenskiold*. Mesa Verde National Park CO: Mesa Verde Museum Association.

Dillon, Diane. 2008. "Indians and 'Indianicity' at the 1893 World's Fair." In *George de Forest Brush: The Indian Paintings*, ed. Nancy K. Anderson, 101–29. Washington DC: National Gallery of Art, in association with Lund Humphries, Hampshire U.K.

Dilworth, Leah. 1996. *Imagining Indians in the Southwest: Persistent Visions of a Primitive Past*. Washington DC: Smithsonian Institution Press.

Dixon, Roland B. 1930. "Anthropology, 1866–1929." In *The Development of Harvard University since the Inauguration of President Eliot, 1869–1929*, ed. Samuel Eliot Morrison, 202–15. Cambridge: Harvard University Press.

Dobbs, David. 2005. *Reef Madness: Charles Darwin, Alexander Agassiz, and the Meaning of Coral*. New York: Pantheon Books.

Dodge, Richard E. 1900. Dodge to "Hyde," August 27. File 89L A3.043.2. Archives, Laboratory of Anthropology, Museum of Indian Arts and Cultures, Santa Fe.

———. 1922. Dodge to Neil M. Judd, December 15. Pueblo Bonito Correspondence, Neal Merton Judd Papers. National Anthropological Archives, Smithsonian Institution.

Dorsey, George Amos. 1900. "The Department of Anthropology of the Field Columbian Museum—A Review of Six Years." *American Anthropologist* n.s. 2: 247–65.
———. 1907a. "The Aim of a Public Museum." *Proceedings of the American Association of Museums* 1: 98–100.
———. 1907b. "The Anthropological Exhibits of the American Museum of Natural History." *Science* 25, no. 641: 584–89.
———. 1923. *Why We Behave Like Human Beings*. New York: Blue Ribbon Books.
———. 1925. "Review of *Anthropology* by A. L. Kroeber." *American Anthropologist* 27, no. 4): 558–60.
Draper, Joan E. 1989. "The White City and Its Interpreters: Historians, Critics, and the Chicago World's Columbian Exposition of 1893." In Daniel H. Burnham, *The Final Official Report of the Director of Works of the World's Columbian Exposition*, ix–xix. New York: Garland Publishing.
Dyson, Stephen L. 1999. "Brahmins and Bureaucrats: Some Reflections on the History of American Classical Archaeology." In *Assembling the Past: Studies in the Professionalization of Archaeology*, ed. Alice B. Kehoe and Mary Beth Emmerichs, 103–16. Albuquerque: University of New Mexico Press.
———. 2002. "The Archaeological Institute of America between the Wars." In *Excavating our Past: Perspectives on the History of the Archaeological Institute of America*, ed. Susan Heuck Allen, 157–68. Boston: Archaeological Institute of America.
Eakins, Thomas. 2005. *A Drawing Manual*. Edited and with an introduction by Kathleen A. Foster and an essay by Amy B. Werbel. Philadelphia: Philadelphia Museum of Art, in association with Yale University Press.
Edwards, Elizabeth. 1990. "Photographic 'Types': The Pursuit of Method." *Visual Anthropology* 3, nos. 2–3: 235–58.
Evans, Brad. 2005. *Before Cultures: The Ethnographic Imagination in American Literature, 1865–1920*. Chicago: University of Chicago Press.
Evans, Christopher. 2004. "Modelling Monuments and Excavations." In *Models: The Third Dimension of Science*, ed. Soraya de Chadarevian and Nick Hopwood, 109–37. Stanford CA: Stanford University Press.
Evans, Nancy L. 1987. "Frederick Starr: Missionary for Anthropology." Unpublished MA thesis, Department of Anthropology, Indiana University.
Evans, R. Tripp. 2004. *Romancing the Maya: Mexican Antiquity in the American Imagination 1820–1915*. Austin: University of Texas Press.
Everdell, William R. 1997. *The First Moderns*. Chicago: University of Chicago Press.
Ewers, John C. 1959. "A Century of American Indian Exhibits in the Smithsonian Institution." *Annual Report of the Smithsonian Institution for 1958*: 513–25.
———. 1978. *Murals in the Round: Painted Tipis of the Kiowa and Kiowa-Apache Indians. An Exhibition of Tipi Models Made for James Mooney of the Smithsonian Institution during his Field Studies of Indian History and Art in Southwestern Oklahoma, 1891–1904*. Washington DC: Smithsonian Institution Press.

Fagin, Nancy L. 1984. "Closed Collections and Open Appeals: The Two Anthropology Exhibits at the Chicago World's Columbian Exposition of 1893." *Curator* 27, no. 4: 249–64.

———. 1988. "The James Mooney Collection of Cheyenne Tipi Models at Field Museum of Natural History." *Plains Anthropologist* 33, no. 120: 261–78.

Fairchild, David. 1931. *Exploring for Plants*. New York: Macmillan.

Fane, Diana. 1993. "Reproducing the Pre-Columbian Past: Casts and Models in Exhibitions of Ancient America, 1824–1935." In *Collecting the Pre-Columbian Past: A Symposium at Dumbarton Oaks, 6th and 7th October 1990*, ed. Elizabeth Hill Boone, 141–76. Washington DC: Dumbarton Oaks Research Library and Collection.

Farrington, Oliver C. 1930. "A Brief History of the Field Museum from 1893 to 1930." *Field Museum News* 1–2. Chicago: Field Museum of Natural History.

Fash, Barbara W. 2004. "Cast Aside: Revisiting the Plaster Cast Collection from Mesoamerica." *Visual Resources* 20, no. 1: 3–17.

Fear-Segal, Jacqueline. 2007. *White Man's Club: Schools, Race, and the Struggle of Indian Acculturation*. Lincoln: University of Nebraska Press.

Fernlund, Kevin J. 2000. *William Henry Holmes and the Rediscovery of the American West*. Albuquerque: University of New Mexico Press.

Fewkes, J. Walter, Ales Hrdlicka, William H. Dall, James W. Gidley, Austin Hobart Clarke, William H. Holmes, Alice C. Fletcher, Walter Hough, Stansbury Hagar, Paul Bartsch, Alexander F. Chamberlain, and Roland B. Dixon. 1912. "The Problems of the Unity or Plurality and the Probable Place of Origin of the American Aborigines." *American Anthropologist* 14: 1–59.

Fitzhugh, William W. 1997. "Ambassadors in Sealskins: Exhibiting Eskimos at the Smithsonian." In *Exhibiting Dilemmas: Issues of Representation at the Smithsonian*, ed. Amy Henderson and Adrienne L. Kaeppler, 206–45. Washington DC: Smithsonian Institution Press.

Flack, James K. 1975. *Desideratum in Washington: The Intellectual Community in the Capital City, 1870–1900*. Cambridge: Schenkman Publishing Company.

Fleming, Paula Richardson, and Judith Luskey. 1986. *The North American Indians in Early Photographs*. New York: Harper and Row.

Fletcher, Alice C. 1915. *Indian Games and Dances with Native Songs*. Boston: C. C. Birchard Publishers.

Fletcher, Maurine S., ed. 1977. *The Wetherills of the Mesa Verde: Autobiography of Benjamin Alfred Wetherill*. Lincoln: University of Nebraska Press.

Flinn, John J., comp. 1893a. *Official Guide to the Midway Plaisance*. Chicago: Columbian Guide Company.

———. 1893b. *Official Guide to the World's Columbian Exposition*. Chicago: Columbian Guide Company.

Fogelson, Raymond D. 1991. "The Red Man in the White City." In *The Spanish Borderlands in Pan-American Perspective*, ed. David H. Thomas, 73–90. Columbian Consequences 3. Washington DC: Smithsonian Institution Press.

Foster, Kathleen A. 1997. *Thomas Eakins Rediscovered: Charles Bregler's Thomas Eakins Collection at the Pennsylvania Academy of the Fine Arts.* New Haven: Yale University Press; Philadelphia: Pennsylvania Academy of the Fine Arts.

Foster, Michael K. 1996. "Language and the Culture History of North America." In *Handbook of North American Indians,* 17: *Languages,* ed. Ives Goddard, 64–110. Washington DC: Smithsonian Institution Press.

Fowke, Gerard. 1910. "Antiquities of Central and Southeastern Missouri." *Bureau of American Ethnology Bulletin* no. 37. Washington DC: Government Printing Office.

Fowler, Don D. 1975. "Notes on Inquiries in Anthropology: A Bibliographic Essay." In *Toward a Science of Man: Essays in the History of Anthropology,* ed. Timothy H. Thoreson, 16–32. The Hague: Mouton.

———. 1989. *The Western Photographs of John K. Hillers: "Myself in the Water."* Washington DC: Smithsonian Institution Press.

———. 1999. "Harvard vs. Hewett: The Contest for Control of Southwestern Archaeology, 1904–1930." In *Assembling the Past: Studies in the Professionalization of Archaeology,* ed. Alice B. Kehoe and Mary Beth Emmerichs, 165–211. Albuquerque: University of New Mexico Press.

———. 2000. *A Laboratory for Anthropology: Science and Romanticism in the North American Southwest, 1846–1930.* Albuquerque: University of New Mexico Press.

Fowler, Don D., and Nancy J. Parezo. 1999. "Nomenclature and Numbers: The 'Washington Establishment' and the Definition of Americanist Anthropology." Paper delivered at Symposium on Coming of Age in Chicago: Studies in Archaeology and Anthropology at the 1893 World's Fair, Annual Meeting of the Society for American Archaeology, Chicago.

Fowler, Don D., and David R. Wilcox. 1999. "From Thomas Jefferson to the Pecos Conference: Changing Anthropological Agendas in the North American Southwest." In *Surveying the Record: North American Scientific Exploration to 1930,* ed. Edward C. Carter II, 197–224. Memoirs of the American Philosophical Society 231. Philadelphia: American Philosophical Society.

———. 2003. *Philadelphia and the Development of Americanist Archaeology.* Tuscaloosa: University of Alabama Press.

Frazar, George B. 1891. Letter to Frederic W. Putnam, December 29. Putnam, F. W.-World's Columbian Exposition—Correspondence A–Z. HUG 1717.2.12, Harvard University Archives.

Freed, Stanley A. 2012. *Anthropology Unmasked: Museums, Science, and Politics in New York City.* Volume 1: *The Putnam-Boas Era.* Wilmington OH: Orange Frazer Press.

Freed, Stanley, Ruth S. Freed, and Laila Williamson. 1988a. "American Museum's Jesup North Pacific Expedition." In *Crossroads of Continents: Cultures of Siberia and Alaska,* ed. William W. Fitzhugh and Aron Cromwell, 97–103. Washington DC: Smithsonian Institution Press.

———. 1988b. "Capitalist Philanthropy and Russian Revolutionaries: The Jesup North Pacific Expedition (1897–1902)." *American Anthropologist* 90, no. 1: 7–24.

Fuller, Henry Blake. 1893. *The Cliff-Dwellers*. New York: Harper and Brothers.
Gabriel, Kathryn, ed. 1992. *Marietta Wetherill: Reflections on Life with the Navahos in Chaco Canyon*. Boulder: Johnson Books.
Gale, Robert L. 1992. *The Gay Nineties in America: A Cultural Dictionary*. Westport CT: Greenwood Press.
Gallatin, Albert. 1845. "Notes on the Semi-Civilized Nations of Mexico, Yucatan, and Central-America." *American Ethnological Society Transactions* 1: 1–352.
———. 1848a. "Ancient Semi-Civilization of New Mexico." *American Ethnological Society Transactions* 2: iii–xcvii.
Gardner, Helen. 2008. "The Origin of Kinship in Oceania: Lewis Henry Morgan and Lorimer Fison." *Oceana*, July 1, www.thefreelibrary.com, accessed May 26, 2011.
Gay, Peter. 2008. *Modernism: The Lure of Heresy from Baudelaire to Beckett and Beyond*. New York: W. W. Norton.
Geertz, Clifford. 1973. "Religion as a Cultural System." In *The Interpretation of Cultures*, 87–125. New York: Basic Books.
Genoways, Hugh H., and Mary Anne Andrei, eds. 2008. *Museum Origins: Readings in Early Museum History and Philosophy*. Walnut Creek CA: Left Coast Press.
Gilbert, James. 1991. *Perfect Cities: Chicago's Utopias of 1893*. Chicago: University of Chicago Press.
———. 1993. On the Two Texts of the Fair. Paper presented at the Chicago Historical Society, January.
Gilbert, Paul, and Charles Lee Bryson. 1929. *Chicago and Its Makers*. Chicago: Felix Medelsohn.
Giberti, Bruno. 2002. *Designing the Centennial: A History of the 1876 International Exhibition in Philadelphia*. Lexington: University Press of Kentucky.
Gilliland, Marion Spjut. 1975. *The Material Culture of Key Marco, Florida*. Gainesville: University of Florida Press.
———. 1989. *Key Marco's Buried Treasure: Archaeology and Adventure in the Nineteenth Century*. Gainesville: University of Florida Press.
Gillmor, Frances, and Louisa Wade Wetherill. 1934. *Traders to the Navahos: The Story of the Wetherills of Kayenta*. Boston: Houghton Mifflin.
Gioia, Ted. 1997. *The History of Jazz*. New York: Oxford University Press.
Glass, Aaron. 2009. "Frozen Poses: Hamat'sa Dioramas, Recursive Representation, and the Making of a Kwakwa̱ka'wakw Icon." In *Photography, Anthropology and History: Expanding the Frame*, ed. Christopher Morton and Elizabeth Edwards, 89–116. Farnham, U.K.: Ashgate Publishing.
Gleach, Frederick W. 2007. "Cushing at Cornell: The Early Years of a Pioneering Anthropologist." *Histories of Anthropology Annual* 3: 99–120.
Glotzhober, Robert C., and Bradley T. Lepper. 1994. *Serpent Mound: Ohio's Enigmatic Effigy Mound*. Columbus: Ohio Historical Society.
Godoy, Ricardo. 1977. "Franz Boas and His Plans for an International School of American Archaeology and Ethnography in Mexico." *International Journal of the History of the Behavioral Sciences* 13: 22–42.

Goldstein, Daniel. 1994. "'Yours for Science': The Smithsonian Institution's Correspondents and the Shape of the Scientific Community in Nineteenth Century America." *Isis* 85, no. 4: 573–99.

Goode, George Brown. 1991 [1888]. "Museum-History and Museums of History." Paper read before the American Historical Association, Washington DC, 26–28 December 1888. Reprinted in *The Origins of Natural Science in America: Essays of George Brown Goode*, ed. Sally Gregory Kohlstedt, 297–319. Washington DC: Smithsonian Institution Press.

———. 1892. "First Draft of a System of Classification for the World's Columbian Exposition." In *Annual Report of the United States National Museum, Year Ending June 30, 1891*, 649–60. Washington DC: Government Printing Office.

———. 1895a. "The Principles of Museum Administration." In *Annual Report of the Museums Association of Great Britain*, 1–73. York: Coultas and Volans.

———. 1895b. "Recent Advances in Museum Method." In *Annual Report of the United States National Museum for the Year Ending June 30, 1893*, 21–58. Washington DC: Government Printing Office.

Graham, Ian. 1993. "Three Early Collectors in Mesoamerica." In *Collecting the Pre-Columbian Past: A Symposium at Dumbarton Oaks, 6th and 7th October 1990*, ed. Elizabeth Hill Boone, 49–80. Washington DC: Dumbarton Oaks Research Library and Collection.

———. 2002. *Alfred Maudslay and the Maya: A Biography*. London: British Museum; Norman: University of Oklahoma Press.

Grandin, Madame Léon. 2010. *A Parisienne in Chicago: Impressions of the World's Columbian Exposition*. Edited by Mary Beth Raycraft. Urbana: University of Illinois Press.

Grant, Madison. 1916. *The Passing of the Great Race: The Racial Basis of European History*. New York: Charles Scribner's Sons.

Green, C. H. 1893. Letter to Putnam, December 12. Putnam, F. W.-World's Columbian Exposition—Correspondence A–Z. HUG 1717.2.12, Harvard University Archives.

Green, Jesse, ed. 1979. *Zuñi: Selected Writings of Frank Hamilton Cushing*. Lincoln: University of Nebraska Press.

———. 1990. *Cushing at Zuñi. The Correspondence and Journals of Frank Hamilton Cushing, 1879–1884*. Albuquerque: University of New Mexico Press.

Green, Martin. 1979. *Dreams of Adventure, Deeds of Empire*. New York: Marboro Books.

Greenberg, Joseph H. 1987. *Language in the Americas*. Stanford: Stanford University Press.

Greenberg, Henry, and Georgia Greenberg. 1984. *Carl Gorman's World*. Albuquerque: University of New Mexico Press.

Greenberg, Joseph H., Christy H. Turner II, and Stephen Zegura. 1986. "The Settlement of the Americas." *Current Anthropology* 27: 477–97.

Greenhalgh, Paul. 1988. *Ephemeral Vistas: The Expositions Universelles, Great Exhibitions, and World's Fairs, 1851–1939*. Manchester: Manchester University Press.

Griffin, James B., David J. Meltzer, Bruce D. Smith, and William C. Sturtevant. 1988. "A Mammoth Fraud in Science." *American Antiquity* 53, no. 3: 578–82.
Griffiths, Alison. 2002. *Wondrous Difference: Cinema, Anthropology and Turn-of-the-Century Visual Culture*. New York: Columbia University Press.
Guthrie, Kimberley, and Stacy Lathrop. 2002. "The More Things Change, the More They Stay the Same." *Anthropology News* (American Anthropological Association), March: 15–16.
H. Jay Smith Exploring Company. 1893. *Catalogue of Cliff Dwellers Exhibit, World's Columbian Exposition*. Chicago: La Monte, O'Donnell and Company.
Haas, Mary. 1969. "Grammar or Lexikon? The American Indian Side of the Question from Duponceau to Powell." *International Journal of American Linguistics* 3: 239–55.
Hallowell, A. Irving. 1960. "The Beginnings of Anthropology in America." In *Selected Papers from the American Anthropologist, 1888–1920*, ed. Frederica de Laguna, 1–90. Evanston: Row, Peterson.
Hammond, George Peter, and Agipeto Rey, eds. 1953. *Don Juan de Oñate: Colonizer of New Mexico, 1595–1628*. Vol. 2. Albuquerque: University of New Mexico Press.
Handy, Moses P., ed. 1893. *The Official Directory of the World's Columbian Exposition, May 1st to October 30th, 1893. A Reference Book of Exhibitors and Exhibits; of the Officers and Members of the World's Columbian Commission*. Chicago: W. B. Conkey.
Hardacre, Emma C. 1878. "The Cliff-Dwellers." *Scribner's Monthly* 17, no. 2: 266–76.
Harper, William Hudson, ed. 1921. *Chicago: History and Forecast*. Chicago: Chicago Association of Commerce.
Harrell, David. 1987. "'We contacted Smithsonian': The Wetherills at Mesa Verde." *New Mexico Historical Review* 62, no. 3: 229–48.
———. 1992. *From Mesa Verde to the Professor's House*. Albuquerque: University of New Mexico Press.
Harris, Charles H., III, and Louis R. Sadler. 2003. *The Archaeologist Was a Spy*. Albuquerque: University of New Mexico Press.
Harris, Neil. 1978. "Museums, Merchandising, and Popular Taste: The Struggle for Influence." In *Material Culture and the Study of American Life*, ed. Ian M. G. Quimby, 140–74 New York: W. W. Norton.
———. 1983. "The Gilded Age Reconsidered Once Again." *Archives of American Art Journal* 23: 8–18.
———. 1990. *Cultural Excursions: Marketing Appetites and Cultural Tastes in Modern America*. Chicago: University of Chicago Press.
———. 1993. "Memory and the White City." In *Grand Illusions: Chicago's World's Fair of 1893*, ed. Neil Harris, Wim de Wit, James Gilbert, and Robert W. Rydell, 3–32. Chicago: Chicago Historical Society.
Harris, Neil, Wim de Wit, James Gilbert, and Robert W. Rydell, eds. 1993. *Grand Illusions: Chicago's World's Fair of 1893*. Chicago: Chicago Historical Society.

Hauptman, Laurence M. 1993. *The Iroquois in the Civil War: From Battlefield to Reservation.* Syracuse: Syracuse University Press.
Hawley, Florence. 1936. *Field Manual of Prehistoric Southwestern Pottery Types.* New Mexico Bulletin, Anthropological Series 1(4). Albuquerque: University of New Mexico Press.
Hawthorne, Julian. 1893a. *Humors of the Fair.* With illustrations by Will E. Chapin. Chicago: E. A. Weeks and Company.
———. 1893b. "Foreign Folk at the Fair." In *A World's Fair 1893: A Special Issue of Cosmopolitan Magazine*, vol. 15, no 5: 567–76, www.archive.org/stream/worldsfair 1893worl/worldsfair189300worl_djvu.txt, accessed June 9, 2011.
Hayes, Ann. 1993. "The Chicago Connection: 100 Years in the Life of the C. H. Green Collection." In *Anasazi Basketmaker: Papers from the 1990 Wetherill-Grand Gulch Symposium*, ed. Victoria M. Atkins, 121–41. Cultural Resources Series 24. Salt Lake City: United States Department of the Interior, Bureau of Land Management.
Hays, Samuel. 1959. *Conservation and the Gospel of Efficiency: The Progressive Conservation Movement, 1890–1920.* Cambridge MA: Harvard University Press.
Henderson, Palmer. 1893. "Cliff-Dwellers' Houses." *American Antiquarian* 15, no. 3: 170–73.
Hewitt, J. N. B. 1895. "James Owen Dorsey." *American Anthropologist* o.s. 8: 180–83.
Hicks, Dan. 2013. "Four-Field Anthropology: Charter Myths and Time Warps, from St. Louis to Oxford." *Current Anthropology* 54(6): 753–63.
Hieb, Louis A. 1993. "Elsie Clews Parsons in the Southwest." In *Hidden Scholars: Women Anthropologists and the Native American Southwest*, ed. Nancy J. Parezo, 63–75. Albuquerque: University of New Mexico Press.
Higinbotham, Harlow N. 1896. Letter to Frederic W. Putnam, February 17. Putnam, F. W.-General Correspondence, 1851–1947. HUG 1717.2.1, Harvard University Archives.
Hill, Errol G., and James V. Hatch. 2003. *A History of African American Theatre.* Cambridge: Cambridge University Press.
Hines, Thomas S. 1979. *Burnham of Chicago, Architect and Planner.* New York: Oxford University Press.
Hinsley, Curtis M. 1976. "Amateurs and Professionals in Washington Anthropology, 1879 to 1903." In *American Anthropology: The Early Years*, ed. John V. Murra, 36–68. Proceedings of the American Ethnological Society for 1974. New York: West Publishing.
———. 1981. *Savages and Scientists: The Smithsonian Institution and the Development of American Anthropology, 1846–1910.* Washington DC: Smithsonian Institution Press.
———. 1984. "Wanted: One Good Man to Discover Central American History." *Harvard Magazine*, November–December, 64A–H.

———. 1985. "From Shell-heaps to Stelae: Early Anthropology at the Peabody Museum." In *Objects and Others: Essays on Museums and Material Culture*, ed. George W. Stocking Jr., 49–74. Madison: University of Wisconsin Press.

———. 1986. "Edgar Lee Hewett and the School of American Research in Santa Fe, 1906–1912." In *American Archaeology Past and Future*, ed. David J. Meltzer, Don D. Fowler, and Jeremy A. Sabloff, 217–36. Washington DC: Smithsonian Institution Press.

———. 1991. "The World as Marketplace: Commodification of the Exotic at the World's Columbian Exposition, Chicago, 1893." In *Exhibiting Cultures: The Poetics and Politics of Museum Display*, ed. Ivan Karp and Steven D. Lavine, 344–65. Washington DC: Smithsonian Institution Press.

———. 1992. "The Museum Origins of Harvard Anthropology, 1866–1915." In *Science at Harvard University: Historical Perspectives*, ed. Clark A. Elliott and Margaret W. Rossiter, 121–45. Bethlehem: Lehigh University Press.

———. 1996a. "Digging for Identity: Reflections on the Cultural Background of Collecting." *American Indian Quarterly* 20: 180–96.

———. 1996b. *The Smithsonian and the American Indian: Making a Moral Anthropology in Victorian America*. Washington DC: Smithsonian Institution Press.

———. 1996c. "Strolling through the Colonies." In *Walter Benjamin and the Demands of History*, ed. Michael P. Steinberg, 119–40. Ithaca: Cornell University Press.

———. 1999. "Frederic Ward Putnam (1839–1915)." *Encyclopedia of Archaeology: The Great Archaeologists*, 1: 141–54. Santa Barbara: ABC-CLIO.

———. 2002. "Founding the AA 100 Years Ago." *Anthropology News* (American Anthropological Association), March: 13–14.

———. 2003. "Drab Doves Take Flight: The Dilemmas of Early Americanist Archaeology in Philadelphia, 1889–1900." In *Philadelphia and the Development of Americanist Archaeology*, ed. Don D. Fowler and David R. Wilcox, 1–20. Tuscaloosa: University of Alabama Press.

Hinsley, Curtis M. Jr., and Bill Holm. 1976. "A Cannibal in the National Museum: The Early Career of Franz Boas in America." *American Anthropologist* 78, no. 2: 306–16.

Hinsley, Curtis M., and David R. Wilcox, eds. 1995. *A Hemenway Portfolio: Journal of the Southwest* 37, no. 4.

———. 1996. *The Southwest in the American Imagination: The Writings of Sylvester Baxter, 1881–1889*. Tucson: University of Arizona Press.

———. 1999. "Coming of Age in Chicago: Studies in Archaeology and Anthropology at the 1893 World's Fair," symposium organized for 64th Annual Meeting of the Society for American Archaeology, Chicago, March 26.

———. 2002. *The Lost Itinerary of Frank Hamilton Cushing*. [Frank Hamilton Cushing and the Hemenway Southwestern Archaeological Expedition, 1886–1889, 2.] Tucson: University of Arizona Press.

———. n.d. a. *First Dreams, New Opportunities: Cushing's Hemenway Correspondence, 1885–1887*. [Frank Hamilton Cushing and the Hemenway Southwestern

    Archaeological Expedition, 1886–1889, 4.] Tucson: University of Arizona Press (in preparation).

———. n.d. b. *Archaeological Camping in Arizona: Comparative Fieldwork from September, 1887, to May, 1888.* [*Frank Hamilton Cushing and the Hemenway Southwestern Archaeological Expedition, 1886–1889*, 5] Tucson: University of Arizona Press. (in preparation).

Hitchcock, Ripley, ed. 1895. *The Art of the World Illustrated in the Paintings, Statuary, and Architecture of the World's Columbian Exposition.* New York: D. Appleton.

Hodge, Frederick W., ed. 1907–10. *Handbook of American Indians North of Mexico*, 2 vols. Bureau of American Ethnology Bulletin 30, Parts I–II. Washington DC: Government Printing Office.

———. 1916. *Holmes Anniversary Volume: Anthropological Essays Presented to William Henry Holmes in Honor of his Seventieth Birthday, December 1, 1916.* Washington DC: Privately Printed.

Hofmann, Charles, ed. 1968. *Frances Densmore and American Indian Music: A Memorial Volume.* Contributions from the Museum of the American Indian, Heye Foundation 23. New York: Museum of the American Indian, Heye Foundation.

Hofstader, Richard. 1944. *Social Darwinism in American Thought.* Philadelphia: University of Pennsylvania Press.

Holmes, W. H. 1878. "Report on the Ancient Ruins of Southwestern Colorado, Examined during the Summers of 1875 and 1876." In *10th Annual Report of the United States Geological and Geographical Survey of the Territories*, 383–408. Washington DC: Government Printing Office.

———. 1893. "The World's Fair Congress of Anthropology." *American Anthropologist* o.s. 6: 423–48.

———. 1895. *Archaeological Studies among the Ancient Cities of Mexico, Part I: Monuments of Yucatan.* Field Columbian Museum Publication 8. Anthropological Series 1(1). Chicago: Field Columbian Museum.

———. 1897a. *Archaeological Studies among the Ancient Cities of Mexico, Part II: Monuments of Chiapas, Oaxaca and the Valley of Mexico.* Field Columbian Museum Publication 16. Anthropological Series 1(2). Chicago: Field Columbian Museum.

———. 1897b. "Stone Implements of the Potomac-Chesapeake Tidewater Province." In *15th Annual Report of the Bureau of American Ethnology for 1893-94*, 13–152. Washington DC: Smithsonian Institution.

———. 1898. "Museum Presentation of Anthropology." *Proceedings of the American Association of Science* 47: 485–88.

———. 1902. "Classification and Arrangement of the Exhibits of an Anthropological Museum." *Science* 16: 487–504.

———. 1903. "The Exhibit of the Department of Anthropology, Report on the Exhibits of the U.S. National Museum at the Pan-American Exposition, Buffalo, New York, 1901." *Annual Report of the U.S. National Museum for 1901*: 200–218.

———. N.d. "Random Records of a Lifetime, 1846–1931." Scrapbooks, 10 vols. National Museum of American Art, Smithsonian Institution.

Holmes, William H., and Otis T. Mason. 1902. "Instructions to Collectors of Historical and Anthropological Specimens. Especially Designed for Collectors in the Insular Possessions of the United States." *U. S. National Museum Bulletin* 39, part Q.

Horowitz, Helen Lefkowitz. 1976. *Culture and the City: Cultural Philanthropy in Chicago from the 1880s to 1917.* Chicago: University of Chicago Press.

Hough, Walter. 1908. "Otis Tufton Mason." *American Anthropologist* 10: 660–67.

———. 1922. "Racial Groups and Figures in the Natural History Building of the United States National Museum." *Smithsonian Institution Annual Report for 1920*: 611–56.

Howard, Kathleen L. 2002. Creating an Enchanted Land: Curio Entrepreneurs Promote and Sell the Indian Southwest, 1880–1940. PhD dissertation, Arizona State University, Tempe.

Howe, Kathleen Stewart. 2003. "Primordial Stones: Reading Ancient Mesoamerica." In *The New World's Old World: Photographic Views of Ancient America*, ed. May Castleberry, 32–61. Albuquerque: University of New Mexico Press.

Howells, William Dean. 1961 [1894]. *Letters of an Altrurian Traveller, 1893–94.* Edited by Clara M. Kirk and Rudolf Kirk. Gainesville: Scholars' Facsimiles and Reprints.

Hoxie, Fred. 1984. *A Final Promise: The Campaign to Assimilate the Indians, 1880–1920.* Lincoln: University of Nebraska Press.

Huntington, Ellsworth. 1914. *The Climatic Factor as Illustrated in Arid America.* Carnegie Institution of Washington Publication 192. Washington DC: Carnegie Institution.

Hymes, Dell. 1961. "Alfred Louis Kroeber." *Language* 37: 1–28.

Isaac, Gwyneira. 2011. "Whose Idea Was This?: Museums, Replicas and the Reproduction of Knowledge." *Current Anthropology* 52, no. 2: 211–33.

———. 2013. "We'wha goes to Washington." In *Reassembling the Collection: Ethnographic Museums and Indigenous Agency*, ed. Rodney Harrison, Sarah Byrne, and Anne Clarke, 143–69. Santa Fe: SAR Press.

Ives, Halsey C., ed. 1893. *The Dream City: A Portfolio of Photographic Views of the World's Columbian Exposition.* St. Louis: N. D. Thompson Publishing Company.

Jacknis, Ira. 1984. "Franz Boas and Photography." *Studies in Visual Communication* 10, no. 1: 2–60.

———. 1985. "Franz Boas and Exhibits: On the Limitations of the Museum Method of Anthropology." In *Objects and Others: Essays on Museums and Material Culture*, ed. George W. Stocking Jr., 75–111. Madison: University of Wisconsin Press.

———. 1990. "James Mooney as an Ethnographic Photographer." *Visual Anthropology* 3, nos. 2–3: 179–212.

———. 1991a. "Northwest Coast Indian Culture and the World's Columbian Exposition." In *The Spanish Borderlands in Pan-American Perspective*, ed. David H. Thomas, 91–118. Washington DC: Smithsonian Institution Press.

———. 1991b. "George Hunt, Collector of Indian Specimens." In *Chiefly Feasts: The Enduring Kwakiutl Potlatch*, ed. Aldona Jonaitis, 177–226. Seattle: University of Washington Press.

———. 1996. "The Ethnographic Object and the Object of Ethnology in the Early Career of Franz Boas." In *Volksgeist as Method and Ethic: Essays on Boasian Ethnography and the German Anthropological Tradition*, ed. George W. Stocking Jr., 185–214. Madison: University of Wisconsin Press.

———. 1999. "Patrons, Potters, and Painters: Phoebe Hearst's Collections from the American Southwest." In *Collecting Native America, 1870–1960*, ed. Shepard Krech III and Barbara A. Hail, 139–71. Washington DC: Smithsonian Institution Press.

———. 2002a. "The First Boasian: Alfred Kroeber and Franz Boas, 1896–1905." *American Anthropologist* 104, no. 2: 520–32.

———. 2002b. *The Storage Box of Tradition: Kwakiutl Art, Anthropologists, and Museums, 1881–1981*. Washington DC: Smithsonian Institution Press.

———. 2008. "A New Thing?: The National Museum of the American Indian in Historical and Institutional Perspective." In *The National Museum of the American Indian: Critical Conversations*, ed. Amy Lonetree and Amanda J. Cobb, 3–42. Lincoln: University of Nebraska Press.

———. 2015. "In the Field/*En Plein Air*: The Art of Anthropological Display at the American Museum of Natural History, 1905–30." In *Anthropology of Expeditions: Travel, Visualities, After-Lives,* ed. Erin L. Hasinoff and Joshua Bell, 120–74. New York and Ann Arbor: Bard Graduate Center and the University of Michigan Press.

Jenkins, David. 1994. "Object Lessons and Ethnographic Displays: Museum Exhibitions and the Making of American Anthropology." *Comparative Studies in Society and History* 36, no. 2 (April): 242–70.

Johnson, Rossiter, ed. 1897–98. *A History of the World's Columbian Exposition, Held in Chicago in 1893*. 4 vols. New York: D. Appleton and Company.

Jonaitis, Aldona. 1992. "Franz Boas, John Swanton, and the New Haida Sculpture at the American Museum of Natural History." In *The Early Years of Native American Art History: The Politics of Scholarship and Collecting*, ed. Janet Catherine Berlo, 22–61. Seattle: University of Washington Press; Vancouver: UBC Press.

Judd, Neil M. 1920. Letter to George Pepper, April 12. Pueblo Bonito Correspondence, Neal Merton Judd Papers. National Anthropological Archives, Smithsonian Institution.

Jonnes, Jill. 2004. *Empires of Light: Edison, Tesla, Westinghouse, and the Race to Electrify the World*. New York: Random House.

Joyce, Thomas A. 1914. *An Introduction to the Archaeology of the Mexican and Mayan Civilizations of Pre-Spanish America*. New York: G. P. Putnam's Sons.

Kagan, Robert. 2007. *Dangerous Nation: America's Foreign Policy from Its Earliest Days to the Dawn of the Twentieth Century*. New York: Vintage Books.

Karlowicz, Titus M. 1970. "D. H. Burnham's Role in the Selection of Architects for the World's Columbian Exposition." *Society of Architectural Historians Journal* 29: 247–54.

Karp, Walter. 2003 [1979]. *The Politics of War: The Story of Two Wars Which Altered Forever the Political Life of the American Republic (1890–1920)*. New York: Franklin Square Press.

Kavanagh, Thomas W. 1990. "A Brief Illustrated History of the Manikins, Statues, Lay-Figures, and Life Groups Illustrating American Ethnology in the National Museum of Natural History." Manuscript no. 7502. National Anthropological Archives, Smithsonian Institution.

Kennedy, John Michael. 1969. *Philanthropy and Science in New York City: The American Museum of Natural History, 1868–1968*. Ann Arbor: University Microfilms.

Kennedy, Paul. 1987. *The Rise and Fall of the Great Powers: Economic Change and Military Conflict from 1500 to 2000*. New York: Random House.

Kessner, Thomas. 2003. *Capital City: New York City and the Men Behind America's Rise to Economic Dominance, 1860–1900*. New York: Simon and Schuster.

Kevles, Daniel J. 1995. *In the Name of Eugenics: Genetics and the Uses of Human Heredity*. Cambridge: Harvard University Press.

Kidder, A. V. 1936. "Speculations in New World Prehistory." In *Essays in Anthropology*, ed. Robert H. Lowie, 143–52. Berkeley: University of California Press.

Kidwell, Clara Sue. 1999. "Every Last Dishcloth: The Prodigious Collecting of George Gustav Heye." In *Collecting Native America, 1870–1960*, ed. Shepard Krech III and Barbara A. Hail, 232–58. Washington DC: Smithsonian Institution Press.

Kim, Kyung-Man. 1994. *Explaining Scientific Consensus: The Case of Mendelian Genetics*. New York: Guiliford Press.

Kirshenblatt-Gimblett, Barbara. 1998. "Objects of Ethnography." In *Destination Culture: Tourism, Museums, and Heritage*, 17–79. Berkeley: University of California Press.

Knell, Simon J. 2000. *The Culture of English Geology, 1815–1851*. Farnham, U.K.: Ashgate Publishing.

Knipmeyer, James. 2006. *In Search of a Lost Race: The Illustrated American Exploring Expedition*. Xlibris.com.

Kohler, Robert E. 1996 [1990]. "The Ph.D. Machine: Building on the Collegiate Base." In *Scientific Enterprise in America: Readings from Isis*, ed. Ronald L. Numbers and Charles E. Rosenberg, 98–122. Chicago: University of Chicago Press.

———. 1994. *Lords of the Fly: Drosophila Genetics and the Experimental Life*. Chicago: University of Chicago Press.

Kohlstedt, Sally Gregory. 1976. *The Formation of the American Scientific Community: The American Association for the Advancement of Science, 1848–1860*. Urbana: University of Illinois Press.

———. 1991. *The Origins of Natural Science in America: The Essays of George Brown Goode*. Washington DC: Smithsonian Institution Press.

———. 2008. "Otis T. Mason's Tour of Europe: Observation, Exchange, and Standardization in Public Museums, 1889." *Journal of Museum History* 1, no. 2: 181–207.
Kohlstedt, Sally Gregory, Michael M. Sokal, and Bruce V. Lewenstein, eds. 1999. *The Establishment of Science in America: 150 Years of the American Association for the Advancement of Science.* New Brunswick: Rutgers University Press.
Kolianos, Phyllis E., and Brent R. Weisman, eds. 2005a. *The Florida Journals of Frank Hamilton Cushing.* Gainesville: University Press of Florida.
———. 2005b. *The Lost Florida Manuscript of Frank Hamilton Cushing.* Gainesville: University Press of Florida.
Kroeber, A. L. 1909. "Classificatory Systems of Relationship." *Journal of the Royal Anthropological Institute of Great Britain and Ireland* 39: 77–84.
———. 1916. "Inheritance by Magic." *American Anthropologist* 18: 19–40.
———. 1917. "The Superorganic." *American Anthropologist* 19: 163–213.
———. 1918. "Heredity, Environment, and Civilization." *American Museum Journal* 18, no. 5: 351–59.
———. 1923. *Anthropology.* New York: Harcourt-Brace.
———. 1925a. *Handbook of the Indians of California.* Bureau of American Ethnology Bulletin no. 78. Washington DC: Government Printing Office.
———. 1925b. "Archaic Culture Horizons in the Valley of Mexico." *University of California Publications in American Archaeology and Ethnology* 17, no. 7: 373–408.
———. 1926. "Archaeological Exploration in Peru. Part I, Ancient Pottery from Trujillo." *Field Museum of Natural History Anthropological Memoirs* 2, no. 1: 1–44.
———. 1935. "History and Science in Anthropology." *American Anthropologist* 37, no. 4: 539–69.
———. 1944. *Configurations of Culture Growth.* Berkeley: University of California Press.
———. 1952. *The Nature of Culture.* Chicago: University of Chicago Press.
Kroeber, Theodora. 1970. *Alfred Kroeber: A Personal Configuration.* Berkeley: University of California Press.
Kuhn, Thomas S. 1970. *The Structure of Scientific Revolutions*, 2nd edition. Chicago: University of Chicago Press.
Kuklick, Bruce. 1993. *Puritans in Babylon: The Ancient Near East and American Intellectual Life, 1880–1930.* Princeton: Princeton University Press.
Kuklick, Henrika. 1993. *The Savage Within: The Social History of British Anthropology, 1885–1945.* Cambridge: Cambridge University Press.
Kuper, Adam. 1996. *Anthropology and Anthropologists: The Modern British School,* 3rd edition. New York: Routledge.
Kurtz, Charles M. 1893. *Official Illustrations from the Art Gallery of the World's Columbian Exposition.* Philadelphia: George Barrie.
Lacey, Michael J. 1979. The Mysteries of Earth-Making Dissolve: A Study of Washington's Intellectual Community and the Origins of American Environmentalism in the Late Nineteenth Century. PhD dissertation, George Washington University.

Lakatos, Imre, and Alan Musgrave, eds. 1970. *Criticism and the Growth of Knowledge*. Cambridge: Cambridge University Press.

Lamb, Daniel S. 1906. "The Story of the Anthropological Society of Washington." *American Anthropologist* 8: 564–79.

Lange, Charles H., and Carroll L. Riley. 1996. *The Life and Adventures of Adolph Bandelier, American Archaeologist and Scientist*. Salt Lake City: University of Utah Press.

Lange, Charles H., Carroll L. Riley, and Elizabeth M. Lange, eds. 1984. *The Southwestern Journals of Adolph F. Bandelier, 1889–1892*. Vol. 4. Albuquerque: University of New Mexico Press, and Santa Fe: School of American Research.

Lange, Patricia Fogelman. 1998. "Cultural Collecting Fever in New Mexico: Figurines and Governor L. Bradford Prince." *Journal of the Southwest* 40, no. 2: 217–42.

Larson, Erik. 2003. *The Devil in the White City: Murder, Magic, and Madness at the Fair That Changed America*. New York: Crown Publishers.

Laufer, Berthold, ed. 1906. *Boas Anniversary Volume: Anthropological Essays Presented to Franz Boas*. Lancaster PA: New Era Printing.

———. 1919. "Review of *Korean Buddhism, History—Conditions—Art: Three Lectures by Frederic Starr*." *American Anthropologist* 21, no. 1: 84–86.

Laylander, Don, ed. 2004. *Listening to the Raven: The Southern California Ethnography of Constance Goddard Dubois*. Salinas CA: Coyote Press.

Lears, T. J. Jackson. 1981. *No Place of Grace: Antimodernism and the Transformation of American Culture, 1880–1920*. New York: Pantheon Books.

Leja, Michael. 2004. *Looking Askance: Skepticism and American Art from Eakins to Duchamp*. Berkeley: University of California Press.

Lesser, Alexander. 2004. "Franz Boas." In *Totems and Teachers: Key Figures in the History of Anthropology*, ed. Sydel Silverman, 1–25. Walnut Creek: AltaMira Press.

Lewis, Arnold. 1997. *An Early Encounter with Tomorrow: Europeans, Chicago's Loop, and the World's Columbian Exposition*. Urbana: University of Illinois Press.

Lewis, David Levering. 1997. *When Harlem Was in Vogue*. New York: Penguin Books.

Lewis, Russell. 1983. "Everything Under One Roof: World's Fairs and Department Stores in Paris and Chicago." *Chicago Historical Review* 12: 29–43.

Lightman, Bernard. 2007. *Victorian Popularizers of Science: Designing Nature for New Audiences*. Chicago: University of Chicago Press.

Lister, Robert H., and Florence C. Lister. 1985. "The Wetherills: Vandals, Pothunters, or Archaeologists." In *Prehistory and History of the Southwest: Papers in Honor of Alden C. Hayes*, ed. Nancy C. Fox, 147–53. Albuquerque: Archaeological Society of New Mexico.

———. 1990. *Aztec Ruins National Monument: Administrative History of an Archaeological Preserve*. Southwest Cultural Resources Center, Professional Papers 24. Santa Fe: National Park Service.

Llorente, Tina Marie. 1996. "The World's Fairs of 1889 and 1893: Antecedents to Maya Revival Style Architecture." MA thesis, University of California, Santa Barbara.

Lockwood, Frank C. 1929. *The Life of Edward E. Ayer*. Chicago: A. C. McClurg.
Longacre, William A. 1999. "Why Did the BAE Hire an Architect?" *Journal of the Southwest* 41, no. 3: 359–69.
Longstreth, Richard. 1983. *On the Edge of the World: Four Architects in San Francisco at the Turn of the Century*. Berkeley: University of California Press.
———. 1991. *The Mall in Washington, 1791–1991*. Washington DC: National Gallery of Art.
Lovell, Margaretta M. 1996. "Picturing 'A City for a Single Summer': Paintings of the World's Columbian Exposition." *Art Bulletin* 78, no. 1: 40–55.
Low, Jean. 1977. "George Thornton Emmons." *Alaska Journal* 7, no. 1: 2–11.
Lowie, Robert H. 1920. *Primitive Society*. New York: Liveright.
———. 1933. "Report of the Editor." *American Anthropologist* 36: 278–80.
———. 1956. "Reminiscences of Anthropological Currents in America Half a Century Ago." *American Anthropologist* 58, no. 6: 995–1016.
———. 1959. *Robert H. Lowie, Ethnologist: A Personal Record*. Berkeley: University of California Press.
Lurie, Edward. 1960. *Louis Agassiz: A Life in Science*. Chicago: University of Chicago Press.
———. 1974. *Nature and the American Mind: Louis Agassiz and the Culture of Science*. New York: Science History Publications.
Lurie, Nancy O. 1966. "Women in Early American Anthropology." In *Pioneers of American Anthropology: The Uses of Biography*, ed. June Helm, 43–54. Seattle: University of Washington Press.
Lutz, Catherine A., and Jane L. Collins. 1993. *Reading National Geographic*. Chicago: University of Chicago Press.
Lyman, Stanford M. 1982. "Two Neglected Pioneers of Civilizational Analysis: Perspectives of R. Stewart Culin and Frank Hamilton Cushing." *Social Research* (Autumn): 694–729.
———. 1990. *Civilization, Contents, Discontents, Malcontents, and Other Essays in Social Theory*. Fayetteville: University of Arkansas Press.
MacDonald, George F. 1983. *Haida Monumental Art: Villages of the Queen Charlotte Islands*. Vancouver: University of British Columbia Press.
Mack, John. 2007. *The Art of Small Things*. Cambridge: Harvard University Press.
Malinowski, Bronislaw. 1922. *Argonauts of the Western Pacific*. New York: Dutton.
Mark, Joan T. 1980. *Four Anthropologists: An American Science in Its Early Years*. New York: Science History Publications.
———. 1988. *A Stranger in Her Native Land: Alice Fletcher and the American Indians*. Lincoln: University of Nebraska Press.
Martin, Geoffrey J. 1973. *Ellsworth Huntington, His Life and Thought*. Hamden CT: Archon Books.
Martinko, Whitney A. 2009. "'So Majestic a Monument of Antiquity': Landscape, Knowledge, and Authority in the Early National West." *Buildings and Landscapes* 16, no. 1: 29–61.

Mason, Otis T. 1875. *Ethnological Directions Relative to the Indian Tribes of the United States*. Washington DC: Government Printing Office.

———. 1883. "What Is Anthropology?" Washington DC: Smithsonian Saturday Lectures.

———. 1884. "The Scope and Value of Anthropological Studies." *Proceedings of the American Association for the Advancement of Science for 1884*: 365–83.

———. 1889a. Letters to George Brown Goode, August 16, 26, and 31. In "Letters from Europe. Written by Otis T. Mason to Dr. Goode and the Mason Family, July 17–Oct. 7, 1889." Smithsonian Institution Archives, Washington.

———. 1889b. Letter to Sallie Mason (wife), September 7. In "Letters from Europe. Written by Otis T. Mason to Dr. Goode and the Mason Family, July 17–Oct. 7, 1889." Smithsonian Institution Archives, Washington.

———. 1890. "Anthropology in Paris during the Exposition of 1889." *American Anthropologist* o.s. 3: 27–36.

———. 1894. "Ethnological Exhibit of the Smithsonian Institution at the World's Columbian Exposition." In *Memoirs of the International Congress of Anthropology*, ed. C. Staniland Wake, 208–16. Chicago: Schute Publishing Company.

———. 1895. "Department of Ethnology." *Annual Report of the U. S. National Museum for 1893*: 125–30.

———. 1906. Letter to Arthur P. Rice, May 18. Otis T. Mason Papers, National Anthropological Archives.

Mathews, Nancy Mowll, Charles Musser, and Marta Braun, eds. 2005. *Moving Pictures: American Art and Early Film, 1880–1910*. Manchester VT: Hudson Hills Press, with Williams College Museum of Art.

Matthews, Washington, Jacob L. Wortman, and John S. Billings. 1893. Human Bones in the Hemenway Collection in the U. S. Army Medical Museum. *Memoirs of the National Academy of Sciences* 6: 141–286.

Maudslay, Alfred P. 1893. "Paper Mouldings of Monuments or 'Squeezes.'" In *Hints to Travellers, Scientific and General*, ed. Douglas W. Freshfield and W. J. L. Wharton, 7th edition, revised and enlarged, 455–60. London: Royal Geographical Society.

May, Henry. 1994 [1959]. *The End of American Innocence*. Chicago: Quadrangle Books.

Mayer, Henry. 1998. *All on Fire: William Lloyd Garrison and the Abolition of Slavery*. New York: St. Martin's Press.

McCarthy, Kathleen D. 1982. *Noblesse Oblige: Charity and Cultural Philanthropy in Chicago, 1849–1929*. Chicago: University of Chicago Press.

McCusick, Marshall. 1991. *The Davenport Conspiracy Revisited*. Ames: Iowa State University Press.

McFeely, Eliza. 2001. *Zuni and the American Imagination*. New York: Hill and Wang.

McGee, W. J. 1888. Letter to Eugene W. Hilgard, July 17. W. J. McGee Papers, Library of Congress.

———. 1893. "Anthropology at the Madison Meeting." *American Anthropologist* o.s. 6: 435–48.

———. 1895. "Robert Henry Lamborn: Obituary." *American Anthropologist* o.s. 5(8): 175–76.

———. 1896. "Review of W. H. Holmes, *Archaeological Studies among the Ancient Cities of Mexico*." *American Anthropologist* o.s. 9: 137–40.

McNitt, Frank. 1957. *Richard Wetherill, Anasazi: Pioneer Explorer of Southwestern Ruins.* Albuquerque: University of New Mexico Press.

———. 1962. *Indian Traders.* Norman: University of Oklahoma Press.

———. 1966. *Richard Wetherill, Anasazi.* Albuquerque: University of New Mexico Press.

McVicker, Donald. 1986. "Frederick Starr and the Walker Museum." *Council for Museum Anthropology Newsletter* 10, no. 1: 6–14.

———. 1989. "Parallels and Rivalries: Encounters between Boas and Starr." *Curator* 32, no. 3: 212–28.

———. 1992a. "The Matter of Saville: Franz Boas and the Anthropological Definition of Archaeology." In *Rediscovering Our Past: Essays on the History of American Archaeology*, ed. J. E. Reyman, 145–59. Aldershot, U.K.: Avebury.

———. 1992b. "The Field Museum Collections from Mexico." In *México la Vision del Cosmos: Three Thousand Years of Creativity*, ed. Donald McVicker, 65–70. Chicago: Mexican Fine Arts Center Museum.

———. 1999. "Buying a Curator: Establishing Anthropology at Field Columbian Museum." In *Assembling the Past: Studies in the Professionalization of Archaeology*, ed. Alice B. Kehoe and Mary Beth Emmerichs, 37–52. Albuquerque: University of New Mexico Press.

———. 2003. "A Tale of Two Thompsons: The Contributions of Edward H. Thompson and J. Eric S. Thompson to Anthropology at the Field Museum." In *Curators, Collections and Contexts: Anthropology at the Field Museum, 1893–2002*, ed. Stephen E. Nash and Gary M. Feinman, 139–52. Fieldiana: Publication no. 1525, Anthropology New Series no. 36. Chicago: Field Museum of Natural History.

———. 2004. "All the King's Horsemen and All the King's Men: Putting Old Collections Together Again." *Museum Anthropology* 27, nos. 1–2: 49–62.

———. 2007. "Elephant Pipes and Israelite Tablets: The Controversy between the United States Bureau of Ethnology and the Davenport Academy of Natural Sciences." *Bulletin of the History of Archaeology* 17, no. 1: 9–17.

———. 2012. *Frederick Starr: Popularizer of Anthropology, Public Intellectual, and Genuine Eccentric.* Lanham MD: AltaMira Press.

McVicker, Mary F. 2005. *Adela Breton: A Victorian Artist amid Mexico's Ruins.* Albuquerque: University of New Mexico Press.

Meltzer, David J. 1993. *Search for the First Americans.* Washington DC: Smithsonian Institution.

———. 2003. "In the Heat of Controversy: C. C. Abbott, the American Paleolithic, and the University Museum, 1889–1893." In *Philadelphia and the Development* of *Americanist Archaeology*, ed. Don D. Fowler and David R. Wilcox, 48–87. Tuscaloosa: University of Alabama Press.

———. 2009. *First Peoples in a New World: Colonizing Ice Age America*. Berkeley: University of California Press.

———. 2010. "When Destiny Takes a Turn for the Worse: William Henry Holmes and, Incidentally, Franz Boas in Chicago, 1892–97." *Histories of Anthropology* 6: 171–224.

Meltzer, David J., and Robert C. Dunnell, eds. 1992. *The Archaeology of William Henry Holmes*. Washington DC: Smithsonian Institution Press.

Menand, Louis. 2001. *The Metaphysical Club: A Story of Ideas in America*. New York: Farrar, Straus and Giroux.

Merriam, C. Hart. 1930. Letter, August 29. *American Anthropologist* 33 [1931]: 104.

Metz, Charles L. 1884a. Letter to Frederic W. Putnam, March 18. Peabody Museum Papers, Harvard University Archives.

———. 1884b. Letter to Frederic W. Putnam, August 26. Peabody Museum Papers, Harvard University Archives.

Michaelson, Scott. 1999. *The Limits of Multiculturalism*. Minneapolis: University of Minnesota Press.

Milanich, Jerald T. 2001. "A Peek at the Past." *Archaeology* 54, no. 5: 38–39.

Militello, Theresa. 2009. "Horatio Nelson Rust and His Contributions to American Archaeology." *Pacific Coast Archaeological Quarterly* 41(1): 1ff.

Miller, Darlis A. 2007. *Matilda Coxe Stevenson, Pioneering Anthropologist*. Norman: University of Oklahoma Press.

Miller, Donald L. 1996. *City of the Century: The Epic of Chicago and the Making of America*. New York: Touchstone–Simon and Schuster.

Minton, Maurice K. 1890. Letter to Warren K. Moorehead, December 22. Warren K. Moorehead Papers, Correspondence, 1885–1908, box 4–8. MSS 106. Ohio State Historical Society, Columbus.

———. 1891. Letter to Frederic W. Putnam, December 28. Putnam, F. W.-General Correspondence, 1851–1947. HUG 1717.2.1, Harvard University Archives.

———. 1892. Letter to Warren K. Moorehead, March 12. Warren K. Moorehead Papers, Correspondence, 1885–1908, box 4–8. MSS 106. Ohio State Historical Society, Columbus.

Modell, Judith Schachter. 1983. *Ruth Benedict: Patterns of a Life*. Philadelphia: University of Pennsylvania Press.

Mooney, James A. 1893. "Indian Bread Makers." Unprovenienced newspaper clipping, May 26. Newspaper clippings, Frank Hamilton Cushing Collection, Braun Research Library, Southwest Museum, Los Angeles.

———. 1894. Outline Plan for Ethnologic Museum Collections. Manuscript, file no. 4788. Smithsonian Institution, National Anthropological Archives.

———. 1896. *The Ghost-Dance Religion and the Sioux Outbreak of 1890*. Annual Report of the Bureau of Ethnology for 1893, part 2. Washington DC: Government Printing Office.

———. 2013. *In Sun's Likeness and Power: Cheyenne Accounts of Shield and Tipi Heraldry*. Transcribed and edited by Father Peter J. Powell. 2 vols. Lincoln: University of Nebraska Press.

Moore, Charles. 1913. "Lessons of the Chicago World's Fair: An Interview with the Late Daniel H. Burnham." *Architectural Record* 33: 35–44.

———. 1921. *Daniel H. Burnham: Architect, Planner of Cities*. Boston: Houghton Mifflin.

Moorehead, Warren K. 1884. "Ancient Fortifications near Granville, Ohio." *Young Mineralogist and Antiquarian* 1: 72.

———. 1890. *Wanneta, the Sioux*. New York: Dodd, Mead.

———. 1891. Diary vol. XXII, September 4. Warren K. Moorehead Papers, Journals etc., box 20. MSS 106. Ohio State Historical Society, Columbus.

———. 1892a. Diary Vol. XXII, March 16. Warren K. Moorehead Papers, Journals etc., box 20. MSS 106. Ohio State Historical Society, Columbus.

———. 1892b. Diary Vol. XXII, March 23. Warren K. Moorehead Papers, Journals etc., box 20. MSS 106. Ohio State Historical Society, Columbus.

———. 1892c. Diary vol. XXII, May 17. Warren K. Moorehead Papers, Journals etc., box 20. MSS 106. Ohio State Historical Society, Columbus.

———. 1892d. Diary vol. XXII, May 25. Warren K. Moorehead Papers, Journals etc., box 20. MSS 106. Ohio State Historical Society, Columbus.

———. 1892e. Letter to Frederic W. Putnam, April 4. Warren K. Moorehead Papers, Correspondence, 1885–1908, box 4–8. MSS 106. Ohio State Historical Society, Columbus.

———. 1892f. Diary vol. XXII, June 3. Warren K. Moorehead Papers, Journals etc., box 20. MSS 106. Ohio State Historical Society, Columbus.

———. 1892g. Diary vol. XXII, May 2. Warren K. Moorehead Papers, Journals etc., box 20. MSS 106. Ohio State Historical Society, Columbus.

———. 1893a. Diary vol. XXII, May 5. Warren K. Moorehead Papers, Journals etc., box 20. MSS 106. Ohio State Historical Society, Columbus.

———. 1893b. Diary vol. XXII, September 14. Warren K. Moorehead Papers, Journals etc., box 20. MSS 106. Ohio State Historical Society, Columbus.

———. 1893c. Diary vol. XXII, May 8. Warren K. Moorehead Papers, Journals etc., box 20. MSS 106. Ohio State Historical Society, Columbus.

———. 1893d. Diary vol. XXII, July 24. Warren K. Moorehead Papers, Journals etc., box 20. MSS 106. Ohio State Historical Society, Columbus.

———. 1893e. Letter to "the Attorney General, World's Columbian Exposition, Chicago," November 4. Warren K. Moorehead Papers, Correspondence 1885–1908, box 4–8. MSS 106. Ohio State Historical Society, Columbus.

———. 1897a. Letter to Robert S. Peabody, May 4. Warren K. Moorehead Papers, Correspondence 1885–1908, box 4–8. MSS 106. Ohio State Historical Society, Columbus.

———. 1897b. Letter to Robert S. Peabody, May 18. Warren K. Moorehead Papers, Correspondence 1885–1908, box 4–8. MSS 106. Ohio State Historical Society, Columbus.

———. 1897c. Letter to Peabody, June 11. Warren K. Moorehead Papers, Correspondence 1885–1908, box 4–8. MSS 106. Ohio State Historical Society, Columbus.

———. 1898. Diary Vol. XXII Dec. 28. Warren K. Moorehead Papers, Journals etc., box 20. MSS 106. Ohio State Historical Society, Columbus.

———. 1903–4. "The Field Diary of a Archaeological Collector." *American Inventor* March 1903–April 1904.

———. 1906a. "A Brief Account of the Founding of the Department of Archaeology at Phillips Academy." *Department of Archaeology Bulletin* (Phillips Academy, Andover), vol. 3: 17–25.

———. 1906b. "A Narrative of Explorations in New Mexico, Arizona, Indiana, etc." *Department of Archaeology Bulletin* (Phillips Academy, Andover), vol. 3: 30–199.

———. 1922. *The Hopewell Mound Group of Ohio*. Field Museum of Natural History Publication 211. Anthropological Series 6, no. 5. Chicago: Field Museum.

Morgan, Lewis H. 1877. *Ancient Society, or, Researches in the lines of Human Progress from Savagery through Barbarism to Civilization*. New York: Henry Holt.

———. 1881. *Houses and House-Life of the American Aborigines*. Contributions to North American Ethnology 4. Washington DC: U. S. Geological Survey.

Morgan, Thomas J. 1892. Notes of a Meeting with F. W. Putnam and Alice C. Fletcher regarding Indian Office Exhibit. January 30. F. W. Putnam Papers, box 34, Harvard University Archives.

Morris, Charles R. 2005. *The Tycoons; How Andrew Carnegie, John D. Rockefeller, Jay Gould, and J. P. Morgan Invented the American Supereconomy*. New York: Henry Holt.

Moses, L. G. 1984. *The Indian Man: A Biography of James Mooney*. Urbana: University of Illinois Press.

———. 1996. *Wild West Shows and the Images of American Indians, 1883–1939*. Albuquerque: University of New Mexico Press.

Mullins, Nicholas C. 1973. *Theories and Theory Groups in Contemporary American Sociology*. New York: Harper and Row.

Munro, Jane. 2014. *Silent Partners: Artist and Mannequin from Function to Fetish*. Cambridge, U. K: Fitzwilliam Museum, and New Haven: Yale University Press.

Munson, Marit K., ed. 2007. *Kenneth Chapman's Santa Fe: Artists and Archaeologists, 1907–1931*. Santa Fe: School for Advanced Research.

Murphy, Robert F. 1972. *Robert H. Lowie*. New York: Columbia University Press.

Murphey, Stephen O. 1993. *Theory Groups and the Study of Language in North America*. Amsterdam: John Benjamins.

Nabokov, Peter. 1989. "Introduction." *A Study of Pueblo Architecture in Tusayan and Cibola*, by Victor Mindeleff, ix–xli. Classics of Smithsonian Anthropology. Washington DC: Smithsonian Institution Press.

Nash, Stephen E., and Gary M. Feinman, eds. 2003. *Curators, Collections, and Contexts: Anthropology at the Field Museum, 1893-2002*. Fieldiana: Publication no. 1525, Anthropology New Series no. 36. Chicago: Field Museum of Natural History.

Newcomb, Franc Johnson. 1964. *Hosteen Klah, Navaho Medicine Man and Sand Painter*. Norman: University of Oklahoma Press.

Nisbet, Robert. 1992. *Teachers and Scholars, A Memoir of Berkeley in Depression and War*. New Brunswick: Transaction Publishers.

Nye, David E. 1990. *Electrifying America: Social Meanings of a New Technology, 1880-1940*. Cambridge: MIT Press.

O'Brien, Michael J. 1996. *Paradigms of the Past: The Story of Missouri Archaeology*. Columbia, Missouri: University of Missouri Press.

O'Brien, Michael J., and R. Lee Lyman. 2001. "The National Research Council and Midwestern Archaeology: The St. Louis Meeting of 1929." *Missouri Archaeologist* 62: 107–37.

Orvell, Miles. 1989. *The Real Thing: Imitation and Authenticity in American Culture, 1880-1940*. Chapel Hill: University of North Carolina Press.

Parezo, Nancy J. 1987. "The Formation of Ethnographic Collections: The Smithsonian Institution in the American Southwest." *Advances in Archaeological Method and Theory* (Orlando: Academic Press), vol. 10: 1–47.

———. 1993. *Hidden Scholars: Women Anthropologists and the Native American Southwest*. Albuquerque: University of New Mexico Press.

Parezo, Nancy J., and Don D. Fowler. 2007. *Anthropology Goes to the Fair: The 1904 Louisiana Purchase Exposition*. Lincoln: University of Nebraska Press.

Parmenter, Ross. 1966. "Glimpses of a Friendship: Zelia Nuttall and Franz Boas." In *Pioneers of American Anthropology: The Uses of Biography*, ed. June Helm, 83–148. Seattle: University of Washington Press.

Parr, Albert E. 1959. "The Habitat Group." *Curator* 2: 107–28.

Patterson, Michelle Wick. 2010. *Natalie Curtis Burlin: A Life in Native and African American Music*. Lincoln: University of Nebraska Press.

Pauly, Philip J. 1994. "Modernist Practice in American Biology." In *Modernist Impulses in the Human Sciences, 1870-1930*, ed. Dorothy Ross, 272–89. Baltimore: Johns Hopkins University Press.

———. 2000. *Biologists and the Promise of American Life: From Meriwether Lewis to Alfred Kinsey*. Princeton: Princeton University Press.

Peabody, Robert S. 1897. Letter to Warren K. Moorehead, May 12. Warren K. Moorehead Papers, Correspondence 1885–1908, box 4–8. MSS 106. Ohio State Historical Society, Columbus.

Peabody, Selim H. 1896. Letter to Frederic W. Putnam, January 14. Putnam, F. W.-World's Columbian Exposition—Correspondence A–Z. HUG 1717.2.12, Harvard University Archives.

Peabody, Selim, and Stanley Wood, ed. 1894. *The White City (As It Was): The Story of the World's Columbian Exposition. Illustrated by a Series of Eighty Perfect Pictures from Photographs by W. H. Jackson*. Chicago: White City Art Company. No pagination.

Peet, Stephen D. 1896. Letter to Frederic W. Putnam, February 17. Putnam, F. W.- General Correspondence, 1851–1947. HUG 1717.2.1, Harvard University Archives.

Phillips, Ann. 1993. "Archaeological Expeditions into Southeastern Utah and Southwestern Colorado between 1888 and 1898 and the Dispersal of the Collections." In *Anasazi Basketmaker: Papers from the 1990 Wetherill-Grand Gulch Symposium*, ed. Victoria M. Atkins, 103–18. Cultural Resources Series 24. Salt Lake City: United States Department of the Interior, Bureau of Land Management.

Pillsbury, Joanne, ed. 2012. *Past Presented: Archaeological Illustration and the Ancient Americas*. Washington DC: Dumbarton Oaks Research Library and Collections.

Pinsky, Valerie. 1992. "Archaeology, Politics, and Boundary Formation: The Boas Censure (1919) and the Development of American Archaeology during the Inter-War Years." In *Rediscovering Our Past: Essays on the History of American Archaeology*, ed. Jonathan E. Reyman, 161–90. Aldershot, U.K.: Avebury.

Plummer, E. H. 1893. Letter to F. W. Putnam, September 2. F. W. Putnam Papers, box 34, Harvard University Archives.

Poole, Robert M. 2004. *Explorer's House: National Geographic and the World It Made*. New York: Penguin Press.

Powell, John Wesley. 1882–83. "Human Evolution." *Transactions of the Anthropological Society of Washington* 2: 176–208.

———. 1883. "Introductory." Bureau of Ethnology *Second Annual Report (1880–1881)*: xxvii, xxx–xxxiii. Washington DC: Government Printing Office.

———. 1890a. "Prehistoric Man in America. *Forum* 8: 489–503.

———. 1890b. "Problems of American Archaeology." *Forum* 8: 638–52.

Prudden, T. Michell. 1906. *On the Great American Plateau: Wanderings Among Canyons and Buttes, in the Land of the Cliff-Dweller, and the Indian of To-Day*. New York: G. P. Putnam's.

Putnam, Frederic W. 1879. "Introduction." *Reports upon Archaeological and Ethnological Collections from Vicinity of Santa Barbara, California, and from Ruined Pueblos of Arizona and New Mexico, and Certain Interior Tribes*. Report of the United States Geographical Surveys West of the One Hundredth Meridian. Vol. VII.: Archaeology. 1–21, 317–19. Washington DC: Government Printing Office:,

———. 1882. Letter to Charles L. Metz, September 13. Charles Metz Papers, Cincinnati Historical Society.

———. 1887. "Obituary of Miss Cordelia A. Studley." *Proceedings of the Boston Society of Natural History* 23: 419–20.

———. 1890. "American Ethnology: An Interesting Suggestion for the Columbian Exposition." *Chicago Tribune*, May 30: p. 12, col. 1.

———. 1891a. Letter to Warren K. Moorehead, March 18. Warren K. Moorehead Papers, Correspondence 1885–1908, box 4–8. MSS 106. Ohio State Historical Society, Columbus

———. 1891b. Letter to Conrad Viets, April 9. Putnam, F. W.-General Correspondence, 1851–1947. HUG 1717.2.1, Harvard University Archives.

———. 1891c. Letter to Cornelius C. Cusick, June 13. F. W. Putnam Papers, box 31, Harvard University Archives.

———. 1891d. Monthly Report to the Director-General for June. July 4. F. W. Putnam Papers, box 34, Harvard University Archives.

———. 1891e. Letter to Cornelius C. Cusick, July 20. F. W. Putnam Papers, box 31, Harvard University Archives.

———. 1891f. Letter to Cornelius C. Cusick, July 29. F. W. Putnam Papers, box 31, Harvard University Archives.

———. 1891g. Monthly Report to the Director-General for July. August 5. F. W. Putnam Papers, box 34, Harvard University Archives.

———. 1891h. Draft of speech to Committee on the Liberal Arts, September 21. F. W. Putnam Papers, Harvard University Archives.

———. 1891i. Monthly Report to the Director-General for September. October 14. F. W. Putnam Papers, box 34, Harvard University Archives.

———. 1891j. Letter to William E. Curtis, October 17. F. W. Putnam Papers, box 34, Harvard University Archives.

———. 1891k. The Columbus Memorial Museum [Commercial Club Address]. November 28. Typescript. F. W. Putnam File, Field Museum Archives.

———. 1891l. Monthly Report to the Director-General for November (n.d.). F. W. Putnam Papers, box 34, Harvard University Archives.

———. 1892a. Monthly Report to the Director-General for November. December 8. F. W. Putnam Papers, box 34, Harvard University Archives.

———. 1892b. Monthly Report to the Director-General for August. September 8. F. W. Putnam Papers, box 34, Harvard University Archives.

———. 1892c. Letter to Antonio Apache, May 13. F. W. Putnam Papers, box 31, Harvard University Archives.

———. 1892d. Letter to Antonio Apache, August 4. F. W. Putnam Papers, box 31, Harvard University Archives.

———. 1892e. Monthly Report to the Director-General for January. February 8. F. W. Putnam Papers, box 34, Harvard University Archives.

———. 1892f. Monthly Report to the Director-General for June. July 1. F. W. Putnam Papers, box 34, Harvard University Archives.

———. 1892g. Monthly Report to the Director-General for July. August 9. F. W. Putnam Papers, box 34, Harvard University Archives.

———. 1892h. Letter to Moorehead, May 24. Warren K. Moorehead Papers, Correspondence 1885–1908, box 4–8. MSS 106. Ohio State Historical Society, Columbus.

———. 1893a. Letter, April 17. *Essex Institute Historical Collections* 30: 186–89.

———. 1893b. "Ethnology, Anthropology, Archaeology." In *The World's Columbian Exposition*, ed. Trumbull White and William Igleheart, 415–22. Philadelphia: International Publishing Company.

———. 1893c. Letter to Selim H. Peabody, October 9. Putnam File, Field Museum Archives.

———. 1893d. Monthly Report to the Director-General for September. October 5. F. W. Putnam Papers, box 34, Harvard University Archives.

———. 1893e. Monthly Report to the Director-General for December, 1892. January 5. F. W. Putnam Papers, box 34, Harvard University Archives.

———. 1893f. Letter to Charles L. Hutchinson, October 3. F. W. Putnam Papers, box 31, Harvard University Archives.

———. 1893g. Letter to Jesse W. Fewkes. April 3. F. W. Putnam Papers, box 31, F. W. Putnam Papers, Harvard University Archives.

———. 1893h. "Ethnology, Anthropology, Archaeology." In *The World's Columbian Exposition, Chicago, 1893: A Complete History of the Enterprise*, ed. Trumbull White and William Igleheart, 423–35. Philadelphia: International Publishing Company.

———. 1893i. Letter to Daniel M. Browning, September 29. F. W. Putnam Papers, box 34, Harvard University Archives.

———. 1893j. Monthly Report to the Director-General for June, 1893. July 1. F. W. Putnam Papers, box 34, Harvard University Archives.

———. 1893k. Monthly Report to the Director-General for August, 1893. September 1. F. W. Putnam Papers, box 34, Harvard University Archives.

———. 1893l. Letter to Daniel M. Browning. August 25. F. W. Putnam Papers, box 34, Harvard University Archives.

———. 1893m. Letter to Edward Brown, December (n.d.). F. W. Putnam Papers, box 31, Harvard University Archives.

———. 1893n. Letter to Edward E. Ayer, December 31. F. W. Putnam Papers, box 34, Harvard University Archives.

———. 1893o. Letter to George Davis, March (n.d.). Putnam Papers, box 35, Harvard University Archives.

———. 1893p. Letter to Green, December 2. Putnam, F. W.-World's Columbian Exposition—Correspondence A–Z. HUG 1717.2.12, Harvard University Archives.

———. 1893q. Letter to Peabody, October 9. Putnam, F. W.-World's Columbian Exposition—Correspondence A–Z. HUG 1717.2.12, Harvard University Archives.

———. 1893r. Letter to W. H. Holcomb, June 23. Putnam, F. W.-World's Columbian Exposition—Correspondence A–Z. HUG 1717.2.12, Harvard University Archives.

———. 1893s. Letter to E. H. Plummer, December 1. Putnam, F. W.-World's Columbian Exposition—Correspondence A–Z. HUG 1717.2.12, Harvard University Archives.

———. 1893t. Letter to Charles W. Eliot, October 15. F. W. Putnam Papers, box 34, Harvard University Archives.

———. 1894. Letter to Samuel A. Crawford. March 7. Boas Papers, American Philosophical Society.

———. 1894a. Letter to Edward H. Thompson, May 19. F. W. Putnam Papers, box 31, Harvard University Archives.

———. 1894b. Letter to Boas, March 7. Putnam, F. W.–General Correspondence, 1851–1947. HUG 1717.2.1, Harvard University Archives.

———. 1895. Letter to Adolph Bandelier, February 18. Ralph W. Dexter Papers, Kent State University Archives, Kent, Ohio.

———. 1896. Letter to Francis C. Lowell, January 7. Putnam, F. W.–General Correspondence, 1851–1947. HUG 1717.2.1, Harvard University Archives.

———. 1897. Letter to Charles W. Eliot, December 31. Charles W. Eliot Papers, box 118, Harvard University Archives.

———. 1898. Letter to Charles W. Eliot, June 22. Charles W. Eliot Papers, Harvard University Archives.

———. 1901. "A Problem in American Anthropology." *Annual Report of the Smithsonian Institution for 1899*, 473–86. Washington DC: Government Printing Office.

———. 1907. Letter to Clark, February 23. Putnam, F. W.–General Correspondence, 1851–1947. HUG 1717.2.1, Harvard University Archives.

Qureshi, Sadiah. 2011. *Peoples on Parade: Exhibitions, Empire, and Anthropology in Nineteenth-Century Britain*. Chicago: University of Chicago Press.

Radcliffe-Brown, A. R. 1923. "Methods of Ethnology and Social Anthropology." *South African Journal of Science* 20:124–47.

Raibmon, Paige. 2005. *Authentic Indians: Episodes of Encounter from the Late Nineteenth-Century Northwest Coast*. Durham: Duke University Press.

Rainger, Ronald. 1991. *An Agenda for Antiquity: Henry Fairfield Osborn and Vertebrate Paleontology at the American Museum of Natural History, 1890–1935*. Tuscaloosa: University of Alabama Press.

Ralph, Julian. 1893. *Harper's Chicago and the World's Fair: The Chapters on the Exposition Being Collated from Official Sources and Approved by the Department of Publicity and Promotion of the World's Columbian Exposition*. New York: Harper and Brothers Publishers.

Recchiuti, John Louis. 2007. *Civic Engagement: Social Science and Progressive-Era Reform in New York City*. Philadelphia: University of Pennsylvania Press.

Reed, Christopher Robert. 2000. *"All The World Is Here!" The Black Presence at White City*. Bloomington: Indiana University Press.

Reinelt, Janelle G., and Joseph R. Roach, eds. 1992. *Critical Theory and Performance*. Ann Arbor: University of Michigan Press.

Reingold, Nathan. 1991 [1976]. "Definitions and Speculations: The Professionalization of Science in America in the Nineteenth Century." In *Science, American Style*, ed. Nathan Reingold. New Brunswick: Rutgers University Press.

Rivers, W. H. R. 1914. *Kinship and Social Organization*. London: Constable.
Robertson, Imogene C. S., and A. Edmere Cabana Barcellona. 1939. *Seventy-Five Years: A History of the Buffalo Society of Natural Sciences, 1861–1936*. Buffalo Society of Natural Sciences Bulletin 18.
Rohde, Joy Elizabeth. 2004. "It Was No 'Pink Tea': Gender and American Anthropology, 1885–1903." In *Significant Others: Interpersonal and Professional Commitments in Anthropology*, ed. Richard Handler, 261–90. History of Anthropology 10. Madison: University of Wisconsin Press.
Roscoe, Will. 1988. "We'wha and Klah: The American Indian Berdache as Artist and Priest." *American Indian Quarterly* 12, no. 2: 127–50.
———. 1991. *The Zuni Man-Woman*. Albuquerque: University of New Mexico Press.
Rosenberg, Chaim M. 2008. *America at the Fair: Chicago's 1893 World's Columbian Exposition*. Charleston: Arcadia Publishing.
Rosenberg, Charles E. 1996 [1983]. "Science in American Society: A Generation of Historical Debate, with Headnote and Afterword." In *The Scientific Enterprise in America: Readings from Isis*, ed. Ronald L. Numbers and Charles E. Rosenberg, 123–40. Chicago: University of Chicago Press.
———. 1997 [1976]. *No Other Gods: On Science and American Social Thought*. Revised and expanded edition. Baltimore: Johns Hopkins University Press.
Rosenzweig, Phyllis. 1977. *The Thomas Eakins Collection of the Hirschhorn Museum and Sculpture Garden*. Washington DC: Smithsonian Institution Press.
Rossiter, Margaret W. 1996 [1980]. "'Women's Work' in Science, 1880–1910." In *The Scientific Enterprise in America: Readings from Isis*, ed. Ronald L. Numbers and Charles E. Rosenberg, 2–20. Chicago: University of Chicago Press.
———. 1982. *Women Scientists in America: Struggles and Strategies to 1940*. Baltimore: John Hopkins University Press.
Roth, Walter. 2000. "Sol Bloom, the Music Man." *Chicago Jewish History* 24, no. 3: 4–7.
Rowe, John Howland. 1962. "Alfred Louis Kroeber, 1976–1960." *American Antiquity* 27, no. 3: 395–415.
Ruhlen, Merritt. 1991. "The Amerind Phylum and the Prehistory of the New World." In *Sprung from Some Common Source: Investigations into the Prehistory of Languages*, ed. Sydney M. Lamb and E. Douglas Mitchell, 328–50. Stanford: Stanford University Press.
Russell, Frank. 1901. Letter to W. J. McGee, March 4. Bureau of American Ethnology Papers, Letters Received. National Anthropological Archives, Smithsonian Institution.
Russell, Teresa. 1903. Letter to William H. Holmes, December 3. Bureau of American Ethnology Papers, Letters Received. National Anthropological Archives, Smithsonian Institution.
Rydell, Robert W. 1984. *All the World's a Fair: Visions of Empire at American International Expositions, 1876–1916*. Chicago: University of Chicago Press.
———. 1993. "A Cultural Frankenstein? The Chicago World's Columbian Exposition of 1893." In *Grand Illusions: Chicago's World's Fair of 1893*, ed. Neil Harris,

Wim de Wit, James Gilbert, and Robert W. Rydell, 143–70. Chicago: Chicago Historical Society.

———. 1999. "'Darkest Africa': African Shows at America's World's Fairs." In *Africans on Stage: Studies in Ethnological Show Business*, ed. Bernth Lindfors, 135–55. Bloomington: Indiana University Press.

———. 2006. "World's Fairs and Museums." In *A Companion to Museum Studies*, ed. Sharon Macdonald, 135–51. Malden MA: Blackwell.

Rydell, Robert W., and Rob Kroes. 2005. *Buffalo Bill in Bologna: The Americanization of the World, 1869–1922*. Chicago: University of Chicago Press.

Salisbury, Stephen. 1875. Letter to Robert C. Winthrop, February 12. Salisbury Family Papers, American Antiquarian Society, Worcester, Massachusetts.

Sandberg, Mark B. 2003. *Living Pictures, Missing Persons: Mannequins, Museums, and Modernity*. Princeton: Princeton University Press.

Sapir, Edward. 1916. *Time Perspective in Aboriginal American Culture: A Study in Method*. Ottawa: Government Printing Bureau.

———. 1925. "Sound Patterns in Language." *Language* 1:37–51.

Saville, Marshall. 1894. Letter to Putnam, September 10. Putnam, F. W.-General Correspondence, 1851–1947. HUG 1717.2.1, Harvard University Archives.

Schaffer, Kristen. 2010. "'The Beautiful and Useful Laws of God': Burnham's Swedenborgianism and the *Plan of Chicago*." *Planning Perspectives* 25, no. 2: 243–52.

Schaffer, Kristen, Scott J. Tilden, and Paul Rocheleau. 2003. *Daniel H. Burnham: Visionary Architect and Planner*. New York: Rizzoli.

Scharnhorst, Gary. 2008. *Kate Field: The Many Lives of a Nineteenth-Century American Journalist*. Syracuse NY: Syracuse University Press.

Scherer, Joanna C. 1975. "You Can't Believe Your Eyes: Inaccuracies in Photographs of North American Indians." *Studies in the Anthropology of Visual Communication* 2, no. 2: 67–79.

———. 2014. "Artifact Identification Using Historical Photographs: The Case of Red Cloud's Manikin." *Visual Anthropology* 27, no. 3: 217–47.

Schwartz, James. 2008. *In Pursuit of the Gene: From Darwin to DNA*. Cambridge MA: Harvard University Press.

Schwartz, Vanessa R., and Jeannene M. Przyblyski, eds. 2004. *The Nineteenth-Century Visual Culture Reader*. New York: Routledge.

Scott, Gertrude. 1991. Village Performance: Villages at the World's Columbian Exposition, 1893. PhD dissertation, New York University.

Scott, Walter Dill, and Robert B. Harshe. 1929. *Charles Deering, 1852–1927: An Appreciation*. Boston: Privately Printed.

Service, Elman R. 1985. *A Century of Controversy: Ethnological Issues from 1860 to 1960*. New York: Academic Press.

Sewell, Darrel, et al. 2001. *Thomas Eakins*. Philadelphia: Philadelphia Museum of Art, with Yale University Press.

Shapiro, Emma D. 2008. "'A Purpose in Every Stroke': Brush's Images of Indian Artisanry." In *George de Forest Brush: The Indian Paintings*, ed. Nancy K. Anderson, 83–99. Washington DC: National Gallery of Art, with Lund Humphries, Hampshire, U.K.

Shaul, D. Leedom. 1999. "Linguistic Natural History: John Wesley Powell and the Classification of American Languages." *Journal of the Southwest* 41, no. 3: 297–310.

Shepp, James W., and Daniel B. Shepp. 1893. *Shepp's World's Fair Photographed. Being a Collection of Original Copyrighted Photographs Authorized and Permitted by the Management of the World's Columbian Exposition . . . All Described in Crisp and Beautiful Language.* Chicago: Globe Bible Publishing Company.

Singh, Simon. 2004. *The Big Bang: The Origin of the Universe.* New York: Harper Perennial.

Skrupskelis, Ignas K., and Elizabeth M. Berkeley, eds. 1997. *William and Henry James: Selected Letters.* Charlottesville: University of Virginia Press.

Smith, Carl S. 2006. *The Plan of Chicago; Daniel Burnham and the Remaking of the American City.* Chicago: University of Chicago Press.

Smith, Duane A. 1988. *Mesa Verde National Park: Shadows of the Centuries.* Lawrence: University Press of Kansas.

———. 2005. *Women to the Rescue: Creating Mesa Verde National Park.* Durango: Durango Herald Small Press.

Smith, H. Jay. 1893. *The Cliff Dwellers.* Chicago: H. Jay Smith Exploring Company, World's Columbian Exposition.

Smith, Laurel. 1994. "In the Museum Case of Otis Mason: Natural History, Anthropology, and the Nature of Display at the United States National Museum." MA thesis, University of Oklahoma.

Smyk, E. A. 2012. "John Dyneley Prince: Profile of an Ivy League Scholar in Politics." *The Historic County: Newsletter of the Passaic County Historical Society* 12(1–2): 1, 3–5.

Snead, James E. 1999. "Science, Commerce, and Control: Patronage and the Development of Anthropological Archaeology in the Americas." *American Anthropologist* 101, no. 2: 1–16.

———. 2001. *Ruins and Rivals: The Making of Southwest Archaeology.* Tucson: University of Arizona Press.

———. 2002a. "Lessons of the Ages: Archaeology and the Construction of Cultural Identity in the American Southwest." *Journal of the Southwest* 44, no. 1: 17–34.

———. 2002b. "The 'Western Idea': Local Societies and American Archaeology." In *Excavating Our Past: Perspectives on the History of the Archaeological Institute of America,* ed. Susan Hueck Allen, 123–40. Boston: Archaeological Institute of America.

———. 2011. "'The Three Axes were from Canyon del Muerto': The Relic Hunting Economy in the Late 19th Century Southwest." Paper presented at the 51st Annual Meeting of the Western History Association, Oakland, October 13–16.

———. N.d. (forthcoming). *Relic Hunters: Encounters with Antiquity in 19th Century America.* Oxford: Oxford University Press.

Spencer, Frank. 1997. *A History of Physical Anthropology: An Encyclopedia*. 2 vols. New York: Garland Publishing.
Spencer, Herbert. 1880. *First Principles*. Reprinted from 5th London edition. London: A. L. Burt.
Spier, Leslie. 1913. "Results of an Archeological Survey of the State of New Jersey." *American Anthropologist* 15(4): 675–79.
——— 1917. *An Outline for a Chronology of Zuñi Ruins*. American Museum of Natural History Anthropological Papers 18 (3): 207–331. New York: American Museum of Natural History.
Spinden, Herbert J. 1913. *A Study of Maya Art*. Cambridge: Harvard University Press.
Spiro, Jonathan Peter. 2009. *Defending the Master Race: Conservation, Eugenics, and the Legacy of Madison Grant*. Burlington: University of Vermont Press.
Squier, Ephraim George. 1852. *Nicaragua: Its People, Scenery and Monuments and the Proposed Interoceanic Canal*. New York: D. Appleton.
———. 1973 [1877]. *Peru: Incidents of Travel and Exploration in the Land of the Incas*. New York: AMS Press.
Stansell, Christine. 2010. *American Moderns: Bohemian New York and the Creation of a New Century*. Princeton: Princeton University Press.
Starr, Frederick. 1893. "Anthropology at the World's Fair." *Popular Science Monthly* 43, no. 5: 610–21.
Stegner, Wallace, ed. 2004. "Editor's Introduction." In *The Arid Lands*, by John Wesley Powell, xii–xxxi. Lincoln: University of Nebraska Press.
Stephens, John Lloyd. 1841. *Incidents of Travel in Central America, Chiapas, and Yucatan*. New York: Harper and Brothers.
———. 1843. *Incidents of Travel in Yucatan*. New York: Harper and Brothers.
Steward, Julian H. 1961. "Alfred Louis Kroeber, 1976–1960." *American Anthropologist* 63: 1038–87.
Stevenson, James. 1883. "Illustrated Catalog of the Collections Obtained from the Indians of New Mexico and Arizona in 1880." *Second Annual Report of the Bureau of Ethnology, 1880–1881*: 423–65. Washington DC: Government Printing Office.
Stewart, Susan. 1984. *On Longing: Narratives of the Miniature, the Gigantic, the Souvenir, the Collection*. Baltimore: Johns Hopkins University Press.
Stocking, George W., Jr. 1960. "Franz Boas and the Founding of the American Anthropological Association." *American Anthropologist* 62: 1–17.
———. 1968. *Race, Culture, and Evolution: Essays in the History of Anthropology*. New York: Free Press.
———. 1974. *A Franz Boas Reader: The Shaping of American Anthropology, 1883–1911*. Chicago: University of Chicago Press.
———. 1976. "Ideas and Institutions in American Anthropology: Toward a History of the Inter War Period." In *Selected Papers from the American Anthropologist, 1921–1945*, ed. G. W. Stocking Jr., 1–53. Washington DC: American Anthropological Association.

——. 1979. *Anthropology at Chicago: Tradition, Discipline, Department*. Chicago: University of Chicago Library.
——. 1985. *Objects and Others: Essays on Museums and Material Culture*. Madison: University of Wisconsin Press.
——. 1987. *Victorian Anthropology*. New York: Free Press.
——. 1988. "Guardians of the Sacred Bundle: The American Anthropological Association and the Representation of Holistic Anthropology." In *Learned Societies and the Evolution of Disciplines*, ed. S. B. Cohen, D. Bromwich, and George W. Stocking Jr., 17–25. American Council of Learned Societies Occasional Paper No. 5. New York: ACLS.
Storr, Richard J. 1966. *A History of the University of Chicago: Harper's University, the Beginnings*. Chicago: University of Chicago Press.
Strain, Ellen. 2003. *Public Places, Private Journeys: Ethnography, Entertainment, and the Tourist Gaze*. New Brunswick: Rutgers University Press.
Strathern, Paul. 1999. *Locke in 90 Minutes*. Chicago: Ivan R. Dee.
Tenorio-Trillo, Mauricio. 1996. *Mexico at the World's Fairs: Crafting a Modern Nation*. Berkeley: University of California Press.
Terhune, Anne Gregory, and Elizabeth Johns. 2006. *Thomas Hovenden: His Life and Art*. Philadelphia: University of Pennsylvania Press.
Terry, Robert James. 1956. "Memories of a Long Life in St. Louis." *Missouri Historical Society Bulletin* (January 1956): 147–62.
Thatcher, John B. 1894. Letter to Warren K. Moorehead, May 17. Warren K. Moorehead Papers, Correspondence 1885–1908, box 4–8. MSS 106. Ohio State Historical Society, Columbus.
Thomas, Northcote Whitridge, and Barbara W Freire-Marreco, eds. 1907. *Anthropological Essays Presented to Edward Burnett Tylor in Honour of his 75th birthday, Oct. 2, 1907*. Oxford: Clarendon Press. Available at http://www.worldcat.org/.
Thompson, Edward H. 1929. "Forty Years of Research and Exploration in Yucatan." *Proceedings of the American Antiquarian Society* 39: 41–42.
——. 1932. *People of the Serpent: Life and Adventures among the Maya*. Boston: Houghton Mifflin.
Thompson, Mark. 2001. *American Character: The Curious Life of Charles Fletcher Lummis and the Rediscovery of the Southwest*. New York: Arcade Publishing.
Thompson, Raymond Harris. 2005. "Anthropology at the University of Arizona, 1893–2005." *Journal of the Southwest* 47, no. 1: 327–74.
Thoresen, Timothy. 1973. "Folkloristics in A. L. Kroeber's Early Theory of Culture." *Journal of the Folklore Institute* 10: 41–55.
——. 1975. "Paying the Piper and Calling the Tune: The Beginnings of Academic Anthropology in California." *Journal of the History of Behavioral Sciences* 11: 257–75.
Timreck, Ted W. 1980. *Franz Boas, 1858–1942*. Odyssey film biography. Boston: Public Broadcasting Associates, WGBH.

Tomkins, Calvin. 1970. *Merchants and Masterpieces: The Story of the Metropolitan Museum of Art*. New York: E. P. Dutton.

Towner, Lawrence W. 1970. *An Uncommon Collection of Uncommon Collections: The Newberry Library*. Chicago: Newberry Library Associates.

Tozzer, Alfred M. 1933. "Zelia Nuttall." *American Anthropologist* 31: 475–82.

Trachtenberg, Alan. 1982. *The Incorporation of America: Culture and Society in the Gilded Age*. New York: Hill and Wang.

Traubel, Henry. 1961 [1905]. *With Walt Whitman in Camden*. Vol. 1. New York: Rowman and Littlefield.

Trennert, Robert A. 1987a. "Fairs, Expositions, and the Changing Image of Southwestern Indians, 1876–1904." *New Mexico Historical Review* 62, no. 2: 127–50.

———. 1987b. "Selling Indian Education at World's Fairs and Expositions, 1893–1904." *American Indian Quarterly* 11, no. 3: 203–20.

Treuttner, William H. 1985. "Dressing the Part: Thomas Eakins's Portrait of Frank Hamilton Cushing." *American Art Journal* 17, no. 2: 48–72.

Truman, Ben C. 1893. *History of the World's Fair*. Philadelphia: Mammoth Publishing Company.

Trump, Erik. 1998. "Primitive Woman—Domestic(ated) Woman: The Image of the Primitive Woman at the 1893 World's Columbian Exposition." *Women's Studies* 27: 215–58.

Turner, James. 1999. *The Liberal Education of Charles Eliot Norton*. Baltimore: Johns Hopkins University Press.

Twyman, Robert W. 1954. *History of Marshall Field & Co., 1852–1906*. Philadelphia: University of Pennsylvania Press.

van Brunt, Henry. 1892. "Architecture at the World's Columbian Exposition." *Century Magazine* n.s. 22: 81–99; 24: 385–99; 24: 540–48; 24: 720–31; 24: 897–907.

———. 1894. "The Architectural Event of Our Times." *Engineering Magazine* (January): 432–33.

Viets, Conrad. 1891. Letter to Frederic W. Putnam, August 22. Putnam, F. W.–General Correspondence, 1851–1947. HUG 1717.2.1, Harvard University Archives.

Visweswaran, Kamala. 1998. "'Wild West' Anthropology and the Disciplining of Gender." In *Gender and American Social Science: The Formative Years*, ed. Helene Silverberg, 86–126. Princeton: Princeton University Press.

Wade, Edwin L. 1985. "The Ethnic Art Market in the American Southwest, 1880–1980." In *Objects and Others: Essays on Museums and Material Culture*, ed. George W. Stocking Jr., 167–91. Madison: University of Wisconsin Press.

Wade, Edwin L., and Lea S. McChesney. 1980. *America's Great Lost Expedition: The Thomas Keam Collection of Pottery from the Second Hemenway Expedition, 1890–1894*. Phoenix: Heard Museum.

Wake, C. Staniland. 1894a. Letter to Frederic W. Putnam. January 8. F. W. Putnam Papers, box 35, Harvard University Archives.

———. 1894b. *Memoirs of the International Congress of Anthropology*. Chicago: Schulte Publishing Company.

Waldon, William. 1893. *World's Columbian Exposition Art and Architecture*. 3 vols. Philadelphia: George Barrie.

Walker, John Brisben. 1893. "Introductory: The World's College of Democracy." *A World's Fair 1893: A Special Issue of Cosmopolitan Magazine, 1894*, ed. J. B. Walker, 519–28, http://archive.org/stream/worldsfair189300worl/worldsfair189300 worl_djvu.txt, accessed 9 June 2011.

Walker, William S. 2008. "John C. Ewers and the Problem of Cultural History: Displaying American Indians at the Smithsonian in the Fifties." *Museum History Journal* 1, no. 1: 51–74.

Ward, Lester. 1968 [1883]. *Dynamic Sociology; or Applied Social Science*. 2 vols. New York: Greenwood Press.

Warren, Louis S. 2005. *Buffalo Bill's America: William Cody and the Wild West Show*. New York: Vintage Books.

Webber, E. Leland. 1984. "Books, Business, and Buckskin." *Field Museum Bulletin* 55, no. 7: 5–10.

Wedel, Waldo. 1977. "The Education of a Plains Archaeologist." *Plains Anthropologist* 22, no. 75: 1–12.

Weimann, Jeanne Madeline. 1981. *The Fair Women: The Story of the Woman's Building, World's Columbian Exposition, Chicago, 1893*. Chicago: Academy Chicago.

Welsch, Robert L. 2003. "Albert Buell Lewis: Realizing George Amos Dorsey's Vision." In *Curators, Collections and Contexts: Anthropology at the Field Museum, 1893–2002*, ed. Stephen E. Nash and Gary M. Feinman, 99–115. Fieldiana: Publication no. 1525, Anthropology New Series no. 36. Chicago: Field Museum of Natural History.

Wetherill, Richard. 1893a. Letter to Talbot Hyde, November 12. Accession File 1894–45. Folder: "Pueblo Bonito, N.M. George Pepper, Collector and 2nd Wetherill Collection Utah & Arizona." Department of Anthropology Archives, American Museum of Natural History.

———. 1893b. Letter to Putnam, November 12. Putnam, F. W.–General Correspondence, 1851–1947. HUG 1717.2.1, Harvard University Archives.

———. 1894. Letter to Putnam, May 3. Putnam, F. W.–General Correspondence, 1851–1947. HUG 1717.2.1, Harvard University Archives.

———. 1896. Letter to Talbot Hyde, October 1. Accession File 1894–45. Folder: "Pueblo Bonito, N.M. George Pepper, Collector and 2nd Wetherill Collection Utah & Arizona." Department of Anthropology Archives, American Museum of Natural History.

———. 1897a. Letter to Hyde, October 24. Accession File 1894–45. Folder: "Pueblo Bonito, N.M. George Pepper, Collector and 2nd Wetherill Collection Utah & Arizona." Department of Anthropology Archives, American Museum of Natural History.

———. 1897b. Letter to Talbot Hyde, February 15. Accession File 1894–45. Folder: "Pueblo Bonito, N.M. George Pepper, Collector and 2nd Wetherill Collection

Utah & Arizona." Department of Anthropology Archives, American Museum of Natural History.

———. 1897c. Letter to Hyde, October 24. Accession File 1894–45. Folder:"Pueblo Bonito, N.M. George Pepper, Collector and 2nd Wetherill Collection Utah & Arizona." Department of Anthropology Archives, American Museum of Natural History.

———. 1897d. "The Sandal Last." *Antiquarian* 1, no. 9: 247.

White, Trumbull, and William Igleheart, eds. 1893. *The World's Columbian Exposition, Chicago, 1893: A Complete History of the Enterprise*. Philadelphia: International Publishing Company.

Wiebe, Robert H. 1967. *The Search for Order, 1877–1920*. New York: Hill and Wang.

Wilcox, David R. 1999. "The Chicago 'Triumph' of Frank Hamilton Cushing in 1893." Paper presented at the 64th Annual Meeting of the Society for American Archaeology, Chicago, March 26.

———. 2003a. "Creating Field Anthropology: Why Remembering Matters." In *Curators, Collections, and Change: A History of Field Museum Anthropology 1893–2002*, ed. Stephen E. Nash and Gary M. Feinman, 31–47. Fieldiana: Publication no. 1525, Anthropology New Series no. 36. Chicago: Field Museum of Natural History.

———. 2003b. "Restoring Authenticity: Judging Frank Hamilton Cushing's Veracity." In *Philadelphia and the Development of Americanist Archaeology*, ed. Don D. Fowler and David R. Wilcox, 88–112. Tuscaloosa: University of Alabama Press.

———. 2004. "Looking for Middle Ground: Archaeology on the Colorado Plateau Today." In *The Colorado Plateau: Cultural, Biological, and Physical Research*, ed. Charles van Riper III, and Kenneth Cole, 11–18. Tucson: University of Arizona Press.

———. 2005. "Creating a Firm Foundation: The Early Years of the Arizona State Museum." *Journal of the Southwest* 47, no. 1: 375–410.

———. 2010. "The Early AA and AAA: An Archaeological Approach." MS on file, Department of Anthropology, Museum of Northern Arizona, Flagstaff.

Wilcox, David R., and Don D. Fowler. 2002. "The Beginnings of Anthropological Archaeology in the North American Southwest: From Thomas Jefferson to the Pecos Conference." *Journal of the Southwest* 44: 121–234.

Wilcox, David R., Phil C. Weigand, J. Scott Wood, and Jerry B. Howard. 2008. "Ancient Cultural Interplay of the American Southwest in the Mexican Northwest." *Journal of the Southwest* 50(2): 103–206.

Willey, Gordon R., and Jeremy A. Sabloff. 1974. *A History of American Archaeology*. San Francisco: W. H. Freeman.

Willoughby, Charles C. 1898. *Prehistoric Burial Places in Maine*. Archaeological and Ethnological Papers of the Peabody Museum 1, no. 6.

———. 1919. "The Serpent Mound of Adams County, Ohio." *American Anthropologist* 21, no. 2: 153–63.

Wilmarth, A. F. 1893. Letter to Antonio Apache, September 11. F. W. Putnam Papers, box 34, Harvard University Archives.

Wilson, Thomas. 1891. "Anthropology at the Paris Exposition in 1899." *Annual Report of the United States National Museum for the Year Ending June 30, 1890*: 641–80.

———. 1894. Letter to Warren K. Moorehead, October 11. Warren K. Moorehead Papers, Correspondence 1885–1908, box 4–8. MSS 106. Ohio State Historical Society, Columbus.

———. 1897. Letter to Moorehead, April 28. Warren K. Moorehead Papers, Correspondence 1885–1908, box 4–8. MSS 106. Ohio State Historical Society, Columbus.

Wilson, William H. 1989. *The City Beautiful Movement*. Baltimore: Johns Hopkins University Press.

Winser, John H. 1893. Letter to Warren K. Moorehead, October 20. Warren K. Moorehead Papers, Correspondence 1885–1908, box 4–8. MSS 106. Ohio State Historical Society, Columbus.

Winship, George Parker. 1896. "The Coronado Expedition, 1540–1542." *Annual Report of the Bureau of American Ethnology, 1892–93*: 329–613.

Winslow, Helen M. 1893. "Met on the Midway." *Frank Leslie's Popular Monthly* 38: 501–504.

Wissler, Clark. 1917. "The New Archaeology." *American Museum Journal* 17, no. 2: 100–101.

Woodbury, Richard B. 1993. *60 Years of Southwestern Archaeology: A History of the Pecos Conference*. Albuquerque: University of New Mexico Press.

Woodbury, Richard B., and Nathalie F. S. Woodbury. 1999. "The Rise and Fall of the Bureau of American Ethnology." *Journal of the Southwest* 41, no. 3: 283–96.

Wonders, Karen. 1993. *Habitat Dioramas: Illusions of Wilderness in Museums of Natural History*. Acta Universitatis Upsaliensis; Figura; nova ser. 25. Uppsala, Sweden: Almqvist and Wiksell International.

World's Columbian Exposition. 1898. *Report of the President to the Board of Directors of the World's Columbian Exposition*. Chicago: Rand McNally and Company.

World's Columbian Exposition Illustrated (WCEI). 1891–94. 4 vols. Chicago: James B. Campbell.

Wright, Robin K. 2001. *Northern Haida Master Carvers*. Seattle: University of Washington Press; Vancouver: Douglas and McIntyre.

———. 2009. "Zacherias and the Chicago Settee: Connecting the Masterpiece to the Master." *American Indian Art Magazine* 35, no. 1: 68–75.

———. 2015. "Skidegate Haida House Models." In *Sharing Our Knowledge: The Tlingit and Their Coastal Neighbors*, ed. Sergei Kan, 381–93. Lincoln: University of Nebraska Press.

Zimmermann, Warren. 2002. *First Great Triumph, How Five Americans Made Their Country a World Power*. New York: Farrar, Straus and Giroux.

Zumwalt, Rosemary. 1988. *American Folklore Scholarship: A Dialogue of Dissent*. Bloomington: Indiana University Press.

Zwerdling, Alex. 1998. *Improvised Europeans: American Literary Expatriates and the Siege of London.* New York: Basic Books.

Zwick, Jim. 2006. *Inuit Entertainers in the United States: From the Chicago World's Fair through the Birth of Hollywood.* West Conshohocken PA: Infinity Publishing Company.

CONTRIBUTORS

Curtis M. Hinsley is Regents' Professor Emeritus at Northern Arizona University. He has written or edited numerous books and articles on the history of American anthropology and archaeology, with special attention to the American Southwest. He lives in Sedona, Arizona, with his wife, Victoria Enders.

Ira Jacknis (1952–2021) was a research anthropologist at the Phoebe A. Hearst Museum of Anthropology, University of California, Berkeley. His research specialties included the arts and culture of Native North America, modes of ethnographic representation (photography, film, sound recording), museums, and the history of anthropology.

Donald McVicker (1934–2015) held a PhD in anthropology from the University of Chicago and was a professor emeritus of anthropology at North Central College. Until his death in 2015 he was a research affiliate in anthropology at the Field Museum. His many publications on the history of American anthropology include the biography (2012) of Frederick Starr, the first anthropologist at the University of Chicago.

James E. Snead is professor of anthropology and curator of the archaeological repository at California State University, Northridge. He has published widely on the history of archaeology in North America with works such as *Ruins and Rivals: The Making of Southwest Archaeology* and *Relic Hunters: Archaeology and the Public in Nineteenth-Century America*.

An independent itinerant scholar, **David R. Wilcox** (1944–2022) collaborated with Curtis Hinsley for over thirty years on a documentary history of the Hemenway Southwestern Archaeological Expedition, editing with him "A Hemenway Portfolio" (*Journal of the Southwest*, 1995) and the first two volumes of the history (1996, 2002) as well as related essays. With Don D. Fowler he published "The Beginnings of Anthropological Archaeology in the North American Southwest: From Thomas Jefferson to the Pecos Conference" (2002) and co-edited *Philadelphia and the Development of Americanist Archaeology* (2003). Wilcox is also the author of a history of anthropology at the Field Museum, "Creating Field Anthropology: Why Remembering Matters" (2003), and other essays in the history of southwestern anthropology. He co-edited *The Mesoamerican Ballgame* (1991) and *Zuni Origins: Toward a New Synthesis of Southwestern Archaeology* (2007), among his numerous monographs and essays on southwestern archaeology.

INDEX

Page numbers in italic indicate illustrations.

Abbott, Charles C., 4
Abel, Karl, 113
Academy of Natural Sciences (Philadelphia), xx–xxi, xxiv, 86
Adams, Edward Dean, 437
Adams, Henry, xxxiii
Adams, Mary Newbury, 113
Administration Building, 42, 157, 159
Africa collections, 63, 64–65, 98, 174. *See also* Dahomey Village
African Americans, 63
Agassiz, Alexander, 117
Agassiz, Louis, 19, 381; and Putnam, 2–3, 4, 11
Agricultural Building, 159, 187
Alamo Ranch, 340, 342, 348–49, 356
Alaska exhibit, 168, 203n39
Albion NY, 148n10, 153, 201n21, 205n54
Alder, Cyrus, 111
Algerian-Tunisian Village, 59, 67–68, 69
Algonquians, 307, 334n52
Alliot, Hector, 163–64, 169, 201n26, 206n56
Ambrosetti, Juan Bautista, 421, 450n8
American Anthropological Association (AAA), xix, xxiv, 148n9, 420; Boas and, 421, 425, 452n19; "fleeting members" of, 444–46; formation of, xxxiv, 421, 425, 446, 494; "interested members" of, 438–44; membership of, 431–33, 434–37
American Anthropologist, xln8, 146; American Anthropological Association and, 420, 425; Anthropological Society of Washington and, xxii; Boas and, xix, 420, 426, 430, 446, 456; contributors to, 420, 430–31, 455–58; creation of, 129, 414; Goddard and, 424, 426, 429; Henshaw and, xxii, 418, 456; Hodge and, 148n9, 420, 424, 429, 456; leadership committees of, xxii, 421, 424, 429; reorganization in 1898 of, xxxiv, 420; review of International Congress of Anthropology in, 99–100, 120–23
American Antiquarian, xx
American Association for the Advancement of Science (AAAS), xxi, 417; and *American Anthropologist*, 420, 446; annual meetings of, xxxiv–xxxv, 100, 285; Putnam and, xxxiv, 9, 148n7
American Breeders Association, 423
American Ethnological Society (AES), 425, 438, 440, 446, 453n24
American Folklore Society (AFS), 450n5; Boas and, xxiii–xxiv, 379, 414, 422, 428; Chicago Folk-Lore Society conflict with, xli (n13), 199n4, 379; founding of, xxiii, 413; organizational model of, xxxiv–xxxv
American Illustrated Magazine, 344, 347, 350
American Museum of Natural History (AMNH), xxi, 321, 352, 400, 424, 428; Boas and, 264, 335n68, 386–87, 395, 415; establishment of anthropology at, 74, 264, 414–15, 419, 447; expeditions sponsored by, 106, 494; Putnam and, 7, 21, 74, 148n7, 264, 273, 353, 414–15, 419, 447
American Naturalist, xl (n8), 9, 148n7, 208n75, 400
American Philosophical Society, xx–xxi, xxiv, 149n13
American Society of Naturalists, 9

549

Ames, Eric, 58
Ami, Henry M., 437
Amsterdam Exposition (International Colonial and Export Trade Exhibition, 1883), 56
anatomical laboratories, 82–83
Ancient Society (Morgan), 104, 119n8, 426
Ancon necropolis, 8, 81, 330n17
Andree, Richard, 466–67, 477
Anfänge der Kunst (Grosse), 468
animals: Chicago World's Fair exhibits of, 58, 181–82, 208n72; domestication of, 219–20; humans and, 56, 479
Annanuck, Mary Dookshoode, 252
Anthropological Society of St. Louis, 453n25
Anthropological Society of Washington (ASW), 148n9, 420, 446; and *American Anthropologist*, xxii, 425; formation of, xxi, 128, 413; and International Congress of Anthropology, 100, 110; Mason and, xxi, xxiii, 149n14; membership of, 431–32; role and orientation of, xxii–xxiii, 431
anthropology (American): in 1894–98, 418–20; in 1899–1903, 420–22; in 1904–9, 422–23; in 1910–15, 423–25; in 1916–20, 425–26; in 1921–25, 426–30; authority structure in, 268–69, 492; Boas place in, xxxiv, 266, 403, 418; Boston and, xxiii–xxiv, 264, 273, 430; Brinton place in, xix, 1–2, 414, 447; Chicago and, xxi, 74–75, 383–84; Chicago World's Fair and development of, xxxix, 106–7, 123, 130–31, 263–64, 266, 413, 414, 417–18, 492; cultural philanthropists and, 375–76; differences with European, 106–7, 128–29, 460; and diversity, xl (n9), 428, 438, 447, 448, 449n1; founding fathers of, xix, xx, 1–2, 74–75, 131, 266, 414, 447; Hodge place in, 418, 421, 424; Holmes place in, 266, 418; internationalization of, 421–22; journals' role in, xx, xl (n8); Kroeber place in, 427, 428; Mason place in, xxiii, 266; museum institutionalization of, 263–64, 266; new directions of, xxxiv, 430, 494–95; New York and, xxi, 13–14, 439, 453n24; outside employment of scientists in, 266–67; periodization scheme for, xxxix, 415–16, 429; Philadelphia and, xx, xx–xxi, xxiv, xxxiii, 414; polarities and tensions within, 108; Powell place in, xix, 1, 266, 414, 447; prior to Chicago World's Fair, xix–xxiv, xxxiii–xxxv, 128–31; professional collaboration in, 3–4, 389–90, 446–47; professional generations of, 104–5, 131, 266, 418; professionalization of, xxi, xxxviii, 359, 376, 380–81, 383–84, 389, 413–14, 416–17, 425, 436, 437; Putnam place in, xix, 1, 74–75, 266, 414, 447; relic hunting and, 339, 342, 359n1; Santa Fe and, xxi, 422–23; spatial and institutional analysis of, 430–34; subfields of, xix, 93, 100, 130, 273, 417, 460, 491; Washington and, xxi–xxii, 128–29, 264, 273
Anthropology (Kroeber), 427, 430, 434
anthropology (science): applied, 472–73; Brinton on aims of, 146, 459–75; comparative, 16, 94, 106, 146, 269, 273, 315, 330n10, 476–87; "criminal," 448n1, 452n17, 453n24; cultural, xxxiv, 273; and eugenics, 129, 423, 425–26, 428, 447, 451n17; Field Museum and, 88, 400–401; popular images of, 240–43, 384; research aims in, 482–83; role of evidence in, 10, 102, 463–64; stratigraphic analysis in, 423–24; training in, xxxv, 464, 491; university departments of, xxxv, 21, 264, 426–27, 431, 434; women in, xxi, xl (n5), 3, 4, 425, 427–28. *See also* International Congress of Anthropology
Anthropology Building (Department of Ethnology displays), 91–98, 369–74, 492; anthropometric statues in, 286, 331n25; arrangement of exhibits within, 269, 270–71, 317; Cushing visits to, 179–80, 181, 192, 194; delays in completion of, 23–24, 162, 271, 347; games exhibit in, 208n76, 330n10; and Government Building displays, 267, 268–69, 270, 271, 370; inside plan of, 93–94, 270–71; labeling of exhibits in, 271–72; La Rabida relics at, 92, 202n34; life group exhibits in, 298, 332n38; "Man and His Works" as motto of, 17, 93; Mesoamerican exhibits at, 92–

550

Index

93, 95, 287, 289, 290–92, 372; Ohio mound exhibits in, 79–80, 96, 283–87, 294, 349, 350, 372–73; opening of, 24, 349; Peruvian exhibit in, 97, 220–24, 287, 370–71; photos and drawings of, *249, 271, 279*; plaster casts used at, 274–75; and private collectors, 339; Putnam given control of, 23–25; southwestern artifacts at, 348, 362–68, 372. *See also* Department of Ethnology; exhibits, anthropological

Antiquarian, 358

Antonio Apache, 28, *253*, 348; biographical note on, 203n37; and Cushing, 163, 167, 168, 176; and recruitment of Navajo representatives, 36–40

Apaches, 29, 37, 253

Arawak exhibit, 46, 95

Archaeological Institute of America (AIA), xl (n4), 422–23, 433, 453–54n28; formation of, xxi, xxxiv, 413

Archaeological Society of Washington, 445

Archaeological Studies among the Ancient Cities of Mexico (Holmes), 396–97

The Archaeologist, 352

archaeology, 452n20; American, 337–38, 357; Boas on, 79–81; Brinton and, 103, 461–62; and ethnography, 379–80; and ethnology, 452n21; "New Archaeology," 424; professional-amateur collaboration in, 449n4; Putnam fieldwork in, 4–8; as subfield of anthropology, xix, 273, 491. *See also* exhibits, anthropological

architecture, 147–48n5, 278, 321; of Chicago World's Fair buildings, 126–27, 262, 276, 277; Native American, 48, 276–95

Armour, Allison Vincent, xxxviii, 419; and Field Museum, 391, 394, 396, 397, 402; and Holmes, 386, 394–95, 396–97; patronage of archaeological expeditions by, 376, 397, 494; as personal patron, 386, 395, 397

Armour, George, 395

Armour, Philip D., 391, 395–96, 402

Armstrong, Maitland, *139*

Arnold, Benjamin Walworth, 444–45

art, Native American, 221–22, 223, 235–36, 277–78, 305, 480

Art and Archaeology, 452n18

Artes, Charles Friedrich Sebastian, 113

Art Galleries. *See* Fine Arts Palace

Art Institute of Chicago, 84, 375, 396, 399

Atlanta exposition (1895), 318, 320

avant-garde movement, 113, 128, 415, 447

Ayer, Edward Everett, 110; biographical information, 151n21, 397–99; donations to Field Museum by, 151n20, 383, 398, 494; and Field Museum management, 72, 139, 391, 398, 400, 409, 410; and Marshall Field, 71, 110, 139, 390, 402; and Newberry Library, 151n21, 398, 402, 494; as patron and philanthropist, xxxviii, 386, 397, 398–99, 401–2, 437, 494; photo of, *391*

Aymé, Louis, 47–48

Aztecs, 229, 230n4, 467

Baird, Spencer Fullerton, xviii, xxii, 380–81

Baker, Frank, 111, 418

Baker, Lee, 103

Baker, William T., 19

Baldwin, C. C., 374

Ballantyne, Robert Michael, 113

Bancroft, George, 102

Bancroft, Hubert H., 51

Bandelier, Adolph F., 425, 457; and Chicago World's Fair exhibits, 7–8; fieldwork by, 102–3, 419; and Morgan, xxi, 3

Barkan, Louis, 416, 452n19

Barrett, Samuel A., 320

Barrows, David Prescott, 111, 421–22

basket-making, 214, 365–66

Bassett, Fletcher Stewart, 113, 379

Bassett, Helen Wheeler, 379

Bastian, Adolf, 466–67, 477, 479

Bates, Oric, 437

Battle, Elizabeth Burns, 113

Baum, Henry Mason, 436

Baxter, Sylvester, 132, 136, 183, 208n73

bead-making and drilling, 213

Beals, Ralph, 426

Beckwith, Hiram William, 110

Bell, Alexander Graham, xl (n9), 423, 446, 449n1

Bell, Robert, 113–14

Beloit College, 210n98, 434

Bender, Thomas, xx

Index 551

Benedict, Ruth, 428, 430, 452n20
Benham, James W., 438
Benjamin, Walter, xvi
Bennett, Tony, xvi
Berchtold, Frederick, 114
Bergmann, Carl F. W., 155, 199n7, 299, 332n35
Besant, Annie Wood, 183, 208n73
Besant, Walter, 168, 169, 203n42
Bickford, F. T., 177, 206n62
Bidlake, John, 70–71
Billings, John Shaw, 442
biology, 449n3, 460
Bishop, Mrs. Thomas Bringham, 440
Bixby, William Keeney, 437, 453n26
Blackmar, Frank Wilson, 444
Blackstone, Mrs. Timothy B., 401
Blake, William Phipps, 156, 161, 201n23
Bloembergen, Marieke, 57
Bloom, Sol, 64, 67–71
Boas, Franz: and American Anthropological Association, 421, 425, 452n19; and *American Anthropologist*, xix, 420, 426, 430, 446, 456; and American Folklore Society, xxiii–xxiv, 379, 414, 422, 428; and American Museum of Natural History, 264, 335n68, 386–87, 395, 415; on anthropology as science, 130, 316, 376, 482–83; and "Boasians," 428–29, 430, 447; and Brinton, xxxiii–xxxiv, 107–8, 129, 417, 477; and Chicago World's Fair displays, 24, 78–83, 130–31, 135, 267–68, 317, 318, 385; and Columbia University, 264, 419, 447; comparative anthropology opposed by, 146, 476–87; cultural relativism of, 129, 266; and Cushing, 135; on customs and beliefs, 482–84; diversity embraced by, 428, 447; on environmental conditions' influence, 318, 482–83, 484–85; and ethnographic village, 27, 28, 31, 34; eugenics movement opposed by, 423, 425–26; family of, 491; on fathers of American anthropology, xix, xx, 1, 131, 414; and Field Museum, 71, 390–91, 394; fieldwork by, 106, 319–20, 322–23, 325, 335n68, 427; and Goddard, 424, 426; and Holmes, 389; and human exhibits, 34, 46, 47, 81–82; at International Congress of Anthropology, 100, 107, 110, 111, 131, 187, 190, 191; and Kroeber, 428–29, 447, 452–53n21; on linguistics, 107, 424, 426, 479; and Mason, 269, 296, 484; and McGee, 421, 446; and methodological fallibility, 451n15; on Moorehead, 352; and Newell, xxiii–xxiv, 414; opposition to, 425, 426, 448–49; physical anthropology work by, 370, 388, 448; place of in American anthropology, xxxiv, 266, 403, 418; posing for photographs by, 310, 320, 334n57; and Putnam, 4, 73, 74, 352, 386, 419, 484; on race, 82–83; regional ethnography of, 269; and *Science*, xxii; social and cultural evolutionism opposed by, xxxiii–xxxiv, 104–5; and Starr, 377, 379, 402–3; on Tylor, 477, 484; and women in anthropology, 427–28
—works: "Classification of the Languages of the North Pacific Coast," 107; "Ethnology at the Exposition," 78–83, 492; "The Limitations of the Comparative Method of Anthropology," xxxiii–xxxiv, 476–87; *The Mind of Primitive Man*, xxxiv; *Race, Language and Culture*, 453n23; *The Social Organization and the Secret Societies of the Kwakiutl Indians*, 320
Boas, Marie, 114, 491
Boehm, Lisa, 12, 15
Bolivia, 81, 97
Bolton, Henry Carrington, 168, 204n43
Bonaparte, Prince Roland, 349, 437
Bonny, C. C., 120
Boston-Cambridge MA, 45; as American anthropology center, xxiii–xxiv, 264, 273, 430
Boston Globe, 41
Boston Herald, 132
botany, 88, 397
Bourke, John Gregory, 253, 480; biographical note on, 202n34; and Cushing, 165, 170, 184; at International Congress of Anthropology, 111, 184
Bowditch, Charles Pickering, xxiii, 287, 419, 437, 494
Bowman, Blanche, 196
Boyer, Emanuel Roth, 114

Boyle, David, 421, 450n9
Brace, Charles Loring, 439
Brace, Elizabeth Mead Hyde, 439
Brace, Robert Neill, 439
Braddock, Alan, 327
Brady, James E., 114
Branner, John Casper, 439
Braudel, Fernand, 413
Braverman, Max, 114
Brazil, 81, 94
bread making, 154, 214–15, *296*, *297*, 306
Breasted, James Henry, 147n3
Brinkman, Paul, 72
Brinton, Daniel Garrison, xxxvi, 99–109; as American anthropology father, xix, 1–2, 414, 447; and archaeology, 103, 461–62; biographical information, 101, 420; Boas polemics with, xxxiii–xxxiv, 107–8, 129, 417, 477; and Cushing, 108–9, 122, 132, 135, 136, 146, 176, 180, 189, 193, 194, 198, 207n69, 209n79; dispersal of energies by, xxiv; Eakins portrait of, *xxvii*, 261, 329n1; as evolutionist, 1–2, 103; on fieldwork, 101–2; as International Congress of Anthropology chairman, 100, 110, 184, 191, 446; linguistics work of, 107, 190, 370, 448, 468; and Morgan, 103, 104, 105, 119n8; papers to International Congress of Anthropology by, 103–7, 119n8, 121–22, 185; on race, 103, 460, 469–71; on results of International Congress of Anthropology, 100, 191; university teaching posts of, xxxv, 264; works: "The Aims of Anthropology," xxxiii, 459–75; *Library of Aboriginal American Literature*, 103; "The 'Nation' as an Element in Anthropology," xxxvi, 104–5, 119n8, 121; *Notes on the Floridian Peninsula*, 101; "On Various Supposed Relations between the American and Asian Races," 105–7, 121–22, 185
Brinton, John H., 329n1
Brinton, Sarah M. Tillson, 180, 207n69
Brinton, Sarah Ward, 329n1
British Columbia, 81–82, 97, 277, 319–20
British Guiana, 46, 81, 95
British Museum, 233, 294, 331–32nn28–29
Brohough, Gustav Olsen, 114

Bronson, Clark H., 114
Brookings, Robert, 453n26
Brooklyn Institute of Arts and Sciences, 206n59, 414
Brooklyn Museum, 202n31, 321, 331–32n29
Brooks, Van Wyck, 14
Browman, David L., xxiii, 4, 7
Brown, Charles E., 436
Brown, Julie K., 36
Brown, Mrs. William Wallace, 114
Brown, Theodora Krakow, 426
Browning, Daniel M., 33, 34, 38
Brühl, Gustav, 111
Bryan, Thomas B., 410
Bryant, Henry Grier, 438
Bryant, William Clement, 203n35
Bryn Mawr College, 431
Buffalo exposition (Pan-American Exposition, 1901), xvi, 64–65, 301, 318, 489
Buffalo Society for Natural History, 64
Bullene, Mrs. Egbert Frank (née Emma Jay), 438–39
Bureau of American Ethnology (BAE) [and Bureau of Ethnology], 148n9, 200n11, 225; about, xx, xxii; and Chicago World's Fair displays, 153, 199n3, 212–28, 268, 323, 379; and field expeditions, 131, 136, 234, 281, 372; formation of, xxi, 128, 264, 413; Holmes and, 200n11, 386, 394, 419, 421, 422; name change to, 419; Powell and, xx, xxii, xxxv, 1, 131, 380. *See also* Government Building (Smithsonian displays)
Bureau of Indian Affairs, 30, 31, 32, 33, 35, 295
Burnham, Clara Louise, 50–51, 493
Burnham, Daniel Hudson, 54, 151n20; architectural work by, 126–27, 147–48n5, 276; biographical information, 147n4, 205n53; and Chicago World's Fair construction, 67, 69, 276; and Cushing, 133, 137, 139, 176, 177–78, 179; and Millet, 136–37, 150n18, 205n53; photo and portrait of, *xxxi*, *139*
Burnham, Margaret, 137, 177, 178–79, 205n53
Burrows, Herbert, 183, 208n73
Bushnell, David Ives, Jr., 457
Busnhell, David Ives, Sr., 445, 453n26

Index 553

Butler, Amos William, 439

Cahokia IL, 96
Cahokia Mound Association, 453n25
Cairo Street. *See* Street in Cairo
Cairo Street Waltz, *xxxii*
calendar, 228–30
Cammann, Hermann Henry, 437
Canada, 46, 81; exhibits from, 28, 94, 95, 272, 372
Cantrill, Mary Cecil, 136, 150n17, 177, 193, 195
Captain Gold's house, 278, *280*, *281*
Carnegie, Andrew, 13
Carnegie Institution of Washington, 48, 114, 421, 424, 428
Carroll, Mitchell Alexander, 445–46, 452n18
Castañeda, Pedro de, 323
Catherwood, Frederick, 291, 293
Catlin, George, 307
Cauldwell, Walter I., 114
Centennial Exposition. *See* Philadelphia Centennial Exposition (1876)
Centennial Exposition of the Ohio (Cincinnati, 1888), 343, 448n1
Century Magazine, 132, 203n41
Cesnola, Palma di, 385
Ceylonese pavilion, 167, 175
Chaco Canyon, 353–54, 356–57, 419, 494
Chamberlain, Alexander Francis, 430, 455
Chamberlin, Thomas C., 72–73, 394
Chapin, Will E., 49, 52, 243
Chapman, Carl, 453n25
Chapman, Kenneth, 325
Charnay, Désiré, 96, 290, 292, 331n26
Chatelain, Heli, 114
Chavero, Alfredo, 421, 450–51n10
Chicago Academy of Sciences, 403–4n1; Museum of, 18–19, 85
Chicago Folk-Lore Society, xli (n13), 199n4, 379
Chicago Herald: cartoons from, *24*, *249*, *250*, *251*; on Columbian Museum opening, 405–11; coverage of Chicago World's Fair by, 240–41; on ethnological exhibits, 91–98

Chicago Historical Society, 84, 395, 410
Chicago IL: and American anthropology, xxi, 74–75, 383–84; boosterism in, 375, 383; fairs in, 12–13; growth of, 11–12, 126; image of, 65, 68; Putnam vision for museum in, 12, 17–18, 19, 73, 84–90, 273, 388; selected as site for WCE, xvii, 13–15, 68; wealthy elite of, 12, 133, 384–85. *See also* Field Columbian Museum
Chicago World's Fair. *See* World's Columbian Exposition (WCE)
Chichén Itzá, 290, 331n24; displays from, 48, 292, 331n28; fieldwork in, 74, 376, 395, 396
Chick, E. E., 290
Chinese Joss House and Wah mee Exhibit, 172–73
Christenson, Andrew L., 449n4
Cincinnati Art Museum, 373
Cincinnati exposition (1888), 343, 448n1
Cincinnati Society of Natural History, 373
City Beautiful movement, 127, 147n5
Civic Federation (Chicago), 12
Clark, May S., 157, 200n15
Clark University, 431
Clements, Forest, 426
Cleveland, Grover, 33
cliffdweller exhibits, 216–20, 362–68; arrangement of, 280–81; attraction of, 48, 348; Boas on, 80; creation of structure for, 278–83; Cushing visits to, 156, 161, 163, 174, 216; location of, 40, 201n22; misrepresentations in, 171–72; origin of collection, 205–6n56; photo of, *349*; subsequent fate of, 494; and Utah pavilion collection, 347
cliffdwellers, 96, 161, 363–68; basketry of, 214, 365–66; games of, 189; from Mancos region, 216, 217, 219, 220; and Mesa Verde site, 276, 340, *341*, 342, 348–49; pottery of, 188–89, 216–17, 231n6, 365, 366–67; textiles of, 367–68. *See also* Zuni Pueblo
The Cliffdwellers (Fuller), 68
Closson, Carlos Carleton, Jr., 114
Codman, Henry Sargent, *139*
Cody, William "Buffalo Bill," 30, 170, 277
Cohn, Isaac, *255*
Colburn, Richard T., 114

Cole, Douglas, 4, 20, 24, 47, 381
Cole, Fay-Cooper, 7, 401, 426–27, 450n5
Colojo, "Giant," 382
Colorado Cliffdweller Exhibit. *See* cliffdweller exhibits
Colorado State Exhibit, 38, 347
Colorado State Historical Society, 340–41
Columbia Building, 171
Columbian Historical Exposition (Madrid, 1892), 265, 275, 285, 293
Columbian Museum. *See* Field Columbian Museum
Columbia University, xxi; anthropology department at, 421, 431; Boas association with, 264, 419, 447
Columbus, 89–90, 92, 490
Comanche, 310, *311*, *312*
Commercial Club of Chicago, 12; Putnam address to, 84–90
comparative anthropology, 16, 94, 269, 273, 330n10; Boas opposition to, 146, 476–87; Cushing and, 105, 315
Conger, Cornelia, 395
Congo, 387
Conn, Steven, 10
Conquest of Mexico (Prescott), 397
Cook, George, 162
Copán, Honduras, 210n99, 290, 292–93, 316
Copeland, John Hoeny, 114
Cornell University, xx, 437
Corson (Corbes), Juliet, 197, 211n102
Cosmopolitan, 54–55, 163, 201n27
Costa Rica, 80, 94, 167
Coulter, John M., 399
Crane, E. H., 114
Crane, Erma, 181, 208n71
Crane, Richard Teller, Jr., 151n22
Cree, 28, 46, 82, 372
Cregier, DeWitt C., xvii, 13
Cresson, Hilborne T., 345, 360n5
criminal anthropology, 448n1, 452n17, 453n24
Croffutt, William Augustus, 155, 157, 168, 172, 199n8
Cross, John, 277
Crystal Palace (London), 263, 298, 332n33

Culin, Helen Bunker, 114, 205n52; Cushing diary on, 172, 174, 176, 180, 181, 196–97
Culin, Robert Stewart, 108, 264, 266, 329n1, 420; biographical notes on, 149n12, 202n31; and cliffdweller exhibit, 348, 362; on comparative games, 105, 145–46, 208n76, 225, 330n40; Cushing diary on, 165, 166, 171, 172, 173, 174, 175, 181, 182, 185, 189, 193, 194, 196, 197; Cushing friendship with, 132, 136, 145, 163, 176, 202n31, 316; and folklore, 330n10, 372; *Games of the North American Indians*, 132; at International Congress of Anthropology, 111, 176; knowledge of Chinese by, 149n12, 165, 173; photo of, *133*
cultural anthropology, xxxiv, 273
cultural evolutionism, xxii, xxxiii, 266
cultural hybridity, 315–16
cultural relativism, 129, 266
culture areas, 317–18
Cummings, Byron, 325, 446
Cummings, Edward Estlin, 114
Curtis, Fannie E. Coann, 166, 173, 192, 203n36
Curtis, Natalie Burlin, 325
Curtis, Pearl Coann, 169, 204n44
Curtis, William E., 70, 73
Cushing, Emma Tennison Magill: biographical note on, 198–99n1; Cushing diary on, 154, 156, 157, 158, 159, 160–61, 163, 164, 165, 166, 167, 168, 169, 170, 171, 172, 173, 174, 175, 176, 179, 180, 181, 182, 192; family of, 153
Cushing, Frank Hamilton: accusations against, 132, 136; on anthropological museums, 316, 335n63; and Antonio Apache, 163, 167, 168, 176; and Boas, 135; and Brinton, 108–9, 122, 132, 135, 136, 146, 176, 180, 189, 193, 194, 198, 207n69, 209n79; and Burnham, 133, 137, 139, 176, 177–78, 179; and cliffdweller exhibits, xxxviii, 161, 163, 171–72, 174, 216–20, 280–81, 348, 362; on cliffdwellers' life and culture, 188–89, 216–20, 363–68; and comparative cultures, 105, 315; Culin friendship with, 132, 136, 145, 163, 176, 202n31, 316; diary of, xxxvii, 125, 147n1, 153–98, 389; Eakins, portrait of, 149n10,

Index

555

Cushing, Frank Hamilton (*continued*) 151n24, 261, 326–27; and evolutionism, 104–5, 141, 144, 266; fieldwork among Zuni by, 102, 131–32, 233–34, 306, 307, 333n46, 372; and Fletcher, 135, 136, 177, 180, 193, 194; friendships and networking by, 131, 136–37, 139–40, 148–49n10, 170, 414; on games, 105, 145–46, 184, 185, 189, 224–26; Government Building display work by, xxxvii, 135, 153, 154, 156, 165, 166, 167, 168, 169, 170, 172, 177, 179, 194, 212–13, 267, 268, 329–30n8, 446; and Hazzard, 162–63, 174, 195–96, 198; health of, 132, 199n2; and Hemenway Expedition, 131–32, 153–54, 221, 316, 335n63; and Hodge, 132, 153, 157, 166; and Holmes, 135, 154, 156, 162, 165, 167, 168, 171, 179, 180, 193, 212, 314–15, 389–90, 490; Hovenden portrait of, *xxviii*, 144, 151n24; at International Congress of Anthropology, 105–6, 111, 122, 135–36, 176–77, 184–91, 209n79; and Kate Field, 145, 169, 171, 204n45; knowledge of Zuni language by, 131, 178, 236; and Kunz, 156, 161, 163–64, 165–66, 167, 168; and life group displays, 299, 305, 306, 309, 312–15, 319; and Mason, 134, 135, 158, 329–30n8; and Matthews, 165, 170, 171, 176, 180–81; on Mexican calendar, 228–30; at Midway Plaisance, 61, 156, 158, 159, 181–82; and Millet, 136–37, 173, 176, 183–84; on Native American ceremonies and beliefs, 141, 144, 169, 170–71, 186, 187, 195, 214–15, 218, 305; on Native American industries, 213–14; and Nuttall, 135, 136, 177, 180, 194; personal qualities of, 141, 144; on Peruvian collections, 220–24; photo poses by, 310, 311, *312*; as popularizer and showman, 312–15, 404n2; and Powell, 132, 145, 154–55, 170, 171, 172, 173, 174; and Putnam, 6–7, 106, 136, 185; and Rorer, 136, 170, 175, 177, 181, 193, 195; on ruins in Yucatán, 161, 390; and Stevenson, 132, 149n13; on symbolism, 226–28; and U.S. National Museum, 135, 265, 316; works: "The Arrow," 146; "Monthly Report," 212–30; "My Adventures at Zuñi," 132; "Outlines of Zuñi Creation Myths," 153; *Zuñi Breadstuff*, 132, 136, 306

Cushing, Milo, 170
Cushing, Thomas, 170
Cusick, Cornelius C., 28
Cutler, Robert E., 114

Dahomey Village, 61–64, 191, 277
Dall, William Healy, 111
Dana, Charles A., 14
dances: Kwakiutl, 34–35, 161–62, 169; at Street in Cairo, 59, 75–76, 191, 385
Darnell, Regna, 1, 101–2, 108, 275, 404n2
Davenport, Charles Benedict, 423
Davenport Academy of Natural Sciences, 380, 443
Davis, George R., 15, 17, 19–20, 23
Davis, Linda, 196
Davis, William, xl (n9)
Dawes Act, 29
Dawson, Charles Mercer, 420, 450n6
Day, David Fisher, 166, 167, 175, 202–3n35
Deans, James, 114, 277
Debbas, G. K., 59
"Decorative Art of British New Guinea" (Haddon), 468
Deer, Francisca Examiner, 45
Deer, Tom, 44
Deering, Charles, *142*, 151n23; and Cushing, 141, 170, 204n46
De Ford, Henry "Buckskin Joe," 39
de Laguna, Frederica, 100
The Delight Makers (Bandelier), 103
Dellenbaugh, Frederick Samuel, 439
Deloria, Philip, 310, 334n56
Deming, Edwin Willard, 445
Densmore, Frances, 325
Department of Ethnology (Department M): collections obtained by, 22–23, 95, 271; exhibits of, 78–83, 91–98, 276–77, 295, 371–72; funding of, 22, 271; practical problems faced by, 271–72; Putnam and, 2, 17, 46–47, 68, 79, 91, 122, 374; Sickles and, 33–35. *See also* Anthropology Building (Department of Ethnology displays)
Dewey, Alvin Hiram, 440
Dexter, Ralph, 20, 22

De Young, Michael H., 67, 69
Dimock, George Edward, 439
Dinwiddie, William, 319
Dittmer, Chris F., 114–15
diversity: American anthropology and, xl (n9), 438, 448, 449n1; Boas embrace of, 428, 447; Midway Plaisance and cultural, 50, 52–53, 55, 75, 447; of Native American cultures, 129–30, 379; tolerance of, xxxvi; White City marginalization of, 328, 447
Dixon, Roland B., 74, 457
Dodge, Richard E., 356–57
Dodge, William Earl, Jr., 444
domestic labor, 304–5
Donaldson, Henry Herbert, 111, 440
Donehoo, George Patterson, 440–41
Dorsey, George Amos, xxxviii, 316; and *American Anthropologist*, 420, 457; biographical notes on, 209n83, 449–50n5; and Field Museum, 9, 352, 381, 398, 400–401, 419, 424, 449–50n5; fieldwork in Peru and Bolivia by, 274–75, 370–71; as first Harvard anthropology PhD, 8, 419; at International Congress of Anthropology, 111, 186; and life group displays, 315, 320; and Moorehead, 343, 352, 360n4; and Peruvian exhibit, 7, 97, 220, 223; photo of, 382; as popularizer, 376, 377, 381, 383, 434; as professional anthropologist, 436, 437; and Putnam, 8–9, 74, 210n99, 425; and Starr, 381, 387, 388
Dorsey, Ida Chadsey, 198, 211n103
Dorsey, James Owen, 154, 456
double-handled pitchers, 363–64
Douglass, Frederick, 63
Dowling, Thomas, Jr., 115
drama, evolution of, 191, 193
DuBois, Constance Goddard, 436–37
Duke, Charles F., 44
Dunbar, U. S. J., 299

Eakins, Thomas, 327; portrait of Brinton by, *xxvii*, 261, 329n1; portrait of Cushing by, 149n10, 151n24, 261, 326–27; technique of, 304, 326
Earll, Robert Edward, 158, 159, 174, 197–98, 201n20

Echlin, Henry Magiford, 115
Edison, Thomas, 325
Edwards, Charles Lincoln, 115
Egyptian Temple, 59
Electricity Building, 126, 160
Eliot, Charles W., 3, 21
Ellsworth, James William, 110
Emmons, George Thornton, 168, 203n39, 441
Eneutseak, Esther (Helene Columbia Palmer), 42, *43*, 45–46
Engerrand, G. C. [Jorge], 423
environmental determinism, 129, 427, 451n17
Escuela Internacional de Arquelogía y Etnología, 423–24
Eskimos. *See* Inuit exhibit
Esquimaux Village, 40–46; photo of, *41*
Essex Institute, 2, 9, 148n7
ethnographic village, 25–35; Esquimaux Village, 40–46; location of, 26–27; Penobscot Village, 27, 46, 276, 277; recruitment of Native peoples for, 27–28, 29, 31–33
ethnography, 40, 294, 324; and archaeology, 379–80, 401; vs. art, 376–78; Cushing and, 136, 266–67, 299, 311–12; Mooney and, 307, 311–12, 317
Ethnological Report on the Native Tribes of Southeast Alaska (Emmons), 441
ethnology, 452n20; and archaeology, 452n21; Boas on, 479–81; Brinton on, 103, 464–73; International Congress of Anthropology discussion of, 121–22; as subfield of anthropology, xix, 93, 100, 491
eugenics movement, 129, 428, 447, 451n17, 452n19; opposition to, 423, 425–26
Evans, Christopher, 282
Evans, R. Tripp, 287
Evanston IL, 139, 176, 177, 182
evolution doctrine, 128–29, 466
evolutionism, xxxiii, 128–29, 269; Boas on, xxxiii, xxxiii–xxxiv, 104–5; Brinton on, 1–2, 103; cultural, xxii, xxxiii, 266; social, xviii–xix, 57, 62–63, 104, 473
exhibits, anthropological, 22–35, 212–28; African, 63, 64–65, 98, 174; Algerian-Tunisian Village, 59, 67–68, 69; of

Index 557

exhibits (*continued*)
animals, 58, 181–82, 208n72; Anthropology Building arrangement of, 269, 270–71, 317; of basketry, 214, 365–66; Boas and, 24, 78–83, 130–31, 135, 267–68, 317, 318, 385; Boas review of, 78–83; of bread making, 154, 214–15, 296, 297, 301; *Chicago Herald* review of, 91–98; cliffdweller collections, 40, 48, 80, 156, 161, 163, 171–72, 174, 201n22, 216–20, 278–83, 348, 362–68; collaboration in preparation of, 268; commercial side to, 22–23, 29, 30, 36, 46, 54–55, 67, 69, 385, 403; comparison of at Anthropology and Government buildings, 267, 268–69, 270, 271, 370; country exhibits, 94–95; Cushing work on, xxxvii, 135, 153, 154, 156, 165, 166, 167, 168, 169, 170, 172, 177, 179, 194, 212–13, 267, 268, 329–30n8, 446; Dahomey Village, 61–64, 191, 277; display techniques, xxxvii, 22, 265, 295, 298–99; from Egypt and Palestine, 98; entrepreneurs and, 58; ethnocentrism and racism in, 55, 305, 306, 493; German Village, 184, 191, 193, 395; Government Building arrangement of, 269–70, 272, 317, 379–80; Holmes and, 154, 208n76, 212, 268, 276, 299, 307, 319, 329n8, 335n66, 370, 446; illustrative of ceremonials, 154, 214–15, 302, 319, 324; Inuit exhibit, 40–46, 81, 252, 276, 277; Iroquois exhibit, 26, 28, 82, 97, 276–77; Javanese Village, 156, 158, 159, 191, 230n4; labeling of, 275, 306, 312–13; life groups, 295–316; linguistic map, 107, 130, 265, 268, 273, 275, 370, 379; Lorillard Expedition collection, 96–97; Mayan collection, 47–48, 79, 80, 92–93, 96, 130, 161, 267, 273, 275, 283, 287–88, 290–94, 321, 331n27, 372; Ohio mound collection, 79–80, 96, 97, 267, 275, 283–87, 349, 350, 372–74; Penobscot Village, 27, 46, 276, 277; Peruvian collection, 80–81, 220–24, 270–371, 294; photography used in, 274–75, 290–94, 309–10, 335n54; plans for, xvii–xviii; of pottery, 154, 175, 214, 216–17, 231n6, 266–67, 371; at previous fairs and expositions, 55–57, 60, 62, 67–68, 265, 275, 285, 298, 369; public reception of, 76–77, 388, 493; of silversmithing, 154, 177, 179, 213, 301, *303*, 304–5; South Sea Islands village, 77, 82, 98; of spinning and weaving, 154, 213–14, 222–23, 230n4, 304; Street in Cairo, 52, 59–61, 75–76, 174, 191, 246, 247, 277, 385; subsequent fate of collections in, 85–86, 264, 321–22, 331–32n29, 331n19, 331n26, 335n66, 374, 414, 446–47; Turkish Village, 59, 255. *See also* Department of Ethnology; human exhibits

Fagin, Nancy L., 269, 332n38, 335n64
Fairchild, David, 397
family structure, 303, 482
Fane, Diana, 290
Farabee, William C., 84, 429
Farny, Henry F., 306
Farrand, Livingston, 436
Faye, Paul-Louis, 437
Ferris Wheel, 64, *65*, 135, 157, 200n17
Fewkes, Jesse Walter, 210n99, 418; and *American Anthropologist*, 429, 430, 455; biographical note on, 207n68; and Cushing, 179, 197; at International Congress of Anthropology, 111, 187; work among Pueblos by, 372, 480
Field, Marshall: endowment for Columbia Museum by, xxxviii–xxxix, 71, 110, 126, 139, 390, 402; at museum dedication ceremony, 408–9, 410; photo of, *393*
Field, Mary Katherine Keemle "Kate": biographical note on, 204n45; and Cushing, 145, 169, 171, 204n45; reports on Chicago World's Fair by, 1, 49, 243
Field Columbian Museum: A. V. Armour and, 391, 394, 396, 397, 402; Ayer and management of, 72, 139, 391, 398, 400, 409, 410; Ayer donations and support to, 151n20, 383, 398, 494; board of, 391, 396; Boas and, 71, 390–91, 394; Burnham and, 151n20; ceremony to inaugurate, 408–11; declared mission of, 390, 400, 405; Dorsey and, 9, 352, 381, 398, 400–401, 419, 424, 449–50n5; founding of, 264, 390–91, 394, 405–11; Higinbotham and, 139–40, 390, 391; Holmes and, 73, 394, 399, 419; initial management team of, 72–73;

Laufer and, 394, 400–401, 403, 425; Marshall Field and, xxxviii–xxxix, 71, 110, 126, 139, 390, 402, 408–9, 410; Putnam relationship to, 19–20, 71–73, 351, 361n10, 390–91, 394; Putnam vision of, 12, 17–18, 19, 20, 73, 84–90, 273, 388; scientists' dissatisfaction with, 399–400; Skiff and, 21, 391, 399, 400; Southwestern Expedition sponsored by, 421; staffing of, 394; Starr and, 387, 388; WCE collections given to, 85–86, 264, 331n19, 331n26, 331–32n29, 335n66, 374, 414, 446–47
field inscriptions, 294
Fillmore, John Comfort, 111, 186, 209n80, 325
film, 324–25
Fine Arts Palace, 158–59, 167, 174, 390, 407
Finsch, Otto, 98
Fisheries Building, 272
Fletcher, Alice Cunningham, 30; biographical information, 150n15, 207n70; and Cushing, 135, 136, 177, 180, 193, 194; *Indian Games and Dances*, 425; at International Congress of Anthropology, 100, 110, 111, 185–86, 209n80; and Putnam, 4, 32, 150n15
Fletcher, Robert, 456
Flint, Weston, 156, 200n12
folklore, xli (n13), 379, 462. *See also* American Folklore Society
forced sterilization, 423
Ford, James Bishop, 437
Fort Ancient, 5, 344, 345
Fort Hill, 283, 374
Fournier, Alex, 348
Fowke, Gerard, 350
France, 95, 96–97
Frank Leslie's Popular Monthly, 63
Franklin, Benjamin, xxiv
Franklin Institute for the Promotion of the Mechanic Arts, xxiv
Franz Boas: 1858–1942 (Hinsley), 388
Free Museum of Science and Art, xxiv, 414, 420
French-Sheldon, Mary, 111, 186
Freud, Sigmund, 423
Fryer, John, 437

Fuller, Henry Blake, 68, *143*, 207n65; and Cushing, 141, 178, 183
Furness, William Henry, III, 441
fylfot, 185, 226–28

Gallatin, Albert, 107
games: Culin work on, 105, 145–46, 208n76, 225, 330n40; Cushing on Native American, 105, 184, 185, 189, 224–26; exhibits devoted to, 82, 330n10
Games of the North American Indians (Culin), 132
Gamio, Manuel, 423
Ganon, Ela, 59
Garrison, William Lloyd, 451–52n17
Gaston, W. E., 115
Gates, Peter Goddard, 437
Gatschet, Albert Samuel, 456
Geertz, Clifford, 262
gender, 304, 333n46; and women in anthropology, xxi, xl, 3, 4, 425, 427–28
genetics, 451n15
geographical environment, 478, 484–85
geology, 106, 240, 387; Putnam on, 88
geometrical designs, 480–81
Geraldine, Dion, *139*
German Village, 184, 191, 193, 395
Gibbs, George, 107
Giddings, Franklin H., 112
Gifford, E. W., 428, 429
Gilbert, James, 493
Gilder, Richard Watson, 168, 169, 203n41
Gill, DeLancey, 164, 165, 167, 202n30, 334n52
Gillard, William H., 115
Gilman, Benjamin I., 325
Glenny, Bryant Burwell and William Henry, 203n35
Glenny, John Clark, 203n35
Goddard, Pliny Earle, 424, 426, 429
Goethe, Johann Wolfgang von, 472
Goldenweiser, Alexander A., 436, 437, 458
Goode, George Brown: biographical note on, 230n1; and Chicago World's Fair exhibits, xviii, 66–67, 213, 272, 301; display techniques of, 66–67, 275, 295; on public museums' role, xviii, xl (n1), 18; and science of anthropology, 10, 266

Goodyear, William Henry, 175, 206n59, 331n29
Gordon, George Byron, 316, 425
Gould, Marcia Louise Towndrow, 170, 204n48
Gouldy, Mary E., 115
Government Building (Smithsonian displays), 212–28, 274, 275, 295, 492; and Anthropology Building displays, 267, 268–69, 270, 271, 370; arrangement of exhibits in, 269–70, 272, 317, 379–80; costumed mannequins used in, 298–99, 332n38; Cushing work in, 154, 156, 165, 166, 167, 168, 169, 170, 172, 177, 179, 194, 212; inaccuracies in, 315, 335n59; photo of, *270*; principal sources for, 306, 379; space restrictions in, 272; U.S. National Museum preparation of displays for, 154, 212, 232–33, 264, 267–68, 283, 347, 379. *See also* exhibits, anthropological
Grabill, John H., 323
Graham, Charles Carey, 341
Graham, Douglas D., 174, 175, 176, 206n58
Graham, E. R., *139*
Graham, Henry E., 115
Grand Basin, 167
Grant, Madison, 426, 428
Gray, Asa, 2
Grayton, Anna, 426
Green, C. H., 342, 347, 351
Green, Jesse, 147n1
Greene, Henry, 276
Greenhalgh, Paul, xvi, 55, 56, 62
Greenlee, William Brooks, 115
Grosse, Ernst, 468
Grubbe, Emile Herman, 115
Grumbling, C. M., 115
Guerreiro, João Verissimo Mendes, 115
Gulliver, Frederic Putnam, 115
Gunsaulus, Frank W., 409
Guyot, Arnold Henry, 478

Haddon, Alfred Cort, 468
Hagar, Stansbury, 457
Hagenbeck, Carl, 58, 182, 208n72
Haida, 276–78, 325
Hale, Horatio, 107, 484

Hammond, John Hays, 439
Hammond, Natalie Harris, 439
Handbook of North American Indians (Hodge), 423
Handbook of the Indians of California (Kroeber), 427
Handy, Moses P., 49, 242
Handy, Mrs. Henry Hunter Smith, 441
Harper, William Hudson, 76–77
Harper, William Rainey, 73, 147n3, 377
Harper's Monthly, 50, 76, 243, 260
Harriman, Mrs. E. H., 423
Harris, Neil, 239
Harris, William Torrey, 132, 149n11
Harrison, Benjamin, 14, 15, 30, 68
Harrison, Carter Henry, III, 71, 115
Harrison, Charles Custus, 440
Harrison, Mrs. Ralph Chandler, 441
Hart, Ernest Abraham, 115
Hartman, Carl Vilhelm, 196, 210–11n100
Harvard University, xx, 448; anthropology program at, 8, 418–19, 431; and Chicago World's Fair displays, 21, 286, 331n25; Copán expedition of, 292–93, 316; Putnam professorship at, xxxv, 2, 8, 74, 264, 273. *See also* Peabody Museum of Archaeology and Ethnology
Hassler, Emil, 112
Hastings, William, 437
Hatmaker, Benjamin J., 167, 203n38
Hawthorne, Julian, 49, 52–53, 76, 243, 493
Haynie, James H., 20
Hazelius, Artur, 298
Hazzard, Charles D.: biographical note on, 205–6n56; and cliffdweller exhibit, 201n24, 348; collections assembled by, 280, 342, 351; and Cushing, 162–63, 174, 195–96, 198
Hazzard Cliffdweller collection. *See* cliffdweller exhibits
Hearst, Phoebe Apperson, 74, 208n70, 419, 427, 437; and Hazzard collection, 351, 494; and UC Berkeley, 21, 208n70, 264, 351, 420
Heaven, Sophie, 187, 209n89
Hemenway, Augustus, 132
Hemenway, Mary Tileston, xxiii, 131, 149, 325, 494; and Cushing, 133–34, 136, 316; death of, 207n68, 418

Hemenway Southwestern Archaeological Expedition, 148n9, 149n11, 207n68; Cushing and, 131–32, 153–54, 221, 316, 335n63; Putnam and, 6–7
Henderson, Alice Palmer, 164, 175, 201n28
Henderson, Palmer, 161, 164, 201n24
Henry, Joseph, 18, 380–81
Henshaw, Henry Wetherbee, 307; and *American Anthropologist*, xxii, 418, 456; and Chicago World's Fair, 268, 329n5; training of, xxxv, xl (n6)
Herrman, Esther, 437
Hewett, Edgar Lee, 358, 433, 436, 446, 452n18, 457; and School of American Archaeology, xxi, 422–23
Hewitt, J. N. B., 436–37
Heye, George Gustav, 361n13, 395, 494
Hicks, Frederick Charles, 115
Higinbotham, Harlow Niles, 39, 69, 396, 399; biographical note on, 151n22; and Chicago World's Fair authority structure, 15, 23; and Field Museum, 139–40, 390, 391; photo of, *392*; and Putnam, 24, 72, 394
Hill, W. W., 426
Hiller, F. L. L., 115, 186, 209n81
Hillers, John K., 275, 282, 306, 309
Hindoo jugglers, 35, 191
H. Jay Smith Exploring Company, 205–6n56, 278. *See also* cliffdweller exhibits; Smith Exploring Company, H. Jay
Hjetland, John Hans, 115–16
Hodge, Frederick Webb, 306; and *American Anthropologist*, 420, 424, 429, 456; and American anthropology, 418, 421, 424; biographical notes on, 148n9, 200n14; and Cushing, 132, 153, 157, 166; *Handbook of North American Indians*, 423
Hoffman, Walter James, 266, 307, 330n8, 456; and life group displays, 299, 305, 333n47; posing for photo by, 310, *314*
Holland, William Jacob, 441
Holmes, Bayard Taylor, 116
Holmes, William Henry: and *American Anthropologist*, 430, 455; and Armour, 386, 394–95, 396–97, 419; and *Art and Archeology*, 452n18; Ayer as admirer of, 398; biographical note on, 199n3; and Boas, 389, 421; and Bureau of American Ethnology, 200n11, 386, 394, 419, 421, 422; and Chicago World's Fair exhibits, 154, 208n76, 212, 268, 276, 299, 307, 319, 329n8, 335n66, 370, 446; and Cushing, 135, 162, 212, 314–15; Cushing diary on, 154, 156, 165, 167, 168, 171, 179, 180, 193, 389–90, 490; and development of American anthropology, 266, 418; and Field Museum, 73, 394, 399, 419; fieldwork by, 307, 419; at International Congress of Anthropology, 100, 110, 112, 119n1, 186; and life group displays, 299, 301, 307, 314–15, 319, 335n66; museum display theories of, 318; and National Gallery of Art, 427, 453–54n28; on Powell, 1; and Putnam, 7; review of International Congress of Anthropology by, 99–100, 120–23; at U.S. National Museum, 265, 359n1, 422; as visualist and artist, 266, 267; works: *Archaeological Studies among the Ancient Cities of Mexico*, 396–97; *Stone Implements of the Potomac-Chesapeake Tidewater Province*, 319
homosexuality, 304
Hondon, H., 255
Hooper, Franklin William, 414, 444
Hooton, A. E., 453n24
Hopewell Group, 283
Hopi: bread makers, 154, *296*, *297*, 301, 305; fieldwork among, 307, 308–9, 310
Hopkins, Louis J., 441–42
Horowitz, Helen Lefkowitz, 386
Horticultural Building, 158
Hough, Walter, 112, 266, 429, 456
Houghton, Frederick Boies, 203n35
House of the Stormy Sea, 277, 330n18, 331n20
Houses and House-Life of the American Aborigines (Morgan), 36, 276
Hovenden, Thomas: biographical note on, 147n2; *Breaking Home Ties* painting by, *xxix*, 125–26; portrait of Cushing by, *xxviii*, 144, 151n24
Hovey, Horace Carter, 192, 210n96
Howell, Helen Sarah Norton, 116

Howells, William Dean, 49, 54–55, 243
Howland, Henry Raymond, 203n35
Hoxie, Fred, 33
Hrdlicka, Ales, 457
Hubbard, Gardiner Greene, 449n1
Hubbell, John Lorenzo, 438
Huckel, J. F., 438
human agency, 36, 129
human exhibits, 35–47, 76–77, 295, 490; of Africans, 61–64; anthropologists and, 57–58; Boas and, 34, 46, 47, 81–82; history of, xvi, 55–59, 332n31; of Inuit, 40–46; of Kwakiutl, 34–35, 161–62, 169, 385; and life group dioramas, 295, 332n31; of Navajo and Apache, 36–40, 46, 91–92, 161; Putnam and, 36–39, 46–47; recruitment of subjects for, 27–28, 31–33, 36–37, 62–63
Humboldt, Alexander von, 105, 230
Humors of the Fair, 52–53, 243, 259
Hunt, Gaillard, 171, 204n49
Hunt, George: at International Congress of Anthropology, 112, 187, 209n87; and Kwakiutl, 46, 209n87, 277, 322–23
Hunt, Jimmy, 411
Hunter, Annie, 293
Huntington, Archer Milton, 422, 437
Huntington, Ellsworth, 427
Huntington Survey, 424
Hurd, Henry Mills, 178, 206n64, 442
Hutchinson, Charles L., 20, 151n20, 399
Hyatt, Alpheus, 6, 9
Hyde, Benjamin Talbot Babbitt, 437
Hyde, Frederick, xxxviii, 348–49, 355, 419, 494
Hyde, Talbot, xxxviii, 355, 361n13, 419, 494; Wetherill and, 351, 357
Hyde Exploring Expedition, 351, 353–55, 357, 359, 419, 494

imperialism, xvi, xix, 75, 420
Incas, 220, 223, 371
Indian Games and Dances (Fletcher), 425
International Congress of Americanists, 100, 105, 421
International Congress of Anthropology (1888), 448n1

International Congress of Anthropology (1893), 339, 379, 494; attendance at, 110–18; Boas at, 100, 107, 110, 111, 131, 187, 190, 191; Brinton as chairman of, 100, 110, 184, 191, 446; Brinton on results of, 100, 191; Brinton papers and addresses at, xxxvi, 1, 103–7, 119n8, 121–22, 185; Cushing diary account of, 184–91; Cushing participation in, 135–36, 176–77; Cushing presentations to, 106, 184, 185, 186, 187, 191, 209n79; goals of, 100; Holmes review of, 99–100, 120–23; schedule of, 99, 120–21; significance of, 99–100, 492
International Folk-Lore Congress, xli (n13), 202nn33–34
International Journal of American Linguistics, 426
Inter-State Industrial Exposition, 13
An Introduction to the Study of Southwestern Archaeology (Kidder), 452n20
Inuit exhibit, 40–46, 81, 252, 276, 277
Iroquois exhibit, 26, 28, 82, 97, 276–77
Ives, Halsey Cooley, 168, 203n40

Jackson, Alice Hooker Day, 442
Jackson, John L., 116
Jackson, Percy, 442
Jackson, William Henry, 276
Jacobi, Abraham, 442
Jacobsen, Johan Adrian, 58, 112
Jahn, Ulrich, 116
James, George Wharton, 436–37
James, William, xxxiii, 11
Japanese pavilion, 26, 40, 70, 158, 276
Jastrow, Joseph, 112, 172, 204n50, 372
Jastrow, Morris, Jr., 172, 204n50; at International Congress of Anthropology, 112, 189, 210n94
Javanese Village, 156, 158, 159, 191, 230n4
Jayne, Horace Fort, 439
Jenks, Albert Ernest, 421–22
Jesup, Morris K., 21, 74, 395, 419
Jesup North Pacific Expedition, 106, 419, 492
Johns Hopkins University, xx, 442
Johnson, Albert, 428
Jones, William, 445

Jordan, David Starr, 439
Journal of American Folk-Lore, xx, 422, 428, 430
Joyce, Thomas A., 424
Judd, Neil, 361n13
Jung, Carl, 423

Kaiser, Arthur, 116
Kallenberg, Henry Frederick, 116
Kane, Elisha Kent, 298
Karr, William Wesley, 158
Keam, Thomas V., 308, 309
Keasby, Lindley Miller, 444
Kedzie [Jones], Nellie Sawyer, 116
Kelley, Isabel, 426
Keppler, Joseph F., 239–40
Kerr, William Wesley, 200n19
Kersey, Charles Anselm, 116
Kidder, A. V., 424, 452n20
Kiowa, 267, 303, 304, 305; Mooney and, 307–8, 317, 335n64
Kipling, Rudyard, 65
Kirkham, William Barri, 442
Kiva ceremonials, 218, 231n7
Klah, Hosteen, 304, 333n46
Knapp, William J., 379
Knell, Simon, 338
Knowles, Frances Howe Seymour, 437
Kopta, Emery, 443
Korean Buddhism (Starr), 401
Kotuktooka (Evilina Cooper), 41
Kroeber, Alfred Louis, 3, 422, 425, 451n15; as *American Anthropologist* contributor, 430, 456; and Boas, 428–29, 447, 452–53n21; opposition to eugenics movement by, 423, 426; role of in American anthropology, 427, 428; works: *Anthropology*, 427, 430, 434; *Handbook of the Indians of California*, 427
Kunz, George Frederick, 453n27; biographical note on, 201n23; and Cushing, 156, 161, 163–64, 165–66, 167, 168; at International Congress of Anthropology, 112, 187
Kurtz, Charles, 161, 201n22
Kwakiutl, 34, 46, 156, 257, 276–77; Boas fieldwork among, 322–23; "cannibal ceremony" of, 385; dances of, 34–35, 161–62, 169; hamatsa ceremony of, 302, 319–20, 324

labeling, exhibit, 275, 306, 312–13
Labná ruins, 287, 290; display based on, 47, 93, 95, *288*, *289*, 292, 388
Lacey, Michael, 129
LaGarde, Louis Anatole, 100, 110
Laguna, Fredericka de, 441
Lamborn, Robert Henry, 165, 202n31
Land of Sunshine (Lummis), 445
Lane-Fox Pitt Rivers, Augustus H., 287
La Rabida, 92, 165, 167, 202n34, 253
Laufer, Berthold, 421, 429, 457; and Field Museum, 394, 400–401, 403, 425
Learned, William, 203n35
Leather and Shoe Trades Building, 26, 27, 324
Lemmon, John Gill, 116
Lemmon, Sara Allen Plummer, 116
Lenz, Rodolfo, 421, 451n12
León, Nicolás, 421, 451n14
Le Plongeon, Augustus, 292
Levasseur, Pierre Emile, 112
Leverson, Montegue Richard, 116
Levi, Monahan, 241, *255*
Lévi-Strauss, Claude, 76
Levy, Robert, 59
Lewis, Samuel S., 116
Liberal Arts Building, 16, 23, 159, 166–67, 286, 331n25
Library of Aboriginal American Literature (Brinton), 103
life groups, 295–316, 332n35; about, 295, 298; Chicago World's Fair innovation in, 300–302; documentary sources for, 306–9; errors made in preparation of, 313, 315–16, 334–35nn58–59; labeling of, 306, 312–13; and living human displays, 295, 332n31; photographs of, 26, *297*, *302*, *320*, *321*, *322*; production process to create, 299–300, 332–33nn38–39; refraction in, 295, 304, 309, 315–16, 324, 328; and semi-habitat dioramas, 301, 333n43; at Smithsonian Institution, 298–99, 332n36; social action depicted in, 302–3, 304–5; state of arrested motion in, 296–97, 326;

life groups (*continued*)
  subsequent fate of, 318–19, 321–22; as *tableaux vivants*, 297–98; tribal range of, 300, 305–6, 333n40
Lightman, Bernard, 376
Ling, Reamer, 445
linguistics, 452n20; as anthropology subfield, 187, 273; Boas on, 107, 424, 426, 479; Brinton on, 107, 190, 370, 448, 468; Powell language map, 107, 130, 265, 268, 273, 275, 370, 379
Linguistic Society of America, 452n20
Little Egypt dance performances, 59, 385
Lloyd, Henry Demarest, 141, 183, 208n74
Lloyd, Jessie Bross, 141, 183, 208n74
Lobingie(r), Charles Sumner, 116
Locke, John, 451n17
Lockwood, Daniel Newton, 203n35
Lockwood, Frank C., 398
Logan, John H., 132
London exposition (Crystal Palace, 1861), 263
London exposition (Imperial International Exhibition, 1909), 62
Lord, George S. and Eda, 141, 178, 182–83, 206–7n64
Loubat, Joseph Florimond M. le Duc de, 395, 419, 437
Louisiana Purchase Exposition (St. Louis, 1904), xvi, 30, 318, 321, 422, 433, 444, 489
Lovell, Margaretta, 261
Low, Charles F., 5
Lowie, Robert H., 426, 428; and *American Anthropologist*, 424, 434, 458; and Boas, 429, 430
Lumholtz, Carl Sophus, 112, 184–85, 191, 208n75
Lummis, Charles F., 422, 445
Lurie, Ed, 3

MacCurdy, George Grant, 430, 455
MacFarland, Henry, 12
MacVeagh, Frederick, 151n20
Madrid Exposition (1892), 265, 275, 285, 293
Madrid Exposition (1894), 360n7
Magill, Charles, 156, 158, 160, 169, 175, 184, 196, 197, 199n5

Magill, George L., 176, 180, 184, 192, 196, 206n61
Magill, Julia Groves, 164, 165, 166, 168, 174, 202n29
Magill, Mary, 155, 156, 160, 169, 175, 196, 197, 199n5
Magill, Ned, 156
Magill, Samuel Edward ("Ned"), 156, 164, 165, 166, 168, 174, 202n29
Maler, Teobert, 292
Manak, Columbia Susan, 41
Manny, Frank Addison, 117
Manufactures and Liberal Arts Building, 22, 23, 26
Manwarren, Wilfred Hamilton, 117
Mark, Edward Laurens, 117
Mark, Joan, 3, 30
Martin, Paul Sidney, 147n3
masks, 481
Mason, Edward G., 410
Mason, John Alden, 436
Mason, Otis Tufton, 265, 266, 350; and *American Anthropologist*, 420, 430, 455; and American anthropology's development, xxiii, 266; and Anthropological Society of Washington, xxi, xxiii; biographical notes on, 149–50n14, 200n19; and Boas, 269, 296, 484; and Chicago World's Fair exhibits, xvii–xviii, 268, 269, 272, 298, 317–18, 329n8, 370; on culture areas, 269, 317–18; and Cushing, 134, 135, 158, 329–30n8; at International Congress of Anthropology, 100, 106, 110, 112, 122, 190–91; and life group displays, 298, 315, 332n31; on Paris 1889 Exposition, xvii, 67, 106–7; and Smithsonian annual reviews, xl (n8)
mastodon, 97
Matthews, Washington, 308, 348, 456, 480; biographical note on, 202n33; Cushing and, 165, 170, 171, 176, 180–81
Maudslay, Alfred, 316; in photographs, 291, 292; use of photos by, 290, 292, 293–94, 331n28
Mayan ruins, 79, 80, 96, 130, 267, 273, 283, 372; architectural models of, 287–88, 321;

and Chichén Itzá site, 48, 74, 290, 292, 331n24, 331n28, 376, 395; Cushing diary on, 161; photographic presentations of, 275, 290–94; plaster casts of, 92–93, 161, 275, 287–88, 290–94, 321, 331n27; Thompson and, 47–48, 95, 287–88, 290, 331n24, 372, 386, 388
Mayas, 376, 451n13; architecture of, 47–48, 287–88
Maybeck, Bernard, 441
Maynard, George W., *139*
McAdams, William, 116–17
McChesney, Augusta, 155, 199n6
McCormick, Stanley, 421, 437
McCown, Theodore, 426
McDowell, Henry Burden, 145, 151–52n25
McDowell, Irvin G., 152n25
McGee, Anita Newcomb, 112
McGee, William John, xv, xxxv, 30, 112, 156, 418; and *American Anthropologist*, xix–xx, 420, 446, 456; anthropological perspective of, 129, 478; biographical information, 200n11, 422; and Boas, 421, 446; and St. Louis, 422, 453n26, 489
McGuire, Joseph Deakins, 457
McKim, Charles F., *139*
McLoyd, Charles, 340–41, 342, 346
Mead, Margaret, 452n20
Meltzer, David J., 399
Menand, Louis, xxxiii
Mendel, Gregor, 451n15
Mepham, George, 453n26
Mercer, Henry Chapman, 112, 184, 208n75
Merriam, C. Hart, xl (n6)
Merriam, John C., 428
Mesa Verde ruins, 276, 340, *341*, 342, 348–49
Mesher, Peter, 44
Metcalf, Willard Leroy, *xxx*, 174, 206n57, 306
methodological fallibility, 451n15
Metropolitan Museum of Art, 223, 385, 444
Metz, Charles L.: Ohio mound fieldwork by, 97, 283–84, 372–73; and Putnam, 5, 6, 7
Mexican Archaeology (Joyce), 424
Mexican calendar, 228–30

Mexican studies, 422–23
Midway Plaisance, xxxvi, 48–59, 64; architecture of, 276, 277; Boas on, 82; commercial nature of, 29, 54–55, 67, 69, 295; constructed chaos of, 385, 493; cultural diversity of, 50, 52–53, 55, 75, 447; Cushing visits to, 156, 158, 159, 181–82; Dahomey Village exhibit along, 61–64, 191, 277; human displays along, 295, 322, 372; Javanese Village along, 156, 158, 159, 191, 230n4; management of, 65–71; photos and drawings of, *66*, 76, *260*; and popular science, 17, 376; reviews and narratives of, 50–55; Street in Cairo exhibit along, 52, 59–61, 75–76, 174, 191, 246, 247, 277, 386; theatrical performances at, 64–65; White City contrasted to, 54, 385, 447
Mill, John Stuart, 473
Miller, Milo George, 442
Millet, Francis Davis "Frank": biographical notes on, 150–51n18, 205n53; and Cushing, 136–37, 173, 176, 183–84; photos of, *139*, *140*
Millet, Lucia, 173, 205n53
Mills, Theodore A., 299, 332–33n39
Millspaugh, Charles, 397, 399
Milwaukee Public Museum, 320
Mindeleff, Victor and Cosmos, 234, 281–83, 294
The Mind of Primitive Man (Boas), xxxiv
Miniter, P. J., 117
Minton, Maurice K., 344, 347
Missouri Archaeological Society, 453n25
Molera, Eusebio Joseph, 439
Monsen, Frederick, 437
Montes, Emilo, 112
Montez collection, 220–21, 223
Mooney, James A., xxxv, 33, 176, 266, 306, 456; anthropological perspective of, 104–5, 266, 315, 335n62; biographical note on, 206n60; field photographs by, *303*, 310, 334n54; fieldwork by, 307–9, 317, 334n52, 335n64; and life group displays, 299, 308, 312–13, 314, 330n8, 370; museum display scheme of, 316–17
Moore, Clarence Bloomfield, 442

Index 565

Moorehead, Warren King, xxxviii, 163, 316, 343–47; anthropologists' dissatisfaction with, 360–61n9; biographical information, 343–44, 352–53, 360n3; Boas on, 352; at Chicago World's Fair, 349–50; and Chicago World's Fair exhibits, 97, 284, 347, 369–74; patrons of, 345–46, 354–55; and Peabody, 358, 361n13, 422; photo of, *344*; and Putnam, xxxviii, 344–47, 352, 361n10; relic-hunting scheme of, 346, 360n6; and Wetherill, 353–54, 355, 357, 358–59; and Wilson, 343, 349, 352, 354

Moorehouse, Georg Wilton, 117

Moorish Palace, 59, 174

Moqui Shoshonis, 188

Morgan, Lewis Henry: Bandelier and, xxi, 3; Brinton and, 103, 104, 105, 119n8; Powell and, 129, 281; works: *Ancient Society*, 104, 119n8, 426; *Houses and House-Life of the American Aborigines*, 36, 276; *Systems of Consanguinity and Affinity in the Human Family*, 104

Morgan, Thomas Jefferson, 30–31, 32, 35

Morley, Sylvanus Griswold, 48, 423, 424

Morse, Edward Sylvester, 9, 486; at International Congress of Anthropology, 106, 112, 185

Mosconas, Demetrius, 59

Moses, George, 29, 69

Mullins, Nicholas C., xxii, 428

mummies, 93, 97, 130, 221, 281, 371

Muniz, Manuel Antonio, 117

Murie, James, 437

Museum of the Chicago Academy of Sciences, 18–19, 85

museums, natural history: Chicago World's Fair legacy for, 316–19; department store-type displays at, 263; educational role of, 10, 126; exclusion of working people from, 128, 385; gifts and bequests to, 71, 87, 351, 383, 494; growth of public, xviii, xl (n1), 18; and institutionalization of anthropology, 263–64; management of, 86–88; mission of, 84–85, 90, 386; Putnam vision of, 10, 12, 17–18, 19, 73, 84–90, 273, 388; structure of, 88–89; as visual medium, 264–65

music, Native American, 185–86

Muybridge, Eadweard, 297, 304, 325, 326, 336n74

mythology, 186, 187, 215, 236, 237, 468–69

Nabokov, Peter, 283

Nashville fair (1897), 317, 318

National Academy of Sciences Biographical Memoirs, 3

National Anthropological Archives (NAA), 147n1

National Association for the Advancement of Colored People, 423

National Gallery of Art, 427, 453–54n28

National Geographic Society, xl (n9), 421, 449n1

National Origins Act, 428, 452n19

Native Americans: architecture of, 48, 276–95; art of, 221–22, 223, 235–36, 277–78, 305, 480; and cultural hybridity, 313–16; diversity of, 129–30, 379; and education, 372; games of, 105, 184, 185, 189, 224–26; human exhibits of, 27–28, 31–46, 81–82, 91–92, 161–62, 169, 385; Indian Affairs Bureau and, 30–31, 32, 33, 35, 295; labor activities of, 97, 154, 188–89, 213, 216–17, 301, 304–5, 365–67; music and song of, 185–86; and "playing Indian," 310–11; Sickles dispute with Putnam over, 33–35; stereotypes of, 305, 306; as theme at Chicago World's Fair, 272; tribal range for life groups, 300, 305–6, 333n40; U.S. treatment of, 29–30

Navajo: human displays of, 36–40, 46, 161; Mooney fieldwork among, 308, 309, 310; silversmithing by, 154, 213, 301, *303*, 304–5; and Smithsonian collections, 305; spinning and weaving by, 154, 213, 230n4, 304; symbols of, 226–27; totems of, 480

Nelson, Nels, 424

"New Archaeology," 424

Newberry Library, 375; Ayer and, 151n21, 398, 402, 494

Newcombe, Charles F., 329

Newell, William Wells, xx, 197; biographical note on, 209n85; and Boas, xxiii–xxiv, 414, 453n27; at International Congress of Anthropology, 110, 112, 187

New Mexico pavilion, 304, 347
New School of Social Research, 434
New York Academy of Anthropology, 445, 448, 453n24
New York NY, xxi, 13–14, 416, 439, 453n24
New York Times, 34, 60, 127
Nicholas, Zacherias, 278, *281*
Nicholson, Grace A., 443
Nies, James Buchanan, 442–43
Nisbet, Robert, 428
Noble, John W., 33
Nordenskiold, Gustav, 342, 347, 360n7
Norton, Charles Eliot, xxi, 126, 128
Norway, 95
Notes on the Floridian Peninsula (Brinton), 101
Nuttall, Zelia Maria Magdalena Parrott, 427; biographical notes on, 150n15, 207–8n70; and Cushing, 135, 136, 177, 180, 194; at International Congress of Anthropology, 112, 186, 189, 209n84; Mexican anthropological work by, 98, 189, 228, 229, 230, 275

Ogden, Althea Abbey, 117
Ohio Historical Society, 283, 374
Ohio mound exhibit, 96, 97, 267, 275, 349, 350, 372–74; architecture miniatures prepared for, 283–87; Boas on, 79–80; photos of, *284, 285*; Serpent Mound, xxiii, 5, 96, 283–86, 374, 493
Ojibwa scribe, 306, 310, *313*
Olmsted, Frederick Law, 26
Olsen, Ronald, 426
Omaha exposition (1898), 318
Oñate, Juan de, 187, 209n88
O'Neale, Lila, 426
Orvell, Miles, 263
Osborn, Frederick, 428
Osborn, Henry Fairfield, 428
Owen, Charles, 436
Owen, Mary Alicia (Julia Scott), 439–40
Owens, John G., 8, 194, 210n99, 290, 292

Packard, A. S., 9
Palenque, 290, 292, 395
Palliser, Christopher Columbus, 41–42, 45
Palmer, Bertha Honoré (Mrs. Potter Palmer), 42, *44*, 45, 395

Palmer, Edward, 306
Palmer, Walter, 187, 209n90
Pan-American Exposition (Buffalo, 1901), xvi, 64–65, 301, 318, 489
Pangolo, George, 60
Paraguay, 81, 94
parallelism, 462, 467
Paris Exposition (1867), 55
Paris Exposition (1878), xvi, xvii, 55–56
Paris Exposition (1889), 51, 100, 298; and Chicago World's Fair, xvi–xvii; human displays at, 56–57, 60, 62, 67–68, 265, 332n31
Parsons, Elsie Clews, 415, 424, 427, 428, 430–31, 458
The Passing of the Great Race (Grant), 426
patolli, 105, 145, 467
patrons and patronage, xxxviii–xxxix, 384–88; and anthropology, 375–76, 402; Armour and, 376, 386, 395, 397, 494; Ayer and, xxxviii, 383, 386, 397, 398–99, 401–2, 437, 494; and benefactor control issue, 386; Chicago World's Fair and, 338, 493–94; danger of dependency on, 386–87; Hearst and, 208n70, 264, 351, 419, 420, 437, 494; of institutions and associations, 264, 351, 383, 385, 386, 402, 420, 494; Moorehead and, 345–46, 354–55; patron-client relationship, 350, 358, 361n13, 386, 402–3; personal patron type, 385–86, 394, 395, 397; philanthropist types, 386; professional patron type, 386, 389–90; and relic hunting, 351–52; sponsorship of expeditions by, xxiii, 106, 345–46, 354–55, 376, 397, 419–20, 493–94
Pauly, Philip J., 449n3
Payne, Eleanor ("Nellie") Magill, 153, 155, 186, 192, 199n9
Payne, George C., 155, 199n9
Payne, James G., 199n10
Peabody, Charles, 422, 436, 457
Peabody, George, 354
Peabody, Lucy Evelyn, 440
Peabody, Robert Singleton, 354, 355, 361n12, 422
Peabody, Selim, 351
Peabody Museum (Salem), 2, 9, 148n7

Peabody Museum of Archaeology and Ethnology (Cambridge), xx, 210n98, 316, 321, 400, 448; art vs. ethnography conundrum at, 376; fieldwork sponsorship by, 325, 388–89; management of, 86; and Ohio mounds, 283, 284–85, 286, 289; Putnam and, xx, xxiii, 2, 4, 9, 21, 214, 263–64, 359, 376. *See also* Harvard University

Peale Museum, xxiv

Peary, Robert, 40

Pecos Conference, 452n20

Peet, Stephen Dennison, xx, 360–61n9; biographical note on, 209n78; at International Congress of Anthropology, 12, 105, 110, 185, 189

Peñafiel, Antonio, 421, 451n13

Peñasco Blanco village, *282*

Pené, Xavier, 62–64

Pennsylvania Academy of the Fine Arts, xxiv

Penobscot Village, 27, 46, 276, *277*

Pepper, George, 355, 395

Pepper, William, xxiv, 132, 148–49n10, 204–5n51, 336n74

Peralta, Manuel de, 189, 210n92

Peristyle, 159, 160, 184

Perkins, George Henry, 112

Persian Palace, 59–60

Peruvian collection, 294, 370–71; Boas on, 80–81; Cushing on, 220–24; of mummies, 93, 97, 130, 221, 371

Peshlakai, Atsidi, 38, 39–40, *303*, 304

Philadelphia Centennial Exposition (1876), 55, 65, 285, 295, 298, 325; Chicago World's Fair and, xvii, 369; Smithsonian displays at, 131, 265, 275; and U.S. National Museum, xviii, 17–18, 264

Philadelphia PA: and American anthropology, xx, xx–xxi, xxiv, xxxiii, 414; University Museum of, xxiv, 136, 206n56, 316, 351, 414, 420, 422, 446

Philippines, 421–22

Philips, Walter Alison, 141

Phillips (William Abbott or J. Wallace), 178, 186, 194, 207n66

Phillips Academy, 422, 424, 431

photography: field photos, 292–93, 304, 309–10, 334n54; and life groups, 297, 309–10; metaphoric-metonymic relationship in, 328; photo albums and souvenirs, 45, 48, 49, 53, 241–42, 323, 348; positive-negative method in, 274–75, 293–94; used in Chicago World's Fair exhibits, 274–75, 290–94, 309–10, 335n54

physical anthropology: Boas and, 27, 268, 269, 370, 448; Brinton and, xxiv, 103, 104; Chicago World's Fair laboratory of, 94, 273, 388, 492; as subfield of anthropology, xix, 93, 100, 273, 460, 491

Pickett, M. B., *139*

Pimas, 226–27

plaster casts, 274–75, 283, 293, 328, 330nn13–14; creation of, 290, *291*, *292*

"playing Indian," 310–11

Plummer, E. H., 28

Pomiuk, "Prince," 45

popular culture, xx, 416

popular education, xxxvi, 75–76

popular science, 1, 376, 377–84, 404n3

Popular Science Monthly, xx, xxii, xxxiii, xl (n8)

Portrait Types of the Midway Plaisance, 60, 76; about, 241–42; excerpts from, 252, *253*, *254*, *255*

Post, A. H., 466–67, 477

Post, George B., *139*

pottery, 153, 175, 214, 371; of cliffdwellers, 188–89, 216–17, 231n6, 365, 366–67

Powell, John Wesley, 106, 448, 456; as American anthropology father, xix, 1, 266, 414, 447; as archaeologist, xxi, xl (n4), 306, 414; and Bureau of American Ethnology, xx, xxii, xxxv, 1, 131, 380; and Chicago World's Fair exhibits, 321, 446; and Cushing, 132, 145, 154–55, 170, 171, 172, 173, 174; and Henshaw, xl (n6); Holmes on, 1; language map of, 107, 130, 265, 268, 273, 275, 370, 379; Morgan's influence on, 129, 281; photo of, *xxv*; as professionalizer, xxi, 380–81

Powhatan quarry men, 305, 307, 319, *320*, *321*, *322*

Prescott, William H., 102, 397

568 *Index*

Preston, May Wilson, 173, 205n55
Primitive Society (Lowie), 426
Prince, John Dyneley, 440
professionalization and professionalism: amateurs and, 380, 385, 404n1, 413, 449n4; of American anthropology, xxi, xxxviii, 359, 376, 380–81, 383–84, 389, 413–14, 416–17, 425, 436, 437; in archaeology, 338, 449n4; collaboration and, 3–4, 389–90, 446–47; of museum anthropology, 263; patrons and, 386, 389–90; popularization and, 376, 377–84, 418, 434
Prudden, T. Mitchell, 342, 357
The Psychic History of the Cliff Dwellers (Bullene), 438–39
Puck. See *World's Fair Puck*
Pueblo Bonito, 353–54, 355–56, 357, 358
Pueblos. *See* Zuni Pueblo
Putnam, Alice Edmands, 117
Putnam, Charles, 380
Putnam, Eben, 9–10
Putnam, Edward Kirby, 443
Putnam, Elizabeth Duncan, 443
Putnam, Esther O. Clarke, 6
Putnam, Frederic Ward, xxxvi, 2–9, 71–77; and AAAS, xxxiv, 9, 148n7; address to Commercial Club of Chicago, 84–90; and Agassiz, 2–3, 4, 11; as American anthropology father, xix, 1, 74–75, 266, 414, 447; and American Museum of Natural History, 7, 21, 74, 148n7, 264, 273, 353, 414–15, 419, 447; and anthropological expeditions, 287, 353, 355, 388–89, 419; and Anthropology Building, 23–25; biographical information, 2–3, 148n7, 422, 425; and Boas, 4, 73, 74, 352, 386, 419, 484; and Chicago World's Fair displays, 22–35, 267, 283–84, 285, 294, 317, 339–40, 369–74; commercial ambitions of, 9–10; and Cushing, 6–7, 106, 136, 185; and Dorsey, 8–9, 74, 210n99, 425; on ethnological study in America, xxi, xl (n4); Field Museum relationship to, 19–20, 71–73, 351, 361n10, 390–91, 394; fieldwork by, 4–8, 337, 357; and Fletcher, 4, 32, 150n15; Harvard professorship of, xxxv, 2, 8, 74, 264, 273; as head of Department of Ethnology, xxxvi, 55, 68, 79, 94, 95, 446; and Higinbotham, 24, 72, 394; Holmes on, 7; and human displays, 36–39, 46–47; at International Congress of Anthropology, 100, 105, 106, 110, 112, 120–21, 122, 185, 188, 191; introduction to *Portrait Types of the Midway Plaisance* by, 75, 241; and Metz, 5, 6, 7; and Midway Plaisance, xxxvi, 67, 71; and Moorehead, xxxviii, 344–47, 352, 361n10; on museums' dependence on patronage, 386–87; on museums' mission, 84–85, 90; and Peabody Museum, xx, xxiii, 2, 9, 214, 263–64, 359, 376; photo of, *xxvi*; and popular education, xxxvi, 75–76; and professionalism of science, 383–84, 389; promotional activities by, 9; on science of anthropology, xv, 9, 359, 417, 480; and Sickles, 33–35; and Skiff, 39, 384; and Starr, 377–79, 389; students of, 4, 74, 425; teaching by, 8–9, 74, 148n7, 264; vision of anthropology at Chicago Fair, 11, 12, 15–22, 75–76, 130, 337; vision of museum in Chicago, 12, 17–18, 19, 73, 84–90, 273, 388; and women in anthropology, 4
Putnam, George Palmer, 442
Putnam, Henry W., 9
Putnam, Mary Corina, 442

race, 328, 425–26; Boas on, 82–83; Brinton on, 103, 460, 469–71
racism, 55, 103, 452n17, 493; and racial caricatures, 52–53, 63, *246*
Radcliffe-Brown, Alfred Reginald, 452–53n21
Radin, Paul, 436, 437
railroad station, 157–58
Ralph, Julian, 49, 50, 243
Ranck, D. H., 136
Ratzel, Friedrich, 478, 484
Raymond, Jerome Hall, 117
Reardon, James A., 453n26
Reed, Christopher Robert, 63
refraction definition, 262
Reid, Whitelaw, 441
Reingold, Nathan, 436
Reisner, George Andrew, 420–21

Index 569

Reiss, Wilhelm, 371
relic hunting, xxxvii–xxxviii; and antiquities market, 337–39, 340–41, 346; Chicago World's Fair and, 339–40, 347–50; Moorehead and, 343–47; patronage for, 351–53; Wetherill and, 340–43
religion, 141, 144, 224, 235–36, 305; Boas on, 482–84
Rex, Frank C., 117
Rice, Edward, *139*
Riggs, Chauncey Wales, 165, 202n32
Ritter, Karl, 478
Rivers, W. H. R., 426
Robson, John, 277, 278, 331n20
Roddy, Thomas, 39
Rorer, Sarah Tyson: biographical notes on, 150n16, 204n48; and Cushing, 136, 170, 175, 177, 181, 193, 195; "Mrs. Rorer's Corn Recipe's Cookbook" by, *138*; portrait of, *137*
Rosenberg, Charles E., 415
Rossiter, Margaret, 3
Royce, Sophia Wells, 148n10
Russell, Frank, 74, 361n11
Rust, Horatio Nelson, 194, 196, 210n98
Ryan, W. A., 117
Rydell, Robert W., xviii, 62, 403
Ryerson, Martin A., 151n20, 387, 398

Sabloff, Jeremy A., 424
sacredness, 223–24, 468–69
Safford, William E., 274–75
Saint-Gaudens, Augustus, *139*
Salem MA, 2–3, 133–34, 494
Salem Press, 9–10
Salisbury, Mr., 170, 204n47
Salisbury, Stephen, III, 117
Samoan Village, 191, 254
San Diego exposition (1915), 321
Santa Fe NM, xxi, 422–23
Sapir, Edward, 424, 425, 452n20, 458; and Boas, 426, 453n22
Sargent, Dudley Allen, 83, 445
Saturday Review, 376
Sauer, Carl, 451n16
Saville, Marshall H., 8, 290, 292, 316, 352, 395

Sawyer, Wells Moses, 224, 231n9
Scammon, Ariana, 117
Schiff, Jacob Henry, 421
School of American Archaeology, xxi, 422–23
Schurtz, Carl, 442
Science, xxii, xl (n8), 269
Scientific American, 192
scientific integrity, xxxvi, 425
Scott, Gertrude, 64–65
Seidmore, Eliza Ruhnmah, 169, 171, 204n44
Seler, Eduard, 423
Selig, William N., 383
semi-habitat dioramas, 301, 333n43
Sergel, Charles Hubbard, 117
Serpent Mound, xxiii, 5, 96, 283–86, 374, 493; photos of model, *284*, *285*
Service, Elman, 426
Seven Cities of Cibola, 102, 219–20
Sewall, May Eliza Wright, 173, 205n55
Shields, Thomas Edward, 117
Shoe and Leather Building, 167, 272
Shoshoneans, 216, 217
Sickles, Emma C., 33–34, 35
Siflico, A., 59
silversmithing exhibits, 154, 177, 179, 213, 301, *303*, 304–5
Simms, Stephen Chapman, 436–37
Skidegate, 277, 278, *279*, 331n19
Skiff, Frederick J. V.: at Columbian Museum opening, xxxix, 409–10; as Field Museum director, 21, 391, 399, 400; and Putnam, 39, 384
Skiles, J. W., 40
Skinner, Alanson B., 458
skyscrapers, 147–48n5
Small, Albion Woodbury, 112
Smith, Harlan Ingersoll, 112, 316; biographical note on, 203n40; and Cushing, 163, 168, 198
Smith, Herbert Wood, 117–18
Smith, H. Jay: biographical note on, 201n24; and cliffdweller exhibit, 171–72, 348; and Cushing, 161, 162–64, 165–66, 167, 171–72
Smith, Lee Herbert, 203n35
Smith College, 434

Smith Exploring Company, H. Jay, 205–6n56, 278. *See also* cliffdweller exhibits; H. Jay Smith Exploring Company

Smithsonian Institution, xviii, xxi, 64, 298, 327; Bureau of Ethnology within, 128; Chicago World's Fair legacy for, 316–17; library of, 239; life group displays at, 319, 321–22, 335n65; U.S. National Museum established within, 264. *See also* Government Building (Smithsonian displays); U.S. National Museum

social evolutionism, xviii–xix, 57, 62–63, 104, 473

The Social Organization and the Secret Societies of the Kwakiutl Indians (Boas), 320

sociology, 121, 472

song, Native American, 185–86

sound recordings, 324–25

South Sea Islands village, 77, 82, 98

souvenir photo albums, 45, 48, 49, 53, 241–42, 323, 348

Spanish-American War, 420, 421

Spaulding, Charles Warren, 118

Speck, Frank G., 264, 425, 429, 430

Spencer, Herbert, xxxiii, 128–29, 477

Spier, Leslie, 424

Spinden, Herbert J., 424

spinning and weaving, 213, 230nn2–3

Spiro, Jonathan Peter, 452n19

Sprigge, S. S., 169, 204n45

Springer, Frank, 452n18

Squier, Ephraim George, 371

Starr, Frederick V., xxxviii, 110, 379, 390, 457; and Boas, 377, 379, 402–3; and Dorsey, 381, 387, 388, 402–3; and Field Museum, 387, 388; fieldwork by, 387; and patrons, 380, 383, 388; photo of, 278; as popularizer of science, 376, 377, 379, 383; and Putnam, 377–79, 389; at University of Chicago, 147n3, 383, 387, 401, 426–27; works: *Korean Buddhism*, 401; *The Truth about the Congo*, 387

State Archaeological Association of Ohio, 285

state pavilions, 180, 272, 373

Statue of Industry, 242, 258

Steinmates, Benjamin F., 118

Steinmetz, S. R., 466–67

Stephen, Alexander M., 308

Stephens, John Lloyd, 291

stereotypes, 13, 243, 305, 306

Stetson, George Rochford, 436–37

Stevenson, James, 305, 306

Stevenson, Matilda Coxe, 113, 190, 305, 306

Stevenson, Sara Yorke, 264; biographical notes on, 149n13, 210n95; at International Congress of Anthropology, 113, 190; portrait of, 134

Steward, Julian, 426

St. Louis Art Museum, 433, 453–54n28

St. Louis MO, 433, 453n26

St. Louis Public Museum, 422, 453n26

St. Louis World's Fair (Louisiana Purchase Exposition, 1904), xvi, 30, 318, 321, 422, 433, 444, 489

Stocking, George, xxxiii, 263, 324, 383

Stoll, Otto, 478

Stone Implements of the Potomac-Chesapeake Tidewater Province (Holmes), 319

stratigraphic analysis, 423–24

Street in Cairo, 174, 191, 277; appeal of, 60–61; dance performances at, 59, 75–76, 191, 385; description of, 52, 59–61, 75; drawings of, 246, 247

Strong, William Duncan, 426

Stubel, Alphons, 371

Studley, Cornelia, 4

A Study of Maya Art (Spinden), 424

Sudanese Village, 174

Sullivan, Louis R., 458

Sumner, William Graham, xxxiii

Sun Dance, 34–35

Swanton, John R., 74, 321, 331n20; and *American Anthropologist*, 424, 429, 457

swastika, 185, 226–28, 468

Sweet, Henry N., 292

Sweet Clover (Burnham), 50–51, 493

symbolism, 185, 188, 226–28, 468

Systems of Consanguinity and Affinity in the Human Family (Morgan), 104

Taber, Ralph G., 40, 45

tableaux vivants, 297–98
Taft, William Howard, 127
tapestry weaving, 213–14, 222–23, 230n4
Ten Kate, Hermann F. C., 105
Terrell, Isaiah Mulligan, 118
Terry, Robert James, 453nn25–26
textiles: cliffdwellers and, 218–19, 367–68; Peruvian, 221–22, 223
Thaw, Benjamin, 437
Thomas, Cyrus, 456
Thompson, Edward H., 74, 384; and Allison V. Armour, 395, 396; and Mayan ruins exhibit, 47, 48, 95, 287–88, 290, 331n24, 372, 386, 388
Thruston, Yates P., 118
Tiffany Pavilion, 165, 168, 187
Time Perspective in Aboriginal American Culture (Sapir), 425
tipis, 276, 277, 317, 335n64
The Tlingit Indians (Emmons and Laguna), 441
Topinard, Paul, 57–58
totemic organization, 229, 480
totem poles, 81–82, 161, 265, 277, 321, 325, 372; drawing of exhibit, *257*
Tozzer, Alfred, 74, 423
Transportation Building, 272
Trenton gravels controversy, 424
Trevor, John Bond, Jr., 428
Tristes Tropiques (Lévi-Strauss), 76
The Truth about the Congo (Starr), 387
turkeys, 219–20
Turkish Village, 59, 255
Turner, Frederick Jackson, 448n1
Turner, William W., 107
Turner Group, 5, 283, 374
Tylor, Edward Burnett, 105, 423; biographical note on, 152n26; Boas on, 477, 484; Cushing on, 145, 230
Tyschudi, John James von, 371

Uhle, Max, 419, 420
universities: anthropology departments at, xxxv, 21, 264, 426–27, 431, 434; rise of urban, xx, 126
University of Arizona, 434
University of California at Berkeley, xxi; anthropology program at, 74, 148n7, 359, 426, 428, 431, 434, 447; Hearst philanthropy toward, 264, 351, 420–21
University of Chicago, xxi; anthropology program at, xxxviii, 147n3, 377, 383, 387, 401, 426–27; Ayer gifts to, 398–99; founding of, 126; Starr and, 147n3, 383, 387, 401, 426–27; Walker Museum and, 387, 398–99
University of Denver, 434
University of Michigan, 434
University of Minnesota, 434
University of Nebraska, 434
University of Pennsylvania: anthropology department at, 264, 424–25, 434; as center, xx, xxiv; University Museum of, xxiv, 136, 206n56, 316, 351, 414, 420, 422, 446
University of Texas, 434
University of Washington, 434
U.S. Army Medical Museum, 100, 110
U.S. Geological Survey, xx, 1, 148n6
U.S. National Museum, xviii, xxii, 338; Chicago Fair displays prepared by, 154, 212, 232–33, 264, 267–68, 283, 347, 379; Cushing and, 135, 265, 316; donation of Chicago Fair collections to, 154, 213; establishment and growth of, xviii, xx, 17–18, 264; exhibits in, 154, 213, 233, 234–35, 265, 272, 318, 332n32; Holmes and, 199n3, 265, 359n1, 422; life groups in, 295, 296, 320, 322, 332n32; and Philadelphia Centennial Exposition, xviii, 17–18, 230n1, 264
Utah pavilion, 196, 347
Uxmal ruins, 95, 287, 292; plaster casts made from, 47, *288*, 388

Van Brunt, Henry, *139*
Vancouver Indian Settlement, 35, 161
Victorianism, 263, 376
Viets, Conrad, 346–47
Viking ship, 95, 169
Villard, Henry, 419
Vincent, W. D., 40, 45
Virchow, Rudolph, 105
Vistas of the Fair, 76, 242; drawings from, *256*, *257*, *258*
vital statistics, 463

Volk, Ernest, 97, 113, 189, 210n93
Von Buschan, Vaschide, N., 470
von Ihering, Hermann, 421, 451n11
Voth, Hermann, 421

Wake, Charles Staniland, 73; biographical note on, 119n2; at International Congress of Anthropology, 100, 110, 113
Walcott, Charles D., 73
Walker, George C., 387
Walker, John Brisben, 163, 201n27
Walker Museum, 387, 398–99
Wallis, Willson Dallum, 458
Ward, Lester Frank, 129, 148n6
Warfield, John Ogle, 443
Warner, Lloyd, 426
Washington Academy of Sciences, 420
Washington DC: and American anthropology, xxi–xxii, 128–29, 264, 273; Burnham architecture in, 127; Cushing home in, 176, 180, 181, 182, 197–98
Washington Post, xxvii, 208n73, 232–37
Washington University in St. Louis, 434
Waterman, T. T., 436, 437
waxworks, 298
The Way of the Eskimo, 45–46
Ways and Means Committee, 40, 62, 67
weaving, 213–14, 222–23, 230n4, 304
Webber, E. Leland, 398, 402
Weber, Max, 305
Wedel, Waldo, 427, 451n16
Weeks, Joseph Dame, 168, 169, 203n41
Weidler, Z. A., 118
Wellcome, Henry Solomon, 118
Wells, Ida B., 63
West, George Arbor, 437
West, Gerald Montgomery, 113
Western Reserve Historical Society, 373
Wetherill, Richard, xxxviii, 340–43, 347; and Chaco Canyon excavations, 353, 355–57, 358; at Chicago Fair, 348–49, 490; and Moorehead, 353–54, 355, 357, 358–59; and patrons, 342, 351–52; photo of, *341*
We'wha, 333n45
Wharton, Anne Hollingsworth, 172, 205n52
Wheatland, Henry, 2, 3–4, 9, 10
Whepley, Henry Milton, 443–44, 453n26

White, Henry S., 118
White, John, 307
White City, *49*; architecture of, 126–27, 128, 276, 328; Cushing observation on, 159; destruction of, xv, 406; marginalization of diversity in, 328, 447; Midway Plaisance contrasted to, 54, 385, 447; utopian vision of, xv, 490, 493
The White City (As It Was), 51–52
Whiteley, Eliza Lawton, 118
Whitman, Walt, xxiv, 469
Whitney, Henry Payne, 118
Wickersham, James, 440
Wilcox, Gordon F., 203n35
Wilder, George Durand, 118
Wild West shows, 29, 30, 33, 170, 277
Willey, Gordon R., 424
William (Samoan), *254*
Williams, G. P., 118
Williams, Stephen, xxiii
Williams, Talcott, 148–49n10; biographical note on, 204–5n51; Cushing diary on, 172, 173, 174, 175, 176
Willoughby, Charles C., 194, 210n98, 286, 316, 457
Wilmarth, A. F., 39, 342–43, 360n7
Wilmarth collection, 347, 348, 360n7
Wilson, James, 423
Wilson, Thomas, 360n5, 370; and Moorehead, 343, 349, 352, 354
Wingate, Hannah S., 118
Winnetka IL, 183
Wisconsin pavilion, 96, 97
Wissler, Clark, 422, 424, 457
Wistar Institute, 431, 439
With the Procession (Fuller), 68
Woman's Building, 169, 170–71, 181, 195
women in anthropology, xxi, xl (n5), 3, 4, 425, 427–28
Women's Anthropological Society of America (WASA), xl (n5), 100, 110
Wood, John George, 404n3
Wooded Isle, 25–26, 40, 158, 174, *256*
Woodyatt, Clara Lillian Burnham, 177, 178, 179, 182, 183, 206n63
Worcester, Dean Conant, 421
Worcester, Joseph, 139, 179, 207n67

world fairs and expositions, xvi–xvii, 12, 13, 58–59, 265

World's Columbian Exposition (WCE): and African Americans, 63; and American anthropology's development, xxxix, 106–7, 123, 130–31, 263–64, 266, 413, 414, 417–18, 492; and American cultural history, xv–xvi, xviii–xix, 129, 262–63; architecture of, 126–27, 129, 262, 276; attendance at, 24, 239, 446; books on, 49–52, 323; Chicago's selection to host, xvii, 13–15, 68; classification scheme of, 66–67; closing of, 71; commercial side to, 22–23, 29, 30, 36, 46, 54–55, 67, 69, 385, 403; Cushing at, 135, 136–41, 144, 153–98; destruction of, xv, 128; diversity at, 50, 52–54, 55, 75, 447, 493; drawings and paintings of, xxx, 261; dual authority structure of, 15, 23; as ethnographic site, 322–25; funding for exhibits at, 388–89; income from, 348; lasting impact of, 489–90; newspapers and magazines on, 52–53, 76; preparations for, 388–89; professional interaction at, 337–38, 389–90; Putnam vision of, 15–22, 75–76; and relic hunting, 339–40, 357–58; representational legacies of, 316–25; scientific purposes in, 17, 75, 384; souvenir albums and guidebooks from, 45, 48, 49–51, 53, 241–42, 323, 348; visual images of, xxxix, 239–43, 245–60, 262. See also exhibits, anthropological

World's Columbian Exposition Illustrated (WCEI), 26, 50

World's Fair Puck, 49, 63; about, 239–40; covers of, 245, 246, 247

World War I, 416

Wotts, Charley, 173

Wounded Knee, 29, 33

Wright, Frank Lloyd, 276

Wright, George Frederick, 113, 374

Wright, Robin, 331n19

Wyman, Jeffries, 2, 10

Wyman, Walter and Edward, 141, 178, 179, 186, 194, 196, 207n64

Yale University, 431, 443

Youman, Edward L., xx, xxii, xxxiii

Yucatán ruins. See Mayan ruins

Zacharias (Inuit), 46

zoology, 88

Zorn, Anders, 183

Zuñi Breadstuff (Cushing), 132, 136, 306

Zuni Pueblo, 232–37, 372, 427; animal fetishes of, 218; calendar of, 229; ceremonies of, 187, 215; Chicago World's Fair exhibits of, 169, 275, 372; cliffdwellers as ancestors of, 188, 216, 220, 221; Cult Societies of, 229; cultural region of, 217, 231n5; Cushing fieldwork among, 102, 131–32, 233–34, 306, 307, 333n46, 372; games of, 184, 189, 225; life group displays of, 299, 304; mythology of, 195, 236, 237; pottery of, 154, 188; religious beliefs of, 144, 218, 221; social organization of, 190; and turkeys, 219–20. See also cliffdwellers

Zwick, Jim, 44–45

www.ingramcontent.com/pod-product-compliance
Lightning Source LLC
Chambersburg PA
CBHW021713300426
44114CB00009B/121